Foodservice Procurement

Purchasing for Profit

Foodservice Procurement

Purchasing for Profit

Marian C. Spears

Professor Emerita, Kansas State University

Merrill,
an imprint of Prentice Hall
Upper Saddle River, New Jersey   Columbus, Ohio

Library of Congress Cataloging-in-Publication Data

Spears, Marian C.
    Foodservice procurement: purchasing for profit / Marian C.
Spears
       p.   cm.
    Includes bibliographical references and index.
    ISBN 0-02-414241-7
    1. Food service purchasing.   I. Title
TX911.3.P8S64   1999
647.95'068'7—dc21   98-3280
                                                   CIP

Cover photo: © 1998 John Burwell, Washington DC
Editor: Kevin M. Davis
Production Editor: Linda Hillis Bayma
Production Coordination: Carlisle Publishers Services
Design Coordinator: Diane C. Lorenzo
Cover Designer: Dan Eckel
Insert Designer: Rod Harris
Insert Coordinator: Tracey B. Ward
Production Manager: Laura Messerly
Illustrations: Carlisle Communications, Ltd.
Director of Marketing: Kevin Flanagan
Marketing Manager: Suzanne Stanton
Advertising/Marketing Coordinator: Krista Groshong

This book was set in Garamond by Carlisle Communications, Ltd. and was printed and bound by R.R. Donnelley & Sons Company. The cover was printed by Phoenix Color Corp.

 © 1999 by Prentice-Hall, Inc.
Simon & Schuster/A Viacom Company
Upper Saddle River, New Jersey 07458

Printed in the United States of America

10 9 8 7 6 5 4 3 2

ISBN: 0-02-414241-7

Prentice-Hall International (UK) Limited, *London*
Prentice-Hall of Australia Pty. Limited, *Sydney*
Prentice-Hall of Canada, Inc., *Toronto*
Prentice-Hall Hispanoamericana, S. A., *Mexico*
Prentice-Hall of India Private Limited, *New Delhi*
Prentice-Hall of Japan, Inc., *Tokyo*
Simon & Schuster Asia Pte. Ltd., *Singapore*
Editora Prentice-Hall do Brasil, Ltda., *Rio de Janeiro*

Foodservice Procurement: Purchasing for Profit is designed as a textbook for undergraduate students in hospitality and dietetics programs. It is much more than a purchasing book that focuses on how much of a product should be purchased to feed a given number of customers. Purchasing in many foodservice operations is handled by a cook, many of whom do an excellent job, or another employee who may not know the product. More and more, purchasing is assigned to college graduates who are making purchasing part of their career. Purchasing for a foodservice operation involves much more expertise than just buying products. With so many products available on the market today, buyers must decide which products meet the quality standards required by customers and at the same time find the lowest possible price for a product.

Purchasing is now considered a profession of the same stature as teaching, nursing, or business management. Buyers must have a body of knowledge and skills acquired through education and training. A small foodservice operation might have one person in charge of purchasing, receiving, and storage, but in most cases the manager does the purchasing while a cook is responsible for receiving and storing products and perhaps inventory as well. A large operation, however, usually has a purchasing department with many buyers, each of whom purchases a specific product, such as meat, seafood, produce, equipment, or cleaning and sanitation supplies. Students choosing purchasing as a career are finding out that they need to be specialized to further their career. Also, persons interested in making purchasing their career should be members of professional purchasing organizations. Sharing knowledge and experiences with professional peers is critical to continuing education and advancement. In today's technological environment, computer skills and interpersonal communication skills are essential. With all of this technology, foodservice buyers must not lose sight of the products they are purchasing and therefore should keep updated on what is available on the market that will meet their customers' needs. They also should be able to justify the cost effectiveness of each purchase. Thus, a significant portion of this textbook is devoted to learning about the products.

Organization of the Text

The text is divided into four parts. Part 1, "Purchasing for Profit," discusses the status of foodservice purchasing and how it fits into the procurement unit of a foodservice operation. If a foodservice operation is to generate a profit, the goal of its manager should be to make purchasing a profit center instead of a cost center. This is followed by a discussion of the marketing channel where a change in ownership from the producer to the customer occurs. Part 2, "Procurement Procedures," emphasizes the purchasing, receiving, storage, and inventory control practices that are critical to cost control and profit generation. "Purchasing Food Products," Part 3, is the "meat and potatoes" of this book. Because customers are so concerned about healthful foods today, the Food Guide Pyramid is used as the conceptual framework for this part of the textbook. Grain foods are the base of the Food Guide Pyramid and therefore are discussed first. These food products are followed by fresh and processed fruits and vegetables on the second level and by meat and dairy products on the third level. The foodservice buyer must be knowledgeable about the nutritional value of food. Customers also demand microbiologically safe food, so the use of the Hazard Analysis Critical Control Point system is emphasized. The last, but very important, section of the book, Part 4, is "Purchasing Nonfood Products," which addresses primarily production and service equipment. Without question, equipment is the most expensive expenditure in the foodservice operation. Purchasing equipment is quite different from purchasing food because it is a capital investment that must last many years.

Acknowledgments

This textbook would not have been finished without the help of Jennifer Rettele, a senior level student in the Coordinated Program in Dietetics at Kansas State University. She worked with the author many hours each week in preparing the manuscript for publication. Jenny is a computer whiz who bailed out the author whenever she had computer troubles. Preparing outlines, reference lists, figures, and permission forms, making corrections in the chapters, and taking materials to a copy center were a few of her responsibilities. She organized files and the author's desk frequently. In addition to these tasks, Jenny would critique the chapters to determine if she understood them. Up to this time, she has never had a foodservice purchasing course, which puts her on the same level as students are when they begin reading this text. She pointed out to the author statements that were not clear to her.

Special thanks go to Ed Becker, Santee/Becker Associates, Food Facility Design Consultants in Mission, Kansas, who contributed many hours of his time to Chapter 15, "Production Equipment." He served as a consultant to the author and helped her choose the basic pieces of equipment needed in a foodservice operation. He also suggested manufacturers and distributors who were willing to share their knowledge and color photographs of equipment.

Because foodservice purchasing is a hands-on profession, very little research is available, and current textbooks on the topic are scarce. Most of the information about products came from manufacturers, processors, distributors, and suppliers. This textbook could not have been written without their willingness to share their knowledge and expertise with students who are entering the field. They provided information from years of experience in the field and illustrations and photographs that were used in figures. All in all, they were very cooperative and a pleasure to know.

Also, foodservice industry trade magazines provided much information on purchasing. The author keeps current in the field by reviewing *Nation's Restaurant*

News, Restaurants and Institutions, Restaurants USA, Food Management, and *Fresh Cut,* the magazine for value-added produce. These magazines are valuable because they keep readers up-to-date on what is really happening in the foodservice industry. Professional journals such as *The Journal of The American Dietetic Association* and *School Foodservice & Nutrition* provide research in the area.

I would also like to gratefully acknowledge the following reviewers for their insightful suggestions: Evelina W. Cross, Louisiana State University; Cathy Hsu, Iowa State University; William Jaffe, Purdue University; Erna Marquis, Johnson & Wales University; James R. McClain, California State University, Fullerton; Jerry Vincent, Johnston County Community College; and Lea Wikoff, California State Polytechnic University.

Finally, I want to thank my Merrill/Prentice Hall editor Kevin Davis for his help in preparing the text for publication. His assistant, Holly Jennings, also was very helpful.

Marian C. Spears

About the Author

Marian C. Spears, Ph.D., R.D., Professor Emerita, Kansas State University, formerly head of the Department of Hotel, Restaurant, Institution Management and Dietetics, is a native of Ohio. She holds bachelor's and master's degrees from Case Western Reserve University, followed some years later by a doctorate from the University of Missouri-Columbia. Her seventeen years of professional practice before entering academe included positions as manager of a commercial cafeteria, chief dietitian of a nationally known children's home, and chief dietitian of a private hospital, all in Cleveland. She later was associate director of dietetics at Barnes Hospital, St. Louis. Her academic experience began as assistant professor of home economics at the University of Arkansas, Fayetteville, in 1959. During the years in Arkansas, she and her husband maintained an extensive consulting practice in the design and operation of foodservice facilities. In 1971, she became associate professor and director of education, Food Systems Management Coordinated Program in Dietetics at the University of Missouri-Columbia. She taught undergraduate purchasing courses in Arkansas and Missouri and a graduate level procurement course while department head at Kansas State University.

Dr. Spears' professional memberships include The American Dietetic Association, the American School Food Service Association, the Council of Hotel, Restaurant, Institutional Education, the National Restaurant Association, and the Academy of Management. She has authored and coauthored numerous publications in refereed journals. Honors include Sigma Xi, Phi Kappa Phi, Gamma Sigma Delta, and Omicron Nu. Dr. Spears received The American Dietetic Association Marjory Hulsizer Copher award in 1989. This is the highest honor conferred upon one of 60,000 members. She also is listed in *Who's Who in America.*

Brief Contents

Contents

xi

Part 2 Procurement Procedures   93

Part 3 Purchasing Food Products   161

PART 1

Purchasing for Profit

This textbook is divided into four parts:

- **Purchasing for Profit**
- **Procurement Procedures**
- **Purchasing Food Products**
- **Purchasing Nonfood Products**

The four chapters in Part 1 provide an overview of purchasing and its essential role in the foodservice industry.

- **Chapter 1, Status of Foodservice Purchasing.** Purchasing managers currently have the opportunity to become professionals by certification in a national foodservice organization. The goal of managers should be to make purchasing a profit center instead of a cost center if the operation is to generate a profit. Emphasizing the needs and desires of the customer and the requirements of the foodservice operation can help accomplish this outcome.

- **Chapter 2, Procurement.** As the first unit in a foodservice operation, procurement is defined as the managerial process of acquiring food and nonfood materials for production. Several activities—purchasing, receiving, storage, and inventory control—exist within the unit. Managing food safety by using the Hazard Analysis Critical Control Point program illustrates management skills needed by procurement managers.

- **Chapter 3, The Market.** Market is defined as the medium through which a change in ownership occurs and products move through the marketing channel from producer to customer. The food industry is the most controlled industry in the United States today because it is covered by comprehensive and complex federal regulations.

- **Chapter 4, Product Selection.** The primary function of the foodservice buyer is to procure the required products for the desired use at minimum cost. The buyer must know the quality and quantity of products to buy, techniques for analyzing value, and the rationale for making or buying products.

1

1

Status of Foodservice Purchasing

Purchasing for a foodservice operation, be it a hotel restaurant, hamburger chain, elementary school cafeteria, nursing home, or hospital, is a tremendous challenge! Food budgets are being cut, food prices are experiencing inflationary increases, customers are demanding more for their money, and employees are unhappy that salaries are not keeping up with the cost of living. Specifications for food and supplies change constantly as old standbys become "new and improved." The number of food products in the market increases daily, making choices by the purchaser more complex. With all of these problems, management is under pressure to increase profits by reducing costs.

Interestingly, the National Restaurant Association (NRA) has forecast that the total restaurant industry will spend $119.4 billion in 1998 on food and drink purchases. As the industry continues to expand, the amount of money spent by restaurateurs for these purchases will increase. Full service, limited-service (often referred to as fast-food or quick-service), and food contractors will spend more than $70 billion as shown in Figure 1.1. In 1998, quick-service restaurants, which make up 46% of the

Figure 1.1. Restaurant-industry food-and-drink purchases projected for 1998.* Food-and-drink purchases should exceed $119 billion in 1998.

Group I—Commercial Restaurant Services**	Estimated Food-and-Drink Purchases ($000)	Group II—Institutional Restaurant Services—Business, Educational, Governmental or Institutional Organizations That Operate Their Own Foodservice	Estimated Food-and-Drink Purchases ($000)
Eating Places		Employee foodservice	$537,947
Fullservice restaurants	$34,715,530	Public & parochial elementary,	
Limited-service restaurants	32,383,691	secondary schools	4,424,756
Commercial cafeterias	1,255,086	Colleges & universities	1,721,194
Social caterers	905,031	Transportation	526,399
Ice-cream, frozen-custard, yogurt stands	741,427	Hospitals	4,133,595
Total—Eating Places	**$70,000,765**	Nursing homes; homes for the aged, blind,	
Bars & taverns***	536,425	orphans, mentally & physically disabled	3,067,959
		Clubs, sporting & recreational camps	1,166,981
Total—Eating-and-Drinking Places	**$70,537,190**	Community centers	1,416,972
Food Contractors			
Manufacturing & industrial plants	$2,325,287	**Total—Group II**	**$16,995,803**
Commercial & office buildings	686,262	**Total—Groups I and II**	**$109,472,768**
Hospitals & nursing homes	809,123		
Colleges & universities	1,530,329	Food furnished foodservice employees	
Primary & secondary schools	732,204	(FSE) in Groups I and II	6,909,293
In-transit restaurant services (airlines)***	1,023,856		
Recreation & sports centers	906,107	**Total—Groups I, II and FSE**	**$116,382,061**
Total—Food Contractors	**$8,013,168**	**Group III—Military Restaurant Services**	
Lodging Places		Defense personnel	$1,845,162
Hotel restaurants	$4,904,993	Officers' & NCO clubs ("Open Mess")	781,714
Motor-hotel restaurants	124,200	Foodservice—military exchanges	383,286
Motel restaurants	181,251		
Total—Lodging Places	**$5,210,444**	**Total—Group III**	**$3,010,162**
		Grand Total	**$119,392,223**
Other Commercial			
Retail-host restaurants	$4,797,182	*"Purchases" refers to expenditures by	
Recreation & sports centers	1,387,885	establishments for their food-and-drink supplies.	
Mobile caterers	339,558	**Data are given only for establishments with payroll.	
Vending & nonstore retailers	2,191,538	***Food purchases only.	
Total—Other Commercial	**$8,716,163**		
Total—Group I	**$92,476,965**		

Source: Restaurants USA. Used with the permission of the National Restaurant Association.

total eating places in the United States, should purchase approximately $32.3 billion for food and drinks. This corresponds with increased customer purchases of these items. Purchases by food contractors will increase, too. They are expected to reach $8.0 billion in 1998, the result of greater penetration into noncommercial operations such as schools, colleges and universities, and nursing homes.

To illustrate the magnitude of purchasing in foodservice operations, Reid and Riegal (1989) conducted a survey in 61 multiunit foodservice firms, including retail restaurants, lodging foodservices, and noncommercial foodservices. They found that the number of persons employed in the purchasing department ranged from a single staff member to a high of 300. The number of buyers in these departments ranged from 1 to 123. A better measure of the size of these departments is the size and number of purchase orders issued in a year. More than one fourth of the firms reported that the average purchase order was more than $8,000, and approximately two thirds said it was more than $2,000. One third of the firms reported that more than 8,000 purchase orders were issued each year.

An example of this volume of purchased products is the Aramark's Olympic Grocery List for the 1996 Olympic games in Atlanta. Aramark is a world leader in managed service partnerships and nine-time veteran of Olympic Games foodservices. In more than 100,000 hours of initial planning, Aramark chefs and nutritionists developed a "World Menu" with more than 550 recipes designed to meet the needs of athletes from different countries, different ethnic and religious backgrounds, and varying nutritional needs to help them achieve their best in the Olympics. The challenges were to

- Prepare and serve more than 5 million meals in 33 days
- Serve the needs of 15,000 athletes, coaches, staff, and officials from 197 countries
- Perform all foodservices at the Olympic Village, 8 Olympic venues, and 1,900 points of service
- Provide foodservice in the Olympic Village 24 hours a day
- Recruit and train more than 6,500 people to meet these challenges

Aramark's (partial) grocery list for service inside the Olympic Village included:

- 15,498 pounds of fresh asparagus
- 61,958 strip steaks
- 46,560 bunches of green onions
- 3,333 pounds of black-eyed peas
- 23,342 pints of strawberries
- 9,057 pounds of shredded cheddar cheese
- 48,000 dozen fresh eggs
- 25,000 pounds of fresh mushrooms
- 30,000 pounds of radicchio lettuce
- 2,656 coconut custard pies
- 34,000 pounds of rice (dry weight)
- 7,850 pounds of spaghetti (dry weight)
- 32,800 pounds of margarine
- 10,827 bunches of fresh parsley
- 17,998 pounds of fresh tomatoes
- 11,000 French baguettes
- 665 pounds of anchovies
- 20,000 French rolls

Not many people have the opportunity to be involved in a purchasing role of this scope. But whether you are in a small or large foodservice operation, you must still be familiar with the products and purchasing procedures. The purpose of this text, therefore, is to prepare students to manage the purchasing activity in a for-profit foodservice operation and to become familiar with the various food and nonfood products available on the market. Before this purpose can be met, however, purchasing must be described as a profession.

PURCHASING AS A PROFESSION

"The purchasing field is no longer viewed as a functionary profession delegated to a dusty employee located in the most obscure part of the organizational chart. Instead, it is dynamic, strategic, and vital to the good health of any company's profitability, growth, and staying power." This statement comes from a past chairperson of the Foodservice Purchasing Managers (FPM) professional organization of the National Restaurant Association. Another past FPM chairperson stated that "foodservice purchasing is no longer a field for retiring operators. It has become a professional field. We're bringing in young people who are making foodservice purchasing a career. Professionalism is what we are all about. Purchasing is more than a seat-of-the-pants activity today. Purchasing is one of the major contributors to an operation's efficiency and fiscal health" (Patterson, 1991).

Purchasing is really a semiprofession, sometimes called an occupation. Other examples of semiprofessions include school teaching, nursing, librarianship, pharmacy, stockbrokering, advertising and business management (Goode, 1957). Semiprofessions are different than the four great established professions of the clergy, medicine, university teaching, and law and, therefore, will never reach the levels of knowledge and dedication to service that society considers necessary for a profession. Today, however, many semiprofessions are considered professions because characteristics other than knowledge and service have become requirements for belonging to these unique groups. Purchasing, therefore, is considered a profession and as such should have the same status in an organization as other professions.

In this text, purchasing is considered a profession, and purchasing managers are professionals because they have met the qualifications established for the role. A purchasing manager may be the foodservice manager, the kitchen manager, or even the cook, depending upon the type and size of the operation. In large operations, purchasing is a department staffed by many employees with expertise in purchasing, record keeping, and/or clerical tasks. Examples of these purchasing departments are in the corporate offices of chain restaurants, district offices of school lunch programs, medical centers, and university foodservices. In privately owned restaurants, the owner, kitchen manager, or chef might be delegated the purchasing responsibility. In individual school lunch programs or small hospitals, the buyer often is the foodservice manager. One person could be the manager, cook, and buyer in the smallest operations. Regardless of the situation, buyers have the opportunity to become professionals. Those who want to make a career of purchasing need to pursue specialized education, on-the-job experience, and membership in the appropriate organization that includes research and a code of ethics.

Specialized Education and Experience

The professional possesses a specialized body of knowledge and skills acquired during education and training in a university or community college setting. For those who do not have this opportunity, workshops or seminars on purchasing are available. The role of a purchasing professional requires awareness of the needs of the customer, ability to equate value to cost, and participation on the top-level management team. The educational experience most often occurs in a university or community college setting because of the variety of disciplines available. In addition to purchasing courses, purchasing professionals need courses in consumerism, communications, accounting, finance, business law, and management. Courses also are suggested in industrial engineering, in which concepts of materials management and inventory control are explored, and foreign languages, which will give a bilingual purchasing manager an advantage in international trade.

Even though recent graduates seldom become purchasing managers, some choose purchasing as a career after gaining foodservice experience. For individuals who finally choose foodservice purchasing as a career, more specialization is highly recommended. Basic courses in food selection, purchasing, production, and safety will give credence to managers and make their jobs easier. The current emphasis on the safe handling of seafood, meat, poultry, eggs, and many other foods indicates that a university course in microbiology should be a requirement. A sanitation course also is necessary because receiving and storage equipment and areas must be spotless to prevent contamination of foods.

More and more, a college education is required for purchasing managers. A study with a 55% response rate from chief purchasing executives in selected organizations indicated that 3% of food and beverage purchasing executives had only a high school education, 52% a bachelor's degree, and 45% a graduate degree (Fearon, 1988). Without question, a minimum of a bachelor's degree is required for a purchasing manager striving to be on the top management team of an organization. In addition to education, experience in the field is a prerequisite for top level positions in purchasing. For that reason, a major part of this textbook is devoted to knowing your products.

Professional Organizations

Professional organizations develop certification and continuing education programs, conduct self-motivated research, and support a code of ethics. The National Association of Purchasing Management (NAPM) is the professional organization for purchasing. As a group affiliated with the National Restaurant Association, Food Purchasing Managers is the organization specifically for foodservice.

National Association of Purchasing Management

Founded in 1915, NAPM is committed to providing national and international leadership in purchasing and materials management education and research. Membership in the association is increasing (currently more than 38,000 professional members) because the concept of purchasing as a profit generator in organizations is increasingly emphasized. Certification, research, and a code of ethics are all components of NAPM.

The Certified Purchasing Manager (CPM) program focuses on the managerial, administrative, strategic, and tactical aspects of the purchasing, materials, and supply management function. Certification requires

- passing the CPM exam,
- 5 years purchasing/materials management experience or 3 years experience and a 4-year college degree, and
- accumulating 35 CPM continuing education points.

The exam consists of four modules:

- Module 1: Purchasing
- Module 2: Administration
- Module 3: Supply
- Module 4: Current Issues

Recertification has been an important part of the CPM program since its beginning in 1974. Lifelong learning has taken on new meaning in society today. Yesterday's knowledge may not be adequate for today's performance requirements. CPMs recertify every 5 years by earning 12 CPM points through continuing education and contributions to the profession.

The Accreditation Purchasing Practitioner (APP) program established in 1995 is designed to serve buyers who are primarily engaged in the tactical and operational side of the purchasing, materials, and supply management functions. To qualify for the APP program, an individual must earn 2 years of work experience or 1 year of work experience in addition to an associate's degree at minimum. Exam requirements for the APP require that modules 1 and 4 of the CPM exam must be completed successfully. The APP is a stand-alone accreditation program, in that the person who holds this credential has met the requirements established by NAPM for performing the work of buyers. The APP can be used as a step toward completion of the CPM program. Reaccreditation also is an important part of the APP program. APPs reaccredit every 5 years by earning 42 hours of continuing education in purchasing, materials, management, and business-related subject areas.

Foodservice Purchasing Managers

The Foodservice Purchasing Managers (FPM) group was formed under the auspices of the National Restaurant Association (NRA) in 1977 and is dedicated to purchasing professionalism through industry communication and education. Because foodservice is 100% customer driven, especially in commercial operations, membership in FPM should be a prerequisite for purchasers in the field. FPM is considered "one of the industry's best-kept secrets" (Patterson, 1991). Members must have a full-time purchasing position with a NRA operator member. No restriction is placed on the type of operation members represent. For example, members purchase for chains, hotels, colleges and universities, and independent restaurants.

The FPM group established a certificate program to measure and recognize excellence in foodservice purchasing. The Certified Foodservice Purchasing Manager Program (CFMP) begins with the CPM program, which measures standards representing levels of formal education, knowledge, experience, and contributions to the purchasing field. Upon completion of the CPM program, a member of the FPM group can become a CFMP by passing an 800-question exam in 4 hours or less.

National Association of Food Equipment Manufacturers

The National Association of Food Equipment Manufacturers (NAFEM) is an organization of manufacturers that makes equipment for the foodservice industry. A number of foodservice purchasing managers are members of NAFEM because much of their time is spent purchasing equipment. It supports all of the equipment-oriented organizations: Foodservice Consultants Society International, Marketing Agents for Foodservice Industry, Foodservice Equipment Distributors Association, and Commercial Food Equipment Service Association (Patterson, 1992). Many foodservice managers and buyers attend NAFEM conventions, especially if they are building or renovating foodservice facilities.

The Certified Foodservice Professional (CFSP) program administered by NAFEM raises professional standards through continuing education and encourages members to establish personal goals and participate in self-assessment. The certification process includes completing a personal data form on education, foodservice experience, and industry-related experiences. Certification requires successful completion of a written exam. In addition, NAFEM holds professional seminars on senior management, sales management, and selling skills to help CFSP candidates achieve certification.

Research

Self-motivated research is encouraged by professional organizations and must occur if the profession is to survive. Informal research occurs every time a decision is made, but formal research is much more scientific and must be planned. Of the three professional organizations previously discussed, NAPM is most involved in formal research. An avenue for reporting and sharing research results is NAPM's *International Journal of Purchasing and Materials Management*.

The Center for Advanced Purchasing Studies (CAPS) began in 1986 when leading purchasing and materials management professionals from NAPM requested that research critical to their organization and profession be provided. An affiliation agreement between NAPM and Arizona State University's College of Business resulted in CAPS, the only national not-for-profit research center in purchasing and materials management. CAPS has a unique position as a bridge between private industry and the academic community, integrating business experience with advanced research. As purchasers expand their strategic role in industries, the demand for accurate information on vital research issues increases.

The goals of CAPS are to provide research that identifies trends, analyzes issues, and suggests solutions for problems. Research goals are accomplished through three main programs:

- **Major Research.** Seven reports on critical purchasing issues, including "Purchasing Practices of Large Foodservice Firms" by Reid and Reigel (1989), have been published since 1986. Another research study, "Purchasing Education and Training Requirements and Resources" (Kolchin & Giunipero, 1993), should be of interest to foodservice purchasing managers. The objectives of this study are to specify the common body of knowledge for purchasing, to project the changing professional requirements to the year 2000, to determine specific skills for various procurement positions in the typical organization, and to determine nationally what training resources currently are available to meet identified needs.
- **Benchmarking Reports.** CAPS provides objective purchasing performance data annually on more than 20 industries, including purchasing performance benchmarks for the U.S. foodservice industry. A **benchmark,** or

point of reference in measuring or judging quality or value, gives purchasing professionals the objective reference point they need to evaluate their own performance.

- **Executive Purchasing Roundtable.** Key purchasing professionals from Fortune 500 and international firms meet annually in a face-to-face forum to identify and assess the most current critical purchasing issues on which research is needed. Two members of the planning committee are from foodservice organizations.

Code of Ethics

To support their profession, organizations must have a code of ethics to which members subscribe. Many businesses also have a code of ethics. A **code** is a set of rules for standards of professional practice or behavior established by a group, and **ethics** have been defined as the principles of conduct governing an individual or a business. A **code of ethics** is influenced by personal codes of individuals, but the major emphasis is on the relationships within professional organizations and businesses. Standards are the result of the managerial process of planning and are defined as the measurement of what is expected to happen. NAPM, FSM, and NAFEM all have codes of ethics or standards of practice.

Many businesses currently are changing from a code of ethics to standards of practice. For example, NAPM changed to standards of practice in January 1992. The ideal method of purchasing would be based on price, quality, and delivery from the supplier, offering the best possible combination of all three. A **supplier,** often identified as a seller or vendor, is a person who offers products for sale. Supplier is the term used by NAPM in the *International Journal of Purchasing and Materials Management* and therefore will be used in this text. This ideal method is not always an easy task because salespersons might have their own ideas of price and quality and buyers might favor certain suppliers over others. A **buyer,** often called a purchaser, is responsible for selecting and purchasing products. The difficulties of buying objectively have led NAPM to develop Principles and Standards of Purchasing Practice to serve as a guide (Figure 1.2).

FPM has its own code of ethics, as shown in Figure 1.3. This code was developed to promote and encourage ethical practices in the foodservice industry. To give further credence to the code, the purchasing group agreed that each member should indicate support for the principles by signing the code of ethics document.

The Certified Foodservice Professional (CFP) program administered by NAFEM also has a code of ethics (Figure 1.4). One of the prerequisites for CFP candidates is that the candidate must reflect a commitment to the value system inherent in the CFP code of ethics. Any CFP may be suspended or expelled from the program if the Certification Board of Governors determines the individual has violated the code of ethics.

FOODSERVICE AS A CUSTOMER-DRIVEN OPERATION

The foodservice industry is customer driven in the current information and service society. Quality food and service for customer satisfaction are required to make a profit. The foodservice manager should understand segmentation of the industry and

Figure 1.2. NAPM's Principles and Standards of Purchasing Practice.

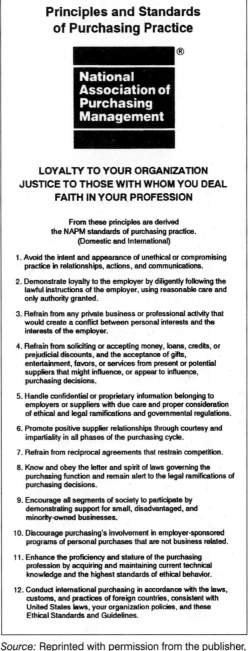

Principles and Standards of Purchasing Practice

National Association of Purchasing Management ®

**LOYALTY TO YOUR ORGANIZATION
JUSTICE TO THOSE WITH WHOM YOU DEAL
FAITH IN YOUR PROFESSION**

From these principles are derived
the NAPM standards of purchasing practice.
(Domestic and International)

1. Avoid the intent and appearance of unethical or compromising practice in relationships, actions, and communications.

2. Demonstrate loyalty to the employer by diligently following the lawful instructions of the employer, using reasonable care and only authority granted.

3. Refrain from any private business or professional activity that would create a conflict between personal interests and the interests of the employer.

4. Refrain from soliciting or accepting money, loans, credits, or prejudicial discounts, and the acceptance of gifts, entertainment, favors, or services from present or potential suppliers that might influence, or appear to influence, purchasing decisions.

5. Handle confidential or proprietary information belonging to employers or suppliers with due care and proper consideration of ethical and legal ramifications and governmental regulations.

6. Promote positive supplier relationships through courtesy and impartiality in all phases of the purchasing cycle.

7. Refrain from reciprocal agreements that restrain competition.

8. Know and obey the letter and spirit of laws governing the purchasing function and remain alert to the legal ramifications of purchasing decisions.

9. Encourage all segments of society to participate by demonstrating support for small, disadvantaged, and minority-owned businesses.

10. Discourage purchasing's involvement in employer-sponsored programs of personal purchases that are not business related.

11. Enhance the proficiency and stature of the purchasing profession by acquiring and maintaining current technical knowledge and the highest standards of ethical behavior.

12. Conduct international purchasing in accordance with the laws, customs, and practices of foreign countries, consistent with United States laws, your organization policies, and these Ethical Standards and Guidelines.

Source: Reprinted with permission from the publisher, the National Association of Purchasing Management, Principles & Standards of Purchasing Practice, adopted January 1992.

Figure 1.3. Code of ethics of Foodservice Purchasing Managers Group.

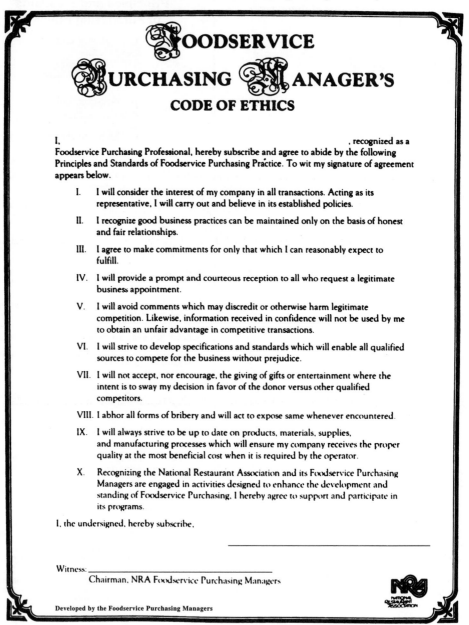

FOODSERVICE
PURCHASING MANAGER'S
CODE OF ETHICS

I, _____, recognized as a
Foodservice Purchasing Professional, hereby subscribe and agree to abide by the following
Principles and Standards of Foodservice Purchasing Practice. To wit my signature of agreement
appears below.

I.   I will consider the interest of my company in all transactions. Acting as its representative, I will carry out and believe in its established policies.

II.   I recognize good business practices can be maintained only on the basis of honest and fair relationships.

III.   I agree to make commitments for only that which I can reasonably expect to fulfill.

IV.   I will provide a prompt and courteous reception to all who request a legitimate business appointment.

V.   I will avoid comments which may discredit or otherwise harm legitimate competition. Likewise, information received in confidence will not be used by me to obtain an unfair advantage in competitive transactions.

VI.   I will strive to develop specifications and standards which will enable all qualified sources to compete for the business without prejudice.

VII.   I will not accept, nor encourage, the giving of gifts or entertainment where the intent is to sway my decision in favor of the donor versus other qualified competitors.

VIII.   I abhor all forms of bribery and will act to expose same whenever encountered.

IX.   I will always strive to be up to date on products, materials, supplies, and manufacturing processes which will ensure my company receives the proper quality at the most beneficial cost when it is required by the operator.

X.   Recognizing the National Restaurant Association and its Foodservice Purchasing Managers are engaged in activities designed to enhance the development and standing of Foodservice Purchasing, I hereby agree to support and participate in its programs.

I, the undersigned, hereby subscribe,

_____

Witness: _____
Chairman, NRA Foodservice Purchasing Managers

NRA
NATIONAL
RESTAURANT
ASSOCIATION

Developed by the Foodservice Purchasing Managers

Source: National Restaurant Association. Used by permission.

Figure 1.4.   Code of ethics of the National Association of Food Equipment Manufacturers.

C*ode of Ethics*

The code of ethics for the Certified Foodservice Professional program has been adopted to promote and maintain the highest standards of service and personal conduct among its members. Adherence to these standards is required for acceptance in the program and serves to ensure public confidence in the integrity and service of the CFSP. As a Certified Foodservice Professional, I pledge to:

1. Maintain the highest standard of personal conduct;
2. Promote and encourage the highest level of ethics within the industry;
3. Maintain loyalty to the organization that employs me and pursue its objectives in ways that are consistent with industry interests;
4. Recognize and discharge my responsibility and that of my industry to uphold all laws and regulations relating to the CFSP policies and activities;
5. Strive for excellence in all aspects of the foodservice industry;
6. Use only legal and ethical means in all activities;
7. Accept no personal compensation for foodservice-related activities except with the knowledge and consent of my organization's management;
8. Maintain the confidentiality of privileged information entrusted or known to me by virtue of my position;
9. Refuse to engage in, or countenance, activities for personal gain at the expense of my organization or the foodservice industry;
10. Always communicate internal and external statements in a truthful and accurate manner;
11. Cooperate in every reasonable and proper way with industry colleagues and work with them in the advancement of the foodservice profession; and
12. Use every opportunity to improve public understanding of the foodservice industry.

National Association of Food Equipment Manufacturers
401 N. Michigan Ave.
Chicago, IL 60611-4267
312/644-6610
FAX 312/321-6869

Source: Code of Ethics, Certified Food Service Professioal Program, North American Association of Food Equipment Manufacturers. Used by permission.

how to target the customer market. The manager also should realize that the menu, or plan of the operation, must meet the needs of customers who want value for the lowest cost if a profit is to be made. The person doing the purchasing has a crucial role in creating customer satisfaction while at the same time aiding management in making the foodservice operation profitable.

Industry Segmentation

The foodservice industry often is divided into two segments: commercial and institutional, which is called noncommercial in this text. Regardless of whether the foodservice operation is commercial or noncommercial, buyers today should know the goals of their operations and purchase accordingly. The commercial segment is concerned about the bottom line because profit is required to keep the business operating. This segment includes quick-service and full-service restaurants, lodging, recreational centers, supermarkets, convenience stores, and retail outlets.

The noncommercial segment, although formerly considered a not-for-profit part of the foodservice industry, must be careful that expenses do not exceed income. This segment includes employee meals, schools, hospitals, correctional facilities, colleges and universities, military, nursing homes, transportation, and child care, life care, and elder care centers. The line between commercial and noncommercial foodservice has almost disappeared. The days of not-for-profit operations are gone because of the pressure of budget cuts, dwindling subsidies, and increased competition. Noncommercial foodservice managers are taking risks and being creative not only to break even, but also to make a profit. Many schools and universities have installed pizzerias and are making their own pizza. Hospitals sell take-home food to employees and visitors, operate vending machines, and provide catering for special events to reduce expenses. Today, almost all noncommercial foodservices must produce revenue to survive. Management must determine customers' needs and expectations and satisfy them.

Target Market

The word **market** has numerous meanings. In this text it refers to the medium through which a change in ownership moves products from producer to customer. Customers must need a particular product and have the ability to purchase it, which is a function of buying power or money. Customers also should be willing to use their buying power and have the authority to buy specific products. An example is the teenager who has the desire, money, and willingness to buy beer but is prohibited by law from making the purchase.

Swinyard and Struman (1986) suggest that separating customers into "natural" market groups provides the basis for successful strategy development in marketing a restaurant. The menu and marketing can be designed to match the needs of one of these groups and suppress competition. Managers can identify target customers through characteristics such as lifestyle, age, gender, income, and education. Purchasing for these market groups takes an understanding of what customers are willing to buy. Even a simple product, such as ground coffee beans, requires that the manager samples various brands within an acceptable price range and asks customers often for their opinions before a purchasing decision can be made.

Customer Needs

Management should determine customers' needs and expectations and satisfy them. Customers usually are associated with a profit operation, but today's healthcare managers also have discovered that patients have opinions about the care they expect to receive. Healthcare was a seller's market a decade ago, when the physician decided where the patient would be sent for treatment. Today, healthcare is a buyer's market, and patients assume the role of primary decision makers, choosing where they want to go for treatment. This scenario also applies to most noncommercial foodservice operations, including schools, colleges and universities, and day and eldercare centers.

Knowing customers and their needs can produce repeat business, and customers who are dissatisfied with the competition are excellent prospects. For example, customers who patronize a quick-service restaurant probably want to eat and run, dress casually, and keep the cost of the meal low. Needs of these customers are quite different than those of customers who consider dining a social event. The astute manager knows that customer satisfaction is essential for the success of *any* foodservice. Well-planned menus, value, and low prices might all contribute to satisfaction, but the ultimate measure of success is whether the customer returns. The goals of buyers for foodservice operations are essentially the same. All purchasers are interested in buying products that meet the needs of their customers at the lowest total cost possible.

The Menu

The **menu,** a list of food items, serves as the primary control of the operation and the core of everything that happens in the foodservice. The menu controls each function in the operation and is the major determinant for the budget (Spears, 1995). Cooks are responsible for preparing menu items and communicating with the storeroom the amount of each ingredient needed for a recipe. The wait staff then has the responsibility to serve the items on the menu.

Menu planning is a complicated process whether it be a **static menu,** one in which the same menu items are offered every day, or a **cycle menu,** a series of menus offering different items daily on a weekly, biweekly, or some other basis (Spears, 1995). Most restaurants use a static menu and noncommercial operations use a cycle menu, although many hospitals are using a static menu because of short patient stays. Menus generally are planned by a team that gives input into the process. The foodservice manager, dietitian, kitchen manager, cook, buyer, and perhaps a customer all may be valuable members of the team. The purchasing professional knows the market, products and their availability, packaging alternatives, product shelf life, prices, suppliers, and transportation costs, all of which are critical data for menu planning decisions. These concepts will be discussed in later chapters.

Menu planning is much more complicated today than in the past as customers voice their needs and preferences. Customers have become increasingly aware of the relationship between diet and health in recent years and realize that food eaten away from home is an important component of their overall diet. Menus are less effective in meeting the nutrition needs of customers, especially children, if products are purchased before the menu is planned. The product, rather than nutrition needs, controls the decision-making process (Gunn, 1992). Customers are demanding that food producers, processors, and foodservice operators provide nutritious and healthful products. Customers' concern for nutrition has convinced food processors to promote food products on the basis of nutritional benefits.

Buyers for foodservice operations would benefit from a course in basic nutrition, because as of May 1993, claims about the nutritional value of a food product must be documented on the labels of cans or packages. As customers demand nutritious food, buyers are responsible for purchasing products that meet their demands. Concern for the environment also has affected the packaging industry and industries manufacturing disposable products for foodservice operations. Buyers not only have to know products, but they also need to check the packaging, which can become waste in the environment. These and many other customer concerns have made purchasing a much more sophisticated profession than it was a decade ago.

Value

The goal of any foodservice establishment is to serve quality food while maximizing value for both the operation and customer. NAPM has defined value as "a systematic study of the function of an item or system for the purpose of identifying unnecessary cost, which can be eliminated without impairing the capacity of the item or system to perform as required." In simple terms, **value** is the perceived relationship between quality and price; as these relationships change, perceived value changes (Virts, 1987). Buying in the foodservice sector is no different than in the industrial sector. The goal for both is to attain maximum value for each dollar expended.

The customer evaluates quality and price of food to determine if the meal has enough value to make a return visit. Quality can be measured by the food, pleasant atmosphere, service cleanliness, menu variety, convenient location, and dining experience. If the quality is good and the price is right, the customer probably will be loyal and return. To satisfy the customer, the suppliers, foodservice operator, and employees must work together to encourage customers to be loyal to their operation. The *Value Equation,* developed by Pillsbury Brands and shown in Figure 1.5, illustrates this concept. In choosing a supplier, the operator should check the breadth of the product line, competitiveness of price, quality of products, relationships with each other, and service. Knowledgeable employees also are required to make the equation work (Grand Metropolitan Foodservice, Inc., 1993).

Figure 1.6 illustrates the *Value Chain.* Several factors, from merchandising support to caring employees, influence customers' dining experience. Each link along the value chain is vital in making this experience a positive one. The key to unlocking profits, of course, is satisfied customers (Grand Metropolitan Foodservice, Inc., 1993).

An improvement in quality tends to increase the value, and an increase in price tends to lower the perceived value by the customer. Value is simply the perception by the customer that they are getting more than they paid for. Value in any foodservice operation must be based on the needs and expectations of the target market. Because the foodservice industry is customer driven, customers' perceptions of value are extremely important. A 99-cent hamburger on a bun may be a great value for one target market just as a $100 dinner with vintage wine is for another target market.

Value will not go away in the quick-service segment, at least not any time soon (Kramer, 1996). Not only do the value trendsetters like McDonald's and Taco Bell continue to feature hot prices on products, but others, such as Subway, are emphasizing value in a big way for the first time. No longer can customers be sold on price only because now value equals big portions with big flavors and high quality, all for the value prices that customers expect. Add to that customer expectations for speedy service and convenience. Burger King, which faced tough times in the early '90s, has developed a back-to-basics value strategy based on what they do best: burgers, fries, and Coke. Subway kicked off 1996 with a new campaign selling meatball subs for 96 cents. Subway has been known more for its lunch-meat sandwiches than hot beef items but wants to be more competitive with its

Figure 1.5. The value equation.

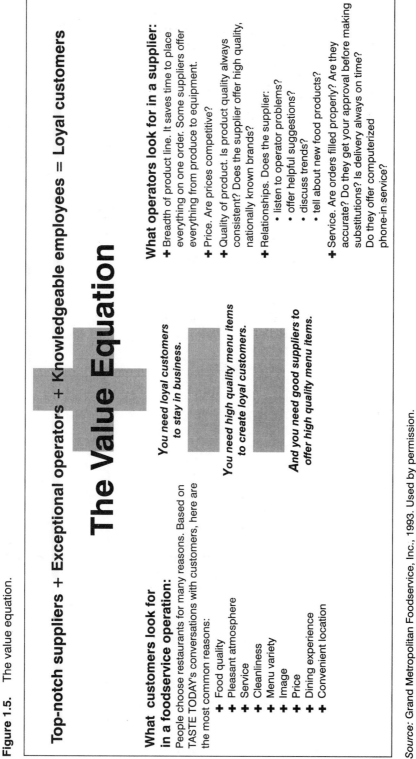

Top-notch suppliers + Exceptional operators + Knowledgeable employees = Loyal customers

The Value Equation

What customers look for in a foodservice operation:

People choose restaurants for many reasons. Based on TASTE TODAY's conversations with customers, here are the most common reasons:

+ Food quality
+ Pleasant atmosphere
+ Service
+ Cleanliness
+ Menu variety
+ Image
+ Price
+ Dining experience
+ Convenient location

You need loyal customers to stay in business.

You need high quality menu items to create loyal customers.

And you need good suppliers to offer high quality menu items.

What operators look for in a supplier:

+ Breadth of product line. It saves time to place everything on one order. Some suppliers offer everything from produce to equipment.
+ Price. Are prices competitive?
+ Quality of product. Is product quality always consistent? Does the supplier offer high quality, nationally known brands?
+ Relationships. Does the supplier:
  • listen to operator problems?
  • offer helpful suggestions?
  • discuss trends?
  • tell about new food products?
+ Service. Are orders filled properly? Are they accurate? Do they get your approval before making substitutions? Is delivery always on time? Do they offer computerized phone-in service?

Source: Grand Metropolitan Foodservice, Inc., 1993. Used by permission.

Figure 1.6. The value chain.

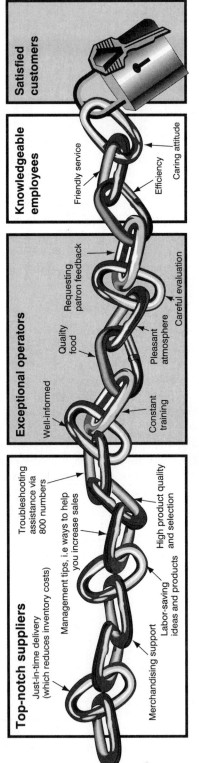

Top-notch suppliers

Just-in-time delivery
(which reduces inventory costs)

Troubleshooting
assistance via
800 numbers

Management tips, i.e ways to help
you increase sales

High product quality
and selection

Merchandising support

Labor-saving
ideas and products

Exceptional operators

Well-informed

Quality
food

Requesting
patron feedback

Pleasant
atmosphere

Careful evaluation

Constant
training

**Knowledgeable
employees**

Friendly service

Efficiency

Caring attitude

**Satisfied
customers**

Source: Grand Metropolitan Foodservice, Inc., 1993. Used by permission.

burger-selling rivals. Big-flavored products such as Taco Bell's Burrito Supreme & Wendy's Fajita Wrap are getting a lot of attention recently. Pizza, chicken, and seafood quick-service restaurants also are emphasizing value to increase sales and profit.

Price

The customer wants quality food at the lowest price, which means the foodservice operation must control costs. Price must be placed in true perspective in relation to cost, of which price is only one element. Purchasing managers believe the supplier should be paid a fair price, which is the lowest price that ensures a continuous supply of the desired quality (Leenders, Fearon, & England, 1989). A continuous supply of a product is possible only from a supplier making a reasonable profit. The product no longer could be offered by the supplier if it did not produce a profit.

Total costs, including overhead and profit, must be covered by sales. Direct costs generally consist of the price of materials and labor. Indirect costs are rent, property taxes, equipment depreciation, computerization, and energy. **Direct costs** usually are defined as those that can be specifically and accurately assigned to a given unit of production (Leenders et al., 1989); in foodservice operations, this would be the menu item served to the customer. **Indirect costs** are those incurred in the operation that cannot be related directly to any unit of production; in foodservice, this would include costs of occupying and operating the facility. Factors such as transportation, receiving, storage, and inventory are expenses purchasers also must add to the price to determine ultimate cost. In addition, quality, obsolescence, spoilage, and other factors need to be considered in determining ultimate cost, although to evaluate and convert those costs to dollars and cents may be more difficult. A supplier has many costs, including profit, which become the price charged to purchasers of food. Converting the food to a product for sale incurs many costs, including profit, which become the price charged to the customer. For example, a supplier may charge $3.50 for a T-bone steak, which includes profit, but the purchaser might charge the customer $7.00, which includes food, labor, and preparation costs as well as profit.

Although many similarities are found in buying practices between the foodservice and industrial sectors, differences also are apparent. For example, certain characteristics of products and services in foodservice are more difficult to handle than in industry. One major issue in the purchase of most food items is that of perishability. Shelf life of foods is extremely critical; thus produce and dairy products must be purchased locally. Another issue is the market fluctuation in raw food prices. Seasonality, weather disasters, or transportation strikes make pricing menu items a difficult task for the foodservice manager. Customers will become unhappy if menu prices change daily. Many foodservice managers use a standard cost for menu items and base the price to the customer on that. For some items such as fresh lobster, the menu might state, "Priced according to daily market cost."

PURCHASING AS A PROFIT GENERATOR

Well-managed companies almost always set specific targets for profits in relation to both sales and net worth. One of the easiest ways to achieve this objective is to set selling prices high enough to guarantee success. For many years, prevailing wisdom in most manufacturing firms was that a purchasing department could not make or break a company. This thought has changed because today quite the opposite is true. Reck and Long (1983) conducted research on organizing purchasing as a profit center in the *International Journal of Purchasing and Materials Management*. One of the major reasons for this change is the fact that the average manufacturing firm today spends more than half its sales revenue for purchases.

Granted that purchasing for a foodservice operation is different than purchasing for a manufacturing operation, better purchasing saves dollars paid to suppliers for needed materials, supplies, and services. These savings go directly to the bottom line, before taxes, on the profit and loss statement (Leenders et al., 1989). If the same amount of money saved is made in increased sales, however, the contribution to profit, assuming a 5% profit margin before taxes, would be only half of the amount saved by astute purchasing. Purchase dollars are high-powered dollars! Reducing purchasing costs should be an objective of a foodservice operation. Savings from using good purchasing techniques have a greater effect on the profit and loss statement than increasing sales. Since increased sales already have received attention in foodservice operations, purchasing may be the last untapped profit producer.

COMPUTERIZATION OF PURCHASING PROCEDURES

Computer software purchasing programs are readily available, but finding the one that best suits the needs of a specific foodservice operation can be difficult. Most foodservice operators choose a program that fits their purchasing practices and then modify it to meet their needs. A software purchasing program can be a great tool for a foodservice buyer who also might be the top manager, unit manager, chef, or kitchen manager. Although differences exist between software programs, most perform such basic tasks as managing inventory, food costing, and ordering from suppliers.

Large foodservice operations have been using computers for purchasing for many years; relatively small operations also use a computer as an aid in making managerial decisions. However, computers can only work with the information provided by managers. If the information is incorrect, the output also is incorrect. Hence the saying, "garbage in, garbage out." Computers cannot make judgments (Kotschevar & Donnelly, 1999). Foodservice managers, therefore, should have reasons for investing in a computer system and understand what a computer can do to make purchasing more efficient in their operations.

Reasons for Computerization

A foodservice manager should know how to operate a computer and understand the various functions it can perform. Computer systems are effective in relieving managers of repetitive, routine tasks, thus enabling them to use their time and skills for planning and decision making. As the costs of personal computers decrease, this technology is more accessible to foodservice operations. For most managers, time saved, increased accuracy, reduction of paper and supplies costs, and labor saved have more than made up for the initial investment in a computerized system (Stefanelli, 1992).

Computers have made information more accurate and quicker and easier to retrieve than ever before (Kotschevar & Donnelly, 1999). The computer, in combination with a good software program, can help managers become more efficient while making the job easier. Software purchasing programs that reduce clerical, computational, and recording tasks previously done manually are available.

For example, many software companies, aware that school foodservice is a big and growing business, are producing packages specifically for these operations. One package allows a central county or regional buying co-op to establish specifications, gather purchasing needs from each school district, solicit bids and quotes, and generate orders. All of this is accomplished with personal computers using data transfer, faxes, and fax modems. Specifications and item lists are uniform among school districts, and the orders are clear, concise, and economical. Another package permits school foodservice directors to establish their own item list with specifications and pack sizes, obtain supplier prices, and place orders by fax, modem, or direct wire.

Purchasing Efficiency

Without question, a well-planned computerized purchasing system increases the efficiency of the entire foodservice operation. Numerous foodservice operation files are required to accomplish this task. Inventory files especially are required to keep costs under control and make purchasing profitable.

Operation Files

Menu, recipe, ingredient, forecasting, and other files can be created on disks to make the information available to the computer. A **file** has been defined as a collection of logically arranged, related data or records (Kotschevar & Donnelly, 1999). The number of files and amount of information in each depends on the size of the foodservice operation and the capacity of the computer. Each item in a file is identified by a code, usually a number. Entering information in the files takes time, but the payoff is great in terms of managerial efficiency. Managers have current information immediately on what to purchase and how much the ingredients cost so they can make efficient purchasing decisions.

The *menu file* contains all food items that might be on a menu. Although menus can be planned on the computer, the many constraints involved in devising a menu make this a difficult program to develop. For example, menu planners must consider the number and kind of items in a group (entrées, vegetables, desserts) color of food items (avoid all white or brown), flavor to balance between strong and mild foods, nutritional balance to meet dietary guidelines, and cost to stay within a budget. Managers make the final decisions, and they can override the computer and add, delete, or change the selected menu items.

A *recipe file* is required to produce the items in the menu file. Developing this file requires the expertise of a person who understands standardizing recipes and programming for a computer. The yield of a recipe can be increased or decreased, but someone experienced in food production should determine if the modified recipe still produces an acceptable product. The use of these computerized recipes for the correct quantity eliminates waste and therefore increases profit.

The *ingredient file* is a complete list of all food items in inventory or needed for a recipe. Ingredient costs need to be current for menu pricing. When the inventory for an ingredient reaches a predetermined level, the computer generates purchase orders for suppliers. In some operations, the purchaser's computer is connected directly by telephone lines to the supplier's computer for placing orders, thus eliminating the need for salespersons or order takers. Managers can spend more of their time talking to customers, thus improving service—and profits.

The *forecasting file* contains historical data such as number of portions of a menu item sold when it is on the menu with a popular or unpopular item. For example, fried chicken sales differ when listed with lasagna or with liver and onions. Often a cook or a chef makes the decision based on what happened the last time the item was served. Research results from various mathematical models can help managers make better decisions on the number of portions to be prepared at a future time. The foodservice manager either accepts the forecasts or overrides them when something unusual happens, such as a snowstorm, football game, or holiday.

Bid analysis software generates prices for comparisons of competing suppliers, thus aiding the buyer in making supplier selection decisions. Specifications for food products also can be stored in files. A bidding form, including the items to be bid upon plus complete specifications, ensures that each supplier is bidding on the same product.

Inventory Files

Inventory control is a requirement for an efficient operation. Because public funds are involved, managers of publicly owned noncommercial foodservice operations, such as hospitals or schools, are required by the government to have records indicating the amount of food on hand at the beginning of a month, plus the amount ordered, minus the amount served and wasted, to equal the amount left at the end of the period. The inventory record is then checked against actual supplies. A small percentage of errors is unavoidable, but it should remain fairly constant. If a major variation occurs, theft or poor record keeping may be a problem. Large commercial operations, especially chains, have similar requirements.

Surprisingly, many privately owned operations have no formal inventory records and literally operate in the dark. Computerization of the inventory can alleviate many problems by letting the manager know how much money is tied up in storage. An accurate inventory in many operations is difficult, however, because food products probably are in many different areas, including dry, refrigerated, freezer, and point-of-use storerooms. A computer can simplify the task by generating an inventory form by location. Weekly inventories may be more useful than monthly checks for some managers.

Bar code and scanning technology permit managers to conduct a physical inventory and calculate the value of stock more quickly than a manual operation. The adoption of the **Universal Product Code (UPC)** in 1973 transformed a technological curiosity into a standardized system for designating products (Seideman, 1993). The UPC is a system for uniquely identifying the thousands of different suppliers and millions of different products that are warehoused, sold, delivered, and billed throughout retail and commercial channels of distribution. It provides an accurate, efficient, and economical means of controlling the flow of products through the use of an all-numeric product identification system. Up until 1973, some companies used letters, some used numbers, some used both, and a few had no codes at all. When the UPC was established, these companies had to give up their individual methods and register with a new Uniform Code Council (UCC).

Figure 1.7. Universal Product Code (UPC) and symbol.

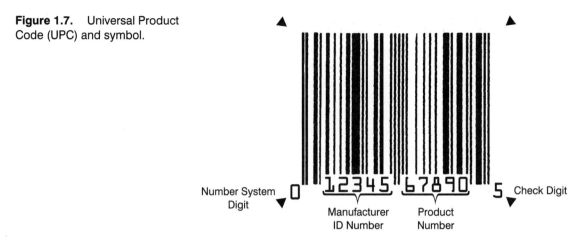

The UPC is the rectangular box with black vertical lines of various widths identifying the contents of the package, carton, and case (Figure 1.7). The code is split into two halves of six digits each. The first digit (number system digit) is always zero except for products like meat and produce that have variable weight. The next five are the manufacturer's or processor's code, followed by a five-digit product code. The final number is a *check digit* used to verify that the preceding digits have been scanned properly. Manufacturers register with the UCC to get an identifier code for their company and then register each of their products. Thus each package has its own unique identification number. After many years of research, scanning is currently done by a microchip. UPC has been used in retail grocery stores for some time and currently is being introduced into wholesale food operations serving foodservice operations. Manufacturers, processors, and distributors must contend with multiple distribution channels and conflicting industry standards. Adoption of UCC standards by trade associations has helped minimize industry-specific standards. Use of the UPC numbers simplifies the ordering procedure by making the buyer's file interface with that of the suppliers. Use of this technology helps buyers achieve more accurate ordering, receiving, and inventory control. In large operations, electronic scanners are used, but in small ones, hand scanners are adequate.

SUMMARY

Purchasing is considered a profession and as such should have the same status in an organization as other professions. Most purchasing managers are professionals with a specialized education, on-the-job experience, and membership in a professional organization. The National Association of Purchasing Management is the professional organization for purchasers in all types of industries, and the organization specifically for foodservice is the Foodservice Purchasing Managers group of the National Restaurant Association. The National Association of Food Equipment Manufacturers focuses on the equipment side of the foodservice industry. Certification, continuing education, and research are important parts of membership in these organizations. A code of ethics to which members adhere also is a hallmark of a professional organization.

The foodservice industry is customer driven. Quality food and service for customer satisfaction are required to make a profit. The industry is divided into two segments:

commercial and noncommercial foodservice operations. Customers can be separated into target markets by their needs. Well-planned menus, value, and low prices contribute to customer satisfaction.

Purchasing can be a profit generator in a foodservice operation. Savings from using good purchasing techniques have a greater effect on the profit and loss statement than increasing sales. A software purchasing program can be a great tool in making the purchasing department a profit generator. A well-planned computerized purchasing system increases the efficiency of the entire foodservice operation. Menu, recipe, ingredient, forecasting, and inventory are some of the computer files that can be created to help manage a foodservice operation.

REFERENCES

Fearon, H. E. (1988). *Purchasing organizational relationships.* Tempe, AZ: National Association of Purchasing Management.

Goode, W. J. (1957, April). Community within a community: The professions. *American Sociological Review, 22,* 194.

Grand Metropolitan Foodservice, Inc. (1993). Taste Today. *The Value Chain.* Minneapolis, MN.

Gunn, M. (1992). Professionalism in purchasing. *School Food Service Journal, 46*(9), 32–34.

Kolchin, M. G. & Giunipero, L. (1993). *Purchasing education and training requirements and resources.* Center for Advanced Purchasing Studies, Tempe, AZ: National Association for Purchasing Management.

Kotschevar, L. H., & Donnelly, R. (1999). *Quantity food purchasing* (4th ed.). Upper Saddle River, NJ: Merrill/Prentice Hall.

Kramer, L. (1996). Sandwich rivals adding size, taste, dual-brand lures to 'value' equation. *Nation's Restaurant News, 30*(17), 72, 76.

Leenders, M. C., Fearon, H. E., & England, W. B. (1997). *Purchasing and supply management* (11th ed.). Homewood, IL: Irwin.

Patterson, P. (1991). Purchasing manager's group: One of industry's best-kept secrets. *Nation's Restaurant News, 25*(48), 40.

Patterson, P. (1992). Certification adds professionalism to purchasing. *Nation's Restaurant News, 26*(12), 36.

Reck, R. R., & Long, B. G. (1983, Winter). Organizing purchasing as a profit center. *International Journal of Purchasing and Materials Management, 19,* 2–6.

Reid, R. D., & Riegel, C. D. (1989). *Purchasing practices of large foodservice firms.* Tempe, AZ: National Association of Purchasing Management.

____. (1998) Food-and-drink purchases could top $119 billion in 1998. *Restaurants USA, 18*(1), 42–43

Seideman, T. (1993). Bar codes sweep the world. *American Heritage Invention and Technology, 8*(4), 56–63.

Spears, M. C. (1995). *Foodservice organizations: A managerial and systems approach* (3rd ed.). Upper Saddle River, NJ: Merrill/Prentice Hall.

Stefanelli, J. M. (1997). *Purchasing: Selection and procurement for the hospitality industry* (3rd ed.). New York: Wiley.

Swinyard, W. R., & Struman, K. D. (1986). Market segmentation: Finding the heart of your restaurant's market. *The Cornell Hotel & Restaurant Administration Quarterly, 27*(1), 89–96.

Virts, W. B. (1987). *Purchasing for hospitality operations.* East Lansing, MI: Educational Institute of the American Hotel and Motel Association.

2

Procurement

The goal of any foodservice operation is to serve quality meals while maximizing value for both the foodservice and the customer. As we discussed in chapter 1, value is the perceived relationship between quality and price. As those relationships change, so does perceived value (Virts, 1987). According to McCarthy (1991), "value is simply the perception by customers that they are getting more than they paid for." To attain this goal, the necessary raw or processed food must be procured, preprocessed, and produced as menu items before it can be served to the customer.

Spears (1995) conceptualized the foodservice operation as a foodservice system. A foodservice systems model, which is the conceptual framework of an operation, can be used to analyze a foodservice operation. The model is based on the basic open systems model of an organization that includes input of resources, transformation, and output or goals. Components of control, memory, and feedback also are integral parts of the foodservice systems model.

Transformation is a critical element in the system. Food is the major resource brought into the foodservice operation. It must be changed into a quality menu item that satisfies the customer and therefore makes a profit for management. Knowledge of the various units in a foodservice operation and functions of management is necessary to understand the role of procurement. Management is responsible for what happens in the transformation of food products to menu items.

UNITS OF A FOODSERVICE OPERATION

The major units of a foodservice operation, classified according to their purpose or function, are procurement, production, distribution and service, and sanitation and maintenance. Because very few foodservice operations currently have a preparation unit between procurement and production, it is not included in this text. More and more food products can be purchased peeled, sliced, or portioned, and the few that are not can be prepared by cooks in the production unit. Note in Figure 2.1 that each unit overlaps the other three, denoting their interdependence.

Procurement

The first unit in the foodservice operation, as shown in Figure 2.1, is **procurement,** which is defined as the managerial process of acquiring material for production. Material includes nonfood items such as detergent and disposable tableware, but the chief material is food. Materials brought into the foodservice operation must meet the needs of the cooks in the production area. The quality of purchased food affects the quality of the menu item, and the cost of the item affects the profit.

Figure 2.1.   Functional units of a foodservice operation.

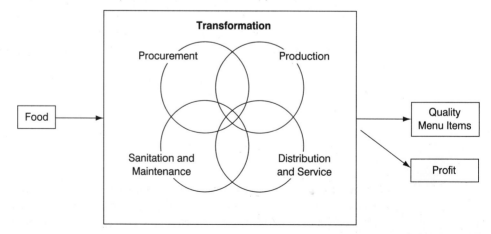

Production

The next unit in the foodservice operation, **production,** is defined as the process by which goods and services are created. Raw food must be prepared and cooked. Many persons believe the objective of a foodservice is to produce the highest possible quality food. In this text, however, the objective of production is to produce quality menu items that satisfy the expectations, desires, and needs of customers, clients, or patients at the lowest possible cost.

Distribution and Service

Distribution and service usually are considered together although these processes may represent two distinct but interrelated functions. **Distribution** is the process of transporting food from the production unit to the service area. **Service** has many definitions but has been defined best by Shames and Glover (1988) as the attempt of a person to fulfill the perceived needs of another within a particular social environment.

Distribution and service in hospitals are very complex and difficult to control; the appropriate food at the correct temperature and quality must be delivered to patients in many locations. Food contractors providing meals for airlines also have many problems to solve, such as varying numbers of passengers and delayed and canceled flights. Because the industry is customer driven, quality of service can make or break a foodservice establishment. Food may be excellent and sanitation above reproach, but if service is lacking the customer will rate the operation as poor. The opposite can occur if the food is mediocre but the waitress or waiter provides high quality service.

Sanitation and Maintenance

Sanitation and maintenance are the fourth unit in Figure 2.1, but they are very much interrelated with the other three. Sanitation and maintenance of the facility and equipment are the two major components of a sanitation program. **Sanitation** is defined by the Food and Drug Administration (FDA) as the use of heat or chemicals to destroy 99.99% of the disease-causing microorganisms on a food-contact surface. **Maintenance,** usually identified as preventive maintenance, is the act of keeping the facility and equipment in a state of repair or efficiency. A facility must be more than clean: It must also be sanitary. **Clean** means *free of visible soil,* while **sanitary** means *free of harmful levels of contamination.* Cleaning and sanitizing are both issues of concern in the maintenance of facilities and equipment. Preventive maintenance has two aspects: regular cleaning schedules and standard procedures and the preventive and corrective maintenance of foodservice equipment and facilities.

PROCUREMENT MANAGEMENT

Management can be defined as a process whereby unrelated resources are integrated for accomplishing organizational goals. Management also has been described as the primary force that coordinates everything happening in the organization. Managers get

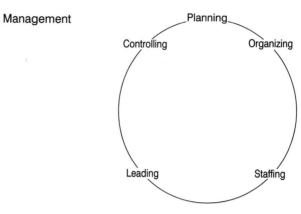

Figure 2.2. Management functions.

things done by working with people and other resources to meet the goals of the operation. Management functions include planning, organizing, staffing, leading, and controlling, as shown in Figure 2.2. Managers of procurement in foodservice operations perform these functions in coordinating all activities of employees. For example, the menu is a basic plan prepared by a manager that indicates the organization of the procurement unit (organizing), the number (staffing) and assignments (leading) of employees, and the quality and cost of the purchased items (controlling). Figure 2.3, developed from a survey of procurement managers and their superiors in multiunit commercial foodservice establishments (Loecker, Spears, & Vaden, 1983), is a model job description for a procurement unit head. Note that the head manages all procurement activities, from purchasing to receiving to storage to inventory control. The objective of the procurement unit is to obtain the best value at the lowest price consistent with established quality standards for products served to customers. In small operations, the foodservice manager often serves as the procurement, production, and service unit heads, but in large operations separate personnel function in these roles.

Figure 2.4 is an abbreviated generic organization chart showing employee positions in the four units of a school foodservice operation. Menu items are prepared in a central kitchen responsible for providing lunches to children in three schools. Note the director of foodservice communicates vertically with the four unit heads in the central kitchen, who communicate horizontally with each other. The heads are responsible for managing their own areas and assigning job activities to their employees. Also, note the placement of the personnel, financial management, materials management, and maintenance departments between the director of foodservice and the four unit heads. The personnel in these departments really serve as consultants to the director and unit heads. Employee, budget, transportation, and maintenance problems and decisions can be discussed and solved by asking for advice from personnel in these departments.

Food Safety Programs

As everyone working in foodservice knows, serving wholesome, tasty, safe food to customers is one of the foodservice manager's primary goals. Nervous restaurant operators turned to the Educational Foundation of NRA for help when illnesses and

Figure 2.3. Procurement manager: commercial foodservice position description.

Purchasing/Procurement
- Obtain the best value at the lowest price consistent with established quality standards and delivery schedules.
- Forecast market conditions, availability of materials, and economic conditions.
- Develop specifications for materials and services in cooperation with personnel responsible for production, including make-or-buy decisions.
- Authorize rejection of materials that fail to meet specifications.
- Maintain files or supplier stock lists, catalogs, price sheets, and discounts.
- Negotiate contracts for food, supplies, and services.
- Determine whether open market or contract is preferable for purchasing various materials and services.
- Coordinate review of purchase contracts by legal counsel and/or other appropriate personnel.
- Determine the cost of deliveries and the best method of transportation.
- Issue purchasing orders for needed materials and services.
- Monitor purchase orders to determine if deliveries are correct.
- Handle communication concerning overshipment, shortages, price changes, etc.

Vendor/Supplier Relations
- Establish a system for supplier selection and rating.
- Select suppliers and negotiate reasonable terms.
- Compare suppliers' product quality, services, dependability, and cost.
- Act as a liaison between suppliers and other departments in your organization in solving problems.
- Oversee distribution of bids and receipt of quotations.
- Create goodwill for your organization through cordial trade relations.
- Work with sales representatives to identify new products, materials, processes, etc.
- Investigate suppliers' facilities, when appropriate.

Inventory/Warehouse Management
- Determine necessary stock levels to provide adequate food and supplies and minimize capital investment.
- Minimize operating costs for storage of food and supplies.
- Monitor records of inventory, materials on order, and potential demands for food and supplies.

Personnel Management
- Determine staffing needs, develop position descriptions, and select qualified personnel for purchasing and storage functions.
- Train and manage purchasing and storeroom personnel.
- Promote good relations between purchasing and other personnel in the organization.

General Management
- Establish priorities for meeting objectives.
- Serve on policy-making team of the organization.
- Monitor flow of materials through the system, from selection to production to service.
- Develop and monitor budget for operations within scope of responsibility.
- Support a program of data processing.
- Promote energy conservation in all operations within scope of responsibility.

Figure 2.4.   Abbreviated organization chart for a school foodservice operation.

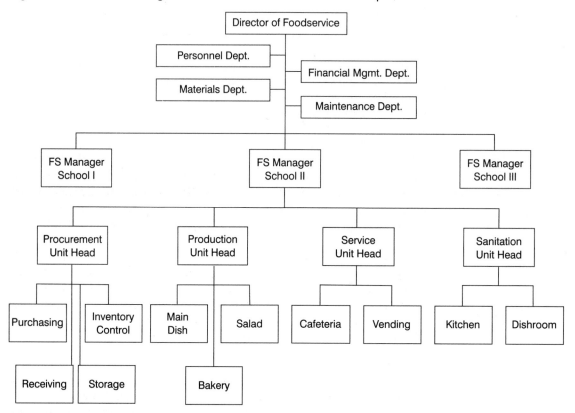

Source: Loecker, Spears, & Vaden (1983).

deaths of customers served undercooked hamburgers in quick-service restaurants made headlines in the early 1990s. Foodservice managers must do much planning, organizing, staffing, leading, and controlling to meet the goal of serving safe food to customers.

ServSafe®

In response to pleas from restaurant operators, NRA's Educational Foundation developed a Serving Safe Food certification course to help leaders in the foodservice industry meet this goal based on the Hazard Analysis Critical Control Point (HACCP) program. The ServSafe® program emphasizes the foodservice manager's role in measuring risks, setting policies, and training and supervising employees. The course includes employee study guides, videos, a leader's guide, and other teaching aids for foodservice employees. Employees who successfully complete the ServSafe® course and examination receive a certificate that is accepted in most areas where training in food safety is required for foodservice employees.

HACCP

Food is the primary resource in a foodservice operation. In the early 1970s developments in food technology influenced changes in food product flow through procurement, production, and distribution and service (Spears, 1995). **Food product flow** refers to the alternative paths within the operation that food products and menu items may follow, beginning with receiving and ending with service to the customer. Physical, chemical, and microbiological changes occurring in food throughout all stages of procurement, production, and service must be controlled to ensure the quality and safety of the finished menu items.

HACCP is the systematic analysis of all process steps in the foodservice units, from food products from suppliers to consumption of menu items by the customer. Analysis is applied throughout food product flow to establish critical controls and eliminate hazardous conditions and procedures. **Hazard analysis** identifies which specific foods are at risk and the locations in the food product flow where mishandling is likely to occur. Critical control points are established to ensure that hazards are corrected.

Food in a foodservice operation flows through receiving, storage, preparation, cooking, holding and service, cooling, and reheating. The illustration on the cover of the NRA ServSafe® certification course book, as shown in Figure 2.5, shows this cycle from receiving food at the loading dock to serving it to customers. Note the "danger zone" warning with the clock and thermometer to emphasize the importance of the time-temperature relationship required from receiving to storage to keep food safe.

Management Functions

Because most students are familiar with management functions, only their application to a real situation will be given. Establishing a food safety program in a foodservice operation probably has been on managers' agendas more often than any other topic. NRA figures show that an outbreak of foodborne illness can cost an operation more than $75,000 (NRA, Educational Foundation, 1992). Cases involving death and serious injury can cost much more. By serving safe food, a manager can avoid:

- legal fees
- medical claims
- employees' lost wages
- cleaning and sanitizing costs

Before applying management functions to a real situation, available food safety programs must be reviewed.

Planning

Planning is defined as determining in advance what should happen in the future. Planning is essential if a manager wants to organize, staff, lead, and control a food safety program. Both short-range and long-range plans must be made depending upon the time required for accomplishment. Planning is paramount in preventing food safety problems.

Figure 2.5.   Serving Safe Food
Certification Coursebook cover.

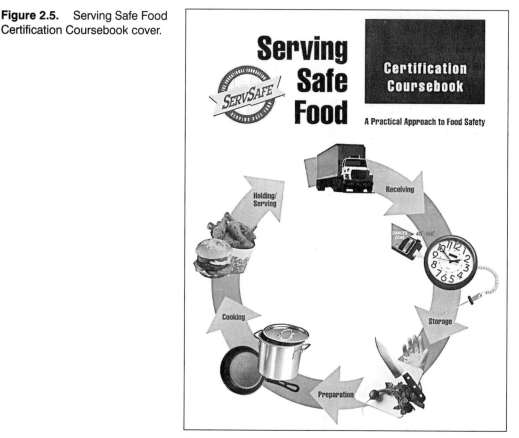

Short-range plans usually cover one year or less. The menu generally is considered a short-range plan because it is controlled primarily by the changing needs of the customer. It becomes the basic plan for the entire foodservice operation; therefore, representatives from each unit should be on the menu planning team.

The operating budget for the procurement unit is another example of short-range planning. The procurement head submits an annual budget to the foodservice manager for the next year that includes employee salaries, maintenance costs, cleaning materials, and clerical supplies to operate the unit. Planning a budget for food products is a difficult task in many commercial foodservice operations because the amount of food purchased depends on the menu and the customer count. A noncommercial operation budget at a school, nursing home, or hospital is much easier to plan because the number of people eating meals is stable and often a cycle menu is used. A budget is a requirement in these operations because funds must be allocated in advance of their usage.

Long-range planning in most foodservice operations encompasses a five-year cycle and begins with an assessment of the current conditions and projections about changes. Food safety and food quality are critical to the bottom line, and sanitary handling of food products is a major factor in both assessments. The foodservice manager is responsible for serving safe food to customers and training employees on a continual basis. The first project, which a manager might approach as a short-term plan, is to develop a sanitation training program for employees. Clean and sanitary equipment and facilities are required before a food safety program is initiated. Then an employee food safety program must be planned and presented as quickly as possible. Long-range planning is necessary to establish a thorough food safety program in the procurement, production, and service units. HACCP is the food safety and self-inspection program that provides managers the tools they need to develop a cost-effective program.

To adopt a ServSafe®/HACCP program in a foodservice operation, unit heads must assume responsibility for planning flow charts for food products that are at risk. The procurement unit head is responsible for receiving and storage. This is an ongoing process because once the various risks for contamination are determined, procedures for the flow of foods must be identified and recorded in the receiving and storage section of the flowchart, as shown in Table 2.1. The HACCP program for purchasing and storing frozen ground beef for use in chili is illustrated. The hazard in purchasing, receiving, and storing frozen ground beef, listed in the second column, is followed by the standards below which the ground beef would be unacceptable. How to monitor the product and the corrective action if the standard is not met also must be spelled out. Finally, results are recorded. Unit heads need to organize their unit to meet the food safety goal by adequately staffing the unit, leading employees, and controlling the quality and cost of the menu items served to the customer.

Organizing

Once planning is accomplished, a unit head should activate the plans. This usually requires development of an organization chart of the entire operation. **Organizing** is the process of grouping activities, delegating authority to accomplish activities, and providing for coordination of relationships, both horizontally and vertically. Figure 2.4 is an abbreviated generic organization chart showing employee positions in the four units of a foodservice operation. Note that the director of foodservice communicates vertically with the four unit heads, who communicate horizontally with each other. The four unit heads are responsible for managing their own areas and assigning job activities to their employees. Also, note the placement of the personnel, financial management, materials management, and maintenance departments between the foodservice manager and unit heads. Staff members in these departments work with both the manager and the heads.

The procurement unit must be organized to accomplish goals through short-range and long-range plans. Employees who are responsible for purchasing food products are ideal members of the menu planning team because they know the availability and price of food. They also can provide good input to the budgeting process through their knowledge of market conditions. Representatives from purchasing, receiving, and storing definitely must be involved in the development of a ServSafe®/HACCP program in the foodservice operation. They are responsibile for

Table 2.1. HACCP flowchart for purchasing, receiving, and storing frozen ground beef for chili.

Operational Step	Hazard CCP	Standard (Criteria)	Type of Monitoring	Corrective Action If Standard Not Met	Records
Purchasing and receiving frozen ground beef	Bacterial growth and survival; chemical or physical contamination	Product obtained from an approved source	Shift manager checks purchase specifications upon receipt of product and invoice	Reject delivery; obtain product from an approved source	Certificate of conformance and invoice
		Accept product at 0°F (−17.8°C) or lower	Shift manager measures temperature with a thermocouple or thermometer	Reject delivery	Receiving log
		Packaging intact	Observation	Reject delivery	
Storing frozen ground beef	Bacterial growth and survival	Store frozen patties in freezer at a unit temperature of 0°F (−17.8°C) or lower	Shift manager measures frozen product temperatures with a thermocouple or thermometer	Move to freezer unit capable of maintaining temperature at 0°F (−17.8°C) or lower until ready to thaw or prepare	Daily inspection audit
		Label, date, and use FIFO method of stock rotation	Check that product is covered and packaging intact	Discard if maximum storage time is exceeded	

creating receiving and storing flowcharts for foods at risk of contamination. The purchasing unit head should inspect wholesale operations for cleanliness and handling of food products in the facility and during transport to the foodservice operation. Employees in receiving must check products delivered to the operation for correct temperatures and clean and unbroken packaging, and storage personnel monitor temperatures and sanitation of storage areas.

Staffing

Among the most critical tasks of a manager is **staffing:** the recruitment, selection, training, and development of employees who will be most effective in helping the foodservice operation meet its goals. In the organizing process, various job positions are defined. In many operations, staffing is carried out primarily by a personnel department that handles routine procedures such as advertising, recruiting, and hiring and serves in an advisory capacity to all departments. Unit heads, who also serve as line managers, are responsible for training and development of employees. Training is an ongoing process and must never be neglected. Incorporating the ServSafe®/HACCP program into the foodservice operation will require additional training for all employees in the four units. The foodservice manager probably will meet with all employees to explain the program before delegating training to the unit heads.

Leading

The leading function of management involves directing and channeling human effort to accomplish objectives. **Leading** is the human resource function particularly concerned with individual and group behavior. Leading is primarily concerned with creating an environment in which employees are motivated to contribute to achieving goals. In the procurement unit, the head and employees decide which products need receiving and storing flowcharts and the critical procedures for each. A minimum of weekly management and employee training sessions on the system are essential.

Controlling

Controlling is the process of ensuring that plans are followed. It involves comparing what should be done with what was done and then taking corrective action, if necessary.

Referring back to the ServSafe®/HACCP program, the desired objective of the procurement unit is to obtain the best value at the lowest price consistent with established quality standards, the most important of which is food safety. The receiving clerk is responsible for taking the temperature of raw meat and checking the packaging for tears at time of delivery. If the temperature is above 40°F for fresh raw meat or 0°F for frozen ground beef or if the package is torn, the shipment is rejected and credit is given to the foodservice operation. Neither of these are within acceptable limits and the corrective action is to reject delivery. The storage employee is responsible for preventing cross-contamination of other foods and stores the meat on the lower shelf of the refrigerator to prevent contamination of foods from meat drippings. The internal temperature of the package should remain at 0°F or lower and be checked often. If the temperature starts to increase, the meat should be moved to a refrigerator for thawing and cooked immediately when it reaches 40°F or discarded if it has been above that level for more than four hours.

MANAGERIAL ASPECTS OF PROCUREMENT

Many management practices proven successful in industry have been adapted for foodservice operations with positive results. Examples include resource management, management of a profit center, strategic planning, and materials management.

Resources

Meeting goals of the organization has top priority for managers. The goal of a foodservice operation is specific: serving quality meals at an acceptable cost to meet the needs of the customer while making a profit and satisfying employees. Managers use the following four resources to meet the goal of the foodservice operation.

- *Human:* Labor and skill
- *Materials:* Food and supplies
- *Facilities:* Space and equipment
- *Operational:* Money, time, utilities, and information

Human

Operational goals cannot be met without employees, the most valuable resource of any industry. Controlling and reducing labor costs and simultaneously increasing labor productivity is a challenge for foodservice managers. Labor cost recently has emerged as the predominant cost in hospitality operations (Keiser & DeMicco, 1993), surpassing food as the biggest expense. If management is to generate a profit for commercial operations or generate revenue for noncommercial, labor control is inevitable. The foodservice industry has some unique labor problems, including high turnover. Employee salaries are lower than in many other industries, and hours may be long and scheduled at times that other working people have social activities. Scheduling and staffing become top priorities for many foodservice managers. In the personnel management section of the procurement unit head position description (Figure 2.3), staffing needs, position descriptions, selection of qualified personnel, training and management, and good relationships with personnel in other units are emphasized. Lowering labor costs by improving productivity and providing satisfactory wages that attract and retain competent employees becomes a monumental challenge for the foodservice manager.

As shown in the ServSave/HACCP long-range planning example, introducing a new project in the procurement unit does not mean that additional employees will be hired. Job positions must be examined and unnecessary tasks eliminated.

Purchasing products that are ready to serve except for final heating decreases labor costs in the production unit. Torn lettuce, potatoes cut for french fries, chopped onions, frozen avocado pulp, portion cut meat and poultry, and baked products all are labor savers for the entire operation. Purchasing these products, however, requires suppliers to communicate up-to-date information to buyers.

Materials

Materials, the resource that makes a foodservice operation unique, include food and supplies. The procurement head or foodservice manager must have a tremendous amount of knowledge about the materials resource because the quality and cost of food and other supplies affect customer satisfaction. Purchasing for a foodservice operation is highly specialized. Procurement unit heads must not only know the products to be purchased but also understand the market, the movement of materials through the market, and federal legislation, which are discussed in Chapter 3. In addition, they must forecast, plan, organize, control, and perform other managerial functions. Buyers also are involved in decision making using techniques adapted from industry, such as value analysis and make-or-buy decisions, which are covered in Chapter 4. The first three sections of the position description in Figure 2.3 pertain to materials management.

Facilities

Space and equipment for materials handling are resources needed for any type of industry. **Materials handling** refers to the movement and storage of materials as they proceed through the foodservice operation. Good design of materials movement increases efficiency. The amount of materials handling often depends on the location and arrangement of receiving, storage, and production areas and on the type of equipment available. Foodservice managers must understand that well-planned space and well-designed equipment are required for an efficient operation. The design and size of the facility have a great effect on the types of food products that must be purchased. If space is not allocated for pre-preparation, frozen, not fresh, vegetables, more ready-prepared menu items, and pies, cakes, and cookies might be purchased.

Operational

Resources essential for the functioning of the foodservice operation are identified as **operational resources** and include money, time, utilities, and information. These resources are the nuts and bolts of making an operation work.

Money.   Because money is essential for operating any kind of business, a budget must be developed to be sure it is spent wisely. A **budget** is a plan for operating a business expressed in financial terms or a plan to control expenses and profit in relation to sales. Expenditures in relation to the projected level of revenues should be estimated for food, labor, and other operational expenses. Each unit manager should submit a budget to the foodservice manager for projected expenses. The procurement head then projects the labor costs and other expenses, such as a new computer, a refrigerator to replace an old one, and clerical supplies. The procurement head bases estimates of food costs on the menu and customer census. The menu planning team should be responsible for the final food budget. The profit objective of the organization also must be considered. The projected profit from a given volume of sales can be estimated and the ability to attain the profit determined.

Time.   Management of time is a constant concern for the manager. Everything that happens in a foodservice operation, from procurement to placing an order before the customer, is geared to meal times. In restaurants in which only fresh fish and seafood are served, buyers become anxious if the delivery is delayed. Canned and frozen products and staples generally are ordered weeks before they are used. Fresh meat, poultry, seafood, and produce might be ordered a week or more in advance, but delivery time needs to be as close to use as possible.

Utilities.   Utilities include gas, electricity, and water, all of which are needed for operating a foodservice establishment. The foodservice industry depends on steady sources of energy just as many manufacturing industries do. The final product, food ready to eat, depends greatly upon energy consuming equipment: refrigerators, freezers, ovens, ranges, dish machines, and water heaters. The space in which employees work and customers are served must be lighted, heated, cooled, and ventilated. To illustrate the dependence of the operation on energy, consider the crises the manager faces when confronted with a power failure at a critical time during production or service. Loss of power, if prolonged, also has tremendous implications for the procurement and supplier storage units because of potential loss of food stored in refrigerators or freezers. Also, storerooms seldom have windows; if the lights go out, work ceases.

A 1984-85 study of seven East Coast quick-service to full-service restaurants found the following energy use (Burman, 1988):

28.0% for climate control

17.8% for hot water

13.5% for lighting

5.8% for refrigeration

34.9% for cooking equipment

In many operations, management has not given sufficient priority to reducing energy usage. Energy costs usually are of limited concern if profit margins are at projected levels.

Information.   Transfer of information that is meaningful to those involved is identified as *communication*. Over the past several decades, use of electronic data processing has increased in foodservice and hospitality operations, driven by the need for more rapid information retrieval to attain effective planning and control. Before the advent of computers, managers frequently lost much valuable information about the operation's activities. Management information functions are the most frequently used computer applications by noncommercial foodservice managers (McCool & Garand, 1986). Preparation of payroll, budget, and food cost reports are applications most frequently cited. Today, almost all foodservice operations have computerized their purchasing and inventory systems.

Profit and Cost Centers

A large percentage of the sales revenue in a foodservice establishment is spent for purchases. Purchasing, therefore, contributes to the profit of the operation. Until recently, purchasing in a large organization, such as a hospital, was considered a service to other departments, and top management considered it as a cost center rather than a profit generator. Some research has been conducted on purchasing as a profit center but none on how to organize and operate a purchasing department as a profit center with measurable bottom-line responsibilities.

However, Reck and Long (1983) discussed the procedures for organizing the purchasing activity to make it a profit center. A **profit center** is any department assigned both revenue and expense responsibilities. It is expected to manage expenses while creating profit for an organization. A **cost center** is a department expected to manage expenses but not generate profits for the organization; it is designed to help other departments contribute to the creation of profit.

The profit center concept is most successful in an organization with a centralized purchasing department that is responsible for all major purchases. Other departments need authority to purchase items and services directly from suppliers if significant cost savings can be achieved. The purchasing department can make a profit by charging a transfer price when selling the items or services to other departments. For example, if the centralized purchasing department is responsible for purchasing canned fruits and vegetables for the foodservice operation, it adds a percentage to the cost of the product to cover the overhead and labor for handling the transaction and to make a profit. A buyer can produce a profit by negotiating for lower prices, consolidating orders from several departments into one large order, developing long-term supply agreements with suppliers in return for larger discounts, and searching for low-cost suppliers and substitute materials.

Even though small foodservice operations seldom have access to centralized purchasing, managers can very easily develop purchasing into a profit center by establishing procedures to reduce costs and thus contribute to profits. Managerial decisions on cost reduction need to include such concerns as geographic location, number of suppliers, storage space, size of inventory, and cost of each purchasing transaction. The procurement unit adds costs to the purchase price of an item as do production, service, and sanitation. These costs, plus a profit margin, become the ultimate cost to the customer. Any savings in the units can be added to profits rather than penalizing the customer if profit increase is the objective. Strategic planning is required to meet this objective.

Strategic Planning

According to Fearon (1988), purchasing is becoming broader in scope and responsibility, requiring the purchasing manager to have a more varied background with a wider range of experience. Because procurement in foodservice operations is considered a profit generator, as it is in other industries, those responsible should be members of the top management team and involved in high-level decision making. The procurement unit should contribute to the goals, one of which is profit, of the foodservice operation. Purchasing managers should set priorities that are most important strategically. Reck and Long (1988) have placed the development of the purchasing activity on a continuum from no direction to being full integration into the strategic planning process.

According to Kast and Rosenzweig (1985), planning is always long range or strategic. Both types of plans are an integral part of the total planning process and establish the basic framework on which more detailed programming and operational planning take place. As stated previously, long-range planning generally encompasses a five-year cycle and begins with an assessment of current conditions and projections about changes. **Strategic planning,** however, concentrates on decisions, not on documented plans, analyses, forecasts, and goals. Strategic planning deals with decisions regarding the broad technological and competitive aspects of the organization, the allocation of resources over an extended period, and the eventual integration of the foodservice operation within the environment. The operation must develop a competitive edge over its rivals by planning effective use of human, materials, facilities, and operational resources. The outcome of the strategic planning process is a brief working document that unifies action of participants toward achievement.

If procurement generally is recognized as an important element of strategic planning, then procurement should be involved in strategic planning and strategic decision making. In a study on purchasing practices, Reid and Riegel (1989) found that 85 percent of 61 multiunit foodservice operations, including retail restaurants, lodging, and noncommercial, indicated that purchasing was involved to one degree or another in strategic planning.

In major decision making, such as changing the concept of a foodservice operation, all management personnel must be involved. The procurement unit is responsible for scanning the market for food items required for a new menu item and finding a processor or wholesaler who can handle the volume. Specialized equipment and serving containers for the new menu items probably need to be purchased. Specifications must be written and prices solicited for food products and equipment. A strategic decision, such as this example, involves everyone in the foodservice operation and must be well planned.

Materials Management

The concept of **materials management** has been well expressed by Dillon (1973) as the unifying force that gives interrelated functional units a sense of common direction. The goal is to transform materials into an output that meets definite standards for quantity and quality. An organization using the concept has a single manager responsible for the planning, organizing, motivating, and controlling of all activities principally concerned with the flow of materials into an organization (Leenders, Fearon, & England, 1993). Materials management expressed in operational terms is an organizational concept of centralizing responsibility for those activities involved in moving materials into and in some cases through the organization. Functions usually include purchasing, receiving, storage, inventory control, and traffic, with production control and related activities sometimes included. Procurement therefore is a critical component of the materials management concept.

The need to control the overall cost of materials and to minimize excessive inventories has started a trend to use the materials management concept in foodservice industries. A materials manager has a crucial role in Stouffer's frozen food division. A number of hospitals, both small and large, now have a materials manager in a staff position with advisory responsibilities for all material resources. In Figure 2.4, the materials manager position is shown as a staff position giving advice to both top management and the procurement manager. A materials manager is a consultant to all departments or units on the movement of materials through the organization. In smaller operations that cannot justify an additional staff person, the materials management function could be performed by top level management.

PROCUREMENT ACTIVITIES

Several important activities exist within the procurement unit: purchasing, receiving, storing, and inventory control. Each of these activities has distinctive definitions and components. **Purchasing** is an activity concerned with the acquisition of goods; it is often described as obtaining the right product in the right amount, at the right time, and at the right price. To do this, food and supply buyers must know the market and the products and possess general business know-how. They also need to rely on sales representatives for advice on purchasing decisions and valuable information about available food items and new products. Within the purview of purchasing, procedures must be developed for selecting products, choosing a purchasing method, selecting and evaluating suppliers, completing purchase records, and establishing a code of ethics (Spears, 1995). As purchasing becomes broader in scope and responsibility, it requires a purchasing manager with a more varied background and a wider range of experience (Fearon, 1988).

Receiving can be defined as a process for ensuring that products delivered by suppliers are those that were ordered by the purchasing department. After food and supplies have been received properly, they must be placed in appropriate **storage,** which is the holding of goods under proper conditions to ensure quality until time of use. **Inventory** is a record of food and supply assets owned by the organization, and **inventory control** is the technique of maintaining items in storage at desired quantity levels (Spears, 1995). Good management techniques must be applied to all these activities for efficient foodservice operation.

SUMMARY

The goal of a foodservice operation is to serve quality meals while maximizing value both for the foodservice and the customer. Raw food or food in various stages of preparation is transformed through the procurement, production, distribution and service, and sanitation and maintenance units of the foodservice operation into a quality menu item that satisfies the customer and makes a profit. Management is responsible for what happens in the change of food products to menu items.

Management is a process whereby unrelated resources are integrated for accomplishing the goal of a foodservice operation, which is to serve quality meals at an acceptable cost to meet the needs of the customer while making a profit and satisfying employees. Four resources are available for meeting the goal: human (labor and skill), materials (food and supplies), facilities (space and equipment), and operational (money, time, utilities, and information).

Purchasing should be managed as a profit center, not a cost center. Strategic planning that concentrates on decisions regarding the technological and competitive aspects and eventual integration of the organization into the environment is required if profit increase is the objective. Materials management is the unifying force that gives interrelated functional units a sense of common direction. Responsibility for moving materials through purchasing, receiving, storage, inventory control, and traffic is centralized; often production control and related activities are included.

Several activities exist within the procurement function. Purchasing is an activity concerned with the acquisition of goods. It is often described as obtaining the right product in the right amount, at the right time, and at the right price. Receiving is a process for ensuring that products delivered by suppliers are those that were ordered by the purchasing department, and storage is the holding of goods under proper conditions to ensure quality until time of use. Inventory is a record of food and supplies owned by the operation, and inventory control is the technique of maintaining items in storage at desired quantity levels.

REFERENCES

Burman, J. (1988). Keeping an edge on energy costs. *Restaurants USA, 8*(7), 20–23.

Dillon, T. F. (1973). Materials management: A convert tells why. *Purchasing, 74*(5), 43.

Fearon, H. E. (1988). *Purchasing organizational relationships.* Tempe, AZ: National Association of Purchasing Management.

Kast, F. E., & Rosenzweig, J. E. (1985). *Organization and management: a system and contingency approach* (4th ed.). New York: McGraw-Hill.

Keiser, J., & DeMicco, F. M. (1993). *Controlling and analyzing costs in food service operations* (2nd ed.). Upper Saddle River, NJ: Merrill/Prentice Hall.

Leenders, M. C., Fearon, H. E., & England, W. B. (1997). *Purchasing and supply management* (11th ed.). Homewood, IL: Irwin.

Loecker, K. A., Spears, M. C., & Vaden, A. G. (1983). Purchasing managers in commercial foodservice organizations: Clarifying the role. *Professional, 2*(1), 9–16.

McCarthy, T. (1991). The definitions of value. *Nation's Restaurant News, 25*(4), 40.

McCool, A. C., & Garand, M. M. (1986). Computer technology in institutional foodservice. *Journal of the American Dietetic Association, 86,* 48–56.

National Restaurant Association, The Educational Foundation. (1992). *Applied foodservice sanitation* (4th ed.). Chicago: Author.

National Restaurant Association, The Educational Foundation. (1995). *Serving safe food, certification coursebook.* Chicago, IL.

Reck, R. R., & Long, B. G. (1983). Organizing purchasing as a profit center. *Journal of Purchasing and Materials Management, 19*(Winter), 2–6.

Reck, R. R., & Long, B. G. (1988). Purchasing: A competitive weapon. *Journal of Purchasing and Materials Management, 24*(3), 2–8.

Reid, R. D., & Riegel, C. D. (1989). *Purchasing practices of large foodservice firms.* Tempe, AZ: National Association of Purchasing Management.

Shames, G., & Glover, G. (1988). Service management as if culture exists. *International Journal of Hospitality Management, 7*(1), 5–7.

Spears, M. C. (1995). *Foodservice organizations: A managerial and systems approach* (3rd ed.). Upper Saddle River, NJ: Merrill/Prentice Hall.

Virts, W. B. (1987). *Purchasing for hospitality operations.* East Lansing, MI: Educational Institute of the American Hotel and Motel Association.

3

The Market

"Going to market" is a phrase often used by chefs who pride themselves on serving only the freshest vegetables they pick up daily at the local farmer's market. French women have special baskets which they use to shop for a "loaf of bread, a hunk of cheese, and a bottle of wine" at the town square market. These markets often are identified as places in which food items are sold—a building or an outdoor stand, for example. For professionals who purchase food items in large quantities, however, the market has a different meaning. The **market** is defined as the medium through which a change in ownership moves products from producer to customer.

PURVEYORS get stuff to market

KINDS OF MARKETS

We all have heard the childhood rhyme, "to market, to market, to buy a fat pig." Of course, today with the emphasis on low fat foods, the pig would be lean. Foodservice operations use many kinds of markets, all of which can be classified by

44

type of material or location. Foodservice markets may be meat or fresh produce establishments or locations in Chicago or Mexico.

Type of Material

Material resources in a foodservice operation consist of food products and nonfood products identified as supplies. Food markets are those in which food products are sold, including grains; fresh or processed vegetables and fruits; meat, seafood, poultry and eggs; milk and cheese; and beverages. The buyer should have knowledge not only about these various food products but also how long their shelf life is and how each has been stored before purchasing.

Nonfood products for a foodservice operation include such items as large and small equipment, tableware, uniforms, and disposables. Contracts for such services as entertainment, equipment rental, laundry, maintenance, and pest control are becoming more prevalent and therefore must also be discussed. Contracts are purchased as are any nonfood products.

Geographic Location

Markets often were identified as primary, secondary, or local by their location, but these terms are no longer used because a more practical system for getting perishable food to the supplier has been developed. Primary markets used to be the major sources of supply not only in the United States but also in the world. Prices were set in primary markets, quality standards determined, and other factors essential for promoting the movement and sale of products analyzed. A strong transportation network was needed to move perishable products quickly from primary to secondary to local markets. For many years, Chicago was the primary market for meats, particularly beef, but it no longer has stockyards or slaughterhouses. Cattle were sent there to be fattened and slaughtered before being shipped as carcasses to secondary markets for fabrication before sending the meat to local markets. All that is left is the Chicago Mercantile Exchange, which deals with futures trading as a hedge against price increases.

Currently, cattle raised on ranches in the Midwest—Kansas, Nebraska, North Dakota, Oklahoma, and Texas—are sent to feed lots and processors nearer to the ranch. The same pattern is followed with lamb raised in Texas, California, and the Rocky Mountain states; with seafood from the Atlantic and Pacific Oceans and the Gulf of Mexico; and fresh vegetables and fruits in California, Florida, Texas, and Mexico. Processing is occurring as close to the source of these and other products as possible, thus reducing transportation costs and shortening the time before products reach the customer.

Local markets receive products from local farms or processors and sell them to customers in a specific geographic area. Prices are not set or standards established by the local market. Rather, the local market responds to the needs of local customers who expect certain products. Today, with the emphasis on providing fresh food to customers, farmers and seafood markets have become very popular because of their accessibility to chefs and cooks.

MARKETING CHANNEL

Today's buyer has a powerful influence on the world food distribution system. The buyer is the one who listens to the desires of customers, who determines what is grown and packaged, and who understands how items are processed or manufactured, shipped, sold, and consumed. If an item cannot be sold, it will not be grown or manufactured or marketed.

Therefore, this exchange of ownership of a product occurs in the marketing channel, sometimes called the distribution channel, as shown in Figure 3.1. The **marketing channel** indicates the exchange of ownership of a product from the producer through the manufacturer or processor and the distributor to the customer. Products are distributed through the channel from the producer to the customer and procured by reversing the path of the product from the customer to the producer.

Components

The marketing channel has five major components: producers, manufacturers or processors, distributors, suppliers, and customers. Value and cost are added to the product in each of these components and are reflected in the final price paid by the customer.

Figure 3.1.   The marketing channel.

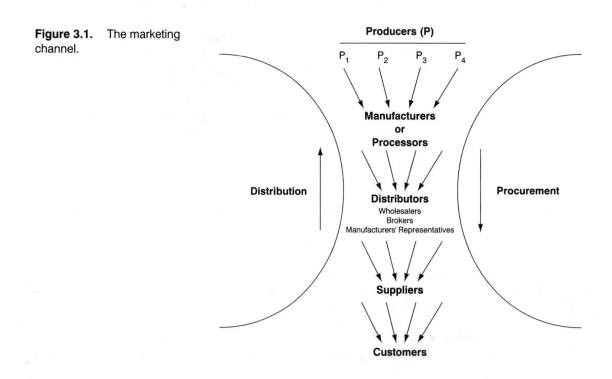

Producers

Producers, generally farmers or ranchers, produce raw food to sell to manufactur- ←
ers or processors, who sell to distributors or directly to the foodservice operation. ←
The products are then sold to customers. The abundance of food in the United States ←
is not caused by more people, animals, and land on today's farms, but is rather the
result of increased efficiency in agricultural operations resulting from application of
advances in science and technology. The amount of land used for producing food
has not really expanded, but the amount of food produced per acre has increased
tremendously. This increase results from improvements in production methods, animal and plant genetics, and farm mechanization. Each year more food for more people is produced by fewer farmers. In 1940, one farmer produced food for about 12
people. Today one farmer can produce food for more than 80 people.

Processors

The food supply in the United States is marketed not only by quantity but also by
quality, variety, and convenience (Potter, 1986). In the early 1900s, food spoiled
quickly and variety was limited because most products were seasonal. In contrast,
today supermarkets stock more than 12,000 items and distributors vie for shelf space
in heavy traffic aisles. The processor is responsible for the many forms of a food
available to the customer.

For example, ranchers raise calves to a weight of 500 to 600 pounds before transferring them to a feed lot, which functions as a feed growing area, where their weight is
brought up to 1,000 to 1,200 pounds. The cattle are then sold directly to a meat packing plant near the feed lot in which cattle are slaughtered and the meat is processed,
portioned, and packaged in plastic film before boxing it. The boxes are then shipped
to all parts of the country in refrigerated trucks in 50,000-pound loads to warehouses.
Distributors store the meat temporarily under refrigeration before selling it to the supplier, which sells it to a commercial or noncommercial foodservice operation, which
converts it to menu items and sells it to the customer. Another example is an equipment
manufacturer who buys stainless steel from a producer to manufacture dish machines
to sell to a foodservice operation through a distributor and supplier.

Buyers for large foodservice operations—quick-service restaurant chains, for example—often bypass distributors by purchasing directly from the producer or
processor and then act as their own wholesalers. Buyers for a chicken chain might
purchase chickens directly from a producer that meets their specifications and then
transfer the chickens to a processor that prepares them for cooking in the operations.
Many of these chains own or subsidize a number of producers for the entire lot of
chickens; the buyer is assured of a constant flow of chickens even at times of a shortage. The foodservice manager should evaluate carefully the cost of transferring this
responsibility to the buyer; often money is not saved.

Distributors

Distributors, the third component in the marketing channel, are persons who are
responsible for transferring products from the processor or manufacturer to the

supplier. They are classified as wholesalers (including superdistributors), brokers, and manufacturer's representatives. Some small manufacturing or processing plants sell products directly to the foodservice operation, but the large size of most plants precludes this type of selling. These operations must rely on distributors, especially if they do not have their own salespeople.

Wholesalers.   **Wholesalers** are distributors who purchase from various manufacturers or processors, provide storage, sell, and deliver products to suppliers. The wholesaler protects the quality of a product from the time it is purchased to the time it is delivered to the foodservice operation. For example, the wholesaler learns from agents in the field the best time to purchase products, the grade, packaging, and handling of products before delivery and storage in the wholesale warehouse. Wholesalers can be either full or broadline, specialty, or special breed distributors (Gunn, 1995). **Full or broadline wholesalers** generally carry large amounts of stock, permitting the buyer to purchase everything from frozen and canned products to kitchen equipment and furniture. **Specialty wholesalers** deal in a particular product category, such as meat, produce, dairy, paper, or detergent. Milk and bread companies are specialty manufacturers and distributors.

Many of the large multiunit foodservice corporations serve as wholesalers by establishing food and nonfood warehouses and selling and distributing products to the units. Only bread, milk, and produce must be purchased locally. Some multiunit corporations have a commissary in which raw food is converted to products in various stages of production for selling to the individual units. Centralizing production can decrease labor costs and control quality.

Services beyond delivery that help a manager do a better job are expected by foodservice managers. Distributors who provide such services at no additional cost differentiate themselves from their competition, giving foodservice managers more incentive to do business with them. These extra services could include merchandising advice for menu items or products, seminars, order entry and inventory control options, nutritional analysis of food products, quality testing, and salad bar merchandising. Probably the most appreciated service is product education to introduce new products and exciting ways to present them to customers.

Special breed distributors are purchasing and product movement specialists whose customers are restaurant chains that purchase food directly from processors and hire a distributor to deliver the products. These distribution companies include such industry giants as Martin-Brower Company with 26 warehouses delivering more than $3 billion worth of food a year and Golden State Foods, the second largest, delivering $990 million a year. More than 30 of these companies deliver at least 13 percent of all food sold wholesale. Many special breed companies were formed with assistance from large chains to deliver products to their individual restaurants. If the ownership of a restaurant changes or the chain files for bankruptcy, the need for products also changes, resulting in financial losses for many special breed distributors. The 1990s also saw the emergence of a global economy affecting the foodservice distribution industry. Managers of a large noncommercial foodservice operation, such as a city school lunch program, should be aware of special breed distributors as potential suppliers.

Another type of distribution company, which has become very popular in the United States, is the wholesale club or supermarket. These companies started in big cities but have extended to smaller communities. Not only do they carry food products in household sizes, but they also have large sizes, such as number 10 cans of vegetables and fruits, 10-pound bags of chicken breasts, and 25-pound bags of detergent. Many small foodservice operators purchase most of their supplies from these wholesale clubs because the large distributors could not justify the cost effectiveness of delivering to them. The one disadvantage is that purchases are cash and carry, but the advantage is that the price is competitive with the large distribution companies because transportation costs are eliminated.

Brokers. **Brokers** are independent sales and marketing representatives who contract with manufacturers, processors, or prime source producers to both sell and conduct local marketing programs with wholesalers, suppliers, or foodservice operators, according to the National Food Brokers Association (NFBA). They represent a variety of products. Buyers often seek out brokers when they are "sourcing out" a new or existing product. Brokers do not take title to the products they sell. They are retained by manufacturers, processors, or producers who contract and pay a commission for their services. The NFBA does not consider the broker a distributor but rather an aid to sales and marketing in an operation. Brokers are not employed by or affiliated with the buyer to whom they sell and are not subject to the buyer's direct or indirect control. In the marketing channel, however, they are classified as distributors.

Today's brokerage firm is a sophisticated business employing staff with a variety of responsibilities, including account management, marketing, retail service, menu planning, foodservice promotion concepts, and technical support. Brokers vary in size from small firms with fewer than 10 employees to large regional companies with hundreds of employees. Processors of products needed by foodservice operations can go through regional managers who manage a number of brokers in a geographic area. Brokers often have test kitchens in which products for the foodservice market are prepared and tested. Foodservice brokers must be aware of their customers' needs and must know their products to find the right one for restaurant owners, dietitians, and chefs. For example, potato producers have been using the services of brokers for many years. The broker seeks out growers with one-pound baking potatoes to sell to a wholesaler or directly to a restaurant with a potato bar. A different kind of potato is needed for a french fry processing plant or a quick-service restaurant chain, in which case the broker would have to test different kinds of potatoes to find the best ones for frying.

Manufacturers' Representatives. **Manufacturers' representatives** do not take title, bill, or set prices. They usually represent small manufacturing companies, often including foodservice equipment manufacturers. The companies pay a flat commission on sales volume. This method of selling is probably the most economical because the company does not have to maintain sales offices in every area their customers are. Manufacturers' representatives are not empowered to enter into contracts on behalf of the companies they represent and can only make small decisions. They have fewer and more specialized lines than a broker and a minimum number of manufacturers. They have greater product expertise than brokers. For example, they might represent a manufacturer of ranges and ovens, refrigerators and freezers, transport carts, or dishmachines. Often they represent two or more of these products.

Suppliers

Suppliers are the fourth component in the marketing channel. They sell products to the ultimate buyer, the customer. The foodservice manager generally will buy more often from the supplier than from a wholesaler, broker, or manufacturer's representative because of the convenience of doing one-stop shopping by dealing with a prime supplier, often referred to as a single source supplier. This type of supplier is used for most purchases. Most foodservice managers favor the "don't put all your eggs in one basket" approach, preferring instead to bid out individual line items. By doing so, they believe, they get the most competitive prices and avoid being at the mercy of one particular supplier (Savidge, 1996). Some managers, especially in small operations, like the more personalized service prime suppliers give them. They agree that using this type of supplier is not necessarily the cheapest way to buy, but it certainly makes purchasing a simpler process. In the long run, it pays off.

However, the co-op/prime supplier arrangement often used in school foodservices offers advantages to both the supplier and buyer. Suppliers enjoy a guaranteed portion of a big school foodservice pie, while school districts enjoy the lower costs associated with volume purchasing along with the ease of dealing with one supplier. Savidge warned that despite the pluses of relationships with one supplier, risks are still possible: when the bottom falls out, as in a market crash, the destruction of crops by bad weather, or the supplier going bankrupt, you could lose everything.

Customers

The **customer,** anyone who is affected by a product or service, is the fifth component of the marketing channel. According to the NRA (National Restaurant Association, 1997), almost half of all adults were foodservice patrons on a typical day during 1995. Men eat out more than women: an average of 4.6 meals per week versus 3.8 per week in 1995. Customer satisfaction becomes the goal of the foodservice industry, and purchasing quality food and related products should be the first objective for the foodservice operation.

Value-Added

The cost of taking food products through the marketing channel often equals or even exceeds the initial cost of the products. Value is added to products at each step in the marketing channel, not solely due to what happens in the channel. **Value-added** is the increase in value caused by both processing or manufacturing and marketing or distributing, exclusive of the cost of materials, packaging, or overhead. The objective of value-added is to increase the marketing value of raw and semiprocessed products.

Processing flour to adapt it for specific baking purposes is an example of the value-added concept. Research has proven that wheat flour after original milling is not satisfactory for products such as bread, rolls, biscuits, cakes, doughnuts, pie crust, crackers, pasta, and thickening agents for sauces and puddings. An example of modification of wheat flour is cake flour in which the amount of gluten is reduced to produce a fine-textured cake. The value-added cost of a special purpose flour includes the miller, research scientist, necessary production facilities, and distribution of the product.

Produce distributors have been increasing the market value of fresh fruits and vegetables for some time and are constantly coming up with new ideas for the foodservice manager to control labor costs while improving quality. Peeled oranges are available, as are grapefruit sections and fresh pineapple chunks. Peeled potatoes have virtually eliminated potato peeler equipment, which was a necessity in every foodservice operation not too many years ago. Not only are peeled potatoes available but potatoes can be purchased cut into any shape the operation needs. Lettuce heads still can be purchased, but many operators now buy lettuce torn or chopped. A tossed salad mix currently is a popular product. Caterers are putting more of their labor dollars into service rather than production. For example, watermelons are now carved into baskets that can be filled with a large assortment of fruits cut into various shapes.

Pricing

Occasionally, the wholesale price of a food item may be more than the "bargain special" at the local supermarket. For example, a large chain-affiliated supermarket may bypass distributors by purchasing hundreds of pounds of frozen turkeys directly from the processor. The supermarket price then can be much less than the restaurant or school foodservice buyer pays to the wholesaler. Such price differentials are part of buyers' concerns but are usually beyond their control.

Every foodservice manager believes suppliers should be paid a fair price for purchased materials. What is a fair price? According to Leenders, Fearon, & England (1989), a **fair price** is the lowest price that ensures a continuous supply of the proper quality where and when needed. Of course, continuous supply is possible only if the supplier is making a profit from sales.

An important part of price determination involves discounts and paybacks available on given purchases. Cash and quantity discounts are the most common given by suppliers to foodservice operations, and occasionally a promotional discount is available. Paybacks on quantity purchases in cash or prizes generally are given by processors.

A **cash discount** refers to a percentage reduction in the price of a product if the bill is paid within a specific time period before, at the time, or shortly after the product is delivered. Suppliers offer cash discounts that vary both in the amount allowed and the period during which the discount can be taken. The most common cash discount is stated as *2/10, net 30:* if the buyer pays for the products within 10 days of delivery, a 2% discount can be deducted from the price on the invoice. If the payment is delayed beyond 10 days, the amount on the invoice must be paid. If, however, the bill is not paid within 30 days, the supplier may start collection procedures and often will add interest for the extended period. In some foodservice operations, the accounting department may have payment of bills on a different schedule and buyers cannot bargain for discounts.

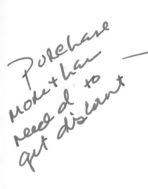

A **quantity discount** refers to a percentage reduction in the price of a product if the amount ordered exceeds the amount established by the supplier. For example, a case price is set for each canned product, but if a foodservice orders a full pallet of 56 cases of one product, the distributor may give a 3% discount.

Rebates from processors are another form of discounting for quantity. Special promotions by a processor might be available to foodservice operations. Promotions change annually. For example, if the foodservice buyer purchases 1,000 cases of the processor's products this year, 25 cents per case could be refunded to the operation. Rebates often are in the form of prizes; for instance, three bicycles might be given to a foodservice operation during Nutrition Week if it purchases 500 cases of the processor's products.

The supplier or processor usually justifies such discounts and paybacks on the basis of savings realized from selling in large quantities. Also, the savings in marketing expenses are no greater for a large order than for a small one, and the billing expense is the same. Substantial savings in processing costs are possible if orders are placed in advance of production. From the buyer's viewpoint, the cost of storing a large quantity of canned goods for a long time might be greater than the savings. The money could be invested instead of tying it up in products sitting on the shelf.

A **promotional discount** refers to a reduction in the price of a product if the product is featured in the operation. For example, a brand name mentioned on the menu might result in a discount from the processor.

Buyers often have difficulties in evaluating the price of a product without knowing how much value was added in the marketing channel. Many factors affect fair price, including supply and demand, competition, and perceived value.

Supply and Demand

Supply and demand is a basic economic concept that greatly influences the price paid for a product. The greater the supply and the smaller the demand, the lower the prices. Conversely, the smaller the supply and the greater the demand, the higher the prices. Generally when supply is high, quality of the product is high and the price is low; the highest quality and the lowest prices of fresh vegetables and fruits or seafood are available when the supply is the greatest.

Seasonality, the time when the quality of raw food products is highest, always has been a prime factor in supply and demand. The quality and greatest supply of broccoli in the United States is from February through April, of tomatoes July through October, and of cantaloupe June through August. Seafood also is seasonal in the area in which it is caught; for example, North Pacific king salmon is at its peak from April to August and New England lobsters from May to December. Today with the popularity of salad bars and seafood restaurants, the demand curve is flattening and prices are a little more stable during seasons when supply is lower. This change in the demand curve has caused distributors to seek out new sources of supply for off-season.

For example, tomatoes are imported to the United States from Mexico and grapes from Chile because customers want these products all year. Foodservice managers need to know when the greatest number of animals are sent to market because meat prices will be the lowest at these times. In the fall, prices tend to drop, and they increase in late winter and spring. Prices for pork decrease in June and January because young pigs are six months old and ready for the market at those times.

If supply and demand were the only factors controlling prices, farmers would have no control over prices that could be charged for foods sold. Economic and political conditions and the influence of the business community can have a great effect on prices. A pricing plan under the authority of the Agricultural Marketing Act of 1937 has established prices for three classifications of dairy products: fluid milk (milk, skim milk, buttermilk), soft milk products (cream, yogurt, cottage cheese, ice cream), and hard milk products (cheese, butter, dry milk) (Kotschevar & Donnelly, 1999). Milk supply is constant and customers can purchase as much milk as they desire at a reasonable price. Congress has established funds for purchasing dairy herds to control the number of products on the market; these animals are slaughtered and sold often as lower grade meat.

Probably more control by states is put on alcoholic beverages than any other consumable product in the market (Kotschevar et al., 1999). Some states dictate brands that purveyors carry or billing, shipping, and receiving procedures. Prices usually are controlled by local, county, state, and federal regulations; if not, trade associations or suppliers often restrict free purchasing, or purchasing without controls.

Suppliers also participate in the supply and demand concept. If a supplier has a large amount of a product on hand, price cutting might be the solution. Holding the product on a shelf costs the supplier money that could be drawing interest in the bank. Shelf space is very expensive. Suppliers quite often will forfeit profit by reducing the price to the buyer, thus creating a demand by the buyer.

Competition

Competition, the act of winning out over other suppliers, comes into action. Suppliers generally emphasize the overall value of the product. We have previously cited Virts' (1987) definition of value as "the perceived relationship between quality and price; as these relationships change, perceived value changes." Virts emphasized that *perceived value* should be used because value means different things to different people. He developed an equation to show that *perceived value* is directly related to *perceived quality* and *perceived supplier services* but inversely related to *perceived as-served cost* of food or beverages or *perceived as-used cost* of supplies.

$$\text{Perceived value} = \frac{\text{perceived quality} + \text{perceived supplier services}}{\text{perceived as-served or as-used cost}}$$

If the quality and supplier services costs remain the same and the as-served cost decreases, the value of the product increases. If, however, quality decreases and supplier services and as-served costs remain the same, the value of the product decreases. Supply and demand creates a price level that includes profit for the supplier even though prices can vary among them.

Most products enter the marketing channel in their basic form, such as wheat, cattle, or fruits and vegetables. These products are processed in a variety of ways, adding different levels of value to the basic form, and then are sold to distributors who sell them to the customer. The final product should be equated with the price before the customer makes a decision.

An excellent example of the supply and demand theory was given by the restaurant analyst at Prudential Securities in New York who wrote the comprehensive report "Where Is the Beef and Where Is It Going?" (Papiernik, 1996). The report stated that "1996 is apt to be a transition year from beef-cost declines to flat-to-higher beef costs, which could pose a problem depending on the trends in other costs." A correlation was found between grain prices and what was happening in the beef industry; changes in one area of commodity pricing ripple through the entire food-pricing arena. For instance, though soaring grain prices increased the cost of flour and thus baked goods, pizza, and pasta, these prices were triggering cattle ranchers to sell off their herds for earlier slaughtering. Ranchers did so because the cost of continuing to feed cattle was higher than the price they could get by fattening them up. The mass move toward disposal of cattle led to an oversupply in the market, triggering even lower prices for beef and resulting in lower costs for foodservice operators, which helps to offset increases in other food products. This could all lead to a depletion of cattle in future years by triggering a beef shortage and higher prices as the cattle supply is built up.

The analyst gave some examples by going into the effect of higher prices on various foodservice operations. She postulated that chain companies like McDonald's, in which lower beef prices have encouraged a sales strategy built on value pricing, could face pressure. For instance, a chain like Wendy's focuses on product quality rather than low pricing. Wendy's uses fresh beef for hamburgers instead of the frozen beef its competitors use. Frozen hamburgers can be contracted when price of beef is low, but fresh beef is more susceptible to market price swings. If, however, beef prices across the board force competitors to raise prices, then the gap between Wendy's and the others would narrow. Because Wendy's has a high quality product, they might sell more hamburgers and take over the market. McDonald's already is beginning to cover its bases against such an event by taking advantage of low beef prices and coming up with specials. For example, the Arch Deluxe was recently replaced with the Mega Mac, which will probably be replaced when sales decline or beef prices increase. Promotion of this adult-sized sandwich stresses both quality and low cost. The old cliché is that a vicious cycle could occur.

FEDERAL LEGISLATION

The purpose of federal legislation is to protect the consumer without stifling industry and, therefore, national economic growth. Government, industry, and the consumer need to interact to accomplish this purpose; each is interdependent and mutually affects the performance of the other two, as shown in Figure 3.2. Government is responsible for enacting legislation that safeguards the consumer and at the same time promotes competition among industries. With the ultimate goal of satisfying the consumer while making a profit, industry is responsible for

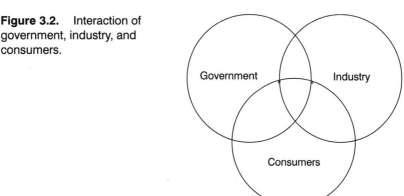

Figure 3.2. Interaction of government, industry, and consumers.

complying with this legislation. Consumers, who are becoming increasingly vocal about such issues as food safety, nutrition, and the environment, alert government about their concerns and expect industry to produce appropriate products.

Legislation Promoting Competition

The U.S. government seeks to support competition by preventing either the buyer or supplier from taking advantage of the other in pricing a product unfairly or using collusion. The four most important federal laws protecting pricing and competition are the Sherman Antitrust, Federal Trade Commission, Clayton, and Robinson-Patman Acts.

Sherman Act

[handwritten: Promotes Competition]

Any combination, conspiracy, or collusion with the intent of restricting trade in interstate commerce is illegal under the Sherman Antitrust Act of 1890. The government was given the power to break up monopolies. The act concerns agreements between buyers and sellers or competitors that prevent either from making decisions on their own. If suppliers band together to fix prices or boycott certain other suppliers, their action is deemed illegal.

Federal Trade Commission Act

[handwritten: Prevents (tie in) tie in purchasing]

The federal government controls antitrust violations through the Federal Trade Commission and the Clayton Act, both established in 1914. The commission has the power to pursue companies engaging in unfair competition through deceptive advertising and promotions or monopolies in the market. The commission clarifies and increases the power of the Sherman Act.

Clayton Act

An extension of the Sherman Act is the Clayton Act, which outlaws tie-in sales that occur when a supplier requires the buyer to purchase one product before purchasing another one. Sometimes a manufacturer or processor will make a deal so good on the purchase of two products that the buyer cannot refuse it. A hypothetical example is requiring customers to buy a turkey before they can buy the stuffing mix or cajoling them into buying both products because the price is good. Because of the Federal Trade Commission and Clayton Acts, this unfair practice is seldom found in foodservice operations.

Robinson-Patman Act

Unfair pricing methods were restricted by the Robinson-Patman Act of 1936. A supplier must not discriminate prices between customers purchasing the same product in the same quantity. Exceptions are discounting for large quantities, lowering prices for products that are obsolete or have a short shelf life, and meeting lower prices by competitors in the same area.

Legislation Related to the Foodservice Industry

Comprehensive and complex federal regulations make the food industry the most controlled industry in the United States. Although many federal agencies are responsible for regulations that directly affect the industry, the U.S. Department of Health and Human Services (DHHS) and the U.S. Department of Agriculture (USDA) are the most often involved. The U.S. Department of Commerce also is becoming involved because of the great concern for the microbiological safety of seafood for human consumption.

U.S. Department of Health and Human Services

The Federal Food, Drug, and Cosmetic Act was passed in 1938 and is enforced by the Food and Drug Administration (FDA), a DHHS agency. The Public Health Service Act is administered by the same department.

Federal Food, Drug, and Cosmetic Act.   The purpose of the **Federal Food, Drug, and Cosmetic Act** is to ensure that foods other than meat, poultry, and fish are pure and wholesome, safe to eat, and produced under sanitary conditions. The law also specifies that packaging and labeling agree with the contents.

   Mandatory Standards.   The act provides three mandatory standards—identity, quality, and fill of container—for products shipped across state lines. **Standards of identity** establish what a given food product contains. Certain ingredients must be present in a specific percentage before the standard name may be used. For example, the consumer is assured that any product labeled mayonnaise, regardless of its manufacturer, contains 65 percent by weight of vegetable oil, along with vinegar or lemon juice and egg yolk. Products labeled mayonnaise that do not contain egg yolk violate FDA regulations. For example, low-cholesterol mayonnaise that contains only egg white with an added stabilizer does not meet this standard of identity. The FDA has initiated a review of standards of identity for such products that will include public hearings resulting in either a change in regulations or prosecution of current violators.

If a food does not meet the FDA quality standards, it must be labeled "Below Standard of Quality" and can bear an explanation such as "Good Food–Not High Grade," "Excessively Broken," or "Excessive Peel." **Standards of fill** tell the packer ← how full a container must be to avoid a charge of deception. ← (False packaging)

Amendments. Two major amendments to the Federal Food, Drug, and Cosmetic Act are the Food Additive (1958) and Color Additive (1960) amendments, both of which safeguard the consumer against adulteration and misbranding of foods. **Adulterated food** contains substances injurious to health, is prepared or held under unsanitary conditions, or is filthy, decomposed, or contains portions of diseased animals. Another addition was the Miller Pesticide Amendment of 1954, which provides procedures for establishing tolerances for residues of insecticides used with both domestic and imported agricultural products. Tolerances of permitted residues are established by the Environmental Protection Agency, but the FDA is responsible for their enforcement. The FDA samples dairy products, fish, fresh and processed fruits and vegetables, and animal foods for unsafe residue levels.

Food irradiation is classified as a food additive and is regulated by the FDA. **Irradiation** refers to exposure of substances to gamma rays or radiant energy. The process for some foods has been approved since the 1960s, followed in 1985 by approval of irradiation to control trichina in pork and, in 1992, to control foodborne pathogens and other bacteria in frozen poultry, including ground poultry products (Derr, 1993). The position of the ADA adopted on October 29, 1995, is that food irradiation is one way to enhance the safety and quality of the food supply. The ADA encourages the government, food manufacturers, food commodity groups, and qualified dietetics professionals to continue working together in educating consumers about this technology. Ionizing radiation has energy high enough to change atoms by knocking an electron from them to form an ion, but not high enough to split atoms and cause foods to become radioactive. The amount of energy absorbed by a food is measured in units called *kilograys* (kGy). Less than one kGy inhibits the sprouting of tubers in potatoes, delays the ripening of some fruits and vegetables, controls insects in fruits and stored grains, and reduces the problems of parasites in foods of animal origin. One to 10 kGy control microbes responsible for foodborne illness and extend the shelf life of refrigerated foods. More than 10 kGy are used only on spices and dried vegetable seasonings.

Genetically Engineered Food. In May 1992, the FDA proposed that the same policy for regulating the safety of all other foods be used for genetically engineered foods. The policy should be based on the characteristics of the food and not the processes used to produce them (FDA Issues, 1992). **Genetically engineered food** is food that can be altered to reduce spoilage and improve flavor by splicing in new genes or eliminating existing genes. To bring these new foods to the market more quickly, FDA announced that genetically engineered fruits and vegetables produced through a process known as *recombinant DNA*, a new combination of genes, would need no special testing or labeling. By splicing in new genes or suppressing or eliminating existing genes, the genetic makeup of a food can be altered (Cheney, 1992). The gene that activates the enzyme causing rotting in a tomato does not act until the tomato is mature. Scientists at Calgene have found a way to "turn off" that gene, creating the Flavr Savr tomato introduced to the public in 1993.

When genetically altered foods were introduced, more than 1,000 chefs pledged to boycott them. They did not want to give their customers food that might cause allergic reactions or concerns for people of certain religions (pork genes for Jewish or Muslim customers) or vegetarians (flounder genes in tomatoes) (Allen, 1992). The American Dietetic Association has taken the position that "the techniques of biotechnology are useful in enhancing the quality, nutritional value, and variety of food available for human consumption and in increasing the efficiency of food production, processing, distribution, and waste management" (Position of The American Dietetic Association, 1993).

GRAS List.   The government publishes a **Generally Recognized as Safe** (GRAS) list of safe substances, authorized by trained scientific experts, that may be added to foods. In enacting the 1958 Food Additives Amendment, Congress had to consider how to classify the hundreds of food ingredients already on the market, which had been used safely for many years. Congress exempted two categories of substances from the food additive regulation process. The first category applies to substances the FDA or USDA had determined were safe to use in food prior to 1958. The second category was GRAS substances in use before 1958; the most widely recognized example is food flavorings. Because flavorings are such a small portion of a product's ingredients, GRAS review of flavors had a low priority (GRAS status, 1992).

In 1959, the Flavor and Extract Manufacturers Association established an expert panel to determine the GRAS status of several hundred flavor substances. A requirement for determining GRAS status is that safety information about the substance is available in the scientific literature for public review. Only two decisions have been challenged. The FDA even submitted a list of several hundred natural flavor substances for evaluation. Many companies file a petition with the FDA for GRAS approval of a substance. If the petition contains the required information, the FDA will accept it and publish a notice in the *Federal Register* (GRAS status, 1992).

The Delaney Amendment requires that food additives suspected of being carcinogenic be removed from the market. Sulfur dioxide, the fumes of which are used to prevent darkening of dried potatoes and some dried fruits, and sodium nitrate, used in preserving and keeping the color in hams, are suspected carcinogens. These substances are still on the GRAS list, but the government requires that the addition of sulfites be stated on the label. Sulfites are not permitted to be used in produce.

Labeling of Food.   A food is considered misbranded if the label does not include adequate or mandatory information or provides misleading information. The objective of the **Fair Packaging and Labeling Act** of 1967 is to ensure that the consumer can obtain accurate quantity and content information from a food label, thus permitting value comparison.

Nutritional information is mandatory on labels only for foods for which a nutritional claim is made or that have added vitamins, minerals, or protein (Pennington and Hubbard, 1997). Nutrition labeling information for other foods up to this time is voluntary. Many food processors, however, provide nutritional information upon request. Since 1986, sodium content must be listed on all processed foods regulated by FDA that have nutrition labeling.

Public Health Service Act.   The most rigid control for food is placed on the production, processing, and distribution of Grade A milk. The Public Health Service standard for Grade A milk is largely a standard of wholesomeness. Grade A on fresh milk means that it has met state or local requirements equal to or exceeding federal requirements.

U.S. Department of Agriculture

The USDA has an important role in the food regulatory process. It is authorized to make public food regulations by Federal Meat Inspection, Poultry Inspection, Egg Products Inspection, and Agricultural Marketing Acts. One of its most important functions, authorized by the Agricultural Marketing Act, is the grading, inspection, and certification of all agricultural products. U.S. grades are levels of quality, and U.S. grade standards define the requirements met by a product to obtain a particular grade. The use of U.S. grades, however, is voluntary. The **Food Safety and Inspection Service** (FSIS) of the USDA is responsible for ensuring that meat and poultry products destined for interstate commerce and human consumption are wholesome, unadulterated, and properly labeled. Those products must not pose any health hazards.

The USDA has established grade standards for fruits, vegetables, eggs, dairy products, poultry, and meat products. The varying terminology in standard grades has led to much consumer confusion, and many believe a uniform grade terminology is needed. A summary of grades in use today is shown in Table 3.1.

The USDA also is responsible for enforcing four federal acts. The **Meat Inspection Act** provides for the destruction of diseased and unfit meat, regulates sanitation in meat plants, requires stamping of inspected meat, prevents addition of harmful substances in meat products, and eliminates false or deceptive labeling. The Meat Inspection Act was amended by the **Wholesome Meat Act of 1967,** which requires inspection of all meat if it is moved within or between states and inspection of foreign processing plants exporting meats to the United States.

The Poultry Products Inspection Act was amended in 1968 and designated as the **Wholesome Poultry Products Act,** which requires inspectors to assess the cleanliness of plants and maintenance of equipment. Inspection procedures for poultry are similar to those required for meat. Labels on poultry and poultry parts also must be approved. Under the Egg Products Inspection Act (1978), plants that break and further process shell eggs into liquid or dried egg products are similarly inspected. In all three acts, monetary and technical assistance is provided to aid plants in meeting federal requirements.

The USDA **Agricultural Marketing Service,** in cooperation with state agencies, offers official grading or inspection for quality of processed dairy products, poultry and eggs, fresh and processed fruits and vegetables, and meat and meat products. Grading is based on U.S. grade standards developed by the USDA for these products. The **food acceptance service,** developed by the USDA, is included in the grading and inspection programs and provides impartial evaluation and certification that food purchases meet contract specifications. Any healthcare organization, commercial foodservice, governmental agency, educational institution, or public or private groups

Table 3.1. Summary of major grades of food categories.

Product	Products Graded	Grading Criteria	Quality Grades Highest ⟶ Lowest					
Beef	54%[a]	Eating quality Color of flesh Firmness and marbling	Prime, Choice, Select, Standard, Commercial, Utility, Cutter, Canner					
Veal	na[b]	Eating quality Flesh and bone color	Prime	Choice	Good	Standard	Utility	Cull
Lamb	na	Eating quality Bone-to-meat ratio Flesh color Firmness and marbling	Prime	Choice	Good		Utility	Cull
Pork	na	Primarily yield	No. 1	No. 2	No. 3	No. 4	Utility	
Poultry	89% turkey 67% chicken and other	Confirmation Fleshing Fat covering	Grade A		Grade B			Grade C
Eggs	40%	Appearance of shell Size of air cell Condition of yolk and white	Grade AA	Grade A	Grade B			Grade C
Fish	na	Appearance Uniformity Absence of defects Texture Flavor and odor	Grade A		Grade B			Grade C

Product	Percent of products sold[a]	Quality factors	Grades (highest to lowest)
Milk, fluid	na[b]	Bacterial count; Sanitary conditions	Grade A (only grade for human consumption); Grade B
Milk, nonfat dry	na	Flavor and odor; Bacterial count; Scorched particle content; Lumpiness; Solubility	U.S. Extra; U.S. Standard
Milk, whole dry	na	Moisture content	U.S. Premium; U.S. Extra; U.S. Standard
Butter	63%	Flavor and odor; Freshness; Plasticity; Texture	Grade AA; Grade A; Grade B
Cheese (Cheddar, Swiss, Colby, Monterey Jack)	na	Flavor and odor; Texture; Body; Appearance; Finish; Color	Grade AA; Grade A; Grade B; Grade C
Produce — Frozen	55%	Maturity; Shape; Color; Size; Uniformity; Texture; Presence of defects	U.S. Fancy; U.S. No.1; U.S. No. 2; U.S. No. 3
Produce — Fresh	45%		(USDA reports 156 different grades for fruits, vegetables, and nuts)
Produce — Canned	35%		

[a] Percent of products sold, Agricultural Marketing Service, USDA, 1987.
[b] na = data not available

buying food in large quantities may use the service on request. Suppliers often use the acceptance service to ensure that they meet contract specifications.

If purchases are to be certified by the USDA acceptance service, contracts with suppliers should include this provision. The supplier is then responsible for obtaining certification, which, like all grading services, is provided for a fee. Contract specifications for the products can either be based on USDA grade standards or tailored to meet the buyer's needs. They may include USDA grades, condition, type of refrigeration, cut, trim, size, packaging, weight, shape, and color.

To provide the acceptance service, an official grader employed by the Agricultural Marketing Service or a cooperating state agency examines the product at the manufacturing, processing, or packing plant or at the supplier's warehouse. If the product meets contract specifications, the grader uses an official stamp on the package or case to certify that the product is accepted. The grader also issues certificates indicating that the products comply with the contract specifications.

U.S. Department of Commerce

Public attention has been focused on the fact that fish and seafood are not subject to mandatory continuous inspection as are meat and poultry. Reports concerning the safety of seafood have been appearing on television and radio and in newspapers. Some restaurateurs have noticed a decline in seafood sales as a result of the negative publicity. Customers and the seafood industry are asking for a national inspection program. Prominent chefs and restaurant owners have been lobbying in an effort to convince Congress to toughen existing seafood inspection standards (Walkup, 1992).

The **U.S. Department of Commerce** was established in 1903 to promote American businesses and trades; one of its responsibilities is to expand U.S. efforts. The **National Marine Fisheries Service,** under the Department of Commerce, offers a voluntary inspection program. The FDA is responsible for inspection and sanitation of U.S. fish and seafood plants; it also monitors imports and interstate shipments for compliance with the Federal Food, Drug, and Cosmetic Act. Some consumer groups have advocated a mandatory seafood inspection program. The U.S. General Accounting Office (GAO) indicated that the following concerns need special attention:

- Improved tests to measure microbiological contamination in shellfish
- Increased public awareness of risks of consuming raw mollusks
- Greater enforcement of bans on harvesting shellfish from closed or contaminated areas
- Additional research on chemical contamination of seafood

Congress has directed the National Oceanic and Atmospheric Administration to review current fish inspection programs and recommend needed changes. Until inspections are required, foodservice operators should be sure that fish is fresh and purchased from a reputable source and that fresh oysters, clams, and mussels from out of state have a certified shipper's tag on which the number of the bed where the shellfish was grown and harvested is identified.

Imported Food Regulations

The FSIS is responsible for the safety of meat and poultry imported into the United States. Foreign countries must impose inspection requirements at least equal to those in the United States to make products eligible for import. The point of entry inspection includes examination of net weight, condition of the container, incubation of bacteria in canned products, and the label. A laboratory analysis is performed, including testing for drug and chemical residues.

Nonmeat and poultry items in packages and requiring no further processing are under FDA jurisdiction. The FDA has limited authority to inspect foreign manufacturing and processing facilities. The FDA has a low sampling rate of products but is improving inspection of imported foods with a computer system called the Import Support and Information System (ISIS) that will be able to profile firms, products, and countries of origin to identify problems and detect trends.

SUMMARY

Market is defined as the medium through which a change in ownership moves products from producer to consumer. Markets can be identified in a foodservice operation by type of material, food or nonfood products, agent, wholesaler and others, and geographic location.

The exchange of ownership of a product occurs in the marketing channel. The producer sends products to processors or manufacturers, which sell the items to distributors, which then sell to the customer. Value and cost are added to the product in each component and are reflected in the price the consumer has to pay. Many factors affect fair price, including supply and demand, competition, and perceived value.

The food industry is the most controlled industry in the United States today. The Federal Food, Drug, and Cosmetic Act of 1938 is enforced by the Food and Drug Administration, an agency within the Department of Health and Human Services. The act ensures that foods other than meat, poultry, and fish are pure and wholesome, safe to eat, and produced under sanitary conditions and that packaging and labeling accurately reflect the contents.

The USDA is authorized to make public food regulations by the Federal Meat Inspection, the Poultry Products Inspection, and the Agricultural Marketing Acts responsible for grading, inspection, and certification of all agricultural products. The Food Safety and Inspection Service (FSIS) is responsible for ensuring that meat and poultry products destined for interstate commerce and human consumption are wholesome, unadulterated, properly labeled, and not hazardous to health. The USDA Agricultural Marketing Service, in cooperation with state agencies, offers official grading or inspection for quality of manufactured dairy products, poultry and eggs, fresh and process fruits and vegetables, and meat and meat products. The National Marine Fisheries Service, under the Department of Commerce, offers a voluntary inspection program for fish and seafood, which are not subject to mandatory continuous inspection as are meat and poultry.

REFERENCES

Allen, R. L. (1992). New York chefs speak out against genetic engineering. *Nation's Restaurant News, 26*(24), 3, 75.

Cheney, K. (1992, Oct. 7). Cooking up controversy. *Restaurants & Institutions,* 14–15.

Derr, D. D. (1993). Food irradiation: What is it? Where is it going? *Food & Nutrition News, 65*(1), 5–6.

FDA issues food biotech guidelines. (1992, July/August). *Food Insight,* 6.

GRAS status: What's in a name? (1992, July/August). *Food Insight,* 6–7.

Gunn, M. (1995). *First choice, a purchasing systems manual for school foodservice.* National Foodservice Management Institute. University, MI.

Kotschevar, L. H., & Donnelly, R. (1999). *Quantity food purchasing* (5th ed.). Upper Saddle River, NJ: Merrill/Prentice Hall.

Leenders, M. C., Fearon, H. E., & England, W. B. (1997). *Purchasing and supply management* (11th ed.). Homewood, IL: Irwin.

National Dairy Council. (1997). Newer knowledge of milk and other fluid dairy products.

National Restaurant Association. (1997). 1995 National Restaurant Association foodservice industry pocket factbook. *Restaurants USA, 14*(11), attachment.

Papiernik, R. L. (1996). Where's the beef? You might find it in your margins. *Nation's Restaurant News, 30*(21), 11, 59.

Pennington, J. A. T. & Hubbard, J. S. (1997). *Journal of the American Dietetic Association,* 97: 1407–1412.

Position of The American Dietetic Association: Biotechnology and the future of food. (1993). *Journal of The American Dietetic Association, 93*(2), 189–192.

Position of the American Dietetic Association: Food Irradiation. (1996). *Journal of the American Dietetic Association, 96*(1), 69–72.

Potter, N. N. (1986). *Food science* (4th ed.). Westport, CT: Avi Publishing Company.

Savidge, T. F. (1996). Putting your eggs in one basket. *School Foodservice & Nutrition, 50*(4), 26–28.

Virts, W. B. (1987). *Purchasing for hospitality operations.* East Lansing, MI: Educational Institute of the American Hotel and Motel Association.

Walkup, C. (1992). Group of chefs joins chorus for seafood inspection. *Nation's Restaurant News, 26*(11), 3.

4

Product Selection

Purchasing for a foodservice operation is a highly specialized job function. Buyers must know not only the products to be purchased but also the quality of the products, quantity to purchase, technique for analyzing value, and rationale for making or buying the menu items. The primary function of the buyer is to procure the required products for the desired use at minimum cost. Accomplishing this function involves planning, organizing, controlling, and research by the buyer to aid in decision making.

QUALITY CONTROL

The word *quality* has different meanings to different people. The objective of a foodservice operation often is stated as the production of the highest possible quality food. This leads to the difficult problem of defining quality. David (1979) suggested that quality may be a fancy name for whatever one likes; quality tells you where you ought to go. If we believe that the objective of a foodservice is to satisfy the expectations, desires, and needs of customers, clients, or patients, we begin to realize that quality has a different meaning to each of these groups (Spears, 1995). For example, hamburgers sold at a quick-service restaurant have a different quality of meat than does broiled or grilled chopped sirloin steak served in an expensive restaurant. Both, however, have the desired quality expected by the customer for the price. Price cannot be separated from value primarily because value is the over-all impact a product makes upon a customer's quality of life.

In essence, **quality control** in a foodservice operation assures day-in, day-out consistency in each product selected to serve to the customer. Controlling, one of the management functions discussed in chapter 2, is the process of ensuring that plans are followed. Standards, specifications, and the sensory analysis process all serve as controls in purchasing products with the quality desired by the customer and the price required by the foodservice manager.

Standards

Standards are a result of the managerial process of planning. In the discussion in chapter 2 on the managerial function of controlling, these standards were defined as the measurement of what is expected to happen. **Standards,** therefore, provide the basis for monitoring performance of the foodservice operation and taking any cor-rective action deemed necessary. Most standards are established by the federal gov-ernment for food, microbiological safety, facility sanitation, and nutrition.

Food

The role of the Food and Drug Administration (FDA) in enforcing the Federal Food, Drug, and Cosmetic Act is discussed in depth in chapter 3. Standards of identity, quality, and fill of container for processed food items crossing state lines are estab-lished. The role of the U.S. Department of Agriculture (USDA), also discussed in chapter 3, is to assure wholesomeness of agricultural products consumed by the pub-lic. The USDA has a voluntary quality grading service for wholesome products sup-ported by standards for each grade.

Referring back to Table 3.1, note the grading criteria for each food group. These criteria are standards that denote limitations for the various levels of quality. For ex-ample, eating quality of beef can vary from fine to coarse and firm to flabby texture. The color of the meat and the amount of marbling also are indicators of quality.

Microbiological Safety of Food

The ultimate goal of a foodservice sanitation program is to protect the customer from foodborne illness. Achievement of that goal requires a two-pronged strategy: pro-tecting food from contamination and reducing the effect of existing contamination (National Restaurant Association [NRA], Educational Foundation, 1992).

Possibilities for contamination of food before it is purchased include contaminated equipment, infected pests and animals, untreated sewage, unsafe water, and soil, as shown in Figure 4.1. After purchase, possibilities of contamination exist in storage, preparation, and service of food. Following human consumption, illness occurs and

Figure 4.1.   Transformation of a foodborne illness.

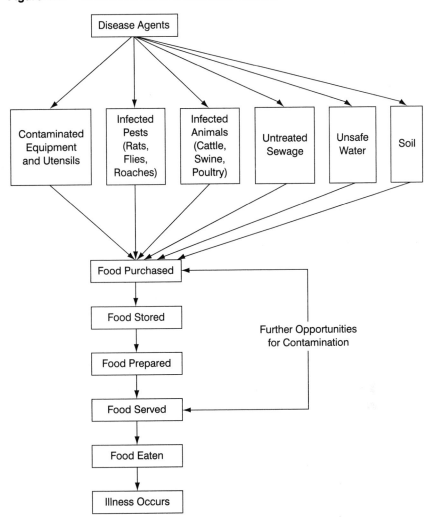

Source: From National Restaurant Association, Educational Foundation, 1985.

can be transmitted from infected persons through respiratory tract discharges, open sores, cuts, and boils or through hands soiled with feces into food being prepared. The consumed food then completes the transmission to other persons.

Reducing the effect of contamination is largely a matter of temperature control in the storage, production, and service of food. The **food danger zone** is between 40°F and 140°F, temperatures at which bacteria multiply rapidly (Figure 4.2). Four hours is the longest time food can safely remain in this zone, although food should not be in the 60°F to 100°F temperature zone longer than two hours. Both time and temperature are important in handling food to preserve microbiological quality.

Control of the microbiological quality of food must focus on the food itself, employees and patrons involved in handling food, and the facilities, including both

Figure 4.2. Important temperatures in sanitation and food protection.

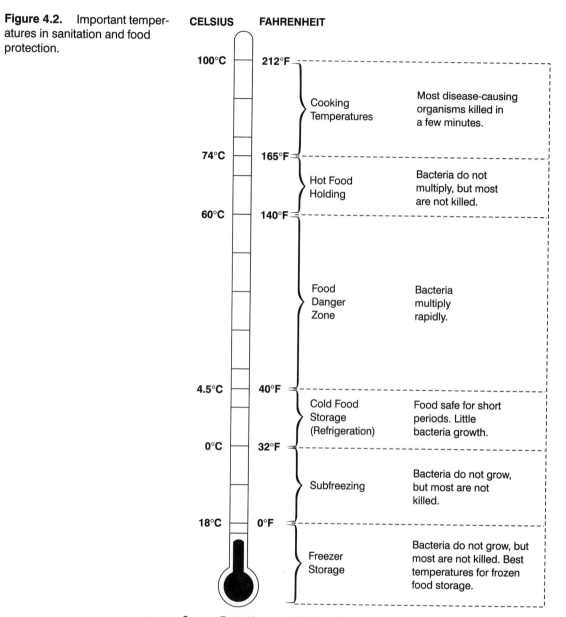

Source: From *Home and Garden Bulletin No. 162,* USDA, 1970, Washington, DC: USDA.

large and small equipment. Clearly, the condition of food brought into a facility is a critical aspect to consider as are practices during storage, production, and service.

The Hazard Analysis Critical Control Point (HACCP) program was developed in 1971 by the Pillsbury Company for the National Aeronautics and Space Administration (NASA) to be sure food fed to astronauts in outer space is absolutely safe. The system had to ensure zero defects in handling food during processing. It had to correct errors before they happened rather than sample finished products to identify those with high levels of contamination (NRA, Educational Foundation, 1992). The ServSafe® course developed by NRA was based on HACCP.

At each step in the flow of food through the operation, a **risk,** which is a chance that a condition in foodservice will lead to a hazard, can occur. A **hazard** is considered an unacceptable contamination. As risks are determined, procurement unit heads need to identify in the receiving and storage areas **critical control points,** defined as procedures by which a preventive or control measure can be applied to prevent hazards.

With the exception of certain cultured foods, such as blue veined cheeses and yogurt, only pathogen-free ingredients with low levels of microbial count should be purchased. The purchasing manager should check sanitary practices in warehouse and transportation vehicles before selecting a supplier. If food safety is not monitored before purchasing, other areas may use contaminated products that will affect the safety of products served to customers.

Increased numbers of highly processed foods used in some foodservice operations have caused concern about potential hazards to public health. The FDA, responsible for the establishment of microbiological quality standards, has set acceptable microbial levels for food products to protect customers.

Protection of the food supply available to the customer is the responsibility of governmental agencies at the federal, state, and local levels. The U.S. Public Health Service (PHS) and its subdivision, the FDA, both of which are agencies with the U.S. Department of Health and Human Services (DHHS), are charged specifically with promoting the health of every American and the safety of the nation's food supply. Two agencies within the PHS related to sanitation standards and regulation are the Centers for Disease Control (CDC) and FDA. The CDC is charged with protecting public health by providing leadership and direction in the control of diseases and other preventable hazards. The CDC is responsible for identifying causes of foodborne illnesses and the FDA for protecting the nation's health from unsafe and impure foods.

Facility Sanitation

Many state and local governments have adopted PHS codes in establishing standards of performance in sanitation for foodservice establishments. State and local health agencies act to ensure that foodservice establishments:

- are equipped, maintained, and operated to offer minimal opportunities for food hazards to develop;
- use food products that are wholesome and safe; and
- are operated under the supervision of a person knowledgeable in sanitary food handling practices (Longree & Armbruster, 1987).

The government has been interested in securing the sanitary quality of food for many years. Periodic inspections are made by officials of state or local agencies to compare performance of foodservice operations with standards of cleanliness and sanitation. The FDA has developed a Model Food Service Sanitation Ordinance to assist health departments in developing regulations for a foodservice inspection program. Some state and local agencies develop their own codes. The FDA recommends inspections at least every six months, although the frequency is determined by the local agency.

A **sanitarian,** often referred to as the health official or inspector, is an individual trained in sanitation principles and methods and public health (NRA, Educational Foundation, 1992). The foodservice manager and unit head should accompany the sanitarian during inspection. They should take advantage of the experience and expertise of the sanitarian by asking questions; employees should be encouraged to do the same. They should take notes during the inspection and be willing to correct problems, such as no thermometers in refrigerators or freezers and cases of food on the floor in the storage area. Based on their years of experience, sanitarians generally can offer advice on correcting violations. Foodservice managers and employees should welcome a visit from the sanitarian and not resent it if they are truly dedicated to serving safe food to customers.

The receiving area should be designed for ease in cleaning. The floor should be of material that can be easily scrubbed and rinsed and have adequate drains and a water connection nearby to permit hosing down the area. Storage for cleaning supplies should be located conveniently. Since insects tend to congregate near loading docks, adequate screening must be provided. Outdoor zappers are electrocutor traps used to destroy flying insects and should carry the Underwriters Laboratory (UL) seal for electrical safety. The Underwriters Laboratory® is an organization responsible for the compliance of equipment with electrical safety standards. The light produced by the zapper attracts insects and therefore should be mounted in the loading dock area but not near the exit door (NRA, Educational Foundation, 1992).

Floors in the dry storage area must be easy to clean and slip resistant to prevent accidents. External walls and subfloors should be well constructed, insect- and rodent-proof, and insulated. Walls and ceilings should be painted light colors, have a smooth surface that is impervious to moisture, and be easy to wash and repair. Products never can be stored on the floor; they should be stored on shelves or pallets to permit frequent floor cleaning. If steam lines, duct work, and hot water lines must pass through the dry storage area, they should be insulated.

Cleanability that promotes sanitation is a significant need in walk-in refrigerators and freezers. Hard-surface, easy-to-clean floors, walls, and fixtures should be of smooth, nonabsorbent material. Drains to remove scrubbing water and condensate should be located inside walk-ins. Finally, uniform ventilation and adequate lighting should be provided in these units as an aid in maintaining sanitary conditions. Any deficiencies must be corrected before the next inspection. Local health agencies generally have authority to close an operation that has an inordinate number of deficiencies in meeting sanitation standards. Immediate action also is required if violation is extremely dangerous.

A number of other organizations are active in upgrading and maintaining the sanitary quality of various food products and establishing standards for foodservice operations. The NRA Educational Foundation has taken leadership in developing standards and promoting training in foodservice sanitation. The foundation has been a major contributor to the upgrading of sanitation practices through its national uniform sanitation, training, and certification plan for foodservice managers. A course was developed in 1974 and revised in 1978, followed by a certification plan under contract with the FDA. All students who complete the course and pass an examination receive an Educational Foundation Certificate of Completion.

NSF International, formerly called the National Sanitation Foundation, is one of the most influential agencies concerned with sanitation. **NSF International** is a non-profit, noncommercial organization that seeks solutions to problems involving cleanliness and sanitation. It is dedicated to public health safety and environmental protection by developing standards, providing education and superior third-party conformity assessment services, and representing the interest of all stakeholders. On the basis of research results, NSF develops minimum sanitation standards for equipment, products, and devices. Manufacturers can request that NSF evaluate their equipment, and they receive an NSF Testing Laboratory Seal of Approval for equipment meeting NSF standards. Purchasers for noncommercial foodservice operations generally specify that equipment be approved by NSF. Increasing numbers of commercial operations also have this requirement.

Nutrition

Foodservice managers can no longer afford to ignore customer demand for nutritionally adequate menu offerings. Nutritional needs of customers should be a primary concern in all foodservice operations, especially in those that provide the greatest percentage of their customers' daily nutrients. Restaurant managers do not have this problem because very few customers eat the majority of their meals in one restaurant. However, restaurants must meet the demands of a growing number of customers for foods lower in fat, salt, and sugar if a profit is to be made. "Heart Healthy" foods are featured on many restaurant menus. Even chefs who have been notorious for preparing food items rich with butter, cream, and eggs are learning to modify recipes. The Culinary Institute of America in Hyde Park, N.Y., considered one of the finest chef training schools in the country, not only has a nutrition component in the curriculum but has an entire building designated as the General Foods Nutrition Center with a registered dietitian (RD) on staff.

Nutrition Guidelines.   The USDA's illustration of the *1995 Dietary Guidelines for Americans,* developed by the USDA and DHHS, is an abstract diagram of seven colored rings (Figure 4.3) that are designed to answer the question, What should Americans eat to stay healthy? They provide advice for healthy Americans ages two years and older about food choices that promote health and prevent disease. To meet the guidelines, choose a diet with most of the calories from grain products, vegetables, fruits, lowfat milk products, lean meats, fish, poultry, and dry beans. Choose fewer calories from fats and sweets. Many people would have difficulty in converting the statements into servings of familiar food items.

The NRA supports the 1995 guidelines and highlights a statement that delights many consumers and restaurateurs: The new recommendations state that drinking alcohol not only can enhance meals but also might have health benefits if consumed in moderation (Ruggiero, 1996). The second notable change is the emphasis on daily moderate physical activity and the suggestion that adults should strive for a healthy weight. Instead of saying that adults should "use" sugars, salt, and sodium in moderation, the guidelines now say that people should "choose a diet moderate in sugars, salt, and sodium." The guidelines also include instructions about ways to use the Food Guide Pyramid and the Nutrition Facts Label.

Figure 4.3. Dietary guidelines for Americans.

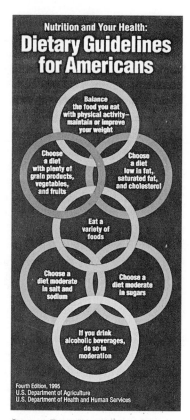

Source: From "Nutrition and Your Health: Dietary Guidelines for Americans" by USDA and DHHS, 1995, *Home and Garden Bulletin No. 232,* Washington, DC: USDA and DHHS.

In the spring of 1992, the USDA launched the Food Guide Pyramid (Figure 4.4 and Plate 1), the first official attempt to illustrate dietary guidelines in a meaningful way. The **Food Guide Pyramid** is a complex illustration with many different food and nutrition messages: dietary variety; moderation of fats, oils, and sugars; and the relative amount of food from each major group determined by the number of recommended daily servings. The pyramid does not include all dietary guidelines; salt or sodium, alcohol, and weight are not included. The pyramid augments, but does not replace, the guidelines. The Purchasing Food Products section of this book is based on the Food Guide Pyramid.

Foodservice Responsibilities.   What effect does this customer interest in nutrition have on the responsibilities of the foodservice buyer? A whole new facet has been added to the buyer's duties. Knowledge of the nutritional value of foods is crucial in making purchasing decisions. Customers are concerned about the amount of fat in their diets. Meat trimmed of fat and skinless chicken parts can be specified by the buyer. Polyunsaturated oils can replace saturated oils in salad dressings, and

Figure 4.4.   USDA Food Guide Pyramid.

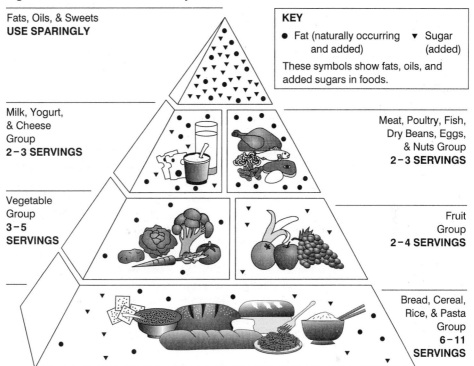

Source: From "USDA Food Guide Pyramid" prepared by Human Nutrition Information Service, August 1992, *Home and Garden Bulletin No. 252,* Washington, DC: USDA and DHHS.

egg substitutes can replace whole eggs in baked products to reduce the amount of cholesterol.

Lower calorie products, such as canned fruit packed in fruit juice or beverages, yogurt, or baked products prepared with sugar substitutes might be purchased to meet customer demands. On the other hand, in spite of the emphasis on low calorie desserts, foodservice operations offering high calorie foods such as pie, doughnuts, ice cream, and anything chocolate and rich are enjoying high sales volumes. Also, use of herbs and spices other than salt for seasoning has increased tremendously.

Customers also are requesting high fiber products, linked to reduced incidence of cancer. Vegetarian diets are no longer uninteresting. As a result, dried beans, lentils, peas, and other legumes are featured on many menus. Excellent pasta, bean, or rice entrées often are offered as alternatives to meat. Cereal has become a staple on menus and variety is unbelievable. Bread items also are very popular, especially those prepared with whole grains.

Alcoholic beverage consumption has decreased in this country. When customers do drink, however, they order more premium brands of spirits, wines, and beer than ever before. Driving while under the influence (DUI) of alcohol is dangerous and carries stiff penalties upon arrest and conviction. A "designated driver" who drinks only nonalcoholic beverages is an increasingly common solution. Consequently, nonalcoholic beverages, such as colas, sparkling spring waters, and fruit and vegetable juices, are growing in popularity.

Customers are demanding more fresh than processed foods, and some insist on organically grown products. Fresh fruits and vegetables rather than canned or frozen products are featured in many restaurants. An increasing number of restaurants are advertising that only fresh fish is served. *Fresh* translates as *nutritious* to many customers. The result is that produce and fish orders probably will be placed more often, and deliveries will occur more frequently.

Nutrition Labeling.   The **Nutrition Labeling and Education Act** of 1990 lays out the regulations that went into effect in 1994 for nutrition labeling for most foods sold in grocery stores. Voluntary programs for nutrition information for many raw foods, including the 20 most frequently eaten raw fruits, vegetables, and fish and the 45 best-selling cuts of meat, are encouraged by FDA. Under the act, some foods are exempt from nutrition labeling. These include:

- Food served for immediate consumption, such as that served in hospital cafeterias, airplanes, and mall cookie counters
- Ready-to-eat food that is not for immediate consumption but is prepared on site, including bakery, deli, and candy store items
- Food shipped in bulk, as long as it is not for sale in that form to consumers
- Medical foods, such as those used for nutritional needs of patients with certain diseases
- Plain coffee and tea, some spices, and other foods that contain no significant amounts of nutrients

The current regulations require that nutrition information be available for health or nutrient-content claims made on placards and signs. The FDA also proposed similar requirements for restaurant menu items making such claims. Restaurants would have to provide a reasonable basis for making claims, such as relying on recipes endorsed by medical or dietary groups. Even though foodservice operations are not required to have nutrition labeling on menu items, managers would be wise to understand the labels and be able to answer any questions customers might ask. Buyers also need to understand the labels to help them make purchasing decisions. If they purchase for hospitals, schools, or nursing homes, dietitians can order enriched cereals or lowfat milk. Even large restaurant chains have a dietitian on staff to ensure the menu items meet dietary guidelines.

The FDA and USDA agreed on new food labeling regulations in November 1992. All processed foods had new labels by May 1994, and processed meat and poultry items, which are under USDA jurisdiction, had new labels by July 1994 (Figure 4.5). The FDA and USDA considered the health issues of greatest concern to the general public and identified nutrient information that must appear on the package label and other optional data. Required nutrient information includes total calories, calories from fat, total fat, saturated fat, cholesterol, sodium, total carbohydrates, dietary fiber, sugars (mono- and disaccharides), protein, vitamins A and C, calcium, and iron. If a processor makes a claim about any other nutrient—that a product is enriched or fortified with thiamin or niacin, for example—information about that nutrient also is mandatory.

Nutrient content per serving appears on the label as % Daily Value (DV) and includes Daily Reference Values (DRVs) and Reference Daily Intakes (RDIs). Some of the figures are based on the number of calories consumed per day, with 2,000 calories established as the reference. These numbers help consumers assess how a food fits into a healthy diet and should help prevent confusion about quantitative values.

Specifications

Quality has become the watchword in the foodservice industry. Quality food depends upon the development of and adherence to rigorous purchasing specifications based on standards. Standards and specifications are not the same although they may overlap (Patterson, 1993). A **food standard** most commonly describes characteristics for a specified product and provides a quality reference, usually indicated by a grade, such as Choice, A, No. 1, or Fancy (see Table 3.1). It can also be a standard of identity, discussed under the Federal Food, Drug, and Cosmetic Act in chapter 3, which spells out what may be contained in a processed product such as mayonnaise. A food standard is set by a government agency, such as the USDA, which establishes quality standards, or the FDA, which makes public the standards of identity. The USDA sets quality standards for meat, poultry, eggs, dairy products, fruits, vegetables, and nuts. The U.S. Commerce Department sets quality standards for fish and seafood.

Figure 4.5.   Generic nutrition label.

Nutrition Facts	
Serving Size ½ cup (114g)	
Servings Per Container 4	
Amount Per Serving	
Calories 90	Calories from Fat 30
	% Daily Value*
Total Fat 3g*	**5%**
Saturated Fat 0g	**0%**
Cholesterol 0mg	**0%**
Sodium 300mg	**13%**
Total Carbohydrate 13g	**4%**
Dietary Fiber 3g	**12%**
Sugars 3g	
Protein 3g	
Vitamin A 90% • Vitamin C 60%	
Calcium 4% • Iron 4%	

* Percent Daily Values are based on a 2,000 calorie diet. Your daily values may be higher or lower depending on your calorie needs:

	Calories:	2,000	2,500
Total Fat	Less than	85g	90g
Sat Fat	Less than	20g	25g
Cholesterol	Less than	300mg	300mg
Sodium	Less than	2,400mg	2,400mg
Total Carbohydrate		300g	375g
Dietary Fiber		25g	30g

Calories per gram:
Fat 3 • Carbohydrate 4 • Protein 4

Source: From the FDA and the USDA Food Safety and Inspection Service, 1992.

A specification establishes the specific requirement for what the buyer wants. The root of the word specification is "specific," which means that criteria must be met. The primary safeguard of foodservice quality is adherence to specifications. A **specification** has been defined in many different ways, but it is essentially a statement readily understood by both buyers and suppliers of the required qualities of the product, including allowable limits of tolerance. In the simplest terms, a specification, or "spec," may be described as a list of detailed characteristics of a product for a specific use (Spears, 1995). Specifications should be tailored to the menu, recipes, and operation. They should be developed by the buyer and checked by the foodservice manager. Buyers often ask suppliers to help write specifications, and most are willing to do so.

Types

Three types of specifications used in foodservice are technical, approved brand, and performance. One of these types, or a combination of two or all three, is selected on the basis of the product—food, supplies, or equipment—to be purchased.

Technical specifications are used for products in which quality can be measured objectively and impartially by testing instruments. For example, graded food items for which a national standard exists require a technical specification. Other examples are metals used in custom-made equipment, such as stainless steel and aluminum, for which thickness is measured by gauges. This type of specification also can be written for detergents and cleaning compounds that can be chemically analyzed. Technical specifications are used most often for food products purchased by schools, colleges and universities, large healthcare facilities, and multiunit commercial operations.

Approved brand specifications indicate quality by designating a product of known desirable characteristics, such as a manufacturer's specification for a convection oven or a processor's formula for frozen pizza. Paper and plastic disposable items also could be identified by brand name. The brand name specification often is used in smaller foodservice operations in which a cook or chef might be responsible for purchasing in addition to operational duties. Nothing captures customers' attention and enthusiasm more than branded products that meet their expectation for quality. Brand names are used on menus or on individual packets of condiments as a status symbol. Examples include packets of Heinz Ketchup, Grey Poupon Mustard, or Mrs. Dash no salt seasonings. Pepsi and Coca Cola compete fiercely to keep their brand names in front of the public. Alcoholic beverages are purchased almost exclusively by brand names.

To buy everything by brand name, however, can cause many problems (Patterson, 1991). Often a number of distributors must service the account, which is not as profitable for the supplier as one big delivery would be. The foodservice operation probably must pay more because bargaining power for only one product is greatly diminished. Thus, the profit made by purchasing decreases. Even if the purchaser buys primarily by brand, specifications should be reviewed periodically. A new product could come on the market that is far superior to the brand now in use.

Performance specifications measure quality by the effective functioning of small or large equipment, disposable paper and plastic items, or detergents.

Examples include the minimum and maximum number of pounds to be weighed on a scale, the number of dishes to be washed per minute, the minutes coffee will remain at serving temperature in a styrofoam cup, or the pH level of detergents. A specification for a particular product also might combine technical and performance criteria.

Specification Writing Criteria

Buyers for a foodservice operation must have written specifications to be effective. With written specifications, suppliers, the receiving clerk, and the foodservice manager all can determine if the products received are what was ordered. Despite those advantages, writing specifications can be time consuming and labor intensive, especially for small operations. Writing specifications for high-priced products, such as meats and seafood, first will make it easier to write specs for other products. This process requires a team approach and generally includes the foodservice manager, dietitian, procurement and production unit heads, buyer, cook or chef, and financial manager. A written specification describing food or nonfood products to be purchased must be developed to ensure desired quality standards are met. A specification can be simple or complex. The brand name type is the simplest and the technical is the most complicated.

Good specifications are

- clear, simple, and sufficiently specific so both buyer and supplier can readily identify all provisions required
- consistent with products or grades currently on the market
- verifiable by label statements, USDA grades, weight determination, etc.
- realistic quality standards that would find at least some products acceptable
- fair to the supplier and protective of the buyer's interests
- capable of being met by several bidders to encourage competition

Suppliers can provide useful advice in writing specifications. Once the specifications team decides upon a product that best meets its qualifications, it can ask a supplier to describe it. This information then can be incorporated into a brief draft specification to be reviewed by other suppliers who also sell the product. Once a consensus is reached, a specification is written and entered into a computer. Then it can be used each time an order for the product is placed.

Information Included

All specifications for food products should include the following information:

- name of product (trade or brand) or standard
- federal grade, brand, or other quality designation
- size of container (such as weight or can size)
- count per container or approximate number per pound (number of pieces per container, if applicable)
- unit on which price will be based

Information that would describe the product in more detail might include:

- product use (in salads or soups, for instance)
- product test procedures used by the foodservice to determine quality compliance (such as taking temperatures or weighing)
- detailed description (degree of ripeness, flavor characteristics, etc.)
- quality tolerance limits (number of substandard products in a container, usually for produce)
- weight tolerance limits (range of acceptable weight, usually in meat, poultry, or seafood)

Any other information that helps to describe the product should be included. Some examples:

- Canned goods: type or style, pack, syrup density, size, specific gravity
- Meat and meat products: age, exact cutting instructions, weight tolerance limit, composition, condition upon receipt of product, fat content, cut of meat to be used, market class
- Fresh fruits and vegetables: variety, weight, degree of ripeness or maturity, quality tolerance limit, geographical origin
- Frozen foods: temperature during delivery and upon receipt, variety, sugar ratio
- Dairy products: temperature during delivery and upon receipt, milk fat content, milk solids, bacteria count

Were it not for the availability of nationally accepted grades and other criteria developed by the USDA, writing a specification would be an almost unsurmountable task for the buyer and a difficult order for the supplier to interpret. Buyers can now write definite specifications by citing a standard, which is in itself a rigorous specification. These standards constitute a common technical language for buyers and suppliers. For example, if a buyer orders a USDA choice grade round of beef, the supplier knows immediately the expected quality. The same is true for Grade A chickens, Grade AA eggs, and many other food groups outlined in Table 3.1. Sample specifications and reference materials for various food and nonfood items are included in later chapters that deal with those specific items.

Sensory Analysis

Food quality is evaluated by sensory methods to determine if foods differ in such qualities as taste, odor, juiciness, tenderness, or texture. **Sensory analysis** is a science that measures the texture, aroma, flavor, and appearance of food products through human senses. Foodservice operations should use sensory evaluation for purchasing new food items and for maintaining quality of existing items (Spears, 1995). Buyers have a critical role in the sensory analysis process. First, they know the market better than anyone in the foodservice and have a responsibility to let the manager know if new products are available. In most large operations, a panel of customers or managers are selected to evaluate the product. The buyer needs to have a sample of the product on hand for that evaluation. Once the decision is made, the buyer orders the selected product from the supplier. In small operations, the buyer and manager might make the decision together.

Sensory evaluation of new food products usually is conducted by a sensory or consumer panel before a purchasing decision is made. Sensory panels are small, ranging from 6 to 12 people trained to judge quality characteristics and differences among food items. Panel members must be experienced in the use of score cards and in the vocabulary of food descriptions; they also must be able to distinguish among various levels of basic tastes (sweet, salt, sour, and bitter) and to repeat their assessments with reasonable precision. A consumer panel usually includes 50 to 100 people who are representative of the target market. The objective of **consumer panels** is to evaluate acceptance of, or preference for, a food product.

Analytical and affective sensory tests are used for product evaluation. In an **analytical test** a trained panel evaluates differences and similarities of quality and quantity of sensory characteristics. An untrained panel of consumers performs an **affective test** by evaluating preference, acceptance, and opinions of a product.

Before purchasing a new menu item, a quality standard should be developed for the product. An example of a standard for carrot cake with cream cheese icing is shown in Figure 4.6. Samples of cakes from various distributors should be available for sensory tests. Unless the foodservice operation is very large, untrained panels generally are used to discriminate among the cakes and to determine customer acceptance and preference.

For discriminatory tests, such as difference tests and ranking, panelists do not need extensive training and large panels are not required. The paired comparison test can be used to differentiate between a pair of coded samples on the basis of some specified characteristic, such as sweetness, crumbliness, moistness when chewing, lightness, or degree of browning. Figure 4.7 is an example of a comparison of the moistness of two samples of carrot cake. The ranking test extends the paired comparison test to three or more coded samples. Panelists are asked to rank them by intensity of the characteristics that differentiate the products. An example of this type of questionnaire is provided in Figure 4.8.

Panelists should receive the samples for all tests in a random order to avoid order biases in the testing. Ten to 12 panelists are sufficient. Results of the discrimination testing can be compared to affective testing of acceptance or preference to decide which cake is preferred. The goal of such tests is to determine the response of the customer to the product. If too few customers are used, the results can be questionable. Approximately 20 to 40 customers should give an acceptable response.

QUANTITY DEMAND

Food items served to the customer are dictated by the menu. The foodservice manager projects the number of customers or clients expected at each meal and tells the production manager how much of each menu item will be needed by using **forecasting,** which is the art and science of estimating future events. Some managers determine the number of portions by looking at historical or past records. A more sophisticated approach is to incorporate historical information into forecasting models, thus providing a more scientific technique. Regardless of the method used to determine quantities, intuition should not be downplayed. Many experienced managers,

Figure 4.6. Example of a standard for carrot cake with cream cheese icing.

Carrot Cake with Cream Cheese Icing

Carrot cake should have a soft crust with barely noticeable browning. The interior should be a cinnamon brown color and very moist and compact. Grated carrots are difficult to detect but add body and moisture to the product. Chopped nuts and cinnamon flavor should be identifiable. The cake usually is topped with a mild-flavored cream cheese icing that blends with the positive cinnamon flavor.

Cream cheese icing should be smooth and easy to spread. It should be fluffy yet maintain its shape and adhere to the cake. A cream cheese color and flavor should be evident.

Figure 4.7. Example of paired comparison form.

Name of Panelist _____ Date _____
Product _____
Evaluate the moistness of the two samples of carrot cake. Taste the cake sample on the left first. Indicate which has the greatest moistness when chewing.

     Code number 181   Code number 213

      _____   _____

Comments:

Figure 4.8. Example of ranking test form.

Name of Panelist_____ Date _____

Rank the four samples of carrot cake for crumb moistness as you chew them. The least moist sample is ranked first and the most moist is ranked fourth. Place the code numbers on the appropriate lines. Test the samples of the coded cakes in the following order: 181, 213, 345, 409.

    _____   _____   _____   _____
     1   2   3   4

cooks, and chefs intuitively know if the quantity is correct for a special situation, such as a holiday, a weather change, or an important event across town, and accordingly make adjustments in the number of portions. For example, an upscale restaurant might greatly increase its stock of Beef Wellington entrées and Cherries Jubilee desserts for Wednesday, February 14. The restaurateur has kept records for the last year on the number of these items served on Wednesdays and can determine how much to buy under ordinary circumstances. The extra customers expected for Valentine's Day, however, will require the restaurateur to use intuition in determining how many additional servings of this entrée and dessert will be needed.

Historical Records

Historical records are written accounts of previous events, such as purchase orders, census sheets, and inventory statements, which become the base for most forecasting processes. This is especially true of foodservices in which these records were used to determine food production quantities long before forecasting techniques were available. In fact, such historical records are the root of most of these procedures. If these records are not accurate and complete, they cannot be used for forecasting with any reliability.

Records contain pertinent information applicable to forecasting: date and day of week, meal or hour of service, special event or holiday, and even applicable weather conditions. Although the production record includes vital information on food items served to customers, production is by no means the only organizational unit that should keep records. Only by cross-referencing records of sales with those of production can a reliable historical base for forecasting be made. Sales records yield customer count patterns that can be useful for forecasting in foodservice operations in which meals are sold, as in restaurants, hospital employee and guest cafeterias, and schools. Forecasting provides a data base for decision making and planning. Historical records in the production unit should be correlated with those kept by purchasing, including names and performance of suppliers and food prices.

Forecasting Models

The time is long past when the manager of a small foodservice could run to the corner grocery store or when the purchasing manager of a large operation could make an emergency appeal to a wholesaler if a shortage occurs. Today, business is too complex for such hand-to-mouth existence, and forecasting is essential. Foodservice managers must make good forecasts by using current data to determine future needs, regardless of the size or type of operation. Forecasts vary in sophistication, from those based on historical records and intuition to complex models requiring large amounts of data and computer time. A **forecasting model** is a mathematical formula to predict future needs, which are used as an aid in determining quantity. Managers must be careful to choose a forecasting model that is suitable for a particular situation.

Forecasting techniques have been categorized in numerous ways, but the most common classification for models used in foodservice is the **time series model,** which assumes that actual occurrences follow a identifiable pattern over time. For example, the number of cartons of milk required each day in a school foodservice operation will be higher in the spring semester than in fall. To make past data useful, variations must be reduced to a trend line that can be extended into the future and smooths the data. Moving average and exponential smoothing, both time series models, are used frequently with foodservice data.

Moving Average

The most common and easiest of the smoothing procedures is the **moving average method,** which uses a repetitive process for developing a trend line. It is used only on the same menu item. The process begins by taking the average number of portions for each menu item sold for the last five or more times as the first point on the trend line. The second point on the line is the new average, made by dropping the first number and adding the most recent number of portions sold to the bottom of the list before taking another average.

An example of the moving average method is shown in Figure 4.9. Data for grilled, marinated, boneless, skinless chicken breasts cover a 10-day period in the past. A 5-day moving average is used. The first 5-day moving average is calculated by adding the demands for days 1 through 5 and dividing by 5, giving an average of 105 servings. The next moving average is calculated by adding the demands for days 2 through 6 and dividing by 5. The procedure is repeated by dropping the earliest day's data and adding the next for a total of 5 days. Demand data values and moving average values plotted on the graph (Figure 4.10) illustrate the smoothing effect of the method. Note that the smoothed data curve eliminates daily variations in demand and thus indicates a trend based on the past. This averaging process, when continued, yields data points that smooth out the data to a comparatively constant pattern for use in the forecast.

Exponential Smoothing

The **exponential smoothing method** is a popular time series model in which an exponentially decreasing set of weights is used, giving recent values more weight than older ones. It can be set up on a computer spreadsheet and is very similar to the moving average model except that it does not uniformly weigh past observations. Also, the only data required are the weight (alpha) that is applied to the most recent value, the most recent forecast, and the most recent actual value or customer demand, thus eliminating the need to store historical data (Wheelwright & Makridakis, 1989). The alpha component of the model is the judgment factor, or smoothing coefficient, which indicates how well the manager believes past data represent current customer count.

The judgment factor, alpha, is a number between 0 and 1 and is used to adjust for any errors in previous forecasts. Alpha is the weight assigned to the most recent customer demand, and 1–alpha is the weight for the most recent forecast (Messersmith & Miller, 1992). The exponential smoothing model in simple terms is:

$$\text{New forecast} = \left\{ \begin{matrix} \text{judgment} \\ \text{factor} \end{matrix} \right\} \left\{ \begin{matrix} \text{last} \\ \text{demand} \end{matrix} \right\} + \left\{ \begin{matrix} 1-\text{judgment} \\ \text{factor} \end{matrix} \right\} \left\{ \begin{matrix} \text{last} \\ \text{forecast} \end{matrix} \right\}$$

In forecasting for foodservice, alpha is usually 0.3 and 1–alpha is 0.7. If the last demand for hamburgers dropped to 150 because of student illnesses from the 300 usually forecast for the school lunch program, only 255 would be prepared the next time hamburgers are on the menu.

New forecast = [0.3 × 150] + [0.7 × 300] or 255 hamburgers

Figure 4.9. Example of moving average.

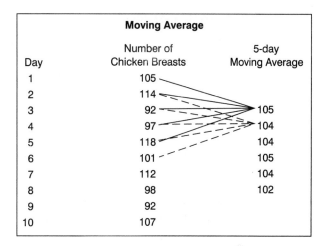

	Moving Average	
Day	Number of Chicken Breasts	5-day Moving Average
1	105	
2	114	
3	92	105
4	97	104
5	118	104
6	101	105
7	112	104
8	98	102
9	92	
10	107	

Figure 4.10. Graph illustrating moving average smoothing effect.

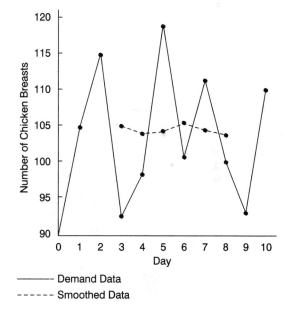

——— Demand Data

----- Smoothed Data

The next time hamburgers are on the menu, however, students are back in school and eager to have hamburgers for lunch. Intuition indicates that greater reliance should be placed on the most recent forecast. The alpha value for customer demand was decreased to 0.1 and 1–alpha increased to 0.9. The new forecast is 285 hamburgers, a much more realistic number.

New forecast = [0.1 × 150] + [0.9 × 300] or 285 hamburgers

If no children are absent from school on the day hamburgers are on the menu, the cook probably would prepare 300 hamburgers. Intuition of cooks or managers remains a crucial component of forecasting.

PURCHASING DECISIONS

Purchasing for commercial and noncommercial foodservice operations is a highly specialized job function. Buyers must have knowledge about products to be purchased, the market, buying procedures, and market trends. They must understand how products are produced, processed, and moved to market. In addition, they must be able to forecast, plan, organize, control, and perform other management functions.

The primary function of the buyer is to procure the required products for the desired use at minimum cost. Not only should foodservice managers be concerned about the price of raw products, but they also should keep in mind the difference between the *as purchased* cost and the cost of the edible portion of the product. Efficient buyers can be of great assistance to foodservice managers in determining the product yield of many raw food products. Buyers also can conduct basic research to aid in decision making. They can use industry techniques, such as value analysis, make-or-buy decisions, and cost effectiveness to make these important decisions (Spears, 1995).

Product Yield

Yield is the amount of product resulting at the completion of the various phases of the procurement/production/service cycle. It usually is expressed as a definite weight, volume, or serving size. For most foods, losses in volume or weight occur in each phase, although a few foods, such as rice and pasta, increase in volume during production. **As purchased** (AP) is the amount of food bought before processing to give the number of edible portions required to serve a specific number of customers. The AP weight of meat, fish, and poultry decreases before being cooked for many reasons, such as the removal of skin and bones or trimming of fat. What results is the **edible portion** (EP), which is the weight of a menu item without skin, bones, and fat available for eating by the customer after it is cooked. During cooking, shrinkage occurs, up to 35% for a roast. Carving subtracts another 5% before serving to the customer (Kotschevar & Donnelly, 1999). Buyers must factor in these losses to determine the as served (AS) yield, which is important for menu item pricing. Only delicatessen cold meat and poultry products are 100% edible; the cost of bones, skin, and cooking loss is included in the purchase price. The *Food Buying Guide* (1984), published by the USDA for use in child nutrition programs, provides data on the edible yield percentages of various foods to assist food buyers in planning amounts to purchase. The cooked yields of selected meat, poultry, and fish products are shown below.

Product	Yield
Ground beef (less than 30% fat)	42%
Barbecued pork ribs	45%
Chicken breast (skin and bones)	66%
Turkey roll	66%
Breaded fish sticks (fried)	56%

As an example, if a 4-ounce grilled boneless and skinless chicken breast is desired, a 6.1-ounce breast with rib bones and skin should be purchased. To calculate the amount of chicken breast with rib bones and skin to purchase, divide the 4-ounce EP by the 66% (0.66) yield.

4-ounces EP ÷ 0.66 = 6.1-ounces AP

The EP price is important to the foodservice manager. The AP price of the chicken breast with bones and skin is $0.126 per ounce, or $0.77 for 6.1 ounces. To calculate the EP price of the 6.1-ounce chicken breast, divide the AP price ($0.77) by the EP yield percentage (66%).

AP price ÷ EP yield % = EP price

or

$0.77 ÷ 0.66 = $1.17

Fresh fruits and vegetables, which often are peeled, seeded, and cooked, decrease in weight before being consumed, as shown in this chart.

Product	Yield
Apples, cored and peeled	80%
Bananas	65%
Cantaloupe	52%
Watermelon	57%
Pears	78%
Broccoli	81%
Carrots	70%
Carrots, cooked	60%
Corn on the cob, cooked	55%
Iceberg lettuce	76%

The recipe in *Food for Fifty* (Molt, 1997) for seven 9-inch apple pies (56 servings) requires 12 pounds of peeled, cored apple slices. A raw apple has an 80% yield. To calculate the number of pounds of whole apples to purchase for the recipe, divide 12 pounds of apples by 80%, or 0.80.

12 lbs apples EP ÷ 0.80 = 15 lbs apples AP

If the AP price for one pound of apples is $0.45, the buyer then can calculate the EP price.

EP price = $0.45 ÷ 0.80 = $0.56 per pound

Value Analysis

The value concept crosses over all functional units of a foodservice, especially procurement, production, and service. It creates a new purchasing activity—value analysis. To measure value, managers must balance the value of the product received in a purchase with the price of the product. Suppliers sell buyers the quality of the product requested in the specification. Buyers then need to use their purchasing skills to procure the specified quality at a minimum price. The essence of quality is suitability (Heinritz, Farrell, Giunipero, & Kolchin, 1991). Perhaps part of the price is for quality features that do not contribute substantially to the suitability of the product for foodservice. That makes the expenditure wasteful. A prime example is the purchase of an expensive, sophisticated software package for an operation in which the manager has no idea what is needed and has no employees trained to use the software. Many of the software features will go unused. A simple package likely would be adequate, and it certainly would be less expensive.

The purpose or function for which the product is purchased needs to be reviewed and the quality component in the specification revised to reduce costs without impairing suitability (Heinritz et al., 1991). This process is identified as value analysis, which should become a routine part of the purchasing process. Value analysis is an important element of scientific purchasing and, as such, has brought about the realization that purchasing is a profit-making function. The concept of value analysis is critical in enhancing efficiency and profitability (Williams, Lacy, & Smith, 1992). Reductions in purchasing costs by making the process more efficient exert great impact on profitability, which is quite different than increasing profit by selling more products.

Definition

Value analysis is the methodical investigation of all components of an existing product or service with the goal of discovering and eliminating unnecessary costs without interfering with the effectiveness of the product or service (Miles, 1972). This practice grew out of manufacturing, but it has broad implications for foodservice as well. For example, a value analysis of a menu item may reveal that some quality features may be limited without detracting from the final product. Quality should depend on the form in which the final product will be used. An example is the use of whole, colossal black olives rather than lower cost pieces when the recipe for beef enchiladas calls for pitted, chopped black olives. This change not only would reduce product cost but also labor time for pitting and chopping.

As stated previously, **value** is the relationship between the price paid for a particular item and its utility in the function it fulfills. Value depends on what is being measured and who is doing the measuring. For example, a food specification prepared by the foodservice manager may be viewed differently by the purchasing manager. Two common results of conducting a value analysis are a change in the specification or the supplier. Value analysis has been described as a new approach to the "best buy" problem in purchasing (Spears, 1995).

Foodservice Application

Although value analysis is employed in the development of new products, it is used more frequently in evaluating existing product specifications. Thus, it is readily applicable to foodservice. For example, a new menu item, a grilled, marinated, boneless, skinless chicken breast, was introduced recently into a large quick-service chain of restaurants. Shortly after the introduction, sales declined rapidly in approximately half of the restaurants. Customers complained that the grilled breasts were dry and the flavor bland. Upper-level management decided to conduct a value analysis on a minimum of four grilled chicken breasts in different stages of preparation in the corporate headquarters test kitchen. Company policy is to have as much purchasing and preparation as possible occur in each restaurant. However, management is reviewing this policy because the scarcity and cost of qualified employees is a big concern.

The company decided to serve a 4-ounce grilled chicken breast in all restaurants and to make comparisons based on this cooked weight. To meet this standard, 5-ounce raw boneless, skinless breasts were purchased for grilling. If raw chicken breasts with rib bones and skin were purchased, however, the weight would be 6.1 ounces because the edible portion yield of the grilled breast is 66% of the AP weight, as noted earlier. Chicken breasts were purchased in various stages of preparation and were prepared in the corporate test kitchen. A consumer panel evaluated each product for quality while management conducted a cost analysis. Results of these evaluations and recommendations were given to the decision makers in corporate headquarters.

Report to Management

A brief value analysis report for corporate headquarters based on the chain restaurant example of grilled boneless, skinless chicken breasts is shown in Figure 4.11. This example illustrates a primary requirement for reporting to management—brevity! Complete data on the test procedure and results should be prepared as a reference and excerpted for the report to management. Value analysis results for quality and cost and recommendations are of major interest to management and therefore should be concise in the report.

The example of grilled, marinated, boneless, skinless chicken breasts illustrates a good approach to a primary and secondary problem. The primary problem, customer dissatisfaction, was solved by comparing the moistness, flavor, and appearance of the prepared-on-premises product to a commercial frozen product. The boneless, skinless chicken breast marinated and grilled on premise (Product 2) ranked highest in moistness and flavor. The secondary problem, labor intensity, required a cost analysis to determine if the higher price of a commercial frozen product could be justified. Product 1, which had to be boned, skinned, marinated, and grilled on premise, had the lowest raw food cost and the highest labor cost. Boning and skinning chicken breasts by inexperienced cooks with improper equipment is more time consuming than if it were done in an efficient processing plant. Cost effectiveness is a key consideration in the decision whether to make or buy boneless, skinless, marinated chicken breasts for grilling.

Make-or-Buy Decisions

The procedure of deciding whether to purchase from oneself (make) or purchase from suppliers (buy) is a continuing process, and make-or-buy decisions should be reviewed periodically. A foodservice manager has three basic choices for production of a menu item:

- Produce the item completely, starting with basic raw ingredients.
- Purchase all ingredients and assemble them.
- Purchase the item ready to cook or serve from a wholesaler.

Few foodservice managers consider the first alternative because of labor cost. Purchasing whole chickens, removing the breast halves from the ribs, and skinning

Figure 4.11. Example of a value analysis report.

VALUE ANALYSIS
Report to Administration

Product Evaluated: Grilled, marinated, boneless,   **Evaluator:** Mike Jones
               skinless chicken breast   **Date:** June 1, 1998

Statement of Problem
- Customers complained grilled chicken breasts were dry and too spicy.
- Management is concerned about cost, especially labor, of the product.

Products Evaluated
1. Raw 6.1-ounce chicken breast boned, skinned, marinated, and grilled on premise.
2. Raw boneless and skinless 5-ounce chicken breast marinated and grilled on premise.
3. Frozen marinated, raw, boneless, and skinless 5-ounce chicken breast grilled on premise.
4. Frozen grilled, marinated, boneless, and skinless 4-ounce chicken breast microwaved on premise.

Methodology
- *Preparation of product*
  Chicken breasts with or without rib bones, skin, or marinade were purchased. Products 1, 2, & 3 were purchased raw, and 4 was purchased grilled. Products 3 & 4 were purchased frozen. Products 1 & 2 were marinated on premise; all but Product 4 were grilled on premise. Product 4 was microwaved on premise.
- *Test procedure*
  The four products, each identified by a number, were cut into sample size portions. Each product was rated on flavor, moistness, and appearance by a taste panel consisting of 12 foodservice managers, 12 foodservice employees, and 12 customers.

Value Analysis Results
- *Cost Evaluation*

Cost items	Product 1	Product 2	Product 3	Product 4
		cost per portion		
Food	$ .77	$ .97	$ 1.43	$ 1.48
Labor	1.19	.68	.41	.34
Total	$ 1.96	$ 1.65	$ 1.84	$ 1.82

- *Quality Evaluation*
  Product 2 ranked highest in moistness and flavor, and Product 3 ranked second highest. Product 4 was missing the "hot off the grill" flavor and appearance. The selling price of Product 1 would be too high for the target customer because of labor cost.

Recommendation
- Product 2 should be used for this quick-service chain of restaurants, but a few boxes of Product 3 should be kept in the freezer for emergencies.

---

and shaping each would take a tremendous amount of time. In addition, the remainder of the chicken would have to be used to keep costs under control. Even a modified version of this decision, purchasing chicken breasts with the rib bone and skin, requires a lot of labor. With the chicken breasts in the value analysis example, the most logical choices were the last two alternatives in Figure 4.11. Purchasing boneless, skinless chicken breasts and marinating them before grilling was compared to commercial frozen products, which were boneless, skinless, and marinated.

Decision

Make-or-buy decisions are procedures for deciding whether to purchase from oneself (make) or purchase from suppliers (buy). These decisions can be accomplished in a variety of ways (Zenz, 1981):

- Suppliers may propose an alternative and submit quotations on a product they can produce.
- Suppliers may perform unsatisfactorily, creating emergencies because of delivery problems or poor quality.
- Unreasonable supplier price increases can trigger an investigation.
- A new product may be added or an existing one substantially modified.
- A value analysis study of an existing product may require a make-or-buy evaluation.
- Reduced sales and idle equipment or employees may encourage a manager to make items previously purchased from outside suppliers.

Foodservice Decisions

Decision factors in foodservice are quality, quantity, service, and cost. The serving of **quality** food is a prime consideration in all foodservices, whether menu items are made in the operation or purchased ready to serve from the processor. Quality standards have become well established among most processors. However, many variations, especially in seasonings, are evident. In the grilled chicken breast example (Figure 4.11), the chicken breast was tender and juicy, but the seasonings masked the flavor of the chicken, making the product unacceptable to the customer. The standard was that the flavor of the marinade should not overpower the subtle flavor of the chicken.

Quantity is part of the decision process when the ability to produce in the desired amount is required. Quantity to be produced must be considered in the make-or-buy decision. The quantity may be too large for a make decision or too small for the processor to consider. Many chain restaurants cannot afford to increase the size of the kitchen by decreasing the number of tables for customers. Processors cannot afford to buy additional equipment to produce a menu item that has limited sales. As a result, many foodservice operations, especially chains, are working with processors to produce menu items acceptable to customers. The volume sold to these restaurants makes expansion of processing facilities profitable.

Service includes a wide variety of intangible factors that influence the buyer's satisfaction. Two important factors in the decision process are reliable delivery and predictable service. Foodservices operate on a rigid time schedule, and a late delivery of a menu item cannot be tolerated. The dependability of a supplier in all circumstances

Figure 4.12.   Structure of choice model with an example.

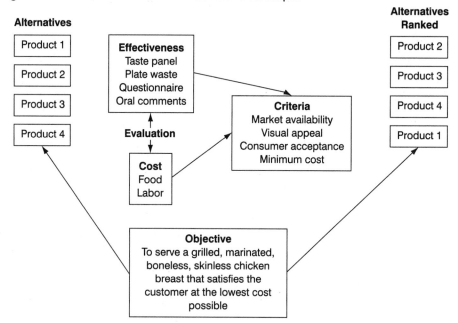

must be assured. Clues to suppliers' reliability may be their record of labor relations and reputation in the industry, including opinions of other customers. The geographic proximity of a supplier to a foodservice operation also should be considered.

When quality, quantity, and service are equal, a make-or-buy decision is made by comparing known cost from the supplier with the estimated cost of making the product. The cost of raw food is easily determined, but costs of labor, energy, equipment depreciation, and overhead may be more difficult to calculate.

Set policies for reaching make-or-buy decisions should be avoided because these decisions are influenced by a number of factors. What is critical today may not be critical tomorrow. The buyer must strike a fine balance among all factors and make a cost-effective choice on what is best for a particular foodservice operation.

Cost Effectiveness

Cost effectiveness is a technique that provides a comparison of alternative courses of action in terms of their cost and effectiveness in attaining a specific objective (Spears, 1995). Cost is quantitative, in dollars and cents, while effectiveness is qualitative. Cost effectiveness is generally used to minimize the dollar cost of a product. The structure of choice model, shown in Figure 4.12, can be used to explain the cost effectiveness concept as it applies to the grilled, marinated, boneless, skinless chicken breast example. The pathway from the desired objective—to serve a grilled marinated, boneless, skinless chicken breast that satisfies the customer at the lowest cost possible—to the final choice of one of the alternatives is shown in Figure 4.12: Products 1, 2, 3, or 4.

Each alternative must be evaluated for effectiveness and cost. Some of the techniques for evaluating quality are consumer taste panels, studies on plate waste, questionnaires, and oral comments. Evaluation for cost is much easier. The two most important cost elements are food and labor. The next step is to examine each of the evaluated alternatives to see how they meet the established criteria. Suggestions for criteria are market availability, visual appeal, consumer acceptance, and minimum cost. After this examination, the alternatives in our example were ranked in the value analysis as follows: Product 2, 3, 4, and 1. Product 2—raw, boneless, skinless 5-ounce chicken breast marinated and grilled on premise—had the lowest total cost and ranked highest in quality, moistness, and flavor. It was the first choice of the consumer panel. Product 3—frozen marinated, raw, boneless, skinless 5-ounce chicken breast grilled on premise—was the second choice based solely on quality because the cost was the highest of all four products. The recommendation was that Product 2 should be the choice for the quick-service chain and that for emergencies a few boxes of Product 3 should be kept in the freezer.

The alternative selected may not be the least expensive because potential effectiveness is a major consideration. The lowest AP price does not necessarily indicate the lowest EP cost as in the case of Product 1 (raw 6.1-ounce chicken breast boned, skinned, marinated, and grilled on premise), in which food cost is the lowest but labor cost is the highest. The total cost of Product 1 was the highest of all alternatives.

SUMMARY

Foodservice buyers must know the quality and quantity of food products to purchase, techniques for analyzing value, and the rationale for making or buying them. The primary function of the buyer is to procure the required products for the desired use at minimum cost.

Quality control in a foodservice operation assures consistency in each product offered for service. Standards, specifications, and the sensory analysis process all serve as controls in purchasing products with the quality desired by customers and the price required by the foodservice manager. Standards, usually established by federal agencies, set benchmarks for food, microbiological safety, facility sanitation, and nutrition. A specification is a list of detailed characteristics in a product for a specific use. Three types of specifications used in foodservice are technical, approved brand, and performance. Sensory analysis is a science that measures the texture, aroma, flavor, and appearance of food products through human senses.

The amount of food that needs to be prepared is determined by forecasting, the art and science of estimating future events. Forecasts vary from those based on historical records and intuition to complex models requiring large amounts of data and computer time. The moving average and exponential smoothing models are used most frequently with foodservice data.

Foodservice managers should be concerned about the difference between the as purchased price (AP) and the cost of the edible portion (EP). Buyers can be of great assistance in figuring product yield of raw foods. Buyers also should use industry techniques, value analysis, make-or-buy decisions, and cost effectiveness. Value analysis is the methodical investigation of all components of an existing product or service with the goal of discovering or eliminating unnecessary costs without interfering with the effectiveness of the product. The procedure of deciding whether to purchase from oneself (make) or purchase from suppliers (buy) is a continuing process, and make-or-buy decisions should be reviewed periodically. Cost effectiveness is a technique that provides a comparison of alternative courses of action in terms of their cost and effectiveness in attaining a specific objective.

REFERENCES

David, B. D. (1979). Quality and standards—the dietitian's heritage. *Journal of The American Dietetic Association, 75,* 408–413.

FDA/USDA announce labeling proposals. (1992). *Journal of the American Dietetic Association, 2*(1), 29.

Food buying guide for child nutrition programs (Program Aid No. 1331). (1984). Washington, DC: U.S. Department of Agriculture, Food and Nutrition Service.

Heinritz, S., Farrell, P. V., Giunipero, L., & Kolchin, M. (1991). *Purchasing: Principles and applications* (8th ed.). Englewood Cliffs, NJ: Prentice Hall.

Kotschevar, L. H., & Donnelly, R. (1999). *Quantity food purchasing* (5th ed.). Upper Saddle River, NJ: Merrill/Prentice Hall.

Longree, K., & Armbruster, G. (1987). *Quantity food sanitation* (4th ed.). New York: Wiley.

Messersmith, A. M., & Miller, J. L. (1992). *Forecasting in foodservice.* New York: Wiley.

Miles, L. D. (1972). *Techniques of value analysis and engineering.* New York: McGraw-Hill.

Molt, M. (1997). *Food for fifty* (10th ed.). Englewood Cliffs, NJ: Prentice Hall.

National Restaurant Association, Educational Foundation. (1992). *Applied foodservice sanitation* (3rd ed.). Chicago: Author.

Patterson, P. (1991). Specifications: The key to effective buying. *Nation's Restaurant News, 25*(10), 57.

Patterson, P. (1993). Differentiating between standards and specifications. *Nation's Restaurant News, 27*(42), 20.

Ruggiero, T. (1996). The new dietary guidelines: Triumph of science and reason. *Restaurants USA, 16*(4), 12.

Spears, M. C. (1995). *Foodservice organizations: A managerial and systems approach* (3rd ed.). Upper Saddle River, NJ: Merrill/Prentice Hall.

USDA. (1970). Important temperatures in sanitation and food protection. *Home and Garden Bulletin No. 162.* Washington, DC: Author.

USDA and Department of Health and Human Services, prepared by Human Nutrition Information Service. (1992, August). USDA Food Guide Pyramid. *Home and Garden Bulletin No. 252.* Washington, DC: USDA and DHHS.

USDA and DHHS. (1995). Nutrition and your health: Dietary guidelines for Americans (4th ed.). *Home and Garden Bulletin No. 232.* Washington, DC: USDA and DHHS.

Wheelwright, S. C., & Makridakis, S. (1989). *Forecasting methods for management* (5th ed.). New York: Wiley.

Williams, A. J., Lacy, S., & Smith, W. C. (1992). Purchasing's role in value analysis: Lessons from creative problem solving. *International Journal of Purchasing and Materials Management, 28*(2), 37–42.

Zenz, G. J. (1981). *Purchasing and the management of materials* (5th ed.). New York: Wiley.

PART 2

Procurement Procedures

Procurement is the first unit in the foodservice operation, and the first activity in it is purchasing.

- **Chapter 5. Purchasing.** Good purchasing practices are critical to cost control and profit generation. The purchasing process includes procedures, records, and selection of effective suppliers. Astute purchasing managers guard against ethical problems that occur more often in purchasing than in any other activity in the foodservice operation.

- **Chapter 6. Receiving, Storage, and Inventory Control.** Receiving, storage, and inventory control are the other activities included in the procurement unit because they are as critical to cost control and profit generation as is purchasing.

Purchasing

"Of any task school foodservice professionals perform, effective purchasing has the single greatest impact on the quality of food we serve," contended Marlene Gunn (1992b) at the National Food Service Management Institute's conference, "Impact of Food Procurement on the Implementation of the Dietary Guidelines for Americans in Child Nutrition Programs." Gunn noted that menus are less effective in meeting the nutrition needs of children if products are purchased before the menu is planned. When that happens, the product usually dictates menu decision making. The menu serves as the primary control of the operation and is at the core of all that happens in the foodservice. The menu controls procurement, production, distribution and service, and sanitation and maintenance in both commercial and noncommercial foodservice operations.

Purchasing also is critical in a restaurant because the quality of menu items depends upon the raw ingredients used to produce them (Stefanelli, 1993). A smooth-running restaurant generally has a management staff capable of implementing and performing the restaurant industry's purchasing principles and procedures. Managers usually prepare product specifications based on the restaurant's production requirements. Being right the first time is important because correcting a purchasing mistake is difficult. For instance, determining the correct amount to order is a challenge for buyers. If they overbuy, excess stock increases the restaurant's storage costs. If they underbuy, a stock-out produces customer dissatisfaction. The unpredictability of a typical restaurant's business complicates the task of computing orders. If the foodservice caters exclusively to banquet customers or to a school or other captive audience, determining how much to buy is relatively easy. Buyers must know suppliers' delivery schedules to determine how much to order. Frequent deliveries usually are preferred because most menu items are perishable and expensive and tie up too much capital while sitting on a storage shelf.

As an activity concerned with the acquisition of products, purchasing plays a central role in the procurement functional unit. Procurement is defined as the managerial process of acquiring material for production. That material includes nonfood items, such as detergent and disposable tableware, but the chief material is food. Purchasing is intertwined with receiving, storage, and inventory control activities. Foodservice buyers must have a thorough understanding of the various purchasing methods, supplier selection, the process, and transportation decisions. Buyers serve as agents authorized to act on behalf of the principal, which is the organization. Suppliers provide products and services to an organization. Essential to all these important components of the purchasing activity is the ethical behavior of buyers and the operation.

PURCHASING METHODS

Purchasing methods used by foodservice operations have the greatest influence on the price of food (Gunn, 1992a). The foodservice manager projects the number of customers expected for a specific meal and forecasts the required number of servings for each menu item. The production unit then orders the amount of food needed for each item from the storeroom. The buyer checks the stock on hand and uses it or, if not available, places an order based on previously written specifications. This is a very simplified explanation of the purchasing activity. In large operations, the ordering procedure is computerized; seldom is emergency ordering required because menus are planned in advance and the food is in stock. Regardless of the operation's size, purchasing can be either informal or formal.

Informal

Informal verbal or written price quotations received by telephone or personally with a salesperson are often used when time is an important factor. Informal purchasing generally occurs under the following circumstances:

- Amount of the purchase is so small that the time required for formal purchasing practices cannot be justified.
- A product can be obtained only from one or two sources of supply.
- The need is urgent and immediate delivery is required.
- Stability of market (and prices) is uncertain.
- Size of the operation is too small to justify more formal procedures.

A minimum of two prices for each item should be obtained because informal quotations, usually oral, have little legal protection. Prices quoted by telephone should be recorded by the buyer and then checked against the invoice at the time of delivery. Federal, state, or local laws often determine conditions under which informal purchasing can be used for tax-supported institutions (Spears, 1995).

Formal

Tax-supported institutions usually are required to use competitive bidding, which is optional for private institutions and commercial foodservices. Competitive bidding very often culminates in a formal contract between the buyer and supplier. Understanding the legal implications of contract buying is important for both parties. These legal considerations apply equally to buying for a single independent unit, a department within an organization, several departments of an organization, or a group of organizations.

Bid Buying

Bid buying occurs when a number of suppliers are willing to compete over price quotes on the buyer's specifications. Buyers generally use the fixed bid or the daily bid procedure.

The **fixed bid** often is chosen for large quantities, particularly for nonperishable items purchased over a long period of time. Suppliers prefer to avoid committing to long-term bids because of potential price fluctuations. Buyers select several suppliers and give them specifications and bidding forms for desired products, which they complete and return. Figure 5.1 is an example of a bid request form.

The **daily bid** often is used for perishable products that last only a few days. Sometimes this bid is referred to as *daily quotation buying*. Daily bids usually are made by telephone and followed by a written confirmation before the buyer accepts the bid. The buyer records bids quoted by telephone on a quotation form similar to that in Figure 5.2.

Whether fixed or daily bids are used, there are two basic methods for selecting a supplier.

- **Line-item bidding.** Each supplier bids on each product on the buyer's list, and the one offering the lowest price receives the order for that product. Foodservice buyers must consider the size of orders wholesalers are required to deliver. According to Gunn (1992b), the typical wholesaler needs a guarantee of a $600 minimum order to realize a return on investment. The line-item bid is much more time consuming than the bottom-line bid and costs more

Figure 5.1. Example of a bid request form.

BID REQUEST

Bids will be received until   November 24, 1998

Issued by:	Community Hospital	*Address:*	100 North Street Sunnyvale, OK
Date issued:	September 29, 1998	*Date to be delivered:*	Weekly as ordered between 12/30/98 to 6/30/99

Increases in quantity up to 20% will be binding at the discretion of the buyer. All items are to be officially certified by the U.S. Department of Agriculture for acceptance no earlier than 2 days before delivery; costs of such service to be borne by the supplier.

Item No.	Description	Quantity	Unit	Unit Price	Amount
1	Tomatoes, whole or in pieces, U.S. Grade B, #10 cans, 6/cs.	100	cs.		
2	Sweet Potatoes, vacuum pack, U.S. Grade B, #3 vacuum cans (enamel lined), 24/cs.	50	cs.		
3	Asparagus, all green, cuts and tips, U.S. Grade A, #10 cans, 6/cs.	50	cs.		
4	Corn, Cream Style, golden, U.S. Grade A, #10 cans (enamel lined), 6/cs.	50	cs.		
5	Blueberries, light syrup, U.S. Grade B, #10 cans (enamel lined), 6/cs.	20	cs.		

Supplier _____

Figure 5.2.   Example of a form for telephone bids.

**COMMUNITY HOSPITAL
QUOTATION RECORD FORM**

Date: Wed., 8/25/98

Delivery Date: Fri., 8/27/98

Circle accepted price quotation.

					Price Quotations			
Item	Specifications	Amount Needed	Amount on Hand	Amount to Order	Supplier Jones per unit	Jones total	Supplier L. & M. per unit	L. & M. total
Tomatoes	U.S. #1, 20# lug, 5 × 6	4 lugs	1	3	$10.50	$31.50	$10.75	$32.25
Lettuce	U.S. #1, Untrimmed Iceberg, 40% hard head, 24 heads, 1 crate	4	1	3	12.00	36.00	11.70	35.10
Potatoes	U.S. #1, Long Russet Bakers 100 count (50# box)	6	2	4	8.82	35.28	9.07	36.28
Onions	U.S. #1, Yellow, med. size, 50# sack	1	0	1	10.25	10.25	10.00	10.00
Watermelon	U.S. #1, Red flesh	400#	0	400#	.18/#	72.00	.155/#	62.00
						$185.03		($175.63)

for both the supplier and the buyer. Note in Figure 5.3, the potential supplier A will deliver the peaches, B the sugar, and C the pears. The price offered on each item is considered independently.

- **Bottom-line bidding.** This type of bidding, often referred to as the *all-or-nothing approach,* requires suppliers to bid the best price on a complete list of items. Milk bids in school foodservice operations have been awarded on a bottom-line basis for a long time. Can you imagine having one dairy deliver 2-percent unflavored milk while another delivers whole and skim milk, and maybe a third dairy delivers cottage cheese and yogurt? The foodservice manager would have to receive three deliveries and process three invoices. Bottom-line bidding on peaches, pears, and sugar is illustrated in Figure 5.4. The quantity of each item and the extended price (unit price multiplied by quantity) are shown. To compare prices by potential suppliers, unit price for each item is multiplied by quantity and extended prices are added.

Purchasing managers for federal, state, and local institutions must allow bidding by all qualified suppliers, although private institutions and commercial foodservices may select any supplier they want to submit bids. A bid request form, on which the specification and date for closing the bids are indicated, is used to solicit bids from prospective suppliers. Bids usually must be submitted in an unmarked, sealed

Figure 5.3.   Example of a line-item bid.

Product Name	Potential Supplier A	Potential Supplier B	Potential Supplier C
Peaches	($20.36)	$22.94	$23.41
Pears	$22.49	$23.95	($22.46)
Sugar	$19.06	($18.75)	$21.45

Source: From *First Choice, A Purchasing Systems Manual for School Foodservice* (p. 97) by M. Gunn, 1995, University, MS: National Food Service Management Institute.

Figure 5.4.   Example of a bottom-line bid.

Product Name	Quantity	Potential Unit Price	Supplier A Extended	Potential Unit Price	Supplier B Extended	Potential Unit Price	Supplier C Extended
Peaches	25 cs	$20.19	$504.75	$22.02	$550.50	$21.50	$537.50
Pears	10 cs	$20.94	$209.40	$20.48	$204.80	$21.50	$215.00
Sugar	15 bags	$15.98	$239.70	$16.63	$249.45	$14.10	$211.50
Bottomline Total			($953.85)		$1,004.75		$964.00

Source: From *First Choice, A Purchasing Systems Manual for School Foodservice* (p. 97) by M. Gunn, 1995, University, MS: National Food Service Management Institute.

envelope and are opened at a specified time. Government purchasing policies require that this be done publicly and that the award should be made to the lowest bidder. Once a method of bidding is decided, the pricing mechanism for products should be determined.

Pricing Mechanisms

Price is the final piece of information the buyer needs to choose a product. Quality standards have been met by using well-written specifications, and all that remains is to find the lowest price for a specific product. Various pricing mechanisms are available, but the two most common are a firm price for a specified period of time and a reimbursable cost plus fixed fee for service price (Gunn, 1995).

The simplest method is requesting a firm price on a product for a specified period of time. **Firm price** contracts should be limited to one-time delivery or short-term contracts. The price on canned fruits and vegetables usually remains constant for a year or until the next harvest. Late summer and early fall are the height of the canning season for most produce. Prices quoted in the fall remain stable throughout the year unless the wholesaler is overstocked on some items and reduces prices at the end of the season. If suppliers are understocked, however, prices might increase.

Pricing meat and fresh produce is quite different and generally is updated daily. A firm price on meat is seldom quoted and is never quoted on fresh produce. Meat prices are determined by buyers and suppliers in the marketing channel and produce prices by supply and demand.

Hiemstra & Stix (1990) studied cost plus fixed fee purchasing in six Indiana school districts as an alternative to the competitive bid method. The **cost plus fixed fee** buyer reimburses the supplier for the actual cost of the product and freight and pays a predetermined set fee for delivery, warehousing, financing the inventory, and profit (Gunn, 1992b) either to the supplier or a distributor (Gunn, 1995). This type of purchasing for schools includes the following characteristics (Hiemstra & Stix, 1990; Hiemstra, 1992):

- A one-year contract is drawn up based on a competitive bid for the wholesale price of specified groups of products from one supplier, and a fixed fee per case is set.
- Prices paid by the foodservice operation vary directly with those of the supplier, thus permitting suppliers to pass on to customers any changes in market prices.
- The fee per case must remain the same even if the price increases to prevent suppliers from making additional profit. The fixed service fee makes the procedure legal for government contracts because it removes profitability of price increases for the suppliers and helps protect the buyer from price gouging (Hiemstra & Stix, 1990).
- Suppliers must allow the schools to audit all invoices before increasing prices.

In summary, the cost plus fixed fee method of purchasing is less expensive and easier to operate. It provides better service and somewhat higher quality products than the traditional bid system during a period of rising prices and product changes. Further study on this method is needed before foodservice operations adopt it en masse. Many schools are examining other alternatives because of freight deregulation, which is discussed later in this chapter (Gunn, 1995).

A modification of the cost plus fixed fee method is cost plus a markup percentage on each product. This option is used by practically every restaurant chain in the country (Patterson, 1992). This practice is allowed in the private sector but is not an option for schools, government hospitals, and other public buyers. The restaurant chain goes to a manufacturer or processor and negotiates prices with the understanding that the price is the one paid by the distributor, which makes no profit on the product. Then the restaurant chain negotiates a fixed percentage fee, which includes profit, with the distributor for handling the product. The distributor stores, handles, delivers, and bills the restaurant chain for the total cost of the product. In the cost plus fixed fee method, a product price is contracted for a year at the same time the fee is fixed. In commercial chains, the markup is by percentage. If the product price goes up, the markup price goes up; if the price goes down, the markup price goes down. For example, if canned peach halves are $22.00 a case and markup is 12.5%, the fee would be $2.75 per case, or $275.00 for 100 cases. If, however, peaches are $24.00 a case, markup is $300.00. If peaches are $20.00 a case, markup would be $250.00.

Legal Considerations

Purchasing practices and the relationship between buyer and supplier are usually based more on good faith than on legal considerations. The purchase and sale interchange, however, is a legal and binding commitment covered in the Uniform Commercial Code (UCC), which has been passed by all state legislatures except Louisiana. The **Uniform Commercial Code** provides uniformity of law pertaining to business transactions in eight areas identified as articles. Article 2, which governs purchase/sales transactions, is of prime concern to buyers, because it protects them legally against trickery by suppliers. The major legal areas involve the laws of agency, warranty, and contracts. Therefore, buyers should understand the basic principles of each to avoid litigation.

Law of Agency.   Most purchases involve many laws, but every purchasing transaction is governed by at least one legal requirement, the law of agency. Buyers may involve the foodservice operation and themselves in expensive legal disputes if they do not understand how this law affects the purchasing function. The **law of agency** defines the buyer's authority to act for the organization, the obligation each owes the other, and the extent to which each may be held liable for the other's actions.

Some terms need to be defined before the law can be understood. An **agent** is an individual authorized to act on behalf of another party, known as the principal. The **principal** is a person who needs an agent to work on his or her behalf. The **agency** is a business relationship between the agent and principal. Agents have the power to commit their principals in a purchase contract with suppliers. In large organizations, the power of the agency generally is delegated to the buyer, but in small organizations this authority may have developed over years without ever being recorded in a written agreement.

Often the buyer deals with a salesperson and not the supplier. Generally, salespeople are considered to be special agents empowered to solicit business for their principal or company. The primary interest of most salespeople, quite rightfully, is to make as many sales as possible. Most companies protect themselves and their customers by specifying in sales agreements that they are not bound by a salesperson's promises unless they are in writing in a contract approved by an authorized person in the supplier's office.

Law of Warranty.   The **law of warranty** is a guarantee by the supplier that an item will perform in a specified way (Kotschevar & Donnelly, 1999). The UCC recognizes three types of warranties (Leenders, Fearon, & England, 1993):

- Express warranty—promises, specifications, samples, and descriptions of goods that are under negotiation
- Implied warranty of merchantability—suppliers inflate the virtues of their products for the purpose of making a sale and are guilty of a breach of warranty
- Implied warranty of fitness for a particular purpose—buyer relies on the supplier's skill or judgment to select or furnish suitable goods

The UCC provides that if the supplier knows the particular purpose for which the goods are required and the buyer is relying on the supplier's skill or judgment to select or furnish suitable goods, the implied warranty is that the goods shall be fit for such purpose. If, however, the buyer provides detailed specifications for the item, the supplier is relieved of any warranty of fitness for a particular purpose.

Law of Contract.   The **law of contract** is an agreement between two or more parties. Because contracts constitute an agent's primary source of liability, buyers should always be certain that each contract bearing their signature is legally sound. A contract must fulfill five basic requirements to be considered valid and enforceable: the offer, acceptance of the offer, consideration, competent parties, and legality of subject matter.

- *Offer.* The first step in entering into a contract is making an offer, usually by the buyer. A purchase order becomes a buyer's final offer to do business. When the supplier agrees to terms, a contractual relationship is in force. A contract does not exist until both parties agree to the terms stipulated therein.
- *Acceptance.* The next step is the acceptance of the offer by the supplier. Generally, a clause is included that requires the supplier to indicate acceptance of purchase order terms. Two copies of the order are sent to the supplier, one for the supplier and the other to be signed and returned to the buyer.
- *Consideration.* Consideration is the value, in money and materials, that each party pays in return for fulfillment of the other party's contract promise. Failure to do so usually means that the contract is not legally enforceable. Buyer and supplier must agree on quantity, price, and time of delivery. Difficulties often occur because the parties do not define precisely the exact quantity to be purchased. The contract requires the supplier to deliver the quantity of materials specified in the agreement and the buyer is bound to purchase that amount. A price usually is stipulated, but occasionally a statement may be included that the price should not be higher than that of the last shipment. Time of delivery also should be specified for contract orders. The supplier is obligated to meet the delivery date, and failure to do so leaves the supplier liable for damages.
- *Competent parties and legality.* The final two requirements of a contract are competency and legality. *Competency* means that the agreement was reached by persons having full capacity and authority to enter into a contract. *Legality* means that a valid contract cannot conflict with any existing federal, state, or local regulations or laws.

An example of a contract award form for purchasing by a school district is shown in Figure 5.5.

Independent and Organizational Purchasing

Buying methods and legal concerns are just as applicable to an independent foodservice operation as they are to organizations. Buyers must be legally authorized to act as agents of those for whom they purchase.

Figure 5.5. Example of a contract award form.

Contract Award

Board of Education or School _____   Contract Award No. _____
_____   Date Awarded _____
Address   Date Bid Opened _____
_____

This is a notice of the acceptance of Bid # _____ for the period of _____
19_____ to _____ 19_____.

Delivery
Delivery is to be made in two shipments: Week of _____ and _____ between
_____ a.m. and _____ p.m.

Notice to Contractors
This notice of award is an order to ship. Orders against contract are listed by _____ and invoices shall be rendered direct to the _____. The price basis, unless otherwise noted,
_____ includes delivery and transportation charges fully prepaid F.O.B. agency. No extra charge
to be made for packing or packages.

Names and Addresses of Successful Bidders

Offer
In compliance with the above award, and subject to all terms and conditions listed on the Bid Request, the
undersigned offers and agrees to sell to _____ the items listed on the attached schedule.

Bidder_____
_____
Address

By _____
      Signature of person authorized to sign this contract

Title _____

Accepted as to items numbered _____   Accepted by _____

By _____   Date _____

Title _____

Independent Purchasing

Independent purchasing is done by a person who has been authorized to purchase food and supplies for the foodservice department in a restaurant, hospital, or school. In the simplest situation, a restaurant owner might be both manager and buyer and would have full legal authority to execute binding contracts. In small hospitals, the head of the dietetics department may have the authority for foodservice purchasing and thus becomes the agent for the principal, which is the hospital. A similar scenario might exist in a school lunch program in which the foodservice manager buys food and supplies.

Organizational Purchasing

Organizational purchasing usually is done by a committee authorized to purchase food and supplies for many foodservices within a specific category of foodservice operations, such as a restaurant chain, a nursing home chain, or all universities in a state system. Organizational purchasing that includes centralized, group, and cooperative purchasing is not always clear-cut and might overlap, depending on needs of the foodservice operations. Warehouse club purchasing is not as restricted.

Centralized Purchasing.   One person or department handles **centralized purchasing.** In these operations the head of the department usually reports directly to top management, which has the overall responsibility for making a profit. Advantages of centralized purchasing include:

- Better control with one department responsible for purchasing and one complete set of records for purchase transactions and expenditures
- Development of personnel with specialized knowledge, skills, and procedures that result in more efficient and economical purchasing
- Better performance in other departments when managers are relieved of purchasing and of the interruptions and interviews incidental to purchasing
- Economic and profit potentials of purchasing to make it a profit rather than a cost center (Heinritz, Farrell, Giunipero, & Kolchin, 1991)

The purchasing office staff purchases for all departments. The purchasing staff sees suppliers on a regular basis, thus saving valuable time for other departments. The staff, however, will arrange appointments with the appropriate department personnel if a supplier needs to discuss users' concerns or introduce a new product. Generally, centralized receiving and storage are part of the purchasing office, although in some operations the receiving clerk reports directly to the controller. The various departments purchase materials from the storeroom. The price a department pays for a product equals the ultimate cost to the purchasing office. In simple terms, the actual price of the product plus operating costs of the purchasing office and a small percentage for profit is billed to the buyer.

Most hospitals have used centralized purchasing for many years. The foodservice department purchases canned and frozen products, staples, paper goods, and detergents from the central storeroom. In most cases, perishable foods, such as fresh fruits and vegetables and meat, are purchased and stored in refrigerators or freezers in the foodservice. Buyers of these products generally have foodservice experience and understand the quality required to satisfy customers. Even though specifications have been sent to suppliers, a person with expertise in the field can prevent many problems. More than one delivery per week is necessary if freshness is emphasized on menus. For example, salad greens should be crisp, fresh seafood should be delivered the same day it is served, and ground meat should be cooked as soon as possible. The buyer also must be able to make substitutions after conferring with the manager if a product is not available and to adjust quantities according to forecasts. Dairy products and fresh baked products, including bread, generally are on contract. Quantities often cannot be determined until the morning of delivery, and only a person in the foodservice operation can make the decision.

Such an in-house purchasing department in a self-contained organization is the clearest example of centralized purchasing. Widely dispersed units under one central management, however, may also use centralized purchasing. An example is a school foodservice operation in which a central purchasing office, usually with warehouse facilities, meets the requirements for all schools in the district. Warehousing and delivery costs are added to the purchasing budget, but these costs may be somewhat offset by lower prices from suppliers that do not have to make individual deliveries to all schools in the district.

Group Purchasing.   Often erroneously lumped with centralized purchasing, **group purchasing** involves bringing together foodservice managers from different operations, most often noncommercial, for joint purchasing. The economic advantage of group purchasing is that the volume of purchases is large enough to warrant volume discounts.

A site is selected for the group purchasing office, and purchasing personnel are hired by the group of managers and paid from group funds. Warehouse space is not required because products are delivered directly to the foodservice operation by a distributor on a cost-plus basis. Participating managers serve as an advisory committee to the purchasing personnel and also have some decision-making power. An example is their agreement on specifications for each item to be purchased. Obviously, wide variations in specifications defeat the purpose of group purchasing because the amount of each product would be decreased, thus decreasing high-volume savings.

Foodservice managers or their representatives, often production dietitians or chefs, make joint decisions in the selection of canned products by attending can cuttings. Group purchasing is done for most of the food groups. Meat, poultry, seafood, and produce are included because of the large volume. Nonfood products are also purchased jointly. In large group purchasing operations, personnel with expertise in the various areas are on staff.

The best example of group purchasing is found in health care organizations, particularly hospitals (Lorenzini, 1991). Since volume purchasing has been shown to bring food costs down anywhere from 3% to 10%, the number of hospitals organizing or joining purchasing groups has been increasing steadily. Some foodservice consultants estimate that close to 80% of hospitals in the United States belong to purchasing groups and that about 160 such groups exist.

The earliest group purchasing program was started in 1918 by the Greater Cleveland Hospital Association and was supported by hospitals in a 100-mile radius of Cleveland. Currently, many cities (including Cincinnati, Chicago, Los Angeles, and Philadelphia) and states (Connecticut, Idaho, Mississippi, and Missouri) have group purchasing organizations. Large medical centers and small hospitals can profit from group purchasing. Members of health care purchasing groups bought $15.4 billion in goods and services in 1991, according to a 1992 survey (Wagner, 1992). These group purchasing organizations have contracts for products or services with various companies. The most widely used contracts continue to be those for medical/surgical supplies, followed by medical equipment and pharmaceuticals. Group purchasing has become so large that it has its own professional group.

Healthcare Procurement Services, Inc. (HPSI) is the largest group purchasing service in the United States and has a membership of 5,500 facilities in 45 states. This service provides cost containment and improves the bottom line in participating hospitals and nursing homes. It also has developed a menu service and many other programs to help facilities meet regulations and improve the dining experience for their clients. HPSI has more than 3,700 accounts and 40 sales field staff who visit each account on a quarterly basis to meet with each department head to make sure their suppliers are providing satisfactory service and product quality. A fee is charged for this service. Purchasing is done for every department in each facility, including medical, housekeeping, maintenance, and foodservice. Most products are purchased nationally, but some perishable items, such as dairy products, fresh meat, and bread, are purchased locally. Purchasers are given two suppliers in most major product categories from which to choose. HPSI can negotiate for the lowest prices because of the volume of participation. At the same time, the supplier makes a good profit.

University Health System Consortium (UHC) is a member-driven alliance of 77 academic health centers in the United States with a mission to strengthen the competitive position of the 60 basic members and 30 associate members in their respective markets. A component of UHC is the Group Purchasing Program, designed to enhance the purchasing value to participants by using the collective power of UHC members to develop favorable national purchasing agreements. UHC has a potential purchasing volume in excess of $5 billion annually.

The Group Purchasing Program offers food and nutrition services purchasing as a distinct program. It has agreements to purchase food items, foodservice small wares, foodservice capital equipment, and branded foods. The process of purchasing includes competitive bids. Because it is a member-driven program, UHC members determine which suppliers are awarded the bid.

Cooperative Purchasing.   Primarily used in school foodservice operations, cooperative purchasing is not new (McLaren, 1996). Some well-known school foodservice cooperatives have been in operation 10 years. **Cooperative purchasing** is a large organization owned by and operated for the benefit of those using its services. The typical foodservice operation purchases more than 400 food items to meet the demands of the customer (Gunn, 1995). One person cannot keep up with available products because the manufacturing process or ingredients constantly change. Even restaurant chains do not develop specifications in local franchised units. Each unit pays a fee for the expertise of the corporate headquarters staff that is responsible for purchasing for all the units. Most other multiunit foodservice operations do not have a headquarters staff but have a purchasing cooperative.

The formation of a purchasing cooperative is a time-consuming process and usually takes a minimum of two years before receiving the first delivery (Gunn, 1995). For school foodservice operations, state laws should be researched because most states require some type of formal agreement between districts that join a cooperative. The most critical decision is choosing an administrative unit to make decisions and solve problems. For example, will orders for food and supplies, and the resulting billing and payment, go directly from each school district to the distributor? Will the cooperative operate a warehouse or have just-in-time delivery direct to the sites?

An example is the California-based Partners in Nutrition Cooperative (PINCO) (McLaren, 1996). It has a formal structure with an elected board that meets every 6 to 8 weeks. Members purchase everything from food to paper goods through the cooperative, which has an automated system and owns a warehouse. Approximately 46 small school districts that serve 247,000 meals a day belong to the cooperative. PINCO handles every step of purchasing from bidding to ordering to delivery. Members are required to order at least one of the bid items for large-volume products, such as burritos, but the cooperative also will order any nonbid items for school districts. Orders are sent by modem from schools and delivered by a PINCO-owned truck to individual schools or a central warehouse.

Fees are based on usage and are figured on the number of cases ordered, the number of deliveries each week, and the distance from the PINCO warehouse. Each district deposits funds in a PINCO account, and once the order is received, it is paid for from the fund. One of the school districts is responsible for the paperwork, and a formal audit of the district is conducted each year to verify that proper procedures are being followed.

Warehouse Club.   Warehouse clubs offer self-service, cash-and-carry, and wholesale prices (Geisse, 1988). A growing number of restaurateurs are discovering substantial savings and product offerings by buying from these clubs. Many other small foodservice operations are also using them for the same reasons. Products remain in original cartons stacked on pallets or metal shelves separated by wide aisles. A wide variety of brand name items, including food, cleaning supplies, furniture, and electronic equipment needed for operating restaurants, are stocked in plain and unfinished warehouses. Personnel is not available to assist customers. Markups on most products average 10% over wholesale cost, but food products have an even lower percentage markup. These clubs, which now number more than 200 in the United States, have been a boon to single restaurants. Owners of more than one restaurant also can benefit from this type of purchasing.

SUPPLIER SELECTION

Supplier selection may be the single most important decision made in purchasing. The National Association of Purchasing Management uses the term *supplier* to describe a person who offers products for sale. The trend to fewer suppliers, more "buy" than "make" decisions, electronic data interchange, and continuing improvement in quality, price, and service requires greater communication between buyers and suppliers than ever before. Thus, improving buyer and supplier relationships is a key concern in selecting suppliers (Leenders et al., 1993).

Traditionally, the supplier seeks out the buyer, but for the purchasing professional, this leaves too much to chance. Few foodservice managers need to be convinced of the advantages of consolidating most purchases with a **primary wholesale food-service distributor,** defined as a purchasing and product movement specialist in chapter 3. Gone are the days when buyers had many suppliers or distributors to supply their needs. The obvious savings in purchasing from wholesale distributors rather than a long list of suppliers are apparent. Managers can expect better service and reliability. The buyer and supplier should regard their business dealings as a partnership in which both parties cooperate to the fullest extent for their mutual benefits.

Because of mounting competitive pressures, every manager should pay careful attention not only to selecting a wholesale distributor but maintaining the relationship that ensues. The selection process consists of the inquiry and survey stages followed by an evaluation.

The Survey Stage

The purpose of a supplier survey is to explore all possible outlets for a product. Sources of valuable and reliable information include personal experience and business contacts. All information should be kept in complete and up-to-date supplier files in the purchasing office. These files should contain the name and address of every supplier with whom a foodservice operation has transacted business, plus information on the products purchased from the supplier. Additional helpful information would be reliability in meeting delivery dates, willingness to handle emergency orders, and number of times orders are incorrect. The supplier file can be cross-referenced with a file of products listing from whom they were purchased and prices paid, which also could be helpful in selecting a supplier.

Members of professional organizations with similar interests can be helpful in selection. Also, state and national trade shows and exhibitions provide up-to-the-minute information on new products and suppliers who sell them. Finally, the business pages of the local telephone directory should not be ignored as a source of information. The local Chamber of Commerce also may give some assistance. For information on new products, developments, methods, and suppliers, trade publications are an excellent source. A conscientious purchasing agent will read and keep a file of appropriate publications.

The Inquiry Stage

In the inquiry stage of the supplier selection process, the field is narrowed from possible sources to acceptable sources. In general, this process involves comparing the ability of potential suppliers to provide the right quality and needed quantity at the right time, all at the right price with the desired degree of service. Evaluate each supplier as to quality, service, and price (Lynn, 1996). Assess the product itself along with the supplementary service and support systems the company provides. Confirm that the supplier has the resources to meet your operation's needs from both a production and delivery perspective. Remember, a great product at a good price is no bargain if the supplier cannot make enough of the product or get it to you on time.

Geographic location combined with transportation capabilities are major concerns in evaluating a supplier's service. Certainly, shorter delivery distances offer better opportunities for satisfactory service. The kinds and quantities of products available to suppliers also are important considerations in selecting a supplier capable of meeting the foodservice operation's requirements. The selected supplier should keep current with technological developments, provide new and improved products as they become available, and maintain quality control standards that ensure inspection and storage methods adhere to FDA and USDA standards.

Warranty and service offered by an equipment supplier is a vital concern for the buyer, and such information generally has to come from talking to other customers. A telephone call usually is adequate, although some buyers ask former or current customers to complete a confidential questionnaire.

Another factor to consider is that the financial condition of a supplier is vital for maintaining a satisfactory business relationship. Verify the company's claims before making a commitment to purchase (Lynn, 1996). Ask for references and do a credit check on the supplier, just as the supplier probably will do on your operation. In general, the controller or credit manager of the buyer's organization can provide a credit report. A credit check will tell the operator how well the supplier pays distributors. If a supplier is not paying its distributors, it may have trouble getting raw materials, which could delay delivery of your order. When feasible, visit the prospective supplier's warehouse facilities to verify the efficiency and general cleanliness associated with a good business. The visit gives the buyer an opportunity to observe personnel and order-handling procedures in the operation.

After the survey and inquiry stages of selection, the buyer should have a few suppliers from which to choose one or more. The selection process is relatively subjective; more objective evaluations can be made after an order is placed and the product delivered. An evaluation process needs to be developed that can be used for both newly selected suppliers and those who have been servicing the operation for some time.

Supplier Performance Evaluation

Evaluation of suppliers is a continuing purchasing task (Leenders et al., 1993). Current suppliers should be monitored to be sure they are meeting performance expectations, and new ones need to be screened to determine if they should be seriously considered in the future. Although buyers tend to use suppliers with a track record for reliability, new suppliers should be given the opportunity to make a few deliveries so their performance can be evaluated. Selecting a supplier performance evaluation instrument that is fair but really evaluates performance can be difficult. Many foodservice managers develop their own forms. Figure 5.6 is an example of an evaluation form that a foodservice manager could modify and use.

Evaluations should be conducted periodically to keep the supplier's record file up to date. Suppliers who have good evaluations will appreciate knowing the results. Suppliers who do not rate well should be told why before the business relationship is severed.

Figure 5.6. Example of a supplier evaluation form.

SUPPLIER PERFORMANCE EVALUATION

*Supplier:*_____ *Date:*_____

Company	Excellent	Good	Fair	Poor
Size and/or capacity				
Financial strength				
Technical service				
Geographical locations				
Management				
Labor relations				
Trade relations				
Products				
Quality				
Price				
Packaging				
Uniformity				
Service				
Delivers on time				
Condition on arrival				
Follows instructions				
Number of rejections				
Handling of complaints				
Technical assistance				
Emergency deliveries				
Supplies price changes promptly				

PURCHASING PROCESS

Procurement in any foodservice operation requires procedures to accomplish the routine purchasing transaction as quickly and accurately as possible. Undoubtedly, each foodservice has its own procedures unique to its individual needs, but very likely these procedures are similar to the basic pattern followed by other operations. The adoption of definite purchasing procedures implies utilization of appropriate records for each phase in the purchasing process.

Purchasing Procedures

Several basic *procedures* are found in some form in every foodservice purchasing unit (Figure 5.7). These procedures are simple and should be adapted to the special needs of an organization's various departments. Buyers can add, delete, or modify these procedures to fit their operation. In this text, the eight basic procedures used by most foodservice operations will be discussed.

Recognition of a Need

The production unit is most often the first place to recognize a need. The second location is the storage area, where the objective is to have on hand when needed the right products in the right quantity at the right time. A third location in a large organization is the centralized purchasing department, which has inventory responsibility. Recognition of a need should be followed by action to remedy the deficiency by preparing a requisition.

Figure 5.7.   Basic procedures of purchasing.

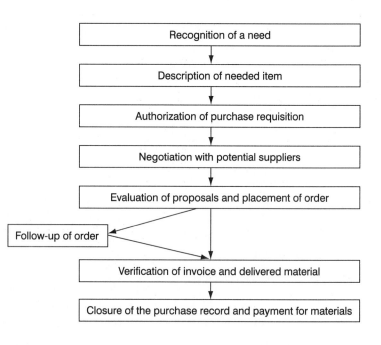

Description of the Needed Item

In most foodservice operations, when cooks in the production unit recognize a need, they initiate a requisition, preferably written, to the storeroom for the required amount of the product. If the storeroom has an adequate inventory, the requisition can be honored. If honoring the requisition brings the inventory stock below the acceptable minimum, storeroom personnel initiate another requisition to purchasing for replenishment of the product to the desired inventory level. In any case, the requisition must contain an accurate description of the desired product and needed quantity. Correction or alteration of the requisition by other than initiating personnel is inappropriate unless approved by supervisory personnel. The necessity for accuracy in requisitions cannot be overemphasized.

Authorization of the Purchase Requisition

The third step in the purchasing process is authorizing the purchasing requisition. In every foodservice, a policy should be established to indicate who has the authority to requisition food, supplies, and equipment. No requisition should be honored unless the person submitting it has the authority to do so. Furthermore, suppliers should know the names of persons authorized to issue purchase orders and should not accept orders not signed by authorized personnel.

Negotiation with Potential Suppliers

Negotiation in purchasing is the process of working out a purchasing and sales agreement that is mutually satisfactory to both buyer and supplier and reaching a common understanding of the essential elements of a contract. This is a crucial procurement function. Some important considerations when negotiating supplier agreements include the cost of the item itself, quantity discounts, add-ons such as freight and insurance, and payment terms (Lynn, 1996). To determine the true value of a quantity discount, calculate how long you can expect to store the material and what your cost will be for carrying the inventory. Payment terms also are an important contract consideration. Some suppliers offer discounts for early payment; others extend what amounts to an interest-free, short-term loan by offering lengthier terms. Negotiation usually establishes such vital details as qualifications of a supplier, fair and reasonable prices to be paid for needed products, delivery dates agreeable to both the buyer and the supplier, and renegotiated contract terms when conditions change.

Evaluation of Proposals and Placement of Order

All supplier proposals are evaluated for compliance with the preceding four basic procedures in purchasing (Figure 5.7). Following evaluation of proposals is the actual placement of an order. Ideally, all orders should be in writing, but if an order is placed by telephone, confirmation in writing should be made promptly. A written record of every purchase should always be on file.

Follow-Up of Order

Theoretically, a follow-up after the order has been placed and accepted by the supplier should not be necessary. However, follow-up is justified when a specific delivery time of certain items is critical to a banquet or other occasion. Most foodservice managers have a purchase checking procedure, usually involving color-coded copies of the purchase order. Forms for this purpose are discussed later in this chapter.

Verification of Invoice and Delivered Material

The invoice is the supplier's statement of what is being shipped to the buyer and what payment is expected. The invoice should be checked against the purchase order for quality, quantity, and price. Delivery and condition of materials should agree with the purchase order and invoice. Any differences require immediate action by the buyer. For example, the condition of fresh meat should be verified, and any indication of high temperatures is a cause for rejection and immediate communication with the supplier.

Closure of the Purchase Record

Closing the purchase record consists of the clerical process of assembling the written records of the purchase process, filing them in appropriate places, and authorizing payment for the goods delivered. The filing system need not be complex; its only purpose is to provide an adequate historical record of these business transactions.

Purchasing Records

The essential records for the purchasing process are the requisition and purchase order, originating with the buyer, and the invoice, prepared by the supplier. These records differ among foodservice operations but all have the same essential information (Spears, 1995).

Purchase Requisition

The requisition is the first document used in the purchasing process. It may originate in any one of a number of units in the foodservice operation. Most requisitions, however, originate in the production unit when the head cook sends a list of the amount of each ingredient for a recipe to the storeroom. An example is shown in Figure 5.8. Five basic items of information generally are included on all requisitions:

- *Requisition number.* This number is necessary for identification and control purposes and generally is accompanied by a code for the originating department.
- *Delivery date.* The date on which the item should be in the storeroom for use by cooks should allow sufficient time to secure competitive bids and completion of the purchase transaction, if at all possible.
- *Budget account number.* This number indicates the account to which the purchase cost will be charged.

Figure 5.8.   Example of a purchase requisition.

COMMUNITY HOSPITAL
PURCHASE REQUISITION

To: _____ Purchasing Office _____   *Requisition No.:* _____ FS1201 _____

Date: _____ August 17, 1998 _____   *Purchase Order No.:* _____ 1842 _____

From: _____ Foodservice _____   *Date Required:* _____ September 14, 1998 _____

Budget Account No.: _____ FS 1101 _____

Total Quantity	Unit	Description	Supplier	Unit Cost	Total Cost
20	Cases	Tomatoes, diced, U.S. Grade B (Extra Standard) #10 cans, 6/case	L. & M. Wholesale Grocers	$13.86	$277.20

Requested by _____   Approved by _____   Date Ordered _____ 8/20/98 _____

- *Quantity needed.* Quantities should be expressed in a common shipping unit, such as cases, along with the number of items in a unit. For example, the entry on the requisition is for 25 cases of cherry pie filling, with 6 No. 10 cans to a case.
- *Description of the item.* The description and quantity needed are the two most important pieces of information on the requisition form and therefore are given the most space. The description information may include the product specification, brand, or catalog number.

In addition to the above information, which is provided by the person responsible for the requisition, the buyer adds the name and address of the supplier and the details of the purchase, including the purchase order number, price, and date ordered.

Purchase Order

A purchase order is the document, based on the information in the requisition, completed by the buyer who gives it to the supplier. It states in specific terms the purchase and sales agreement between the buyer and supplier. Before acceptance, the purchase order represents an offer to do business under certain terms. Once accepted by a supplier, it becomes a legal contract. An example is shown in Figure 5.9.

Figure 5.9. Example of a purchase order.

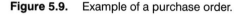

COMMUNITY HOSPITAL
1010 Main Street
Sioux City, Oklahoma

To: L. & M. Wholesale Grocers

200 South Street

Sunnyvale, OK

Purchase Order No.: _____ 1842 _____

Please refer to the above number on <u>all</u> invoices, two copies required.

Date: _____ August 24, 1998 _____

Requisition No.: _____ FS1201 _____

Dept.: _____ Foodservice _____

Date Required: _____ September 12, 1994 _____

Ship to: _____   F.O.B.: _____   Via: _____   Terms: _____

Total Quantity	Unit	Description	Supplier	Unit Cost	Total Cost
20	Cases	Tomatoes, diced, U.S. Grade B (Extra Standard) #10 cans, 6/case	L. & M. Wholesale Grocers	$13.86	$277.20

Approved by _____
Title: Director of Purchasing
                Community Hospital

Format of Purchase Order.   The purchase order, like the requisition, exists in a wide variety of formats that have been developed to meet the needs of individual foodservice operations. The principal reason for this variety is that the purchase order is a legal document; the terms presented in it are intended to protect the buyer's interests, which differ from one operation to another. However, almost every purchase order includes these items:

- Name and address of the foodservice operation at the top of the purchase order for easy identification
- Name and address of the supplier, usually typed in a box in the upper left of the form

liability - if sign for
order agreeing to pay

- Identification numbers, including purchase order and purchase requisition numbers, usually in a box in the upper right side of the form. Frequently these numbers are accompanied by instructions to the supplier to use them on all invoices and correspondence with the buyer.
- General instructions to the supplier, such as information on the marking of shipments, number of invoices to be sent, delivery date required, and shipping instructions
- Complete description of purchase item, including quantity and quality. Quantity to be purchased should be in a separate column and stated in specific pricing units, such as per case or per unit. Quality descriptions, especially in bid or contract buying, should be as brief as possible because specifications have already been agreed upon.
- Price data and all applicable discounts
- Buyer's signature and title indicating approval of the purchase order. This assures the supplier that the order was placed by a legal agent of the operation and that requirements of purchasing law are met.

Required Number of Copies.   Three copies of the purchase order are sufficient for basic ordering: the original, which is sent to the supplier; an acknowledgment copy, which functions as a formal acceptance that the supplier returns to the buyer; and a file copy for the buyer's record. This simplified plan offers minimum control and should not be used in larger operations.

Ordering for large foodservice operations requires six copies of the purchase order. The additional three copies are given to the following individuals or departments:

- *Receiving copy.* This copy informs receiving personnel that a delivery is scheduled on or before a certain date and is intended to alert them to be prepared to count and inspect the shipment on arrival.
- *Accounting copy.* This copy is sent to the accounting office as notification of the commitment to purchase and to allow accounting to reconcile the purchase order with the original requisition and receiving report. If all the essential forms are in order, the purchase is approved for payment.
- *Requisitioner's copy.* Quite often, purchasing sends a copy of the order to the requisitioner as notification that the requisition has been honored and the order placed.

Invoice

The *invoice* prepared by the supplier contains the same essential information as the purchase order: quantities, description of items, and price. When the products are delivered, the supplier's invoice must be compared with the purchase order and quantity received. Any discrepancies or rejections at the receiving point should be noted immediately. In some operations, these problems are handled by the receiving clerk, who notes the discrepancy on the invoice and has the supplier's delivery person initial it. Such notations often are overlooked by the bookkeeper or are unclear and require time to check them. A verbal agreement between the receiving clerk and the delivery person can be even more problematic. The best solution to these problems is the use of a credit memo that provides a written record of adjustments made on the invoice (Dietary Managers Association, 1991).When a problem is noted at the time of delivery, a formal correction should be made on a credit memo. Examples of these problems include:

- wrong price charged
- back order if the product is not delivered or only a small quantity is delivered
- items rejected because of unacceptable quality
- short weight or count

A credit memo is required to adjust the delivery invoice and reflect the change in the amount of the bill. If the delivery person does not have a credit memo form, the receiving clerk should supply it. The credit memo, as shown in Figure 5.10, informs the supplier that the bill must be credited to show only the price of products received. Processing credit memos include special concerns.

- Delivery person must sign and receive a copy of the form.
- Supplier should be called to be sure the credit will be on the next statement sent to the foodservice operation.
- When the invoice is filed for payment, the adjustment must be made on the specific delivery invoice.
- Bills should be adjusted for any applicable credit memos before the foodservice pays.

Audit Trail

Foodservice managers need to understand the accounting aspects of purchasing because products brought into the operation must be paid for. The role of the accounting department in purchasing deserves special attention in a foodservice operation. Financial transactions must be verified by conducting an **audit,** a final report following a formal examination of the books of account. The best way to control purchasing is through the establishment of an **audit trail** that creates an organized flow for source documents, including the requisition, purchase order, and invoice.

The auditing branch of accounting is most often associated with the independent external audit, identified as a financial audit. These audits are conducted by certified public accountants who, in addition to auditing finances, usually make recommendations for strengthening internal operating controls.

Today many operations conduct internal audits to review and evaluate internal control systems. **Internal control,** as defined by the American Institute of Certified Public Accountants, is a plan to coordinate methods within a business to safeguard assets, check the accuracy and reliability of its accounting data, promote operational efficiency, and encourage adherence to prescribed managerial policies (Schmidgall, 1986). For example, in a foodservice food should be stored by a storekeeper, requisitioned by a cook, and accounted for by the accounting department. The storekeeper, cook, and accountant are independent of each other, thus preventing fraud and providing reliable accounting data.

In small foodservice operations, the owner who manages may be both the buyer and bill payer. As the operation increases in size, the owner usually hires a manager

Figure 5.10. Example of a credit memo.

CREDIT MEMO   NUMBER ___1070___

From ABC Hospital   To Acme Poultry and Seafood
___1501 Anywhere Street___   (supplier)
___Anytown, USA___   ___1500 Smith Ave.___
                                       ___Anytown, USA___

Credit should be given on the following:

Invoice number ___71071___   Invoice date ___3/18/xx___

Product	Unit	Number	Price/Unit	Total Price
36/42 Shrimp	pound	20	4.15	83.00

Reason: Total ___$83.00___
Product was to be frozen but
was thawed on surface.

___J. Jones___   ___B. Joyce___
(delivery person)   (authorizing signature)

(prepare in duplicate)

who has purchasing responsibilities and a part-time employee for bookkeeping and clerical duties. In large operations, responsibilities for purchasing are given to one person or department, and the accounting department assumes responsibility for receiving and storage. The purchase order and receiving report are checked against the invoice before the bill is paid; inventory values of products in storage must be determined to facilitate preparation of financial statements (Schmidgall, 1986). This system reduces the possibility of theft and fraud that can occur if only one person is responsible for the three activities.

PURCHASING TRANSPORTATION

The purchase price of materials includes many costs that are not apparent to the novice foodservice buyer. Costs for transportation of products from the place grown, mined, or manufactured to the place needed can represent a substantial part of the price of the purchased product. The foodservice supplier has two roles, one as a buyer from foodservice processors or equipment manufacturers and the other as a wholesaler selling products to an operation. For example, the supplier purchases canned and frozen foods from a processor and a dishmachine from a manufacturer to sell to a foodservice operation. Even though food and nonfood products usually are purchased from wholesalers, the consumer ultimately pays for transportation costs from the place of origin to consumption. The foodservice buyer has little control over costs to transport products to the supplier but has some control over transportation costs from the supplier to the foodservice. One of the advantages of using single source distributors is the cost savings of transportation, because products from all over the United States and sometimes the world are combined in one shipment to fill an order from the foodservice operation. The purchase of transportation, therefore, should include the same techniques as those used for purchasing products: evaluation and selection of suppliers, price analysis, value analysis, and aggressive negotiations (Heinritz et al., 1991). Who pays for transportation and what kind of transportation carrier is needed are questions that should be answered by both the supplier and buyer.

Free on Board

Free on board (F.O.B.) means that products are delivered to a specified point or place with all transport charges paid. Once the point is specified, the following questions can be answered:

- Who pays the carrier?
- When is the legal title of the products being shipped given to the buyer?
- Who is responsible for claims with the carrier if products are lost or damaged during shipment?

F.O.B. origin refers to the place from which the product is originally transported; **F.O.B. destination** refers to the place the product is going. If F.O.B. origin is stipulated, the buyer selects the transport company and pays the freight charges, owns the title, and files claims for loss or damage to the products. The title and control of products come to the buyer when the carrier signs for the products at the point of origin. If F.O.B. destination is stipulated, the buyer pays the freight charges, but the supplier owns the products in transit and files claims. The title remains with the supplier until the products are delivered.

For example, if equipment is purchased F.O.B. origin from a manufacturer, the foodservice buyer not only pays the freight charges, owns the title, and files claims for loss or damage, but also hires a transport company to deliver it. Large operations generally prefer this method because their purchasing departments know through experience which carriers and routes give the best service and lowest price. Smaller operations, however, may not have the expertise in these areas and prefer F.O.B. destination, giving the supplier the responsibility. Variations of F.O.B. origin and F.O.B. destination are possible, but the bottom line is that transportation costs are included in the ultimate price of the delivered products to the consumer (Leenders et al., 1993).

Freight Classifications

Deregulation of transportation, which began in the 1970s, is aimed at reducing the number of rules governing carriers and increasing competition in the industry (Heinritz et al., 1991). The processor or manufacturer decides which kind of transportation is required to deliver products to a wholesaler. Carriers used for products going to foodservice operations are usually trains, trucks, or airplanes; the products are transported as rail, motor, or air freight. Rail freight is used most often for large shipments and accounts for almost half of the freight shipped in the United States. Rates for a full carload generally are lower than for any other kind of transportation. Many superdistributors for foodservice operations have either a rail siding adjacent to their plant or an easily accessible freight yard for pickup by truck, which of course adds additional cost. Fresh potatoes often are transported by rail from the producer to the distributor if the load is heavy enough.

Advantages of motor freight include the most flexibility in short hauls and door-to-door service because foodservice operations have docks for loading and unloading. Transportation as motor freight occurs most often with food and nonfood products. Problems facing the trucking industry in the 1990s include congestion of the already overcrowded interstate highway system, pollution from environmentally unsafe fuel, and possible increases in fuel taxes. Air freight often is competitive with rail and motor freight, despite its higher rates. With the new jumbo jets, fresh food products, such as produce and seafood, and kitchen equipment parts have increased the airlines' share of the freight market (Heinritz et al., 1991).

ETHICAL CONSIDERATIONS

Ever since the Watergate scandal resulted in the resignation of a U.S. president, the public, businesses, and professions have become sensitive to what is and what is not ethical and by whose standards people are measured. The news media have kept the word *ethics* in public view with reports of congressional hearings on ethical conduct of appointees to important positions. With all the emphasis on ethics, politicians occasionally are accused of lying and business people of accepting favors "under the table."

Business and professional organizations are updating codes of ethics or standards of practice and emphasizing them to their members. **Ethics** are defined as the principles of conduct governing an individual or business. Personal ethics should be distinguished from business ethics. The source of **personal ethics** lies in a person's religion or philosophy of life and is derived from definite moral standards. **Business ethics** may be defined as a self-generating system of moral standards to which a substantial majority of business executives gives voluntary assent. Those ethics are a force within business that leads to industrywide acceptance of certain standards of practical conduct (Zenz, 1981). Ethics are created by society, while **morals** are an individual's personal belief about what is right or wrong.

Purchasing probably is one of the most suspect activities in foodservice and other business operations. Opportunities for unethical behavior are many. According to Heinritz et al. (1991), the buyer is the custodian of company funds and of the company's reputation for courtesy and fair dealing with suppliers. The relationship between the buyer and supplier involves many situations that are ethical in nature. The Golden Rule, "do unto others as you would have others do unto you," could be modified for supplier relations as "treat the supplier the same way you would like to be treated if you were the supplier" (Dietary Managers Association, 1991). The buyer's personal ethics should not conflict with the business ethics of the organization. The great majority of purchasing professionals are ethical, according to a study for the Center for Advanced Purchasing Studies (Janson, 1988). Educators are beginning to incorporate concepts of ethical behavior in curricula, especially in business and hospitality programs. Ethical considerations in procurement involve buyer and supplier relationships and social concerns about the environment.

Buyer/Supplier Relationships

Seemingly routine decisions about what is acceptable behavior for a buyer can become confusing. Foodservice managers must answer many questions, and a good way to keep those answers straight is a policy statement. A **policy** is a general guide to organizational behavior developed by top-level management. Each time a situation occurs, it should be handled in the same way regardless of which employees are involved. Any questions the buyer has about ethical concerns should be covered by a policy.

- Can I accept gifts from the supplier?
  Policy: Gifts with a value over $10 cannot be accepted.
- Can I accept an invitation to play golf and have dinner with the supplier?
  Policy: Free meals, drinks, or entertainment with a value over $10 cannot be accepted.
- Can I purchase, for personal use, some of the products I purchase for the operation if I pay the supplier directly?
  Policy: Purchasing from suppliers for self or employees at wholesale prices is not permitted.
- What do I do if a board member tells me to purchase from another member who owns a wholesale meat operation even though the quality is lower and the prices are higher than any other company?
  Policy: A supplier cannot be used if a manager, relative, or employee has more than 5% of stock in the supplier's company because of conflict of interest.
- Do I need competitive bids when I know that one company treats me well and is willing to send a product immediately if I forget to order it?
  Policy: An order is awarded to the supplier with the lowest price for a product or service. Only with administrative approval will a one-price quotation be accepted.
- Can I share with a supplier quotations from other suppliers to receive a lower bid on a product and save money for the foodservice operation?
  Policy: All eligible suppliers will be encouraged to bid on products and services and will be treated the same by the buyer.

These policy statements probably would be expanded in actual foodservice operations and could become more lenient or stricter depending upon the ethical standards of upper-level management. For example, a policy might stipulate no gifts, meals, entertainment, or financial interests in a supplier's business. Policies help provide consistency in problem solving, and employees do not have to guess about what management wants. Thus, policies should be shared with employees and suppliers.

Environmental Concerns

A much broader area of ethics involves responsibility to society, often termed social responsiveness. Purchasing managers are becoming actively involved in disposal of hazardous and nonhazardous waste. Buyers need to educate themselves on environmental issues because in many foodservice operations, waste disposal is the responsibility of the purchasing department. They need to explore new alternatives for increasing recycling and other methods for disposing of waste (Heinritz et al., 1991). Environmental buzzwords are appearing more and more frequently in the United States: "Let's not waste the '90s," "greening of America," "environmental health," and "proper waste management."

Rathje (1991) asks if we can preserve both our environment and many of the opportunities afforded by our lifestyle. He answers, "Yes, if we finally become committed to recycling." Landfills are reaching capacity with solid waste, and few new disposal sites have been approved. The U.S. Environmental Protection Agency (EPA) defines **solid waste** as the products and materials discarded after use in homes, commercial establishments, and industrial facilities. Waste is everywhere. If we are not careful, we may be consumed by it.

Packaging often is blamed for solid waste generation and disposal. Without packaging, food would rot on farms and in warehouses and become infested with insects and other vermin. Food poisoning and disease would spread, and food losses would increase total waste. The EPA in 1989 recommended methods for handling **municipal solid waste (MSW),** defined as refuse collected routinely from households, commercial institutions, offices, and light industry by municipal or private haulers or carried to dumpsters or disposal areas by individuals (Testin & Vergano, 1990).

Restaurants, and take-out operations in particular, have been targeted as the cause of the solid waste problem even though this industry produces no more trash than other business sectors. The misconception occurs partly because of the high visibility of restaurants and the fact that customers throw away disposable cups, plates, and napkins with logos after eating either in or outside the restaurant. Foodservice disposables, however, account for a surprisingly small share of landfill volume. If all the paper, plastic, and aluminum from delis, salad bars, schools, households, hospitals, and restaurants were included, these disposables would account for 1.84% of landfill volume. A typical quick-service restaurant meal consisting of hamburgers, fries, and a medium-size drink produces about 3.5 ounces of packaging weight (Foodservice & Packaging Institute, 1991). Source reduction and recycling are the major methods for controlling waste in foodservice operations.

Minimal packaging combined with reduction in cost comes to mind when source reduction is mentioned. The EPA (1989) defines **source reduction** as the design and manufacture of products and packaging with minimum toxic content, minimum volume of material, and a longer useful life. The thickness of the aluminum in a 12-ounce beverage can has been decreased by using new designs that retain strength while lowering the average weight by 26%. The weight of a 2-liter plastic bottle that holds soft drink beverages has been reduced by 21% and a 16-ounce glass container by 30% over a period of 10 or more years (Testin & Vergano, 1990). Technological changes in packaging materials have been responsible for this decrease in weight. Waste stream analysis research conducted in four middle and two elementary schools in Louisiana indicated that changing the milk packaging from half-pint gable-top cartons to polyethylene pouches decreased the volume of waste in gallons significantly. The volume of total solid waste in the service area of the schools also was decreased significantly because of alternative milk packaging (Hollingsworth, Shanklin, Gench, & Hinson, 1992). Foodservice managers can practice source reduction through selective buying habits and reuse of products. They need to reexamine specifications to decide if products with lighter weight and less bulky packaging can be purchased (Shanklin, 1991).

Recycling is the second method for decreasing waste in foodservice operations. The Food Service and Packaging Institute (FPI) defines **recycling** as the act of removing materials from the solid waste stream for reprocessing into valuable new materials and useful products. Traditional packaging materials, including paper, metals, and glass, have been recycled in varying degrees for many years. Recently, the technology for recycling plastic has improved enough that plastics recycling programs are now in place. Aluminum and glass can be recycled many times without destroying their properties, but paper cannot be recycled more than about five times because fibers become shorter each time and finally wash out of the process (Testin & Vergano, 1990).

Although recycling has increased substantially in the 1990s, collecting recyclable materials and developing markets for recycled products remain a challenge. Paper makes up the bulk of recycled materials and plastic is just beginning to be recycled, but many communities do not collect these materials. Aluminum can manufacturers, however, are heavily involved in recycling and pay relatively high rates for recycled aluminum because it saves most of the energy cost of manufacturing it from ore (National Restaurant Association [NRA], 1989). Foodservice operations can support recycling through their buying power by purchasing goods made from recycled material, such as napkins, paper towels, paper bags, bathroom tissue, and cardboard packing cases.

Foodservice managers face several choices in deciding how to help maintain the environment. A good example is the quick-service restaurant with a big take-out clientele. Of course, take-out business requires the use of disposables, but should reusable tableware be used for customers eating on premise? According to the U.S. Public Health Service, one cause of foodborne disease is reusables subjected to poor dishwashing or improper handling after cleaning. Laboratory tests of both, just before serving, show that disposables are far more sanitary than reusables.

The typical cafeteria using disposables saves 70 gallons of fresh water every 100 meals for dishwashing, which is a major consideration in drought areas. Large dishmachines use up to 500 gallons of fresh water an hour. Automatic dishmachines are energy intensive, requiring a large use of electricity to run the equipment and heat the water to 170°F in the sanitizing cycle. The manufacture of reusables and disposables does require water and energy. Paper mills, however, are located in areas where water is plentiful; plastics use very little water in manufacturing. Only 3% of the world supply of oil accounts for all plastic, and foodservice plastics are just a small part of that. The energy contained within plastic and paper can be almost fully recovered in waste-to-energy plants (Foodservice & Packaging Institute, 1991).

Recent EPA statistics indicate that Americans are showing some improvement in decreasing the growth of landfill waste (King, 1993). As of 1990, 17% of all MSW was either recycled or composted as compared to 10% in 1988. Waste sent to landfills was 67%, down from 80% in 1988. However, Americans continue to generate more waste than ever. The public and legislative mandates are demanding that foodservice operators concentrate even more on source reduction and recycling. Many operators are involving employees in designing waste production programs that, in addition to saving the environment, are a source of revenue by cutting down on waste and receiving cash for recyclable materials.

SUMMARY

Purchasing is the major activity in the procurement functional unit of a foodservice operation. Purchasing methods have the greatest influence on the price of food and can be informal or formal, the latter of which requires competitive bidding. Two basic methods for awarding bids are line-item bidding and all-or-nothing bidding. The two most often used pricing mechanisms are a firm price for a specified period of time and a reimbursable cost plus fixed fee for service price. Cost plus a markup percentage is a variation of the cost plus fixed fee method and is used by practically every restaurant chain in the country. The purchase and sale interchange is a legal and binding commitment covered in the Uniform Commercial Code.

Supplier selection can be the most important decision made in purchasing. The buyer needs to complete the survey, inquiry, and performance evaluation stages in selecting a supplier. The purchasing process can be simplified if well-established procedures and use of appropriate records can simplify the purchasing process. Essential records are the requisition, purchase order, and invoice. These records control purchasing by establishing an audit trail.

The purchase price of products includes transportation costs from the place grown, mined, or manufactured to the place needed. Free on Board (F.O.B.) means that products are delivered to a specified place with all transport charges paid. Products usually are transported to foodservice operations as rail, motor, or air freight.

Opportunities for unethical behavior are many in the purchasing field. The relationship between the buyer and the supplier involves many situations that are ethical in nature. Policy statements should be available to assure that each ethical situation is handled consistently. Buyers have a responsibility to society on environmental concerns, especially waste disposal. Foodservice buyers can participate in source reduction and recycling.

REFERENCES

Dietary Managers Association. (1991). *Professional procurement practices: A guide for dietary managers.* Lombard, IL: Author.

Foodservice & Packaging Institute, Inc. (1991). *Foodservice disposables: Should I feel guilty?* Washington, DC: Author.

Geisse, J. (1988). Wholesale warehouses offer no-frills shopping. *Restaurants USA, 8*(11), 15.

Gunn, M. (1992a). Changes in the food distribution chain: Impact on nutrition and cost. *Impact of Food Procurement on the Implementation of the Dietary Guidelines for Americans in Child Nutrition Programs: Conference Proceedings.* University, MS: National Food Service Management Institute, 25–32.

Gunn, M. (1992b). Professionalism in purchasing. *School Food Service Journal, 46*(9), 32–34.

Gunn, M. (1995). *First Choice, a purchasing systems manual for school foodservice.* University, MS: National Food Service Management Institute.

Heinritz, S., Farrell, P. V., Giunipero, L., & Kolchin, M. (1991). *Purchasing: Principles and applications* (8th ed.). Englewood Cliffs, NJ: Prentice Hall.

Hiemstra, S. J. (1992). Methods of purchasing. *Impact of Food Procurement on the Implementation of the Dietary Guidelines for Americans in Child Nutrition Programs: Conference Proceedings.* University, MS: National Food Service Management Institute, 119–131.

Hiemstra, S. J., & Stix, C. L. (1990). Evaluation of cost plus fixed fee procurement methods in Indiana schools. *School Food Service Research Review, 14*(1), 29–33.

Hollingsworth, M. D., Shanklin, C., Gench, B., & Hinson, M. (1992). Composition of waste generated in six selected school food service operations. *School Food Service Research Review, 16*(2), 125–130.

Janson, R. L. (1988). *Purchasing ethical practices.* Tempe, AZ: Center for Advanced Purchasing Studies/National Association of Purchasing Management, Inc.

King, P. (1993). Recycling & source reduction. *Food Management, 28*(1), 54, 55, 58, 60.

Kotschevar, L. H., & Donnelly, R. (1999). *Quantity food purchasing* (5th ed.). New York: Macmillan.

Leenders, M. C., Fearon, H. E., & England, W. B. (1997). *Purchasing and supply management* (11th ed.). Homewood, IL: Irwin.

Lorenzini, B. (1991). Purchasing groups find savings in numbers. *R & I,* [September 18,] A51–A52.

Lynn, J., (1996). Profiting from smart purchasing. *Restaurants USA, 16*(4), 35–38.

McLaren, P. (1996). Strength in numbers. *School Foodservice & Nutrition, 50*(4), 18–20, 22, 24.

National Restaurant Association. (1989). *Current issues report: The solid waste program.* Washington, DC: Author.

Patterson, P. (1992). State of the industry: Purchasing in commercial food service. *Impact of Food Procurement on the Implementation of the Dietary Guidelines for Americans in Child Nutrition Programs: Conference Proceedings.* University, MS: National Food Service Management Institute, 133–141.

Rathje, W. L. (1991). Once and future landfills. *National Geographic, 179*(5), 116–134.

Schmidgall, R. S. (1986). *Hospitality industry managerial accounting.* East Lansing, MI: Educational Institute of the American Hotel and Motel Association.

Shanklin, C. W. (1991). Solid waste management: How will you respond to the challenge? *Journal of the American Dietetic Association, 91,* 663–664.

Spears, M. C. (1995). *Foodservice organizations: A managerial and systems approach* (3rd ed.). Upper Saddle River, NJ: Merrill/Prentice Hall.

Stefanelli, J. (1993). *VNR's Encyclopedia of Hospitality and Tourism.* New York: Van Nostrand Reinhold, 103–108.

Testin, R. F., & Vergano, P. J. (1990). *Packaging in America in the 1990s: Packaging's role in contemporary American society—The benefits and challenges.* Herndon, VA: Institute of Packaging Professionals.

U.S. Environmental Protection Agency, Office of Solid Waste. (1989). The solid waste dilemma: An agenda for action. *Final report of the Municipal Solid Waste Task Force.* Washington, DC: U.S. Government Printing Office. EPA/530-SW-89-019.

Wagner, M. (1992). Group purchasing survey: Purchase groups buy goods worth over $15 billion. *Modern Healthcare* [September 28], 39, 40, 42, 46, 48–50.

Zenz, G. J. (1981). *Purchasing and the management of materials* (5th ed.). New York: Wiley.

Receiving, Storage, and Inventory Control

Procurement is the managerial function of acquiring material for production. To accomplish this function, products must be purchased, received, and stored in the foodservice operation. High-quality meat or fresh fruits and vegetables can become mediocre products if standards for receiving and storage have not been established.

Because the entire procurement process is a profit generator, receiving and storage are as critical to cost control and profit generating as is purchasing. Without proper controls in these two activities, carefully planned menus and good purchasing procedures have little effect on customer satisfaction. Planning and controlling, therefore, are the management functions relevant to receiving and storage (Spears, 1995). Receiving is a process for ensuring that products delivered by suppliers are those that were ordered in purchasing. After food and supplies have been received properly, they must be placed in appropriate storage, which is the holding of products under proper conditions to ensure quality until time of use. Inventory is a record of products owned by the organization, and inventory control is the technique of having the desired quantity of products in storage.

RECEIVING

Receiving has become known as the "missing link" in procurement because quite often food quality problems are caused by breakdowns in receiving procedures (Gunn, 1992). Say, for instance, that a different product arrives on the receiving dock than what was ordered. The receiving process involves more than just acceptance of and signing for delivered products. It also includes verifying that quality, size, and quantity meet specifications, that the price on the invoice agrees with that on the purchase order, and that perishable products are marked or tagged with the receiving date. Finally, the products should be recorded on a daily receiving record and then sent immediately to the appropriate storage or production areas to prevent deterioration.

A large percentage of foodservice revenues are spent on food purchases. The economic advantages gained by competitive purchasing based on complete and thorough specifications can be squandered by poor receiving practices. Good controls in the receiving process ensure management that a dollar value in quantity and quality is received for every dollar spent (Spears, 1995).

Elements of Receiving Practices

Elements of good receiving include competent personnel with specified responsibilities, facilities, equipment, specifications, sanitation, and security. Receiving is the result of purchasing products that meet specifications for quality and purchase orders for quantity and price.

Competent Personnel

In many operations, receiving is entrusted to an employee who happens to be near the loading dock or storage area when shipments arrive. When responsibility for receiving is not assigned and procedures have not been developed, problems can arise, such as a loss in quality, incorrect quantity, and theft and pilferage of products. These losses can cost a foodservice operation more than its annual net profit.

Responsibility for the receiving activity should be assigned to a specific employee. In small operations, this person may have other duties, but if possible, the person responsible for receiving should not be involved in purchasing or production. Separating the duties of purchasing and receiving is basic to a checks and balances system for ensuring adequate control. The owner or foodservice manager should assume responsibility for either purchasing or receiving if sufficient employees are not available. Employees assigned to receiving products should

- know quality specifications for each product
- evaluate quality of products
- understand the process by which products are received
- know what to do if a problem occurs with an incoming shipment
- make time available to perform receiving tasks
- know how to complete internal receiving records (Dietary Managers Association, 1991)

Model Position Descriptions for the Foodservice Industry, from the National Restaurant Association (NRA) (1992), contains 43 positions, one of which is a receiving clerk, as shown in Figure 6.1. These descriptions are generic and vary with different foodservice operations. The "Competencies" listed on the right side of the description were determined by the Secretary's (of Labor) Commission on Achieving Necessary Skills (SCANS), which has established the basis for all types of positions. The five competencies, each with an explanation, are as follows:

Resources	Allocating time, money, materials, space, and staff
Interpersonal	Working on teams, teaching others, serving customers, leading, negotiating, and working well with people from culturally diverse backgrounds
Information	Acquiring and evaluating data, organizing and maintaining files, interpreting and communicating, and using computers to process information
Systems	Understanding social, organizational, and technological systems, monitoring and correcting performance, and designing or improving systems
Technology	Selecting equipment and tools, applying technology to specific tasks, and maintaining and troubleshooting technologies

Foodservice managers are encouraged to develop their own position descriptions based on the format and ideas presented in the models. Tasks required for a particular position should be substituted for those in the model to make the descriptions meaningful to employees. The following requirements with examples for the position should be noted and emphasized:

- *Physical*—walking, bending, kneeling, handling, reaching, lifting, climbing, stooping
- *Sensory*—vision, hearing, tasting, smelling, speaking, touching
- *Intellectual*—reading, math skills, decision making

Because of the specialized skills and knowledge needed to perform these tasks competently, the training of employees assigned to receiving is essential. Many tasks can be explained and demonstrated through on-the-job training. However, learning how to use specifications for evaluating products is more difficult and may require specific training sessions.

Facilities

In many foodservice operations, the receiving area also may be the entrance for employees and salespeople, a place for general storage, and an exit to trash storage, all of which suggest a need for monitoring and good security procedures (Spears, 1995).

Ideally, the receiving area should be located near the delivery door, storeroom, refrigerators, and freezers to minimize the time and effort required for moving food into proper storage. In small operations, a wide hallway may be used as the receiving area; in larger operations, additional space is needed. In either case the receiving area should be located near the delivery door for two reasons: union contracts of delivery persons may stipulate "inside-door" delivery only, and security concerns

Figure 6.1. Model position description for receiving.

POSITION DESCRIPTION

POSITION TITLE: **RECEIVING CLERK**

REPORTS TO: **Assistant Director/Director**

POSITION SUMMARY: Ensures an orderly flow of supplies so that all items are on hand when needed, to keep and maintain an orderly and clean storeroom, coolers, and freezers. Ensures proper rotation of products.

TASKS AND COMPETENCIES:

Tasks	Competencies
1. Receives all food, canned or frozen, and rotates stock using the first in-first out system.	1. Resources 2. Information
2. Carefully counts and/or weighs items received for correct amount and for compliance with purchase specifications.	1. Resources 2. Information 3. Systems
3. Orders all goods and supplies based on department needs, keeping in mind time required for pre-preparation and for special function advanced bookings.	1. Resources 2. Interpersonal 3. Information 4. Systems
4. Ensures that all shelves are clean and items are rotated, are not stored directly on the floor, and meet all sanitation guidelines for storage.	1. Resources 2. Information

PREREQUISITES:

Education: High school graduate or equivalent. Good math skills helpful.

Experience: Knowledge of foodstuffs is essential. This could be through some gained experience in food purchasing, as storeroom attendant, or as chef/assistant chef/cook.

Physical: Subject to wet floors, temperature extremes, and excessive noise. Must be able to bend, stoop, and perform while standing for long periods of time. Must be able to lift up to 50 pounds. Must be able to write legibly as well as read and understand directions and instructions.

Source: From *Model Position Descriptions for the Foodservice Industry* by the National Restaurant Association, 1992, Washington, DC. Used by permission.

arise when persons who are not foodservice employees are permitted in back-of-house areas (Dietary Managers Association, 1991). For example, a delivery person might have to transport products from the outside dock door through areas not belonging to foodservice before reaching the receiving area, thus creating an opportunity for theft.

In large facilities, a receiving office generally is located near the delivery entrance. Enough space should be available to permit all incoming products to be checked at one time. In smaller facilities where an office for the receiving clerk seldom is available, a desk at the receiving entrance facilitates the check-in of products.

The space allocated for receiving should be ample enough to allow all products in a delivery to be inspected at one time. Many products, such as canned goods or bags of flour, require minimal inspection and only need the package and label checked and the quantity counted. Other deliveries, such as meat or lettuce, may require opening boxes to inspect quality and count or weight. Apples and oranges are packed by count and in layers requiring that the bottom and top layers need to be checked. Storage should not begin until the delivery personnel have left, thus eliminating confusion for the receiving clerk in performing two tasks at one time. Time and money can be saved by providing facilities that require minimum handling of products and permit direct transfer to storage or the production unit.

Equipment

The kind and type of equipment needed for the receiving area is determined by the volume of products received or transferred to another area at one time. For example, a hand truck may be adequate in some foodservice operations, but a forklift may be required for pallet deliveries. A **pallet** is a portable wooden or metal platform for handling by a forklift truck and is used for storage of materials in warehouses (Figure 6.2).

Scales used to be a requirement in a receiving area for weighing all products purchased by weight. Today, however, many foodservice managers believe scales are not necessary because the group of products, commonly called "catch weight" or approximate weight products, has diminished to fewer than five in most operations (Gunn, 1995). Many catch weight products are weighed by the processor, and the weight is recorded on the box. The labeling of food products is strictly regulated by government agencies, which makes weighing products seem like a waste of time only to find that 10 pounds, 2 ounces is really in a box marked 10 pounds, 2 ounces. Few processors would risk damaging their reputation by shorting weight on a case of 8-ounce rib-eye steaks. Big operations that buy a large number of whole cuts of beef might need scales that print the weight of the merchandise on the reverse side of the invoice or packing slip or print a tape which can be attached. The same idea applies to fresh produce. A 50-pound sack of potatoes does not always contain exactly 50 pounds but may weigh anywhere between 47 and 53 pounds depending on the season and the growing region. The sack of potatoes is billed and accepted as 50 pounds regardless of actual weight.

A desk and chair is needed for the employee managing the receiving area. A file cabinet should be available to store records and reports, and a calculator should be on hand to verify computations on the invoice. Tools, such as a can opener, crow-

Figure 6.2. Motorized vehicles.

133

bar, and short-blade knife, for opening containers and packages, are needed to inspect deliveries. A thermometer to check if chilled or frozen products are delivered at appropriate temperatures according to specification, clipboards, pencils, and marking and tagging equipment are also necessary.

Specifications

The employee who receives orders should know the standards suppliers must meet and should have a file box of specifications. All deliveries must be checked against these specifications, and nothing below standard should be accepted. Quality standards as stated in the specification need to be checked. For example a special quality standard might be that meat, produce, dairy products, and frozen foods be transported in temperature-controlled trucks or that produce be shipped only in new containers to protect microbiological safety (Produce Marketing Association, 1995). The procedure for checking quantity should be based on the foodservice policy, which may specify that all items be counted or weighed or that only random counting or weighing be done before signing the invoice.

In large operations receiving clerks are given a copy of the purchase order. The purchase order alerts them that a delivery is scheduled on or before a certain date and that they must be prepared to count and inspect the shipments.

Gunn (1992) suggested that the time has come to make drastic changes in school foodservice purchasing systems to improve receiving. She noted that the process will be difficult because everybody in the marketing channel must cooperate. Most school foodservice buyers use complicated specifications that require laboratory equipment to measure whether the food meets the specified standards, such as grams of fat and percent of white meat in processed chicken products. Most schools cannot afford the expensive laboratory equipment or the personnel trained to use it. Specifications should be limited to include only those standards that can be measured at time of receiving, such as product code numbers and brand names of products that meet the specifications. These two items should be all the receivers need to check at delivery time. Each product would have a label with a code number indicating the plant where the product was processed, the processor's product number, and the date and shift when the product was processed. Brand names of products meeting the specified standards also need to be identified. Each purchasing unit should have a quality assurance program that requires samples to be pulled at random and sent to commercial laboratories for testing all quality indicators used in determining acceptable brands. Gunn concluded that "any effort to implement the Dietary Guidelines will be defeated if we specify an acceptable level of fat or sodium but fail to check the product after receipt." Perhaps someday her hopes will become reality.

Sanitation

The receiving area should be designed for easy cleaning. The floor should have material that is easily scrubbed and rinsed and adequate drains and a water connection nearby to permit hosing down the area. Storage for cleaning supplies must be conveniently located.

Screening the outside doors is necessary because insects tend to gather near loading docks. Fans or electrical or chemical devices for destroying insects often are mounted near the outside doors in the delivery area.

Receiving Security

The foodservice manager should monitor and check security in the receiving area at irregular intervals to ensure that established receiving procedures are followed. Weights, quantities, and quality of merchandise received at various times need to be rechecked as part of the control system.

Persons responsible for purchasing should not be responsible for receiving because they could check the quantity on the purchase order but only send part of it to storage. Scheduled hours for receiving and adequate facilities and equipment for performing receiving tasks prevent many security problems. Products should be moved immediately from receiving to storage to prevent temptation by people passing through the area. Another security measure is to keep the loading dock door locked at all times, if possible. A doorbell can be installed to permit salespeople, delivery personnel, and others to signal their arrival. This practice limits access to those authorized to enter.

The Receiving Process

Detailed procedures are important to assure that products are received properly. The steps in the receiving process are outlined in Figure 6.3.

Inspection against the Purchase Order

A written record of all orders must be kept to provide a basis for checking deliveries. This record, the purchase order (Figure 5.9), becomes the first control in the receiving process by including a brief description of the product, quantity, price, and

Figure 6.3. Steps in the receiving process.

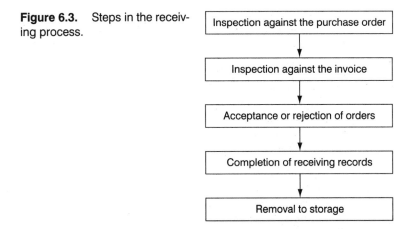

supplier. In small foodservice operations using informal purchasing procedures, this record may be as simple as a notebook for entering the basic ordering information. In large operations with more formal procedures, however, one copy of the purchase order generally is sent to the receiving department as a record of scheduled deliveries (Spears, 1995).

Incoming shipments must be compared with the purchase order to ensure that the products accepted were ordered. The receiving clerk will note if only a partial delivery was made or if a product was not delivered. If a comparison of incoming deliveries with purchase orders indicates that the correct products have been delivered, then quality should be checked.

As stated previously, specialized training of receiving clerks is important to ensure that they understand and can recognize quality standards. Checking products in the presence of the delivery person is essential. All products should be compared with the standards, one of which often is tolerance levels, in the specifications. Without question, the count or weight and quality tolerance levels of all products must be verified before the delivery invoice is signed. Products purchased by count should be counted, and those purchased by weight weighed. For example, a tolerance of two substandard tomatoes in a container might be permitted; 0.5 ounce over or under the specified weight could be acceptable for an 8-ounce steak. When too many products are below the tolerance levels for weight or quality, the receiving clerk should reject the products. A credit memorandum form may be used; one copy with the rejection noted should be signed by the delivery person and the receiving clerk and given to the delivery person to transmit to the supplier. The original credit memo is attached to the invoice by the receiving clerk, who notes the memo number on the invoice and sends it to the accountant for payment. A second copy can be made for the receiving department. Checking products in the presence of the delivery person is essential.

When foodservice operation has a standing order, a specific purchase order or other record is not required for each delivery. In some operations, a quantity level may have been set by the buyer for such products as bread, milk, and coffee. Some foodservice operators permit delivery persons employed by the supplier to check the quantity on hand and deliver enough to meet the quantity level. However, this practice is not recommended (Spears, 1995).

Inspection against the Invoice

After products have been checked against the purchase order and specifications, the delivery must be compared to the invoice prepared by the supplier. The invoice is the supplier's statement of what is being shipped to the foodservice operation and the expected payment.

Checking quantities and prices on the invoice is a critical step in the receiving process. Three receiving methods are used in foodservice operations: invoice, blind, and electronic receiving.

- *Invoice receiving.* The receiving clerk checks the quantity of each product delivered against the purchase order. Any discrepancies are noted on both the purchase order and the invoice. This method is quick but can be unreliable if the receiving clerk does not compare the two records and only checks the delivery invoice.

- *Blind receiving.* The receiving clerk uses an invoice or purchase order with the quantity column blanked out and records on it the quantity of each product received. This method requires that each product be checked since the amount ordered is unknown. This procedure is time consuming and labor intensive for both the receiver and the deliverer.
- *Electronic receiving.* Technology is speeding up the receiving process, although it is still too expensive for small foodservice operations. Tabulator scales, which weigh and automatically print the weight on paper, are being used in large operations as is the Universal Product Code (UPC). Bar codes, originally used on products in grocery stores, currently are appearing on cartons and packages in foodservice operations. Handheld scanners that can read a UPC bar speed up the receiving process.

If the quantities and prices are correct and the receiving employee has checked the quality of the products, the invoice should be signed. Generally two copies of the invoice are required, one for foodservice records and the other for the accounting office. In small operations, only one copy may be required. If errors have been made in delivery or pricing, corrections must be reported on the invoice before it is signed. The delivery person also should initial any correction of errors.

Acceptance or Rejection of Orders

Delivered products become the property of the foodservice operation whenever the purchase order, specifications, and supplier's invoice are in agreement. Payment then will be due at the time agreed upon for products charged on the invoice.

Rejection at the time of delivery is much easier than returning products after they are accepted. If, however, errors are discovered after a delivery has been accepted, the supplier should be contacted immediately. Reputable suppliers generally are willing to correct problems. The foodservice manager should find out why the problem was not detected at time of delivery and revise receiving procedures. Whether products are returned after acceptance or rejected at time of delivery, accounting personnel must be sure credit is given by the supplier.

Occasionally, a substandard product may be accepted because it is needed immediately and time does not permit exchanging it or finding an alternate source. The buyer might try to negotiate a price reduction with the supplier. If a product is not available or only a partial amount is delivered, the buyer needs to decide if it should be backordered.

Completion of Receiving Records

The receiving record provides an accurate list of all deliveries of food and supplies, date of delivery, supplier's name, quantity, and price data. Distribution, either to the kitchen or storeroom, also is indicated. This information is helpful in verifying and paying invoices and provides an important record for cost control of all foods delivered to the storeroom and kitchen.

Products delivered directly to the kitchen are included in that day's food cost, whereas products sent to the storeroom are charged by requisition when removed from stores for production and service. Such a receiving record documents product transfer to storage in facilities in which receiving and storage tasks are performed by different employees and thus provides a checkpoint in the control system. This record usually is prepared in duplicate, one copy to be sent with the invoices to the accounting department and the other retained in the receiving department. If the receiving clerk is responsible for verifying price extensions on invoices, this should be done before the invoice is forwarded to the accounting office. Accounting personnel, however, also should verify the arithmetic extensions on invoices.

Removal to Storage

Products should be transferred immediately from receiving to the secure storage area. Receiving personnel should not be permitted to wait until they have time to move food and supplies to storage. Since the products are now the property of the foodservice, security measures are important to prevent theft and pilferage. Also, spoilage and deterioration may occur if refrigerated and frozen products are held at room temperature for any period of time.

Foodservice operations may have various procedures for marking or tagging products for storage indicated on the receiving record. Marking consists of writing information about delivery date and price directly on the case, can, or bottle before it is placed in storage. Daily food cost calculations can be done quickly because prices do not have to be looked up, and fewer products will spoil on the shelves because the ones with the oldest dates will be used first. Tagging products also facilitates stock rotation to ensure that older products are used first, which is particularly important with perishable food products, such as expensive meat and fish. A two-part card is completed: the tag part is attached to the product before placing it in storage, and the duplicate copy is sent to the person who calculates food cost when the product is issued from storage to production (Figure 6.4). Managers can detect theft because tags identify what should still be in storage. Tagging usually is justified only in large foodservice operations because it is time consuming (Dietary Managers Association, 1991).

Figure 6.4. Sample storage tag.

Tag Number ________	Tag Number ________
Date of Receipt ________	Date Received ________
Weight/Cost	Weight ________
______ (×) ____ = ____ No. of #s Price Cost	Price ________
Name of Supplier: ________________	Cost ________
	Supplier ________
Date of Issue: ________	Date Issued ________

STORAGE

Storage is important to the overall operation of the foodservice because it links receiving and production (Figure 6.5). Proper storage maintenance, temperature control, and cleaning and sanitation therefore are major considerations in ensuring quality of stored foods. Dry and low temperature storage facilities should be accessible to both receiving and food production areas to reduce transport time and corresponding labor costs (Spears, 1995).

Competent personnel are as essential for storage positions as they are for all other foodservice positions. A model storage person position description also has been developed by the NRA (Figure 6.6). Storage employees check in products from the receiving unit, provide security for products, and establish good material handling procedures. Only those employees authorized to store and issue products, check inventory levels, or clean the areas should have access to storage facilities.

Storage Security

Theft in storage facilities is a major problem in a foodservice operation. The sad commentary is that, once again, the customer pays for the problem. Stefanelli (1997) defines **theft** as premeditated burglary and **pilferage** as "inventory shrinkage." Theft occurs when someone drives a truck up to the back door and steals expensive products and equipment. An example of pilferage is the employee who steals a couple steaks before checking out.

Ideally, the storage area should be on the same floor as the production area and visible to the foodservice manager, but this is not always possible. In large operations, the main storage areas often are located on a lower level or in another area of the

Figure 6.5.   Food flow chart.

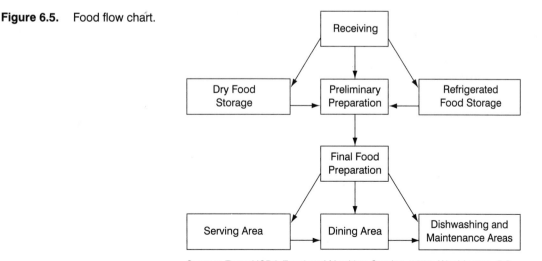

Source: From USDA Food and Nutrition Service, 1975, Washington, DC:
U.S. Government Printing Office.

Figure 6.6. Model position description for storeroom person.

POSITION DESCRIPTION

POSITION TITLE: **STOREROOM PERSON**

REPORTS TO: **Unit Manager**

POSITION SUMMARY: Responsible for the receipt and storage of all food items and equipment received in a unit. The inventory and security of the stored items is under the control of this individual.

TASKS AND COMPETENCIES:

Tasks	Competencies
1. Receives all food, supplies, and materials.	1. Resources
2. Checks incoming merchandise against order sheets for such items as weight count, quality, and specification.	1. Information 2. Systems
3. Ensures items are received and stored at the proper temperatures.	1. Information 2. Resources 3. Technology
4. Maintains delivery and inventory records as prescribed in Manual of Procedures (MOP).	1. Information 2. Systems
5. Keeps all storage areas and inventory in a neat and orderly fashion.	1. Resources
6. Issues stored items to authorized personnel as defined in the MOP.	1. Resources 2. Systems
7. Maintains the overall security of the storage area by ensuring all areas are properly locked and protected.	1. Resources 2. Technology

PREREQUISITES:

Education: High school graduate or equivalent desired. Should be good at basic arithmetic relative to inventory value calculations.

Experience: Prior experience with food items and warehousing techniques desirable.

Physical: Must be capable of strenuous lifting and carrying activity for short periods of time (during deliveries). Should be able to lift up to 50 pounds into storage bins or shelves.

Source: From *Model Position Descriptions for the Foodservice Industry* by the National Restaurant Association, 1992, Washington, DC. Used by permission.

building, making surveillance by the manager difficult. In institutions such as a large hospital, dry storage for food and supplies may be in the central storeroom, and the centralized purchasing department assumes security responsibility. In multiunit restaurant operations, a central warehouse usually is kept for major storage, and a limited storeroom and small refrigerators and freezers for a few days' supply are provided in the individual restaurant operations. Small restaurants often have no designated storage space. Shelves in the kitchen hold extra cans or cartons of food and a refrigerator and freezer hold those that require low temperatures. Everyone becomes suspect when cans of food or pounds of coffee seem to walk out of the kitchen.

Storage areas should be locked and keys given to only those who are in supervisory positions and need access to these areas. Often very expensive items, such as Beluga caviar at $150 a pound or saffron at $50 a pound, are kept locked in a small refrigerator or storage box for which only the foodservice manager or owner has a key. The same method is used to protect expensive silver tableware. Caterers have learned that special locked cupboards for storing silver serving equipment are essential for preventing theft. In some foodservice operations, locks for storage areas are replaced periodically to prevent access with unauthorized duplicate keys. Only authorized people should have access to storage facilities. Adequate lighting is needed in storage areas, not only for sanitation purposes but also to prevent theft. Closed circuit television systems are being used more and more in storage areas and outside exits of buildings.

Types of Storage

All foods should be transferred to storage areas as soon as possible after delivery unless they are to be prepared for service immediately and need to be sent directly to the kitchen. Groceries, canned foods, and staples should be placed in dry storage. Generally, these products are categorized into groups, then arranged either alphabetically or according to frequency of use within the groups. Perishable foods must be placed in refrigerated or frozen storage promptly. In addition, storage areas must be available for china, flatware, trays, utensils, and other nonfood products, such as disposables, detergent, and cleaning products. Coffee and alcoholic beverages should have separate locked storage areas because both often are stolen. Foods that give off odors, such as fresh fish, should be stored separately. New stock, such as dry skim milk or dry cereal, should be placed in back of older stock to prevent loss from deterioration. Foods should be checked periodically for evidence of spoilage, as indicated by bulging or leaking cans, or for changes in appearance, such as freezer burns on meat. Ideally, canned foods should not be kept more than six months even when stored under proper conditions, because the length of time between canning and delivery often is difficult to determine.

Dry Storage

Dry food storage is used for foods not requiring refrigeration or freezing and should provide protection from the elements, insects, rodents, and theft. Cleaning supplies and insect or rat poisons should not be kept in the food storeroom. Instead, a separate locked room should be provided to prevent such items from contaminating food products.

Floors in the dry storage area should be slip resistant and easily cleaned. Walls and ceiling need to be painted light colors and have a smooth surface that is moisture-proof and easy to wash and repair. The number of doors allowing access to the store-room should be limited. A heavy-duty main door needs to be wide enough for equipment to pass through when transporting foods from receiving to dry storage or from dry storage to production areas. This door should lock from the outside; however, a turn-bolt lock or crash bar on the inside of the door permits opening without a key in case someone is locked in. A Dutch door often is used as the main entrance; the lower half is locked at all times except when accepting shipments and the upper door is open during issuing hours.

Good ventilation in dry storage areas is essential for controlling temperature and humidity and preventing musty odors. A thermometer should be mounted in an open area for easy reading. Dry storage temperature should be cool, within a range of 50°F to 70°F. Spices, nuts, and raisins deteriorate if the storage temperature is higher than 52°F, so these products often are kept in a refrigerator. Humidity often is an overlooked factor in storerooms. For most food products, a relative humidity of 50% to 60% is considered satisfactory. Humidity above this level may result in rusting cans, caking of dry and dehydrated products, growth of bacteria and mold, and infestation of insects in the storeroom (Longree & Armbruster, 1987).

Dry storerooms frequently are located in a basement that has all sorts of water, heating, and waste pipes running along the ceiling. Leakage from these pipes is a common source of trouble in basement storerooms, especially leakage from sewer pipes that contaminates food. Hot water and steam pipes may create high temperatures in the storeroom and therefore should be well insulated (Longree & Armbruster, 1987).

Sectional slatted platforms, delivery pallets, and metal platforms with wheels provide a useful type of storage for case lots of canned goods or for products in bags. Their distance from the floor must be in accordance with local health department requirements. Shelving is required whenever less-than-case lots must be stored or when management prefers that canned goods be removed from cases for storage. Adjustable metal shelving is desirable because it allows for various shelf heights and is vermin-proof (Figure 6.7). Shelving must be sturdy to support heavy loads without sagging or collapsing and should be located at least two inches from walls to provide ventilation. If the size and shape of the storeroom permit, shelving should be arranged for accessibility from both sides.

AMCO® has introduced Ultra Density™ Storage shelving, as shown in Figure 6.8, as an alternative to traditional track shelving, which is very expensive to install. Ultra Density™ shelving consists of individual units that fit together in the storage area. These units roll forward or backward. One cart can be rolled to the receiving area and then rolled back to the storeroom. In addition, several people can have access to stored goods instead of just one person in a track shelving area.

Metal or plastic containers with tight-fitting covers can be used for storing cereal products, flour, sugar, dried foods, and broken lots of bulk foods. These containers should be placed on dollies or have built-in wheels for moving from one place to another (Figure 6.9). Aisles between shelves and platforms need to be wide enough for equipment with wheels. Forklift trucks for moving food, supplies, or pallets require much wider aisles than handcarts. Foods should be arranged in the storeroom according to a

Figure 6.7.   Metal shelving for storage area.

Source: InterMetro Industries Corporation. Used by permission.

plan, and every product should be assigned a definite place. Designing forms for checking inventory to match the arrangement of products on shelves saves time.

Low-Temperature Storage

Perishable foods should be held in refrigerated or frozen storage immediately after delivery until use for preservation of quality and nutritive value. The type and amount of low-temperature storage space required in a foodservice varies with the menu and purchasing policies. Too much refrigeration and frozen storage increases capital costs and operating expenses and encourages a tendency to allow leftovers to accumulate and spoil. Astute foodservice managers have found that limiting the amount of low-temperature storage discourages excess purchases and overproduction.

In some foodservice operations, separate refrigerated units are available for meats and poultry, fish and shellfish, dairy products and eggs, and fruits and vegetables. Separate freezers also are available for frozen foods and ice cream. Ideal storage temperatures vary among food groups. The more precise the temperature, the better the quality of the products. Table 6.1 provides a detailed list of recommended storage temperatures and maximum storage times according to type of food, most of which have relatively little processing.

Figure 6.8. Ultra Density™ storage shelving.

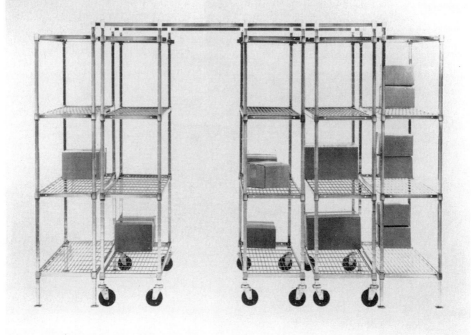

Source: AMCO®. Used by permission.

Low-temperature storage units can be categorized into three types:

- *Refrigerators*—storage units designed to hold the temperature for storing meat and poultry at 30°F to 36°F, fish and shellfish at 30°F to 32°F, dairy products and eggs at 36°F to 40°F, and fruits and vegetables at 40°F to 45°F.
- *Tempering boxes*—separate units for thawing frozen foods, specially designed to maintain a steady temperature of 40°F regardless of room temperature or product load.
- *Storage freezers*—low-temperature units for storing frozen foods that maintain a constant temperature in the range of −10°F to 0°F.

In many foodservice operations, especially small ones, satisfactory storage of various products can be maintained with fewer units kept at the following temperatures:

- Dairy products, eggs, meat, and poultry at 32°F to 40°F
- Fresh fruits and vegetables at 40°F to 45°F
- Frozen foods at −10°F to 0°F

Some operations have only one refrigerator and keep everything but the frozen foods in it. In cases like this, either the lettuce and tomatoes freeze or the dairy products, eggs, meat, and poultry deteriorate quickly. In both cases, quality of the products decreases.

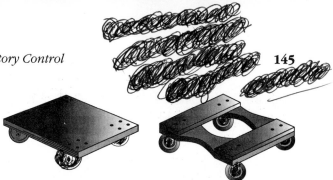

Figure 6.9. Dollies and containers for use in storage facilities.

Platform and Open-Frame Can Dollies

Container on Dolly   Container Equipped with Casters

Source: From USDA Food and Nutrition Service, 1975, Washington, DC: U.S. Government Printing Office.

Humidity control also is important for maintaining food quality in low-temperature storage. A humidity range between 75% and 95% is recommended for most foods. Perishable foods, however, contain a great deal of moisture and therefore a relative humidity of 85% to 95% is recommended. If humidity is not sufficient, evaporation causes deterioration, such as wilting, discoloration, and shrinking.

Low-temperature units are designed as walk-in or reach-in refrigerators or freezers. In large operations, walk-in units generally are located in the storage area with separate reach-in units in the production and service areas for frozen vegetables, dairy products, salad ingredients or salads, and desserts. In small operations, the trend is away from walk-ins and toward reach-ins because less floor space is required and the capital investment generally is lower.

Hard-surface, easily cleaned floors, walls, and shelves should be made of smooth, nonabsorbent material. Shelves for walk-in refrigerators or freezers need to be metal and may be stationary or portable, preferably with wheels for ease of cleaning. The floor level should be the same as that of the area in which the walk-in is located to permit carts to roll in. As with dry storage, food should not be placed on the floor. Drains to remove scrubbing water and condensate should be located inside the low-temperature storage units. Uniform ventilation and adequate lighting are essential in the unit to maintain sanitary conditions. All low-temperature storage units should be cleaned according to manufacturer's instructions on a regular schedule. Most refrigerators and freezers in foodservice operations today are self-defrosting; if not, periodic defrosting of these units must be scheduled.

Table 6.1. Recommended storage temperatures and times.

Food	Refrigerator Storage (32°F–40°F [0°C–4°C])	Freezer Storage (0°F [−18°C] or below)	Dry Storage (30°F–70°F [10°C–21°C])
Roasts, steaks, chops	3–5 days	Beef and lamb: 6 months Pork: 4 months Veal: 4 months Sausage, ham, slab bacon: 2 months Beef liver: 3 months Pork liver: 1–2 months	Never
Ground meat, stew meat	1–2 days	3–4 months	Never
Ham, baked whole	1–3 weeks	4–6 months	Never
Hams, canned	12 months	Not recommended	Never
Chicken and turkey	2–3 days	Chicken: 6–12 months Turkey: 3–6 months Giblets: 2–3 months	Never
Fish or shellfish	30°F–32°F (−1°C–0°C) on ice, 2–3 days	3–6 months	Never
Shell eggs	1–2 weeks	Not recommended	Never
Frozen eggs	1–2 days after thawing	9 months	Never
Dried eggs	6 months	Not recommended	Never
Fresh fruits and vegetables	5–7 days	Not recommended	Never
Frozen fruits and vegetables	—	Variable, depends on kind	Never
Canned fruits and vegetables	—	Not recommended	12 months
Dried fruits and vegetables	Preferred	not recommended	2 weeks
Canned fruit and vegetable juice	—	—	Satisfactory
Regular cornmeal	Required over 60 days	Not recommended	2 months
Whole wheat flour	Required over 60 days	Not recommended	2 months
Degermed cornmeal	Preferred	Not recommended	Satisfactory
All-purpose and bread flour	Preferred	Not recommended	Satisfactory
Rice	Preferred	Not recommended	Satisfactory

Source: Reproduced with permission from *Food Service Manual for Health Care Institutions,* 1994 Edition. Published by American Hospital Publishing, Inc. Copyright 1994.

146

Table 6.2. Foods that give off or absorb odors.

Food	Gives Off Odors	Absorbs Odors
Apples, fresh	Yes	Yes
Butter	No	Yes
Cabbage	Yes	No
Cheese	Yes	Yes
Cornmeal	No	Yes
Eggs, dried	No	Yes
Eggs, fresh shell	No	Yes
Flour	No	Yes
Milk, nonfat dry	No	Yes
Onions	Yes	No
Peaches, fresh	Yes	No
Potatoes	Yes	No
Rice	No	Yes

Source: From USDA Food and Nutrition Service, 1975. *Food Storage Guide for Schools and Institutions,* 27. Washington, DC: U.S. Government Printing Office.

All refrigerators and freezers should have one or more of the following kinds of thermometers:

- Remote reading thermometer, placed outside the unit to permit reading the temperature without opening the door
- Recording thermometer, mounted outside the unit and continuously recording temperatures in the unit
- Bulb thermometer, mounted or hung on a shelf in the warmest area inside the unit

Temperatures in all units must be checked at least twice a day. An employee should be appointed to check and write down temperatures at specified times as a control measure. Some foodservice operations have an alarm or buzzer that is activated when temperatures rise above a certain level. Employees need to be trained to open refrigerator doors as infrequently as possible by obtaining all foods needed at one time to keep temperatures down while conserving energy. When temporary power failures occur, refrigerators and freezers should be opened as seldom as possible.

In both low-temperature and dry storage, foods that absorb odors must be stored away from those that give off odors. Typical foods that emit and absorb odors are listed in Table 6.2.

INVENTORY CONTROL

Inventory in foodservice operations is supported by the presence of products in storage areas. Too large a quantity, or too many products not being used, ties up capital and requires expensive storage space. Most managers try to protect assets while minimizing the capital invested in inventory. Inventory is a record of products owned by the organization, and inventory control is a technique of maintaining assets at desired quantity levels. Issuing products, conducting inventories, and controlling methods all require some type of record keeping.

Issuing Products

Issuing is the process used to supply food to production units after it has been received. Products may be issued directly from the receiving area, especially if planned for that day's menu, but more often food and supplies are issued from dry- or low-temperature storage.

Direct Issues

Products sent directly from receiving to production without going through storage are referred to as *direct issues.* These products usually are used on the day received, and their cost is charged to the food cost for the day. In most foodservice operations, milk and bread are handled as direct issues.

Maintaining accurate food cost records and controlling inventories require that direct issues be processed. If not, food cost will be unrealistically high on the day of delivery and low on the day of actual use.

Storeroom Issues

Foods that are received but not used the day they are purchased are identified as *storeroom issues.* These products are issued from a storage area when needed for production or service. Control of issuing from storage has two important aspects. First, goods should not be removed from the storeroom without proper authorization. Second, only the required quantity for production and service should be issued. A requisition is used to provide these two controls.

The cook or ingredient room employee requisitions from the storeroom person the desired products and quantity and size for each according to a recipe. The **ingredient room** is an area, often a separate room, in which ingredients from storage are measured or weighed according to a recipe before being sent to production. The storeroom person then prepares a daily issue record that contains the daily issue number, issuing storeroom identification, and date of issue. The columns consist of the requisition number, quantity, unit, and product description. In addition, columns for the unit receiving the issue, unit and total prices of products, and identification of the issuing storekeeper are included on the daily issue record (Figure 6.10).

Ingredient rooms are used primarily in noncommercial foodservice operations. Most commercial operations do not have the space to devote to this function. Even large hotel kitchens have downsized. Because space is so expensive, it is used for serving customers, thus increasing revenue.

In foodservice operations that have an inventory control person, the cook or ingredient room employee sends a requisition to this person, who sends it to the storeroom person after checking the availability of the product in inventory. If a computer-assisted inventory system is used, an inventory number for each product is required. Costs would not have to be entered, since these data are available from information stored in the computer. The storeroom requisition also may be generated by the computer. An example of a computer-generated storeroom order form is shown in Figure 6.11.

Figure 6.10. Daily issue record.

Issue Number: 92

Issuing Storeroom: Dry Stores #1   Date of Issue: 9/14/98

Req. No.	Quantity	Unit	Description of Item	Issued to	Unit Price	Total Price	Issued by
823	10	#10 cans	Tomatoes, diced	Cook's unit	$2.31	$23.10	AV
	1	1½# box	Oregano, dried leaf		10.95	10.95	
	1	3# box	Dried, minced onion		4.93	4.93	
	1	1# box	Dried, diced green pepper		7.24	7.24	
	1	20# box	Spaghetti, long thin		10.75	10.75	
	1	1-gal. bag	Catsup		3.18	3.18	
	8	2-oz.can	Bay leaves		3.59	26.32	
	1	11-oz. can	Thyme, grd.		4.99	4.99	
	1	1 gal.	Worcestershire sauce		4.38	4.38	
	1	26-oz. box	Salt, iodized		.26	.26	
	3	#10 can	Tomato puree		2.07	6.21	

Conducting Inventories

Inventory control records must include adequate procedures to permit the foodservice manager to have up-to-date and reliable data on costs of operation. Inventory records have four basic objectives (Spears, 1995):

- provision of accurate information for food and supplies in stock
- determination of purchasing needs
- provision of data for food cost control
- prevention of theft and pilferage

Issuing procedures are only one component of inventory records. A periodic physical count of food and supplies in storage is another requisite element of any inventory control system. More sophisticated records, such as a perpetual inventory, are maintained in many foodservice operations to assist in achieving the objectives.

Physical Inventory

A **physical inventory** is the periodic actual counting and recording of products in stock in all storage areas. Usually, inventories are taken at the end of each month. In large foodservice operations, a complete inventory rarely is taken at one time.

Figure 6.11. Computer-generated order form.

MEAT   - ORDER GROUP

06\06\97 - PITTMAN DATE   06\11\97 -DELIVERY DATE   WEDNESDAY   USAGE PERIOD FRI-SAT

STORAGE LOCATION	CODE	ITEM NAME	BRAND	BIN QT.	ORDER AMOUNT (IN ORDER UNITS)	DELIVERED AMOUNT	NEEDED AMOUNTS LBS.	ORDER UNITS	SUGG ORDER UNITS	INVENTORY ON HAND
13095	0065000803	SAUERKRAUT REFRIG			1 PAIL		9.00	0.5 PAIL	1	
41000	0021010102	EGGS WHOLE FRESH			3 CS		81.00	2.3 CASE	3	
41000	0021020507	EGGS WHOLE LIQUID REFRIG			2 CRTN		37.20	1.9 CARTON	2	
43000	0012113701	GROUND BEEF BULK			29 LB		28.20	28.2 POUND	29	
43000	0012116831	ROAST DINNER INSIDE ROUND			107 LB		106.70	106.7 POUND	107	
47000	0013146025	SAUSAGE BULK			15 LB		15.00	15.0 POUND	15	
47000	0013148028	SAUSAGE LINK 1 OZ			36 LB		36.00	36.0 POUND	36	
47000	0013146108	HAM			13 LB		13.00	13.0 POUND	13	
47500	0013166001	WIENERS BULK			79 LB		78.60	78.6 POUND	79	
47500	0013190083	CHEESE/BROCCOLI STUFFED SHELLS			3 CS		33.80	2.3 CASE	3	
47500	0013198105	BURRITOS			5 CS		80.00	4.4 CASE	5	
47500	0013190156	ENCHILADAS CHEESE			5 CS		67.60	4.5 CASE	5	
48000	0022001000	CHEDDAR CHEESE SHREDDED			24 LB		23.60	23.6 POUND	24	
48000	0022001115	AMERICAN PROCESSED CHEESE RIBBON SLI			0 LB		0.00	0.0 POUND	0	
48000	0022001166	CREAM CHEESE			7 LB		6.20	6.2 POUND	7	
48000	0022001255	FETA CHEESE			2 LB		1.10	1.1 POUND	2	
48000	0022001301	SWISS BIG EYE			5 LB		4.50	4.5 POUND	5	
48000	0022001409	PARMESAN CHEESE GRATED			5 LB		4.30	4.3 POUND	5	
48000	0022001425	PARMESAN CHEESE SHREDDED			8 LB		7.05	7.1 POUND	8	
48000	0022001450	PROVOLONE CHEESE			14 LB		13.05	13.1 POUND	14	
48000	0022001506	MOZZARELLA CHEESE SHREDDED			8 LB		7.05	7.1 POUND	8	
48000	0022001603	BLUE CHEESE			23 LB		22.60	22.6 POUND	23	

Source: From Kansas State University Housing and Dining Services, 1997. Used by permission.

Instead, inventories often are conducted by storage areas or a section of one area each week, with all areas covered by the end of a month.

The process involves two people, one of whom as a control measure is not directly involved with the storeroom. One person counts the products, which should be arranged systematically, and the other person records the data on a physical inventory form, an example of which is shown in Figure 6.12. The form should be designed to match the physical arrangement of the products on the shelves, thereby greatly facilitating the actual physical count. Space should be included to record quantity in stock, unit size, name of food item, item description, unit cost, and total value of the inventory in stock.

In some operations, the price of a product is marked on it before storing. The unit cost then can be recorded at the time of the physical inventory; otherwise, the pricing of the inventory can be completed by the bookkeeper. If the physical inventory

Figure 6.12.   Physical inventory form.

Quantity on Hand	Unit Size	Food Item	Item Description	Unit Cost	Total Inventory Value
	#10	Asparagus	All green cuts and tips, 6/#10/case		
	#10	Beans, green	Cut, 6/#10/case		
	#10	Beans, lima	Fresh green, small, 6/#10/case		
	#10	Beets	Whole, 6/#10/case		
	#10	Carrots	Sliced, medium, 6/#10/case		
	#10	Corn	Whole kernel, 6/#10/case		
	#10	Peas	Sweet peas, 4 sv., 6/#10/case		
	#10	Potatoes, sweet	Whole, 6/#10/case		
	#10	Tomatoes	Whole peeled, juice packed, 6/#10/case		
	46 oz.	Tomato juice	Fancy, 12/46 oz./case		

PHYSICAL INVENTORY

Date _____   Taken by _____   Beginning Inventory $ _____

is computerized, persons taking the inventory only need to record the amount in stock and enter it into the computer for calculating the beginning inventory value. The cost of food for the inventory period can be easily calculated by using the following method:

Beginning inventory
+ Purchases
= Cost of food available
− Ending inventory
= Cost of food used

This method can be satisfactory for small foodservice operations with a small number of products in stock, but for larger operations, a more sophisticated method is needed.

Perpetual Inventory

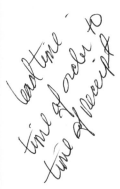

A **perpetual inventory** is a continuous record of all purchases and products in stock. The result is a record of the quantity in stock at any given time along with the value of the food and supply products. An example of a perpetual inventory record is shown in Figure 6.13.

Generally, a perpetual inventory record is restricted to products in dry and frozen storage. Produce, milk, bread, and other fast-moving items usually are not kept on perpetual inventory, but are considered direct issues. Fresh meats, fish, and poultry delivered on the day of use or one or two days in advance also are not recorded on this record but are charged to the food cost for the day on which used. If large quantities of frozen meat are purchased at one time and stored until needed, these products are included on perpetual inventory records. This method of purchasing is a modification of the just-in-time (JIT) manufacturing philosophy introduced into the United States by the Japanese in the late 1970s. **Just-in-time** (JIT) is a philosophy and strategy that has effects on inventory control, purchasing, and suppliers (Heinritz, Farrell, Giunipero, & Kolchin, 1991). The objective of **just-in-time purchasing** is to purchase products just-in-time for production and immediate consumption by the customer without having to record it in inventory. Once a product is put into inventory, capital is tied up. If the product is considered part of daily food cost, the money is not sitting on storeroom shelves making no interest. Buyers must have a good relationship with local suppliers to keep transportation costs low and delivery time short. Although a foodservice is not a manufacturing operation, some business concepts can be useful in decision making. Foodservice managers have many concerns in making a profit and use business concepts to do so. Serving high-quality perishable products at the lowest possible cost is one concern, and using JIT concepts might help.

A business professor at the University of New Hampshire has predicted that **expert systems,** computer programs that build knowledge bases for making decisions, will be integrated into national hamburger chains by the year 2000 (Beasley, 1994). These expert systems will interact with Universal Product Code (UPC) readers and facilitate taking physical inventories. Big central warehouses with large food and supply inventories will be phased out as foodservice operators reduce the capital in inventories. The JIT order and delivery concept will increase in prominence, requiring suppliers to make deliveries as frequently as five times a week directly to production centers. As

Figure 6.13.   Perpetual inventory record.

Item: Tomatoes, diced		*Purchase Unit:* 6/10 cs		*Issue Unit:* #10 can

Issuing Storeroom: Dry Stores #1

Date	Order No. or Requisition No.	Quantity In (purchase unit)	Quantity Out (issue unit)	Quantity on Hand (issue unit)
8/23/94	PO 1842	20 cs		120 cans
8/27/94	R 823		10 cans	110 cans

JIT practices increase, so will computer technology. Foodservice department computers will place orders via phone modems with suppliers' computers.

Perpetual inventories require considerable labor to maintain and are used only in large operations that keep products in stock. However, increasing use of computers makes maintaining a perpetual inventory record much easier. After the computerized inventory control system has been established, the perpetual inventory record can be kept up-to-date simply by recording issues from the storeroom on a daily basis. However it is done, a perpetual inventory record is not sufficient for accurate accounting and control of food and supplies. A physical inventory should be conducted on a monthly basis for verification.

Controlling Methods

The need for inventory control has become very important in all foodservice operations. Methods for accomplishing control are much easier to use today because of computers. The major functions of a control system are to coordinate activities, influence decisions and actions, and assure that objectives are met. In brief, these functions ensure adequate products are available for production and service and at the same time minimize inventory investment (Spears, 1995). Excess inventory is a nonpaying investment.

In foodservice operations, the activities to be coordinated and integrated are those in the procurement, production, and distribution and service units. For example, if homemade bean soup is on the menu and dried beans are not in the storeroom, production is disrupted and service is affected. Decision making can become more routine through the use of computers. However, the manager remains responsible for establishing policies and procedures and for monitoring the foodservice operation to ensure that plans are implemented correctly.

With the increasing size and complexity of foodservice operations, inventory management and control have become more complicated and critical. Several methods are available to assist foodservice managers in determining quantities for purchase, inventory levels, and cost of maintaining inventories.

ABC

In most foodservice operations, a small number of products account for the major portion of the inventory value; therefore, a method for classifying products according to value is needed. This method generally is referred to as the **ABC inventory method** of analysis, shown in Figure 6.14. It is based on the principle that effort, time, and money for inventory control should be allocated to products according to value. Products should be divided into three groups (A,B,C), with the high, "A," and medium value, "B," products given priority.

The "A" products represent only 15% to 20% of the inventory but typically account for 75% to 80% of the value of total inventory. The inventory level of these expensive products, such as frozen lobster tails, should be maintained at an absolute minimum. The "B" products represent 10% to 15% of inventory value and 20% to 25% of the products in inventory. "C" products are those whose dollar value accounts for 5% to 10% of the inventory value but make up 60% to 65% of the inventory.

Figure 6.14.   ABC analysis.

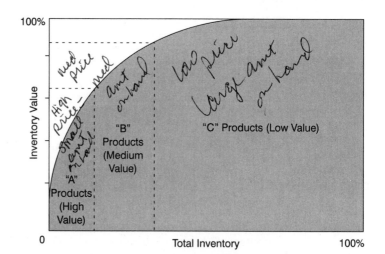

In applying the ABC concept to a foodservice, an analysis and classification of inventory products into the three categories would help the manager decide how much time and effort should be spent in controlling inventory. In a restaurant with both food and beverage operations, liquor would be classified as an "A" product and controlled very closely; breakfast cereals or sugar packets would be classified as "C" products and monitored less closely.

Minimum-Maximum

An often used method for controlling inventory involves the establishment of minimum and maximum inventory levels, commonly called the *mini-max method*. Theoretically, the minimum inventory level could be zero if the last product were used as a new shipment arrived. The maximum inventory level then would be the correct ordering quantity.

In reality, however, this extreme policy is not practical, since it involves running out of a product at a critical time. In the **mini-max method,** a safety stock is established to maintain at a constant level both on the inventory record and in the storerooms. The maximum inventory level consists of the safety stock plus the correct ordering quantity, which is the difference between the safety stock and maximum inventory level. Figure 6.15 is a graphic representation of the mini-max principle.

Safety stock is a backup supply of products to ensure against sudden increases in usage rate, failure to receive products on schedule, receipt of products not meeting specifications, or clerical errors in inventory records. The size of the safety stock depends on the importance of the products, value of the investment, and availability of substitutes on short notice. It is based on lead time and usage rate.

Figure 6.15. Graphic representation of the mini-max principle.

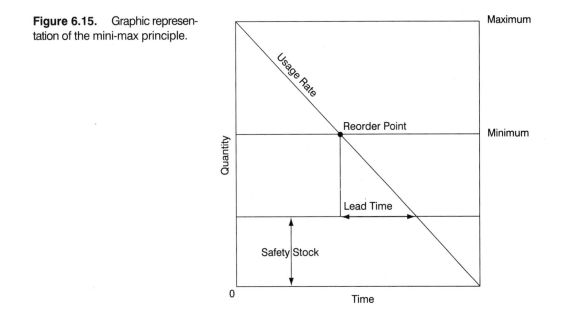

Lead time is the interval between initiation of a requisition and receipt of the product. The shortest lead time occurs when a product is purchased from a local supplier who carries it in stock, and the longest when products are ordered from out-of-town suppliers. Safety stock is part of the quantity on the shelves in the store-room; it must be rotated and is noted only on inventory records. Stock rotation, in which the oldest is used first, should be a policy in the storeroom.

The **usage rate** of a product is determined by past experience and forecasts. The **reorder point,** established from the lead time and usage rate, is the lowest stock level that can safely be maintained to avoid a stock-out or emergency purchasing. The maximum inventory level is equal to estimated usage plus the safety stock.

Economic Order Quantity

The total annual cost of restocking an inventory product depends directly on the number of times it is ordered in a year. To decrease these costs, orders should be placed as seldom as possible by ordering larger quantities. The holding cost of an inventory, however, is directly opposed to the concept of large orders.

The **economic order quantity** (EOQ) concept is derived from a sensible balance of ordering cost and inventory holding cost. The **ordering cost** is defined as the to-tal operating expenses of the purchasing and receiving departments, expenses of purchase orders and invoice payment, and data processing costs for purchasing and inventory. **Holding cost** is the total of all expenses in maintaining an inventory: the cost of capital tied up in inventory, obsolescence of products, storage, insurance, handling taxes, depreciation, deterioration, and breakage.

In Figure 6.16, ordering cost is a curve diminishing as the order quantity increases. The holding cost varies directly with the order quantity and therefore shows as a straight line. The objective of EOQ is to determine the relationship between the or-dering cost and holding cost that yields the minimum total cost, which is the point at which both costs are equal and the two lines intersect. This relationship expressed mathematically yields the formula for EOQ:

$$EOQ = \frac{2 \times \text{ordering cost} \times \text{total annual usage}}{\text{holding cost}}$$

The EOQ method is not practical unless computer assistance is available. Furthermore, the expenditure of large amounts of time and money is not justified on inventory analysis of items that account for very little of total inventory costs. The EOQ method is not suitable for many foodservice operations because of a variable demand for certain food items, seasonal menu changes, and indefinite lead times. EOQ is acceptable, however, for large-scale food processing operations such as com-mercial frozen meals and wholesale bakeries. The quantitative approach to inventory problems requires the knowledge, skill, and judgment of the foodservice manager.

Inventory Valuation Methods

Inventories, which change continually as products are used and replaced, represent a significant portion of current assets owned by the foodservice. In every accounting pe-riod of generally one year, an accounting cycle usually begins and ends each month.

Figure 6.16. Graphic representation of the economic order quantity concept.

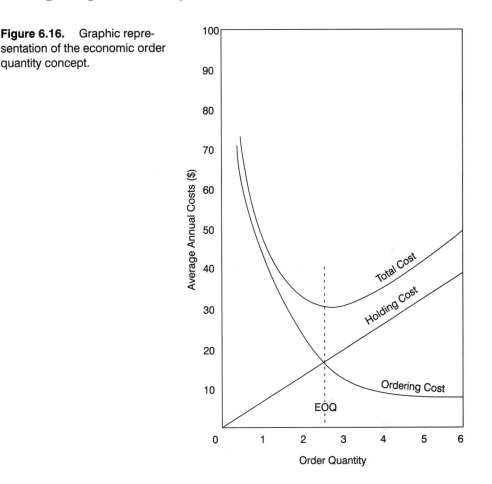

Hence, inventories are taken monthly and the dollar value is included as an asset, a debit, on the monthly balance sheet. A beginning and ending inventory occurs each month; the ending inventory becomes the beginning inventory for the next month.

Rotation of products, using the oldest first, is imperative to maintain food quality. Pricing, or valuing, products does not have to follow this pattern in keeping inventory records. The important factor is that the method of valuing be consistent within an accounting period. The five principal methods of inventory valuation are specific identification, weighted average, FIFO (first in, first out), LIFO (last in, first out), and latest purchase price.

Specific identification involves pricing the inventory at the exact price of each individual product. Marking each product with the purchasing price as it is received is necessary. This method requires detailed record keeping and therefore is used only in very small foodservice operations.

The second method is weighted average, in which a weighted unit cost is used and is based on both the unit purchase price and the number of units in each purchase. Again, cans or packages must be marked with the purchasing price at the time of receipt. For example, four cases of avocado pulp (four 3-pound plastic cartons per case) at $34.50 per case were ordered for guacamole and were still in the freezer at the beginning of the next inventory cycle. Two deliveries of avocado pulp, each at a different price, were made during the month; 12 cases marked at $35.25 each were the first purchase and five cases at $35.75 each were the second. The weighted average purchase price per case for these 21 cases of avocado pulp was $35.23 and calculated as follows.

$$(4 \times \$34.50) + (12 \times \$35.25) + (5 \times \$35.75) \div 21 = \$35.23$$

Inventory valuation using the FIFO method means that pricing closely follows the flow of products through the operation. The older products in the storeroom are used before the newer ones. The ending inventory reflects the current cost of products, since it is valued at the prices for the most recent purchases. If only six cases of avocado pulp were in the freezer when ending inventory was taken, the ending inventory would be valued at $35.67 per case.

$$(5 \times \$35.75) + (1 \times \$35.25) \div 6 = \$35.67$$

LIFO (last in, first out) is based on the assumption that current purchases are largely, if not completely, made for the purpose of meeting current demands of production. Therefore, the purchase price of the oldest stock should be charged out first, valuating the ending inventory at $34.75.

$$(4 \times \$34.50) + (2 \times \$35.25) \div 6 = \$34.75$$

Generally, the value of the inventory will be lowest using LIFO and highest using **FIFO (first in, first out),** which is based on the assumption that current prices will be higher than older ones. Foodservice managers choose LIFO when determining the value of inventory to reduce profit on financial statements to decrease income taxes, particularly in a high inflation period. It minimizes the value of closing inventory, which maximizes food cost for the time period.

The **latest purchase price** method uses the latest purchase price in valuing the ending inventory. This method often is used in foodservice operations because it is simple and fast (Kim, Finley, Fanslow, & Hsu, 1992).

$$(7 \times \$35.75) \div 7 = \$35.75$$

The method chosen for valuing inventory is important because it affects the determination of price of menu items sold, which in turn affects the profit or loss figure. The balance sheet or statement of financial condition of a foodservice operation also is affected, since inventories are a current asset.

SUMMARY

Receiving and storage are as critical to cost control and profit generating as is purchasing. Receiving ensures that products delivered by suppliers are those that were ordered, and storage ensures quality until time of use. Poor receiving practices can defeat the economic benefits gained by competitive purchasing. Competent and well-trained receiving clerks are essential. The receiving area should be near the delivery door and the storage areas to minimize the time and effort required for moving food into proper storage. The most important equipment in the area is the scale for weighing all products purchased by weight. Copies of specifications used by buyers should be available to receiving clerks to check that the products ordered are those that are being received. Security in the receiving area is extremely important; the purchasing person should not be responsible for receiving. Five steps in the receiving process are necessary to assure that products are received properly.

Storage is crucial to the overall operation because it links receiving and production. Dry and low-temperature storage facilities should be accessible to both receiving and food production areas to reduce transport time and labor time. Storage areas should be locked and keys given to only those who need access to the area. Dry storage areas should be cool with controlled humidity. Temperature and humidity control in low-temperature storage are necessary to preserve quality and nutritive value of perishable foods.

Inventory is a record of products owned by the foodservice. Physical inventory, the counting and recording of products in stock, usually is taken each month. Perpetual inventory is a continuous record of the quantity in stock at any given time and the price of the products. The need for inventory control has become important in foodservice operations, and various control tools are available, namely the ABC, minimum-maximum, and economic quantity methods. Inventory is considered an asset on a balance sheet and as such needs to have a dollar value. Different methods of inventory valuation are available, but once one is selected, it should be used consistently within an accounting period.

REFERENCES

American Hospital Publishing Inc. (1994). *Recommended storage temperature and time.*

Beasley, M. A. (1994). Reflections: past, present, future. *Food Management, 29*(1), 54.

Dietary Managers Association. (1991). *Professional procurement practices: A guide for dietary managers.* Lombard, IL: Author.

Heinritz, S., Farrell, P. V., Giunipero, L., & Kolchin, M. (1991). *Purchasing: Principles and applications* (8th ed.). Englewood Cliffs, NJ: Prentice Hall.

Gunn, M. (1992). Professionalism in purchasing. *School Food Service Journal 46*(9), 30–34.

Gunn, M. (1995). *First Choice, a purchasing systems manual for school foodservice.* University, MS: National Food Service Management Institute.

Kim, I. Y., Finley, D. H., Fanslow, A. M., and Hsu, C. H. C. (1992). *Inventory control systems in foodservice organizations: Programmed study guide.* Ames, IA: Iowa State University Press.

Longree, K., & Armbruster, G. (1987). *Quantity food sanitation* (4th ed.). New York: Wiley.

National Restaurant Association. (1992). *Model position descriptions for the foodservice industry.* Washington, DC: Author.

Produce Marketing Association. (1995). The Foodservice Guide to Fresh Produce. Newark, Delaware.

Spears, M. C. (1995). *Foodservice organizations: A managerial and systems approach* (3rd ed.). Upper Saddle River, NJ: Merrill/Prentice Hall.

Stefanelli, J. M. (1997). *Purchasing selection and procurement for the hospitality industry* (4th ed.). New York: Wiley.

USDA Food and Nutrition Service. (1975). Washington, DC: U.S. Government Printing Office.

PART 3

Purchasing Food Products

The eight chapters in part 3 are based on the Food Guide Pyramid, which presents a pattern for what people should be, or are, eating. Since eating right has become a prime concern of consumers, the foodservice buyer should be alert to the nutritional value of food.

- **Chapter 7, Grain Foods.**   Grain foods, which include bread, cereal, rice, and pasta, are the foundation of the Food Guide Pyramid. People should eat more servings, 6 to 11, of these foods than of any other group. Buyers must watch trends in these products.

- **Chapter 8, Fresh Fruits and Vegetables.**   Fresh fruits and vegetables on the second level of the pyramid are the most perishable of all foods and require that the buyer know how to purchase, receive, and store these products. Customers demand that fruits and vegetables be fresh when served.

- **Chapter 9, Processed Fruits and Vegetables.**   Frozen, canned, dried, and dehydrated products also are included on the second level of the pyramid. Customers often prefer processed fruits and vegetables to products that are not fresh. The most exciting technology in processed foods is the value-added concept that processors have developed.

- **Chapter 10, Meats.**   Meat, poultry, fish, dry beans, eggs, and nuts are grouped together on the third level of the Food Guide Pyramid. Buyers who are responsible for purchasing these products need to understand the industry and government regulations. Meat is the highest priced food product in the foodservice operation.

- **Chapter 11, Seafood.**   In seafood operations, purchasing fish, which has become very popular with customers concerned about health, and shellfish often is delegated to one person who understands the product. Freshness, price, and flavor are three critical factors when purchasing frozen or fresh seafood.

- **Chapter 12, Poultry and Eggs.** Customers concerned about their health have increased poultry consumption and buyers have had to gain expertise in purchasing these products. Buyers of poultry and eggs not only need to purchase from reputable suppliers but they must also understand that the products must enter the foodservice at the proper temperature and be carefully monitored during receiving and storage to prevent foodborne illnesses.

- **Chapter 13, Dairy Products.** Dairy products, including milk, cheese, and yogurt, are the other group on the third level of the Food Guide Pyramid. Milk is very perishable but is the most legally controlled of all food items. Purchasing dairy products is not a difficult task once specifications are written.

- **Chapter 14, Beverages.** Beverages are not identified in the Food Guide Pyramid probably because very few have nutritive value. Most of the calories in beverages come from simple carbohydrates. Beverages are either nonalcoholic, such as coffee, tea, and carbonated and bottled water, or alcoholic, including beer, wine, and spirits.

7

Grain Foods

How did bread and other grain-based products, and not vegetables, end up as the foundation for the Food Guide Pyramid (L'Ecuyer, 1996)? In school and other foodservice operations, menu planning under the new meal regulations means starting at the base of the Food Guide Pyramid and looking for creative and innovative ways to reduce fat and increase carbohydrates and fiber without breaking the bottom line—food costs. Grain foods such as bread, cereal, rice, and pasta are highlighted in the Food Guide Pyramid shown in Figure 7.1. The dietary guidelines and the Food Guide Pyramid stress the need for Americans to eat at least 6 to 11 servings of these foods each day. Thus, foodservice buyers have had to learn a lot more about grain products, especially breads, because customers are demanding variety.

The most striking change in the national eating pattern in the past 17 years might be the big increase in grain consumption, according to a U.S. Department of

Figure 7.1. Food Guide Pyramid with bread, cereal, rice, and pasta group highlighted.

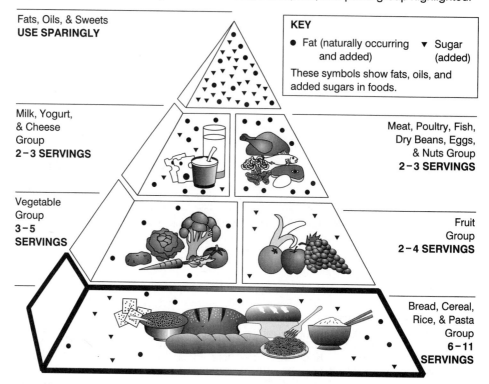

Agriculture (USDA) analysis of current and past nutrition studies as shown in Figure 7.2. The USDA reports that in addition to eating more snack foods and breakfast cereals, people are exploring Mexican and other ethnic grain-based foods.

Baked goods are the first things a customer remembers and tastes when eating away from home (Rogers, 1995). Fresh breads symbolize what a foodservice operation is all about. Now that their appetites are whetted, American customers cannot seem to get enough of the hearty, wholesome, fresh-baked products that bakeries, restaurants, schools, and other noncommercial operations are peddling. One factor fueling their interest is the Food Guide Pyramid.

Another factor really started out as an advertising and marketing campaign for Pillsbury's prepared dough business and ended up as the Poppin' Fresh® Pillsbury Dough Boy. The story of the creation of the Dough Boy was told by a Pillsbury copywriter. He wrote a one-page article titled Happy Birthday and published it in the company's newsletter. In 1965, a small group of advertising people sat around a table and cracked open cans of Pillsbury dough. They really had no clue as to what they were trying to come up with. They just sat there surrounded by cans of dough, trying to find the product's inherent drama. One of the group was a copy writer who was especially interested in the dough itself. With one quick rap on the table, the copywriter made history when he envisioned the image of a dough boy

Figure 7.2. Percent increase in U.S. grain consumption, 1977–1994.

STAFF OF LIFE

What's the most striking change in the national eating pattern in the past 17 years? It may be the big increase in grain consumption, according to a USDA analysis of current and past nutrition studies.

The USDA reports that in addition to eating more snack foods and breakfast cereals, people are exploring ethnic grain-based foods, particularly Mexican.

That was only one of the intriguing analyses that have been announced by USDA so far this year. The analyses combine results from earlier government studies (going as far back as 1977) with findings from 5,500 first-year respondents participating in an ongoing USDA study, "What We Eat in America 1994-1996."

Here's other news:

■ Fruit consumption is up by about 20%, with most of that in the form of juice. Even so, half the country consumes no fruit on any given day. Vegetable consumption is up only slightly.

■ People eat about 6% more calories a day than did those studied in the late '70s; they also weigh 11 or 12 pounds more.

■ More than half the population eats out on a given day, and food eaten away from home accounts for 25% of total calories.

■ The proportion of women and small children eating out is up about 50% since the late '70s. By 1994, half of 3- to 5-year-olds were eating away from home on any given day, up from a third in the '70s.

■ What men buy away from home: soft drinks, salads and coffee, in that order. But restaurant french fries, Mexican foods, and grain mixtures such as pizza were more popular with males than in earlier surveys.

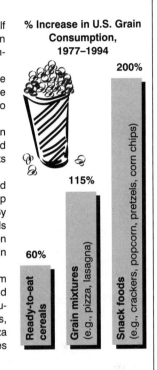

% Increase in U.S. Grain Consumption, 1977–1994

- Ready-to-eat cereals: 60%
- Grain mixtures (e.g., pizza, lasagna): 115%
- Snack foods (e.g., crackers, popcorn, pretzels, corn chips): 200%

Source: USDA Agricultural Research Service.

popping from the can. The Dough Boy has become one of America's most beloved characters (Figure 7.3). Within the first three years of his appearance, he garnered a whopping 87% recognition rate among consumers.

The Dough Boy made his 1965 debut in a commercial for Pillsbury Crescent Rolls, a product he has endorsed for more than a quarter century. For many years, he served as a helper and instructor to family cooks and took a back seat in advertising as product attributes, such as speed and convenience, were emphasized. In the mid '80s, however, the Dough Boy began to regain his superstar status, taking a lead role in several prepared dough commercials. In the early '90s, a fresh new campaign was developed in which the Dough Boy holds center stage in every commercial. Thanks to new technology, his body appears even more flexible and lifelike as he plays his guitar, skips down a stack of books, and reads the Sunday comics.

Another influence is rising global awareness that has expanded customer knowledge of and appetite for ethnic options. The once innocuous bagel, along with other specialty breads, is basking in popularity (*Restaurants & Institutions* Editors, 1996). Although it arrived in America with Jewish immigrants nearly a century ago, only in recent years has much of the country come to enjoy this doughy roll that resembles

Figure 7.3.   Pillsbury Dough Boy.

Source: From Pillsbury Bakeries & Foodservice Inc. Used by permission.

a doughnut in "hole more than in part." Sales in bagel shops and bakeries have increased sharply in recent years.

Factor in the varied flavor and textures of baked products sold at a low cost both to customers and operators, and it is easy to understand why foodservices across the country are firing up their ovens. Underlying these trends is the belief expressed by foodservice buyers that baked products are important to the bottom line of the operation. Purchasing for profit becomes a reality for buyers. Fresh-baked breads are one of the least expensive ways to influence positively a large number of people. One operator said that "breads are the best ways to lower food costs, increase perceived value, and bolster customer satisfaction" (Rogers, 1995).

CEREAL GRAINS

Grains are seeds of the grass family and often are referred to as the foundation of healthy eating (Bennion, 1995). The word *cereal* comes from Ceres, the Roman goddess of grain. The most important cereals in the United States are wheat, corn, rice, oats, rye, and barley. The term **cereal** is not limited to breakfast but applies to a large group of products made from grains, including flours, breads, meals, and pastas. Standards of identity from the Food and Drug Administration (FDA) for cereal flour, macaroni and noodle, and bakery products are listed in the Appendix. Buckwheat often is classified with cereal grains even though it is not a seed of the grass family. Grains are easy to produce, cost very little, and are nutritious. They are staples in the diets of most population groups. In 1993, Americans consumed 54 pounds more per capita of grain products than in 1970, when the consumption was 135 pounds, but they are still not eating the amounts of high-fiber foods, including whole-grain products, legumes, vegetables, and fruit, that are recommended in the Food Guide Pyramid (Putnam & Allshouse, 1994). The nutritive value and structure are similar in all cereal grains.

Nutritive Value

Grains were chosen as the base of the pyramid because Americans should eat at least 50 percent of their total calories in the form of complex carbohydrates. Grain products also are an excellent source of fiber, the major B vitamins, and iron. Today most refined products are enriched with certain nutrients lost during processing; those nutrients are added in amounts that approach their original levels. In addition to being a good source of complex carbohydrates and fiber, bread products have low or moderate sodium content, little or no cholesterol, and a very low percentage of fat and sugar. They are a good source of vitamins and minerals for the calories.

Carbohydrates are either simple or complex. **Simple carbohydrates** are found in sugars such as table sugar, molasses, honey, lactose (in milk), and fructose (in fruits). These carbohydrates break down quickly during digestion and provide an immediate source of energy into the blood stream. **Complex carbohydrates** break down slowly during digestion, giving the body a time-released source of energy. Athletes often eat 60% to 70% of their diet as complex carbohydrates, permitting them to store adequate energy in the muscles for endurance events. The brain also uses complex carbohydrates to function.

Fiber is a general term for the indigestible part of plant foods. It provides almost no energy or calories for the body. Grain products, fruits, vegetables, and legumes are good sources of fiber. Dairy products, meat, poultry, fish, fats, and sweeteners have virtually no fiber. Dietary fiber is either insoluble or soluble. White flour is a good source of soluble fiber, which has been shown to lower blood cholesterol levels. Whole wheat products and bran are sources of insoluble fiber that act as a bulk producer to help prevent constipation.

Structure

The structure of wheat, corn, rice, oats, rye, and barley are similar. We will use a wheat kernel as an example. The kernel of wheat, sometimes called the wheat berry, is the seed from which the wheat plant grows (Figure 7.4). Each tiny seed contains three distinct parts that are separated during the milling process to produce flour. The kernel is a storehouse of nutrients needed and used by man since the dawn of civilization. Kernels of all grains have a starchy endosperm, a bran covering, and a germ.

- Endosperm—about 83% of the kernel weight and the source of white flour. The endosperm contains the greatest share of protein, carbohydrates, and iron, and the major B vitamins, such as riboflavin, niacin, and thiamine. It is also a source of soluble fiber.
- Bran—about 14.5% of the kernel weight. Bran is included in whole wheat flour and can also be purchased separately. The bran contains a small amount of protein, large quantities of the three major B vitamins, trace minerals, and dietary fiber, primarily insoluble.
- Germ—about 2.5% of the kernel weight. The germ is the embryo or sprouting section of the seed, often separated from flour in milling because the fat content (10 percent) limits the shelf life of the flour. The germ contains minimal quantities of high-quality protein and a greater share of B complex vitamins and trace minerals. Wheat germ can be purchased separately and is part of whole wheat flour.

Figure 7.4. A kernel of wheat.

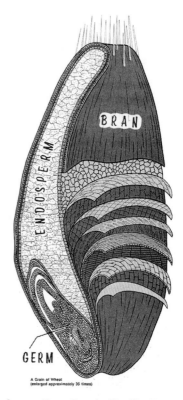

Source: From *Breads: The Significant Edge* by the Wheat Foods Council, 1990, Englewood, CO: Author.

Kinds

Although similar in structure, each grain has its own flavor, color, and texture that gives menu items a certain uniqueness. The total U.S. per capita consumption of wheat products increased from 111 pounds in 1970 to 140 pounds in 1993, of corn from 11 to 22 pounds, of rice from 6.7 to 18 pounds, and of oats from 5 to 9 pounds; rye decreased slightly from 1 pound per capita and barley did the same (Putnam & Allshouse, 1994). Variations in wheat, corn, rice, oats, rye, and barley will be discussed.

Wheat

Kansas is the top wheat-producing state in the United States. Nearly 400 million bushels of hard red winter wheat are harvested annually. This wheat is planted in the fall and harvested in the spring. The seeds root, shoots, and leaves emerge. In the spring, the wheat plants, which have been dormant during the winter, begin to grow again and reach maturity in June and July. **Wheat** is classified as hard or soft, winter or spring, red or white, and durum. Hard red and white winter wheats are used in all-purpose and bread flours for yeast bread and rolls. Soft red and soft white wheats produce flour for making cakes, crackers, cookies, and pastries. Durum wheat is very hard and is used in making pasta, not bread.

Bulgur is a processed form of cracked wheat. Wheat kernels are steam cooked and dried before being cracked. The coarsest grain is used for pilaf, which is traditionally served in Armenian restaurants, the medium for cereal, and the finest for tabbouleh, which is a Middle Eastern menu item that is served cold; the ingredients are bulgur, mint, parsley, onions, and chopped tomatoes mixed with lemon juice and olive oil.

Corn

Corn is a native American plant, and the United States now produces about half of the world's corn crop. Corn kernels are grains that grow on a grass (Margen, 1992). Sweet corn is for eating, while nonsweet field corn is picked at a mature stage then dried and used as livestock feed and, after refining, in many different products, including breakfast cereals, corn oil, cornstarch, whiskey, paper, and plastic. Popcorn is a field corn with thick-walled kernels; when heated, steam is trapped inside the dried kernels causing them to pop. Hominy, which is the endosperm of the corn kernel, is sold whole or is broken in small pieces to make grits. White, yellow, and blue corn are milled into cornmeal. Corn products have become very popular in the last few years because of the popularity of Mexican menu items, such as chips and tortillas.

Rice

White rice is the starchy endosperm of the rice grain; the bran and germ of the grain have been rubbed off by an abrasive process that removes more than half of the minerals and most of the vitamins in the kernel (Bennion, 1995). **Rice** is classified by size as long-grain, medium-grain, and short-grain, which contains more starch than the long- and medium-grains and makes the rice sticky and easy to eat with chop sticks. China produces about 90% of the world's supply of rice. Long-grain rice accounts for 75% of the crops grown in the United States; Arkansas, Louisiana, Mississippi, Missouri, Texas, and California are the major sources of rice. Most white rice is enriched and therefore should not be rinsed before or after cooking. Converted rice, which is parboiled under steam pressure, retains most of its nutrients and increases its keeping qualities. Instant rice is a precooked long-grain rice that is dried by a special process and requires little preparation. Brown rice has had only the husk removed before milling, thus keeping most of its nutritive value. Wild rice is not true rice but the hulled and unmilled grain of a water plant. It is available in limited quantity and is more expensive than white rice. It has been cultivated and is now grown in California and the Great Lakes region (Bennion, 1995).

Oats

Oats have been used primarily to feed animals, especially horses, for centuries. Only in Scotland have oats become a staple food in the human diet. Interest in oats as a food rose recently when researchers found that eating oat bran as part of a lowfat diet helps decrease cholesterol levels in the body, especially if the levels are high. Oats also are an excellent source of complex carbohydrates, protein, minerals, vitamin E, and both soluble and insoluble dietary fiber.

Oats are used in a rolled form by removing the outer hull of the oat kernel, leaving most of the germ and bran with the endosperm. The germ makes the fat content higher than in other cereals. Oat groats are oat kernels with the outer hulls removed. Rolled oats are made by passing groats through rollers to form flakes; groats cut into small pieces and then rolled into thin and small flakes are quick-cooking rolled oats. Oat bran is the outer layer of groats. Granola and Muesli are popular snack foods that contain toasted rolled oats, bran, chopped dry fruit, chopped nuts, or sunflower or pumpkin seeds.

Rye

Rye is similar to wheat except for the color, which is bluish gray (Margen, 1992). It probably originated in Asia and spread into eastern Europe as a weed where it was cultivated as a food. Because it survives best in wet and cold weather, it was grown in eastern Europe, Scandinavia, and Russia. Hardier and more resistant to cold than wheat, this European cereal grain is used mostly for bread baking (Ryan, 1994). Because of its low gluten content, it is usually mixed with wheat flour. Its market forms include mixed wheat and rye flour, whole rye flour, and whole unground rye or berries. It is grown and used in the United States chiefly as a flour-making grain, although rye berries are beginning to be used with other grains for side dishes.

Barley

Barley was one of the first crops to be cultivated by man (Margen, 1992). The United States is the third biggest barley grower in the world. Most of the barley in this country is not eaten as a food; instead, it is either converted into malt for beer production or fed to animals. Pearled barley is the form in which this grain is most often used. Pearling is a process in which the barley grains are scoured six times to remove their outer hull and bran layer, leaving small, round, ivory-colored granules. Pearl barley and mushroom soup is a popular menu item. Quick barley cooks faster than pearl barley because it is precooked by steaming.

Uncommon Grains

A decade ago, the grain most likely to be found on American menus was rice, white and wild, which is not a grain but the seed of an aquatic grass (Ryan, 1994). Today, menus are sprouting more grains than ever before, and the uncommon ones will soon be common on menus.

Amaranth is not a true grain but is related to a weed. It is sacred to the Aztecs, and its name means *immortal*. The grain is small, about the size of a poppy seed, but high in protein, vitamins, and minerals, especially calcium, and low in calories. It is used in pilaf and timbales and is added to pancake, waffle, muffin, and quick-bread batters.

Buckwheat is neither wheat nor grain but the seed of a plant related to rhubarb (Ryan, 1994). It is a plant source of complete protein. Its market forms are buckwheat flour; kasha, or roasted buckwheat groats, whole and in coarse, medium, or fine grinds; and whole white buckwheat, which comes as hulled groats and finely ground cream of buckwheat cereal. Buckwheat flour is used in pancakes and pasta, and kasha is usually used in soups or in stuffings for poultry and meats.

Couscous is the milled endosperm of hard durum wheat, known as semolina. It is traditionally prepared in the Middle East by steaming the semolina over water in three laborious steps that include rolling by hand. Today's market forms include regular bulk couscous and instant and precooked forms.

Millet has long been a staple in Northern Africa and also is eaten in Asia (Margen, 1992). Millet has no gluten and therefore cannot be used in raised breads. Pearl millet, which is the major type grown for human consumption, can be found in health food stores and is always hulled and usually sold in whole-grain form. The tiny, pale yellow or reddish orange beads of millet can be cooked like any other grain.

Quinoa, pronounced KEEN-wah, was called the "mother of all grains" by the Incas (Parseghian, 1995). Actually, it is not a grain but is the fruit of an herb that grows in dry areas at high altitudes in cold weather or hot sunny climates. It does not require rich soil. Its 1,800 varieties cover the color wheel: white, pink, orange, green, red, purple, and black. It is a good source of protein, calcium, and iron. It is boiled in liquid and often toasted before cooking. Chefs are using it in salads with other grains and raw vegetables. The prediction is that it will be found on many menus in the future.

Triticale is a hybrid plant produced by crossing wheat and rye. It is higher in protein than other nonwheat flours but still needs to be combined with a wheat flour to produce a satisfying texture. It is used in some bread products, snack crackers, and noodles.

These grains are the staple in the diets of most population groups. Many basic products are made from them. Two basic categories of processed grains are cereals, or breakfast and snack foods, and flour that is made into breads and pasta.

CEREALS

Breakfast cereals can be ready-to-eat, often called cold cereal, or ready-to-cook, referred to as cooked cereal. According to Putnam and Allshouse (1994), the per capita consumption of ready-to-eat cereals increased from 8.6 pounds in 1970 to 12.3 in 1993 and ready-to-cook cereals from 1.7 pounds in 1970 to 2.7 in 1993.

The emphasis on complex carbohydrates, fiber, lowfat, and cholesterol in the American diet has helped create a new menu for breakfast entrées. Bacon, eggs, and fried potatoes have been replaced by ready-to-eat and cooked cereals.

Ready-to-Eat

Even though cereals have been eaten for thousands of years, cold cereals were not developed until 1894 by Dr. Kellogg, who managed a health sanitarium in Battle Creek, Mich. (Margen, 1992). He developed a wheat-flake cereal and a few years later experimented with corn flakes. In the early 1900s, Kellogg's Corn Flakes and Shredded Wheat and a baked wheat and barley mixture developed by Post, who was a patient at the Battle Creek sanitarium, were on the market. Today more than 100 brands are available to the customer. These cereals not only are eaten at breakfast, but they are used for snacks during the day and at bedtime.

Ready-to-eat cereals contain sweetening agents, salt, flavorings, coloring agents, and antioxidants as preservatives (Bennion, 1995). Most also are fortified with minerals and vitamins. The majority of these cereals are either flaked or puffed. Flaked cereals are made by lightly rolling the grain between smooth rolls to crack the outer layers; sweeteners and flavoring are added before cooking. The product is then dried and flaked on heavy flaking rollers, toasted, cooled, and packaged. Puffed cereals are made by cleaning, conditioning, and putting the whole grain into a pressure chamber in which the pressure is raised to a high level and suddenly released. The expansion of water vapor in the grain on pressure release causes it to puff up several times its original size. The puffed cereal is then dried by toasting, cooled, and packaged.

Cereals that are not flaked or puffed are usually granular or shredded. Granular cereals contain a blend of flours in a yeast-containing dough made into large loaves that are baked and then broken up, dried, and ground to a specific fineness. Shredded cereals are made from a white, starchy wheat. The whole grain is cooked with water until it is soft and rubbery and then cooled, conditioned, and fed into a pair of metal rolls with grooves. The shreds are layered, cut into specified sizes, or spun into little biscuits, baked, dried, cooled, and packaged. Some cereals are extruded into shapes.

Ready-to-Cook

Ready-to-cook cereals are raw and should be cooked before serving. These can be whole grains, such as rice; cracked or crushed grains, such as oatmeal; or granular, made from either the whole grain or endosperm, including farina. The starch in instant cereals, including oatmeal and farina, has been cooked and dried. Adding boiling water to these cereals and stirring the mixture makes the cereal ready-to-eat. Instant rice is precooked by the processor. In the foodservice operation, it is added to boiling water that is brought back to boiling. The pan is removed from the heat and covered until the rice swells. The instant rice is then ready to serve.

FLOUR

Flour is obtained by grinding, then sifting wheat kernels that consist of three distinct parts: bran, germ, and endosperm. During milling, the three parts are separated and recombined accordingly to achieve different types of flours. Wheat has six different classes: hard red winter, hard red spring, soft red winter, hard white, soft white, and durum. Protein and gluten content determine the products that can be made from each type of wheat. The harder the wheat, the higher the amount of protein in the flour. Hard, high-protein wheats are used in breads and quick breads, and durum is used in pasta and noodles. Soft, low-protein wheats are used in cakes, pastries, cookies, and crackers.

Foodservice buyers need to know about flour because it is an important ingredient in basic menu items. After all, bread is called "the staff of life." The buyer needs some basic information about flour to make wise purchasing decisions for such flour products as bread and pasta.

Basic Information

A review of the milling process will further understanding about the type of flour and various wheat flour terms. Without question, white wheat flour is used more often in the United States than any other kind.

Milling Process

The process of milling white flour includes separating the endosperm from the bran and germ and making it into flour. Milling procedures vary from one mill to another, but the basic process is shown in Figure 7.5. A quick overview of the process includes:

- transporting the grain by rail or truck to a grain elevator located near the wheat fields,
- separating the endosperm from the bran and germ,
- washing and scouring the endosperm and then grinding it,
- sifting the ground wheat as often as needed,
- bleaching and enriching the flour, and
- packaging the flour for shipment to various distributors.

Types of Flour

A number of different types of flour are available on the market, and the foodservice buyer needs to know which type will make the best products. Recipes generally specify the type of flour needed; specifications for flour should include the menu items that will be prepared from it. In operations that purchase ready-to-eat breads or pasta for menu items, the responsibility for the type of flour used in these products is on the baker or processor. In those operations that prepare most of the menu items from scratch, however, the buyer needs to know the use of the flour when placing the order. White wheat flour is used more often in the United States than any other kind. It consists of only the ground endosperm of the wheat kernel. The correct type of flour makes a tremendous difference in the quality of the product.

The Wheat Foods Council developed this brief review of various types of flour:

- White flour is the finely ground endosperm of the wheat kernel.
- All-purpose flour is a white flour milled from hard wheats or a blend of hard and soft wheats. It produces the best results for many kinds of products, including some yeast breads, quick breads, cakes, cookies, pastries, and noodles. All-purpose flour is enriched and may be bleached or unbleached. Protein varies from 8% to 11%.
- Bread flour is a white flour that is a blend of hard, high-protein wheats. It has greater gluten strength and protein content than all-purpose flour. Unbleached

Figure 7.5. How flour is milled.

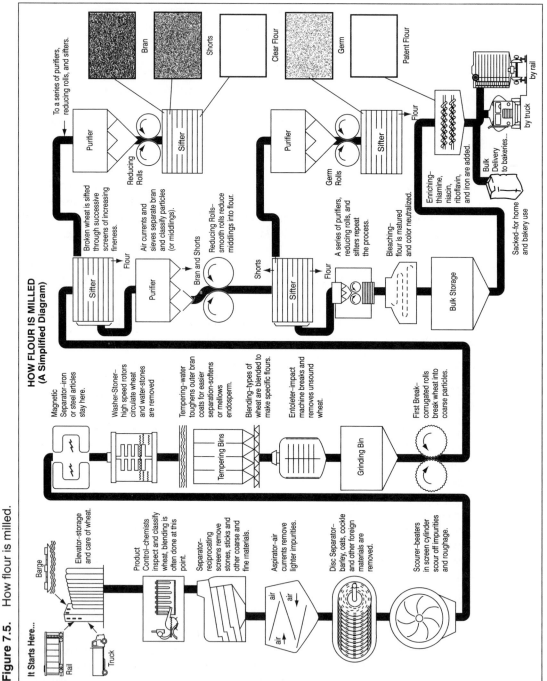

HOW FLOUR IS MILLED
(A Simplified Diagram)

It Starts Here...

Barge

Elevator–storage and care of wheat.

Rail

Truck

Product Control–chemists inspect and classify wheat, blending is often done at this point.

Separator–reciprocating screens remove stones, sticks and other coarse and fine materials.

Aspirator–air currents remove lighter impurities.

Disc Separator–barley, oats, cockle and other foreign materials are removed.

Scourer–beaters in screen cylinder scour off impurities and roughage.

Magnetic Separator–iron or steel articles stay here.

Washer-Stoner–high speed rotors circulate wheat and water–stones are removed.

Tempering–water toughens outer bran coats for easier separation–softens or mellows endosperm.

Blending–types of wheat are blended to make specific flours.

Tempering Bins

Entoleter–impact machine breaks and removes unsound wheat.

Grinding Bin

First Break– corrugated rolls break wheat into coarse particles.

To a series of purifiers, reducing rolls, and sifters.

Purifier

Reducing Rolls

Sifter

Broken wheat is sifted through successive screens of increasing fineness.

Sifter

Flour

Air currents and sieves separate bran and classify particles (or middlings).

Purifier

Bran and Shorts

Reducing Rolls– smooth rolls reduce middlings into flour.

Shorts

Sifter

Flour

Bran

Shorts

Clear Flour

Germ

Purifier

Germ Rolls

Sifter

Flour

A series of purifiers, reducing rolls, and sifters repeat the process.

Bleaching– flour is matured and color neutralized.

Bulk Storage

Enriching– thiamine, niacin, riboflavin, and iron are added.

Patent Flour

Flour

by rail

by truck

Bulk Delivery to bakeries...

Sacked–for home and bakery use

174

Source: From Breads: The Significant Edge by the Wheat Foods Council, 1990, Englewood, CO: Author.

bread flour, sometimes conditioned with ascorbic acid, is milled primarily for commercial bakers. Protein varies from 12% to 14%.

- Cake flour is a fine-textured, silky flour milled from soft wheat with a low-protein content. It is used to make cakes, cookies, crackers, quick breads, and some types of pastry. Cake flour has a greater percentage of starch and less protein than all-purpose flour, which keeps cakes and pastries tender and delicate. Protein varies from 7% to 9%.
- Self-rising flour, also called phosphated flour, is a convenience product made by adding salt and leavening to all-purpose flour. It is used in biscuits but is not recommended for yeast breads. One cup of self-rising flour contains 1½ teaspoons baking powder and ½ teaspoon salt.
- Pastry flour has properties between those of all-purpose and cake flours. It is usually milled from soft wheat for pastry making but can be used for cookies, cakes, crackers, and similar products. It differs from hard wheat flour because it has a finer texture and lighter consistency. Protein varies from 8% to 9%.
- Semolina is the coarsely ground endosperm of durum, a hard spring wheat with high gluten content and golden color. It is hard and granular and resembles sugar. Semolina is enriched and is used to make couscous and pasta products, such as spaghetti, vermicelli, macaroni, and lasagna noodles.
- Durum flour is finely ground semolina. It is enriched and used to make pasta.
- Whole wheat, stone-ground, and graham flours can be used interchangeably. They are produced by either grinding the whole wheat kernel or recombining the white flour, germ, and bran that have been separated during milling. The only differences may be in coarseness and protein content. Insoluble fiber content is higher than in white flours.
- Gluten flour is usually milled from spring wheat and has a high protein (41%), low starch content. It is used primarily for diabetic breads or mixed with other nonwheat or low-protein wheat flours to produce a stronger dough structure.

Wheat Flour Terms

The FDA inspects and approves the use of flour treatments and additives that are used to improve the storage, appearance, and baking performance of flour. The treatments and additives are not harmful (Wheat Foods Council, 1990).

- Enriched flour is supplemented with iron and three B-vitamins (thiamine, niacin, and riboflavin) and may also be supplemented with calcium. No change occurs in taste, color, texture, baking quality, or caloric value of flour.
- Presifted flour is sifted at the mill, making sifting before measuring unnecessary.
- Bleached flour has been bleached chemically to whiten or improve baking qualities. No change occurs in the nutritional value of the flour and no harmful chemical residues remain. Its only effect is to speed up the natural lightening and maturing of flour.
- Unbleached flour is aged and bleached naturally by oxygen in the air. It is more golden in color, generally more expensive, and does not have the consistency

in baking qualities of bleached flour. Unbleached is preferred for yeast breads because bleaching affects gluten strength.

- Patent flour, bleached or unbleached, is the highest grade of flour. It is lower in ash and protein with good color.
- Organic flour is chemical-free and not standardized. Its definition varies from state to state. It may be grown and stored without the use of synthetic herbicides or insecticides. No toxic fumigants were used to kill pests in the grain, and no preservatives were added to the flour, packaging, or food product.
- Gluten is a protein formed when water and wheat flour are mixed. Gluten gives bread dough elasticity, strength, and gas-retaining properties. Wheat is the only grain with sufficient gluten content to make a raised or leavened loaf of bread.

Bread

Fresh bread is perceived as healthful and is a basic menu item on the Food Guide Pyramid. Comfort foods are a big trend, and fresh-baked bread is one of the easiest comfort foods to offer customers. Comfort foods promote a down-home feeling when dining out, and because customers equate home with quality, fresh is perceived as high quality. Customers say they can tell the difference between fresh and frozen baked bread and, of course, they all prefer freshly baked bread. In-house baked breads are on the rise again. Restaurants do not have an exclusive on fresh baked bread. Many hospital, college and university, and school foodservice operations have become known for their bake shops with signature products. Everyone loves fresh baked bread, especially today's younger generation.

For example, Mary Molt, assistant director of Kansas State University Foodservices, augments a large residence hall dining center's in-house baking operation with a small retail bakery (Wheat Foods Council, 1990). Molt explains:

> "The residence hall bakery does the majority of mixing and baking to produce cinnamon rolls, bread, cookies, specialty breads, muffins, and cakes. We use our from-scratch recipes (110 yeast breads in all) and a few yeast bread mixes. We started the retail bakery because students expressed an interest in buying our bakery products. It also presented an opportunity to create campus jobs for students, allowing those with food-related majors to gain work experience."

Since opening the retail store in 1987, $15,000 a year has been added to the student payroll, providing many budding professionals invaluable experience.

According to the USDA's 1993 School Nutrition Dietary Assessment Survey, most grain products, such as bread, rolls, pasta, biscuits, and pizza crusts, currently offered in school are made from refined flour (Friedman et al., 1995). Children who are accustomed to white flour products frequently reject the darker, heartier, whole grain products. A solution to this problem is the development of a hard white wheat through grain breeding and milling techniques that has a lighter color and is milder and less bitter in flavor than the traditional hard red wheat used in most American wheat products. When the whole white grain is ground to an ultrafine flour, it has baking characteristics similar to refined wheat flour, but contains the nutrient profile of traditional whole wheat. This wheat is called *white whole wheat* and has been

PLATE 1

The Food Guide Pyramid

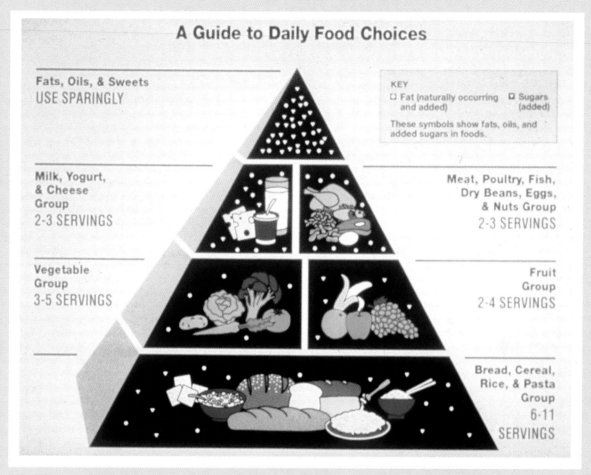

U.S. Department of Agriculture and the U.S. Department of Health and Human Services.

PLATE 2

Bread, Cereal, Rice, and Pasta Group in the Food Guide Pyramid

Courtesy of the Wheat Foods Council.

PLATE 3

Fruit and Vegetable Group
in the Food Guide Pyramid

Courtesy of the National Dairy Council®.

PLATE 4

Meat, Poultry, Fish, Dry Beans, Eggs, and Nuts in the Food Guide Pyramid

Catfish
Courtesy of the
Catfish Institute.

Center Loin Pork Roast
Courtesy of the National
Pork Producers Council.

Egg
Courtesy of the American
Egg Board.

Whole Chicken
USDA.

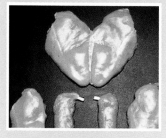

Skinless Chicken
USDA.

Peanuts
Courtesy of the National
Dairy Council®.

Milk, Yogurt, and Cheese Group in the Food Guide Pyramid

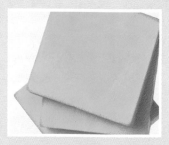

Cheddar Cheese
Courtesy of the National
Dairy Council®.

Plain Yogurt
Courtesy of the National
Dairy Council®.

Reduced Fat Milk
Courtesy of the National
Dairy Council®.

PLATE 5

Foodservice Operations Thermometers

Digital Pocket Test Thermometer, Model DFP450

Refrigerator/Freezer/Dry Storage Thermometer, Model 25HP

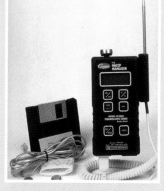

HACCP Manager, Model HT3000

Hot Holding Thermometer, Model 26HP

Meat Thermometer, Model 323

Courtesy of the Cooper Instrument Corporation.

PLATE 6

Moist Heat Equipment

**Steam-Jacketed Kettle,
Model DEE/4T**
Courtesy of Groen, a Dover
Industries Company.

**Pressureless Convection
Steamer, Model 24-CEM-24**
Courtesy of Cleveland
Range Inc.

PLATE 7

Dry Heat Equipment

**Charbroiler,
Model 0836-336A**
Courtesy of U.S. Range.

Clamshell
Courtesy of Lang
Manufacturing Company.

**Deep Fat Fryer,
Model FPH-350C**
Courtesy of Frymaster.

PLATE 7

Dry Heat Equipment

Stack Deck Oven with Separate Heat Source, Model 962
Courtesy of Blodgett.

Convection Oven, Model DFG 100
Courtesy of Blodgett.

Impinger Model, Model 1130
Courtesy of Lincoln.

Microwave Oven, Model NE-2680
Courtesy of Panasonic.

Smoker Oven, Model 150
Courtesy of Cookshack.

Low-temp Cooking and Holding Oven, Model 750-TH-III
Courtesy of Alto-Shaam.

PLATE 8

Multi-Function Equipment

Combi-Oven, Model COS-101S
Courtesy of Blodgett.

Tilting Skillet, Model NHFP
Courtesy of Groen, a Dover Industries
Company.

Convection/Microwave Oven, Model CMA2000
Courtesy of Amana Appliances.

PLATE 9

Refrigeration Equipment

Reach-In, Model 1-1045-01
Courtesy of McCall.

Ice Machine, Model TDE-550
Courtesy of Scotsman.

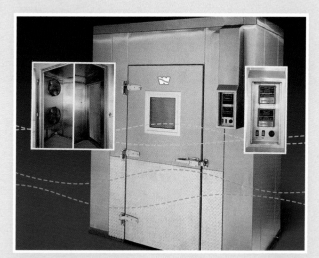

Blast Chiller, Model BC-250-UR
Courtesy of Whirlwind Corporation.

PLATE 10

Warewashing Equipment

Door Dishmachine, Model AM-14C

Rack Conveyor-1 tank, Model C-44A

Rack Conveyor-2 tanks, Model CPW-80A

Courtesy of Hobart Corporation.

PLATE 10

Warewashing Equipment

Power Soak, Model V-1200-L
Courtesy of Metcraft Inc.

PLATE 11

Other Equipment

Mixer, Model A-200

Mixer, Model D-330

Mixer, Model H-600

Courtesy of Hobart Corporation.

PLATE 12

Carts

Utility Cart, Model BC2354-S
Courtesy of Cambro Manufacturing Company.

Service Cart, Model CC1
Courtesy of Carts of Colorado.

**Meal Delivery Cart with System 9"
Unitized Base, Model TDCH-1418-28
and 473-1129**
Courtesy of Seco Products Corporation.

PLATE 13

Service Equipment

Greyson Pattern
Courtesy of Libbey.

Pottery
Courtesy of The Hall China Company.

Fiesta Pottery
Courtesy of The Homer Laughlin
China Company.

PLATE 14

Melamine Compartment Trays

Melamine Dallas Ware®

Courtesy of Carlisle Foodservice Products.

PLATE 15

Holloware

Courtesy of World Tableware, Inc.™

PLATE 16

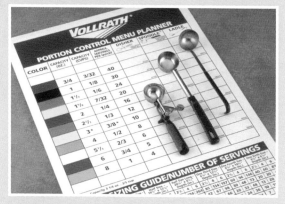

Color Coding System
Courtesy of Vollrath Company, L.L.C.

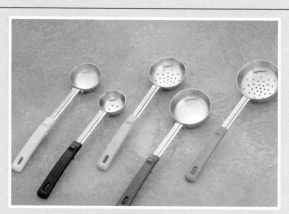

Color Coded Spoodles
Courtesy of Vollrath Company, L.L.C.

Color Coded Ladles
Courtesy of Vollrath Company, L.L.C.

Color Coded Dishers
Courtesy of Vollrath Company, L.L.C.

Disposable Gloves
Courtesy of Foodhandler™.

Table 7.1. "Good sellers," breads identified by *Restaurants & Institutions*.

Commercial		Non-Commercial	
Item	**Index**	**Item**	**Index**
French/Italian bread	137	Bagels	187
Dinner rolls	132	Garlic bread	137
Garlic bread	122	Muffins	132
Focaccia	116	Dinner rolls	124
Sourdough bread	116	Focaccia	116
Breadsticks	107	Soft pretzels	111
Bagels	106	French/Italian bread	108
Nut/fruit bread	105	Breadsticks	104
Muffins	104	Croissants	95
Soft pretzels	101	Cornbread	94
Whole-grain bread	99	Biscuits	90
Biscuits	95	Whole-grain bread	85
Cornbread	93	Nut/fruit bread	85
Pita bread	81	Sourdough bread	83
Croissants	75	Pita bread	70

Most often on menu: Dinner rolls   *Most often on menu:* Dinner rolls

Most added in last year: Focaccia   *Most added in last year:* Breadsticks

Source: From "Breads" by B. A. Johnson, 1995, *Restaurants and Institutions, 105*(26), p. 68. Used by permission.

grown primarily in Australia, India, Pakistan, and China; currently it is being grown in Kansas, Oklahoma, Colorado, Nebraska, and Wyoming. In the study, elementary school children accepted the products made from white whole wheat, causing a foodservice employee to exclaim, "I can't believe it, but their taste buds are changing!"

Good Sellers

The trade journal *Restaurants & Institutions* published a "Good Sellers" list for breads served in commercial and noncommercial foodservice operations (Johnson, 1995). In Table 7.1, various types of bread are ranked from highest to lowest for these two categories. Dinner rolls, probably fresher than in years past, are the most common bread in all operations. These rolls, however, topped the good seller list in only 2 of 13 segment categories: hotels and nursing homes.

Foodservice operators in all segments have added variety to their bread baskets. White tablecloth restaurants have added focaccia, flat bread, and country-style French and Italian breads. Quick-service and family restaurants have added mostly bagels. Casual restaurants, including business and industry operations, have added focaccia, breadsticks, and whole-grain pita breads. Hospitals have added breadsticks, and nursing homes have added fruit or nut bread. Colleges and universities have added focaccia, garlic bread, corn bread, and flat bread. Every commercial operation has a best-seller. Fine dining has focaccia and French or Italian bread; family dining, hotels, and catering have dinner rolls; casual/theme restaurants have either garlic or French bread; and quick-service has soft pretzels. Flat breads definitely are the hottest of the hot, and they are no longer limited to ethnic restaurants (Rogers, 1995). Focaccia, specialty pizzas, pita breads (a staple in the Middle East), tortillas, naan breads, and cracker-like lavash were repeatedly mentioned during discussions with operators around the country.

Bread always has been thought of as the "staff of life," especially in European countries. A wonderful example is a newspaper article by Drozdiak (1995), who asked, "Are the French losing their taste for French bread?" He explains that even today, the beret, the bottle of red wine, and the baguette (a small loaf of French bread) still convey France's primal image to the world. Bread has been the key to social peace and stability for the French government. According to Drozdiak, French supermarkets have forced bakers out of business with their cheap loaves made out of frozen dough that taste so awful that people soon stop buying it. When more than 1,000 of their peers were forced to shut down their ovens last year, French bakers decided to take their case to the streets. Mass demonstrations were staged in the capital urging the president and prime minister to enact emergency measures that would salvage what bakers contend is a cherished part of national heritage and one of the most enduring staples of French culinary arts. The government responded with sympathy and embarked on a crusade to help France's bakers sustain their craft and promised to coax customers back to the virtues of the traditional baguette. The government is preparing a strict law that will regulate the ingredients and five stages required to make authentic bread as distinguished from the imitation products found increasingly in supermarkets.

Purchasing Alternatives

Breads baked on premise from scratch always have had allure for customers. How many times have you heard people say "they bake their own breads" when they are discussing the quality of food served in a specific operation? In small operations with a couple of cooks, rolls or cornbread are made from home recipes that are doubled or tripled, but as the number of customers increase, this method no longer is possible. Many excellent alternatives are available.

From Scratch. Trained bakers and specialized equipment are required to produce consistently high-quality products. The American Institute of Baking in Manhattan, Kan., has excellent courses for training bakers from all over the world. For example, sourdough breads, with their tangy flavor and marvelous texture enhanced by sourdough starters, continue to be in vogue (Rogers, 1995). American bakers enjoy working with sourdough bread because they consider the result a true measure of their expertise. Besides, customers love the product. Some operations place the bakery right in the middle of their dining rooms so the customer can watch what is happening and enjoy the smell of fresh baked products. To make products such as these, a trained baker is required. The advantages and disadvantages of baking from scratch are given in Figure 7.6 (Wheat Foods Council, 1990).

Figure 7.6. Advantages and disadvantages of baking from scratch.

Advantages

- Maximum control, creativity, formula flexibility, freshness, and quality
- Excellent promotion potential
- Lower ingredient costs

Disadvantages

- Training and labor costs
- Need for adequate space
- High initial investment
- Equipment maintenance

Source: From *Breads: The Significant Edge* by the Wheat Food Council, 1990, Englewood, CO: Author.

Purchasing for made-from-scratch, on-premise breads requires expertise by buyers. Not only must they understand buying ingredients in large quantities but also they need to know something about the products they are purchasing. The type of flour, shortening, yeast food, dough conditioners/crumb softeners, and vital wheat gluten can make a lot of difference in the quality of products. Once the products are received, they must be stored correctly and tightly controlled in inventory. This trend is becoming so popular that consultants now make a living helping foodservices set up a bake shop on premises.

Ready-Prepared Products.   Not all foodservice operations can have their own bakeries because the volume of business does not warrant this expenditure. However, successful results can be achieved by purchasing baked products from a local retail baker or beginning with one or more of the available pre-mixed, frozen, brown-and-serve, or par-baked products on the market today. The method to choose should depend upon resources, available space, and personnel.

Local Retail Baker.   Working with a local retail baker is a good alternative to baking in house. They can deliver freshly baked breads and rolls that meet the needs of the operation. They also can develop a signature formula, the term used by bakers for a recipe. The baker chosen should specialize in bread and roll products. Samples should be submitted before decisions are made. Supermarket bakeries could be a source because many have professional bakers on staff and facilities large enough to meet the volume needs of the operation. The foodservice buyer should tell the baker what is needed in specific terms: for example, sandwich buns, dinner rolls, pumpernickel boules (round balls of bread), breadsticks, or cinnamon bread. The size of the product needs to be specified, such as 3- to 4-ounce buns, 1- to 2-ounce dinner rolls, 16- to 18-ounce standard loaves, or 6-inch-long breadsticks.

The buyer should establish a delivery schedule with the baker. Some retail bakers cannot deliver every day because of the distance from the foodservice operation. The buyer needs to check to see that the bread is baked on the same day it is delivered.

Figure 7.7.   Advantages and disadvantages of using a retail baker.

Advantages

- Reliability
- Professional baking expertise eliminates need for on-premise baker(s)
- No additional equipment/repair costs
- No additional labor or inventory
- Reduced storage space
- Cross-marketing advantage—local baker's good reputation could be promoted by you

Disadvantages

- Lack of bakery with needed capabilities
- Delivery logistically not possible
- Order fluctuation poses problem for bakery
- Your needs too specialized for bakery capabilities or profit structure
- Costs too prohibitive

Source: From *Breads: The Significant Edge* by the Wheat Food Council, 1990, Englewood, CO: Author.

Upon delivery, the bread should be wrapped immediately in air-tight, freezer-suitable packaging and stored at 0°F. When needed, the bread should be thawed at room temperature away from drafts or thawed quickly in the wrapper at 95°F to 110°F. Only small amounts of the products should be heated at a time. The bread will never be as good as freshly baked bread, but if handled properly, the quality will not deteriorate much. If the foodservice operation is a large one and close to the retail bakery, fresh bread is often delivered before each meal. Advantages and disadvantages of working with a local retail baker are shown in Figure 7.7.

Premixed.   These products eliminate much of the measuring and weighing of ingredients. Excellent bread, roll, muffin, and other mixes are available. These mixes also can be custom-formulated to create a signature or specialty product. Labor costs might be slightly reduced because a highly trained baker is not needed. The supplier often will train the staff person who makes the products.

Premixes can be either complete mixes or base mixes. Complete mixes contain most of the ingredients necessary to make the desired product. Yeast and water are usually added on premise although some mixes now contain yeast. Base mixes contain only ingredients necessary to produce a specific product. For example, the base mix for whole wheat bread with wheat germ would not contain the white bread flour, liquid, salt, or yeast but would contain the whole wheat flour, wheat germ, and sweetener. Figure 7.8 shows the advantages and disadvantages of using premixes.

Frozen Doughs.   Foodservice operators can use their own creativity and technical assistance from a supplier. Frozen doughs can be the basis for a wide variety of signature breads. Costs of bread dough are about even with scratch and premix prod-

Figure 7.8. Advantages and disadvantages of using premixes.

Advantages

- Uses same equipment as scratch baking
- Products have "from scratch" appearance
- Requires less storage space
- Production time shorter and easier
- Consistency improved—fewer scaling errors
- Training baker necessary, but needs fewer skills, less hours

Disadvantages

- Baking training required
- Ingredient cost slightly higher
- Little formula flexibility
- Mixing flexibility is restricted

Source: From *Breads: The Significant Edge* by the Wheat Food Council, 1990, Englewood, CO: Author.

Figure 7.9. Advantages and disadvantages of using frozen doughs.

Advantages

- Less baking skill needed for dough preparation
- Less waste or staling
- Less preparation and storage space needed
- Shorter production time
- Capital investment for equipment lower
- Smaller labor cost; training still required; still have on-premise baking
- Can produce a wide variety of shapes, textures, and flavors

Disadvantages

- Reduced formula flexibility for signature bread creation. If volume big enough, might have own frozen doughs created.
- Higher dough costs
- Must have tight inventory control
- Timing essential for high quality
- Need correct equipment

Source: From *Breads: The Significant Edge* by the Wheat Food Council, 1990, Englewood, CO: Author.

ucts in which labor and ingredients make up 60% of costs. Frozen dough products cost less than brown-and-serve, but if labor is added, the costs are about the same. Advantages and disadvantages of using frozen doughs are shown in Figure 7.9.

Brown-and-Serve. These products are prebaked just to the point of product stability. They should be stored at room temperature. They then are baked off for 8 to

Figure 7.10. Advantages and disadvantages of using brown-and-serve bread products.

Advantages

- Short production time—bake only
- Still have baked on-premise advantage
- Minimal baking skills needed
- Reduced labor costs
- Equipment investment minimal
- Storage needs minimal
- Produce only as needed

Disadvantages

- Limited choices available
- Limited formula flexibility
- Once baked, product loses quality rapidly; must be served immediately
- Ovens required
- Higher product cost
- Must train staff to handle properly

Source: From *Breads: The Significant Edge* by the Wheat Food Council, 1990, Englewood, CO: Author.

12 minutes to brown the crust. Figure 7.10 gives the advantages and disadvantages of using brown-and-serve bread products.

Prebaked.   These products—loaves, rolls, and pizza crusts—are purchased and held frozen until needed. They are firmer and more completely baked than brown-and-serve products. A baking time of 5 minutes is all that is required because these products are already browned. The advantages and disadvantages are similar to those of brown-and-serve products. Additional freezer space is necessary and the products cannot be held once baked.

Baker's Percent Formula

Bread and roll recipes, called *formulas,* include the amount, usually in pounds, of all the ingredients. *Baker's percent formula* is a recipe for all bread products, in which weights of all ingredients except flour are converted into a percentage of the weight in pounds of the total amount of flour in a recipe. A 100-pound bag of bread flour plus other ingredients produces 180 pounds of dough that makes 160 regular-sized loaves of bread. For example, after much research and experimentation, the amount of gluten required for a loaf of bread that meets certain standards is 2% of the flour weight, or 2 pounds for 100 pounds of flour. If, however, 150 pounds of flour were needed to meet the day's requirement for bread, 2% of the flour weight, or 3 pounds, of gluten would be added to the flour, as shown in Table 7.2. This baker's percent formula remains the same for all amounts of flour in a recipe.

Table 7.2. Baker's percent
formula.

	% of Flour	Flour Weight[b] (lbs.)		
Ingredients[a]	Weight	100	150	200
Gluten	2	2	3	4
Salt	2	2	3	4
Yeast	4	4	6	8
Sucrose	9	9	13.5	18
Shortening	3	3	1.5	6
Milk solids	0.5	0.5	0.75	1
Monoglycerides	4	4	6	8
Water	60	60	90	120

[a]In addition to flour
[b]Flour could be 65% strong enriched flour + 35% multigrain including coarse whole wheat flour, flax seed meal, pumpernickel rye, and rolled oats
Source: From American Institute of Baking, Manhattan, KS.

Pasta

Because pasta is a lowfat, high-carbohydrate food, it fits perfectly with the dietary recommendations of the Food Guide Pyramid. Pasta helps form the foundation of the pyramid as part of the grains group. Pasta is nutritious. Approximately 80% of its calories come from complex carbohydrates, and the remaining calories are mostly protein. It has a fair amount of dietary fiber and little sodium and is virtually fat free. The National Pasta Association promotes pasta as a universally appealing food that makes sense for people of all ages. Fun and flavorful, light, and low in fat, convenient yet very healthful, pasta is the perfect food for pairing with everything from seafood to legumes to fresh fruit. Pasta menu items can be served as appetizers, salads, entrées, side dishes, or desserts. Pasta appeals to every age group.

Good Sellers

Pasta and grains were added to Good Sellers in *Restaurants & Institutions'* Menu Census as a category in 1995 and is shown in Table 7.3 (Frei, 1995). The reason is that pasta especially has come into its own as a main dish, and rice, noodles, and even macaroni and cheese have assumed side-dish status. These menu items are no longer limited by ethnic boundaries, such as pasta by Italian boundaries or rice by Asian. Customer demand for meatless dishes and lighter food also is responsible for the rise of grains on entrée menus. Pasta is on the menu in nearly 100% of business & industry operations and more than 90% of menus in hospitals, healthcare facilities, nursing homes, colleges and universities, and schools. Pasta consumption is still slightly higher in commercial compared to noncommercial segments. Among commercial operations, especially in upscale settings, look for polenta, a cornmeal-based menu item, to shine brightly in coming years not only as a side dish but also as an appetizer and component of main dishes.

Table 7.3. Pasta and grains, good sellers.

Commercial		Non-Commercial	
Item	**Index**	**Item**	**Index**
Pasta	151	Macaroni and cheese	232
Seasoned rice/blends	142	Seasoned rice/blends	148
Wild rice	117	Pasta	138
Macaroni and cheese	112	White rice	127
Dumplings	100	Wild rice	97
White rice	93	Noodles	93
Polenta	80	Dumplings	76
Noodles	80	Hush puppies	58
Hush puppies	77	Other grains	27
Other grains	65	Polenta	27

Most often on menu:
Pasta

Most often on menu:
Pasta

Most added in last year:
Pasta

Most added in last year:
Seasoned rice/blends

Source: From "Pasta and Grains" by B. T. Frei, 1995, *Restaurants & Institutions, 105*(26), p. 92. Used by permission.

History

Pasta usually is thought of as an Italian food, but its origin has never been determined (Margen, 1992). The Chinese may have eaten noodles as early as 5000 B.C. Some historians believe that Marco Polo brought pasta to Italy from the Far East in 1295, but if he did, he was probably comparing it to the pasta that was already there. Evidence is available that pasta was made in Italy as early as 400 B.C. The history of pasta in the United States is much clearer. Thomas Jefferson, while he was the American ambassador to France, brought pasta from Naples in the late 1700s. The first pasta factory in the United States opened in 1848 in Brooklyn, New York, but it did not become popular until Italian immigrants introduced dried pasta in the late 1800s. Italian-style pasta is still the most popular in the United States, but Americans are discovering Asian pastas in the form of noodles and stuffed dumplings.

Pasta Production

All **pasta** is made from a dough, often referred to as a paste; the word *pasta* means paste in Italian (Margen, 1992). The principal ingredient in pasta is semolina, a coarsely ground flour from durum wheat. The carotenoid pigments of the high-protein grain give pasta a golden-color, mellow flavor, and sturdy texture.

Commercially, measured amounts of flour and water are automatically fed into a mixer, which thoroughly blends the ingredients into a dough under vacuum. If any other ingredients are added to the pasta, such as eggs to make egg noodles or spinach or tomato to make red or green pasta, they are added at this stage. Wheat doughs develop gluten when kneaded; more gluten is developed in harder wheats.

Semolina dough is high in gluten and therefore has the resiliency and strength to go through the mechanical pasta-making process and keep its shape during cooking. The dough is kneaded until it reaches the correct consistency. Then it is pushed, or extruded, through a die, a metal disc with holes in it. The size and shape of the holes in the die determine what the shape of the pasta will be. For instance, dies with round or oval holes will produce solid, long shapes of pasta, such as spaghetti. When the extruded pasta reaches the right length, it is cut with sharp blades that rotate beneath the die. The pasta is then sent through large dryers that circulate hot, moist air to slowly dry the pasta. Because different pasta shapes vary in degrees of thickness, they dry for different lengths of time. The dried pasta is packed in bags or boxes. Some of the more fragile pasta shapes, such as lasagna and manicotti, are often packed by hand to protect them from breaking.

Noodles go through a similar process. Egg noodles have whole eggs or yolks added to the dough, which is softer than that used in pasta. The dough is run between rollers to the desired thickness and then automatically cut into various widths and carefully dried. Precooked pasta and quick-cooking noodles are now available on the market. The products are preconditioned by steam to gelatinize the starch and are submitted to high temperatures for a short time. These products can then be quickly reconstituted with boiling water. For example, the dried precooked lasagna noodles can be layered with the sauce and other ingredients and then baked in less than half the time required for regular noodles.

Some chefs make their own pasta although fresh pasta is available on the market. Fresh pasta cooks much more rapidly than dried and is a slightly softer product. For people who like their pasta al dente, dried pasta is best. In Italian *al dente* translates as *to the tooth,* meaning the pasta offers slight resistance when bitten into.

Pasta comes in various shapes and sizes, as shown in Figure 7.11. According to the National Pasta Association, the cook or the chef should choose a pasta shape and sauce that complement each other. Thin, delicate pastas, like angel hair or thin spaghetti, should be served with light, thin sauces. Thicker pasta shapes, like fettuccine, work well with heavier sauces. Pasta shapes with holes or ridges, like mostaccioli or radiatore, are perfect for chunky sauces.

Pasta also can be purchased in various colors and flavors. Spinach pasta is a deep green color, tomato is red, saffron is orange, mushroom is taupe, hot pepper is deep red, and squid ink is black. Customers with a keen taste can identify the flavors.

PURCHASING GRAIN PRODUCTS

Grain products are not as perishable as most other food products and therefore have a longer shelf life. Most grains are sold in boxes or polyethylene bags. The packages should be tightly sealed and dated for freshness. Grains should be clean and dry and have a fresh odor. Grains contain natural oils that can become rancid. Once a package is opened, grain products can become infected with insects and develop mold. Even though they can be stored at room temperature, after a month they will start to deteriorate. In many foodservice operations, they are tightly sealed and stored in

Figure 7.11. Various shapes of pasta.

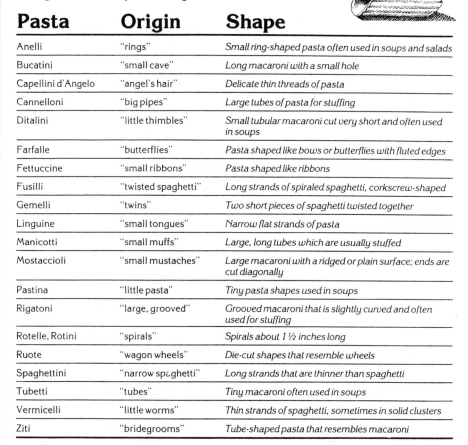

You've Got Pastabilities

With more than 100 different shapes to choose from in the U.S., pasta can help you add new variety to your meals. How many of these shapes have you tried?

Pasta	Origin	Shape
Anelli	"rings"	Small ring-shaped pasta often used in soups and salads
Bucatini	"small cave"	Long macaroni with a small hole
Capellini d'Angelo	"angel's hair"	Delicate thin threads of pasta
Cannelloni	"big pipes"	Large tubes of pasta for stuffing
Ditalini	"little thimbles"	Small tubular macaroni cut very short and often used in soups
Farfalle	"butterflies"	Pasta shaped like bows or butterflies with fluted edges
Fettuccine	"small ribbons"	Pasta shaped like ribbons
Fusilli	"twisted spaghetti"	Long strands of spiraled spaghetti, corkscrew-shaped
Gemelli	"twins"	Two short pieces of spaghetti twisted together
Linguine	"small tongues"	Narrow flat strands of pasta
Manicotti	"small muffs"	Large, long tubes which are usually stuffed
Mostaccioli	"small mustaches"	Large macaroni with a ridged or plain surface; ends are cut diagonally
Pastina	"little pasta"	Tiny pasta shapes used in soups
Rigatoni	"large, grooved"	Grooved macaroni that is slightly curved and often used for stuffing
Rotelle, Rotini	"spirals"	Spirals about 1 ½ inches long
Ruote	"wagon wheels"	Die-cut shapes that resemble wheels
Spaghettini	"narrow spaghetti"	Long strands that are thinner than spaghetti
Tubetti	"tubes"	Tiny macaroni often used in soups
Vermicelli	"little worms"	Thin strands of spaghetti, sometimes in solid clusters
Ziti	"bridegrooms"	Tube-shaped pasta that resembles macaroni

NATIONAL
PASTA
ASSOCIATION

Source: From the National Pasta Association, Arlington, VA. Used by permission.

the refrigerator. They can be stored there for four or five months in moisture-proof containers. Most grains except oats and oat bran, because of their high fat content, can be stored indefinitely in a freezer. The buyer of these products should know the quantity needed for a specific period of time and not overbuy.

Specifications for grain products are not as difficult to write as they are for other products. Most cereals are purchased by brand names that are known by the customer. In restaurants, individual one-serving boxes of specific brands usually are ordered. In other foodservice operations, such as schools, cereals might be put into dispensers for students to serve themselves. Sample specifications follow.

Flour

Origin: northern United States and Canada

Form: hard wheat bread flour

Use: specialty breads and rolls

Composition: minimum of 11% gluten, enriched, bleached

Pack: 50-pound sack

Price: by sack

Cereal

Form: dry

Use: breakfast food and snacks out of a dispenser

Brand: Kellogg's Frosted Flakes

Pack: 4/2½-pound polyethylene bags per case

Price: by case

Pasta

Form: precooked lasagne noodles

Use: baked lasagne casserole

Composition: 100% durum wheat semolina, enriched

Pack: 10-pound carton, hand packed

Price: by the carton

SUMMARY

Grain-based foods form the base for the Food Guide Pyramid because they are often referred to as the foundation of healthy eating. Most grains are seeds, consisting of a starchy endosperm, a bran covering, and a germ, from which the plant grows.

Wheat is the most popular grain in the United States. Other less popular grains are corn, rice, oats, rye, and barley. Two basic categories of processed grains are cereals and flour. Cereals have been thought of as breakfast foods, but today they have become an important part of menu items for all meals. Flour is the base of diets of people around the world. From it bread, often considered "the staff of life," and pasta are made. Flour is the primary ingredient in many varieties of breads and pastas.

The foodservice buyer probably spends less time on purchasing cereals and flour than any other food products. Specifications are not difficult to write because most of these products are purchased by brand names. Quality of flour is determined by the products that are made from it. If the menu items please the customer, the same brand of flour will be ordered again.

REFERENCES

Bennion, M. (1995). *Introductory Foods* (10th ed.). Upper Saddle River, NJ: Merrill/Prentice Hall.

Drozdiak, W. (1995, October 1). Are the French losing their taste for French bread? *The Wichita Eagle*.

Frei, B. T. (1995). Pasta and grains. *Restaurants & Institutions, 105*(26), 92.

Friedman, B. J., Hurd, S., and Cise, N. (1995). Promoting whole grains in school foodservice. *School Foodservice & Nutrition, 49*(6), 70–72, 44, 76.

Johnson, B. A. (1995). Breads. *Restaurants & Institutions, 105*(26), 68.

L'Ecuyer, S. (1996). Grains & the convenience of culture. *School Foodservice & Nutrition, 50*(7), 54–61.

Margen, S. (1992). *The Wellness Encyclopedia of Food and Nutrition*. New York: Rebus.

Parseghian, P. (1995). A grain of truth: Chefs are keen for quinoa. *Nation's Restaurant News, 29*(30), 33.

Putnam, J. J., & Allshouse, J. E. (1994). Food Consumption, Prices, and Expenditures, Food and Consumer Economic Division, Economic Research Service, U.S. Department of Agriculture. Statistical Bulletin No. 915.

Restaurants & Institutions Editors. (1996). Boiled, baked & burgeoning. *Restaurants & Institutions, 106*(17), 18–19, 22.

Rogers, M. (1995). Hot from the oven: A fresh sheet on baking. *Restaurants & Institutions,* supplement to *105*(13).

Ryan, R. R. (1994). All about uncommon grains. *Restaurants & Institutions, 104*(20), 76.

Wheat Foods Council. (1990). Breads: The significant edge. Englewood, CO: Author.

8

Fresh Fruits and Vegetables

Figure 8.1.   Food Guide Pyramid with fruits and vegetables highlighted.

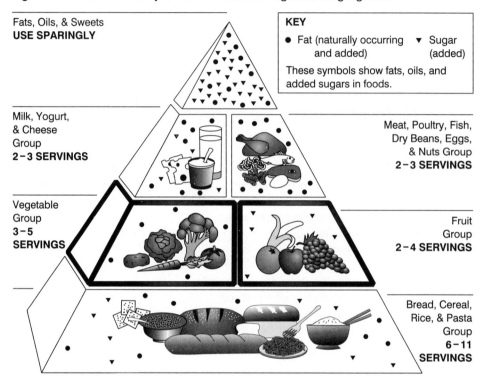

Fruits and vegetables are on the second level of the Food Guide Pyramid and are highlighted in Figure 8.1. An apple, orange, banana, and grapes represent the fruit group, and a potato, carrot, lettuce, broccoli, and tomato represent the vegetable group. Because of similar characteristics, fruits and vegetables are discussed together in this text (Plate 3).

The fresh produce industry in the United States is huge, vital, and constantly changing in response to the needs of the marketplace (Dole Food Company, 1992). From the home gardens in colonial times to today's massive produce farms, the full spectrum of the produce industry has expanded tremendously. Fruit and vegetable production is a dynamic, major segment of the American economy.

THE FARMER'S MARKET

Chefs trained in culinary schools learn a lot about fresh fruits and vegetables. They understand that to serve quality food is to serve fresh food. Alice Waters, founder, chef, and driving force behind the legendary restaurant, Chez Panisse in Berkeley, Calif., has a simple philosophy to use only the freshest and best ingredients and to enhance, not obscure, menu items in their preparation (Fairchild, 1993). Menus in her restaurant are changed each day after the chef brings fresh produce from the market. Apples, oranges, iceberg lettuce, avocados, potatoes, and other produce that ship well and keep their quality for more than a few days are most often purchased from wholesale establishments. If, however, the menu includes seasonal produce, it must be planned daily after a trip to the local market. Quality and flavor are best if seasonal fruits and vegetables, such as corn on the cob, strawberries, tomatoes, and peaches, can be purchased locally. As a result, local farmer's markets have become very popular. A **farmer's market** is a place in which all products, mostly fruits and vegetables, are raised by local growers. The major advantage of purchasing from these markets is that only enough of a product for one or two days needs to be purchased at one time, thus ensuring freshness.

The Union Square Greenmarket is the largest of 19 year-round farmers' markets in Manhattan, Brooklyn, and the Bronx (Kellogg, 1994). Thousands of New York locals, visitors, and chefs shop in these markets every week. More than 600 varieties of fruits, vegetables, and farm-made products can be purchased from 65 farmers. Some farmers even grow special products for customers. Greenmarket was started to help local farmers survive by selling their products directly to customers, not to distributors or suppliers. All products sold in the market must be raised or produced by the growers. Local farmer's markets can be found in most cities, small and large, and they function on the same premise as the Greenmarket. The astute buyer has to know what to look for when purchasing from local markets.

CONSUMPTION OF PRODUCE

Fresh fruits and vegetables are appearing more and more in the American diet, but still are not up to the minimum recommendation in the Food Guide Pyramid. Two to four servings of fruit and three to five servings of vegetables daily are suggested. According to a recent National Cancer Institute telephone survey of American adults, only 23% currently eat five or more servings a day. An adult's daily fruit and vegetable intake is about 3½ servings, or 1½ servings short of the recommended amount (Produce Marketing Association, 1993).

Each year *The Packer,* a produce industry trade publication, conducts a survey of fresh produce consumers. Consumers reported an increased consumption of fruits and vegetables compared to the previous year, and they gave the following reasons for this increase:

- more fruit for snacks (87%)
- concern about diet/nutrition (86%)
- more vegetables in salads (71%)
- more fruit for dessert (59%)
- more vegetables for snacks (52%)
- more vegetable-based meals (41%)
- more microwave vegetables (26%)

Most important to the surveyed consumers were the appearance/condition (97%), taste/flavor (96%), and freshness/ripeness (96%) of fresh fruits and vegetables.

Seventy percent rated price as important, 60% cited nutritional value, and 51% rated highly convenient to eat.

According to a recent survey of college and university foodservice directors, about 15% of the U.S. college students choose a vegetarian option at their dining halls, which is two to three times higher than the percentage of the general population ("Meatless alternatives," 1994). The study, conducted by the National Restaurant Association in cooperation with the National Association of College and University Food Services, found that approximately 97% of all institutions have added meatless items to their menus; 84% intend to expand their vegetarian menu selections in the next 5 years.

NUTRITION

Health authorities recommend that people eat at least five servings of fruits and vegetables every day with a variety of other foods. An apple a day is no longer enough.

Nutrients

The U.S. Department of Health and Human Services, U.S. Department of Agriculture (USDA), and National Academy of Sciences all recommend that Americans should eat a balanced diet low in fat which includes lots of fruits and vegetables. According to the Nutrition and Cancer Prevention Program of the California Department of Health and Services and the California Public Health Foundation, 35% of all cancer deaths may be related to a diet high in fat and low in fiber. Fruits and vegetables help reduce risk of cancer because they are low in fat and are rich sources of vitamin A, vitamin C, and fiber. A lowfat diet that is low in saturated fat and cholesterol and includes plenty of high fiber foods also decreases the risk of heart disease.

Fruits and vegetables high in vitamins A and C and fiber should be eaten daily. Also several servings of vegetables each week should include those from the cabbage family (cruciferous vegetables): bok choy, broccoli, brussel sprouts, cabbage, cauliflower, kale, mustard greens, rutabagas, Swiss chard, and turnips. These vegetables are loaded with vitamins, minerals, and fiber, and experts say they exert a special protective effect against certain kinds of cancer. Fruits and vegetables without added fats have no cholesterol, and almost all are naturally low in calories, fat, and sodium. Some are good sources of other nutrients, such as folacin, potassium, and calcium. Fruits and vegetables also help promote a healthy digestive tract.

Labeling

The Nutrition Labeling and Education Act of 1990 established two deadlines for nutrition labeling of food products (Produce Marketing Association, 1994a). For the 20 most popular raw fruits and vegetables, Congress required the Food and Drug Administration (FDA) to issue final regulations for a voluntary program by November 1991. For all other products, Congress gave until May 8, 1994, to conform to the new nutrition labeling regulations.

Raw fruits and vegetables are still subject to the November 1991 guidelines. The FDA established the current guidelines for voluntary nutrition information in 1991 in accordance with the Nutrition Labeling and Education Act of 1990. Although the law mandates nutrition labeling for almost all processed foods, it allows voluntary point-of-purchase nutrition information for raw fruits, vegetables, and fish as long as a sufficient number of retailers participate. The program is designed to give retail grocers flexibility while ensuring that as many consumers as possible have access to consistent, reliable information. For the first time, consumers at grocery stores across the country will have access to the same basic nutrition information. To meet the guidelines, point-of-purchase nutrition information must include the following:

- name of the fruit or vegetable that has been identified by the FDA as one of the 20 most commonly eaten in the United States (Table 8.1)
- serving size
- calories per serving
- amount of protein, total carbohydrates, total fat, and sodium per serving
- percent of the U.S. Recommended Daily Allowances for iron, calcium, and vitamins A and C per serving

Table 8.1.   Top 20 most commonly eaten fruits and vegetables in the United States.

Order	Fruits	/capita/year (lbs)[b]	Vegetables	/capita/year (lbs)[b]
1	Bananas	26.8	Potatoes	49.1
2	Apples	19.4	Lettuce, head	24.9
3	Watermelon	14.3	Onions	16.2
4	Oranges/temples	14.2	Tomatoes	16.0
5	Cantaloupe	8.3	Carrots	8.0
6	Grapes	7.0	Cabbage	7.9
7	Grapefruit	6.2	Celery	6.4
8	Peaches/nectarines	5.9	Sweet corn	6.2
9	Strawberries	3.5	Bell peppers	5.6
10	Pears	3.4	Cucumbers	5.4
11	Lemons	2.6	Romaine/leaf	5.0
12	Avocados	2.0	Sweet potatoes	3.9
13	Pineapples	2.0	Broccoli	3.3
14	Tangerines/tangelos	1.8	Mushrooms	3.2
15	Honeydews	1.8	Cauliflower	1.8
16	Plums/prunes	1.3	Snap beans	1.4
17	Limes	0.9	Asparagus	0.6
18	Mangos	0.9	Other fresh vegetables[a]	4.4
19	Kiwifruit	0.5		
20	Cherries	0.4		

[a]Garlic, Spinach, Squash, Artichokes, Radishes
[b]1993

Source: From *Food Consumption, Prices, and Expenditures, 1970–1993* by J. J. Putnam and J. E. Allshouse, 1994, Washington, DC: U.S. Department of Agriculture.

Unlike processed, prepackaged food, fresh produce does not lend itself well to individual labeling. Thus, the FDA is allowing retailers to display nutrition information on large placards or to list it in consumer pamphlets or brochures. Of course, retailers are allowed to place nutrition information on individual food wrappers or, when appropriate, on stickers affixed to the outside of a fruit or vegetable.

FRESH PRODUCE MENU TRENDS

Ryan (1994) asked, "What do you get when you combine great American produce and great American chefs?" Her answer: "Incredible vegetable dishes and, sometimes, restaurant legends." Exciting vegetable dishes that appeal to a broad range of customers are reshaping the American restaurant menu today, from upscale dining to limited-menu chains.

Vegetables come in all sizes, shapes, and many shades of green, yellow, orange, red, white, and purple (Margen, 1992). They also have many flavors and textures and can be eaten raw or cooked. Most vegetables are nutrient dense; the amount of nutrients is relatively high for the number of calories. Vegetables, like fruits, should not be washed until time of using to preserve nutrients.

An increased interest in vegetarianism, especially on college campuses, has made foodservice managers find entrées that are not simply meat dishes made without meat (Lorenzini, 1994). Along with this trend comes an interest in organically grown produce (Donovan, 1993). The general assumption about organic products is that they have been grown without chemicals, including synthetic herbicides, pesticides, and fertilizers. Organizations that certify farms require that the land and crops be free of chemicals for a specified period. For example, the Natural Organic Farmers Association requires that no chemical pesticides or herbicides have been used within the past three years. Members of the Culinary Institute of America (CIA) are "going back to the earth" at their West Coast campus, Greystone, in St. Helena, Calif. (Bartlett, 1995). They have been meeting with an expert on organic farming about having an organic farm as part of their vineyard. CIA president Ferdinand Metz emphasized that Greystone is all about picking and touching ingredients and learning how good things can be when used fresh and prepared simply.

Students today want creative lowfat vegetarian menus with unusual grains, rices, sauces, and vegetables. Vegetarian entrées are evolving away from the stigma of steamed, tasteless, diet-inspired, and healthy, thanks to a group of ground-breaking chefs who believe that vegetables deserve the honor of their own cuisine.

Side dishes that used to play second fiddle to center-of-the-plate entrées are becoming the main attraction of a meal (Solomon, 1994). Restaurant operators are beginning to realize that side dishes are great for increasing a check average and decreasing food costs. Side dishes usually sell for $2.95 or $3.95 but only cost 20 or 30 cents to make. A side dish category on the menu is not extra work for the cooks because vegetable accompaniments, such as mashed potatoes, are already prepared to go with entrées. Mashed potatoes served as a side dish might be served with applewood-smoked bacon and sautéed onions or fresh basil with frizzled leeks.

Vegetable medleys are an appealing alternative to the "vegetable of the day," such as broccoli with cheese sauce or buttered carrots. An assortment of fresh, seasonal vegetables—a trio of slivered zucchini, carrots, and sweet peppers, for example—might enhance grilled swordfish or tuna. Winter squash, either pureed, mashed, or combined with other vegetables, is appearing on middle to late autumn menus. Butternut, buttercup, acorn, delicata, spaghetti, and the "best secret in the market," sugarloaf squash, are all readily available.

A side dish of braised greens, so popular in the south for many generations, is finally catching on in the rest of the United States. Collard greens, mustard greens, Swiss chard, and dandelion greens are good accompaniments for fish, chicken, or barbecued ribs. Tops of beets and turnips also can be mixed in with the greens. Kale has a crunchy texture that combines well with other leafy green vegetables. Produce houses are selling large quantities of kale to be used for lining salad bars. It has dark blue-green frilly leaves and remains fresh for many hours. It is now being reproduced in plastic for salad bars.

Solomon (1994), a chef and food consultant, has created many side dishes from tubers. He contended that "the potato is an institution, now and forever, and as a chef, I would be crazed to think otherwise and that mashed potatoes—the lumpy kind—are riding a nostalgia wave." Mashed potatoes are now flavored with spicy ingredients, such as chili peppers, garlic, ginger, fresh herbs, and even sun-dried tomatoes. The baked potato became very popular in the early 1980s. Even though its popularity has diminished somewhat, its flame has been kept alive in college campuses with potato bars and in cafeteria lines with featured-entrée baked and topped potatoes (Ryan, 1994).

Baby vegetables have been appearing on fine dining menus for a few years and have progressed from fad status to a long-term trend (Produce Marketing Association, 1994b). Many varieties—for example, haricot vert (green beans), carrots, and red and yellow teardrop tomatoes—are fully formed when harvested. Others, including beets, corn, and zucchini, are harvested by picking them before they are fully grown. A partial list of miniatures on the market includes artichokes, haricot vert, beets, bok choy, carrots, cauliflower, corn, eggplants, kohlrabi, leeks, lettuce, potatoes, turnips, pattypan squash, and zucchini. As a general rule, root vegetables such as carrots, turnips, beets, and radishes are sold by the bunch. Other items, including pattypan squash, eggplant, and corn, are sold by the pound.

Salad bars are still popular in many restaurants and institutions, but they are changing from simple fare, such as sliced cucumbers, shredded carrots, bacon bits, and iceberg lettuce, to more elegant fare. To permit working people to have a quick lunch while running errands, salad bars are located in the front of many supermarkets. Today, the customer can choose organic salad bars or those that feature mostly healthy grains and vegetables in light olive oil dressings. The more elegant salad bars charge about $5.95 a pound compared to $2.95 a pound in a neighborhood deli. The more expensive salad bars might include roasted vegetables, bean and grain salads like wild rice with black beans and corn, salade nicoise, and Caesar salad.

Spices and herbs are no longer limited to cinnamon, oregano, and chili powder but now run the gamut: cumin, fresh cilantro, fresh basil, fresh red and green chilies, dried chilies, and whole black peppercorns (Straus, 1993). Garlic, a member of the lily family and a close relative of the onion, chive, leek, and shallot, is the herb most commonly identified in entrée descriptions.

PERISHABILITY OF PRODUCE

Most buyers agree that fresh produce causes them more problems than any other food group. The fact that produce is perishable means that the atmosphere and temperature must be controlled and transportation and packaging of products must be carefully monitored.

Controlled Atmosphere Storage

Fresh produce loses quality rapidly because it is a living organism (Kotschevar & Donnelly, 1994). In recent years, the fresh fruit industry has used a long-range storage method known as *controlled atmosphere* (C.A.) (Dole Food Company, 1992). Many fresh fruits ripen after harvesting because they continue to respire, taking in oxygen and generating heat, carbon dioxide, and sometimes ethylene gas while releasing moisture. Such fruits as apples, apricots, cherries, grapes, peaches, and pears emit ethylene gas and should be stored separately. This ripening process may be greatly retarded by the usual cold storage methods, which reduce fruit metabolism, including the rate of respiration.

Under C.A. methods of storage, respiration and ripening may be reduced by lowering the oxygen content of the air. **Controlled atmosphere storage** is a nonchemical process that includes airtight rooms and special equipment to achieve and maintain the desired atmospheric conditions in addition to the requirements of adequate refrigeration and air circulation for regular cold storage. The most successful C.A. fruit storage has been for apples because it keeps their just-picked flavor and crunch all year. Researchers in Washington have been among the leaders in C.A. technology because more than 70% of fresh apples in foodservice distribution channels are from the state. The growth of Washington apples in foodservice is directly attributable to the internal quality standards and long-term storage technology that virtually guarantee consistent, fresh-picked quality all year round. Exact conditions in the rooms are set according to the apple variety, and computers help keep conditions constant. Timing of harvest is critical to good storage results. The apples should be mature but not too ripe. Firmness, skin color, seed color, sugar level, and flesh chlorophyll are tested. Washington apples must remain in the C.A. rooms for a minimum of 90 days to qualify as C.A.-stored apples.

Care should be taken in storing fresh produce because some give off odors, which others absorb. Thus, they need to be stored separately. Fruits and vegetables that give off ethylene gas, which causes color and ripening changes, should definitely be stored separately to avoid odor absorption. Fresh produce also is subject to spoilage from microorganisms, such as bacteria, molds, and yeasts. It must be protected from cuts and bruises that increase the rate of respiration and the possibility of spoilage organisms entering the product.

Temperature Control

Temperatures must be controlled from the time fresh fruits and vegetables are harvested to the time they are served to the customer. **Field heat** in produce needs to be removed as quickly as possible to prevent deterioration of quality prior to shipping or storage. Precooling, the rapid removal of field heat, slows the ripening process in fruit and the breakdown process in vegetables, checks development of molds and bacteria, and prolongs market life. Reducing the temperature of fruit 15°F to 18°F slows the ripening and respiration rate by approximately one half.

Just storing the produce in the refrigerator, the old way of reducing the temperature, was too slow and inefficient and led to loss of quality. Besides, wetting the produce with so much water did not improve the quality. **Vacucooling** is a new dry method of cooling produce by putting it in shipping cartons and then into a tightly sealed chamber in which pressure is reduced by exhausting air, resulting in rapid evaporation and cooling. Vacucooling can reduce the temperature of lettuce 40°F in 30 minutes.

Wax on Produce

Wax labeling regulations became mandatory in May 1994. According to the FDA, retailers must post signs in the produce department indicating all products that are waxed (Washington Apple Commission, 1993). About 75% of all apples grown in the United States are waxed. Apples on the tree secrete their own natural wax to maintain moisture and prevent dehydration. Apples are washed at the fruit packing sheds to remove dust and chemical residues, at which time about half of the original apple wax is lost. If unwaxed apples are left out at room temperature, they lose moisture four times faster than apples with wax, thus losing their characteristic crunch and juiciness.

To combat the loss of moisture, a drop or two of wax is applied after washing the apples. Three types of wax approved by the FDA can be used on produce. The two most common waxes are carnauba wax from the leaves of a Brazilian palm tree and food-grade shellac from an insect found in India and Pakistan. A less frequently used wax is candelilla from desert plants of the genus *Euphorbia*. All of the waxes are derived from natural sources and are within kosher dietary rules. Petroleum or synthetic-based waxes are not used. In addition to apples, about 21 other produce items may have wax applied to them, including avocados, bell peppers, cantaloupes, cucumbers, eggplants, grapefruits, lemons, limes, melons, oranges, parsnips, passion fruit, peaches, pineapples, rutabagas, squash, tomatoes, and turnips.

Transportation

The produce market is being changed by more rapid transportation from farms to the market. Cooled produce, because it is a living organism, needs to be carefully handled in a temperature- and humidity-controlled environment during shipping.

Today, cleaning, trimming, packaging, and weighing products often are completed in the same field where they are harvested.

Traditionally, single items of produce from long distances were transported by rail freight, and rail tracks ran right up to the unloading docks of the receiving terminal. Transportation in the industry changed after chain grocery stores began to operate their own distribution warehouses within a shorter radius of their operations, and central terminal markets began to decline in importance (Dole Food Company, 1992). Today, many chain restaurants, contract foodservice companies, and school foodservice operations are establishing their own warehouses. A trend toward shipping several items in one truck, called a mixer, has taken over in the produce industry. Mixers allow receivers to maintain smaller inventories and usually to sell fresher produce. With mixers, wholesalers receive frequent truck shipments of just enough of a particular item to last a few days until the stock can be replenished. Thus, wholesalers are operating with smaller daily inventories and are selling fresher products. Although it is still relatively expensive, air transport is beginning to be used for transporting cargos of highly perishable products, such as exotic produce and fresh flowers.

Packaging

Ideally, buyers should know how many pieces of fruit or vegetable of a specific size are in a carton. Produce distributors, however, do not always carry a specific pack or carton size. In many cases, packs and counts of the number of fruits and vegetables in a pack vary from growing area to growing area, and the availability of a particular carton may depend upon the distributor's source of supply. The Produce Marketing Association has tried to list those items and packages that are commonly available to the foodservice industry. Those lists are used in this text.

Packaging of produce is causing marketing changes. Automation and standardization processes have improved packaging of all kinds of fresh produce. As a result, specification writing has become easier for the buyer.

Automation

Film and other kinds of wraps have replaced heavy, wooden crates that were difficult to ship and store. These wraps are strong and more protective of the products by holding their freshness, color, and appearance. Polyethylene wraps are used to delay ripening and deterioration. Air is removed from the product and inert gas, like nitrogen or carbon dioxide, replaces it. Bacteriostatic wraps also are being used to reduce the growth of bacteria in sterilized foods; hopefully, wraps will soon be developed to reduce bacterial growth in nonsterilized fruits and vegetables.

The entire packing process has been automated. The packaging process for produce includes washing, sorting, and conveying to the packaging equipment where the product is weighed, poured into the bag, and closed mechanically. More and more waste, such as carrot tops, cauliflower leaves, and pineapple hulls, is being removed from fruits and vegetables before they are packaged. Removing waste can reduce transportation and labor costs.

Standardization

Produce is being sold in smaller units in recyclable packages instead of heavy shipping boxes to make it easier for employees to handle. Much research has been conducted on the development of shipping packages that protect the product and permit easy stacking in a transportation vehicle. Fruits, which bruise easily, should be packed in ways to minimize damage (Fox & Nelson, 1995). Apples, tomatoes, pears, and other delicate produce are either tray-packed or loose-filled. Tray packing entails placing each apple in a fiber tray so that it does not touch any other apple. Correct handling eliminates bruising. The number of apples without bruises is much greater than when using the loose-filled method, in which as many as 30% of the apples would be bruised. The packaging might cost a few cents more but the carton yield would make up for it. Some products are packed by count only and not by case weight. Iceberg lettuce, which is packed 24 to the case, can have varying case weights, anywhere from less than 15 to more than 50 pounds. Case weight should be an important item in produce specifications.

QUALITY, GRADE, AND CONDITION

Quality refers to the characteristics of a product that are permanent, such as maturity, freedom from insect damage, color, and surface blemishes (Dole Food Company, 1992). **Condition** of the product indicates any physical change that might occur in the product before or after harvest that would detract from its acceptability, such as decay, shriveling, or a hollow area around the pit often occurring in peaches and plums. **Grade** refers to the sum of the characteristics of the product at the time it was graded, not sold. As with many products, one lot of fresh produce may barely meet the minimum requirements for a certain grade and another lot may be at the top of the grade.

The USDA reports 156 grades for fresh and processed fruits, vegetables, and nuts. Federal wholesale grades for fresh produce are U.S. No. 1, which is the highest quality, U.S. No. 2, and U.S. No. 3. Most foodservice operations specify U.S. No. 1. Produce also may be graded to meet state minimum grade requirements. Federal and state minimum standards are usually quite broad and flexible. According to the U.S. Marketing Service of the USDA, only about 45% of the fresh produce sold is graded. Some shippers have established a reputation for high quality; they ship only products that meet high-quality standards, such as Sunkist oranges, Dole broccoli, and Chiquita bananas.

PRODUCE IDENTIFICATION

The foodservice buyer cannot know everything about fresh produce but should have enough resources to make good purchasing decisions. The Produce Marketing Association (1995) publishes a *Foodservice Guide to Fresh Produce,* which is especially helpful in writing specifications, as are guidelines from the

United Fresh Fruit and Vegetable Association. *The Buying Guide for Fresh Fruits, Vegetables, Herbs, and Nuts,* produced by the Dole Food Company (1992), has excellent descriptions and colored photographs of each product. Many reference books are available and should be on every foodservice buyer's bookshelves. In addition, growers, boards, and shippers offer in-depth information on almost every product available to the customer.

In many school, college and university, and chain restaurant foodservice operations, the purchasing of produce is a full-time job. In smaller operations, the manager or an employee might handle it. To help potential buyers identify various types of produce, a brief discussion follows of the top 20 (as listed in Figure 8.2) commercially produced fresh fruits and vegetables by per capita consumption (Putnam & Allshouse, 1994). Instead of just ordering 50 apples or 10 pounds of potatoes, the buyer might be able to describe them by characteristics, such as varieties, size, color, and degree of ripeness. In addition, exotic fruits and vegetables, nuts, fresh herbs, and edible flowers will be discussed.

Fresh Fruits

Defining a fruit or a vegetable is sometimes difficult. A tomato technically is a fruit, but it is served most often as a vegetable. **Fruit** botanically is the flesh, or ovary, of a plant that surrounds or contains the seeds of a plant. As such, nuts, cereal grains, olives, corn, tomatoes, and some spices are considered fruits, just as apples and bananas are. Usually, however, only foods that grow on trees and bushes and are succulent, pulpy, sometimes juicy, and either naturally sweet or sweetened before eating are considered fruit. The USDA includes melons in its vegetable data, but the FDA does not. Because most people consider them to be fruits, melons are listed in that category in this text. Fresh fruit consumption gained 22 pounds per capita from 1970 to 119 pounds in 1993. The rise was due entirely to sharp increases in consumption of fresh noncitrus fruits and melons.

Buying fresh fruit is a tremendous challenge for many foodservice operations. Peaches purchased from May through August are luscious, but those in November do not have the same flavor or lusciousness (Johnson, 1996a). Peach season, or any other fruit's season, can come and go in the blink of an eye. Knowing when a fruit is about to peak allows the manager to plan ahead and include it on the menu. The trade journal *Restaurants & Institutions* has devised an excellent chart on fresh fruit availability, as shown in Figure 8.2, to help managers plan ahead.

Bananas

1.   **Bananas** ripen best after they are picked. They are in generous supply all year. They are inexpensive and can be digested easily, making them the most popular fresh fruit in America even though they are grown mostly in Central and South America. Bananas actually are a type of berry that grows on a huge plant, 15 to 30 feet high with a smooth trunk made up of tightly wrapped leaves. One plant produces seven to nine hands, each with 10 to 20 bananas that grow outward and upward, appearing to be upside down (Margen, 1992). Bananas taste better if not tree ripened. They are picked green, shipped, and then ripened in specially equipped warehouse rooms or in sealed packing boxes in which natural ethylene gas emissions cause them to ripen. Bananas generally are purchased by degree of ripeness.

Figure 8.2. Seasonal availability of fruit.

FRUIT	JAN	FEB	MAR	APR	MAY	JUN	JUL	AUG	SEP	OCT	NOV	DEC
Apple*	●	●	●	●	●	○	○	○	●	●	●	●
Apricot	○				○	●	○	○				○
Asian pear*						○	●	●	●	●	○	○
Avocado*	○	●	●	●	●	●	●	●	○	○	○	○
Banana, plantain	○	○	○	○	○	○	○	○	○	○	○	○
Banana, sweet*	○	○	○	○	○	○	○	○	○	○	○	○
Blackberry				○	●	●	●	●	○			
Blueberry	○	○	○	○	○	○	●	●	●	○	○	○
Breadfruit	○	○					○	○	○	○	○	○
Canistel							○	○	○	○	○	
Cherimoya	○	○									○	○
Coconut	○	○	○	○	○	○	○	○	○	○	○	○
Cherry	○	○		○	○	●	●	○				○
Cranberry	○									●	●	●
Date	○	○										○
Durian						○	○	○	○	○		
Feijoa	○	○	○	○	○	○	○	○	○			
Fig	○	○	○	○	○	●	●	●	●	○	○	○
Grapefruit	●	●	●	○	○	○	○	○	○	○	○	●
Grape*	○	○	○	○	●	●	●	●	●	●	●	●
Grape, muscadine								○	○	○		
Guanabana (soursop)	○	○	○	○	○	○	○	○	○	○	○	○
Guava			○	○	○	○	○	○	○			
Kiwano	○	○	○	○	○	○	○	○	○	○	○	○
Kiwifruit	●	○	○	○	○	●	●	○	○	○	○	●
Kumquat	○									○	○	○
Lemon	○	○	○	○	●	●	●	●	○	○	●	●
Lime	●	○	○	○	●	●	●	●	●	○	●	●
Mango	○	○	○	○	○	○	●	●	●	●	●	○
Melon, cantaloupe	○	○	○	○	●	●	●	●	○	○	○	○
Melon, casaba	○	○	○	○	○	○	○	○	●	●	●	○
Melon, Christmas	●									○	○	●
Melon, honeydew	○	○	○	●	●	●	●	●	●	○	○	○
Melon, pepino	○	○	○	○	○							
Melon, Persian						○	●	●	●	○		
Mulberry							○	○	○			
Nectarine	●	●	○	○	○	●	●	●	○	○	○	○
Orange, blood	○	○	○	○	○	○	○	○	○	○	○	○
Orange, moro	○	○	○	○								●
Orange, navel	●	●	●	●	●	○	○	○	○	○	●	●
Orange, temple	○	○	○									○
Orange, Valencia	○	●	●	●	●	●	●	●	●	●	○	○
Papaya, babaco					○	○	○	○	○			

(Continued)

Figure 8.2.   Seasonal availability of fruit.—*Continued*

FRUIT	JAN	FEB	MAR	APR	MAY	JUN	JUL	AUG	SEP	OCT	NOV	DEC
Papaya, Solo	○	○	○	○	●	●	●	●	●	○	○	○
Passion fruit	○	○	○	○	○	○	○	○	○	○	○	○
Peach	●	●	○	○	●	●	●	●	○	○	○	○
Pear*	○	○	○	○	○			●	●	●	●	●
Persimmon	○	○	○	○					○	○	○	○
Pineapple	●	●	●	●	●	●	●	●	●	○	○	●
Plum*	○	○	○	○	●	●	●	●	●	●	○	○
Pomegranate	○	○						○	○	●	●	●
Pomelo	○	○	○	○							○	○
Prickly pear	○	○	○	○					○	○	○	○
Quince										○	○	○
Raspberry	○	○	○	○	●	●	●	●	●	●	●	○
Sapodilla							○	○	○	○	○	
Sapote, black	○	○	○							○	○	○
Sapote, mamey					○	○	○	○				
Sapote, white					○	○	○	○				
Star fruit (carambola)							○	○	○	○	○	○
Strawberry	○	○	●	●	●	●	○	○	○	○	○	○
Sugar apple							○	○	○	○	○	○
Tamarillo					○	○	○	○	○	○		
Tamarind	○	○	○	○	○	○	○	○	○	○	○	○
Tangelo	●	○	○	○							●	●
Tangerine*	●	●	●	○	○	○				○	●	●
Tomatillo	○	○	○	○	○	○	○	○	○	○	○	○
Tomato*	○	○	○	○	○	●	●	●	●	○	○	○
Watermelon*	○	○	●	●	●	●	●	●	○	○	○	○

● peak availability; ○ regular availability; *various species exist but all share the same availability and peak seasons. Those species that differ significantly are listed separately.

Source: "Restaurants & Institutions Guide to Fresh Fruit Availability" by B. A. Johnson, 1996, *Restaurants & Institutions, 106*(7:), pp. 80, 82. Used by permission.

- Turning ripe: slight green color (5 to 6 days to ripen)
- Hard ripe: not green but firm (2 to 3 days to ripen)
- Full ripe: ready to eat now, slightly brown flecked

The edible portion of a banana is 67%. Bananas because they have less water have more carbohydrate and potassium than most fruit.

Jonathan Apples

2.   **Apples** grown in the United States have 2,500 varieties, but only eight of them make up 80% of the volume. The apple is a pome fruit with a central core that has five seeds enclosed in a papery capsule. Favorite varieties are Golden Delicious, Granny Smith, Jonathan, McIntosh, Red Delicious, Rome Beauty, Stayman, and York. The three most popular foodservice varieties are Red Delicious (86% of operators use them), Golden Delicious (26%), and Granny Smith (23%).

Golden or Red Delicious Apples

Extra Fancy and Fancy grades are purchased most often for eating. In 1915, the state of Washington established the first grade standards for apples, followed by the USDA in 1923. More than half of all eating apples come from Washington, which has the most stringent grading standards in the country. A recent action is the adoption of maturity standards for Granny Smith apples. Under statutes enforced by the Washington State Department of Agriculture, Granny Smith apples grown and packed in the state must not exceed a starch level of 1.2% to ensure that customers are buying fully mature fruit, not just cosmetically appealing apples.

Apples can be purchased in cartons that hold 38 to 42 pounds with counts from 48 to 198. They also are packed in bushel baskets, or 3- and 5-pound poly bags. Fragile apples, like Golden Delicious, are packed in a corrugated box, known as a cell carton, with vertical and horizontal dividers for each apple. Apples are a good source of soluble dietary fiber. An eating apple has an edible portion of 76%.

Watermelons

3. **Watermelons** can be round, oblong, or oval and weigh anywhere from 5 to 50 pounds. The flesh generally is a bright red, although orange and yellow species are available. Three varieties are seedless. Ripe melons have a yellowish underside and a dull surface. Watermelons are about 92% water and 8% sugar and are an excellent source of vitamin C and a good source of vitamin A. Two popular varieties are the Charleston, green striped with red meat, and the Black Diamond, dark green and round with red meat. Seedless melons are usually served in restaurants, because removing seeds before serving the customer is difficult. The edible portion of a watermelon is about 47%.

Oranges

4. **Oranges/temples** are most abundant from December to June. Florida, California, and Arizona produce the most oranges, followed by Texas and Mexico. More than 90% of all orange juice produced in the United States comes from Florida. Oranges are an excellent source of vitamin C. Oranges ripen only on the tree and cannot be picked by law until mature. Partially green oranges are not unripe; sometimes warm weather causes regreening as the oranges ripen on the tree. Coloring is sometimes added to the outer skin to make the orange more acceptable to the customer; FDA regulations require that these oranges be stamped "Color Added." The navel, almost seedless and thick skinned, and the Valencia, with few seeds and thinner skin, are the two major varieties of oranges. The 88 count per 40-pound carton of oranges is the most popular of the 48 to 163 counts. The blood orange, when in season, is used by many chefs to enhance the center-of-the-plate menu item because of its appealing red color. The edible portion of an orange is about 60%. Temples are a cross between a tangerine and an orange and have many seeds. They are, however, very sweet and juicy.

Cantaloupe

5. **Cantaloupes** are of the highest quality from May through August. They have a khaki-colored netting with a creamy yellow background and orange color flesh. They should give a little when pressed. Cantaloupes are very perishable and ripen quickly at room temperature. Cantaloupe odor penetrates other foods and also absorbs other odors. They are a good source of beta carotene. Cantaloupes are packed in 42-pound boxes with counts of 9 to 23.

Grapes

6.   **Grapes** are either European, of which 97% sold in the United States are produced in California, or American. European grapes are more popular and versatile. A large proportion of California grapes are made into wine or raisins. Grapes with seeds are thought to be better flavored than seedless, but Americans seem to prefer the convenience of seedless grapes. The Thompson Seedless grape, amber green in color, is the most popular variety grown in the United States, followed by the Emperor, a small-seeded red grape. The Ribier is the most popular black grape. The blue-black Concord grape is the most popular American grape and is used primarily for grape juice and preserves. Grapes are not picked and shipped until ripe, and color can be used as a guide to the sweetest fruit. Green grapes tend toward a yellow-green color, red grapes should be predominantly crimson, and blue grapes should be almost black. A bunch of grapes should have plump fruit tightly attached to moist flexible stems. They are packed in lugs or cartons holding from 10 to 28 pounds. Most grapes are not nutrient rich but are low in calories. They make a good snack food. However, raisins, which are sun-dried grapes, are a concentrated source of calories, sugar, iron, potassium, and B vitamins. They also contain a good amount of dietary fiber (Margen, 1992).

Grapefruit

7.   **Grapefruit** is grown principally in Florida and Texas from December to March, supplemented at other times by grapefruit growing in the deserts of Arizona and California. The Duncan, with yellow skin and many seeds, and the Marsh, seedless and pink-meated with very few seeds, are the most popular. The Ruby Red and Star Red have deep red flesh and sweet flavor. Indian River is a popular brand name in Florida and Rio in Texas. Grapefruit is not picked until fully ripe, but under certain growing conditions, the yellow skin might revert to green after it is ripe. Grapefruits are never artificially colored. They should be round with slightly flattened ends, smooth skinned, and heavy for their size. Grapefruit is a good source of vitamin C and the pink and red varieties of beta carotene. It also is a low-calorie fruit. A peeled and segmented grapefruit has about 47% edible portion.

Peaches

Nectarines

8.   **Peaches and nectarines** are closely related, but the nectarine is not simply a peach without fuzz. The peach has been referred to as "The Queen of Fruits," and Georgia is known as the Peach State although today peaches are grown in more than 30 states, with California as the biggest producer. The two major types of peaches are the freestones, in which the pit separates easily from the flesh when the fruit is mature, and the clingstone, in which the flesh is firmly attached to the pit. Peaches are either yellow-fleshed or white-fleshed and have skins that are creamy or yellowish in color. A glowing blush is not an indication of ripeness or good taste. Peaches are fragile and require careful handling. They are a good source of vitamin C. The edible portion of a peach is 76%.

The nectarine is one of the oldest of all fruits but has gone from a small, fast-softening, white-fleshed fruit to a large, green-, yellow-, or red-skinned, and yellow-fleshed freestone because of cross-breeding with peaches. Like the peach, the nectarine needs to be picked when it is ripe or the taste will be unsatisfactory. Some horticulturists believe that the nectarine will be more popular than the peach in the 21st century. Both peaches and nectarines with counts from 48 to 80 are packed in two-layer cell cartons because these fruits are fragile. Nectarines are a fair source of vitamin A. The edible portion is around 76%, about the same as for a peach.

Strawberries

9. **Strawberries** do not ripen after being picked. They should be plump and firm with good, even color and glossy skins. Green caps should all be in place. Strawberries are the most perishable of all fruits and must be handled carefully. They should not be washed until just before use, and caps should never be removed before washing. Most strawberries are packed in a flat that holds 12 pints and weighs 10 pounds. They are best when eaten the same day they are delivered. Strawberries are the most popular berries on the market and contain more vitamin C than any other berry. The edible portion of a strawberry is about 90%. They are packed in flats, pints, quarts, or 10-pound trays.

Pears

10. **Pears** are related to apples because they are both pome fruits with distinct seeded cores. They are not as hardy as apples and seldom are tree-ripened because the flesh becomes mealy. The most popular varieties are yellow and red Bartletts, Anjou, Bosc, and Comice. Pears are grown mainly in California, Oregon, and Washington. Pears are packed in 44-pound cartons and have counts from 70 to 165. When pears are eaten with their skin, they are a good source of vitamin C and dietary fiber. The edible portion of pears is generally about 78%.

Lemons

11. **Lemons** are available on the market all months of the year and are produced primarily in California and Arizona. They should have a deep yellow color, fine textured skin, and firm heavy fruit with a juice content not less than 30% by volume. Lemons have a count from 75 to 235 and are packed in 40-pound cartons; 165 lemons per carton is the most popular size. Often they can be purchased in 10-pound mini cartons. Lemons are an excellent source of vitamin C if enough are consumed each day. The Ponderosa lemon from Sarasota, Fla., is the size of a grapefruit and is appearing in some markets. The objection to its use is that it is full of seeds.

Avocados

12. **Avocados** have a buttery texture, a nutty flavor, and a large round seed in the middle. They are exceptionally high in fat. In this country, they are grown in California and Florida. The most popular variety is the Hass avocado from California. It weighs about a half pound and has a thick, pebbled skin that changes from green to purplish black as it ripens. Florida avocados are larger than those from California and less buttery but contain less fat and therefore fewer calories. Ripening and softening occur at room temperature. They are packed in one-layer 12½-pound cartons with counts from 6 to 28. Some foodservice managers believe the very presence of avocado on the menu makes it more upscale. It has only a 20% to 25% food cost and increases margin profits considerably.

13. **Pineapples** were given their name because the Spanish thought they resembled a pine cone. No pineapples are grown in the continental United States; the biggest supply comes from the 50th state, Hawaii, followed by Honduras, Mexico, the Dominican Republic, and Costa Rica. Pineapples must be harvested at just the right stage because they do not ripen or become sweeter after they are picked. Next to bananas, pineapples are the second most popular tropical fruit. They should have fresh-looking, dark green crown leaves when purchased. Pulling the leaves easily

Pineapples

does not indicate ripeness. For the greatest economy, pineapples should feel heavy and be as large as possible. They usually are packed in 20-pound half cartons with counts between 4 and 8. Fresh pineapple has a moderate amount of vitamin C and is low in calories. The edible portion of a fresh pineapple is 52%.

Tangerines

14. **Tangerines/tangelos** are actually subgroups of mandarin oranges, a group of citrus fruits that have a loose, easily peeled "zipper" pebbly skin and a distinctive,

Tangelos

Honeydew Melon

Plums

Limes

Mangoes

Kiwifruit

Cherries

slightly tart flavor. They have a nutritive value similar to oranges. Tangerines have a puffy appearance and are heavy for their size. They are highly perishable. Clementine mandarins, often called Algerian tangerines, are considered the finest tangerines on the market. They have a red-orange pebbled rind which peels easily. Florida is the largest producer of tangerines. About 70% of the total year's crop is produced during November, December, and January. Tangelos are a cross between a tangerine and a grapefruit. They look like large oranges with a knob on the stem and have a slight grapefruit flavor. When a whole tangerine or tangelo is peeled, the segments separate easily making them good snack foods. Paperboard cartons holding 56 to 162 tangerines or tangelos are usually purchased for foodservices.

15. **Honeydew melon** rind is usually creamy yellow when ripe and the flesh a pale green, although orange-fleshed honeydews are available. They are ready to eat when the rind feels like satin. Honeydew melons are large, weighing 6 to 7 pounds each with 4 to 12 melons per carton. It is the sweetest of all melons. The edible portion is 57%.

16. **Plums/prunes** are drupes, pitted fruits related to the apricot, nectarine, and peach. However, they have a greater variety of shapes, sizes, and skin colors. More than 75% of the world supply of plums is grown in California. In the United States, 140 or more varieties of plums are available. These varieties are either Japanese, with juicy, yellow or reddish flesh with crimson to black-red skin, never blue or purple, or European, which are always blue or purple with golden yellow flesh. Japanese plums are usually eaten raw and often are called nonprune plums, while European plums are cooked or dried. They are known as prunes and are much smaller and less juicy than the Japanese. Plums are either clingstone or freestone. The largest plums are packed in cell cartons holding 30 pounds. Smaller plums are packed in a tight-fill, 28-pound fiberboard carton. Plums have a high concentration of vitamin A and a fair quantity of vitamin C.

17. **Limes** are produced in California, Florida, and Mexico. They have the same attributes as a lemon except for the color, which is deep green for the Tahiti/Persian limes and yellow-green for those from Mexico. Limes do not hold up as long as lemons. Limes are packed in 10- to 38-pound cartons holding counts of 28 to 72.

18. **Mangoes** are popular in the tropics, and most of them available in the United States are from Mexico, Florida, Haiti, and South and Central American countries. They are either oval or kidney shaped with a fibrous flesh that is orange and a flat stringy pit. They have a flowery aroma and a flavor similar to that of a peach. Their average weight is one pound although some weigh as much as three pounds. They are rich in beta carotene and vitamin C. Mangoes are packed in 10- or 12-pound cartons holding counts of 6 to 14.

19. **Kiwifruit** looks like a fuzzy brown egg and is named for the national treasure of New Zealand, the fuzzy, flightless kiwi bird (Margen, 1992). California kiwifruit is available from November through May and New Zealand from June to October. Kiwifruit is an excellent source of dietary fiber, vitamin C, potassium and has the curious property of tenderizing meat (Dole Food Company, Inc.). They are very popular in school lunch programs. Kiwifruit is packed in 10- or 12-pound cartons.

20. **Cherries** are classified as sweet or sour. Cherries are drupes, or stone fruits, related to plums and more distantly to peaches and nectarines. Cherries picked from the end of May to August are of the best quality. They do not ripen once they are off the trees; they decay. The most popular of sweet cherries is the Bing, a large,

round, extra-sweet cherry with purple-red flesh and a deep red skin that verges on black when fully ripe. The Royal Ann, used for making maraschino cherries, and Rainier, light or white sweet cherries, are milder and sweeter than the Bing, but the light skin emphasizes the slightest bruising. Sour cherries have lower calories and higher amounts of vitamin C and beta carotene than sweet cherries. Cherries are sold in 12-, 18-, or 20-pound lugs.

Fresh Vegetables

A **vegetable** is defined as any edible portion of a plant that either accompanies or is the entrée of a meal. A vegetable may be a leaf (spinach), bud (broccoli), root (carrot), tuber (potato), stem (celery), flower (chive), pod (squash), or seed (legumes such as navy beans or peanuts). Total per capita consumption of 22 major commercial fresh vegetables in 1993 was 104 pounds, which was 32% above the 1970 level (Putnam & Allshouse, 1994).

As with fruits, vegetables are seasonal (Johnson, 1996b). Planning for a banquet often takes months, and knowing the vegetables that will peak at that time is crucial. Corn on the cob is best in the summer but Belgian endive, a gourmet vegetable, is hard to find at that time. Again, "Restaurants & Institutions Guide to Fresh Vegetable Availability" (Figure 8.3) is an excellent resource.

Potatoes

1.   **Potatoes** not only top the 20 fresh vegetables list in the United States but are considered the world's most important vegetable. They also are one of the very few vegetables that originated in the Western hemisphere, probably in the Andean region of South America (Dole Food Company, 1992). They are not native to Ireland and were not even introduced to the Irish until 1585. Their use spread over Europe; the French lovingly called the potato *pomme de terre,* "apple of the earth." When the crop failed in the 1840s in Ireland, the Irish with their potatoes immigrated to the United States.

Botanically, the potato is a succulent, nonwoody annual plant of the nightshade family. It is a tuber, not a root, a swollen underground stem that stores surplus carbohydrates to feed the leafy green plant sprouting above the soil (Margen, 1992). Contrary to popular belief, potatoes are not a fattening food unless they are processed or topped with butter, sour cream, mayonnaise, or gravy. Three ounces of plain boiled potatoes contain 85 calories, but 3 ounces of french fries contain about 345 calories and 3 ounces of hash browns about 240 calories. Most processed potatoes have a high sodium content as well. Fresh unpeeled potatoes are a good source of fiber, vitamin C, potassium, iron, and other minerals. Potatoes are available in the United States all year, but the largest harvest is in the fall and these potatoes can be stored successfully for 9 to 12 months. The most common varieties grown commercially are the

- Long russets: oval-shaped, up to 18 ounces in weight, hard brown skin, and starchy flesh; excellent for baking, mashing, and french frying.
- Long whites: oval-shaped, thin skinned, and waxy when new, starchy and weighing an average 8 ounces when mature; usually best for boiling but some varieties good for baking and frying.
- Round reds: red, smooth skinned, called "new" when first harvested, and when matured are waxy; good for boiling.
- Round whites: multipurpose potatoes, light tan skin, and smaller than long whites; best for boiling but some varieties can be baked or fried.

Figure 8.3. Seasonal availability of vegetables.

VEGETABLE	JAN	FEB	MAR	APR	MAY	JUN	JUL	AUG	SEP	OCT	NOV	DEC
Artichokes	○	○	●	●	●	○	○	○	○	○	○	○
Argula	○	○	○	○	○	○	○	○	○	○	○	○
Asparagus	○	●	●	●	●	○	○	○	○	○	○	○
Bean, green*	○	○	○	○	○	○	○	○	○	○	○	○
Bean, yard-long	○	○	○	○	○	●	●	●	●	○	○	○
Beet	○	○	○	○	○	●	●	●	●	○	○	○
Bok choy	○	○	○	○	○	○	○	○	○	○	○	○
Broccoli	●	●	●	●	○	○	○	○	○	●	●	●
Broccoliflower	○	○	○	○	○	○	○	○	○	○	○	○
Broccoli raab (rape)	●	●	●	●	●	○	○	○	○	●	●	●
Brussels sprouts	●	●	●	●	○	○	○	○	●	●	●	●
Burdock root	○	○	○	○	○	○	○	○	○	○	○	○
Cabbage	○	○	○	○	○	○	○	○	○	○	○	○
Cardoon	●	●	●								●	●
Carrot	○	○	○	○	○	○	○	○	○	○	○	○
Cassava (yuca)	○	○	○	○	○	○	○	○	○	○	○	○
Cauliflower	○	○	○	○	○	○	○	○	○	○	○	○
Celery	○	○	○	○	○	○	○	○	○	○	○	○
Celery root	●	●	●	●	●				●	●	●	●
Chard*	○	○	○	○	○	○	○	○	○	○	○	○
Chayote	○	○	○	○	○	○	○	○	○	○	○	○
Corn	○	○	○	○	●	●	●	●	●	●	○	○
Cucumber	○	○	○	○	●	●	●	●	●	○	○	○
Daikon	○	○	○	○	○	○	○	○	○	○	○	○
Eggplant	○	○	○	○	○	●	●	●	●	○	○	○
Endive, curly	○	○	○	○	○	●	●	●	●	●	●	●
Endive, escarole	○	○	○	○	○	●	●	●	●	●	●	●
Endive, Belgian	●	●	●	●	○				○	○	●	●
Fennel	●	●	●	●	●	○	○	○	○	●	●	●
Garlic	○	○	○	○	○	○	○	○	○	○	○	○
Ginger	○	○	○	○	○	○	○	○	○	○	○	○
Greens*	●	●	●	●	○	○	○	○	○	○	○	○
Herbs, fresh	○	○	○	○	○	○	○	○	○	○	○	○
Horseradish root	○	○	○	●	●	○	○	○	○	●	●	●
Jícama	○	○	○	○	○	○	○	○	○	○	○	○
Kale	●	●	●	○	○	○	○	○	○	○	○	●
Kohlrabi (cabbage turnip)			○	○	○	●	●	○	○	○		
Leek	○	○	○	○	○	○	○	○	●	●	●	●

Figure 8.3.   Seasonal availability of vegetables.—*Continued*

VEGETABLE	JAN	FEB	MAR	APR	MAY	JUN	JUL	AUG	SEP	OCT	NOV	DEC
Lettuce, butterhead	○	●	●	●	●	●	●	●	●	●	○	○
Lettuce, iceberg	○	●	●	●	●	●	●	●	●	●	○	○
Lettuce, leaf	○	○	○	○	○	●	●	●	●	●	○	○
Lettuce, romaine	○	○	○	○	○	○	●	●	●	●	○	○
Lotus root	●	●	○	○	○	○	○	○	○	●	●	●
Mushroom*	○	○	○	○	○	○	○	○	○	○	○	○
Okra	○	○	○	○	●	●	●	●	●	●	○	○
Onion, Bermuda	○	○	●	●	●	●	○	○	○	○	○	○
Onion, Spanish	●	●	●	●	●	○	○	●	●	●	●	●
Onion, Maui				●	●	●	●					
Onion, Vidalia				●	●							
Onion, Wala Wala						●	●	●	●			
Parsnip	●	●	○	○	○	○	○	○	○	●	●	●
Pea, black-eyed	○	○	○	○	○	○	○	○	○	○	●	●
Pea, English	○	○	●	●	●	○	○	●	●	●	●	○
Pea, snow/sugar	○	○	●	●	●	●	○	○	●	●	●	○
Pepper, sweet*	○	○	○	○	○	○	●	●	●	○	○	○
Pepper, chile*	○	○	○	○	○	○	○	○	○	○	○	○
Potato*	○	○	○	○	○	○	○	○	○	○	○	○
Pumpkin									○	●	●	○
Radicchio	○	○	○	○	○	○	○	○	○	○	○	○
Radish	○	○	○	○	○	○	○	○	○	○	○	○
Rhubarb	○	○	○	●	●	●	○	○	○	○	○	○
Rutabaga	●	●	●	●	○	○	○	●	●	●	●	●
Scallion*	○	○	○	●	●	●	●	●	○	○	○	○
Shallot	○	○	○	○	○	○	○	○	○	○	○	○
Spinach	○	○	○	○	○	○	○	○	○	○	○	○
Sprouts*	○	○	○	○	○	○	○	○	○	○	○	○
Squash, summer*	○	○	○	○	●	●	●	●	○	○	○	○
Squash, winter*	●	●	●	○	○	○	○	○	○	●	●	●
Squash, baby*	○	○	○	○	○	●	●	●	○	○	○	○
Sun choke	●	●	●							●	●	●
Sweet potato	○	○	○	○	○	○	○	●	●	●	●	●
Tomatillo	○	○	○	○	○	○	○	○	●	●	●	○
Turnip	○	○	○	○	○	○	○	○	○	○	○	○
Watercress	○	○	○	○	●	●	●	●	○	○	○	○
Yucca	○	○	○	○	○	○	○	○	○	○	○	○
Zucchini	○	○	○	●	●	●	●	○	○	○	○	○

● peak availability; ○ regular availability; *various species exist but all share the same availability and peak seasons.

Source: "Restaurants & Institutions Guide to Fresh Vegetable Availability" by B. A. Johnson, 1996, *Restaurants & Institutions, 106* (14), pp. 82, 88. Used by permission.

Potatoes should never be stored in the refrigerator but in a cool dark area to prevent the starch from turning to sugar. Potatoes are packed in 50-pound cartons with counts from 60 to 120. They also are packed in 100-pound bags or 5-, 10-, and 20-pound film bags. Machine-peeled potatoes have an edible portion of 66%.

Iceberg Lettuce

2. **Iceberg lettuce** continues to be the most widely sold variety of all the different kinds of lettuce available on the market. Lettuce has been cultivated for more than 2,500 years; 1995 was the hundredth anniversary of the development of iceberg lettuce seed. This familiar pale green lettuce forms a cabbage-like head that is firm but springy and gives slightly when squeezed. Iceberg lettuce is available year round due to staggered growing seasons, vacuum-cooling, and rapid transportation. The Produce Marketing Association (1995) recommends that the lettuce should be cored before washing by holding the head core-end down and whacking it on a counter; the core can be twisted and lifted out. Some users believe that the lettuce will be bruised if this method is used. Many foodservice operations are purchasing cored and trimmed lettuce packed 6 heads in a poly bag in 24- or 30-count cartons. The edible portion of iceberg lettuce is 75%.

In addition to the very popular iceberg lettuce, other types of lettuce are being used in foodservice operations. Butterhead lettuce, including Boston and Bibb, has a loose head, a soft, buttery texture, and a sweet, mild flavor. Boston is medium in size with grass green leaves outside and light yellow inside; it resembles a flowering rose. Bibb is a small cup-shaped lettuce with deep, rich, green leaves outside blending into whitish green toward the core. Iceberg is the least nutritious lettuce. The darker green leaf lettuce, butterhead, Boston, and Bibb all have much more vitamin C and beta carotene than iceberg.

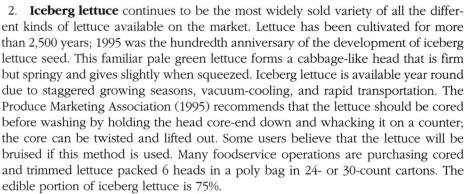

Onions

3. **Onions,** ranked third on the top 20 fresh vegetable list, have been popular since prehistoric times. Onions, leeks, garlic, green onions, chives, and shallots, known botanically as alliums, all belong to the lily family. Many myths about onions persist. Carl Sandburg once said, "Life is like an onion. You peel it off one layer at a time, and sometimes you weep" (Dole Food Company, 1992). In Egypt, a large onion producer, people believe it is a symbol of eternity because it is a sphere within a sphere; Egyptians used to take an oath with their right hand on an onion. The pungency of dry or cured onions depends on climate and soil, not color. The edible portion of dry onions is 89%. Onions can be yellow, deep red or purple, or silver skinned to white in color. Shapes can be round, oval, or flattened. All dry onions should have dry papery skins with small and tight necks. Dry onions are packed in 25- and 50-pound bags; green onions are packed in 15- to 25-pound cartons with counts of 48 bunches. Small foodservice operations can buy half or smaller cartons holding 12 or 24 bunches. Onions are low in calories and most nutrients.

Tomatoes

4. **Tomatoes**, once known as "love apples," botanically are fruits, not vegetables. The tomato is a berry; it is pulpy and contains one or more seeds that are not stones. It is, however, prepared and served as a vegetable. The tomato officially was proclaimed a vegetable in 1893 by the U.S. Supreme Court as the result of a tariff dispute (Margen, 1992). It is a member of the nightshade family as is the potato, bell pepper, and eggplant. Tomatoes are available all year and are grown in all states;

Cherry Tomatoes

Florida is the leading producer, followed closely by California. From January through May, tomatoes are imported from Mexico. The three major categories of tomatoes are the large round slicing, the round and bite-sized cherry, and the small and egg-shaped Italian or Roma. The edible portion of peeled, slicing tomatoes is 96%. In addition to the red varieties, orange and yellow also are available.

The majority of tomatoes are grown in fields, but many are grown in greenhouses either in soil or water (hydroponically). Field tomatoes are picked at a mature green stage when they begin to show a spot of pink at the blossom end. They are called "vine-ripe" tomatoes. If the tomatoes are picked when they are at the red-ripe stage, they would be too tender to stand harvesting, packing, shipping, and machine slicing. Tomatoes never should be refrigerated unless they have ripened too rapidly and then they should be removed an hour before serving to increase their flavor. Since 1991, the USDA has sized tomatoes as small, medium, large, and extra large with a ½2-inch overlap between sizes. Only one size is allowed per container of tomatoes (Produce Marketing Association, 1993). All USDA-inspected tomatoes must be identified with the new size designation stamped on the outside of each container as shown below. A fresh ripe tomato is very rich in vitamins A and C, potassium, and phosphorus.

New Designations	Minimum Diameter	Maximum Diameter
Small*	2$\frac{4}{32}$	2$\frac{9}{32}$
Medium	2$\frac{8}{32}$	2$\frac{17}{32}$
Large	2$\frac{16}{32}$	2$\frac{25}{32}$
Extra Large	2$\frac{24}{32}$	

*Under the federal marketing order, Florida does not ship small tomatoes

Carrots

5. **Carrots** are considered almost a staple in many foodservice operations. Children are often told that eating carrots is good for their eyes because their beta carotene content is converted by the body to vitamin A, a nutrient essential for the functioning of the eye. The feathery tops on carrots usually are removed before they are sold. The leaves indicate that the carrot is a relative of parsley, dill, celery, parsnips, and many other vegetables. Fresh carrots are on the market all year with no distinct peaks and with large supplies. Most carrots are 7 to 9 inches in length and ¾ to 1½ inches in diameter, with an edible portion of 82%. Firm, well-formed, smooth, orange to orange-red carrots with well-trimmed tops should be purchased. Carrots are packed in various sized bags and sometimes in cartons. They are jumbled or placed packed. Jumbo and medium-large carrots are the favorite size. Baby carrots that are pulled from the ground early are sometimes available. Fresh-cut and peeled carrots packaged in a plastic bag often are mistaken for baby carrots because they have been trimmed to 1½- to 2-inch lengths.

Green Cabbage

6. **Cabbage** has been a staple in the diet for hundreds of years. The most popular cabbages in the United States are the light green round or oval heads. Sometimes the outer leaves are tied around the head as the cabbage grows to keep the inside white. This cabbage is packed in 50-pound mesh bags, cartons, and crates with counts from 8 to 16 heads. Red or purple heads and savoy, a yellowish-green head with crinkled

Bok Choy
Cabbage

Napa Cabbage

Celery

leaves, also are available. The edible portion of cabbage heads is approximately 79%. Lemon juice or vinegar should be added to the cooking water to help retain the color of red cabbage. Chinese cabbages are being used by more and more chefs. Bok choy has broad white or greenish-white celery-like stalks topped with loose, dark green leaves and is often called Chinese mustard cabbage because of its slightly sharp tang. Raw leaves have a slightly sharp tang but cooking causes the leaves to be milder and the stalks sweeter. Napa cabbage resembles a head of romaine lettuce with broad-ribbed pale green, strong veined, crinkled leaves. It has a more delicate taste than standard cabbage and is crisp and juicy. Cabbage is a cruciferous vegetable rich in vitamin C and is recommended in diets to reduce the risk of certain types of cancer.

7. **Celery** is available throughout the year. Pascal celery is the most popular and is light green in color and stringless with a crisp texture. It has an edible portion of 75%. Celery hearts are the centers of celery stalks with the outer ribs removed. A bunch of celery, or stalk, is made up of individual ribs that naturally are crisp because of the high water content within the cells. Thus, they are very low in calories. Storage humidity should be between 90% and 95% because otherwise rapid dehydration occurs. Celery is packed in 55- to 65-pound cartons with wire-bound crates with counts between 24 and 48 stalks. Celery hearts are the centers of celery stalks with the outer ribs removed. Precut celery also is available. Celery has a fair amount of vitamins A and B. It is a good snack food because it has few calories. Eaten raw, it is one of the best detergent vegetables that can aid in dental health.

Corn

8. **Sweet corn** on the cob is America's favorite way to eat fresh corn. Consequently, it is appearing on more and more menus in restaurants and other foodservice operations. Corn is available all year with the greatest supply from May through October. California, New York, Pennsylvania, Ohio, and Oregon are major suppliers of sweet corn through the summer, and Florida steps up from November to May. More than 200 varieties of sweet corn are grown in the United States. The most popular are the yellow hybrids, although white, which is popular in southern states, and yellow/white hybrids are becoming more common. Hybrid corns, which remain sweet long after picking, are dominating the market, and many chefs have discovered they prefer serving it raw because it adds a crisp texture and fresh taste to everything from soup to salads.

Corn should be used as quickly as possible after picking. It is one of the most perishable vegetables in terms of taste. If corn must be stored, it should be kept very cold and at high humidity because the sugar in corn turns to starch at higher temperatures. It also has a high respiration rate. Ultra-sweet corn, which contains almost three times as much natural sugar as other types, has a shelf life of up to 10 days; it has become very popular. The buyer should look for husks with well-colored green leaves and fresh stalks. The kernels should be plump, milky, and tender with no space between the rows. Sweet corn is packed in 40-pound crates holding 43 to 48 ears. Yellow corn provides a fair amount of vitamin A and C and other vitamins and minerals.

Bell Peppers

9. **Bell peppers** have three or four lobes and can be green, red, yellow, orange, brown, or purple depending on their degree of maturity and variety (Margen, 1992). Dark green peppers turn scarlet red or gold at full maturity and are considerably sweeter than those at the immature stage. Bell peppers are available all year. They are an excellent source of vitamin C. Their edible portion is 82%. Green peppers usu-

ally are packed in 25-pound cartons with varying counts. The other colored peppers often are packed in smaller cartons.

Cucumbers

10.   **Cucumbers** are available all year with an increase of supply from May through July. The majority of the crop comes from Florida but is supplemented during the winter months from Mexico. The two basic types are those for slicing and eating fresh and those cultivated for pickling. Slicing cucumbers should be about 6 to 9 inches long and have glossy, dark green skin and tapering ends. They are packed in 26- to 28-pound cartons with a count of 24. Because cucumbers have a high water content and respiration rate, they are often covered with a harmless wax to cut down on moisture loss. The edible portion of unpeeled cucumbers is 73%, and peeled is 95%. Greenhouse cucumbers are becoming more available; most originated in Europe and are called European or English. They tend to be thin, smooth skinned, seedless, and 1 to 2 feet in length. "Cool as a cucumber" is not just a catchy phrase (Dole Food Company, 1992). In actual tests, on a hot day, the temperature of the pulp will be 20°F cooler than the outside temperature. An unpaired cucumber contains heavy amounts of vitamin A and iron. It is also a detergent helpful to dental health.

Romaine

11.   **Romaine/leaf** are two types of lettuces that are very popular today and add variety to the salad bowl (Margen, 1992). Romaine, or Cos, the main ingredient in Caesar salad, has long, deep green leaves that form a long head. The leaves appear coarse, but they are tender and sweet. The outer leaves are dark green and the inner ones golden-yellow. Romaine is packed in 32- to 40-pound cartons with counts of 24. Leaf lettuce grows with leaves loosely branching from its stalk and does not form heads. The leaves are green or green shaded to dark red at the edges and are either ruffled or smooth. Both of these are good sources of vitamin C and beta carotene. These lettuces have an edible portion of 67%.

Sweet Potatoes

12.   **Sweet potatoes** are not a member of the white potato family but of the morning glory family, as evidenced by the leafy vines produced from sweet potato cuttings (Margen, 1992). The sweet potato is one of the most nutritious vegetables on the market; it is an excellent source of vitamins A and C and a good source of dietary fiber. It is a native American plant available year round, with the greatest abundance from September through February, thus making it a popular Thanksgiving and Christmas menu item. The two general types of sweet potatoes are:

- soft, moist, orange-red flesh when cooked with whitish-tan to brownish-red skin. Usually very plump in shape, these sweet potatoes often erroneously are referred to as "yams." True yams are ivory or off-white in color and very limited in supply.
- firm, dry, somewhat mealy, light yellow or pale orange when cooked with light yellowish-tan or fawn colored skins. These are not usually as plump as the moist ones.

Sweet potatoes are packed in 25- to 40-pound boxes.

Broccoli

13.   **Broccoli** is considered one of the healthiest foods a person can eat. It contains a rich supply of vitamins, especially C and A, minerals, and dietary fiber; it is a cruciferous vegetable thought to protect the body from certain types of cancer.

Broccoli is available throughout the year, but it is most abundant and therefore less expensive from October through April. Compact, firm heads, consisting of dark green or purplish florets on light green stems, should be purchased. Avoid open, flowering yellow buds, indicating overmaturity, shriveled heads, and woody stems. Broccoli has a 61% edible portion. Florets used on salad bars are available. Broccoli is packed in 22-pound cartons holding 14 to 18 bunches or 9- to 18-pound cardboard boxes holding 3 to 6 plastic mesh bags of florets.

Mushrooms

14.   **Mushrooms** are not really a vegetable but rather a fungus. They have no roots or leaves, do not flower or have seeds, and do not need light to grow. Mushrooms proliferate in the dark and reproduce by releasing billions of spores (Margen, 1992). Mushrooms were always grown in caves or cellars, but today most are grown in specially designed buildings in which the light, temperature, humidity, and ventilation can be controlled. Wild mushrooms can be toxic and have caused deaths; therefore, they should be picked only by experts. The button mushroom is the most popular commercially grown mushroom in the United States. It has a smooth, round-capped top and can be white, off-white, and brown (identified as Cremini). All button mushrooms belong to a single species, Agaricus bisporus. Because mushrooms have no chlorophyll, they lack beta carotene or vitamin C, but they do contain a substantial amount of B vitamins, copper, manganese, and phosphorus and are low in sodium and very low in calories—20 calories per cup of raw mushrooms. They have an edible portion of 97%. They are packed in 3-, 5-, or 10-pound cartons with varying counts. The freshest mushrooms are closed around the stem by a thin veil. Size or color does not affect quality.

Mushrooms must be kept cold and humid and need to be ventilated, not stored in plastic bags. Never peel or scrub mushrooms. Wipe with a dry or damp paper towel. If they have a lot of soil, place them in a colander and rinse quickly just before using them. Other varieties of mushrooms, such as Chanterelle, Shiitake, Oyster, Cremini, and Portobello, are becoming popular. These mushrooms often are packed in 1-pound plastic containers. They are available all year. Truffles are fungi prized for their flavor and are almost impossible to cultivate and to harvest. The plants grow underground by attaching themselves to tree roots, usually hazels or oaks, and have to be sniffed out by pigs or dogs that detect their scent (Margen, 1992). Black truffles come from France and Italy and white from northern Italy; they are in season in the late fall and winter. They are very expensive and therefore are used sparingly in recipes.

Cauliflower

15.   **Cauliflower** is a cultivated descendant of cabbage. The cruciferous vegetable is a compact head, identified as the curd, surrounded by ribbed green leaves that protect it from sunlight and prevent the flower buds from developing chlorophyll (Margen, 1992). If the head does poke through, the grower ties the leaves over it to shield it from the sun. Sunlight discolors the buds and causes them to develop an undesirable flavor. Cauliflower most often is sold in 18- to 25-pound cartons holding from 6 to 16 pretrimmed heads. Raw cauliflower has a large amount of vitamin C. The actual edible portion is 55%. The broccoflower is a cross between cauliflower and broccoli; the curd resembles cauliflower and is chartreuse green rather than dark green like broccoli. Cauliflower florets are available for salad bars.

Snap Beans

Asparagus

16. **Snap beans** have edible pods. The most familiar types are green and yellow wax beans. One way of classifying them is by the way they grow; bush beans and pole beans are the two main varieties. Bush beans are short plants about 1½ feet high that are shaped like a small bush, and pole beans grow on vines that are 8 feet or higher. Bush beans are preferred by commercial growers because they are easier to harvest. These beans should appear fresh, clean, firm, crisp, and free from scars and discoloration. Fresh beans should break with a snap and have no strings. Green beans have a high amount of vitamin A. Most foodservice operations use snap beans in the frozen or canned form because of the labor required to snap off ends before cooking. Snap beans are packed in 28- to 30-pound cartons.

17. **Asparagus** is a member of the lily family, which also includes such plants as onions, garlic, leeks, lilies, tulips, and gladioli. Asparagus is one of two types, green or white, based on the color of the spears. Only green is grown commercially in the United States. White asparagus, which is actually cream colored, is planted and grows under soil, thus blocking sunlight needed to produce chlorophyll. It is more popular in Europe but can be found in U.S. markets or gourmet food shops. White asparagus with green tips also is available. Asparagus deteriorates rapidly if it is not kept cold after harvesting. It usually is quickly cooled through a hydrocooling method at shipping point. Because of its perishability, asparagus is sometimes shipped by jet to assure customers of freshness. A cup of green asparagus provides two-thirds of the daily recommended allowance of vitamin C, one-third of vitamin A, and about one-tenth of the iron needed for an adult. California, New Jersey, Washington, and Michigan are chief sources of supply from mid-February through July. Only asparagus with straight stalks, a fresh appearance, and compact green or purple pointed tips should be purchased.

Information on other fresh vegetables, including artichokes, cooking greens, garlic, radishes, spinach, and squash, is not readily available. The combined per capita use of these vegetables for 1994 was 4.4 pounds.

Exotic Fruits and Vegetables

Produce not familiar to Americans is often labeled as *exotic* (Margen, 1992), *specialty* (Produce Marketing Association, 1993), or *variety* (Dole Food Company, 1992) fruits and vegetables. Most are not new but are being added to center-of-the-plate menu items by adventurous chefs who delight in surprising customers with unusual foods.

Kiwifruit, which has been considered a delicacy for many years, has now been ranked as number 19 on the top 20 list, and the mango is number 18. The carambola, often called Golden Star fruit because it is five-angled, has become more than just a garnish. The cherimoya, referred to as the custard apple because of its smooth texture, has a combination of fresh pineapple, strawberry, and banana flavors (Dole Food Company, 1992). Guava, native to Mexico and South America, can have a pineapple or strawberry color and flavor and adds variety to many menus. Plantains, which look like a rough-skinned, green banana, need to be cooked because of their high starch content; deep-fried plantain chips are considered a delicacy in many restaurants. The ugli fruit, native to Jamaica, also has become popular because it is so miserable looking. It looks like a disfigured grapefruit with light green blemishes that turn orange when ripe, but it is very juicy and has a delightful orange-like flavor.

Vegetables native to other countries are becoming more popular in America now that international foods are emphasized on menus. Such vegetables as bamboo shoots, bean sprouts, bok choy, daikon (a Japanese radish), soybeans, water chestnuts, and the pumpkin-like winter melon are appearing in markets because of their use in Oriental recipes. Taro root, also known as dasheen, is thought to have come from China but is very popular in Hawaii as an ingredient in poi. The increasing popularity of Mexican food has introduced many other vegetables to the American public. For example, nopales, or cactus leaves, are a favorite Mexican vegetable with a flavor and texture like green beans. Jicama, a root tuber used as a potato by the Mexicans, is often served raw as chips for spicy dips in American bars. The tomatillio, or little tomato, is an important ingredient in many salsas.

Nuts

Most nuts are dried fruits or seeds of plants, most often trees. Nuts have a hard shell covering the softer kernels inside. Pumpkin and sunflower seeds, popular snack foods, grow on vegetable or flower plants. Peanuts are really legumes and belong to the pea family, while almonds belong to the peach family (Margen, 1992).

Almonds, the fruit seeds of sweet almond trees, are California's largest tree crop. Brazil nuts are the fruit of a tall evergreen tree and grow in one to three dozen clusters in a hard shell in the Amazon basin. Cashews are part of the cashew apple, and most of them are imported from India. Chestnuts became almost extinct in America at the beginning of the twentieth century when a terrible blight destroyed them; today most are imported from Europe. Coconuts, which are fruit seeds, grow on tropical coconut palms and have a hairy shell lined with a layer of rich white meat that has a high saturated fat content (Margen, 1992). Hazelnuts grow in clusters close to the stem and are bleached from brown to an amber color in bins placed over pots of ignited sulphur. Macadamias have a hard, round shell difficult to remove and therefore usually are sold shelled. They are one of the most popular products of Hawaii. They have a sweet, delicate taste and creamy, rich texture; unfortunately, they contain more fat and calories than any other nut.

Americans eat approximately 12 pounds of peanuts per person per year, and almost half of the peanuts grown are made into peanut butter. Pecans, the oval seeds with a paper-like shell of a North American species of the hickory tree, grow wild but also are cultivated in the southern states. Pine nuts, or pignoli, are small seeds in the pinecone of certain pine trees; they have become very popular because of the Mediterranean influence on menus. Pistachio nuts, which have beige shells and green kernels, are the seeds of half-inch-long red fruits that grow in bunches on evergreen trees in California. Originally, they were imported from Iran and Turkey and often were dyed red to cover up blemishes and make them more attractive to customers. Because people often crack the shells with their teeth, pistachios without the dye might be safer. Walnuts, black or English, have a hard, wrinkled shell inside a thick hull. Black walnut trees usually grow wild and are not raised for commercial use. English walnuts are thought to originate in Persia but by the 1800s were grown commercially in California, making the United States the leading world producer of the nut. The shell of the English walnut is rough and golden-tan in color and splits easily into halves.

Nuts are nutritious. Except for peanuts, they are high in incomplete protein but a well-balanced diet makes up for this deficiency. They also are rich in potassium, iron, and B vitamins, but 70% to 97% of their calories comes from mostly unsaturated fat. The exception is chestnuts, which have only 8% fat calories. Because of their nutritive value, nuts are included with the meat, poultry, fish, and eggs group in the Food Guide Pyramid. They are, however, a fruit and as such are included in this chapter.

Nuts can be purchased in the shell or shelled, except for the cashew, which is sold without shell because the shell contains a caustic oil. Shelled nuts can be purchased whole, chopped, slivered, raw, dry-roasted, or oil-roasted; salted, sugared, spiced, or plain; packaged or loose (Margen, 1992).

Fresh Herbs

Chefs today are using more and more fresh herbs and spices to give flavor to reduced fat menu items. **Herbs** are the stems and leaves of low-growing plants; **spices** are the seeds, bark, roots, and fruit or berries of perennial plants (Margen, 1992). For example, some common herbs are parsley, sage, rosemary, and thyme; some common spices are nutmeg, caraway seeds, cinnamon, and allspice. Herbs can be purchased fresh or dried, while spices generally are dried. Washed and ready-to-use fresh herbs are available through specialist and full-line distributors. Most fresh herbs will keep for a week if refrigerated in sealed plastic bags. The most popular herbs are basil, bay leaves, chives, cilantro, dill, lemon grass, mint, oregano, parsley, rosemary, sage, tarragon, and thyme. Herbs should be fresh-looking, aromatic, and free of slime, browning, or yellowing. They should be added to the menu item just before serving to retain their full flavor.

Edible Flowers

Edible flowers are being used by many chefs as a garnish or in salads. Some, like squash flowers (Figure 8.4), are stuffed and usually deep-fat fried, while others add eye-appeal to platters of food on a buffet table. Herb flowers, such as borage, chives, oregano, and thyme, taste like the herbs and are often used in salads. Other flowers, including daisies, geraniums, lavender, marigolds, nasturtiums, pansies, roses, and violets, are usually used as garnishes. Edible flowers are often sold at farmer's markets or by produce suppliers or are grown by chefs in a small garden next to a restaurant. Flowers should never be picked from a pesticide-sprayed garden or from a field next to a highway because of exhaust fumes or bought from a florist because they usually are sprayed with chemicals. These flowers can be stored in an airtight container in the refrigerator for up to one day.

Figure 8.4.   Squash flowers.

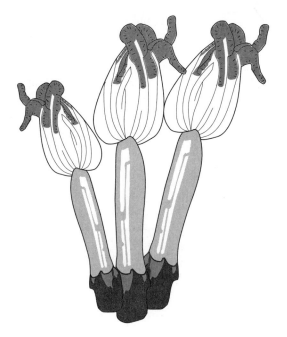

COMMUNICATION BETWEEN BUYER AND SUPPLIER

Communication is critical between the buyer, who in some operations is the food-service manager, and the supplier (Patterson, 1993a). Purchasing is a two-way street and communication should flow both ways.

The Buyer

"Produce is one of the toughest lines for the foodservice buyer. I can see now that to buy produce the most effectively, a foodservice buyer must know a great deal about produce varieties, where they come from, and who handles them." This statement (Patterson, 1993b) came from a certified purchasing manager, a title obtained by passing the certification program of the National Association of Purchasing Management. He was a graduate of one of the leading hotel and restaurant management schools in the United States and had many years of experience as director of purchasing in some of the largest hotels in the country. This buyer accepted a position as a fresh produce specialist with a superdistributor, a supplier to many foodservice operations, and quickly realized the difference between buying produce wholesale for his own operation and buying for resale to many operations. If too much is ordered, the fresh produce specialist is responsible for finding someone to buy it. If too little is ordered, the specialist must try to fill the unexpected demand.

Buyers often do not realize that quality drops off because of growing conditions or switching between growing areas. Many expect to receive the same quality every day when realistically this may not be possible. For buyers who demand picture-perfect produce, the supplier might sort through many cartons of the product hand-selecting exactly the standard the customer demands, which often is much higher than even the USDA requires. The relationship between the buyer and supplier has a strong bearing on how much selection and repacking is done. If the buyer has a contract with only one supplier, that supplier does a lot of it. If, however, the buyer purchases from many suppliers, the price increases for the extra service.

Product knowledge is the main factor in effective produce purchasing. A food buyer should know when the best tomatoes come from California or Florida or Mexico (Patterson, 1993b). At certain times of the year, quality and available quantity decrease and prices go up. When quality and quantity are high, prices go down. Produce prices are volatile because nature is volatile. If a good relationship exists, the supplier will give the buyer advance warning of when these events are likely to occur, thus helping the buyer make good decisions. The buyer should visit the distributor occasionally to see how produce is handled from the time it is received until its delivery to the customer.

The Supplier

At a recent Produce Marketing Association conference, six foodservice operators, three commercial and three noncommercial, told produce suppliers some of their pet peeves about buying produce (Patterson, 1993a). They were eager to have more nutrition information and also better information on how to use the produce they buy. They asked for education programs for the kitchen staff on how to prepare fresh fruits and vegetables. They also wanted to know how to market menu items to their customers. Product information was requested: where the produce comes from, whether it is biogenetically altered, what its pesticide levels are, and whether it is irradiated. Of course, they wanted to know how to trim labor costs and serve more customers at the same time. Because they are responsible for serving safe food to customers, they wanted to know what happens to produce in the marketing channel. Many of them have visited the suppliers' warehouses but wished that more growers and shippers would visit foodservice operations to see if their food safety standards are the same.

The supplier is responsible for quality control. The importance of finding a good supplier cannot be emphasized enough (Patterson, 1993c). A supplier who will work with buyers to make sure they get exactly what they need is a requirement. If the supplier does not have the produce item requested, he or she probably can find it from at least a couple different sources at a higher price. A switch to another grower may result in a difference in the appearance, size, or weight of a product that normally would not meet the specifications. Somewhere out there, however, the product is probably available. The ideal supplier will call the buyer and describe the situation on availability, quality, and price and ask if the substitution will be satisfactory. The buyer then has to decide to accept the product that does not meet the specification or to change the menu item.

PURCHASING, RECEIVING, AND STORAGE

Even though the USDA has developed grade standards for many fresh fruits and vegetables, buyers are not always aware of them. The reason is that grades often are not used in negotiations between the buyer and supplier because they are not as precise as those for other products, such as canned fruits and vegetables or meats. Many experienced buyers establish their own specifications based on USDA standards. Once the supplier delivers the produce, the buyer has to be sure it is stored properly.

Purchasing

The biggest purchasing problem is the great variation in fruits and vegetables from area to area, season to season, and supplier to supplier. Different soils, variations in temperature, amount of moisture in the soil, and variety affect the size, weight, shape, and often the color and flavor of the product.

Produce is grown in many U.S. regions and other countries. Apples are grown in Washington, Oregon, Michigan, Ohio, New York, Pennsylvania, and practically every other state in the country. Large crops of oranges and grapefruits are found in Florida, California, Texas, and Arizona. Different varieties of potatoes are grown in the East, Midwest, and West; tomatoes either are grown locally or come from California, Texas, Florida, or Mexico. Vegetables bought in season are usually lower in price and more likely to be of better quality and flavor. Fresh produce is difficult to buy because it is perishable and shelf life is minimal (Patterson, 1993c).

Some produce buyers depend on certain suppliers to provide the consistency they require, which works most of the time. But even the most consistent supplier is subject to the weather, pests, plant diseases, and natural disasters such as floods, droughts, and storms. Not all produce growers stay put. For example, some California lettuce growers grow lettuce in one area during the summer, move to the San Joaquin Valley for the fall, to Arizona or the Imperial Valley for the winter, back to the San Joaquin Valley for the spring, and then back again to their Central Coast farms for summer (Patterson, 1993c). Yet they use the same label for each of those regions.

Specifications

General guidelines for writing all types of specifications were given in Chapter 4. For fresh produce, the specification might include the variety, weight, degree of ripeness or maturity, quality tolerance limit for defects, and geographical area. Using federal grades as a standard makes specification writing easier. A format for specifications should be established and used for all purchases. Some buyers and their suppliers prefer a paragraph, and others prefer an outline format.

Examples of Specifications

Examples are shown of a fruit and vegetable specification in a paragraph format used by the Kansas State University Foodservice. Specifications sent to suppliers are preceded by the following paragraph.

Kansas State University Foodservice follows the U.S. government standards for the following fruits (or vegetables). Grades indicated as acceptable must be met at the time of delivery, *not* when shipped. Explanations of the acceptable grades are in our specifications to help your shipping and our receiving departments. To allow for variations incident to proper grading and handling, not more than *10%* by count of any lot may be below the requirements of the grade if not otherwise specified. Sometimes sizes will need to be specified according to our use so all sizes are listed.

Following this statement are the specifications. Here is an example for grapefruit and iceberg lettuce.

Grapefruit. 35 lb/carton, 48 count/carton, U.S. No.1, golden pink, or white flesh, peeled E.P. = 47%. Texas, Florida, California, or Arizona varieties. Texas preferred when in season. U.S. No. 1 consists of grapefruit of similar varietal characteristics that include fairly well colored, firm and well formed, mature, and of fairly smooth texture, and are free from bruises, cuts which are not healed, such as decay, growth cracks, dryness or mushy condition, and free from any damage or disease. Tolerances:

- *Florida.* Not more than one third of the surface in the aggregate may be affected by discoloration.
- *California.* Not more than 10 percent may fail to meet the above requirements.
- *Texas.* Not more than one third of the surface may be affected by discoloration.

Lettuce, Iceberg. 40-50 lb/carton, 24 count/carton. U.S. No. 1 heads should be fresh and green, not soft or burst, and free of decay or damage. Each head shall be fairly well trimmed unless specified as closely trimmed. 40% should be hard heads, with the remainder to be firm. E.P. is 75%.

Examples of grapefruit and lettuce specifications in an outline format follow.

Grapefruit

Origin: Texas preferred when in season. If not available, substitute with Florida or California. (Check with buyer.)

Use: breakfast fruit (halves will be served), EP 47%

Preservation form: fresh, delivery in refrigerated truck

Quality: U.S. No. 1, golden pink or white flesh

Tolerance: not more than one third of the surface maybe discolored

Pack: 35 pounds/carton, 48 count/carton

Price: by the box

Lettuce, Iceberg

Origin: California; if quality not good, substitute Arizona, Florida, or Mexico

Use: liner for salads. (Heads need to be fairly well trimmed unless specified as closely trimmed.)

Figure 8.5. Refrigeration temperatures for storing fresh fruits and vegetables.

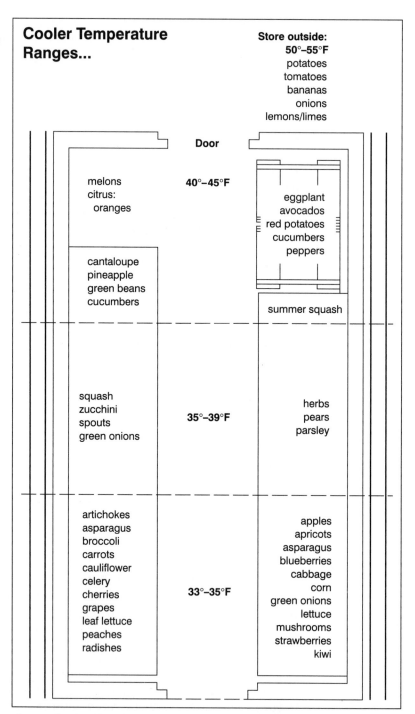

Cooler Temperature Ranges...

Store outside:
50°–55°F
potatoes
tomatoes
bananas
onions
lemons/limes

Door

40°–45°F

melons
citrus:
    oranges

eggplant
avocados
red potatoes
cucumbers
peppers

cantaloupe
pineapple
green beans
cucumbers

summer squash

35°–39°F

squash
zucchini
spouts
green onions

herbs
pears
parsley

33°–35°F

artichokes
asparagus
broccoli
carrots
cauliflower
celery
cherries
grapes
leaf lettuce
peaches
radishes

apples
apricots
asparagus
blueberries
cabbage
corn
green onions
lettuce
mushrooms
strawberries
kiwi

Source: Cambro Manufacturing Company. Used by permission.

Preservation form: delivery in refrigerated truck

Quality: U.S. #1, fresh and green and free of decay or damage

Tolerance: 40% hard heads and 60% firm heads

Pack: 40-50 pounds/carton, 24 count per carton

Price: by carton

Receiving

The person who receives fresh produce should know the specifications, what was ordered, and how it should be stored. Fresh fruits and vegetables are living organisms, and their quality must be protected. The amount ordered should be checked against the amount received. Fresh produce should be delivered in refrigerated trucks to maintain freshness, and a tolerance level should be established for damage or blemishes.

Storage

Regardless of how well specifications are written, if produce is not properly stored and handled in the foodservice, it will never please the customer. Produce is extremely perishable and should be stored as soon as received. Extreme heat, like that on the loading dock, can dry out and damage the products. Extreme cold, on the other hand, freezes produce or changes the ripening process. The stock should be rotated, and the first-in, first-out (FIFO) principal should be used. All fresh produce should be protected from bruising, which causes the products to spoil quickly.

Each type of fresh fruit and vegetable requires a combination of the following factors:

- temperature
- humidity (moisture level in the air)
- amount of light
- other factors, including storage away from other products and gentle handling

Refrigeration temperatures for fresh fruits and vegetables are shown in Figure 8.5.

SUMMARY

The farmer's market has added a new dimension to menus; fresh seasonal produce can be purchased daily instead of semi-weekly from wholesale establishments. The American diet now includes more fruits and vegetables because they are low in saturated fat and cholesterol and high in fiber.

Fresh produce is perishable and loses quality rapidly. The atmosphere and temperatures must be controlled, and transportation and packaging of products must be carefully monitored. The quality and grade of produce needs to be checked before it is purchased. The buyer needs to have enough resources to make good purchasing decisions. In addition to identifying the most popular fresh fruits and vegetables, the produce buyer also is responsible for purchasing exotic produce, nuts, fresh herbs, and edible flowers. Purchasing is a two-way street, and communication is critical between the buyer and supplier. The buyer must write clear specifications for the supplier, and the supplier should do everything possible to provide the buyer with the specified product.

REFERENCES

Bartlett, M. (1995). Ferdinand Metz. *Restaurants & Institutions, 105*(13), 134–136, 138, 140–143.

Dole Food Company, Inc. (1992). *The buying guide for fresh fruits, vegetables, herbs and nuts* (9th ed.). Shepherdstown, WV: Author.

Donovan, M. D. (Ed.). (1993). *The professional chef's® techniques of healthy cooking.* New York: Van Nostrand Reinhold.

Fairchild, B. (1993). Chez Panisse. *Bon Appétit, 38*(11), 142–144, 146–147.

Fox, S., & Nelson, J. (1995). The produce puzzle. *School Food Service & Nutrition, 49*(3), 22–24, 26, 28.

Johnson, B. A. (1996a). Restaurants & Institutions guide to fresh fruit availability. *Restaurants & Institutions, 106*(7), 80, 82.

Johnson, B. A. (1996b). Restaurants & Institutions guide to fresh vegetable availability. *Restaurants & Institutions, 106*(14), 82, 88.

Kellogg, M. A. (1994). Where the big apple buys apples. *Bon Appétit, 39*(10), 106–110.

Kotschevar, L. H., & Donnelly, R. (1991a). *Quantity food purchasing* (5th ed.). Upper Saddle River, NJ: Merrill/Prentice Hall.

Lorenzini, B. (1994). Exceeding expectations: Restaurants & Institutions college and university giants. *Restaurants & Institutions, 104*(20), 12–14, 19.

Margen, S., & Editors of the University of California at Berkeley Wellness Letter. (1992). *The wellness encyclopedia of food and nutrition.* New York: Rebus.

Meatless alternatives offered at vast majority of colleges. (1994). *Washington Weekly, 14*(23), 4.

Patterson, P. (1993a). Communication is critical when buying produce. *Nation's Restaurant News, 27*(30), 48.

Patterson, P. (1993b). A hard sell: Buying produce is no day in the park. *Nation's Restaurant News, 27*(4), 23.

Patterson, P. (1993c). Defining standards eases produce purchasing. *Nation's Restaurant News, 27*(26), 24.

Produce Marketing Association. (1993). Fruit and vegetable consumption: What are Americans eating? *Fruit & Vegetable News, 1*(2), 1, 4.

Produce Marketing Association. (1994a). Nutrition labeling. *Fruit & Vegetable News, 2*(1), 1, 4.

Produce Marketing Association. (1994b). Supplement to Restaurant Business, Inc., Publications. New York, *The New Basics,* 30.

Produce Marketing Association. (1995). *The foodservice guide to fresh produce.* Newark, DE: Author.

Putnam, J. J., & Allshouse, J. E. (1994). *Food consumption, prices, and expenditures, 1970–93.* Statistical Bulletin No. 915. Washington, DC: Food and Economics Division, Economic Research Service, U.S. Department of Agriculture.

Ryan, N. R. (1994). It takes a special kind of culinary magic to transform vegetables into incredible vegetables. *Restaurants & Institutions, 104*(26), 98–99, 104, 110.

Solomon, J. (1994). Side dishes with star potential. *Restaurants USA, 14*(8), 27–29.

Straus, K. (1993). The flavor explosion. *Restaurants & Institutions, 103*(13), 16–17, 24, 26–28.

Washington Apple Commission. (1993). Wax on produce. *Core Facts,* Fall, Issue #1.

9

Processed Fruits and Vegetables

Frozen, canned, and dehydrated fruits and vegetables are modifications of the fresh items that make up the second level of the Food Guide Pyramid (Figure 8.1). In most cases, the processed foods have the same nutritional value as their fresh counterparts because of modern processing technology. Calories can be slightly higher if a sugar syrup is added, but seldom is it significant if only one portion is added to the daily intake.

Foodservice managers once had four sets of menus each year for spring, summer, autumn, and winter. These menus were seasonal, especially for fresh vegetables and fruits, because the managers depended on what was available on the market. For example, strawberry shortcake appeared only on menus in April and May in some parts of the country, grapes from August through September, cucumbers from May to July, and sweet potatoes from October through December. Today, strawberries appear on menus from January through December, and grapes and cucumbers are available all year. Sweet potatoes, usually a Thanksgiving menu item, often accompany baked ham at Easter time. Improvements in transportation have been a major factor in making these fruits and vegetables available all year. Some produce, such as asparagus, iceberg lettuce, broccoli, certain melons, apples, and citrus fruits, does not have to ripen completely before picking and is no longer considered seasonal. The opening of international trade also has increased the length of time that seasonal foods are available. For example, good quality fresh tomatoes from Mexico and melons from South America are found in U.S. markets in January. The biggest factor in this change, however, has been the processing of fresh produce into acceptable products with a much longer shelf life.

Probably one of the greatest advances in the preservation of fresh produce occurred in the last years of the twentieth century. The concept of *value-added* was created. Customers were asking that fresh produce be served when they eat away from home. The foodservice industry's response was the creation of salad bars, which remain popular and have increased customer satisfaction. Foodservice managers had a challenge to keep fresh fruits and vegetables on hand during rush hours. Salad bars were labor intensive because employees had to clean the produce and cut it into bite-size pieces. Produce has a short shelf life, resulting in a great amount of waste. Sanitation also became a problem, and outbreaks of foodborne illnesses among customers were beginning to appear.

Thus, the challenge to the produce industry was to supply to foodservice operations fresh products ready to serve and with a long shelf life. After much research, the industry responded with value-added products. Every day more of these products are available to foodservice operations and consumers. Within the next few years, they will overtake the foodservice industry. The last section of this chapter is devoted to the value-added concept.

PRESERVATION OF FOOD

Before discussing the various processes of preserving food, a review of the marketing channel, discussed in chapter 3, is necessary. The produce buyer must understand why fresh produce is not always the best purchase in terms of quality and cost and why purchasing it in another form may be better and cheaper. Processing fresh products has solved many food spoilage problems for years.

Marketing Channel

Knowledge of the components of the marketing channel (Figure 3.1) is crucial for the buyer of highly perishable fresh produce. The time required to take the produce through the channel and the temperature needed to maintain the quality at the level it was at harvesting are critical. Also, the value added to produce as it goes through the channel increases the marketing value of raw and semi-processed products.

The producer or grower picks the fruits and vegetables, cleans them of soil and insects, packs them for delivery to the processor or wholesaler, and delivers them as quickly as possible. The time required to take produce from the field to the market is decreasing. In many instances, processing really begins in the field as harvesting, cleaning, trimming, packaging, and even weighing are being done there (Kotschevar & Donnelly, 1999). The produce is cooled and sent by controlled temperature and humidity trucks to the processor for freezing, canning, dehydrating, or other processing. Wholesalers generally purchase produce through brokers who are contracted by processors to both sell and conduct local marketing programs for wholesalers or foodservice operators. They are paid a commission by the processor on the dollar value of products sold. Brokers do not take title to the products they sell. Large brokers may represent 20 to 30 processors and products and deal in large units, which in the case of fruits and vegetables is the carload or truckload. Some brokers, such as the potato broker, are specialized.

Processing Food

Preservation of food has been a challenge from the earliest days of civilization. Scarce food supplies at certain times of the year encouraged people to seek preservation methods for food items that are abundant for only a short time. Drying foods such as berries, grains, or nuts when they were in season and then storing them was one of the earliest methods of preservation (Kotschevar & Donnelly, 1999). This was followed by using salt, sugar, acid, smoke, chemicals, and even alcohol as in the preservation of wine. Scientific studies were beginning and scientists like Louis Pasteur, who found that heat or cold prevented food from spoiling, were being recognized. Appert made a great discovery when he found that food heated in containers was safe to eat. The tin can, in which food was sealed and heated, was developed, and manufacturing these cans became an important industry in the twentieth century. Freezing food quickly followed; today frozen foods are competing with canned foods in sales.

Per capita consumption of processed vegetables increased 16% between 1970 and 1993, as vegetables used for freezing rose 37% and for canning 12% (Putnam & Allshouse, 1994). Per capita consumption of vegetables for canning, excluding tomatoes, declined 8% for the same time.

PURCHASING PROCESSED PRODUCE

Without question, purchasing processed fruits and vegetables is a difficult task for the foodservice manager or purchasing agent. According to the Agricultural Marketing Service of the U.S. Department of Agriculture (USDA), only 55% of frozen and 35% of canned produce sold is officially graded. USDA reports 156 different grades for fresh and processed fruits, vegetables, and nuts. Each of these products has its own grade and packaging standards, making specification writing a difficult job. Buyers need to choose suppliers carefully because they often have to depend upon them to provide quality products. The astute buyer will choose a good supplier and purchase most processed produce through that supplier.

Grade Standards

The U.S. Standards for Grades are issued under authority of the **Agricultural Marketing Act** of 1946 by the USDA that provides for the issuance of official U.S. grades to designate different levels of quality. The grade standards for processed fruits and vegetables are designed to assist in marketing by providing a convenient basis for sales and for establishing quality control programs. These standards also serve as a basis for the official grading of these products by USDA Agricultural Graders and are for the voluntary use of processors, suppliers, and buyers. In addition to the U.S. grade standards, grading manuals or instructions for inspection of several processed fruits and vegetables also are available from the USDA Processed Products Branch. A list of U.S. standards and grading manuals for processed fruits, vegetables, and related products is available from the USDA Agricultural Marketing Service.

Few canned fruits and vegetables are USDA graded, but the USDA Agricultural Marketing Service has a voluntary grading system that is available through the Processed Products Branch. This service often is used by suppliers to ensure that the product meets contract specifications. Purchasers should request this certification in the contract. The supplier then asks the marketing service to certify the lot for a fee before the purchaser accepts the product. Contract specifications can be based either on USDA grade standards or the Food and Drug Administration (FDA) standards of identity, quality (see Appendix), and fill. FDA standards can be tailored to meet the purchaser's needs and might include net weight, vacuum readings, drained weight, style, and condition of container, and the USDA Certificate of Quality and Condition, as shown in Figure 9.1. Points are assigned to each FDA standard and are totaled to determine the USDA quality level of the product: 90 to 100 for U.S. Grade A, for USDA Grade Fancy, or for Grade B Choice Extra Standard, 80 to 90 for U.S. Grade B, and 70 to 80 for U.S. Grade C.

Figure 9.1.   Sample USDA Certificate of Quality and Condition.

UNITED STATES DEPARTMENT OF AGRICULTURE
AGRICULTURAL MARKETING SERVICE

**CERTIFICATE OF QUALITY AND CONDITION
(PROCESSED FOODS)**

Please refer to this certificate by number and inspection office.

This certificate is receivable in all courts of the United States as prima facie evidence of the truth of the statements therein contained. It does not excuse failure to comply with any applicable Federal or State laws.
WARNING: *Any person who knowingly falsely make, issue, alter, forge, or counterfeit this certificate, or participate in any such action, is subject to a fine of not more than $1,000 or imprisonment for not more than one year, or both (7U.S.C. 1622 (h)).*
The conduct of all services and the licensing of all personnel under the regulations governing such services shall be accomplished without discrimination as to race, color, religion, sex, or national origin.

Z- 093142

DATE   JANUARY 29, 1996

APPLICANT	ADDRESS
The ABC Company, Inc	Chicago, Illinois

RECEIVER OR BUYER	ADDRESS
The State of USA	Anywhere, USA

SOURCE OF SAMPLES	PRODUCT INSPECTED
OFFICIALLY DRAWN	CANNED WHOLE KERNEL CORN

CODE MARKS ON CONTAINERS

     123
     51, 23, 22........

PRINICIPAL LABEL MARKS

"ABC Company Golden Sweet Whole Kernel Corn, Net Wt. 6lbs. Distributed by the ABC Company, Chicago, IL packed in U.S.A."

Net Weight:	MEETS label declaration
Vacuum Readings:	11 to 12 inches
Drained Weight:	72.4 to 76.8 ounces
	74.3 ounces, Average
Color:	YELLOW

Condition of Container: MEETS applicable U.S. Standards for Condition of Food Containers.

GRADE:

U.S. GRADE A or U.S. FANCY
Average Score 92 points. MEETS requirements as published in the State of Anywhere specifications for Item Number 277-34-0166.

REMARKS:

This certificate covers 3,840 cases 6/No. 10. cans (Applicant's Count). Product packed in beaded enamel lined cans cased in domestic corrugated fiber cases. Lot located in applicant's warehouse, Chicago, Illinois and identified by code marks as shown above. Applicant's written statement indicates product packed August 1995. Cases stamped with USDA "OFFICIALLY SAMPLED" stamp as shown above.

Pursuant to the regulations issued by the Secretary of Agriculture under the Agricultural Marketing Act of 1946, as amended (7 U.S.C. 1621-1627), governing the inspection certification of the product designated herein, I certify that the quality and condition of the product as shown by samples inspected on the above date were as shown, subject to any restrictions specified above.

ADDRESS OF INSPECTION OFFICE	SIGNATURE OF INSPECTOR
218 N. Technology Drive South Bend, IN 46628	I.M. Inspector

FORM FV-146CS (9-92)
☆U.S. GPO: 1992—333-847

Even though most processors do not use USDA grade standards for frozen or canned products, they do have a first, second, and third quality level often identified by a specific color label. For example, the Nugget® brand has a black label for Grade A Fancy, Grade B Choice, or Grade B Choice Extra Standard, red for Grade B Extra Standard, and green for Grade C Standard (Figure 9.2). Equivalent grades for fruits and vegetables are as follows:

Figure 9.2.   Example of use of colored labels to indicate quality choices of canned and frozen fruits and vegetables for a specific brand.

Nugget Black
Grade A — Fancy or B Choice

Nugget Red
Grade B — Extra Standard

Nugget Green
Grade C — Standard

Nugget Black Label

GRADE A FANCY
This is the highest U.S.D.A. grade for fruits and vegetables. Grade A Fancy products are carefully selected for uniformity of size, color, texture and tenderness. Apples, pineapple, beans and corn are examples. Tomato products in this category are selected for the best color, consistency and flavor.

GRADE B CHOICE
For California-packed fruits, this is top of the line. Products with this grade are selected for consistency, style, color, and lack of defects. Peaches, pears and fruit cocktail are examples.

**GRADE B CHOICE
EXTRA STANDARD**
This U.S.D.A. grade of tomatoes is the standard in the foodservice industry. Grade B meets the criteria for the most discriminating customers who require "top of the line" quality.

Nugget Red Label

GRADE B EXTRA STANDARD
The designation "extra standard" applies specifically to vegetables and tomatoes. Grade B vegetables are reasonably uniform in size, color and texture. They are also more mature than Grade A vegetables. Tomato products with this grade have good color, consistency and flavor and have lower total solids than the Grade A Fancy products.

Red label products usually have the greatest appeal among foodservice operators in the "moderately priced" category. Coffee shops, contract feeders or health care facilities may find Nugget Red Label delivers the ideal price/value relationship given their food cost requirements.

Nugget Green Label

GRADE C STANDARD
Tomatoes and vegetable products with this grade are wholesome, nutritious and flavorful but they lack uniformity. Tomato products with this grade level have a lower solid level and are slightly thinner than Grade B. The products are, however, wholesome and nutritious. These products always meet or exceed U.S.D.A. and F.D.A. standard of quality.

Products packed under the Nugget Green Label have a wide application as ingredient foods. They have appeal for foodservice operators on a lower budget, many of whom buy on a bid basis.

Nugget.
BRAND

Source: From Nugget® Brand Distributors, Inc. Stockton, CA

First quality	Choice Fruits (numerical score 80-90)
	Extra Fancy and Fancy Vegetables (numerical score 90-100)
Second quality	Standard Fruits (numerical score 80-90)
	Extra Standard Vegetables (numerical score 80-90)
Third quality	Substandard Fruits (numerical score below 70)
	Standard Vegetables (numerical score 70-80)

Few fruits meet the fancy grade standards. Therefore, Choice, which is really USDA Grade B, fruits are included under the first and second quality labels.

The Nugget® brand also has an Oro Fino label for the upscale line of Italian-style specialty items and a Nutri-Gold label for products with exceptional taste and quality that have reduced fat, sugar, sodium, calories, or cholesterol. The Nutri-Gold label is used only on products that have undergone rigorous testing and meet specific dietary guidelines set by registered dietitians.

Many suppliers argue that their first, second, or third grade products will grade in the upper range of the numerical score. For example the Fancy score is 90 to 100, and their Fancy score is 95. Some processors require that products packed under their label score in the upper range.

Packaging

Probably the biggest problem that foodservice managers have in purchasing processed produce is determining the size package to purchase. Package sizes have not been standardized and obtaining this information is almost impossible. Not too long ago, apples could be purchased by the bushel, half bushel, or peck. Today they might be packed 40 pounds to a case, or 113 individual apples per case. Fruits and vegetables can be purchased in 1-pound No. 303 cans up to 6-pound 9-ounce No. 10 cans. Average can sizes are shown in Figure 9.3.

The supplier is the best source of information on the package size that best suits the buyer's needs. Purchasing on price alone can often lead to higher costs down the road. For example, purchasing 30 pounds of frozen strawberries might be 10 cents a pound cheaper than buying four 5-pound boxes at a higher price. Unless the extra 10 pounds of strawberries are planned in the next day's menu, the 30-pound purchase might be more expensive than the 20-pound option. Thawed strawberries begin to lose their color, firmness, and customer appeal very quickly.

Labeling

The basic laws governing the labeling of canned, frozen, and packaged foods are the Federal Food, Drug, and Cosmetic Act of 1938, the Fair Packaging and Labeling Act of 1967, and the Nutrition Labeling and Education Act of 1990 (The Almanac, 1995). When the food processor ships foods labeled either with the food processor's own labels or with the distributor's labels, the food processor as the shipper has full responsibility to see that the labels comply with the law and regulations. If processed food is found to be adulterated or misbranded, the processor must answer under the law as the party that introduces processed foods into interstate commerce. A food is deemed to be misbranded if

- Its labeling is false or misleading.
- It is offered for sale under the name of another food.
- It is an imitation of another food, unless its label bears the word "imitation" followed by the name of the food imitated.
- Its container is made, formed, or filled as to be misleading.
- The package does not bear the name and place of business of the processor, packer, or distributor.
- The package does not have an accurate statement of the quantity of the contents in terms of weight, measure, or numerical count.
- Any word, statement, or other information required by this Act is not likely to be read or understood by the ordinary individual.
- It represents a food that has a definition and standard of identity prescribed by regulations and does not conform by listing the common names of the specified ingredients on the label.
- It has a standard of quality prescribed by regulations and falls below that standard without noting it on the label.
- It falls below its standard of fill of container without noting it on the label.
- It misrepresents predominance by weight. Ingredients such as spices, flavorings, colorings, and chemical preservatives need not be identified if they are 2% or less by weight.

Figure 9.3. Average can sizes.

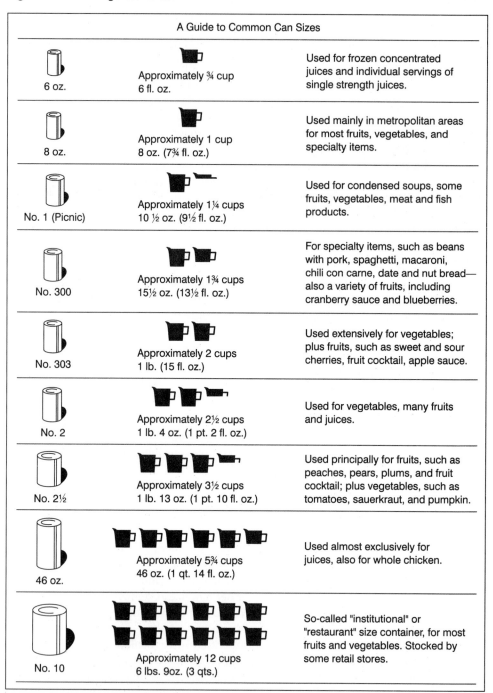

A Guide to Common Can Sizes		
6 oz.	Approximately ¾ cup 6 fl. oz.	Used for frozen concentrated juices and individual servings of single strength juices.
8 oz.	Approximately 1 cup 8 oz. (7¾ fl. oz.)	Used mainly in metropolitan areas for most fruits, vegetables, and specialty items.
No. 1 (Picnic)	Approximately 1¼ cups 10 ½ oz. (9½ fl. oz.)	Used for condensed soups, some fruits, vegetables, meat and fish products.
No. 300	Approximately 1¾ cups 15½ oz. (13½ fl. oz.)	For specialty items, such as beans with pork, spaghetti, macaroni, chili con carne, date and nut bread—also a variety of fruits, including cranberry sauce and blueberries.
No. 303	Approximately 2 cups 1 lb. (15 fl. oz.)	Used extensively for vegetables; plus fruits, such as sweet and sour cherries, fruit cocktail, apple sauce.
No. 2	Approximately 2½ cups 1 lb. 4 oz. (1 pt. 2 fl. oz.)	Used for vegetables, many fruits and juices.
No. 2½	Approximately 3½ cups 1 lb. 13 oz. (1 pt. 10 fl. oz.)	Used principally for fruits, such as peaches, pears, plums, and fruit cocktail; plus vegetables, such as tomatoes, sauerkraut, and pumpkin.
46 oz.	Approximately 5¾ cups 46 oz. (1 qt. 14 fl. oz.)	Used almost exclusively for juices, also for whole chicken.
No. 10	Approximately 12 cups 6 lbs. 9oz. (3 qts.)	So-called "institutional" or "restaurant" size container, for most fruits and vegetables. Stocked by some retail stores.

Source: From the American Can Company.

Figure 9.4.   Nutrition label on a no. 10 can of cut green beans.

The **Allens** **Veri-green**™ Cut Green Beans

Nutrition Facts
Serving Size ½ cup (120g)
Servings Per Container 25

Amount Per Serving

Calories 20	Calories from Fat 0

% Daily Value*

Total Fat 0g	**0%**
Saturated Fat 0g	**0%**
Cholesterol 0mg	**0%**
Sodium 200mg	**8%**
Total Carbohydrate 4g	**1%**
Dietary Fiber 2g	**6%**
Sugars 2g	
Protein 1g	

Vitamin A 8%	•	Vitamin C 2%	
Calcium 2%	•	Iron 6%	

*Percent Daily Values are based on a 2,000 calorie diet. Your daily values may be higher or lower depending on your calorie needs.

	Calories:	2,000	2,500
Total Fat	Less Than	65g	80g
Saturated Fat	Less Than	20g	25g
Cholesterol	Less Than	300mg	300mg
Sodium	Less Than	2,400mg	2,400mg
Total Carbohydrate		300g	375g
Dietary Fiber		25g	30g

Calories per gram:
Fat 9 • Carbohydrate 4 • Protein 4

INGREDIENTS: GREEN BEANS, WATER, SALT, ZINC CHLORIDE ADDED TO STABILIZE COLOR.

ALLEN CANNING CO.
PACKERS AND DISTRIBUTORS
SILOAM SPRINGS, AR 72761-0250 U.S.A.

- It claims to have special dietary uses, but its label contains no information on its vitamin, mineral, and other dietary properties.

The Nutrition Labeling and Education Act of 1990, amended in August 1993, requires that the label must have the following nutrition information, as shown in Figure 9.4, for a No. 10 can of cut green beans:

- serving size customarily consumed and expressed in a common household measure, such as ½ cup or 1 tablespoon

- number of servings per container
- total number of calories derived from any source and from the total fat in each serving size
- amount of total fat, saturated fat, cholesterol, sodium, total carbohydrates, complex carbohydrates, sugars, dietary fiber, and total protein in each serving size

Specifications

Writing specifications for processed foods has been simplified for the buyer, especially for those who primarily use a single source distributor. Specifications should be as simple and clear as possible, thus preventing confusion for the supplier. Many buyers give the suppliers copies of their specifications for review and ask for suggestions before purchasing any products. Buyers often give permission to the distributor to choose the lowest priced product that best fits the specification. If a desired brand is requested, the supplier provides it. Because many processed foods have brand names that customers want, such as Heinz Ketchup, Smucker's Orange Marmalade, or Vlasic Kosher Baby Dill Pickles, specifications might be only the brand name and size of container.

Preserving food today may entail refrigerating, freezing, canning, dehydrating, or irradiating. Each process is unique, but the overall goal is to preserve the food to make it safe for human consumption.

REFRIGERATED PRODUCE

Refrigeration is regarded as minimal processing for most fresh fruits and vegetables. It is needed to extend storage life and is considered the first step in processing for freezing, canning, dehydrating, or irradiating food for preservation. Fresh produce should be refrigerated as quickly as possible after picking. Temperature and humidity must be controlled to prevent fruits and vegetables from wilting and losing quality. Temperatures should be above freezing to prevent decay from chilling injury and still cool enough to delay the growth of microorganisms. Most fruits and vegetables should be stored at temperatures between 32°F and 50°F. Although early recommendations for fresh fruits and vegetables were 85% to 95% relative humidity, the current levels are close to 100%. Lower levels of moisture can cause wilting of leafy vegetables and loss of structure in fruits.

Refrigeration is really a temporary means of preservation because if food is held too long, it spoils. Strawberries held in the refrigerator for more than a day or two lose their flavor and start to decay. Oranges are edible for a longer time, but they too finally mold while in the refrigerator. That is one reason that more frozen, rather than fresh, orange juice is purchased. Other foods, such as meat, milk, and eggs, also need to be stored in refrigerators before further processing.

FROZEN PRODUCE

Quick freezing seldom changes the original quality of the product. Therefore, only sound and wholesome raw materials at an optimum level of maturity and freshness should be frozen.

The Process

Processors must use the proper freezing equipment to minimize physical, biochemical, and microbiological changes (Klein, 1992). The three basic freezing methods in commercial use are freezing in air, by indirect contact with the refrigerant, and by direct immersion in a refrigerating medium. In **air-blast freezing,** air is forced through a tunnel or chamber in which food moves through the area on belts or carts. Cold air, −35°C (−31°F), is blown through or across the thin layer of food in about 15 minutes. Small particles of food, such as peas, corn, and berries, remain separate and can be poured into bags for storage. Individually quick-frozen **(IQF) products** are individually quick-frozen in air so they can be poured into bags. IQF shrimp also is being used in these operations. **Indirect contact freezing** occurs when packaged food is placed between freezer shelves for one to two hours. In **immersion freezing,** or direct contact freezing, food is submerged in a liquid refrigerant or sprayed with the liquid. This expensive process is used most often on shrimp or scallops, not fruits and vegetables.

Neither refrigeration nor freezing substantially reduces the number of microorganisms present. Contaminated food before freezing still is susceptible to microbial spoilage after it is thawed. Freezing does preserve the appearance, color, aroma, and flavor of fruits and vegetables, although changes in texture occur. The freezing point differs between foods and varieties of the same fruit or vegetable and is lowered when salt, sugar, minerals, or proteins are added. For example, the freezing point of orange juice is lower than that of water because it contains sugar and minerals. Unless the freezing temperature is low enough, highly concentrated liquid will remain unfrozen. When this occurs, changes in texture, color, flavor, and aroma will be present. Recommended storage times for frozen fruits and vegetables depend upon temperature. For example, peaches held at −18°C (−4°F) will maintain quality for 12 months, but at −12°C (10.4°F), storage life is less than 2 months.

The texture of fruits and vegetables is affected by the rate of freezing (Klein, 1992). Rapid freezing results in small ice crystals that do not break down the product's cells; slow freezing causes large crystals that rupture cells. Repeated thawing and refreezing of fruits and vegetables also cause the formation of large crystals.

Packaging

The type of packaging has a great influence on the quality of frozen fruits and vegetables that need to be protected from oxygen, light, moisture loss, and contamination (Klein, 1992). For the retail market, paper cartons with a wax or plastic coating and an exterior overwrap to prevent moisture from entering the carton are most often used. For IQF fruits and vegetables, opaque polyethylene bags are used. The same type of packaging is used for foodservice operations, but the amount of frozen food in each carton or bag is increased. For the retail market, frozen food is usually sold in small packages holding less than 16 ounces of a product, but foodservice operations buy by the pound. For example, four 5-pound cartons, or six 6½-pound cartons, or one 30-pound polyethylene bag might be packed in one corrugated case. Buyers need to check with processors or wholesalers on package sizes before writing specifications.

The Frozen Food Roundtable (1992) has developed a code of recommended practices for handling frozen foods. Code II, Packaging and Identification of Frozen Foods, includes these statements:

- Packaging and outer cases for frozen foods should be of good quality in order to prevent contamination, ensure the integrity of the product during normal transit and storage, and minimize dehydration.
- Package coding should be adequate for effective identification.
- Outer case coding is useful to enable proper stock rotation of individual cases.
- Phrases such as "Store at 0°F or colder" should appear on outer cases.

Code V, Transportation, states that all vehicles used to transport frozen food, such as trucks, trailers, railcars, ships, and aircrafts, should be:

- clean and free from dirt, debris, offensive odors, or any substances that could contaminate the food
- constructed, insulated, and equipped with adequate refrigeration capacity and air delivery to continuously maintain product temperature of 0°F or colder
- equipped with tight-fitting doors and suitable closures for drain holes to prevent air leakage
- equipped with an appropriate temperature recording device to accurately measure the air temperature inside the vehicle. The dial should be mounted in a readily visible position.

Boil-in-the-bag vegetables in sauce are packaged in opaque polyethylene bags that can withstand both freezing and boiling temperatures (Klein, 1992). These bags must have seals that are strong enough to endure both boiling and microwaving. Vegetables are blanched sufficiently to the almost cooked stage and then quick frozen. Then they are placed in a bag and sauce is added. A vacuum is drawn and the bag is sealed and rapidly frozen.

Fruits are not blanched before freezing but are often treated with ascorbic or citric acid to prevent browning. Sugar or sugar syrup also is added to most fruit to preserve color, flavor, and sometimes texture before freezing. Syrup helps maintain a firm texture because it diffuses into the fruit tissue.

Popular Menu Items

Per capita use of frozen fruits increased 6% from 1970 to 1993 while canned fruits decreased 16%. Even though people ate approximately 3.5 pounds of frozen fruit and 16 pounds of canned fruit per person in 1993, frozen fruit is gaining in popularity (Putnam & Allshouse, 1994). Strawberries continue to be the most popular frozen fruit, with a per capita consumption of 1.38 pounds per year. Sliced strawberries in dry sugar or a syrup to protect against color and flavor loss and a softened texture are sold to foodservice operations in a carton that contains six 6½-pound packages or one 30-pound polyethylene bag. Whole strawberries in syrup also are available in a 30-pound bag. Strawberries should be barely defrosted when served because if all the ice crystals are thawed, the fruit becomes flabby.

Blackberries, raspberries, blueberries, and other berries are usually sold fresh or frozen. Blackberries that are used primarily for pies and cobblers are packed in

30-pound cans or bags, while blueberries are packed in 10-pound cartons. The blueberry muffin, probably the best-selling muffin in America, is responsible for the popularity of this berry. Red raspberries have always been a favorite, but their short growing season kept them off many menus. Frozen red raspberries finally are appearing on more menus even though they are expensive. They also are very fragile and therefore are packaged in 5-pound cartons, two to a case. Small cartons can be opened as needed, and raspberries should be served slightly frozen.

Cherries are the most popular frozen fruit used in large baking operations, with a 0.69-pound per capita consumption annually, followed by apples, peaches, and apricots. Cherries are packed in 30-pound containers. Frozen apple slices are packed in 30- or 40-pound containers. The bulk of frozen peaches are sliced and most often packed in 30- or 32-pound cartons or six 8.5-pound cartons.

Fruit juices have gained in popularity. According to the USDA food consumption report, the per capita consumption of fruit juices went from 5.64 gallons a year in 1971 to 8.39 in 1993 (Putnam & Allshouse, 1994). Citrus fruit juices, including orange, grapefruit, lemon, and lime, were included along with apple, grape, pineapple, and prune juices. These juices were either frozen or canned. Orange juice had a per capita consumption of 3.64 gallons in 1971 and 5.14 in 1993. Today, most orange juice is concentrated and frozen and can be purchased without pulp, with pulp, and fortified with calcium. Fresh pasteurized orange juice currently is popular.

Use of vegetables for freezing, excluding potatoes, rose 8% to 23 pounds per person in 1993 because of greater use of sweet corn and other vegetables, such as baby lima beans (USDA, 1994). Per capita use of potatoes for freezing has remained stable at 51 pounds annually per person for the last 3 years. With strong economic growth in the general economy and long-running specials on french fries in major quick-service restaurants, per capita use of potatoes for freezing is forecast to remain strong.

Specifications

Frozen vegetables usually are U.S. Grade A (Fancy) or U.S. Grade B (Extra Standard), and fruits are U.S. Grade A (Choice) or U.S. Grade B (Standard). Quality should be stated in the specification. The cut or form of the product needs to be specified—for example, whole strawberries, whole leaf spinach, sliced peaches, sliced potatoes, or onion rings. The size of the container and number per case(s) or carton(s) also are important. Buyers often specify the brand of frozen products that has been the most satisfactory in their operation.

Without question, more variations for french fry potatoes are available than for any other frozen product on the market. In the *Catalog of Food Specifications* (1992), prepared by the Food Industry Services Group in cooperation with the USDA, 44 pages are devoted to frozen french fries. In fact, french fries are so popular that a separate 185-page volume has been prepared on purchasing french fry potatoes. In the *Catalog of Food Specifications,* 28 packers and the type of french fries they handle are listed. The USDA has developed length standards—medium, long, and extra long—for french fried potatoes. It also developed thickness standards, ranging from ¼ to 3½ inches, as shown in Figure 9.5, that need to be specified when ordering frozen french fries. Some variations in french fries are illustrated in Figure 9.6. In addition to size and type, french fries are available that can be oven cooked, deep fat

Figure 9.5. Sketches of thickness of french fried potatoes commonly available from processors.

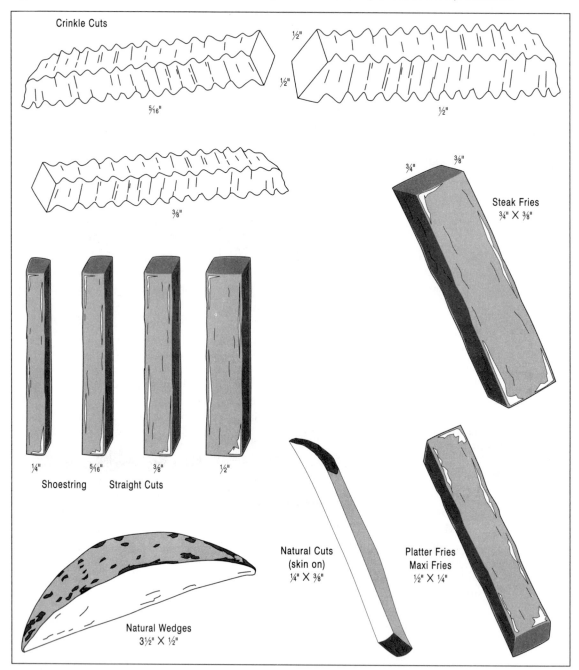

Crinkle Cuts

5/16"

1/2"
1/2"
1/2"

3/8"

Steak Fries
3/4" X 3/8"

3/4"   3/8"

1/4"   5/16"   3/8"   1/2"

Shoestring   Straight Cuts

Natural Cuts
(skin on)
1/4" X 3/8"

Platter Fries
Maxi Fries
1/2" X 1/4"

Natural Wedges
3 1/2" X 1/2"

Source: USDA.

Figure 9.6. Variations in french fried potatoes. Names may vary among processors.

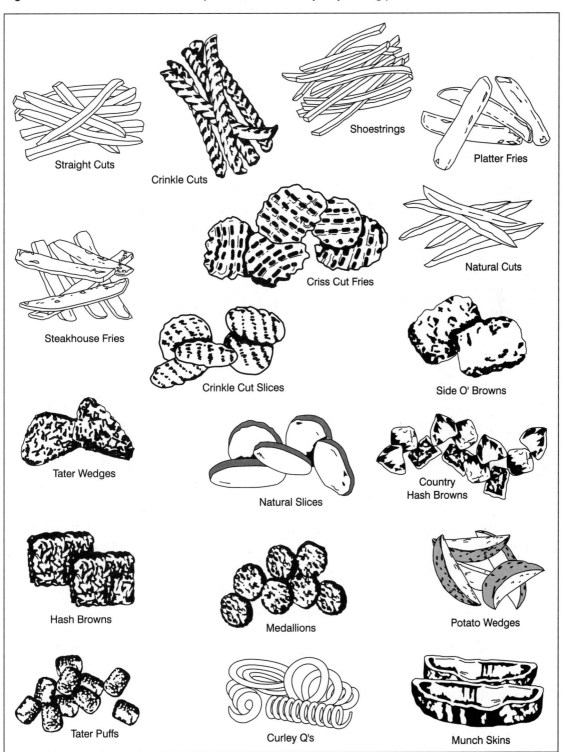

Straight Cuts

Crinkle Cuts

Shoestrings

Platter Fries

Steakhouse Fries

Criss Cut Fries

Natural Cuts

Crinkle Cut Slices

Side O' Browns

Tater Wedges

Natural Slices

Country Hash Browns

Hash Browns

Medallions

Potato Wedges

Tater Puffs

Curley Q's

Munch Skins

Source: USDA.

fried, or seasoned with Cajun or Mexican spices, for example. The buyer must know the customer in order to purchase what will sell best. Will it be straight cuts or crinkle cuts, shoe strings, steakhouse fries, tater puffs, or curly Qs?

Sample specifications for various frozen vegetables and fruits follow:

Potatoes, French Fried, Frozen

Form: crinkle cut, ⅜″ x ⅜″, long

Use: vegetable choice on menu

Quality: U.S. Grade A

Brand: Ore-Ida or Simplot

Preservation form: frozen, 10°F inside carton on delivery in refrigerated truck

Pack: ⅝-pound cartons per case

Price: per carton or case

Green Peas and Pearl Onions, Frozen

Use: vegetable choice on cafeteria line

Quality: U.S. Grade A for peas
U.S. Grade No. 2 or better for pearl onions

Size: 3-4 sieve for peas. Less than ½″ in diameter for pearl onions, minimum of 100 onions per 2½ pound carton

Preservation form: frozen, 10°F inside carton on delivery in refrigerated truck

Pack: 12/2½-pound cartons per case

Price: by carton or case

Strawberries, Frozen

Form: IQF, whole

Size: range from ¾″ to 1″ diameter

Quality: U.S. Grade A

Preservation form: 10°F inside case on delivery in refrigerated trucks

Pack: polyethylene bags inside fiber board cartons, 6/6.5 pounds per case

Price: by carton or case

CANNED PRODUCE

Heat processing is the most popular way of preserving whole fruits to make them available throughout the year (Margen, 1992). Canned fruits lose some vitamin C and beta carotene. Canned vegetables, however, lose a substantial amount of vitamins because they are processed at higher temperatures than fruits. Another concern is the calories in heavy fruit syrup. For instance, the calorie count of heavy syrup is more than double that of light syrup. Canned fruits, however, often are packed in water or unsweetened juices; in the latter form, the nutrients are retained and the increase in calories is far smaller.

The Process

Heat processing is the most common method for preservation of fruits and vegetables. It decreases the number of microorganisms in a food, thus extending the shelf life while keeping the product palatable and acceptable in flavor, color, and texture (Klein, 1992). **Canning** is a highly mechanized industry with washing, sizing, grading, peeling or shelling, trimming, and putting into cans accomplished by machine (Kotschevar & Donnelly, 1994). Canneries generally are located in or nearby the fields, permitting immediate processing after harvesting.

The sequence of activities for a typical vegetable canning operation is as follows: harvesting, receiving, washing, grading, heat blanching, peeling and coring, can filling, exhausting to remove air, sealing, processing, cooling, labeling, and packing. Vegetables can be whole, sliced, cubed, puréed, or made into juice. Most of these modifications also are used in canning fruits.

Most foods, especially vegetables, are blanched before processing. Blanching with either hot water or steam inactivates enzymes, thus preserving sensory and nutritional characteristics of the product (Klein, 1992). Blanching also reduces the microbial load and wilts plant tissues, such as in spinach, to make packing in cans easier. After packing, liquid usually is added leaving some head space to permit the contents to be shaken, and then the cans are closed, vacuum exhausted, and sealed. The cans usually are placed in agitating retorts, or vessels, and heated to 260°F or 270°F at which time moisture is converted into steam and pressure develops within the can. A specific number of minutes is required for each product. Forced convection, which is distribution of heat by the movement of liquid, is necessary to prevent the food from cooking on the sides of the can; head space makes this possible.

Canned fruits and vegetables are considered to be commercially sterile because they have been heat processed for a specific amount of time and at the correct temperature to destroy organisms; which could cause spoilage during handling and storage. Commercially sterile foods have a shelf life of 2 years or more. Longer storage could result in sensory changes, but not in microbiological growth.

Many modifications of this process are made according to the product and type of container. For example, liquids or foods of thin consistency, such as soup or creamed corn, require specific canning equipment (Potter, 1986). Chunks of food, as in chow mein or chicken à la king, require direct steam injection for sterilization. Tomato paste used in Italian cuisine and apricot purée used in bakery products are often sold in 55-gallon drums. If the foods were sterilized in these drums, the center of the food would have to be at the correct sterilization temperature, which would cause the outside to scorch. Instead, drums and lids are sterilized under superheated steam in a large chamber and then filled with the product at the correct temperature and sealed aseptically.

Types of Canned Produce

Almost every fresh fruit and vegetable has been canned or bottled in some form or another. They are available whole, diced, cubed, pickled, puréed, in sauces, in soups, in juices, and in jellies and related products. Most of them have standards of identity as listed in the Appendix. Foodservice buyers depend on knowledgeable distributors who know the new products on the market.

Fruits

Examples of fruits packed in cans or bottles include: apples, solid pack and juice; applesauce; apricots, whole and halves; berries, especially blueberries; red, sour, pitted, and sweet cherries; cranberry sauce and juice; figs, whole; fruit cocktail; grapefruit sections and juice; oranges, mandarin; peaches, halves, slices, and whole spiced; pineapple, sliced, chunks, and crushed; pears, halves and whole spiced; plums, whole; and prunes, dehydrated and then rehydrated. Most fruits are packed in water, juice, or a syrup, and that choice should be noted in a specification. The density of the syrup, which ranges from extra heavy to light, is important information for both supplier and buyer. Syrup density is measured by using a **Brix hydrometer,** an instrument that measures the percent of sucrose, or sugar, in a syrup. Specific values are calibrated in degrees Brix; for example, a light syrup on peaches is between 14° and 19° Brix. A much heavier syrup is added to the fruit during canning, but after standing for a time the fruit dilutes the syrup. Apricots packed in a 55° Brix syrup will come out with a 25° Brix. Generally, the higher the degree of Brix, the higher the price.

Fruit packed in heavy syrup often is used if the fruit is served as-is from the can. Fruit holds its shape better in heavy syrup and therefore is graded the highest; the price of this fruit also is the highest. Fruits in pies and cobblers do not have to be picture perfect, so cheaper canned fruit can be used.

FDA standards of identity for fruit butters, jellies, preserves, and related products are listed in the Appendix. **Fruit butters** have a pastelike consistency that results from cooking the fruit down and putting it through a sieve to make it spread like butter. **Jellies** are made from fruit juices and sugar and are the clear color of the fruit with a sparkling appearance. **Preserves** are jellies with identifiable pieces of fruit; **jams** have mashed fruit. **Marmalades,** usually orange or lemon, are jellies with slices, including the peel, of citrus fruits. These are packed in bulk quantities of 30 gallons, usually for large commercial bakeries, or No. 10 cans for foodservice operations. For customer service, however, individual ½-ounce packets or containers are used.

Olives, botanically classified as a fruit because they have a single stone or pit, are either green or black in color. Green olives are the most popular and can be purchased whole with or without a pit, sliced, or chopped. Pitted olives are most often stuffed with red pimento but also may be stuffed with an almond, anchovy, or pearl onion. Green olives are packed by size; small, medium, large, mammoth, giant, jumbo, and colossal are popular sizes. Olives are packed in brine usually in pint, quart, and gallon glass containers. Black olives often are referred to as ripe olives.

The only ripe black olives, which are small and wrinkled, are the Mission olives brought to California by the Franciscan missionaries. Most black olives identified as ripe olives are really green olives that have been ripened. These are packed by the same sizes as green olives.

Vegetables

Asparagus, green and wax beans, bean sprouts, beets, carrots, corn, hominy, mushrooms, mustard greens, turnip greens, peas, peppers, potatoes, sweet potatoes, pimentos, pumpkin, tomatoes, sauerkraut, and spinach are a few of the common canned vegetables. Tomatoes are available whole, diced, or puréed or made into catsup, juice, paste, or sauce. Cucumbers are processed into sliced, cut, whole dill pickles, sour or sweet pickles, or sour or sweet pickle relish. Various types of dried beans, such as lima, kidney, garbanzo or chickpeas, pinto, and red, are now cooked and packed in brine to save on labor in foodservice operations.

Spoilage

Spoilage of canned fruits and vegetables occurs when certain types of bacteria grow on products that are heat processed (Klein, 1992). The physical and chemical properties of fruits and vegetables affect the type of spoilage. In the United States, the Pure Food Law includes Good Manufacturing Practice (GMP) regulations to help assure food safety and wholesomeness. Low-acid canned and acidified foods are included in the GMP regulations. Safe procedures are required for processing and packaging foods that could support the growth of *Clostridium botulinum,* which produces an extremely dangerous toxin that attacks the nervous system. Improved commercial processing techniques have led to greatly reduced incidents of botulism, although inadequately processed home-canned foods are still frequently associated with the toxin. The temperature and length of food storage also are factors influencing toxin productions and growth. The toxin is stable in acid, but unstable in an alkaline solution. Meats, fish, and low-acid vegetables have been found to support toxin formation and growth.

The safety of low-acid and acidified foods is further ensured through the **Emergency Permit Control** regulations that require processing plants to register themselves and their processes with the FDA (Potter, 1986). Only new processing treatments require FDA approval. Over 100,000 processes have been filed with the FDA. All cans are required to have a code filed with the federal government that identifies the product, cannery, and other information. Contamination of canned foods may result from faulty can seams or jar seals. Water used in the canning process should be microbiologically safe; chlorination of the water is the usual means of control. Canned foods should be destroyed immediately if the cans are leaking or bulging.

Packaging

Materials used for containers include metal, glass, and flexible pouches. Containers must be able to withstand pressure changes during heating and cooling (Klein, 1992). A high temperature is used for processing food and sealing the container, followed by rapid cooling. Today foodservice managers are committed to packaging that can be recycled, and many have established recycling programs within their operation.

Specifications

Technical specifications for canned produce should be on file in every foodservice operation. Guidelines for writing specifications are provided in chapter 4. Standards of identity for many foods are available from the Agricultural Marketing Service (see Appendix). The buyer has to remain in the driver's seat by communicating with the supplier exactly what products are required to meet the needs of the foodservice. Writing technical specifications is the clearest way to communicate. Many buyers find that certain brands of the product meet the specifications and therefore use brand names when ordering. This method eliminates having to communicate the entire specification to the supplier and simplifies ordering. Other buyers, especially those who use a primary supplier, permit the supplier to select the product that best meets the specification; this method often is referred to as *distributor's choice*. Regardless of the method used, a specification is a requirement to make purchasing profitable. Examples of specs for processed produce follow.

Beans, Green

Origin: Oregon blue lake or Northwest

Form: canned

Use: green bean and onion casserole

Quality: U.S. Grade A

Size: 3-4 sieve, cut approximately 2″ in length

Pack: 6/#10 cans per case

Price: per case

Cherries

Form: red sour, pitted

Preservation form: canned, water packed

Use: cherry pie

Quality: U.S. Grade B

Pack: 6/#10 cans per case

Price: per case

Peaches

Form: yellow cling, halves

Use: dessert and salad

Preservation form: canned

Syrup density: light 14°-18° Brix

Quality: U.S. Grade B

Count: 30-40 maximum

Pack: 6/#10 cans per case

Price: per case

Cranberry Juice Cocktail

Form: crystal clear with cranberry red color

Use: beverage

Quality: U.S. Grade A

Enriched: Vitamin C

Ingredients: water, cranberry juice, sugar & inverted sugar, dextrose, vitamin C enriched

Brand: Ocean Spray or Sysco Classic

Pack: 12/46-ounce bottles per case

Price: per case

Jelly

Use: baked products

Variety: 2 apple, 2 blackberry, 2 grape per case

Pack: 6/#10 cans per case

Price: per case

Jam, Strawberry

Use: individual service

Brand: Smuckers

Pack: 200/½-ounce packets per case

Price: per case

DEHYDRATED PRODUCE

Dehydration, or drying, of fruits and vegetables is a means of preservation that decreases bulk and weight and eliminates water that could be used by microorganisms for growth. All food dehydration methods need heat; food, however, is sensitive to heat. The processor must compromise between maximum drying weight and maintenance of food quality.

The Process

The sun removes water from foods growing in fields; cooking and baking also remove water (Potter, 1986). Exposed to the sun, grains dry on the stalk and often require no additional drying for effective preservation. Many spices also are dried naturally. Certain fruits, such as dates and figs, develop high sugar contents while drying on trees. Centuries ago, humans dried thin slices of meat and fish in the air and sun, but the food often spoiled. They discovered ways to use smoke and salt to prevent spoilage.

Sun drying is used less and less, because contamination is a serious problem. Artificial drying with heated air has replaced most sun drying. Food dehydration refers to the almost complete removal of water from foods under controlled conditions that cause minimum, or ideally no other, changes in food properties (Potter, 1986). Most of these foods are dried to a final moisture of about 1% to 5%; examples are dried milk and eggs, potato flakes, instant coffee, and orange juice crystals. These foods can be stored at room temperature for a year or longer. When reconstituted by adding water, the quality of these foods should be very close to the fresh product.

Preservation is the principal, but not only, reason for dehydrating foods. Dehydration decreases the bulk and weight of the food and thus shipping and container costs. The third reason for dehydration is the production of convenience foods, such as instant coffee and instant mashed potatoes which only need water added.

Dehydration basically requires the speedy transfer of heat into the product and of water out of it. Other considerations include the size of the surface of the product. Small particles or thin layers of food hasten the transfer of heat and water. Also, the temperature and velocity of the air, humidity, and atmospheric pressure need to be controlled in the dehydration process. Several basic drying methods are available; the processor must select one based on the type of food to be dried, the quality level desired, and the cost (Potter, 1986). Generally, drying processes that use high temperatures for short times cause less damage to the food than processes that use low temperatures for longer times. Vegetable pieces dried in a well-designed oven for four hours retain higher quality than those sun dried for two days.

Effects on Food

The surface of food dried quickly at high temperatures for short times becomes rigid before the center has dried out. The advantage of this method is that the product will absorb water quickly and resemble the original product, thus pleasing customers who are concerned about the appearance of the product. The disadvantage, however, is that the product is more expensive to package, ship, and store because it is fragile. Products that are dried more slowly at lower temperatures are more dense and easier to package and store better. These dense products often are bought by processors who purchase dehydrated ingredients such as jam for further processing and do not worry about appearance.

Many chemical and physical changes occur during food dehydration that affect the color, flavor, texture, nutritional value, and storage stability. Some of these are specific to the product, while others are the result of the dehydration process that depends upon the composition of the food and the drying method. Although high temperatures are needed in dehydration, they may cause undesirable browning (Klein, 1992). Color deterioration is minimized by dipping cut fruits and vegetables in sodium sulfite. Browning of dehydrated products is generally caused by chemical reactions. Sugar in foods will caramalize if the temperatures are too high. Heat damage also includes reduced rehydration capacity, flavor, and nutritional value. Rehydration often is slowed down because of chemical and physical reactions altering the product's texture. Some loss of flavor can occur, but processors often add flavors from other sources to make the products acceptable to their customers.

Nutritional Value

According to Margen (1992), drying turns such fruits as apples, apricots, bananas, dates, figs, grapes (raisins), peaches, pineapples, and plums (prunes) into concentrated packages of nutrients. Drying reduces the water content usually from 80% to as low as 15%, thus increasing substantially the proportions of minerals, vitamins, and dietary fiber. Of course, sugars and calories also are concentrated, making dried fruits calorie laden.

Some light-colored dried fruits, such as apples, apricots, peaches, and pears, have sulfite preservatives added to avoid browning (Margen, 1992). Processors are required to list preservatives, usually sulfur dioxide, on packages, shipping containers, and bulk bins to alert asthmatics and other people who are allergic to them. Some sulfite-free light-colored dried fruits are now available.

Prunes, which are really dried plums, have been in the spotlight since lowfat menu items have been requested by health-conscious customers. Dried plum purée or dried plum powder is an all-natural fat substitute that enhances rather than diminishes sensory satisfaction. Dried plums are naturally high in fiber, half of which is pectin. During the creaming stage of bakery products, pectin proves to be just as effective as shortening in trapping air. Guidelines for substituting puréed prunes in bakery products, such as muffins and brownies, are usually available from suppliers.

Variations

To compensate for the loss of flavorful fats, several chefs are turning to a new secret ingredient: powder (Parseghian, 1996). Chefs are finding they can cast a spell over diners by using powdered fruits, mushrooms, vegetables, and legumes. The old science of dehydrating foods is coming to the foreground in quantity processing with the new flavored powders. For a tomato product, crispy dried-tomato chips are powdered to give a menu item an intense red color, while spinach powder added to spinach pasta deepens the green color and flavor. Powders, especially bean powders, not only thicken soups and sauces but also intensify the flavor. Powdered porcini, morel, and chanterelle mushroom powders already are very popular. The process of dehydrating intensifies the flavor and sweetness of fruits and vegetables. Herbs and spices, however, tend not to dehydrate well and become bitter when dried.

Concentration and freeze drying of foods are variations of the dehydration process. Both of these methods preserve by removing water and processing the food to protect it from microbial spoilage.

Concentrated

Concentrated foods, such as nonacid fruit and vegetable purées, quickly spoil unless they are processed; sugar syrups and jellies and jams seldom spoil (Potter, 1986). **Concentrated foods** have water drawn from microbial cells by concentrated solutions of sugar or salt, thus preserving the product. Heavy syrups like honey keep indefinitely without refrigeration.

In addition to preservation, the real reason for food concentration is to reduce the weight and bulk of food. Frozen orange juice has replaced fresh orange juice in the United States since it was introduced in 1945. Customers like it so much that production far exceeds all other orange and blended fruit juices. Frozen orange juice is a good example of the complexity of the process.

Buyers should understand the increase in prices of frozen Florida orange juice if a frost occurs in the state. Processors purchase oranges still on the tree from producers; hopefully frost will not damage them (Potter, 1986). Federal and state regulations on the maturity of oranges before harvest focus on solids content and acidity of the juice. Oranges are sent by trucks to the processing plant where they are washed in troughs and then sized and graded. Special machines squeeze the juice from oranges while separating out the oil, which often is bitter. Then the juice is passed through screens to remove pits and pulp. This juice is susceptible to contamination by microorganisms and must be pasteurized before it is concentrated. Fresh orange juice contains about 12% solids, which is increased to approximately 48% in a vacuum evaporator. The concentrate is slush frozen, put into cans, sealed, and solidly frozen in a tunnel freezer before being shipped to customers.

Other products, including concentrated tomato pulp used in spaghetti sauce, soup, or pizza, go through similar processes before reaching customers. Many of these products are sold in bulk rather than in small, expensive cans. Millions of tons of concentrated fruits, juices, vegetables, and milk products are used in foodservice operations. They are a boon to the industry.

Since 1980, bag-in-box packaging developed by Juice Tyme, Inc., has revolutionized many facets of the foodservice industry. Highly concentrated juices and beverages are stored in multilayered, air-proof, light-tight bags that easily connect to automatic dispensers. The products are room temperature and shelf stable for 60 to 90 days, depending upon the product, even after they are connected to dispensing equipment. Beverages are mixed and chilled by the dispenser as they are served. Another advantage is that the products can be located up to 100 feet away from the dispensing site. These products are available in 3- and 5-gallon bag-in-box cartons.

Freeze-Dried

Freeze drying is used to dehydrate expensive liquid foods such as coffee and juices (Potter, 1986). It also is used to dehydrate strawberries, whole shrimp, chicken cubes, mushroom slices, and even large pieces of steak and chops. These foods have a texture and appearance that cannot be preserved by any current drying method. A whole strawberry, for example, is a soft, fragile, almost all-water fruit and would lose its color, flavor, texture, and appearance if dried by any other method. **Freeze drying** prevents food from shrinking by drying it from a solid frozen stage. The principal is that under certain conditions water can go directly from a solid to a gas instead of to a liquid and then a gas. The material is said to *sublime*. The frozen water, or ice, placed in a vacuum chamber under pressure remains frozen because it leaves the solid ice faster than the air can enter the ice and turn it into a liquid. The frozen food remains rigid and the water leaves spaces, resulting in a sponge-like dried structure. Freeze-dried products need specially designed packaging to prevent them from absorbing moisture from the air. The foods reconstitute quickly after the package is opened.

Freeze-dried foods originally were used to feed astronauts on space missions. These foods are lightweight and reconstitute into a very acceptable product. Campers and hikers use them for the same reasons. Freeze-dried coffee, usually referred to as instant coffee, is a staple in many homes. Freeze-dried foods are more expensive than other processed foods and therefore are used only for special occasions.

Specifications

Sample specifications for selected dehydrated products follow.

Raisins

Form: Muscat, seedless

Use: bread and sweet rolls

Quality: U.S. Grade B (Choice)

Pack: 30-pound polyethylene bag inside fiberboard carton

Price: by carton

Orange Juice

Form: frozen, concentrated, unsweetened, calcium enriched

Use: breakfast and snack beverage

Preservation form: frozen, minimum 10°F inside case on delivery in refrigerated truck

Quality: U.S. Grade A

Enrichment: 300 mg. tricalcium phosphate and calcium phosphate per 8 fluid ounces

Dilution: ratio 3/1

Brand: Minute Maid, Coca Cola Co.

Pack: 12/32-ounce cans per case

Price: by case

Figure 9.7. International logo for irradiated foods.

IRRADIATED PRODUCE

Food irradiation is classified as a food additive and therefore is regulated by the FDA. The technical aspect of food irradiation was discussed in chapter 3. Before 1986, irradiation in the United States was restricted to potatoes and onions for prevention of sprouting, and to spices and grains for reducing infestation (Klein, 1992). Then processors were permitted to use low-level irradiation to inhibit growth and maturation of fresh fruits, vegetables, and mushrooms and to eliminate insect infestation. Producers of dehydrated herbs, seeds, spices, and tea also were permitted to use irradiation at a higher level.

A written procedure for each food is required by the FDA to be sure the radiation dose is adequate under commercial processing conditions to achieve its intended effect. The processor also must maintain records for each product that exceed the shelf life of the irradiated food product by one year and make the records available to the FDA. All foods must be labeled with the international logo for irradiated foods, as shown in Figure 9.7, along with either "Treated with radiation" or "Treated by irradiation" and any information required by other regulations.

VALUE-ADDED PRODUCE

Many foodservice managers are going from making all menu items from scratch to value-added products, thus eliminating the prepreparation area in their kitchens. Tasks performed in the operation are taken over by processors.

Value is added to fresh produce at each step in the marketing channel. Value-added is the increase in value caused by both processing or manufacturing and marketing or distributing, exclusive of the cost of materials, packaging, and overhead. According to the Produce Marketing Association (1995):

"Increased demand for ready-to-eat, labor-saving products is propelling the value-added produce industry into the next century. Millions of dollars of fruits and vegetables are processed each year. Other driving forces in the foodservice industry, such as employee turnover, training and employee safety, as well as increased product yields, also are stimulating dramatic growth in this segment of the fresh produce industry."

Benefits

Product yield and employee safety are the most obvious benefits of value-added fresh produce (Produce Marketing Association, 1995). These fresh fruits and vegetables have a 100% yield because they are cleaned, trimmed, cut, and ready to use. Other benefits for foodservice operations include:

- *Portion control and consistent yield.* The same number of portions are in each bag with very little variance.
- *Reduced waste.* Costs of waste disposal are minimal. Packaging wastes are decreased because only poly bags and cardboard cartons are used.
- *Reduced storage space.* Packaging takes up less space in the cooler, resulting in easier inventory control.
- *Product uniformity.* Portion control is simplified.
- *Reduced delivery frequency.* Products require less cooler space and are packaged for maximum shelf life.
- *Consistent supply, quality, and price.* Very little change occurs throughout the year.
- *Reduced training requirements.* The product is ready to use with little or no preparation.
- *Labor redirection.* Employees are not needed for product preparation and can take on other tasks.
- *Employee safety.* Risks for injuries are reduced.

The Industry

The fresh-cut, or value-added, produce processing industry has changed drastically in the last few years. The largest onion processor in the nation, Gills Onions in Oxnard, Calif., wanted to extend the shelf life of fresh whole peeled onions that develop tremendously high plate counts when shipped to the Southeast ("High-tech wash system boosts shelf life," 1995). A voluntary Hazard Analysis Critical Control Point (HACCP) program was developed to monitor bacteria levels in the plant. Various points in the process that could have an influence on quality were identified. Based on the results of the analysis, wash water quality was targeted. A water chemistry control system was installed, and the shelf life of the product doubled. Sanitation in the plant has top priority; the plant (Figure 9.8) looks like a hospital surgery suite. Employees wear white uniforms with long sleeves, a white hair cover, and plastic gloves when handling the onions. Gills now has sliced, diced, and puréed onions of fine, medium, and coarse grinds.

A real breakthrough in technology was the production of "The Original Fresh Cut Artichoke Bottom," touting a shelf life of 15 days by L & O, a fresh-cut producer in Carmel, Calif. This product is marketed to white tablecloth restaurants and small upscale grocery stores ("Fresh trimmed artichoke hearts debut," 1996). The Odello brothers raised high-quality, fresh artichokes from their 300-acre operation for 70

Figure 9.8.   Employees checking onions that are being washed with chemically balanced water.

Source: From *Fresh Cut Magazine for Value-Added Produce.* Courtesy of Joseph Hopkins & Associates, Kingwood, TX.

years. A food technologist and processing consultant helped to perfect the process and set up the facility. Specialized equipment was designed, fabricated, and inspected for areas where bacteria might possibly accumulate. L & O's food safety and sanitation program is patterned after the total quality management concept and has a full-time quality assurance manager monitoring bacteria levels at all times. The artichokes are trimmed in two stages. First the stem and leaves are removed, leaving the heart. Each heart is then hand-carved to its final shape and size, which chefs like because the artichoke heart has a fresh kitchen-prepared look. After a triple wash, the product is vacuum packed and sealed in a bag specially designed to allow respiration to keep the artichoke hearts fresh longer.

Another fresh-cut produce company, Freshway Foods of Sidney, Ohio, is committed to using the HACCP program (Tilton, 1996). The company delivers about 200 different items to foodservice operators in 12 states. A co-owner says HACCP is a way of life at Freshway Foods. It has helped improve sanitation and hygiene practices tremendously and has raised the level of awareness of food safety for every person in the organization. The company's goal is a proactive approach to safety and quality. Quality, food safety, and plant safety teams meet weekly on company time. Everybody in the organization has the same goal. The company has had no product recalls, and HACCP has helped extend the shelf life, appearance, and quality of products. HACCP starts on the dock where the temperatures of produce are taken, and samples are sent to a lab. The products then are put through a complete sensory evaluation test before leaving the dock and going to the processing line. Once produce has been processed and packaged for shipping to a final destination, the same care is taken to assure the quality will still be there upon arrival at the foodservice operation. The company has a fleet of refrigerated trucks and works through a network of distributors to deliver the product to the end user.

Not only has the ready-cut processing industry increased in size; the ready-cut equipment industry is following suit. In the 1995 Processing Equipment Buyer's Guide, a feature in the *Fresh Cut Magazine for Value-Added Produce* (1995), 10 pages were devoted to companies selling ready-cut equipment. Vegetable slicers with a per-hour output up to 23,000 pounds are available. The Opti-Sort II is an efficient piece of equipment used by Valley Fresh Distributing, Inc., in Colorado to eliminate the manual sorting of baby carrots ("Blowing away carrot defects," 1995). Carrots come in from the field and are washed, cleaned, and put into refrigerated storage before their transfer to the packing shed for sizing. They then go into the cutters and emerge in two-inch pieces. The pieces are peeled and polished into small peeled carrots sometimes erroneously called baby carrots. Finally, the carrots go through the Opti-Sort II in which they are examined for defects prior to packaging. The Opti-Sort II achieves consistent high-quality sorting because it inspects all surfaces of the carrot to detect defects. The equipment is washed down each day and is easy to maintain. It also has the unique capacity to handle up to 30,000 pounds of produce per hour.

Equipment is available for bagging, and closing, holding, and sealing bags. In addition to the Opti-Sort II, equipment that specifically cuts cabbage, makes carrot sticks, peels onions, cores and trims lettuce, and accomplishes many other chores is on the market (Figure 9.9). Many companies specialize in equipment and packaging materials. Much research is devoted to developing equipment.

Purchasing

If foodservice managers decide to cut labor costs by purchasing fresh-cut produce, buyers must choose a supplier that keeps up with innovations in those products (Gunn, 1995a). The bottom line is that buyers have to select suppliers by how quickly they get the product to them and how long the products last after receiving them. Regardless of which supplier the buyer chooses, assuring that all needs are met usually means building solid supplier/buyer relationships that flourish through both good times and bad.

The Supplier

The Produce Marketing Association (1995) has organized fresh-cut produce suppliers into these categories:

- *On-site*—companies that process their own products for distribution to customers
- *Local*—companies located in your town with a service area generally less than 100 miles in radius

Figure 9.9. Various types of equipment used in the fresh-cut industry.

Source: From *Fresh Cut Magazine for Value-Added Produce.* Courtesy of Joseph Hopkins & Associates, Kingwood, TX.

- *Regional*—companies with a service/delivery radius of 500 or more miles that usually provide a full line of products and often have a more extensive line of pack sizes than local processors
- *National*—companies located in or near major growing areas that ship products nationwide on commercial transportation to distributors who sell to foodservice operators. Many offer extensive product lines and state-of-the-art processing and packaging systems. A recent trend is for national processors to open regional centers to minimize time in transit and ensure maximum freshness.

The Buyer

The Produce Marketing Association (1995) offers this advice to buyers of fresh-cut produce:

All processors should be carefully evaluated for raw-product quality and sanitation systems. The facility must be clean and cold and food handling equipment sanitized to ensure safe products with acceptable shelf life. Ask about the company's food safety program, microbiological testing procedures, and sanitation guidelines. Also ask about the amount of time products spend in the distribution chain, from packaging to delivery.

The buyer is typically faced with a pair of simple options; regional or national fresh-cut processors (Gunn, 1995b). Regional processors offer personalized service and are often accused of servicing customers to the limit; national processors, often referred to as source processors, say the consistent quality and availability they offer is as important. Regional processors have vegetables shipped to them from West Coast sources and then process and deliver them to customers within a few hundred miles radius. National fresh-cut processors, usually located in all-season western growing regions, have improved technologies for handling and shipping and can send their products all over the United States. This means their processed and fragile products often spend several days en route. While regional processors talk of home-town service and freshness, national processors tout their quality, consistency, volume, and price. Regional processors call their service just-in-time delivery (Gunn, 1995a). They keep tight reins on their inventory and process and deliver fresh-cut produce daily, which also keeps the customer's inventory very low.

Receiving and Inspecting

Value-added products should have an overall fresh appearance when received from the wholesaler (Produce Marketing Association, 1995). If the produce is discolored, wilted, or slimy, it should not be accepted. Employees should be taught how to judge good quality products and recognize when products should not be used. They also should be on the lookout for the following signs of quality loss.

- Cauliflower—dark spots, wet florets
- Shredded cabbage—wet and slimy; excess liquid in the bottom of the bag
- Diced bell peppers—wet and slimy; bag filled with liquid
- Salad mix—brown or reddish-pink color
- Sliced/diced onions—wet and slimy; bag filled with liquid
- Cut carrots (shreds, sticks, coins)—wet and slimy; bag filled with liquid
- Broccoli florets—brown spots, slimy florets
- Chopped/shredded lettuce—brown or reddish-pink color; wet and slimy; excess liquid
- Sliced mushrooms—brown and slimy

Storing and Handling

Value-added vegetables and fruits should be stored at 32°F to 36°F with moderate relative humidity (Produce Marketing Association, 1995). Precut mushrooms, however, should be kept dry. Like all fresh produce, value-added produce should be stored immediately in the proper environment to ensure quality and shelf life. For best quality, value-added produce should be stored in the cooler in original containers and not removed until ready to use.

Leafy products, such as shredded lettuce and salad mix, are susceptible to oxidation if exposed to air. Bags must be handled with care to avoid rips or punctures. If only part of a bag is used, the air should be squeezed out before resealing. Many products have an expiration date, or shelf life information stamped on the individual packages or shipping carton.

Future of Value-Added Produce

The fresh-cut produce industry is still in its infancy and is growing by leaps and bounds. The biggest challenge for the industry is developing the technology for fresh-cut fruit. New peeling and cutting machinery for fresh melons, citrus, and other products promises to transform the emerging fresh-cut fruit field from a cottage industry into a high-volume business that offers customers a true value-added product. Concomitant with this evolution is the development of packaging that would help increase the shelf life of fruit. Because the foodservice industry is customer driven, managers need to put more emphasis on the nutrition value of their menu. Foodservice managers also will be looking at just-in-time purchasing of fresh-cut products.

Fresh-Cut Fruit

Fruit is considered the new and final frontier in the fresh-cut industry. The prediction is that foodservice will spearhead the advancement of fresh-cut fruit (Unrein, 1995). Foodservice managers have been asking for fresh-cut fruit to use as garnishes on buffet platters. Research is focusing on fresh-cut fruit products, processing techniques, packaging, and temperature control. Producers are testing new ways to maintain shelf life for at least 10 days; the industry is committed to not using preservatives. Many processors predict that these items will be available within the next two or three years, but others believe that availability will come sooner. The industry is committed to not using preservatives.

The Washington Apple Commission is pursuing fresh-cut apple wedges and is supporting research at Washington State University. Sales to schools, especially elementary schools, would increase tremendously; whole apples are seldom served because eating an apple is difficult for children who are missing teeth. Research at WSU is still focused on analyzing different treatments that prevent browning without using sulfites.

Already, longer-lasting cantaloupe, honeydew melons, and pineapple cuts are appearing on the market. Stone fruits, such as sliced tree-ripe peaches and nectarines, are breaking new ground in the value-added produce business (Zind, 1995). The use of fresh-cut fruit is growing substantially at the foodservice level. The sales volume in hotels and country clubs of whole peeled melons and melon balls has increased tremendously in the past year. Currently these products last about two days on the shelf, but with new packaging they should soon last four days.

Packaging

Packaging has a vital role in prolonging shelf life and maintaining overall product quality of value-added produce. The object of a good package is to create conditions around the product that are conducive to maintaining its quality. What constitutes proper conditions for a given product depends on its physiology and tolerances. A measured amount of product needs to be put in the bag to permit sufficient surface area for oxygen and carbon dioxide gas exchange (Zagory, 1995). The bag film must be the correct thickness, and temperature must be maintained within the limits of the product and package tolerance. The fruit must be maintained at 38°F to 39°F throughout the production and distribution process. The bag must be strong, clear, flexible, and impervious to leaks. Ideally, bags should be heat-sealed instead of using metal clips or ties which could pose a safety hazard. In addition to film bags, value-added fruits may be packed in plastic containers and glass jars.

The bags and other containers bear a **Best-if-Used-By** date intended to tell the buyer how long the product will retain the best flavor or quality. It allows for two weeks shelf life after packaging fresh-cut products. It is not a safety date, but rather a useful guideline. Some foods may deteriorate more quickly and other foods might last longer than the times suggested. Food products can be eaten after the Best-if-Used-By date if the product has been properly stored and handled and the container is in good condition. For best results, the USDA recommends following the first in-first out inventory control method.

Fresh fruit processing has been limited to natural juice or preservative-based applications because of product perishability. Processors who have made their mark in fresh-cut vegetables are hoping to bring precut fruit in a dry state to the market using the patented FreshHold packaging technology (Zind, 1995). A Fresh Western Marketing Inc. subsidiary is licensing the technology to shippers who will use it for cut melons, strawberries, peaches, and apples. This packaging will allow the fruits to be shipped without juice and will use no preservatives, allowing a totally natural fruit to be shipped. Initial tests gave the products a 10-day shelf life.

Managers at the Dole Food Company, Inc. decided to package fresh-cut pineapple in ripe, refrigerated, ready-to-eat spears and chunks because they realized that foodservice managers like the convenience and time savings of precut fruit, especially since many thought preparing the whole pineapple was difficult ("Dole gets fresh with cut pineapple," 1996). They also preferred the healthy advantage of no added preservatives, sugar, or coloring. The new fresh-cut pineapple line was all part of a corporate strategy to capitalize on prepacked fruit and vegetable products that added value for managers and margins on the bottom line. Dole had to retool packaging lines at its Honolulu packing operation. Pineapple was being cut, bagged, and sealed in a clear, new, flexible package in 12-ounce, 16-ounce, and 5-pound sizes and shipped to distributors shortly after harvest when they began to experience problems with their packaging.

Since the original packaging was not reliable, Dole started from ground zero to find a new packaging supplier. Dole management finally decided after visiting many companies to use Duralam, Inc., a packaging company in Appleton, Wis. Once the decision was made, they worked out the details with Duralam. After years of experience in marketing pineapples, Dole knew that customers need an unobstructed view of the product to reassure them it is ripe and ready to eat. Because the pineapple was packed with no preservatives, shelf life was naturally limited. The highly perishable product required a film structure that would lock in freshness and flavor without leakage or odor transfer. Also, high-quality printing impressions featuring the bold red, blue, and yellow Dole logo were important to create impact at the point of sale. The packaging also had to carry important sales, preparation, and storage information. At the time Dole switched packaging suppliers, Duralam had a limited supply of raw materials available, but it could maintain an inventory in a just-in-time delivery environment.

Just-in-Time Purchasing

The objective of just-in-time (JIT) purchasing in foodservice is to purchase products as needed for production and immediate consumption by the customer without having to store and record it in inventory. The cost of the products is included in daily food costs and capital is not tied up in inventory. Receiving clerks check the food in and then immediately take it to the areas in which it will be used. For example, chopped lettuce, shredded cabbage, and diced fruit go directly to the unit in which employees assemble salads or to the production unit where chefs use fresh-cut vegetables in stir-fry and other menu items. The need for large refrigerated areas for storing fresh produce is eliminated. The ideal situation would be to have reach-in refrigerators in the units using fresh-cut produce for temporary storage until the product is used. More and more suppliers of value-added products are offering daily deliveries or a minimum of two or three deliveries a week to customers.

Customer Trends

Whole-meal selling has become the successful province of quick-service restaurants (McKee, 1995). Supermarket operators are missing an opportunity for sales by not suggesting menus that will meet the customer's desires. Customers want more information about produce, and value-added processors should supply it both to retail and foodservice operators. The 5 A Day program is a great start, but our increasingly health-conscious population cries out for more nutritional good news and direction. The goal of the national 5 A Day program is to increase the per capita consumption of fruits and vegetables in the U.S. from 3.5 to 5 servings per day by the year 2000.

More variety in fruit and vegetable mixtures should be considered by processors, and suggestions for using them (in salads or stir-frys, for example) should be available to the buyer. Salad mixes now on the market include rainbow, caesar, broccoli slaw, tossed green, and baby greens. Salads are now packaged in 25-pound bags for restaurants and institutions. The future of value-added produce holds a world of promise. Beyond the mastery of cutting and blending fruits and vegetables and the search for long shelf life while retaining flavor, texture, and nutrients, the next area of growth in value-added products includes preparation of legumes, grains, and pastas (McKee, 1995). Presoaked, refrigerated, dry beans are already available. Can blanched pastas, presoaked bulgur wheat, and partially cooked potatoes be far behind? Who knows, maybe edible packaging is in the future.

Purchasing for profit becomes a reality when value-added produce products are used in a foodservice operation. Labor costs decrease, and employees are no longer required for preparation of vegetables and fruits. Portion control becomes more exact because the number of portions in each package remains constant. Food waste is minimized when everything in the package is edible. Packaging waste decreases in volume as waste disposal costs drop. The size of storage space can be minimized with just-in-time purchasing. Storage space is expensive; perhaps that space could be used more profitably in the dining area. Finally, capital tied up in inventory can be invested and earn interest. The result is that the savings from using value-added produce can add to the bottom line of the foodservice operation.

SUMMARY

Fresh produce is perishable and expensive when out-of-season, but processing has made it available year-round by increasing shelf life. The processor has an essential role in the marketing channel. Purchasing processed fruits and vegetables can be a challenge for the buyer because 156 different grades, many not official, are available. USDA grade standards and FDA standards of identity, quality, and fill can be used by the buyer as a measuring stick for unofficially graded products. Packaging of processed produce is still in a state of flux; sizes of containers and types of packaging materials have not been standardized. However, regulations for labeling the content and nutritional value of the products are controlled by federal laws. Food can be preserved to make it safe for human consumption by refrigeration, freezing, canning, dehydration, and irradiation.

Refrigeration is considered minimal processing for most fresh produce and is a temporary means of preservation. Shelf life of refrigerated produce is short. Quick freezing requires specialized equipment to minimize physical, biochemical, and microbiological changes. Freezing preserves the appearance, color, aroma, and flavor of vegetables and fruit. Heat processing, or canning, is the most common method for preserving produce. Canning is a highly mechanized industry. Canneries generally are located in or near the fields, permitting immediate processing after harvesting. Dehydration, or drying, is a means of preservation that decreases bulk and weight and eliminates water which could be used by microorganisms for growth. The process is completed under controlled conditions. Food irradiation is classified as a food additive and is regulated by the FDA.

Increased demand for ready-to-eat, labor-saving products is propelling the value-added produce industry into the next century. Value-added fresh fruits and vegetables are eliminating the preparation area in kitchens because the tasks performed in the operation are taken over by processors. As a result, labor costs in the foodservice can be decreased, portion control becomes more exact, food waste is minimized, and just-in-time purchasing is possible.

REFERENCES

Blowing away carrot defects. (1995). *Fresh Cut Magazine for Value-Added Produce, 3* (6), 12, 44.
Catalog of food specifications: A technical assistance manual. (1992). (Vol. I, 5th ed.). Dunnellon, FL: Food Industry Services Group in cooperation with the U.S. Department of Agriculture, Food & Nutrition Service.

Dole gets fresh with cut pineapple. (1996). *Fresh Cut Magazine for Value-Added Produce, 4*(6), 24–25.

Fresh trimmed artichoke hearts debut. (1996). *Fresh Cut Magazine for Value-Added Produce, 4*(8), 14–16.

Frozen Food Roundtable. (1992). *Frozen food handling and merchandising.* Washington, DC.: Hogan & Hartson.

Gunn, J. (1995a). Regional producers customize fresh-cut operations. *Produce Business,* January, 38, 40, 42.

Gunn, J. (1995b). National fresh-cut processors extol consistent quality. *Produce Business,* March, 34–38.

High-tech wash system boosts shelf life. (1995). *Fresh Cut Magazine for Value-Added Produce, 3*(6), 30–31.

Klein, B. P. (1992). Fruits and vegetables. In Bowers, J. (Ed.), *Food theory and applications* (2nd ed.) (pp. 687–766). New York: Macmillan.

Kotschevar, L. H., & Donnelly, R. (1999). *Quantity food purchasing* (5th ed.). Upper Saddle River, NJ: Merrill/Prentice Hall.

Margen, S., & Editors of the University of California at Berkeley Wellness Letter. (1992). *The wellness encyclopedia of food and nutrition.* New York: Rebus.

McKee, M. (1995). How far do consumers want us to go? *Fresh Cut Magazine for Value-Added Produce, 3*(6), 38–39, 42.

1995 processing equipment buyer's guide. (1995). *Fresh Cut Magazine for Value-Added Produce, 3*(6), 14, 16, 18, 20–24, 26–27, 32–35.

Parseghian, P. (1996). The power of powders leaves culinarians spellbound. *Nation's Restaurant News, 30*(33), 27.

Potter, N. N. (1986). *Food science* (4th ed.). Westport, CT: AVI Publishing Co.

Produce Marketing Association. (1995). *The foodservice guide to fresh produce.* Newark, DE: Author.

Putnam, J. J., & Allshouse, J. E. (1994). *Food consumption, prices, and expenditures, 1970–93.* Statistical Bulletin No. 915. Washington, DC: Food and Economics Division, Economic Research Service, U.S. Department of Agriculture.

Tilton, J. L. (1996). HACCP improves safety, quality. *Fresh-Cut Magazine for Value-Added Produce, 4*(4), 14–16, 18–19.

The Almanac of the Canning, Freezing, Preserving Industries. (1995). (78th ed.). Westminster, MD: Edward E. Judge & Sons, Inc.

Unrein, J. (1995, April 10). Precut offers promise for foodservice. *The Packer.*

Zagory, D. (1995). Packaging California's diverse fresh-cut products. *Fresh Cut Magazine for Value-Added Produce, 3*(6), 28–29.

Zind, T. (1995, March 13). Technology expands frontier. *The Packer.*

Meats

Meat Safety
Contamination Prevention
Summary
References

The third level of the Food Guide Pyramid has two food groups: the meat, poultry, fish, dry beans, eggs, and nuts group, as highlighted in Figure 10.1, and the milk, yogurt, and cheese group (Plate 4). Not too long ago, the meat group probably would have been the base of the pyramid because many people thought a meal was not complete unless meat was on the table. Meat usually is the center-of-the-plate menu item around which the meal is planned. In the last few years, however, the lower fat content and cost of poultry and fish have made them very popular. In addition, vegetarianism has increased and grains and beans have been replacing meat menu items. The Food Guide Pyramid suggests two to three 3-ounce servings daily of meat, poultry, fish, dry beans, eggs, or nuts. Of all of these, meat has the greatest amount of government control and is the most expensive menu item. From large restaurant chains to small hospitals, foodservice buyers need a lot of information about meat. In the overall change of dietary habits, nutritionists have declared that meat is still

Figure 10.1.   Food Guide Pyramid with meat, poultry, fish, dry beans, eggs, and nut group highlighted.

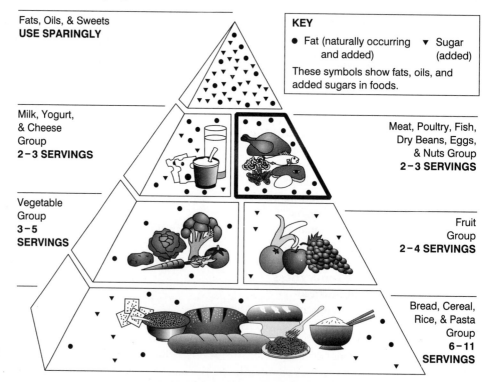

an important nutrient component of menus, but quantities should be in moderation. In this text, nuts and dried beans have been included in the fruit and vegetable chapters even though they are nutritionally similar to foods in this group.

SIGNIFICANCE OF THE MEAT INDUSTRY

The livestock and meat industry has had a significant role in the development of this nation for nearly 500 years (National Live Stock and Meat Board, 1991). This role can be viewed from an historic, economic, and health perspective. Agriculture is the largest industry in the nation today.

Historic Perception

Columbus in the 1490s brought the first cattle with him on his second trip to the West Indies (National Live Stock and Meat Board, 1991). Soon after that, cattle from Spanish stock were brought by ship to Florida and Texas. These cattle quickly acclimated to the hot and dry regions and grew rapidly on any kind of forage. Before railroads, cattle were driven to packing plants near population centers. The first cattle were transported by rail from Abilene, Kan., in 1867. People wanted beef and with the advent of railroads, beef became more available.

Hogs were first brought to Florida by Spanish explorers in 1539 (National Live Stock and Meat Board, 1991). Pork was the most common meat in this country from the early 1500s to the 1800s. The British shipped hogs to the colonies in the early 1600s, and settlers in Virginia were supplying ham and bacon to England. The National Pork Producers Council in its *Pork Industry Progress* brochure serve up a page of "Hog Trivia":

> *How did Uncle Sam come to represent the U.S.Government?*
> "During the War of 1812, a New York pork packer named Uncle Sam Wilson shipped a boatload of several hundred barrels of pork to U.S. troops. Each barrel was stamped 'U.S.' On the docks, it quickly became bantered about that the U.S. stood for Uncle Sam, whose large pork shipment looked to be enough to feed the entire army. Thus did Uncle Sam come to represent the U.S. Government itself."

> *Did you know that . . .*
> "In ancient China fresh pork enjoyed royal status. Around 4000 B.C., the Chinese people were ordered to raise and breed hogs—by a royal decree from the Emperor of China."

> "As much beloved as fresh pork is in America, it is not the United States, but China, that is the number one producer and consumer of fresh pork in the world."

Sheep also were brought to the New World on Columbus' second voyage in 1493 (National Live Stock and Meat Board, 1991). Spanish stock breeders established breeding centers in the Caribbean Islands and Mexico and then in Florida. Sheep raising spread because it was easy and the animals could be used for both food and wool.

Economic Perception

The production of livestock for food is important in the nation's economy (National Livestock and Meat Board, 1991). Cattle and sheep production give cash value to land that would otherwise be unproductive. Cattle, hog, and sheep production requires input from other parts of the economy, giving cash value to croplands and supporting millions of jobs in addition to the farmers and ranchers. Export of meat, meat products, and breeding animals helps to offset the imbalance of trade which the United States suffers. Also, meat makes an important contribution to the health of the nation because it supplies several essential nutrients.

MEAT MENU TRENDS

The Beef Board and Beef Industry Council conducted a $42 million consumer ad campaign to bring home a powerful message to foodservice customers: "Beef, it's what's for dinner." The National Pork Council also conducted a campaign emphasizing "Pork, the other white meat." The American Lamb Council has not developed a logo but has been emphasizing the versatility of lamb in the American diet. The pressure is on to update beef, veal, pork, and lamb entrées without masking them (Ryan, 1994).

Beef

Customers still go to their favorite restaurants for steak, a fact borne out by recent surveys showing that despite economic downturns, steak sales have remained constant. Beef has always been king of meats on both commercial and institutional menus. Americans love real beef—steak and roast beef most of all. On a recent *Restaurants & Institutions* menu census, the hamburger and the cheeseburger were ranked No. 1 and No. 2 best sellers in the sandwich category (Ryan, 1994). According to operators polled in this national survey, the hamburger is offered on 80.6% of all sandwich menus and the cheeseburger is on 79.1%. Even the Japanese, whose appetite has been whetted by the hundreds of McDonald's units in their country, are adopting Americans' fondness for beef.

Since the 1970s, the health craze has been as much a part of American culture as apple pie. Up to the mid '70s, beef Wellington was on the menu of every fine Continental restaurant in America (Ryan, 1994). This rich creation of filet of beef covered with pâté de foie gras wrapped in puff pastry and baked went seriously out of fashion during that time. The Dickens Inn Restaurant and English Pub in Philadelphia now offer beef Wellington with Madeira sauce, and it is the number one best seller. Many customers believe that when they dine out for a special occasion, they can eat what they want and diet tomorrow.

In most cases, however, center-of-the-plate meat entrées today have a lighter, leaner profile. Portions are smaller in response to the public's growing awareness of the U.S. Department of Agriculture (USDA) Dietary Guidelines. Lawry's, The Prime Rib restaurant in California has added to its menu a six-ounce portion of its best-selling prime rib (Dube, 1991). Other popular beef menu items include London broil, pot roast, chicken-fried steak, and barbecued brisket. Signature steak salads have become popular recently; cheese steak salad, an off-shoot of the famous Philadelphia cheese steak sandwich, or a barbecued beef flank steak salad are only two of the salads that have gained recent popularity (Straus, 1992).

Pork

Pork, dubbed "the other white meat" by the National Pork Producers Council, has hit the big time. American consumers are buying pork in record amounts at both the retail and foodservice levels. Thanks to new breeding techniques, pork is leaner and safer to eat than ever before. The old problem of trichinosis, caused by a microscopic parasite that resides as larvae in infected animals or humans, has been virtually eliminated in the U.S. pork industry (Carr, 1992). This means that pork no longer needs to be cooked to the well-done stage to ensure wholesomeness. Today's pork can be cooked quickly to medium doneness, at an internal temperature of 155°F to 160°F, when it is still tender, juicy, and slightly pink in the center.

Pork has a mild flavor that blends well with ethnic menu items. Consider pork bourguignon or pork chops Dijonnaise (French), pork kebabs Anasazi or Pueblo green-chile stew (Southwestern), teriyaki chops or mandarin orange pork salad (Asian), ham biscuits or Louisiana pork Creole (Southern), chile-marinated pork chops or pork tortilla soup (Mexican). Pork can stand up to hearty flavors expected from grilled foods, such as spicy marinades and barbecue sauces, zippy dry spice rubs and sauces, and hickory or mesquite smoke. Some of the most popular meat products in the world are made from pork, from the all-American hotdog to spicy pepperoni, and in between, prosciutto and pancetta, kielbasa and chorizo, braunschweiger and bratwurst, and salami, mortadella, and bologna. Ham, bacon, and sausage are processed pork specialties. The Food and Drug Administration's (FDA) standards of identity for cooked meats, cured meats, unsmoked and smoked sausage, fresh, smoked, and cooked, and luncheon meats, loaves, and jellied products are in the Appendix.

Lamb

Classic menus in fine-dining restaurants often feature rack of lamb, traditionally considered one of the most elegant center-of-the-plate entrées and one of the most expensive. Other less expensive cuts, including leg of lamb, ground lamb, and top round, are economical, versatile, and lean. The Middle East influence on ethnic menu items has increased the use of lamb. Examples are Middle Eastern lamb burgers with apricots, pine nuts, cinnamon, and nutmeg or Greek lamb kebabs, called *souvlaki,* or hickory-smoked barbecue lamb ribs. Lamb pita pizza, a combination of onions, oregano, and feta cheese with ground lamb, all spread on lightly browned pita bread and then baked, is another example of lamb's versatility (American Lamb Council, Undated).

Game Meat

Game meats are appearing on menus more each year. According to the American Deer Farmers Association, Americans are eating 30% more venison today than they were a few years ago (Johnson, 1994). Customers are curious and game animals, such as bear, kangaroo, and ostrich, are an exciting alternative to traditional meats (Figure 10.2). Customers also are concerned about nutrition. Most game meats are low in cholesterol and calories, with almost no calories from fat. **Wild game** is defined as all animals and birds that are hunted (Ursin, 1995). The wild game available

Figure 10.2.   Wild game guide.

Know Your Game

Deer: (Venison.) Includes various species, including elk, moose and caribou. Dark, lean meat with very little marbling and robust flavor. Most common commercial cuts: loin, leg and rack.

Antelope: (Also venison.) Deer-like members of cattle family. Fine-grained meat with stronger flavor than deer. High moisture content; almost no fat.

Wild boar: Close relative to the domesticated pig—not to be confused with *javelina,* a native, wild non-swine pig of the pecary family which is illegal to hunt or sell. Lean with distinctive, rich flavor.

Buffalo: (Also bison.) Wild ox similar to beef. Lean but juicy meat. The hump is considered a delicacy.

Musk ox: Arctic ruminant resembling a cross between ox and sheep. Well-marbled, moist meat with mild flavor.

Bear: Strong-flavored, lean red meat. The paw is one of the Eight Treasures of traditional Chinese cuisine.

Rabbit: Various species. Mild, lean and tender flesh. Similar in flavor to chicken. Easily absorbs cooking fat and flavors.

Kangaroo: Usually from Australia. Very lean meat with strong, full-bodied flavor.

Ostrich: Young birds only (they can live up to 80 years). Protein- and iron-rich red meat with texture of beef.

Duck: 3 to 5 pounds. Many dark-feathered breeds. Dark, lean meat.

Woodcock: Prized French delicacy with 2-foot wingspan. Cooked with entrails intact.

Pheasant: 2 to 5 pounds. Very lean meat, requires moist heat or larding.

Quail: Small species of pheasant. Dark lean breast meat (1 to 2 ounces). Benefits from larding.

Pigeon: ½ to 1 pound. Includes squab, wood pigeon, rock dove and ring dove. Extra-lean dark meat. All but very young birds require larding.

Source: From "Know Your Game" by B. A. Johnson, 1994, *Restaurants & Institutions 104*(29), p. 94. Used by permission.

for commercial foodservice operations in this country usually is not wild because many wild animals are protected and no edible part of any native game animal or bird killed in the wild can be sold for any purpose. For example, kangaroos and bears are specifically raised for the foodservice industry. Much of the game served in foodservice has been farm-raised and often is fed on grain and soy proteins, giving the meat a milder flavor than that from animals fed on juniper berries and yucca roots. The USDA is not required to inspect wild game for wholesomeness because it is not listed in the Federal Meat Act or Federal Poultry Act. Meat not regulated by the USDA automatically is under the jurisdiction of the FDA, which does not inspect raw meat. Anyone selling game meat should submit it for a fee to the USDA for inspection; otherwise the supplier is subject to punitive action from the FDA.

An example of a game meat that is gaining popularity in the United States is the ostrich, dubbed "the other red meat." Ostriches were first commercially domesticated in Cape Colony, South Africa, in the mid-nineteenth century. Restaurateurs are discovering that ostrich is a red-meat alternative for their health-conscious customers who worry about the fat and calories of beef (Somerville, 1996). Ostrich has more in common with the cow than with poultry. The meat of the flightless bird is deep cherry-red with a rich, beefy taste. It has more protein and iron with less fat and fewer calories than beef. The largest bird in the world, with a height of 8 feet or taller, the ostrich weighs as much as 450 pounds. It yields about 75 pounds of meat and 14 square feet of leather, which is used by the shoe and boot industry.

STRUCTURE OF MEAT

Foodservice buyers of meat need to be able to look at a subprimal cut of meat and understand how it can be portioned, cooked, served, and priced to meet the needs of customers. To gain this knowledge, the buyer needs to know something about the physical and chemical composition of meats.

Physical Composition

The word *meat* refers to the edible parts of a carcass, which contains four major tissues: muscle, adipose tissue, bone, and connective tissue. Muscle from cattle becomes beef or veal on the menu. From hogs come pork and further processed products such as ham, bacon, or sausage. From sheep comes lamb.

Skeletal muscle is the major component of the carcass. Muscle consists of bundles of various length fibers interspersed with connective tissue and fat and surrounded by additional connective tissue. The size of the bundles vary in different muscles of the same animal and in different species. Small fiber bundles give a fine-grained meat. Leg and shoulder muscles used for walking and strength have more connective tissue and less tender meat than those in the back, rib, and loin. Other muscles, such as those in the shoulder nearest the rib, in the rump, and in the upper part of the hind leg, provide moderately tender meat.

The amount of fat stored in adipose tissue varies and that quantity of adipose tissue in meat animals increases rapidly with age. Meat contains three types of adipose tissue:

- subcutaneous, or external, located just beneath the skin and often referred to as *finish*
- seam, or intermuscular, located between the muscles
- marbling, or intramuscular, deposited within the muscles and critical to meat quality

As an animal ages, the amount of fat increases and water decreases. External fat and seam fat protect the carcass from shrinking during chilling and help keep the shape of the cuts. Excessive amounts of these fats are not desirable. Increasing quantities of intramuscular fat is partially related to animal age but is almost entirely determined by genetics. Marbling helps make meat juicier, more flavorful, and tender.

Bone, a type of connective tissue that becomes ossified, contains cells and structures and forms the skeleton of the animal. The skeleton protects vital organs and provides a framework for holding up muscles. Bones serve as an indicator of maturity; the USDA uses degree of ossification in animal bones in assigning grades to beef, lamb, veal, and pork. Bones from cattle, sheep, and hogs are almost identical in shape but differ in size.

Chemical Composition

Meat is considered nutrient dense because it supplies a large amount of nutrients to the diet compared to calories. When 5 to 7 ounces of lean meat, trimmed of fat, are eaten every day as recommended by the USDA Human Nutrition Information Service, meat easily fits into diets for preventing and treating heart disease (National Live Stock and Meat Board, 1991). The fibers in lean meat contain approximately 72% water, 20% protein, 7% fat, and 1% carbohydrates, minerals, vitamins, flavoring substances, and other compounds.

Water

Adipose tissue contains little water; the fatter the animal, the lower the water content of its carcass or meat. Beef muscle from mature and fat animals may contain only 45% water but young and lean veal muscle may contain as much as 72% water. Texture, color, and flavor of muscle are affected by the amount of water in muscle tissue (National Live Stock and Meat Board, 1991).

Protein

The protein in meat is high in both quality and quantity (National Live Stock and Meat Board, 1991). Animal foods contain all of the essential amino acids, the basic building blocks of proteins, in amounts and proportions that can be recycled into body protein. Beef, veal, pork, and lamb have high biological value. A cooked, trimmed, boneless, 3-ounce portion of meat contains approximately 25 grams of protein, while lean ground beef contains 21 grams.

Fat

The American Heart Association recommends that no more than 30%, or 600 calories in a 2,000 calorie diet, of the total daily caloric intake should come from fat. Fats are important components of a balanced diet and add flavor, appetite appeal, and satiety to foods. One gram of fat equals 9 calories as compared to 4 calories for one gram of protein or carbohydrate. Fats provide essential fatty acids to the diet, including saturated fats, which are solid at room temperature and tend to raise blood cholesterol levels, and unsaturated fats, which are usually liquid at room temperature and are thought to help lower blood cholesterol levels. Serum, or blood, cholesterol is manufactured by the liver and circulates within the body through the bloodstream. Serum cholesterol is not made from dietary sources, but those fats influence its synthesis. Cholesterol is associated with fats because it is a fat-like sterol in chemical structure and is found only in animal tissues. The way individuals manufacture and respond to dietary sources is influenced by genetics and other physiological factors (National Live Stock and Meat Board, 1991).

Carbohydrates

Approximately 50% of the carbohydrates are stored as glycogen (sugar) in the animal's liver, and the other 50% are in the muscles, blood (usually as glucose), and other tissues, organs, and glands. Excessive animal stress or severe weather changes prior to slaughter may decrease the glycogen, causing a higher muscle pH (less acid) after the carcass is chilled. As a result, a condition called **dark cutting** can occur, turning the meat to a color range from barely evident to black. The dark cutting condition does not affect the eating quality of the cooked meat, but it is aesthetically unacceptable to the customer. Meat may be graded one level lower because of this condition.

Dark cutting meat is a rare occurrence in beef—perhaps 2%—and even rarer in pork and lamb carcasses. Packers and retailers must severely discount prices to sell "dark cutters." Therefore, stress and rough handling of animals are minimized prior to slaughter. After cooking, the color of the meat is the same as that from animals without the condition; thus, some foodservice operations use the meat. One caution is that dark cutting meat has a short shelf life when it is held fresh or thawed and should be chilled until ready for cooking.

Minerals

Meat is a major source of three important minerals: iron, zinc, and phosphorus. Meat contains a significant amount of iron. It is found in hemoglobin, the pigment which gives color to red blood cells, and in myoglobin, which gives meat its red color. Zinc has an important role in DNA synthesis and is essential for protein synthesis and growth and repair of tissues. Meat, particularly organ meat, is one of the best sources of phosphorus in the diet. Phosphorus has an important role in the metabolism of carbohydrates, proteins, and fats. It helps blood and other body tissues maintain a normal acid/base balance and works with calcium and vitamin D in forming teeth and bones.

Vitamins

Meat is a major dietary source of five B-complex vitamins: thiamin, riboflavin, niacin, and vitamins B_6 and B_{12}. Most meat is a good source of thiamin; pork, in recommended serving sizes, provides more thiamin than any other food commonly eaten. Riboflavin is essential for the release of energy from carbohydrates, proteins, and fats. Niacin with other B-vitamins is involved in energy production, and Vitamin B_6 is a component in the enzyme system that converts the amino acid tryptophan to niacin. Vitamin B_{12} is necessary for growth and development.

MEAT INSPECTION

Foodservice purchasing agents want to be sure when purchasing meat that the product is wholesome and safe for human consumption and meets the quality standards that justify its price. Meat must be federally inspected for wholesomeness to protect the customer before a foodservice operation can purchase it.

Federal Inspection

The **Federal Meat Inspection Act** of 1906 required the inspection of all meat crossing state lines. The Wholesome Meat Act of 1967 required that meat sold within a state meets federal inspection standards. The USDA Food Safety and Inspection Service (FSIS) is responsible for federal inspection. State governments are responsible for state inspections and receive some funding from the federal government.

These inspection programs assure buyers that only healthy animals are used and guarantee that facilities and equipment meet sanitation standards. Whenever new or revised regulations are considered, they are published in the Federal Register and in the public press. The public and industry can comment on the regulations before they are implemented.

An official purple round stamp with an abbreviation for "United States Inspected and Passed" and the official number assigned to that packing/processing plant is placed on every primal cut when it passes federal inspection. The stamp also must appear on every prepackaged processed meat product after inspection. If a product is packed in a carton, the inspection stamp must be on the carton and not on the meat. Today much of the fat, with the original primal inspection stamp, is trimmed off the meat. State meat inspection stamps use purple ink and usually a symbol of the state with the establishment number within it. These three stamps are shown in Figure 10.3. The first is used on carcasses, the second is for processed meat, and the third is a stamp used for state inspection.

Kosher Inspection

Some foodservice operations, such as restaurants or retirement centers with a predominantly Jewish population, purchase meat that is kosher, a term meaning "fit and proper" or "properly prepared" (National Live Stock and Meat Board, 1991). Kosher meat must meet the standards of Mosaic and Talmudic laws. It must come from an animal that has split hooves and chews its cud. Because hogs do not meet this requirement, pork, bacon, and ham cannot be kosher. **Kosher meat** is processed under the supervision of a specially trained rabbi who performs the ritual slaughter and drains the blood from the animal. The fresh meat is soaked and salted on all sides and in all cuts and folds to draw out the remaining blood. Biblical law (Leviticus 17:14) states that "You shall not eat the blood of any creature, for the life of every creature is its blood; whoever eats it shall be cut off." Hindquarters cannot be used for kosher meat because the blood cannot be removed completely from them. The rabbi stamps the meat with the kosher symbol, as shown in Figure 10.4, to show that the meat meets the Jewish dietary laws. Kosher meat must still meet all federal or state meat inspection laws before it can be sold.

MEAT IDENTIFICATION

In most foodservice operations, meat is the most expensive food item on the menu, and yet surprisingly many managers know very little about the product. Just a basic understanding of where the various cuts of meat come from on the carcass can give the chef an idea of what cooking method to use to serve the customer a tender, good-flavored entrée. For example, the chuck, or the shoulder, is a well-developed muscle used to support the weight of the animal and to move it from place to place. Chuck is an economical cut to use and very flavorful if it is prepared using a moist heat cooking method. Knowledge about popular processed meats is also important.

Figure 10.3. Meat inspection stamps.

This stamp is used on fresh and cured meat to indicate that it has met the federal inspection requirements for wholesomeness. It is put on all primal cuts, but may not appear on every retail cut.

38
U.S.
INSP'D & P'S'D

This stamp is used on canned and packaged meat products that have met the federal inspection standards.

U.S.
INSPECTED
AND PASSED BY
DEPARTMENT OF
AGRICULTURE
EST. 38

State meat inspection stamps are often in the shape of the state.

444
ILLINOIS
DEPT. OF AGR.
INSP'D &
P'S'D

Note: The number in each stamp identifies the particular meat processing facility.
Source: FSIS, USDA and Illinois Department of Agriculture

Figure 10.4. Kosher meat symbol.

They fit into today's busy lifestyle and are easy to prepare, have little waste, and provide controlled portion sizes. Ready-to-serve or cooked meats are being used more and more and are being purchased by all types of foodservice operations.

Meat Cuts

Meat cuts from cattle, hogs, and sheep are in the same location in all carcasses, as shown in Figure 10.5. Bone, muscle, and fat deposit structures are similar, but size and color can be different. Beef cuts usually are larger than those from hogs and sheep. Also, differences in muscle and fat color, texture, and firmness are a good indicator of the different kinds of meat (Table 10.1).

Processors usually cut a carcass in half and then cut each half into four primal cuts. **Primal cuts** are the chuck, rib, loin, and round of beef, lamb, veal, and pork. The primal cuts of beef are shown in Figure 10.6. Some bone and muscle usually are removed before the cuts are put into separate barrier bags that are then put into separate boxes, referred to as **boxed meat. Barrier bags** are made of four layers of see-through plastic that keep air from entering and water from leaving. The bag also delays the growth of spoilage bacteria. A vacuum pump pulls all air out of the bag and heat seals it. These bags are then labeled and sent to wholesale distributors, who divide the primal cuts into subprimal cuts and usually debone them, except for ribs. For example, the trimmed beef loin, a primal cut, can be broken down into a strip loin, sirloin butt, full tenderloin, and many other **subprimal cuts,** which are small cuts of meat derived from primal cuts. These subprimal cuts then are cut into individual portions either by the wholesaler or the supplier. Because of current labor costs, many foodservice buyers are now purchasing portion-cut meat, such as 54 6-ounce tenderloin filets.

Processed Meat

Processed meat is defined as meat that has been changed by any mechanical, chemical, or enzymatic treatment, altering taste, appearance, and often shelf life (National Live Stock and Meat Board, 1991). Approximately 35% of the beef, veal, pork, and lamb produced in the United States, of which about 75% is pork, is processed. Such popular menu items as bacon and eggs, baked ham, corned beef and cabbage, pastrami and rye bread sandwiches use processed meats. Processed meat is made from wholesome meat that is inspected at every stage of processing. The FSIS approves the sanitation, labeling, packaging, refrigeration temperature, and weight of processed meat from the raw to the finished product.

Ingredients are added to processed meat to extend shelf life, improve the processing technique, and give a distinct flavor and visual appearance to the products. The USDA requires that additives are approved by the FDA and limits the amount that can be used in a product. The USDA also requires that additives be listed on the product label.

Ready-to-Serve Meats

Ready-to-serve meats are precooked meats that only need thawing or heating. They are used in foodservice establishments as a convenience item or a backup for under-

Figure 10.5. Location of meat cuts in animal carcasses.

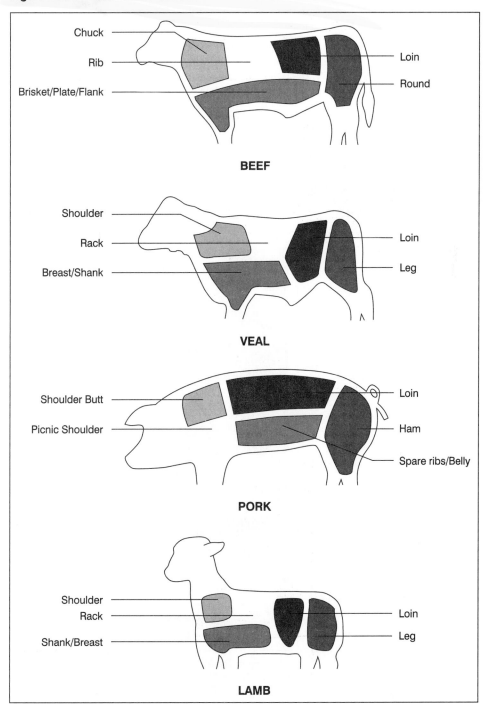

Source: From *The Meat Buyers Guide* by North American Meat Processors Association, 1997. Reston, Virginia. Used by permission.

Table 10.1. Distinguishing characteristics of different kinds of meat.

Kind of Meat	Lean Meat Color	Fat Characteristics
Beef	Bright, cherry-red	White or creamy-white (sometimes yellow) and firm.
Veal	Light pink	Bob veal has little or no fat cover. Special fed veal has white fat.
Pork	(Fresh) Grayish-pink	Characteristically white.
	(Cured) Rose	The fat in pork is soft because it is relatively high in unsaturated fatty acids.
Lamb	Pinkish-red	White, brittle, rather dense, sometimes covered with the "fell," a colorless connective tissue membrane. The fat is harder than the fat in other meat because it is higher in saturated fatty acids.

Source: From the National Live Stock and Meat Board, 1991. Used by permission.

Figure 10.6. Standard primal cuts of beef.

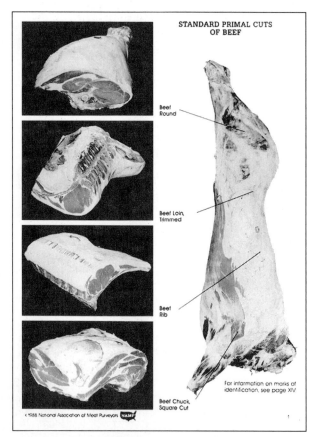

Source: From *The Meat Buyers Guide* by the North American Meat Processors Association, Reston, Virginia 1997. Used by permission.

production of menu items. These products are labor savers in the foodservice operation, but labor cost savings are reflected in the higher price charged by the supplier. The quality of precooked meats is consistent and waste is almost nonexistent. Operations with little kitchen space need only finishing equipment, such as a microwave oven, griddle, and perhaps a convection oven, to survive. Sandwich shops are a common example, and a few hospitals are using this concept in staff and visitor cafeterias.

Top round ready-to-serve beef roasts can be purchased whole, split, or deli-faced, which means it has been marinated before cooking. The roasts are fully cooked using a state-of-the-art process; the meat is stage roasted to guarantee a consistent degree of doneness from end to end. The beef rounds are easy and convenient to serve because they just need to be thawed and heated in a slow oven (275°F) for approximately two hours to an internal temperature of 115°F. They also can be thawed and sliced without heating. Precooked meats have already been cooked to a temperature above the 140°F danger zone.

Precooked items are a real growth area in the pork industry because they offer consistency and convenience. Schools, hospitals, employee feeding, and high-volume commercial foodservices use these items. Heat-and-serve sausage products, ready-to-eat ham, pork chops and loins, and barbecued spare ribs are all available precooked. Tyson advertises versatile, quality-cut boneless pork chops and strips that are quick-frozen in ready-to-cook or fully-cooked forms. Swift Brown 'N Serve Sausage is fully cooked and only needs to be heated or microwaved for a few minutes before serving. It also can be purchased prebrowned and has a fresh, straight-off-the-griddle appearance requiring only heating on a steam table. Armour Swift-Eckrich Foodservice has developed a preblanched bacon that can be finished off on the griddle or convection oven in less than 2 minutes. Hormel Foodservice has a Fast 'N Easy Precooked Bacon on the market that is uniformly sliced and has virtually no shrink.

MEAT QUALITY AND YIELD GRADES

The Meat Grading Branch of the USDA Agricultural Marketing Service is responsible for setting standards, identified as grades for quality and yield of edible meat (Table 10.2), that are used in selling and purchasing meat. Federal grades are available for beef, veal, pork, and lamb. The **quality grade** denotes **palatability,** which refers to the overall taste appeal, tenderness, juiciness, and flavor of cooked lean meat. It is based on two factors: amount of marbling in the meat and the age of the animal. The grades go from best to worst, usually Prime to Cull, and each denotes a specific level of quality as determined by the USDA. The yield grade identifies differences in carcass **cutability,** defined as the amount of salable meat obtained from the carcass as boneless or semiboneless trimmed retail cuts from the round, loin, rib, and chuck. Yield Grade 1 has the leanest carcasses with the greatest yield of edible meat per pound, and Yield Grade 5 has the fattest with the lowest yield. **Yield grades** are based on the amount of external fat, internal fat, size of the rib eye area, and carcass weight. They are not related to quality grades and are used only at the wholesale level.

Even though the grading program is administered by the USDA, participation by packers is voluntary. Processors or packers pay for the grading. As a result of

Table 10.2.   USDA grades for beef, veal, pork, and lamb.

Beef	Veal	Pork	Lamb
Quality Grades	**Quality Grades**	**Quality Grades**	**Quality Grades**
Prime Choice Select Standard Commercial Utility Cutter Canner	Prime Choice Good Standard Utility Cull	Acceptable — quality must be acceptable to qualify for grades 1–4 below. Utility	Prime Choice Good Utility Cull
Yield Grades	**Yield Grades**	**Yield Grades**	**Yield Grades**
1 2 3 4 5	None	U.S. No. 1 U.S. No. 2 U.S. No. 3 U.S. No. 4	1 2 3 4 5

Source: From the National Live Stock and Meat Board, 1991. Used by permission.

grading, livestock owners can produce animals that meet the standards, packers can group meat cuts of similar grade, and retailers can buy the grade of meat required for their customers, who are assured the meat meets standards that predict palatability and cutability (National Live Stock and Meat Board, 1991). Some packers and retailers use their own brand names to designate the quality of meat.

Beef Grading

The buyer may specify quality and yield grades for any beef item. Beef has the greatest number of grades because the variation of age and weight of cattle causes quality and yield to vary more than in any other meat. Grading provides the foodservice manager with an estimate of the tenderness, juiciness, and flavor of cooked beef. The final eating quality of beef can be determined by the age, days in the feedlot, type of diet, and genetics of the animal. The younger the animal, the more likely the meat will be tender. The amount and distribution of fat in lean beef is important in grading. Marbling fat melts during cooking, increases the juiciness of the beef, and contributes to its flavor and tenderness.

Meat from young cattle with the highest amount of marbling is graded Prime, followed by Choice, Select, and Standard as shown in Figure 10.7 and also in Table 10.2. Cattle are divided into two categories: young animals are in Groups A and B and the more mature and older cattle are in Groups C, D, and E. Beef in

Figure 10.7.   Quality grading chart.

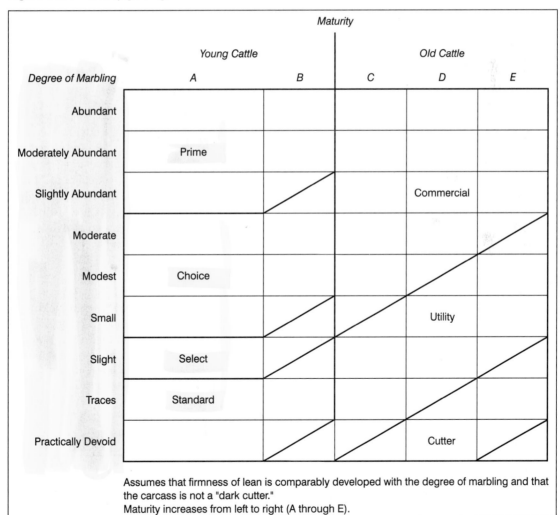

Source: From the American Culinary Federation Educational Institute, 1992. Used by permission.

both categories can have the same degrees of marbling, from *abundant* to *practically devoid*. Notice that beef from only young animals can be graded as Prime, while beef from older animals with slightly abundant marbling can only be graded Commercial. In young animals, muscles are smooth and finely textured; in older animals muscles are coarser, the grade is lower, and the meat is less tender. Yield grades for beef carcasses range from 1, the leanest, to 5, the fattest.

Veal Grading

Veal is the name of meat from calves up to four months of age. The color of veal (class A) is very light pink to a darker pink, and the color of calf (class B) is dark grayish-pink to medium red. The light pink color of veal comes from the youngest calves that are milk-fed or formula-fed. Quality grades of veal are based on the conformation of the carcass and quality of lean meat, which is determined by the amount of fat within the lean between the ribs (feathering) and the amount of fat streaking with the flank muscles. The quality grades (see Table 10.2) of veal are Prime, Choice, Good, Standard, Utility, and Cull; veal has no yield grades.

Pork Grading

The buyer may specify one or a combination of U.S. grades for pork carcasses: U.S. No. 1, U.S. No. 2, U.S. No. 3, U.S. No. 4, Utility. Pork quality is graded differently than other meats. The cutability of the carcass and the quality of meat are the basis for grading pork (see Table 10.2). Pork must have lean quality to qualify for any of the top grades (U.S. No. 1 through 4). The highest cutability comes from the highest grade and the lowest from No. 4. With all the current emphasis on heart-healthy foods, the lean-to-fat ratio in U.S. hogs has improved. Grading standards were revised in 1985 to account for the leaner type of hog produced today.

Lamb Grading

The buyer may specify a quality grade and also a yield grade, although yield grading is seldom used if the lamb is quality graded. Maturity is the most important characteristic in quality grading. The three maturity classes are: A: lamb, class 1; B: yearly mutton, class 2; and C: mutton, class 3. Differences in the development of muscular and skeletal systems are evident between the classes. Grades for lamb are Prime, Choice, Good, Utility, and Cull (Table 10.2).

SPECIFICATIONS

Writing specifications, especially for meat, has always been a difficult task for food-service buyers. Many do not know where various cuts on the carcass come from and why some cuts are more tender than others. However, culinary schools and colleges and universities now require that students take courses on meat purchasing and cooking. Meat suppliers also are willing to help buyers select the right cut for a menu item.

Institutional Meat Purchase Specifications

The **Institutional Meat Purchase Specifications** (IMPS) give an accurate description of standardized cuts of meat. They were developed in the 1940s through the cooperative efforts of the Livestock and Meat Standardization Branch of the USDA's Agricultural Marketing Service, the public, and industry organizations. The **Meat Buyers Guide,** first published in 1961 by the National Association of Meat Purveyors (NAMP, renamed in 1996 to North American Meat Processors), is a pictorial representation of items in the IMPS. The cooperation between the NAMP and the Livestock & Meat Board in producing *The Meat Buyers Guide* indicates how industry organizations can work together for the good of the public and the entire red meat industry. For each type of meat, excellent color photographs of the carcass and primal, subprimal, and portion cuts are shown to help the buyer understand what portion cuts they are purchasing and what the meat should look like when it arrives from the supplier. Every buyer for a foodservice operation needs a copy of the guide to help in meat selection and specification writing.

The IMPS are classified into eight categories, or series, numbered from 100 to 800. Series 100 to 400 contain specifications for beef, lamb, veal, and pork; series 500 to 800 contain specifications for further processed meats and byproducts. The eight series are:

Series 100	Fresh beef
Series 200	Fresh lamb and mutton
Series 300	Fresh veal and calf
Series 400	Fresh pork
Series 500	Cured, cured and smoked, and fully cooked pork products
Series 600	Cured, dried, and smoked beef products
Series 700	Variety meats and edible byproducts
Series 800	Sausage products

The series numbers from 100 through 400 for beef, lamb, veal, and pork include the standardized subprimal cuts for each type of meat. The IMPS and NAMP have a section of specifications for each meat type to help foodservice operators offer their customers a consistently cut product. Portion cuts follow the same numbering scheme as the subprimal but are prefixed with a 1. For example, beef portion cuts start with 1100, lamb with 1200, veal with 1300, and pork with 1400. To illustrate this numbering system, a foodservice manager might have a New York or Kansas City steak on the menu, which are portion cuts of a beef loin. Different parts of the country use the terms New York or Kansas City to refer to either bone-in or boneless beef strip loins. Also, the terms are used to identify steaks cut from these subprimal cuts. The IMPS number 1180 should be used in the specification for loin steaks sent to the supplier.

1180 *Beef Loin, Strip Loin Steak, Short-Cut, Boneless*
The steaks shall be prepared from item Nos. 176 or 180. All bones and cartilages shall be removed and the flank edge shall not exceed 2 inches from the loin eye muscle.

The supplier would know that the steak must be cut from the subprimal cut 180, identified as IMPS 180.

Figure 10.8.   Beef cut information for commercial and noncommercial foodservice operations.

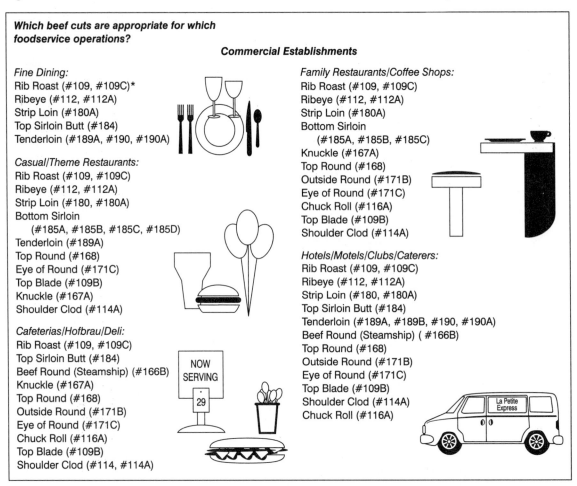

Which beef cuts are appropriate for which foodservice operations?

Commercial Establishments

Fine Dining:
Rib Roast (#109, #109C)*
Ribeye (#112, #112A)
Strip Loin (#180A)
Top Sirloin Butt (#184)
Tenderloin (#189A, #190, #190A)

Casual/Theme Restaurants:
Rib Roast (#109, #109C)
Ribeye (#112, #112A)
Strip Loin (#180, #180A)
Bottom Sirloin
    (#185A, #185B, #185C, #185D)
Tenderloin (#189A)
Top Round (#168)
Eye of Round (#171C)
Top Blade (#109B)
Knuckle (#167A)
Shoulder Clod (#114A)

Cafeterias/Hofbrau/Deli:
Rib Roast (#109, #109C)
Top Sirloin Butt (#184)
Beef Round (Steamship) (#166B)
Knuckle (#167A)
Top Round (#168)
Outside Round (#171B)
Eye of Round (#171C)
Chuck Roll (#116A)
Top Blade (#109B)
Shoulder Clod (#114, #114A)

Family Restaurants/Coffee Shops:
Rib Roast (#109, #109C)
Ribeye (#112, #112A)
Strip Loin (#180A)
Bottom Sirloin
    (#185A, #185B, #185C)
Knuckle (#167A)
Top Round (#168)
Outside Round (#171B)
Eye of Round (#171C)
Chuck Roll (#116A)
Top Blade (#109B)
Shoulder Clod (#114A)

Hotels/Motels/Clubs/Caterers:
Rib Roast (#109, #109C)
Ribeye (#112, #112A)
Strip Loin (#180, #180A)
Top Sirloin Butt (#184)
Tenderloin (#189A, #189B, #190, #190A)
Beef Round (Steamship) (#166B)
Top Round (#168)
Outside Round (#171B)
Eye of Round (#171C)
Top Blade (#109B)
Shoulder Clod (#114A)
Chuck Roll (#116A)

180 *Beef Loin, Strip Loin, Short-Cut, Boneless*
This item is the same as item No. 176, except that the flank edge shall be removed by a straight cut from a point on the rib end which is not more than 3 inches from the outer tip of the loin eye muscle through a point on the sirloin end which is not more than 2 inches from the outer tip of the loin eye muscle.

Identifying the cut, either portion or subprimal, of meat is only one part of a specification. Many other factors need to be defined to purchase the right product for the foodservice operation.

Other Factors

Beef cuts that are appropriate for commercial and noncommercial foodservice operations are shown in Figure 10.8. The subprimal cuts of beef are listed for eight operations, along with the IMPS number. In making buying decisions, the manager must know what customers want and how much they are willing to pay for a meal.

Figure 10.8.   Continued.

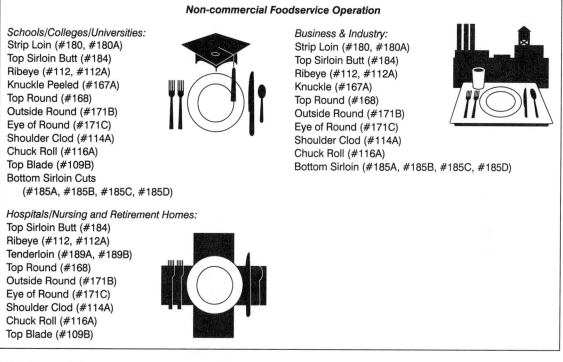

Non-commercial Foodservice Operation

Schools/Colleges/Universities:
Strip Loin (#180, #180A)
Top Sirloin Butt (#184)
Ribeye (#112, #112A)
Knuckle Peeled (#167A)
Top Round (#168)
Outside Round (#171B)
Eye of Round (#171C)
Shoulder Clod (#114A)
Chuck Roll (#116A)
Top Blade (#109B)
Bottom Sirloin Cuts
    (#185A, #185B, #185C, #185D)

Hospitals/Nursing and Retirement Homes:
Top Sirloin Butt (#184)
Ribeye (#112, #112A)
Tenderloin (#189A, #189B)
Top Round (#168)
Outside Round (#171B)
Eye of Round (#171C)
Shoulder Clod (#114A)
Chuck Roll (#116A)
Top Blade (#109B)

Business & Industry:
Strip Loin (#180, #180A)
Top Sirloin Butt (#184)
Ribeye (#112, #112A)
Knuckle (#167A)
Top Round (#168)
Outside Round (#171B)
Eye of Round (#171C)
Shoulder Clod (#114A)
Chuck Roll (#116A)
Bottom Sirloin (#185A, #185B, #185C, #185D)

* # indicates IMPS number for subprimal cuts
Source: From the American Culinary Federation Educational Institute, 1992. Used by permission.

The IMPS saves the buyer many hours of work because the cut of the meat is clearly defined and understood by the supplier. However, the buyer must specify the grade by determining the quality and cutability of meat needed for a recipe. In such cuts as steaks, according to the IMPS, fat must not exceed an average of ¼ inch in thickness, and the thickness at any one point must not exceed ½ inch, unless otherwise specified or unless definite fat limitations are indicated in the detailed item descriptions. Weight range with portion weight tolerances must be specified. If the meat needs to be tenderized, the method should be spelled out. Other factors that should be specified are the type of packaging and the state of refrigeration at the time of delivery to prevent contamination of the meat.

Writing Specifications

Technical specifications are used for most meat items. The USDA measures quality objectively with nationally recognized standards. Many meat packers have used their own brand names and define their own quality standards. Grading by packers closely follows federal grades and standards, but with more flexibility than is allowed by the USDA. The content should be the same for most meat specifications even though the format can be individualized for a specific foodservice operation.

Table 10.3. Specifications for steak menu items for three types of restaurants.

Specification Item	First-Class Hotel or Restaurant	Family-Style Restaurant	Budget Steakhouse
Menu item	New York strip steak, 12-oz. boneless	New York strip steak, 12-oz. with bone	charbroiled strip loin
Product	strip loin	bone-in strip steak	bone-in strip steak
National meat buyers' guide number (NAMP#)	180	1179	1177
Grade	USDA Prime, yield grade two	USDA low Choice (note that this specifies where on the grade)	USDA Commercial (cows only, no bulls)
Trim factor	not to exceed ¼ inch fat with smooth trim	¼ inch to ½ inch fat cover, maximum 2-inch tail	maximum ¾ inch fat, maximum 3-inch tail
Weight range	10 to 12 pounds	12-oz. portion ± half ounce	14 oz. portion ± one oz., minimum ¾ inch thick
Method of tenderization	dry age 14 to 21 days	age whole strips seven to nine days prior to cutting; jackard before cutting	pin whole strip before cutting; individually dip portion steaks in liquid tenderizer
Packaging	wrapped in sanitary paper and tied	individual 12 portions per box, six boxes per case; show date of cutting	multivac, 24 portions per box
Special considerations	eye must be between 2½ and 3½ inches in diameter	¾-inch-thick steaks with vein on both sides are not acceptable	
State of refrigeration	fresh only, ship chilled at temperature between 33 and 40°F	frozen—0°F or less	frozen—0°F or less

Source: From *Foodservice Organizations: A Managerial and Systems Approach* (3rd ed.) by M. C. Spears, 1995, Upper Saddle River, NJ: Merrill/Prentice Hall.

The three sample specifications shown in Table 10.3 are for the steak menu item in three distinct types of restaurants, each with an appropriate menu. The term *strip steaks* has noticeably different specifications in these three restaurant operations. The first specification is for a first-class hotel or restaurant, the second for a family-style restaurant, and the third for a budget steakhouse (Spears, 1995). Note that in each case the NAMP *Meat Buyers Guide* numbers were used to define the meat product. The first-class hotel or restaurant ordered NAMP #180, a whole loin that the chef will cut into portions on the premises. The other two restaurants ordered NAMP #1179, strip loin portioned steaks with the bone in.

The first-class hotel or restaurant specified USDA Prime, the highest quality grade and Yield Grade 2, the second highest out of five grades. As the size of the ribeye area increases, the yield grade decreases. Low USDA Choice was ordered for the family restaurant and USDA commercial; cows only, for the budget steakhouse. Also, as the price to the customer decreases, the amount of fat on the steak increases as does the length of the tail, which is almost all fat with very little meat. Note the fat on the Prime grade steak cannot exceed ¼ inch and the steak for the budget steakhouse can have a maximum of ¾ inch fat.

MEAT TENDERNESS

Muscle fibers become tougher and connective tissues more tender when heat is applied to meat. Choosing the correct cooking process for each cut of meat to make it tender is important to meet the foodservice goal of customer satisfaction. Meat from animals whose muscles have a large amount of collagen-containing connective tissue becomes tender when heat is applied because the collagen is transformed into a water-soluble gel. Cuts of meat such as beef chuck should be cooked by using moist heat, a low temperature, and a relatively low cooking temperature.

Meat cuts such as rib or loin steaks contain small amounts of connective tissues and therefore are most tender when cooked rapidly with dry heat at a higher temperature. These cuts of meats are more tender when cooked to the rare stage rather than well-done because the muscle fibers do not have a chance to toughen. The degree of doneness, however, has been challenged by the FDA ever since an *E. coli* breakout from undercooked hamburgers served in a quick-service restaurant in the early '90s. Meat can be slightly tenderized at home by marinating the meat in a very weak organic acid, usually wine, vinegar, tomatoes, or lemon juice. Marinades penetrate only about ¼ inch into the interior of the meat, thus contributing more to flavor than tenderness. Tenderization requires marinating for at least 6 hours or as long as overnight. Marinating longer than 24 hours causes muscle fibers on the surface to break down, resulting in a mushy texture.

Natural enzyme tenderizers are more effective than marinades. Enzymes are of vegetable origin and include papain from papaya, bromelin from pineapple, and ficin from figs. Using too much of these enzymes also can cause a mushy texture in the meat, thus making the final product unacceptable to the customer.

Processors often tenderize by breaking or cutting the muscle fibers and connective tissues through grinding, chopping, or pounding meat that otherwise would be tough. **Jaccarding** employs a special instrument that pierces the meat with multiple, thin needles and makes small holes visible only in the raw meat.

Retail stores and restaurants use a steak **macerator** to make cubed steaks cut from less tender meat such as chuck or bottom round. Sometimes trimmings and end pieces of steaks are formed together in a macerator to produce high quality cubed steaks.

Aging meat, especially beef, has been the primary method for tenderizing most cuts. **Aging** refers to beef that is held at refrigerated temperatures for an extended period of time to maximize its flavor and tenderness through natural enzymatic processes. **Dry aging** occurs when beef carcasses or wholesale cuts are held at refrigerated temperatures with no protective covering. **Wet aging** refers to storage of wholesale carcasses at refrigerated temperatures in a vacuum package bag. The effect on tenderness is the same with both types of aging.

Enzymatic changes in beef occur within the first 10 days after slaughter because the muscles become more tender due to protein breakdown. In dry aging, referred to as natural aging, beef is held for two to four weeks at temperatures of 34°F to 36°F, and humidity is set at about 70% to keep the exposed meat surfaces dry. This level of humidity causes the moisture to evaporate, resulting in weight loss, which increases the price per pound of aged beef. If a higher level of humidity is used, losses are kept to a minimum, but trimming to remove surface spoilage is greater than the loss from evaporation. Prolonged storage in the presence of air (dry aging) creates an excellent environment for bacterial growth. Foodservice suppliers expect to lose 5% to 10% of the product weight because of dehydration and the need to trim the meat.

Vacuum packaging of beef reduces moisture loss to no more than 1% because spoilage bacteria cannot grow. Some foodservice operators believe that dry aged beef is more flavorful than wet aged, but research has not proven this theory.

Pork, lamb, and veal come from young animals and therefore are usually tender. The meat generally is processed the day after slaughtering. Pork fat is more unsaturated than beef or lamb and develops rancid flavors unless promptly packaged and flavored.

MEAT STORAGE

Proper storage is essential to maintain food safety and quality. In the past, meat was preserved for future use by curing, drying and smoking, and canning and winter freezing. The foodservice manager can tell that meat is spoiled by the color, odor, and texture of the product. Contamination by microorganisms usually cannot be detected by such signs as odor or color.

Meat suppliers and foodservice managers should be able to identify conditions that encourage contamination resulting in foodborne infections. The customer's risk perceptions of food safety hazards and the realities presented by food scientists are quite different, as shown in Table 10.4. Even though the customer ranks chemical residues the highest, the real concern should be bacterial contamination that causes foodborne illness. Over 5 million cases of foodborne illness are reported annually, with millions of additional cases not even identified (Purdum, 1996). Not one single illness caused by chemicals, such as hormones, pesticides, and antibiotics, has been reported when these chemicals were properly administered. Also, knowledge of the type of microorganisms, or pathogens, that cause foodborne illnesses and a plan for prevention of their growth are required to protect customers.

Contamination Conditions

Several types of microorganisms can grow on meat, but bacteria are the most predominant and important to meat quality. Bacteria thrive in conditions which encourage growth, such as specific levels of moisture, temperature, and oxygen as well as the amount of surface exposed and the degree of acidity or alkalinity.

Table 10.4. Customer's perception versus scientist's realities.

Risk Perceptions vs. Reality*	
Customer	**Scientist**
Hormones	Foodborne Illness
Pesticides	Antibiotics
Antibiotics	Pesticides
Foodborne Illness	Hormones

Source: American Culinary Federation Educational Institute, 1992. Used by permission.

Moisture

Microorganisms need moisture to multiply. Bacteria require as least 18% moisture to grow. Fresh meat contains enough moisture to satisfy requirements for bacteria. The moisture level in meat is affected by air flow, humidity, and temperature of the storage area. Air flow increases evaporation losses in unwrapped meat. The humidity in the storage area is responsible for the amount of moisture drawn to the surfaces. When relative humidity is high, condensation occurs. If it is low, moisture evaporates and meat surfaces stay relatively dry, thus inhibiting microbial growth. The correct combination of humidity and temperature levels keeps the meat surfaces dry enough to retard spoilage, yet moist enough to prevent shrinkage and discoloration from dehydration.

Temperature

Most bacteria that can cause foodborne illness cannot grow at low refrigerated temperatures. Temperatures below 40°F prevent most bacterial growth. As the temperature reaches 32°F, the freezing point, few microorganisms grow and reproduction is greatly retarded. For this reason, refrigeration and freezing prolong shelf life. Temperature is a critical factor during meat handling and storage. Meat cannot be held at temperatures higher than 40°F without compromising safety, quality, and appearance.

Oxygen

Microorganisms that require oxygen to grow are called **aerobic** and those that grow only if oxygen is not present are known as **anaerobic.** Others that will grow with or without oxygen are called *facultative.* Aerobic microorganisms grow on the surface or exterior of the meat and anaerobic grow internally. Organisms that live under more than one condition exist mainly on the surface and possibly within meat tissue, usually inside ground meat but never inside intact muscle. Vacuum packaging extends the shelf life of meat—thereby inhibiting aerobic microbial growth—but also allows anaerobes to grow.

Exposed Surface Area

The interior of meat muscle generally is free of microorganisms but the surface is susceptible to contamination and spoilage. Because of its relative size to its weight, a large beef roast has a small amount of surface compared to the same weight of ground beef, which has much more exposed surface around each of many particles. Because of the increased potential for ground beef to become contaminated, handling and storage must be carefully monitored.

Degree of Acidity or Alkalinity

For most bacteria the optimal pH, or acidity, is near neutral, or a pH of 7, with minimum and maximum values between 5.0 and 8.0. A pH below 7 indicates acidity and above 7 alkalinity. Generally, fresh meat has a pH between 5.3 and 6.5, which is within the range favorable for growth of many microorganisms. Vinegar or citric acid is used in food preservation to extend the shelf life of some processed meat. Some bacteria, however, are beneficial and are added to promote lactic acid production to reduce the pH, which produces a controlled fermentation process. Summer sausage is an example of a product that is made using this process.

Foodborne Pathogens

Within the past 15 years, several pathogenic foodborne illnesses, as shown in Table 10.5, have emerged, including Campylobacteriosis infection, *E. coli* 0157:H7 infection/intoxication, and the Norwalk viral illness. Of these, *Esherichia coli* 0157:H7, or *E. coli,* is the most infamous as the result of the January 1993 outbreak of food poisoning in western states. The *E. coli* bacteria can be transmitted by eating raw or undercooked ground beef; it was linked to hamburger patties served in one limited-menu restaurant chain (McLauchlin, 1993). This bacteria is most likely found on the surface of meat and is killed when cuts such as steaks are grilled. Grinding meat, however, transfers the bacteria from the surface to the inside of the product, making *E. coli* more difficult to eradicate. The FDA issued guidelines to federal, state, and local food safety regulators recommending that restaurants cook ground beef products to 155°F until juices run clear and all pink color is gone from the inside. Raw or undercooked ground beef and red meats, including pork and lamb, are the major vehicles of transmission. Thorough cooking and reheating, good sanitation, and refrigeration at 40°F or below are all important ways to prevent growth of the bacteria ("Facts about *E. coli,*" 1993).

Meat Safety

As a result of the *E. coli* outbreak in a quick-service restaurant, the USDA director quickly called for an overhaul of the meat safety program that has become antiquated and suspect (Allen, 1993). As the USDA agency in charge of meat and poultry inspections, the FSIS conducted public hearings and heard from meat suppliers, trade groups, academicians, consumer advocates, and victims of meat-related tragedies. The consensus was that a more scientific approach of looking at risks is needed. The HACCP, hazard analysis critical control point, system or the more recent NRA ServSafe® program was strongly supported. These programs are designed to minimize food safety risks by identifying points at which problems occur and then eliminating them.

Table 10.5. Emerging pathogens that cause foodborne illness.

	Campylobacteriosis Infection	E. Coli 0157:H7 Infection/Intoxication	Norwalk Virus Illness
Pathogen	*Campylobacter jejuni*	*Escherichia coli*	Norwalk and Norwalk-like viral agent
Incubation period	3–5 days	12–72 hours	24–48 hours
Duration of illness	1–4 days	1–3 days	24–48 hours
Symptoms	Diarrhea, fever, nausea, abdominal pain, headache	Bloody diarrhea; severe abdominal pain, nausea, vomiting, diarrhea, and occasionally fever	Nausea, vomiting, diarrhea, abdominal pain, headache, and low-grade fever
Reservoir	Domestic and wild animals	Humans (intestinal tract); animals, particularly cattle	Humans (intestinal tract)
Foods implicated	Raw vegetables, unpasteurized milk and dairy products, poultry, pork, beef, and lamb	Raw and undercooked beef and other red meats, imported cheeses, unpasteurized milk, raw finfish, cream pies, mashed potatoes, and other prepared foods	Raw vegetables, prepared salads, raw shellfish, and water contaminated from human feces
Spore former	No	No	No
Prevention	Avoid cross-contamination, cook foods thoroughly	Cook beef and red meats thoroughly, avoid cross-contamination, use safe food and water supplies, avoid fecal contamination from food handlers by practicing good personal hygiene	Use safe food and water supplies, avoid fecal contamination from food handlers by practicing good personal hygiene, thoroughly cook foods

Source: From *Applied Foodservice Sanitation* (4th ed.). Copyright ©1992 by The Educational Foundation of the National Restaurant Association. Reprinted by permission.

New regulations recently were outlined by President Clinton for changes in the government's meat inspection system for the first time since it was created nearly a century ago. New rules require scientific tests for disease-causing bacteria. The new regulations apply to more than 6,200 meat and poultry slaughter and processing plants and include four major requirements (Allen, 1996).

- Each plant must establish an HACCP plan to meet the approval of USDA inspectors. It must target and eliminate steps in production where hazards might arise.
- All slaughter plants must begin testing for *E. coli* to prevent and reduce the hazards of fecal contamination.
- Plants producing raw ground products must also undergo testing for salmonella.
- All plants must create a written plan for meeting sanitation responsibilities.

Perhaps the single most significant factor in meat safety is temperature control (Hodges, 1996). Every plant will have to identify each temperature-sensitive critical control point, monitor those points constantly, acquire and store the data, and have the capability to retrieve it at any time for analysis. Of course, the cost of these safety measures is significant. The first cost is for equipment. Mechanical or electronic equipment can be purchased, but labor cost for their operation has to be figured into the final cost. Electronic equipment is the most efficient and requires very little labor. Electronic time and temperature recording devices vary in cost from $100 to more than $500 per unit, the software is about $100, and the computer interface costs about $50. A processing plant with 10 temperature-sensitive critical control points will need a recording device costing $200, for a total one-time cost of $2,150. Labor costs are practically nothing. The decision should be to use the best available electronic temperature monitoring technology. It provides overwhelming advantages over mechanical equipment in terms of cost, data accuracy, storage retrieval, and consumer safety.

Foodservice operators have hailed these revamped meat inspection regulations, but they also caution that food safety is still necessary in all kitchens. The 90-year-old system based on sight, smell, and touch is being converted to a science-based system, but operators still have a huge responsibility in serving safe food. The new system will require prevention of food safety problems by processors rather than relying on government inspectors to detect and correct problems after they occur. Foodservice employees still must properly store, handle, and cook meat and poultry products. Many foodservice operators already are taking an active role in ensuring safety in their link of the food supply chain. Since July 1993, the number of foodservice employees certified in the NRA ServSafe® program has jumped 41% to nearly 106,000 (Allen, 1996). Since the inception of the program in 1987, about 590,000 certificates have been earned.

Receiving and storage are critical control points for many foods, especially perishable ones such as raw meat and vegetables. Setting up procedures for inspection and standards for acceptance are necessary to prevent foodborne illness. An HACCP flowchart for safe purchasing, receiving, and storing frozen ground beef used in chili, as discussed in chapter 2 and shown in Table 2.1, should be included in the procedures manual of a foodservice operation as an example for all potentially hazardous foods (National Restaurant Association [NRA], Educational Foundation, 1992). Note that the hazard for receiving and storing these foods is contamination and spoilage, and the corrective action, if the standard is not met, is rejection of delivery or discarding the product. In Figure 10.9, acceptable and unacceptable conditions for receiving fresh beef, lamb, and pork are shown (NRA, Educational Foundation, 1992). The temperature, color, and texture of the meat should be checked before accepting it. Conditions for rejecting it also are given. Many packing plants already use the HACCP program or other risk-control programs, which are not costly to initiate.

The United States is widely acknowledged as having the safest food supply in the world, and meat undergoes more thorough safety inspection than do most foods. Although the number of foodborne illness outbreaks has dropped considerably over the past decade, 77% of those that occur are traced to foodservice operations, 20% to homes, and 3% to food processing plants (Figure 10.10). If any good can come out of the *E. coli* tragedy, it is that the situation has prompted foodservice managers

Figure 10.9.   Acceptable and unacceptable conditions for receiving meat.

Food	Accept	Reject
Fresh meat (Beef, Lamb, Pork)	**Temperature:** at 40°F (4.4°C) or lower	**Color:** brown or greenish; brown, green, or purple blotches; black, white, or green spots
	Beef Color: bright, cherry red	**Texture:** slimy, sticky, or dry
		Cartons are broken; meat wrappers are dirty; packaging is torn
	Lamb Color: light red	
	Pork Color: white fat; pink lean portion	
	Texture: Firm and springs back when touched	

Source: Reprinted with permission from the *Serving Safe Food Employee Guide* (2nd ed.), Copyright © 1995 by The Educational Foundation of the National Restaurant Association. All rights reserved.

across the nation to double- and triple-check their own standards and operating procedures while emphasizing to employees the crucial importance of food safety and sanitation. The basics are to make sure walk-in refrigerator temperatures are cold enough and the cooking temperatures are hot enough. Managers must stress to employees that they must keep clean not only their work areas but also their hands. Overall, it requires complete commitment to specific operational procedures and quality standards that promote health and sanitation.

Contamination Prevention

Meat should be kept clean, covered, and cold to prevent foodborne illness or infection. It must be properly wrapped to keep it clean and covered until it is cooked. Refrigeration and freezing assure that the meat will be kept at a cold enough temperature. Most foodservice buyers purchase meat from suppliers as boxed, vacuum-packaged subprimals to be portioned on premise or as precut, ready-to-cook steaks, chops, and roasts. Because meat goes through physical and biochemical changes during storage and processing, follow these three crucial guidelines:

- Keep meat cold.
- Keep meat clean.
- Keep meat moving.

Figure 10.10.   Sources of foodborne illness.

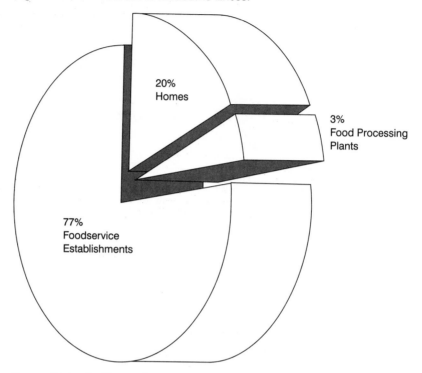

20%
Homes

3%
Food Processing
Plants

77%
Foodservice
Establishments

Source: Centers for Disease Control.

Refrigeration

The ideal temperature to store fresh meat is 28°F to 32°F, although many refrigerators designed to hold a variety of perishable foods are set at 36°F to 40°F. Meat freezes at 28°F. As temperatures increase, shelf life of meat decreases. Health departments require that thermometers be on the outside of refrigerators and freezers and that temperatures be monitored at regular intervals. If meat will not be used within a few days after purchase, it should be frozen as soon as possible to preserve optimal quality. Cured and smoked meat, including luncheon meat and canned hams, is less perishable than fresh meat but should be kept refrigerated in the original packing. Leftover cooked meat should be left whole, wrapped securely, and stored in the coldest part of the refrigerator. It must be used within a day or two. Leaving meat whole prevents dryness and inhibits bacterial growth from recontamination.

Freezing and Thawing

Freezing is the most common method of meat preservation. Many foodservice buyers purchase most meat in the frozen state because processors have blast freezers that use low temperatures and high velocities of air to freeze meat quickly. Meat must

Table 10.6.   Storage chart for fresh and frozen, raw and cooked ground beef.

Type of Product	Storage Temperatures	Storage Times (from date of production)
Fresh Ground Beef	Below 40°F and as close to 28°F as possible	1 to 3 days
Fresh Vacuum Packaged (un-opened) Ground Beef	Below 40°F and as close to 28°F as possible	Up to 14 days (check with supplier)
Frozen Ground Beef	0°F or below	Up to 90 days
Refrigerated Cooked Ground Beef	Below 40°F	2 to 3 days
Frozen Cooked Ground Beef	0°F or below	Up to 90 days

Ground beef products should be properly wrapped with packaging material that is moisture- and vapor-proof.

Source: From Foodservice Ground Beef Safety Guidelines, National Cattleman's Beef Association.

be protected by appropriate packaging; otherwise, the high velocity of air will cause moisture loss on the surface, referred to as *freezer burn,* resulting in a dry, discolored surface that will be tough and taste bland or rancid when cooked. Meat should not be salted prior to freezing because salting draws out moisture and oxidizes meat fat, giving it a rancid flavor and reducing the time meat can be left in the freezer.

Animal fats deteriorate over time and are especially prone to rancidity, resulting in objectionable flavors and odors. Pork, which has more unsaturated fatty acids than other meats, is more perishable than beef and lamb. Therefore, properly wrapped pork should not be kept in the freezer more than 6 months, whereas beef and lamb may be stored for up to 12 months. With good inventory control, meat never should be held in storage for the maximum length of time.

Grinding meat increases the surface area, necessitating a shorter storage time. For this reason, ground meat and sausages cannot be left in the freezer as long as steaks and roasts. Because ground beef, whether fresh or frozen, is easily contaminated, correct storage is crucial. Table 10.6 gives storage temperatures and times for fresh and frozen, raw and cooked, ground beef.

Freezer burn is caused by loss of moisture on the surface of a food (Beef Industry Council and Beef Board, 1992). The two most common causes of this surface dehydration are partial defrosting and refreezing of a frozen product or wrapping the product in such a way that air comes into contact with the surface of the food. When meat is wrapped, if all or most of the air between the surface and wrapping materials is not removed, or, if the package is not tightly sealed, freezer burn will occur.

The most rapid freezing methods, using condensed gases such as liquid nitrogen, are known as **cryogenic freezing** in which very small ice crystals are formed, resulting in minimal damage to the tissue. Cryogenically frozen beef has characteristics similar to those of fresh beef but is a little lighter in color because of the reflection of the light from the small crystals.

FREEZE FAST, THAW SLOW! is the advice in the *Chef's & Foodservice Operator's Guide to BEEF* (Beef Industry Council and Beef Board, 1992). The time-temperature pattern of thawing has the potential to be more detrimental to meat quality than freezing. Thawing occurs more slowly than freezing. The temperature rises rapidly to the freezing point where it remains throughout the process. During thawing, large ice crystals form, and microbial growth occurs when the meat is thawed too quickly at too high a temperature.

Unless meat is cooked from the frozen state, it should be thawed in its original package to prevent dehydration. The ideal method for thawing is to use tempering boxes that are separate units specially designed to maintain a steady temperature of 40°F regardless of room temperature or product load. If a tempering box is not available, the meat should be thawed in the refrigerator. The head cook or chef needs to include on the production schedule when meat should be removed from the freezer and placed in the tempering box to have it thawed or partially thawed for cooking a couple days later.

Packaging

Because bacteria need oxygen to reproduce, vacuum packaging places subprimals or portion cuts of meat in an oxygen-impermeable bag, drawing and sealing a vacuum (Beef Industry Council and Beef Board, 1992). Vacuum packaging inhibits bacterial growth but still allows natural tenderization or aging to continue as usual. Vacuum packaging increases the storage life of refrigerated meat from just a few days to a month if proper storage and handling procedures have been strictly followed.

Leakers

Leakers, or packages that have lost their vacuum, are caused by poor seals on the packages or by mishandling the product during shipping (Beef Industry Council and Beef Board, 1992). Fresh beef usually is a bright cherry-red color but vacuum-packed beef is a deep red or purple color, the normal color of muscle in the absence of oxygen. Fresh beef normally has a very light odor but when vacuum packed, the odor can become sour due to the type of bacteria that are dominant when oxygen is not present. This odor should disappear after exposing the meat to air in about 15 to 30 minutes. *Purge, exudate,* or *weep* are terms to describe the purplish-red fluid found in vacuum or other types of packages of beef cuts.

As meat moves through the marketing channel, especially a modern fabrication/cutting facility, grade identification can be difficult for the foodservice buyer. Often the external fat on the subprimal cuts that has the blue edible ink grade stamp or shield rolled on it has been removed; this could create a problem for the buyer. The USDA is responsible for proper labeling of boxed meat during fabrication or breaking down the subprimal cuts. This processing is done under the watchful eye of a USDA inspector who can certify that what is listed on the label is inside the box, thereby not requiring all cuts to be individually labeled.

SUMMARY

Meat usually is the center-of-the-plate menu item around which the meal is planned. Poultry, fish, and vegetarian entrées have become popular because of their lower fat content and cost and have been replacing meat menu items. Meat is composed of muscle, adipose, bone, and connective tissues. It is considered nutrient dense and contains water, protein, fat, carbohydrates, minerals, and vitamins.

Meat must be federally inspected and stamped for wholesomeness to protect the customer before a foodservice operation can purchase it. Kosher meat is processed under the supervision of a specially trained rabbi and is stamped with the kosher symbol, but it must still meet all federal or state meat inspection laws before it can be sold.

Foodservice managers, chefs and cooks, and buyers should be able to identify various cuts of meat. The carcass usually has four primal cuts that are broken down into smaller cuts, called subprimal, and then portioned before selling to a foodservice operation. Often less tender meat is processed under federal inspection by a mechanical, chemical, or enzymatic treatment to make it more acceptable to the customer.

Grading of meat for quality and yield is available by the federal government but is not required. Most processors or packers have their meat graded, although some do it on their own. Writing specifications for meat has become easier since the Institutional Meat Purchase Specifications have become available.

Proper storage of meat is essential to maintain food safety and quality. Meat should be kept clean, covered, and cold to prevent foodborne illness or infection. Public hearings have been conducted by the Food Safety and Inspection Service to prevent meat-related tragedies, and the consensus was that a more scientific approach of identifying and eliminating risks is needed. The hazard analysis critical control points (HACCP) system and the more recent National Restaurant Association ServSafe® program were strongly supported.

REFERENCES

Allen, R. L. (1993). NCCR creates group to battle food fears. *Nation's Restaurant News, 27*(24), 7.

Allen, R. L. (1996). Operators: Revised meat-inspection law is only the beginning. *Nation's Restaurant News, 30*(30), 3, 155.

American Lamb Council. (Undated). *Recipes & menu ideas*. Englewood, CO: Author.

Beef Board and Beef Industry Council. (Undated). *Beef, it's what they're hungry for.* Brownsdale, MN: Author.

Beef Industry Council and Beef Board. (1992). *Chef's & foodservice operator's guide to BEEF.* St. Augustine, FL: Author.

Carr, T. (1992). *Facts from the Meat Board: Meat science . . . Trichinosis: Risk and prevention.* National Live Stock and Meat Board. (Series No. FS\MS 004). Chicago: Author.

Dube, L. O. (1991). Prime beef leads sales at upscale steakhouses. *Restaurants & Institutions, 101*(23), 125, 130.

Facts about *E. coli*. (1993). *Nutri-facts* (Kansas Beef Council), *19*(Spring), 1.

Hodges, G. (1996). Temperature technology is the wave of the future. *Nation's Restaurant News, 30*(36), 32, 64.

Johnson, B. A. (1994). Know your game. *Restaurants & Institutions, 104*(29), 91, 94, 96.

McLauchlin, A. (1993). Restaurants urged to cook ground beef thoroughly. *Restaurants USA, 13*(3), 7.

National Live Stock and Meat Board. (1991). *The Meat Board's Lessons on MEAT.* Chicago: Author.

National Pork Producers Council. (Undated). *Meat for the '90s PORK*. Des Moines, IA: Author.

National Restaurant Association, Educational Foundation. (1992). *Applied Foodservice Sanitation* (4th ed.). Chicago: Author.

Purdum, T. S. (1996). U.S. meat, poultry inspection system overhauled. New York Times News Service.

Ryan, N. R. (1994). Burgers. *Restaurants & Institutions, 104* (14), 90–91.

Somerville, S. (1996). The flap over ostrich. *Restaurants USA, 16* (6), 34–38.

Spears, M. C. (1995). Foodservice organizations: a managerial and systems approach (3rd ed.). Upper Saddle Ridge, NJ: Merrill/Prentice Hall.

Straus, K. (1992). Make the most of BEEF. *Restaurants & Institutions, 102* (26), 122–123, 126.

Ursin C. (1995). Untamed Tastes. *Restaurants USA, 15* (9), 26–30.

11

Seafood

Customers are falling hook, line, and sinker for seafood, according to a study by the National Restaurant Association (NRA) in conjunction with the National Fisheries Institute (NFI) (Papadopoulos, 1995). Seafood restaurant menu items create a win-win situation for operators and customers. According to the foodservice operators who participated in the study, offering seafood permits restaurateurs to increase profits and at the same time satisfy customers' demands. Offering a variety of seafood on the menu gives customers more choices and allows operators to increase profits because they can take advantage of seasonality and local availability of certain fish and shellfish.

Note that fish is a major component of the meat, poultry, fish, dry beans, eggs, and nuts group on the Food Guide Pyramid (Figure 10.1). Seafood provides enough variety to appeal to many customers. In this study, shrimp was by far the most popular seafood among restaurant diners. Species such as shrimp, crab, haddock, and flounder have universal acceptance. Although little-known varieties, such as skate, hoki, and tilapia, are beginning to appear on menus, traditional and regional varieties remain favorites. Ranked in order of popularity, operators listed shrimp, salmon, and swordfish as the most popular varieties among their customers.

The nutritional value—high in protein and low in fat—of seafood is the major reason for its rise in popularity. Restaurateurs said customers are more concerned with nutritional value, seafood safety, and price than with other issues covered in the survey. Customers have been ordering more grilled and less deep-fried seafood. More than half of the restaurants are offering raw seafood and in those that do, customers are ordering it less. Customers also want to know if the seafood is fresh or frozen. Respondents were more likely to purchase fresh ocean and freshwater fish than frozen but more frozen than fresh shellfish. Restaurateurs in the quick-service business also have to offer customers what they consider is a value at a price they can afford.

Purchasing seafood can be a complex and time-consuming task. In many restaurants featuring seafood, purchasing is delegated to one person who understands the product. Restaurant operators often rely on distributors who specialize in seafood when deciding what is the best purchase on the market that day. Results of the survey indicated that the buyer is more likely to purchase fresh seafood from a seafood-specialty distributor and frozen from a full-line foodservice distributor. Operators rated freshness, price, and flavor as the top three factors they consider when purchasing frozen or fresh seafood. Foodservice operators reported that fresh seafood is better than processed and that customers prefer it.

SEAFOOD IDENTIFICATION

Seafood is the general term for all edible aquatic organisms whether or not they come from the ocean or sea (Gall, 1992). A minimum of 1,000 species of finfish and shellfish are harvested from the wild or raised by aquaculture. Of these, 50 to 100 different species are in the marketplace. These products include

- well-known saltwater fish: cod, flounder, sole, salmon, and tuna
- less widely known and less expensive: hake, cusk, pollock, mackerel, and whiting
- freshwater fish: trout and catfish
- mollusks: mussels, clams, oysters, and scallops
- crustaceans: crabs, lobsters, and shrimp or prawns

Two major categories for the classification of seafood are vertebrate fish and invertebrate shellfish. **Vertebrate fish** have fins and are covered with scales; **invertebrate shellfish** are covered with some type of shell. In *The Seafood List* (Randolph & Snyder, 1993), which is the Food and Drug Administration's (FDA) guide to acceptable market names for seafood sold in interstate commerce, 42 pages are devoted to vertebrate fish species identified alphabetically by market name, followed by their scientific, common, and vernacular names, and 8 pages list invertebrate species identified the same way. For example, under the market name of catfish, 16 species also have scientific names, 14 common names, and 9 vernacular names. Because the nutritional value of seafood is the major reason for its popularity, the buyer needs to have a basic understanding of these values, along with the structure and market forms of finfish and shellfish to better communicate with the supplier.

Nutritional Value

Seafood is a protein-rich food, as are meat and poultry, but it also is lower in calories per 3-ounce cooked serving than other meats (Gall, 1992). Most lowfat species of fish contain less than 100 calories per serving, and fattier fish contain only 200 calories. Buyers can get a general idea about the fat content by looking at the color of the flesh. Lower-fat species, such as cod and flounder, have a white or light color; fattier fish, such as salmon, herring, and mackerel, generally have a much darker color. Protein in seafood contains all the essential amino acids, which are the building blocks the body needs to make protein. A 3-ounce cooked serving of seafood supplies about one third of the average daily recommended amount of protein. Seafood protein is easier to digest because it has less connective tissue than meat and poultry. That is why fish flakes easily when cooked and can be eaten without cutting, making it a good source of protein for people living in retirement homes.

Not only does the amount of fat in seafood need to be evaluated, but the kind of fat also should be considered (Gall, 1992). Fats in food are either **saturated,** which means they are usually solid at room temperature like butter and lard, or **unsaturated,** which are usually liquid at room temperature, such as vegetable oils. Most fat in seafood is polyunsaturated and contains a particular kind known as omega-3 fatty acids, which provides additional *health benefits*. Scientific research suggests that omega-3 fatty acids can help reduce the risk of heart disease by making blood less likely to clot and block blood vessels. Contrary to the belief that shellfish contains high levels of cholesterol, nutritionists now know that it contains less than 100 milligrams of cholesterol per 3-ounce cooked serving.

Fish are naturally low in sodium, but shellfish have a little more. Some processed seafood, such as surimi or imitation shellfish, smoked fish, and canned products, have salt added during processing and therefore contain more sodium.

Nutrition labeling for foods that are not packaged but are sold by weight was not practical. Congress passed legislation requiring the FDA to examine and make changes in the nutritional labeling of foods. The FDA decided that retailers must voluntarily provide nutrition information for fresh seafood, fruits, and vegetables by giving customers access to nutrient charts for the 20 most frequently consumed products in each category.

Fish

Buyers need a thorough understanding of the structure and market forms of fish and shellfish. Fish and shellfish live in the same water, but differences exist between the two.

Structure

Fish have backbones and thus are classified as vertebrates (Margen, 1992). Fish breathe through gills, swim with fins, and usually have scales. Many fish have similar characteristics, making substitutions easy: a fillet from white-fleshed fish is mild in flavor and flaky whether it is cod, flounder, or turbot. Most fish are categorized by their bone and body structure as a round fish or flatfish. A few exceptions are tuna, which has a cross-shaped skeleton, and shark and skate, which have cartilage instead of bones.

Flatfish has a flat, oval body with both eyes on one side of its head; it swims parallel to the ocean floor (Margen, 1992). The backbone divides the fish lengthwise, and two sets of ribs, one fanning up and the other fanning down from the backbone, make the fish look flat. Flatfish have two even rows of fin bones, one from the dorsal fin on top of the body and the other from the ventral on the bottom. These are easily trimmed from the body before preparation. Flounder is the best example of a flatfish (Figure 11.1); each fish produces two very thin fillets. Halibut is the largest flatfish, and the fillets are thick enough to be cut into steaks.

Figure 11.1.   Example of a flat-fish sole.

Source: From *Seafood Buyer's Guide* by the *Alaskan Seafood Marketing Institute* by C. Crapo and H. Pennington, 1995, Juneau, AK: Alaskan Seafood Marketing Institute (ASMI). Used by permission.

Roundfish has a more bullet-shaped body, and its spine lies deeper in the rounded flesh (Figure 11.2). One set of ribs point up from the spine and two sets vertically from the bottom of the backbone. Round fish, such as striped bass, red snapper, and salmon, are more difficult to fillet than flatfish, but the large fish have thicker fillets.

Market Forms

Fish, fresh or frozen, is marketed in various forms, as shown in Figure 11.3. Market forms should be identified in specifications.

- Whole or round: just as it comes from the water. Sometimes it is scaled.
- Drawn: eviscerated through a small opening but not split. Gills and scales usually are removed, but head and tail are left on.
- Dressed or pan-dressed: split, scaled, and eviscerated. Usually head, tail, and fins are removed. Pan-dressed most often refers to small dressed fish, such as rainbow trout, with head on.
- Steaks: thick cross-cut slices of roundfish, such as salmon, or thick flatfish, such as halibut. Skin and backbone are not removed. Portion size should be specified.
- Single fillet: meaty sides of fish cut away from the backbone. Most of the other bones are removed when fish is filleted. Sometimes skin is removed, but often it is left on if the fish is fatty, like salmon, to hold the fish together.

Figure 11.2.   Example of a roundfish: chum salmon.

Source: From *Seafood Buyer's Guide* by the *Alaskan Seafood Marketing Institute* by C. Crapo and H. Pennington, 1995, Juneau, AK: Alaskan Seafood Marketing Institute (ASMI). Used by permission.

Figure 11.3.   Market forms of finfish.

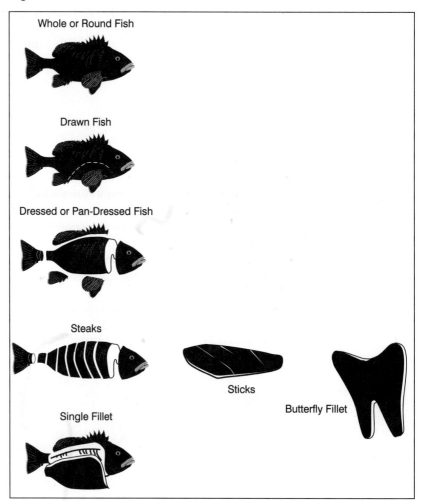

Source: Bureau of Commercial Fisheries, U.S. Department of Interior.

- Sticks: fillets cut lengthwise into pieces, usually of uniform size.
- Butterfly fillet: both sides of the fillet connected at the top.

Shellfish

People who do not like fish often are very fond of shellfish. Shrimp still tops the list of favorite seafoods.

Structure

Edible shellfish are divided into two categories: mollusks and crustaceans. **Mollusks** are animals with no backbones and soft bodies that usually have a shell and are classified into three types:

- univalves: a shell covering a soft underpart. Abalone is an example.
- bivalves: two connected shells. Clams, oysters, mussels, and scallops are examples. A scallop is a large mollusk's adductor muscle that holds the two shells together.
- cephalopods: an internal shell called a quill, ink sacs, and arms with suckers. Squid, octopus, and cuttlefish are examples.

Other edible shellfish are shrimp, crayfish, lobster, spiny lobster, and crab. These are called **crustaceans,** a type of seafood with a soft outer shell and jointed appendages.

Market Forms

Crustaceans are sold either alive or cooked in the shell. Most shrimp, crayfish, and spiny lobsters are marketed headless with the head and thorax removed. Lobster tails are the tails of spiny lobsters, which are much larger than tails of lobsters.

ENVIRONMENTAL FACTORS

The increase in demand for seafood and the decrease in supply is becoming a serious problem in the United States. People are being encouraged to eat more seafood because of its nutritional value, especially its lowfat content and low calorie count. Overfishing and pollution are some of the environmental problems decreasing supply. As a result, seafood prices to the consumer are on a steady increase. One solution to the problem is farm fishing or aquaculture.

Overfishing

As Congress looks for ways to regulate further commercial fishing in its effort to conserve diminishing resources, foodservice operators are preparing for additional short-term price increases and decreases in supply (Walkup, 1993). The House of Representatives voted in late 1995 to reauthorize and strengthen the expired Magnuson Fishery Conservation and Management Act to prevent overfishing and to strengthen marine habitat protection. The Senate has not yet considered its version of the bill. The National Marine Fisheries Service supports the bill because U.S. waters are overfished or seriously depleted of more than 40% of fish species. The fisheries database of the United Nations' Food and Agriculture Organization shows that the catch of some species has decreased by as much as 80% over the last 20 years.

The U.S. Department of Commerce closed a large fishery, which was a leading source of cod, haddock, flounder, and other popular species, located off the coast of Massachusetts. Many foodservice operators in that area agree that such environmentally motivated actions must be taken even though prices will increase and supply will decrease. They are leery of other possible amendments, such as tighter restrictions on fishing quotas or a global ban on fish importation. The problem of overfishing has caused all fresh wild seafood prices to increase in the last few years.

A dramatic decline in the king crab harvest illustrates that overfishing depletes resources (Walkup, 1993). In 1980, 128 million pounds of red crab were harvested from Bristol Bay, Alaska's main king crab fishery; in 1993, only 14.6 million pounds were harvested. The Alaska Department of Fish and Game closed the fishery to commercial fishing in 1994 and 1995 and has not decided whether to reopen it. Foodservice operators have been substituting snow crab, but that supply also is being depleted. Operators have been paying the same price for snow crab as they were for king crab. Several other Alaskan species, especially salmon, currently are being caught in record quantities, which the Alaska Department of Fish and Game has attributed to the state's "wonderful environmental conditions." Washington and Oregon also once produced excellent salmon, but environmental degradation of rivers there have diminished the salmon population.

Pollution

Restaurants that feature regional seafood are having a difficult time in trying to satisfy customer demands (Kapner, 1994). Pollution presents an additional supply problem. Many local oyster fisheries have been closed periodically because of agricultural runoff. Raw oysters and clams on the half-shell remain popular even though signs are posted by foodservice operators telling customers that the restaurant is not responsible for any foodborne illness brought on by these raw delicacies because all seafood is properly handled in that operation. If a problem occurs, the manager is not responsible, but the suppliers are. Many restaurants carry insurance in case lawsuits are filed. Foodservice operators who can afford the expense use independent laboratories to test the safety of their products.

Freshwater fish also suffer from pollution, overfishing, and habitat destruction (Walkup, 1993). The Great Lakes have had serious problems with pollution. Restaurants in that area featured fried perch dinners for most of the twentieth century, and customers would drive many miles to enjoy the local catch. However, state conservation officials in Wisconsin, Illinois, and Indiana recently decreased the allowable catch by two thirds. Many operators are supplementing wild fish with farm-raised fish. Some states are serious about conserving the fish population. Gill net fishing, in which fish are caught by snaring their gills in the meshes of the net, has been banned off the coasts of Florida and Louisiana. California also has outlawed gill net fishing, limiting the supply of fresh local sea bass and snapper. Despite all of these problems, seafood consumption in the United States continues to rise.

Aquaculture

Aquaculture is an elegant name for fish farming. It is the practice of growing fish and shellfish in tanks or in ponds (Moomaw, 1995). It has become increasingly common as a result of the environmental problems of overfishing and pollution. Aquaculture is relatively new to the United States, but not to the world. Aquaculture was practiced as early as 2000 B.C. in the Far East, and Japan and China remain the world leaders. Farm fishing influences the availability of seafood, affects prices, and gives foodservice operations and customers more year-round choices. The U.S.

aquaculture industry has quadrupled from its modest stature in 1980 and now produces close to a billion pounds of seafood a year, which is approximately 15% of the U.S. seafood supply (Moomaw, 1995). The prediction is that farm-raised seafood could soon approach 20% of the world's total production.

Variety of Products

Many of the seafood chains, such as Legal Sea Foods in Boston, Anthony's Fish Grotto and Ghio Seafood in San Diego, and Long John Silver's are using farm-fresh seafood to supplement the wild product. Most wild seafood is seasonal and sporadic. Without a trustworthy knowledge of supply cycles, putting some wild species on the menu can be tricky. Salmon can be served all year, and Long John Silver's supplements wild shrimp with farm-fresh for the several million pounds needed for its 1,435 restaurants annually.

Currently, catfish, trout, sturgeon, salmon, tilapia, clams, oysters, mussels, scallops, shrimp, lobster, and many other types of seafood are being farm raised. More farm-raised catfish is produced and sold each year than all other U.S. aquaculture species combined. Genuine U.S. farmed catfish is ranked the fifth most popular fish consumed in this country, after tuna, Alaskan pollock, cod, and salmon (National Fisheries Institute, 1993). Following is a breakdown of 1994 production and sales figures for the top five aquaculture fish (source USDA):

Species	Pounds Produced (in millions)	Estimated Sales (in millions)
Catfish	439	$374
Crawfish	56	$ 27
Trout	52	$ 53
Salmon	27	$ 60–65
Tilapia	17	$ 18–22

Source: USDA

The Process

Farming begins with the selection and mating of quality brood stock (The Catfish Institute, Undated). A brood fish that produces about 12 years will lay from 3,000 to 4,000 eggs per pound of body weight. Fertilized eggs are collected and placed in controlled hatchery tanks. After 7 days at a temperature of 78°F, the eggs hatch. The young fish are called "sac fry" because of the yolk sacs which supply their food. As the sacs are depleted, the fish begin to swim and are moved to a pond where they grow 4 to 6 inches long and are called fingerlings. They are then transferred into quality-controlled, clay-based ponds filled with pure fresh water pumped from underground wells at the rate of about 4,500 fingerlings per surface acre of water. The average pond, constructed by building above-ground levees to serve as natural barriers, is 10 to 20 land acres and 4 to 6 feet deep. Farm-raised catfish are fed a puffed, high-protein floating food pellet produced by area feed mills. This specially formulated feed is one reason that the farm-raised catfish's subtle taste differs from the muddy taste of the wild catfish. As of January 1, 1995, 144,200 acres of catfish ponds

Figure 11.4. Certified processor seal indicating that the processor has the highest standards set by the catfish institute.

Source: The Catfish Institute, undated. Used by permission.

are in Mississippi, Alabama, Arkansas, and Louisiana. The Certified Processor seal developed by The Catfish Institute (TCI), as shown in Figure 11.4, identifies genuine U.S. farm-raised catfish, the highest quality catfish available on the market today. Processors must meet the following criteria set by TCI to use the seal:

- be located in the United States
- process channel catfish that are farm-raised in the United States, grain-fed, and delivered live to the plant
- be inspected on a minimum weekly basis and then certified as a "sanitary inspected fish establishment" by the U.S. Department of Commerce (USDC)

Currently, more than 90% of U.S. catfish processors are allowed to use the quality seal.

Another result of the effects of overfishing and pollution is the introduction of underutilized species. Foodservice operators are beginning to feature less-known varieties on menus. Chefs are experimenting with various methods of preparation and recipes that make these more plentiful but less familiar species, which cost less than wild seafood, attractive to customers. Tilapia, skate, tautog, wolffish, Cape shark, ling cod, Atlantic mackerel, and rock fish are just a few of the underutilized species on menus today. Educating customers about the state of the world's fisheries is important as is education of waitstaff who must encourage customers to try these menu items. Tilapia is a good example. When it first came on the market, it was difficult to sell, but after recipes were developed and customers were introduced to it, tilapia is finally being accepted as a substitute for better known fish.

Ocean Trust is the country's only national foundation dedicated to protecting the oceans as a food source for humanity ("Cotton, Keogh elected to Ocean Trust," 1995).

It supports education and research on key issues affecting oceans today. The board includes marine scientists interested in environment and technology and seafood industry processors. One mission of the foundation is to form partnerships with foodservice operations to promote the responsible protection, science-based management, and rational use of the oceans as a source of food and livelihood for people around the world.

SEAFOOD MENU TRENDS

According to the National Fisheries Institute, the public spent more than $38 billion on seafood products in 1993, up from $35.2 billion in 1992 (Kindelan, 1995). Sixty-eight percent, or $25.7 billion, was spent at foodservice establishments. The U.S. Department of Agriculture (USDA) reports that per capita consumption of seafood increased from 14.7 pounds in 1992 to 14.9 pounds in 1993.

Menu Analysis

Seafood "good sellers" in 1994 were listed by *Restaurants & Institutions* (Frei, 1995) for commercial and noncommercial foodservice operations (Table 11.1). Even though customer preferences change, some perennial standbys continue strong in the 1990s. Salmon, with the highest sales potential in 1994, also was number one in 1991. Among the noncommercial segments, fried shrimp, number one, and catfish, number two, have maintained their status as popular menu items over the years. Orange roughy, popular in 1991 in the noncommercial operations, did not even make the top 15 list in 1994. Grilled tuna is not as popular in the commercial list as it was in 1991, but still remains in the top 15 list.

Appetizers with fish as the main ingredient were listed on 32% of menus that offered appetizers in 1994, up from 25% in 1989 (Kindelan, 1995). Nine out of 10 menus offering entrées (87%) listed an entrée with fish as the major ingredient in 1994. Out of 10 menus, seven offered appetizers with shellfish as the main ingredient, and shellfish entrées were on 76% of menus offering entrées in 1994.

Top Ten Seafoods

The National Fisheries Institute (NFI) listed America's 1994 top ten seafoods in pounds of edible weight per person (Frumkin, 1995). In addition to the weight of fresh and frozen seafood, the list includes processed products, such as canned fish, fish sticks, or smoked fish. A brief description of each seafood species follows.

1. **Tuna** tops the list, with 3.3 pounds consumed per person of which approximately 95% is canned. Several commercially important species are landed in waters throughout the world (Straus, 1995). Bluefin, yellowfin, and bigeye species are the most sought after, followed by albacore and skipjack. The fresh tuna steak served most often in restaurants is yellowfin or bigeye. Most canned tuna is albacore, skipjack, and some yellowfin, but only canned albacore can be labeled "white meat." The other species must be labeled "light meat."

Table 11.1. Popular seafood choices.

Commercial		Noncommercial	
Item	Index	Item	Index
Salmon	148	Breaded and fried shrimp	209
Mixed seafood platter	139	Catfish	182
Crab cakes	137	Mixed seafood platter	171
Breaded and fried shrimp	127	Breaded and fried	
Calamari	126	fish portions	152
Catfish	121	Boiled/steamed	
Orange roughy	116	whole lobster	141
Grilled/broiled tuna	116	Cod/scrod	138
Grilled/broiled shrimp	115	Scallops	123
Breaded and fried		Grilled/broiled shrimp	121
fish portions	114	Barbecued/Cajun shrimp	120
Cod/scrod	112	Lobster tail	114
Swordfish	112	Oysters	107
Halibut	108	Seafood kebab	104
Whitefish	106	Salmon	102
Boiled/steamed		Flounder	101
whole lobster	105	Crab cakes	99
		Halibut	99

Most often on menu:
Breaded and fried shrimp

Most often on menu:
Breaded and fried fish portions

Most added in last year:
Crab cakes

Most added in last year:
Catfish

Source: From "Fish & Seafood" by B. T. Frei, 1995, *Restaurants & Institutions, 105*(26), p. 80. Used by permission.

The Japanese revere bluefin, the largest of the tuna family at 15 to 80 pounds (although some reach 1,500 pounds), as having the finest meat. They most often serve it raw in sashimi and sushi. As a result of its popularity, bluefin has been overfished, depleting the stock and driving prices sky-high. Bluefin caught in the Pacific go straight to Japan, where customers gladly pay top yen.

Freshness of the meat when purchased is more important than color, which ranges from rich, ruby red to pale pink depending upon the species. The meat should be firm to the touch and smell as fresh as sea air. Tuna, often cut into loins, sometimes has a bloodline running through it. The bloodline has a more distinct flavor than the rest of the meat; some customers prefer to have it cut away.

2. **Shrimp** can be either warm-water or cold-water. U.S. shrimp are caught in the South Atlantic and Gulf of Mexico and also for import in the coastal waters off Latin America and Asia (Margen, 1992). These shrimp are classified by the color of their shells: white, pink, and brown. Cold-water shrimp caught in the North Atlantic and Northern Pacific oceans has a sweeter flavor and firmer meat than those in warm water. Most shrimp are frozen at sea for optimum freshness and practically no loss of quality. They often are thawed for sale and should be labeled "previously frozen." Fresh-

frozen shrimp are sold in bulk, whole, shelled, shelled and deveined, raw or cooked. Frozen cooked shrimp also can be purchased in packages. Shrimp are purchased by size from tiny, 150 to 180 per pound, to colossal, 10 or less per pound. Large shrimp usually are more expensive but taste the same as smaller ones (Margen, 1992).

3. **Alaska pollock** is known for its flavor, texture, color, versatility, availability, and nutritional content (Alaska Seafood Marketing Institute, Undated). It is lean with a tender texture, consistent snow-white color, and excellent flaking qualities. The cold, clear waters of Alaska are the world's largest resource for pollock, which is available year-round. It has proven ideal for every segment of the foodservice market, from quick-service to white tablecloth restaurants. It is equally delicious poached, baked, broiled, steamed, sautéed, or deep-fried. Alaska pollock, a member of the cod family, should never be confused with Atlantic pollock, a different species, which is darker, more oily, and has a fishier flavor. Alaska pollock is available year-round and foodservice operators can count on consistently serving a high-quality whitefish to customers who are increasingly quality conscious. The world's finest surimi seafood products, which are discussed under processed seafood, are made from high-quality Alaska pollock (Crapo & Pennington, 1995).

4. **Cod** is considered to be a perfect choice for a healthy diet because it is low in calories and an excellent source of high-quality protein and essential nutrients. It is found in both the northern Atlantic and Pacific oceans. It is one of the mainstays of New England fisheries. With a firm flaky texture, snow-white color, and mild flavor, it is sold whole but usually as fillets. Haddock and pollock also are members of the cod family. It is often called scrod but should be labeled as "scrod cod" (see page 316 for the definition of scrod).

5. **Salmon** has a unique flavor and color and superior texture that are attributed to the cold, clear waters of the North Pacific with its abundance of natural foods, such as shrimp and other small fish, to feed on (Alaska Seafood Marketing Institute, Undated). They swim upstream in over 2,000 freshwater rivers and lakes each year to spawn. Most fresh salmon and all canned salmon sold in the United States come from the Pacific Ocean. Atlantic salmon comes mostly from Canada and Norway. The following five species of salmon, each with its own characteristics, are available on the market:

- Alaska king or chinook salmon is the largest and least abundant of all five species. It is prized for red flesh, rich flavor, high oil content, and firm texture.
- Alaska sockeye or red salmon is known for its deep red flesh. Sockeye retains its color, firm texture, and distinctive flavor when cooked or processed. It has long been the salmon of choice of the quality-conscious Japanese market.
- Alaska coho or silver salmon has orange-red flesh, superior texture, and excellent eye appeal. It is one of the most commonly used species in foodservice.
- Alaska chum salmon is known for firm pink flesh and moderate fat content, which results in a delicate flavor. It has a strong demand in almost every segment of foodservice.
- Alaska pink salmon is the smallest in size and the most abundant. It is known for light, rose-colored flesh and delicate flavor. Its abundant supply makes it an attractive value.

Figure 11.5.   Promotion for U.S. farm-raised catfish.

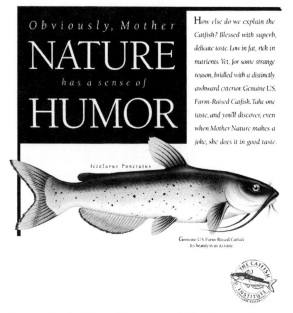

Obviously, Mother

NATURE

has a sense of

HUMOR

How else do we explain the Catfish? Blessed with superb, delicate taste. Low in fat, rich in nutrients. Yet, for some strange reason, bridled with a distinctly awkward exterior. Genuine U.S. Farm-Raised Catfish. Take one taste, and you'll discover, even when Mother Nature makes a joke, she does it in good taste.

Ictalurus Punctatus

Genuine U.S. Farm-Raised Catfish
Its beauty is in its taste.

Source: The Catfish Institute, undated. Used by permission.

6.   **Catfish** is the number-one farmed finfish in America (The Catfish Institute, Undated). More catfish is produced in the United States on a yearly basis than all other farmed-fish combined, and overall production has increased 80-fold since 1970. Catfish have been the brunt of many jokes because of their unique appearance (Figure 11.5). The Catfish Institute promotes its favorite fish with statements like "Obviously, Mother Nature has a sense of humor" and "even when Mother Nature makes a joke, she does it in good taste." Consumers are told that they will discover the true beauty of the catfish in its superb delicate taste. Farm-raised catfish are raised in pure, fresh well waters and fed only natural grains and proteins, making their flesh rich in nutrients and low in fat and proving that looks can indeed be deceiving.

7.   **Flatfish** are found in both North Atlantic and North Pacific waters. Only flounder and sole are in this category. Sole is a flounder with a delicate mild flavor and tender texture. Winter sole, lemon sole, Boston sole, and grey sole come from the Atlantic Ocean. Pacific varieties are rex, petrale, sanddab, and Dover or English sole. The latter two are similar to the excellent English or Dover sole of Europe. Dover sole sometimes is imported fresh or frozen from England, which is reflected in its price. Sole is usually sold whole or as fillets.

8.   **Clams** live in the Atlantic and Pacific oceans and can be either hard-shell or soft-shell. They are bivalves and the edible portions are the muscle that holds the shells together, the siphon through which the bivalve takes in water, and the foot which, when extended from the shell, moves itself through the sand. The largest eastern hard-shell clams, or quahogs, are chewy and are usually cut up and cooked in chowder. Cherrystones, which measure about 3 inches across, and littlenecks, about 2 inches across, are often served raw. New England also produces soft-shell

clams, which are dipped in batter and deep-fat fried. Hard-shell clams, called butter and littleneck clams, are found in the North Pacific. Hard-shell clams should close tightly when tapped; soft-shell clams (Ipswich and longneck) can be slightly agape to accommodate their protruding necks, which should move when touched. Clam meat should be plump and cream-colored and smell fresh. Clams in the shell are purchased alive; dead clams should not be eaten. Chilled shucked clams come from live clams and are delivered within 72 hours after shucking. They should be refrigerated to 38°F or below.

9.   **Crabs** are found in the Atlantic and Pacific waters. These crustaceans are divided into two categories: swimming crabs, such as the blue crab, and walking crabs, such as rock crab. The hard-shell Atlantic blue crab (sold as soft-shell during molting season) is most abundant in the summer and is considered the top variety in the east. Soft-shells are available from May to September. The Florida stone crab is unusual in that only its meaty thick-shelled claws are eaten. Just one leg is removed and the crab is thrown back in the water where it regenerates the missing leg. These crabs are caught from October through March. Dungeness crab is caught from California to Alaska and is one of the larger crabs. Alaska king crab, the largest of all crabs, is unmatched for its sweet flavor and rich, tender texture. It deserves its title, "King of Alaska" (Alaska Seafood Marketing Institute, Undated). Once harvested, it is transported live to processing plants where it is cleaned, cooked, and immediately frozen to preserve its superior quality and natural, fresh-caught flavor and texture. King crab is available in a variety of product forms, from whole or split legs and claws to selected portions. It is ready to serve after thawing. Snow crab is harvested in both the North Atlantic and Pacific oceans. Like king crab, its meat is sold cooked and frozen, making it available all year. Snow crab also is available in a variety of product forms, including cocktail claws, clusters (four legs attached to a piece of the shell on both the right and left side of the large body shell), whole legs, split legs, or lightly scored "Snap 'N Eat" sections. Because of the overfishing of king crab, snow crab has become an excellent substitution.

10.   **Scallops** are usually sold shucked because they deteriorate rapidly out of water (Bennion, 1995). They are the adductor muscle that opens and closes the fan-shaped shell of a large mollusk. Bay scallops, which are found in shallow Northeastern and Gulf coastal waters, are small and have a very delicate flavor. Sea scallops, found in deeper waters, are larger, 100 to 170 per gallon, and more common than bay scallops, 480 to 600 per gallon. Bay scallops are younger and smaller than sea scallops. Meats should have an ivory translucence and feel springy to the touch. A sulfur odor indicates deterioration. Scallops can harbor parasites and should not be eaten raw.

Processed Seafood

Most customers believe that fresh seafood is the best without realizing that fresh seafood does not mean it was harvested recently or is of top quality. It could mean that it has been out of the water for up to 20 days. Seafood quality cannot be improved once the fish leaves the water. It can only be maintained. Fishermen leave port with plenty of ice to keep their catch ice-cold while at sea. The fish is packed immediately and held just above freezing. To ensure freshness and the quickest possible processing, support boats called tenders collect the fresh-caught seafood from several fishing boats and take it back to port. Processing plants usually are located at port where the fish is quickly cleaned, graded, and processed as it comes off the boats.

Freezing and canning are the major processing methods for preserving seafood. Curing by smoking and pickling are other methods that preserve fish to some extent. However, preservation does not eliminate the need for proper storage. Smoked and pickled seafoods need to be refrigerated or canned. Other types of processing are not preservation methods but rather convenience methods. They include portion controlling, breading, and surimi. All processed seafood is under the jurisdiction of the FDA and must meet quality and fill of container identity standards.

Frozen

Seafood should be kept just above 32°F if it is going to be sold fresh, but if it will be sold as frozen, it should be quick-frozen at −20°F or colder, glazed to prevent drying, and then stored at −10°F. Potable water that is safe for drinking must be used for glazing, or covering the fish with a thin layer of ice at 0°F. Both fresh and frozen seafood products can be of high quality if they have been handled and stored properly. For example, the quality of seafood that has been harvested in a remote location and frozen immediately may be superior to that of a similar fresh product that has spent many days en route to its final destination (Gall, 1992). Seafood that has been frozen and then thawed before sale should be labeled "previously frozen."

Canned

The principal kinds of canned seafood are tuna, salmon, sardines, shrimp, crab, clams, and oysters. Not only is canned fish a convenient way to add fish to the diet, but it provides the same health benefits as fresh fish. Canned fish is low in calories, fat, and sodium, and high in protein, B vitamins, and omega-3 fatty acids (Margen, 1992). Of course, fish packed in oil doubles the calories and adds up to 10 times more fat. Much of the canned fish today is water packed. Only 15% of the calories in water-packed tuna comes from fat, compared to over 60% in oil-packed varieties.

One of the nutritional concerns with canned fish is the added salt, which is 4 to 10 times the amount of sodium found naturally in fresh fish. "Low salt" and "no salt added" varieties are available.

Only yellowfin, skipjack, albacore, bluefin, and Oriental tuna species are permitted to be labeled as tuna when in a can (Bennion, 1995). Only albacore may be labeled as white. Other species are labeled as light, dark, or blended. Four styles of packing for canned tuna are solid pack, which is designated as fancy, chunk, flake, and grated, all of which meet standards of identity prescribed by the FDA. The normal color of precooked or canned tuna is very pale to medium pink. Tuna that are tan in color are rejected.

Salmon canning is a big industry in the Pacific Northwest. The two most commonly canned species are the red sockeye salmon and pink salmon. Sockeye is the premier canned salmon. Its bright, deep-red color and firm texture make sockeye an excellent choice for salads or entrées in which color is key to the presentation. Pink salmon has a roselike color with a softer texture and milder flavor and lends itself to a wide array of dishes such as pasta, soups, sandwiches, and casseroles. Cost per serving is less than the sockeye salmon.

Cured

Fish is a very perishable food and requires preservation. Before refrigeration was available, fish was cured primarily by salting, drying, smoking, or pickling. Curing often imparts a distinct flavor that is unique for the variety of fish (Bennion, 1995). Not only do these curing methods preserve the fish, they also alter and enhance texture and flavor. The outer surface hardens and toughens some when the fish is salted, dried, or smoked. Examples of cured fish are salt cod, mackerel, finnan haddie, and kippered herring. **Finnan haddie,** a famous Scottish smoked haddock specialty, is cured in brine to which carotene pigment has been added and later smoked. Lightly cured finnan haddie is preferred but it does not keep well. The same is true with kippered herring cured the same way, but it is often canned to preserve its typical flavor. Herring is most often pickled in wine with onions, and sometimes sour cream is added.

Convenience

Many of today's menu items are sold with partial or complete preparation accomplished before the food is purchased. These convenience foods include the costs of preparation in their prices. In foodservice operations, informed decisions must be made regarding the cost advantages of buying prepared, or partially prepared, food products versus paying labor costs to prepare the foods from scratch in the kitchen (Bennion, 1995). Some foodservice operations have transferred the need for employees with culinary skills and time to prepare menu items from raw products from the kitchen to the processor. Interestingly, more and more quantity food textbooks are including convenience items in recipes. Foodservice operators should analyze cost comparisons between made-on-premises and purchased convenience products. The cost of ingredients should be calculated along with labor and utility costs. Finally, the most important factor to consider in the decision is customer satisfaction. Convenience seafood menu items include fish blocks, breaded seafood, and surimi.

Fish Blocks.   Included in the technological advances in the U.S. seafood industry is the production of deboned, minced raw fish from underutilized species and trimmings from fillets (Bennion, 1995). For example, frozen minced fish blocks are cut into fish sticks and portions that are sold in various forms, such as crunchy breaded pieces, breaded seafood nuggets, and even in the form of breaded little fish. These products can be raw or fully cooked. Raw products usually are breaded and need to be fried or baked, while cooked varieties only require heating before serving.

Breaded Seafood.   In 1991, the Connecticut state government surveyed breaded frozen products and found an average of 33.5% shrimp; the rest were bread crumbs

(Foulke, 1993). The method for breading is included in FDA standard 161.175, revised January 6, 1993, for label declaration of ingredients as follows:

- Frozen raw breaded shrimp is the food prepared by coating one of the following optional forms of shrimp: butterfly or fantail prepared by splitting the shrimp with or without tail fins, round and not split with or without tail fins, pieces consisting of a piece or part of a shrimp, or composite units in which each unit consists of two or more whole shrimp or pieces formed and pressed into a unit.
- The batter and breading ingredients are the fluid constituents and the solid constituents of the coating around the shrimp. These ingredients consist of suitable substances which are not food additives as defined in the Federal Food, Drug, and Cosmetic Act.
- Frozen raw breaded shrimp tests not less than 50% of shrimp material as determined by FDA testing methods. Frozen raw lightly breaded shrimp complies with the same regulations except it contains not less than 65% of shrimp material.

Surimi.   In Japanese, the word **surimi** means *minced fish*. The correct name for the crab, shrimp, lobster, and scallop products produced from surimi is *surimi seafood*. Surimi refers to the raw material from which all surimi seafood is produced. According to the FDA, surimi is an intermediate processed seafood product used in the formulation/fabrication of a variety of finished seafood products. It is minced fish meat (usually pollock) that has been washed to remove fat and undesirable matters, such as blood, pigments, and odorous substances, and mixed with cryoprotectants such as sugar and/or sorbitol. It is passed through a press to remove excess water and then frozen into blocks. In this form, surimi is a colorless and odorless pure protein paste. In making seafood products, surimi is thawed and blended with other ingredients, such as natural shellfish meat or shellfish flavoring, salt, water, and starch, and processed by heat for making fibrous flake, chunk, or other consumer products. For example, surimi seafood is available as (Surimi Seafood Education Center, 1995):

- whole legs that resemble Alaska crab legs, served whole or cut in smaller pieces that are perfect for dipping in a variety of sauces
- mini cuts, bite-size portions that are added to salads, stir-fries, or other cooked menu items
- salad or flake style, cut into appetizing chunks that look and taste like fresh crab meat and used in seafood salads, sandwiches, and pasta salads
- shredded and ready to mix into salads, stuffings, and hot or cold sandwiches and spreads

The finished products are marketed frozen or unfrozen and may be breaded. The FDA has established specific labeling requirements for surimi seafood products. The specific names of all seafoods used in the product must appear in the ingredient statement in descending order of predominance, and all other ingredients must also be declared in descending order.

Menu Items

Many customers have found to their astonishment that the main ingredient in their tuna salad, tuna sandwiches, and tuna noodle casseroles topped with crumbled potato chips actually can be purchased fresh and not just packaged in small, round cans (Frumkin, 1995). According to the National Fisheries Institute, the average American consumed 3.3 pounds of tuna in 1994. Of that tuna total, however, only about 5% is consumed fresh, but that small percentage translates into approximately 4.5 million pounds consumed in 1994. Fresh tuna rapidly has become popular with chefs because of its versatility. Between sandwiches and center-of-the-plate are menu offerings that include grilled tuna burgers, niçoise and Caesar salads topped with grilled tuna strips, tuna tacos, tuna kebabs, appetizers of tuna tartare and sashimi, and tuna soups and stews (Straus, 1995). It can be sautéed, roasted, stir-fried, or grilled. A chef in a Denver restaurant is serving a grilled tuna with a papaya chutney entrée. The tuna fillet is grilled quickly and then served with a housemade chutney prepared from papaya, red onions, ginger root, red peppers, lime juice, honey, olive oil, cumin, coriander, hot sauce, salt, and pepper. The tuna is plated with the chutney and sprinkled with fresh cilantro leaves.

Orange roughy was a trendy fish in the 1980s, but its popularity waned when the market became flooded with it, particularly the frozen product in supermarkets (Walkup, 1993). Tilapia, a farm-raised freshwater fish, sometimes is called the new orange roughy of the 1990s. It is easy to work with because it doesn't dry out easily. It is a mild-flavored fish, a member of the perch family that adapts well to various sauces. One chef gives it a macadamia crust and then sautées it and accompanies it with blood orange and carambola fruit purées. Another chef breads it with sourdough bread crumbs and pan-fries it in olive oil. He accompanies the fish with jicama-orange salsa and tomato-avocado salsa. Another advantage of tilapia is its low price. Skate is another inexpensive fish, abundant due to its large supply and small demand compared with cod, flounder, and sole (Parseghian, 1993). The largest single market for skate is France, but Korean, Chinese, Greek, and other ethnic markets in the United States snag large quantities at low prices. One chef in Los Angeles sautées skate with baby bok choy, brown butter, mushroom sauce, and fried parsnips.

Crab or seafood cakes are not the fish cakes of yore, a Friday staple made with leftover boiled cod and offered as a blue-plate special (Fabricant, 1994a). Good backfin or lump crabmeat, Norwegian salmon, lobster, rock shrimp, and even Dungeness crab are now used (Parseghian, 1996). Crab outsells all other menu items at many restaurants to the point that some chefs have taken the crustacean off the menu to force diners to try other menu items. Most seafood cakes have bread crumbs as an ingredient, but some chefs combine crab with mayonnaise, egg to hold the cakes together, and whole grain mustard, but no spices that will mask the flavor of the crab. These are then baked at 500°F for about 12 minutes.

Crab cakes are offered as entrées or bite-size appetizers with various sauces, such as red pepper, fennel, remoulade, lemon-butter, mustard, or spicy. In one restaurant, jumbo lump crab cakes are served with arugula, grilled corn salad, and roasted red pepper vinaigrette. In another, the cakes are served on creamy corn and fava bean succotash. Salmon also is becoming a favorite for fish cakes. A club in San

Francisco serves a salmon and potato cake with grilled fennel and a citrus vinaigrette. Yet there are throwbacks, shades of the blue-plate special: salmon croquettes with tartar sauce still are a popular menu item in both restaurants and noncommercial foodservice operations.

Fish will never replace bacon, but smoked salmon, trout, and even oysters are taking their place among breakfast meats (Johnson, 1995). Seafood is ideal for breakfast because it cooks quicker than most meats and is bland enough to go with eggs. Anglers have fried up the morning's catch with a couple of eggs in a cast iron skillet over a campfire on the river's edge for many years. For some time, chefs have been trying to update Eggs Benedict, originally a toasted English muffin as a base for grilled Canadian bacon and a poached egg topped with hollandaise sauce, by substituting smoked salmon or crabmeat for the Canadian bacon. Recently, pan-fried cornmeal-crusted trout topped with poached eggs and hollandaise sauce have been added to menus. In the Pacific Northwest, oysters are breaded and pan-fried, then stuffed into omelets. The executive chef at a Philadelphia restaurant was enjoying a bagel with cream cheese in her hotel room and remembered she had a jar of Beluga caviar in her purse as a gift from a friend (Johnson, 1995). She slathered it on the cream cheese and because it was so pedestrian and so decadent at the same time, she knew she had to put it on her new breakfast menu. She could not believe that the first order from the new menu was the $20 bagel with cream cheese and caviar; then and there she knew it would become a best seller.

Squid and octopus are appearing on more and more menus in the United States because of the Mediterranean influence that includes Moroccan, Turkish, Greek, and Middle Eastern. Squid and octopus are cephalopods, a Greek-derived word meaning *headed foot,* and are classified as mollusks with tentacles. Squid, which is sometimes called by its Italian name, calamari, is cut into rings, battered, fried, and served with a spicy sauce, quite often pesto sauce, as an appetizer (Fabricant, 1994b). The purplish-black octopus has a pliable body that consists of tentacles with little buttonlike suctions sprouting directly from its head. Octopus is combined with red wine in many menu items; tender octopus marinated in red wine and grilled over charcoal or braised in red wine and flavored with fennel seeds and cumin are examples. Octopus also lends itself to Greek salads, such as octopus with white beans and caramelized onions, or with string beans in a lemon vinaigrette, or with roasted tomatoes and cucumbers in a red wine vinaigrette, or fava beans, thyme, lemon, and rice dolmas. Chefs have found that calamari is chewy no matter how it is cooked, but to make octopus perfectly tender, it needs to be parboiled for 30 minutes to an hour before marinating, grilling, or braising it to give it flavor.

Many chefs are using chick lobsters that weigh about a pound each because they are more flavorful and tender and cost less than those weighing more than 2 pounds (Parseghian, 1995). Chicks, sometimes called babies even though they are between 4 and 7 years old, are cost effective. Typically yielding 3 ounces of meat, a chick is an ideal portion for appetizers. A cold chick-lobster salad has about a 33% food cost compared to a 55% food cost using a heavier lobster. Menu items using Atlantic Ocean chicks include an appetizer of claw meat and vegetables dipped in tempura batter and deep fried and served with a tomato-mint vinaigrette or a lunch entrée of barley risotto cooked in carrot juice and topped with baby lobster and fried zucchini flowers. Of course, big lobsters harvested on the New England coast weighing between 2.5 to 4 pounds are still considered the big king and can cost the customer as much as $60. Some restaurants use Maine cull lobsters that have one claw missing. The cost drops as much as 30% if cull lobster is served. Because of their attractive price, culls are popular in restaurants. Customers appreciate the savings and agree they really do not need the extra claw since the one left is a good size.

SEAFOOD INSPECTION

Despite public opinion that seafood is not inspected like all other food, it is subject to federal, state, and local government regulations and inspections. Federal legislation has been tightened, and a Hazard Analysis Critical Control Point (HACCP) program has been mandated by the industry.

Federal Legislation

The FDA is primarily responsible for the regulation of seafood at the federal level (Gall, 1992). The agency inspects seafood processing plants and imported seafood, oversees the National Shellfish Sanitation Program, samples and tests seafood products, and enforces labeling requirements. The FDA works with the individual states to implement these regulatory programs. The National Marine Fisheries Service in the U.S. Department of Commerce operates a voluntary grading and seafood inspection and grading program. FDA standards of identity for processed fish and shellfish are in the Appendix. The processor pays a fee for these services.

Even though seafood products have four grades—A, B, C, and Below Standard—grade A is usually requested for foodservice operations. Quality grades are based on appearance, uniformity, absence of defects, texture, and flavor and odor of the seafood. The quality stamp for U.S. Grade A is shown in Figure 11.6. Grades for breaded fish also include the amount of edible fish as compared with the amount of breading and presence of bones in a portion.

To ensure that seafood items are produced under continuous government inspection, the buyer can demand that the seafood has a Packed Under Federal Inspection seal (Figure 11.6), which indicates the seafood is clean, safe, and wholesome. It also indicates that it has been produced by a processing plant that meets all sanitary guidelines of the National Marine Fisheries Service.

Economic Fraud

The FDA has begun to focus more intensely on its mandate to reduce economic fraud in the seafood industry. In 1991, the agency established the Office of Seafood, with a 60% increase in funding for seafood inspection and expanded resources for field offices (Foulke, 1993). Species substitution—selling a cheaper fish as though it

Figure 11.6. Quality and federal inspection stamps for seafood.

were a more expensive one—is one of several kinds of economic fraud involving seafood sales that disturb customers, reputable dealers, and the FDA. Overbreading, another example of economic fraud, has customers paying shrimp prices for bread crumbs, and overglazing shell fish causes customers to pay lobster tail prices for ice. The seafood industry does not condone economic fraud. Its extent is not well documented. The goal of the National Marine Fisheries Service is to combat fraud in the seafood industry to ensure customers full value. Fraud is not always intentional. A misunderstanding or lack of information might lead a seller to buy a misrepresented product. However, even if the seller does not understand the information on the label, the FDA holds the seller responsible.

Species substitution and improper labeling are probably the greatest abuses, especially if the abusers are making a big profit. Purchasing from a reputable dealer is essential. Foulke (1993) has listed some distinguishing characteristics of some popular species.

- Haddock has a dark lateral line along the skin surface.
- Skinless cod fillets have a distinctive white papery membrane along the belly and a white line of fat along the lateral line of the fillet.
- Shark and swordfish look alike, but shark has a dark streak of flesh in the center and rough skin along the edge.
- Red snapper comes only from the southern Atlantic Ocean and the Gulf of Mexico (ask your dealer where the snapper originated).
- Orange roughy comes only from Australia or New Zealand and always arrives frozen. It may be sold thawed, but it must be labeled as previously frozen.
- Scrod is not a type of fish. The term originated in the Boston area to describe the catch of the day. It is a fish under 2½ pounds that is either cod, haddock, or pollock. It should be labeled on a restaurant menu as "scrod cod," "scrod haddock," or "scrod pollock."

The FDA has been very active in finding abusers who substitute less-expensive seafood for high-priced species to make a profit. A few examples are fresh rockfish from Canada labeled as red snapper and oreo dory from New Zealand labeled as orange roughy (Foulke, 1993). If these had not been detained by the FDA, the seller could have made thousands of dollars of profit. The FDA maintains *The Seafood List* (Randolph & Snyder, 1993), which includes the acceptable market, scientific, and regional names of over 1,000 species, in cooperation with the National Marine Fisheries Service.

Adding color additives to the feed of farm-raised fish also is being examined by the FDA. A Vitamin A additive turns trout flesh to the color of salmon, a much higher priced species. It is then marketed as "salmon trout," which is not an acceptable market name. Adding excessive water to seafood is being monitored. Scallops naturally consist of 75% to 79% water, some of which is lost when they are harvested and taken out of the shell. Adding more than is lost and charging scallop prices for it is illegal. The FDA does not object to the industry practice of using a frozen glaze to protect products, such as frozen shrimp and lobster tails. However, that glaze cannot be part of the net weight. Mislabeling a product merits a warning letter from the FDA. Roe (fish eggs) cannot be labeled *caviar* unless it is from the sturgeon species. The current market price for Beluga sturgeon caviar is approximately $85 an ounce, $45 for Ossetra sturgeon, and $35 for Sevruga sturgeon. Roe from other species, such as salmon, is approximately $6 an ounce.

Seafood Safety

Scientists agree that the seafood supply generally meets acceptable safety standards, but potential health risks occur with bacterial or viral contamination, naturally occurring toxins, and chemical contaminants (Gall, 1992). Also, the mandate from the FDA that all seafood processors develop an HACCP program will relieve concerns consumers might have about seafood safety. Note in Figure 11.7 that acceptable conditions for fresh fish, shellfish, and crustacea when received are determined by temperature, which should be below 40°F, and physical attributes such as odor, eyes, and texture. An acceptable and not acceptable quality checklist for fresh and frozen fish is shown in Table 11.2 (National Fisheries Institute, 1993).

Contamination

Improper handling of seafood is the most common problem that leads to foodborne illness. Seafood is a very perishable food that requires proper handling and preparation to maintain quality and ensure safety. The following handling procedures to maintain seafood quality and avoid illness are suggested by Gall (1992):

- Keep seafood cold at all times. Always keep seafood as close to 32°F as possible.
- Avoid cross-contamination. Do not transfer bacteria from one food or food contact surface to another when handling, storing, or preparing seafood.
- Store raw seafood in leakproof containers when possible. Prevent dripping onto other foods and keep seafood from being contaminated by other foods.
- Handle and store raw and cooked seafood separately. Raw foods should not drip or splash on foods that are not going to be cooked again before eating.
- Cook seafood properly. Seafood should be cooked to an internal temperature of at least 145°F (Figure 11.8).
- Cool cooked seafood as quickly as possible. Cooked seafood should be stored in small containers immediately in the refrigerator.
- Thaw seafood properly. Frozen seafood should be thawed in the refrigerator. In an emergency, it should be kept in the package under cold, running water.

Figure 11.7.   Acceptable and unacceptable conditions for fresh seafood.

Food	Accept	Reject
Fresh Fish 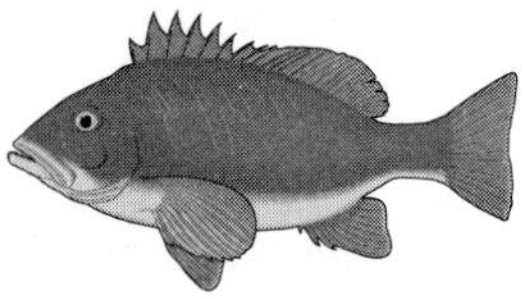	**Temperature:** at 40°F (4.4°C) or lower **Odor:** no fishy odor **Eyes:** bright, clear, and full **Texture:** flesh and belly are firm and spring back when touched Packed in self-draining ice	**Color:** gray or gray-green gills **Odor:** fishy or ammonia odor **Eyes:** sunken, cloudy, or red-bordered **Texture:** dry gills; flesh is soft and gives; if a finger is pressed on the flesh, the fingerprint will stay
Fresh Shellfish (such as clams, mussels, oysters) 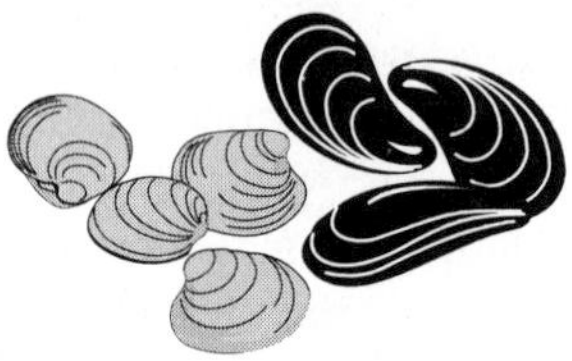	**Temperature:** at 40°F (7.2°C) or lower for live shellfish; 0°F (−17.8°C) for frozen products No strong odor **Shells:** closed **Shipped:** alive Identified by a shell stock tag. Lots should not be mixed up. Record the delivery information, including the dates on the tags. Tags must be kept for 90 days.	**Shells:** if they are partly open and do not close when tapped the clams, mussels, and oysters are dead.
Fresh Crustacea (such as lobsters, shrimp) 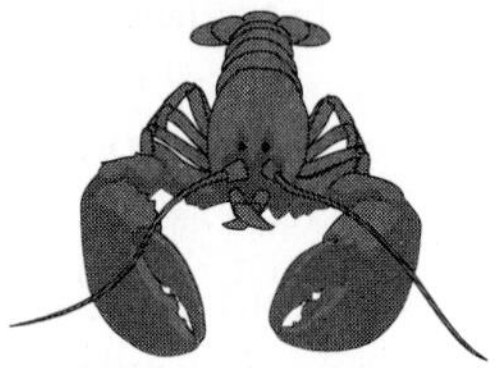	**Temperature:** at 40°F (7.2°C) or lower for live lobsters; 0°F (−17.8°C) for frozen products **Odor:** no strong odor **Shipped:** alive **Lobster shell:** hard and heavy	**Shell:** soft **Odor:** strong

Processor HACCP Program

Foodservice operators have been cheering the FDA's new regulations intended to improve seafood product safety by requiring all processors to have an HACCP program in operation by 1998 (Allen, 1996). This should increase customers' confidence that seafood is safe to eat. The suppliers bear the brunt of this action; many major suppliers already have a system in action. The biggest problem could be that only a couple hundred inspectors are charged with keeping tabs on nearly 6,000 proces-

Table 11.2.   Quality checklist.

	ACCEPTABLE	NOT ACCEPTABLE
Fresh Whole Fish		
Eyes	Clear, bright, bulging, black pupils.	Dull, sunken, cloudy, gray pupils.
Gills	Bright red, free of slime, clear mucus.	Brown to grayish, thick, yellow mucus.
Flesh	Firm and elastic to touch, tight to the bone.	Soft and flabby, separating from the bone.
Smell	Inoffensive; slight ocean scent.	Ammonia, putrid smell.
Skin	Opalescent sheen, scales adhere tightly to skin.	Dull or faded color, scales missing or easily removed.
Belly Cavity	No viscera or blood visible. Lining intact. No bones protruding.	Incomplete evisceration; cuts or protruding bones; off-odor.
Fresh Fillets or Steaks		
Color	Insignificant bruising, blood spotting, or discoloration visible.	Major bruising, red spots or yellow or brown discoloration.
Smell	Ocean-fresh, slight seaweed smell.	Musty, yeast-like, or putrid odors.
Flesh	Consistent texture, firm to touch.	Gaping, soft and mushy, dried edges; excessive bits of skin, fin, scales.
Frozen Fish		
Flesh	Solidly frozen; uniform color. When thawed, meets "fresh" criteria above.	Partially thawed, white or dark spots, freezer burn (yellow or cottony edges); discoloration; tough when cooked.
Packaging	Tight, moisture-proof wrapping.	Loose or non-airtight wrapping; formation of ice crystals.
Ice (On frozen block product)	Clear, clean.	Discolored or cloudy.

Source: From *Seafood Service: 7 Steps to Selling Seafood* by the National Fisheries Institute, 1993, supplement to Restaurant Business Incorporation Publications. Used by permission.

sors. The previous inspection program reacted to problems, but the new system is more proactive by requiring processors to identify and continuously monitor production steps that have the greatest safety hazards, including toxins, chemicals, pesticides, and decay. Processors will be required to show their HACCP plan to FDA inspectors. Former FDA Commissioner David A. Kessler said that "our safety inspections should focus on preventing problems rather than chasing the horses after they're out of the barn." He also asserted that HACCP is a system that makes this possible.

Although fishing vessels, carriers, and retailers are exempt from the regulations, processors are responsible for knowing where the seafood comes from and its condition when it leaves the plant (Allen, 1996). This is an expensive system, but the seafood industry believes it will pay off in the end. Many seafood industries already have an HACCP program in operation and have found it to be cost effective. Long John Silver's, the 1,500-unit, quick-service seafood chain based in Lexington, Ken., trains its suppliers in seafood safety, and company officials make frequent trips to

Figure 11.8.   Seafood temperature danger zone.

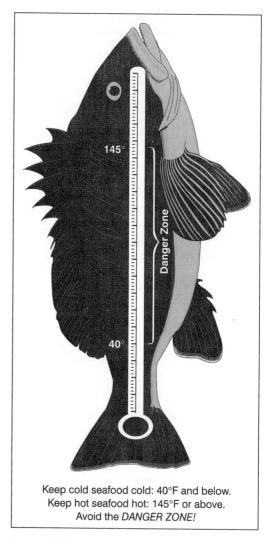

Keep cold seafood cold: 40°F and below.
Keep hot seafood hot: 145°F or above.
Avoid the *DANGER ZONE!*

Source: FDA.

trawlers and factories where their produce is caught and processed. In addition, all products served in their restaurants are tested at one of the company's three seafood audit laboratories.

PURCHASING SEAFOOD

Purchasing seafood can be a complex and time-consuming task. If the foodservice operation is a seafood restaurant, will only fresh-caught seafood be served? If the answer is yes, the menu must change daily, depending upon what is available on the market. If fresh frozen seafood is acceptable when fresh is not available, the menu might not have to be changed so often. If the foodservice operation is in a hospital, cod or haddock might be on the menu and frozen individual portions can be purchased from the full-line supplier.

Supplier and Buyer

The relationship between the distributor and buyer grows best in an atmosphere of open communication and clear expectations. The buyer needs to know about the distributor's operation. If the buyer cannot visit the plant where the fish and shellfish come from, then a visit to the office of the supplier who delivers the seafood is imperative. The supplier can tell the buyer how the distributor handles the seafood, and the buyer can see how the supplier handles the fish and transports it to the foodservice operation. The buyer should select a supplier who fits the buyer's operation. Helping the supplier understand the buyer's operation, preferably with a visit, also is an important part of open communications.

Foodservice operators are in an enviable position when purchasing seafood. Competition among distributors and suppliers is stiff, and service to the operator is important. Like the relationship the operator has with the customer, the relationship between the distributor, supplier, and buyer must be based on trust. The buyer should get a full tour of the supplier's operation and should check the receiving docks, the HACCP checklists, storage and handling procedures, and especially the cutting and packaging areas. Ask questions and keep asking them until you are satisfied with the answers. If shrimp harvests are wiped out by a warm ocean phenomenon that affects shrimp populations, will the distributor be able to offer cost and quality substitutions quickly? How much lead time does the distributor need for orange roughy from Australia, swordfish from Canada, or mahi mahi from Hawaii?

Ask the distributor to tell you before, not after, a price rises significantly for a particular seafood. Ask your distributor for information on new products. Check prices and quality available from other distributors. Some distributors are better equipped than others to run food costs and percentages for you and to give you accurate market and seasonality information before you make a decision. Long-term relationships with suppliers pay off in the end; therefore, choosing your distributor based on service and value, not just price, is the best route.

Specifications

Writing specifications is a two-step process, according to the National Fisheries Institute (1993). First, the seafood buyer has to know what the manager wants on the menu. Second, standards must be set from which smart buying decisions can be made. These steps will be easier if the buyer has a close working relationship with the seafood distributor or processor.

Writing Specifications

Specifications need to be written so everybody, including the distributor, can refer to them. Items to consider when writing specifications include the following:

- *Species.* Appearance, yield, flavor, and cost can vary between king salmon and pink salmon. Taking time to find out the difference between Chinese white shrimp and black tiger shrimp will pay for itself in the future.
- *Origins.* If Mississippi catfish and crab from Chesapeake Bay are on the menu, they must be served. Wild, fresh-frozen, or farm-raised seafood should be noted on the menu and written in the specification. Whether the catch is frozen at sea or delivered daily by fishing boat to a shore-based processor should be specified. These factors affect cost, shelf life, and quality.
- *Product form.* Fillets, steaks, breaded sole, and prebattered shrimp may cost more initially, but save labor time and cost.
- *Yield.* The buyer and supplier should agree on yield specifications first. Decisions on drip-loss and what percentage is acceptable when thawing block-frozen shrimp should be spelled out. If the product is glazed, the percentage of ice allowed should be specified and checked when received.
- *Quality.* The U.S. Department of Commerce (USDC) grade and inspection stamps ensure that the quality of the seafood desired by the buyer is met. If a grade is not available, the seafood brand can be helpful, or the buyer can write in the quality desired.
- *Standards.* Developing useful standards requires clear evaluation techniques. The checklist in Table 11.2 is a guide for developing specific criteria tailored to the operation.
- *Quantity.* Amount of seafood to be purchased should be specified.
- *Processing.* Seafood is sold frozen, canned, cured by smoking or pickling, or ground or flaked and made into preformed products.
- *Additives.* Even though sulfites or tripolyphosphates may improve appearance and lessen drip loss in fillets and shellfish, they must be listed on product labels. Some customers are allergic to these chemicals. If that is a concern, "no additives permitted" must be emphasized on the specification.
- *Pack style and size.* A 5-pound block of frozen Alaska king crab should have 60% body and 40% leg meat and should be specified. A pack style different from an industry standard should be written in the specification. Many distributors will custom-pack to an operator's specifications.
- *Substitutions.* In case of a natural act, such as bad weather or new fishing regulations, a substitution might be made by the distributor with the buyer's consent.

Sample Specifications

As mentioned earlier, the best way to develop specifications is to work with a supplier who is knowledgeable about seafood. Your supplier knows the market and what is available when. The following sample specifications are for portioned fish, breaded fish, live lobster, and cherry stone clams.

Rainbow Trout

Origin: trout farms on the freshwater Snake River, Idaho

Form: dressed (eviscerated and head, tail, fins, and skin removed)

Use: grilled whole fish to be boned at table

Preservation form: fresh, 35°F on delivery in refrigerated truck

Quality: USDC grade A or equivalent

Weight: 8–10 ounces drawn

Pack: 10-pound carton

Price: by the carton

Orange Roughy

Origin: New Zealand waters

Form: boneless and skinless fillets

Use: broiled

Preservation form: frozen, −10°F on delivery in refrigerated truck

Quality: USDC grade A or equivalent

Certification: PUFI seal

Weight: 6–8 ounce fillet without glaze. Tolerance ± 0.5 ounce. Glaze shall not be over 6% of total weight.

Pack: 20-pound carton

Price: by the carton

Breaded fish (pollock) sticks

Origin: Northern Atlantic Ocean

Form: boneless and skinless fish sticks, lightly breaded IQF

Use: oven-baked

Preservation form: frozen, −10°F on delivery in refrigerated truck

Quality: Van de Kamp's breaded fish sticks or equal

Weight: 0.67-ounce/stick, 65% solid fish, 35% breading

Pack: 10-pound carton

Price: by the carton

Mussels

Origin: farm raised

Form: live, in-shell, debearded

Use: steamed

Preservation form: fresh, 35°F–40°F on delivery in refrigerated truck

Quality: shells should be clean and reasonably free of dirt and debris and should close tightly when tapped

Weight: 45–55 pounds/bushel
Pack: bushel
Price: by the bushel

RECEIVING SEAFOOD

Inspect seafood immediately when delivered and keep it cold during the inspection process. Two employees often are appointed to conduct the inspection, because it must be completed before the truck leaves the premises. One employee checks the items against the invoice and the other puts them in refrigerated storage immediately. Damaged boxes, leakage, or moisture-damaged exteriors should be noted on the delivery log. Receivers should have instant-read thermometers to check the temperature of the seafood products as soon as they are unloaded from the truck. Temperature for fresh fish should be 30°F to 38°F and for frozen fish 0°F to 10°F. Live shellfish, such as lobsters and crabs, should be packed in mesh nets or in other packing materials that keep temperatures around 40°F, moisture high, and oxygen available. Temperatures for mollusks, including clams, mussels, and scallops, should be no more than 40°F.

Weights need to be checked while the delivery person is present. When finfish or shrimp are glazed, the glazed product should be weighed and then the glaze rinsed off under cold water and drained for 2 minutes before weighing a second time to determine the net weight. The net weight should be divided into the difference between the net and glazed weight to find the percentage of glaze on the product. If the difference as stated in the specification is more than 10%, the price needs to be adjusted accordingly. For example, 5 pounds of shrimp is glazed into a block with a resultant weight of 5.6 pounds.

$$5 \text{ pounds} \div 0.6 \text{ pounds} = 0.12 \text{ or } 12\%$$

Because this is 2% more than specified, either the price should be reduced or more shrimp added.

The odor of fresh seafood is the first indication of its quality. Top quality finfish and shellfish should have a saltwater scent that is fresh and not "fishy," stale, sour, or sharp with ammonia. The flesh should be firm and resilient if pressed with a finger. If finfish is a whole fish, the eyes must be bright, clear, and bulging. The skin is moist, bright, shiny, and metallic with scales that adhere tightly to the skin. Gills are bright pink or red and not slimy. Steaks and fillets have no browning around the edges, which often occurs with poor handling.

Dead or live shellfish with cracked shells should be rejected. Standards for good quality shellfish are specific. Open shells on mollusks close when tapped, lobster tails curl under when the animal is picked up, and crabs move when touched. Shells of live clams, oysters, and mussels are clean and reasonably free of dirt and debris (Gall, 1992). Soft-shell clams cannot completely close their shells, but they move when touched. The meat of freshly shucked clams, oysters, and mussels is plump and covered with liquid that is relatively clear, not cloudy or milky, and reasonably free of grit. Cooked whole lobsters, crabs, and crayfish are bright red in color, moist, and free of strong odor.

Frozen seafood needs to be frozen solid. Signs of thawing and refreezing include dryness, portions sticking together, water damage on the carton, or ice crystals that adhere to the inside of the package. Use products with an expiration date on the package by that date. Good packaging protects the seafood from freezer burn that causes discoloration and drying.

Contaminated canned seafood can be dangerous. The cans should show no signs of rust, dents, dirt, or swelling. A predetermined number of cartons containing canned seafood need to be opened and inspected by receiving personnel before signing the invoice.

Smoked fish has a bright and glossy appearance and no signs of mold or unusual odor. Smoked seafood requires refrigeration. Cross-contamination with raw products must be avoided because smoked fish seldom is cooked before it is eaten.

Proper storage is essential to prevent contamination and spoilage of seafood. The following tips for storing seafood come from the National Fisheries Institute (1993).

- Use a cloth or plastic wrap between ice and exposed cuts of fish, both fillets and steaks, to retain flavor and moisture. Thawed or fresh shell-on shrimp can be placed directly on flaked ice.
- Store whole, cleaned fish in a stainless steel pan with a perforated bottom rack for drainage. Cover fish with a clean towel and pile ice on top and around it. Fresh fish is stored at 32°F to 35°F.
- Live shellfish is stored in a cool, damp atmosphere between 35°F and 40°F.
- Keep frozen seafood at −18°F to −29°F.
- Stack frozen food cartons away from walls and off the floor for better air circulation.
- Mark the date on each box or package as it enters the storage area. Rotate stock on a first in, first out (FIFO) basis.
- Pasteurized seafoods, such as crabmeat or lobster meat, are refrigerated. Canned seafood or heat-sterilized seafood in sealed containers do not require refrigeration. The ideal temperature for this storeroom is 50°F to 70°F.
- Keep raw and cooked seafoods separated at all times.
- Constantly check temperatures in storage areas.

SUMMARY

Purchasing seafood can be a complex and time-consuming task. The two categories of seafood are finfish and shellfish. Most seafood is a high-protein food that is lower in calories, total fat, and saturated fat when compared to other protein-rich animal foods. A large proportion of the fat is polyunsaturated and contains omega-3 fatty acids. The increase in demand and the decrease in supply is becoming a serious problem. Overfishing and pollution of waters are two environmental problems decreasing supply; farm fishing, or aquaculture, is growing in popularity as a result.

Freezing and canning are the major processing methods for preserving seafood. Most seafood has been partially or completely prepared before purchasing for use in food-service operations. Federal legislation has been tightened and a Hazard Analysis Critical Control Point program is now required for the industry. Economic fraud, especially species substitution and improper labeling, in the seafood industry is being scrutinized by the Federal Drug Administration. In purchasing seafood, a good relationship between the supplier and buyer is important; the supplier also can give a great deal of help in writing specifications. Because fish is very perishable, good receiving and storage practices are necessary.

REFERENCES

Alaska Seafood Marketing Institute, (1997).

Allen, R. L. (1996). Foodservice operators cheer FDA's new HACCP seafood-safety program. *Nation's Restaurant News, 30*(2)3, 61.

Bennion, M. (1995). *Introductory foods* (10th ed.). Upper Saddle River, NJ: Prentice Hall.

The Catfish Institute. (Undated). *Catfish, the cultured fish.* Belzoni, MS: Author.

Cotton, Keogh elected to Ocean Trust foundation board. (1995). *Nation's Restaurant News, 29*(45), 26.

Crapo, C., & Pennington, H. (1995). *Seafood buyer's guide by the Alaskan Seafood Marketing Institute.* Juneau, AK: Alaskan Seafood Marketing Institute.

Fabricant, F. (1994a). Fish cakes swim up the food chain. *Nation's Restaurant News, 28*(41), 37.

Fabricant, F. (1994b). Octopus comes out of hiding. *Nation's Restaurant News, 28*(30), 75.

Foulke, J. E. (1993). Is something fishy going on? *1993 FDA Consumer.* Publication No. (FDA) 94-2274.

Frei, B. T. (1995). Fish & seafood. *Restaurants & Institutions, 105*(26), 80.

Frumkin, P. (1995). Hot tuna. *Nation's Restaurant News, 29*(32), 41.

Gall, K. (1992). *Seafood savvy: A consumer's guide to seafood nutrition, safety, handling, and preparation.* Information Bulletin 1041B226. Ithaca, NY: Cornell Cooperative Extension Publication.

Get Hooked on Seafood Safety. (1993). U.S. Food and Drug Administration.

Hedden, J. (1996). The row over fish. *Restaurants USA, 16*(9)17–19.

Johnson, B. A. (1995). Catch of the morning. *Restaurants & Institutions, 105*(15), 126,128.

Kapner, S. (1994). The raw deal on shellfish. *Nation's Restaurant News, 18*(32), 43,49.

Kindelan, A. (1995). Seafood reels in customers. *Restaurants USA, 15*(5), 43–45.

Margen, S. & Editors of the University of California at Berkeley Wellness Letter. (1992). *The wellness encyclopedia of food and nutrition.* New York: Rebus.

Moomaw, P. (1995). Catch of the day: Farm-fresh fish. *Restaurants USA, 15*(5), 26–30.

National Fisheries Institute. (1993). *Seafood service. 7 steps to selling seafood.* A supplement to Restaurant Business Incorporation Publications.

National Restaurant Association, Educational Foundation. (1995). *Serving safe food, certification coursebook.* Chicago: Author.

Papadopoulos, H. (1995). Fish tales—operators reel in diners with seafood. *Restaurants USA, 15*(10), 43–46.

Parseghian, P. (1993). Skate takes wings. *Nation's Restaurant News, 27*(1), 25.

Parseghian, P. (1995). Lobster tales. *Nation's Restaurant News, 29*(30), 69.

Parseghian, P. (1996). Crab cracks top menus, claws way to crustacean heights. *Nation's Restaurant News, 3*(4), 23.

Randolph, S., & Snyder, M. (1993). The seafood list. Washington, DC: U.S. Government Printing Office.

Straus, K. (1995). All about tuna. *Restaurants & Institutions, 105*(103), 96.

Surimi Seafood Education Center, National Fisheries Institute. (1995). *Surimi Seafood.* National Fisheries Institute. Arlington, VA: Author.

Walkup, C. (1993). Restaurateurs brace for seafood supply decreases. *Nation's Restaurant News, 29*(40), 1, 64.

Poultry and Eggs

The Food Guide Pyramid recommends two to three daily servings of meat, poultry, fish, dry beans, eggs, or nuts, but the size of the poultry in the pyramid is the biggest in that group. Could the reason be that Americans driven by health concerns and lower prices have literally tripled their consumption of poultry, especially chicken, in the last 20 years? In 1960, approximately 30 pounds of poultry per person were consumed, compared with approximately 90 pounds today. In addition, note that eggs are included in this group as an alternative to lean meat, poultry, or fish. A whole egg is counted as one third of a serving because its protein is of the same high quality as the other products. This chapter is divided into two parts: poultry and eggs.

POULTRY

The term **poultry** is used to describe all domesticated birds that are intended for human consumption (Bennion, 1995). These include chickens, turkeys, ducks, geese, and lesser known birds.

Turkey is a truly American food, as demonstrated by these facts from the National Turkey Federation (1995).

- Turkeys originated in the Americas millions of years ago. When the Pilgrims and native Americans had their first Thanksgiving dinner, four wild turkeys were served.
- More Americans serve turkey on Thanksgiving than any other entrée; 425 to 450 millions of pounds of turkey are served, which is about 2 pounds per person. No wonder there are leftovers!
- Over the last two decades, turkey consumption has increased 133%, probably because of convenience and nutritional awareness.
- Turkey sandwiches account for 48% of all turkey consumption.
- According to 1990 USDA data, Israel consumes more turkey per capita than any other country; the United States ranks a close second.
- When Neil Armstrong and Edwin Aldrin had dinner on the moon, turkey was on the menu.
- Ben Franklin wanted to name the turkey, rather than the eagle, the national bird.

Popularity

Many quick-service restaurants specializing in hamburgers have added chicken products to their menus because customers are demanding tasty, lowfat substitutes. Chicken has always been popular and probably will remain so because it is relatively cheap, readily available, and easy to prepare in a variety of ways.

Nutritional Value

In the United States, the estimated per capita consumption of poultry in 1990 was almost equal to that of 64 pounds of boneless and trimmed beef (Bennion, 1995). Approximately 49 pounds of chicken and 14 pounds of turkey were consumed in that time period. Poultry's lower fat content is responsible for its rising popularity.

People are eating less red meat and more poultry to cut down on the amount of fat in their diets. Cooked chicken breast without skin is anywhere from 30% to 80% leaner than beef that has been trimmed of fat. However, cooked chicken has the same amount and quality of protein, minerals, and vitamins that cooked beef has. Only iron and zinc are slightly higher in beef. Eating chicken with the skin more than doubles the amount of fat and saturated fat. Chicken dark meat without skin is higher in fat and cholesterol than white meat without skin.

Turkey breast is the leanest of all meat, with just 135 calories and less than 1 gram of fat per 3½-ounce serving. Almost all the fat is in the skin as it is in chicken. Turkey dark meat is higher in fat than the white meat but is still relatively lean. Turkey is high in the same nutrients as other meat. It is high in protein, niacin, vitamin B_6, vitamin B_{12}, and phosphorus and provides good amounts of iron, zinc, riboflavin, and magnesium.

Duck is all dark meat. Approximately 50% of the calories in duck comes from fat; if the skin is eaten, 75% comes from fat. Most of the fat is found in a thick layer under the skin, making duck high in calories and resulting in a greasy taste. The skin should be thoroughly pricked while duck is roasting. It is high in B vitamins and iron. Goose also is all dark meat. It is very similar to duck in calories and should be cooked the same way.

Purchase Price

Chicken is a rare bird in that it is an equally favorite food of creative chefs, cost-conscious customers, and knowledgeable nutritionists. In the 1930s during the Great Depression, poultry was considered an expensive menu item and was served only on very special occasions such as Thanksgiving and Christmas. If a business was surviving, management would reward employees by giving them a fresh turkey for Christmas.

The poultry business is highly regulated, from state laws restricting truck weight to federal inspectors who work beside employees in plants. The poultry business has always been cyclical. In 1965, Tyson Foods, Inc., in Springdale, Ark., the largest poultry producer and processor in the world, sought refuge from the boom-or-bust cycles by inventing **Rock Cornish game hens,** named for the cross-breeding of the Cornish game cock with the White Plymouth Rock chicken. They are 5- to 6-week-old, plump-breasted birds, very low in fat, weighing 1 or 2 pounds. Tyson sold them to markets as specialty items for 50 cents each at a higher profit than chickens sold by the pound.

Today, chicken and turkey are available year-round because of modern technology. Whole chicken and turkey are usually sold frozen, and the price per pound generally is much less than that of red meat. According to the U.S. Department of Agriculture (USDA), currently ready-to-cook turkey is ranked as one of the top economical meat buys. The more processing that is done—for example, boning and skinning—the higher the price, but the price per edible pound still is less than that for meat. The price of duck and goose per edible pound is much higher than for chicken and turkey. The demand for duck and goose is less and so is the yield.

Menu Trends

According to the 1995 *Restaurants & Institutions* menu census, rotisserie chicken had the biggest gain in popularity in both commercial and noncommercial foodservice operations (Frei, 1995). It did not even appear on the magazine's 1991 menu census. Many foodservice operators in all segments of the industry, including hospitals, colleges, restaurants, and supermarkets, have added rotisserie chicken to their menus in the past year. Rotisserie chicken comes in all flavors—plain, Cajun, lemon, and many others that please the customer's palate. Executives at Boston Chicken decided to give their rotisserie chicken concept a new and distinctive foodservice mission: to satisfy the cravings of people seeking a "home-meal replacement" (Nation's Restaurant News Editorial Board, 1994). Even though this meal can be eaten in a restaurant, Boston Chicken executives came up with the bright idea that customers might like to take home a freshly prepared nutritious meal that can be eaten at their own table on their own plates with their own knives and forks. Their idea has been so successful it is being copied by other foodservice operations.

KFC replaced its Colonel's Rotisserie Gold product because it proved to be too difficult to handle at the store level (Kramer, 1996). The new Tender Roast product is cooked and sold by the piece rather than as a whole, half, or quarter chicken, in keeping with the way KFC sells its fried chicken products. The rotisserie equipment purchased for Rotisserie Gold has been retrofitted to cook the Tender Roast chicken pieces. Like Rotisserie Gold, Tender Roast is marinated with a flavored coating, but the cooking time is shorter and easier for employees to handle.

Baked chicken is very popular in noncommercial foodservices, except for schools where chicken nuggets are very popular (Frei, 1995). Roast turkey, considered a comfort food, is found on many menus, and turkey pot pie is a rising star as are duck and quail and chicken/turkey sausage. Although duck has been served primarily in fine dining rooms, it is beginning to appear in hospital and college foodservices; quail also has made inroads in fine dining menus and Cornish hens in hotel and motel dining rooms.

Grilled chicken breast leads all poultry items in popularity, followed by broiled/grilled chicken, as shown in Table 12.1. Baked chicken appears on almost 100% of menus in all but one segment, schools, of noncommercial good sellers; chicken nuggets were at the top and were the best sellers at about half of schools

Table 12.1. Popular poultry entrées.

Commercial		Noncommercial	
Item	**Index**	**Item**	**Index**
Grilled chicken breast	177	Fried chicken	181
Broiled/grilled chicken	152	Roast turkey	166
Roast turkey	141	Grilled chicken breast	162
Turkey breast	139	Chicken nuggets	149
Fried chicken	138	Broiled/grilled chicken	148
Baked chicken	121	Baked chicken	140
Chicken pot pie	114	Turkey breast	139
Spicy chicken	108	Chicken patties	133
Rotisserie chicken	107	Barbecued chicken	113
Chicken nuggets	100	Rotisserie chicken	104
Other turkey	100	Chicken *cordon bleu*	103
Barbecued chicken	99	Other turkey	90
Chicken *cordon bleu*	97	Spicy chicken	79
Turkey pot pie	92	Turkey pot pie	77
Duck	83	Other game birds	73

Most often on menu:
Grilled chicken breast

Most often on menu:
Baked chicken

Most added in last year:
Chicken pot pie,
barbecued chicken

Most added in last year:
Rotisserie chicken

Source: From "Poultry" by B. T. Frei, 1995, *Restaurants & Institutions, 105*(26), p. 76. Used by permission.

surveyed. Chicken nuggets also are being served in more nursing homes and spicy chicken in more colleges and universities.

Many of the nation's most innovative chefs are exercising their creativity with turkey (Rogers, 1994). The one drawback to turkey is that people think of it only as a Thanksgiving bird. The rationale behind all-turkey restaurants that are cropping up in several parts of the country is that if one or two turkey menu items are good, then an all-turkey menu is even better. Although turkey tastes great and is nutritious, its convenience seems to account most for its growing popularity. Turkey sandwiches are especially popular. New products are coming out on the market, such as turkey tenderloin. Menu items include turkey kiev, blackened turkey ribeye, smoked turkey chops with black bean mango relish, and broiled turkey bone-in chops with cranberry salsa. Ground turkey is being used in place of ground meat in some foodservices, especially noncommercial operations. From tempting tacos to pizza toppings, meatloaf, and burgers, ground turkey is used increasingly because it is lean and protein-rich.

Classification

Poultry is classified by the kind and age of bird. The first way is by kind: chicken, turkey, duck, goose, guinea, or pigeon. The second criteria is by class that indicates the age of the bird and tenderness of the meat (USDA Agricultural Marketing Service, 1995a). The class, in turn, influences the cooking method which should be used for the maximum flavor and tenderness.

Young birds provide tender-meated poultry suitable for all cooking methods, especially broiling, roasting, or frying. They are labeled as:

- chicken: young chicken, Rock Cornish game hen, broiler, fryer, roaster, or capon
- turkey: young turkey, fryer-roaster, young hen, or young tom
- duck: duckling, young duckling, broiler duckling, fryer duckling, or roaster duckling
- goose and guinea: young goose or guinea
- pigeon: squab

Most of the young birds are either sex with the exception of the **capon chicken,** which is a surgically desexed male chicken.

Mature birds provide less tender-meated poultry that is suitable for moist heat cooking such as stewing or baking. This meat may be preferred for soups, casseroles, salads, or sandwiches. They may be labeled as:

- chicken: mature chicken, hen, fowl, baking chicken, or stewing chicken
- turkey: mature turkey, yearling turkey, or old turkey, either hen or tom
- duck, goose, and guinea: mature or old duck, goose, or guinea
- pigeon: pigeon

Inspection

Wholesomeness, quality, class, nutritive value, cost, convenience, and informative labeling are some of the points to consider when purchasing poultry. The USDA is responsible for the wholesomeness and quality assurance of both raw and processed products.

Wholesomeness

Federal legislation of poultry started with the 1957 Poultry Products Inspection Act, which was amended in 1968 and designated as the **Wholesome Poultry Products Act.** It requires inspectors to assess the procedures and cleanliness of plants and the maintenance of equipment. It applies to all raw poultry and processed products, such as canned soup or frozen chicken dinners, sold in interstate commerce. Some states have their own inspection service, which must be at least as stringent as the federal program. If only a state inspection program is used, the poultry cannot be sent to other states.

Inspection procedures for poultry are similar to those required for meat. Labels on poultry and poultry parts must be approved. The USDA Food Safety and Inspection Service (FSIS) is responsible for the wholesomeness of both meat and poultry. The mandatory inspection mark, as shown in Figure 12.1, indicates that the product has been inspected by FSIS to assure product wholesomeness and processing, handling, packaging, and labeling in accordance with the Poultry Products Inspection Act of 1957. It is printed on a tag and attached to the wing or on the carton in which the poultry is packed.

Quality Assurance

Grading involves evaluating poultry in terms of quality standards. The USDA grades apply to six kinds of poultry: chicken, turkey, duck, goose, guinea, and pigeon. The shield with the **USDA poultry voluntary grade stamp,** shown in Figure 12.2, indicates that the poultry has been graded by the Agricultural Marketing Service (AMS) according to quality factors established by grade standards. It appears on any chilled, frozen, or ready-to-cook poultry or poultry parts, either on a section of the carcass or the packaging. The AMS provides the grading service on a voluntary basis to poultry processors and others who request and pay a fee for it. Grading may also be done in cooperation with a state, in which case the official grade shield may include the words "Federal-State Graded."

Poultry may be graded A, B, or C depending upon the confirmation and amount of flesh and fat on the bird, along with freedom from pinfeathers and blemishes. The

Figure 12.1.   USDA mandatory inspection mark.

Figure 12.2. USDA poultry voluntary grade stamp.

top grade A is used for most poultry entrées, and grade B is used for soup stocks and menu items in which poultry is one of many ingredients, such as chicken stew. Grades B and C usually are used in further-processed products in which the poultry meat is cut up, chopped, or ground.

Most foodservice operations use only U.S. Grade A poultry products. According to the USDA, U.S. Grade A poultry whole carcasses and bone-in parts

- are fully fleshed and meaty;
- have a good conformation, a normal shape;
- are free of disjointed or broken bones;
- have a well-developed and well-distributed layer of fat in the skin;
- are free of pinfeathers, exposed flesh, and discolorations; and,
- in the case of whole carcasses, have no missing parts.

Grade A boneless poultry products are free of bone, cartilage, tendons, bruises, and blood clots. Grade A frozen poultry products must be free of freezing defects, such as dehydration or excess moisture.

Safety

One foodservice director admits to using a scare tactic when it comes to handling poultry (Lorenzini, 1994). She tells each and every employee to assume that the poultry they handle carries salmonella. If they do not take care every step of the way from receiving to serving, they could make someone very ill. Scare tactic or not, food safety experts recommend that employees assume that chicken is contaminated.

Buyers of poultry should understand that about 25% of chickens leave processing plants with some detectable salmonella bacteria. The FSIS has approved using trisodium phosphate (TSP) to reduce the incidence of this bacteria on chickens. After inspection and chilling, the chicken may be dipped into a TSP solution. The number of birds containing salmonellae has been reduced to less than 5%. Flavor, texture, taste, and appearance are not affected. Just dipping into a solution, however, is not enough to protect poultry from contamination. Safe handling of poultry after it is purchased is still necessary.

The USDA suggests these rules to follow after poultry is purchased (USDA Agricultural Marketing Service, 1995a):

Figure 12.3.   Acceptable and unacceptable conditions for receiving poultry.

Food	Accept	Reject
Fresh Poultry 	**Temperature:** at 40°F (4.4°C) or lower **Color:** no discolorations **Texture:** firm and springs back when touched Should be surrounded by crushed, self-draining ice	**Color:** purplish or greenish or green discoloration around the neck, darkened wing tips **Odor:** abnormal odor **Texture:** stickiness under wings and around joints; soft, flabby flesh

Source: Reprinted with permission from *Serving Safe Food Employee Guide,* 2nd ed. Copyright © 1995 by The Educational Foundation of the National Restaurant Association. All rights reserved.

- Wash hands, cutting board, utensils, and work surface with hot, soapy water before and after handling raw and cooked poultry.
- Keep raw poultry in the refrigerator at 40°F. Cook within 1 to 2 days or freeze it.
- Keep frozen poultry in the freezer at 0°F. Cook promptly after thawing. Thaw in the refrigerator or in cold water, changing the water every 30 minutes, or in a microwave oven.
- Keep cooked poultry in the refrigerator. Use within 4 days or freeze it.
- Completely cook poultry at one time. Never partially cook, then store and finish cooking later.
- Whole birds should be stuffed just before cooking. Mix dry ingredients with other ingredients (for example, margarine, onion, and broth) just before stuffing the bird. Remove the stuffing from the bird immediately after cooking. Store stuffing separately in the refrigerator.
- When serving poultry, never leave it out of the refrigerator more than 2 hours.
- Put cooked poultry on a clean plate, never on a plate that held raw poultry unless it has been washed thoroughly.

Although critical control points are not necessary at every stage in the flow of food, they are necessary at one or more stages. Raw chicken may carry salmonella when it is received, even if it is received at the proper temperature. Because the salmonella may not be eliminated, reduced, or minimized, receiving is only one control point at which the raw chicken is checked for proper temperature; it also must be refrigerated immediately to hold the temperature, which is another control point. It is later in the flow of food during the cooking process that salmonella is eliminated. Note in Figure 12.3 that acceptable conditions for fresh poultry when it is received are determined by its temperature, color, and texture; unacceptable conditions are determined by odor, color, and texture. Critical control points for receiving fresh poultry must include checking these conditions and rejecting the product if these conditions are not met.

Processed Poultry

By the time poultry is purchased for a foodservice operation, most of it has gone through some type of processing. Value has been added to the live product to make

Figure 12.4.   A USDA poultry inspector in a processing plant examining chickens for contamination.

Source: USDA.

it more attractive to the customer. This value increases food costs at the same time it decreases labor costs.

Processing Industry

Processed chicken was Tyson's biggest boom. Employees debone it, marinate it, cut it into pieces, press it into patties, roll it into nuggets, bread it, batter it, cook it, and freeze it. In return, processed products command a premium price over fresh chicken.

Modern processing plants are a far cry from grabbing a chicken by the neck and whacking off its head. Today live chickens are put on a conveyor belt that leads to a dark room where employees hang them upside down and stun them with electrical shock. Their throats are slit by machine, and they move through boiling water to loosen the feathers. Machines then massage off the feathers, eviscerate the birds, wash them inside and out, and cut them into portions. Seventy birds a minute move down the line, the maximum allowed by the USDA. Government inspectors work beside the employees and inspect the chickens to be sure they are free from disease as they move toward breading, cooking, and freezing operations (Figure 12.4). Nothing is wasted. Feathers, heads, blood, and internal organs are collected and sent to a rendering plant to become ingredients in chicken and cattle feed and pet food. Chicken feet are shipped to China for use in soups and appetizers. Approximately 71% of Tyson's sales are from processed chicken, and the remainder are from fresh and chilled pieces and whole birds.

Figure 12.5.   Popular retail cuts of poultry.

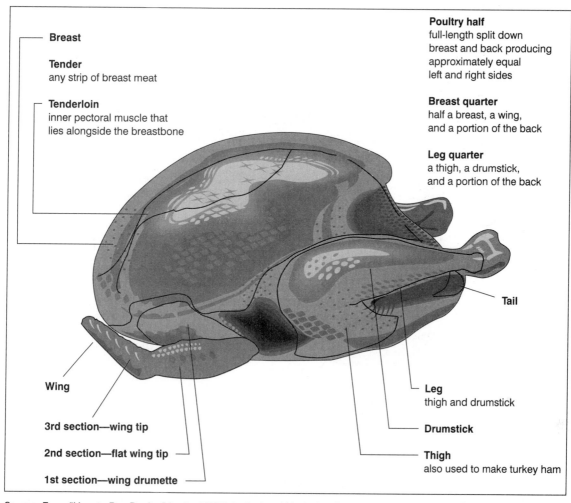

Breast

Tender
any strip of breast meat

Tenderloin
inner pectoral muscle that
lies alongside the breastbone

Poultry half
full-length split down
breast and back producing
approximately equal
left and right sides

Breast quarter
half a breast, a wing,
and a portion of the back

Leg quarter
a thigh, a drumstick,
and a portion of the back

Tail

Wing

3rd section—wing tip

2nd section—flat wing tip

1st section—wing drumette

Leg
thigh and drumstick

Drumstick

Thigh
also used to make turkey ham

Source: From "How to Buy Poultry" by the USDA Agricultural Marketing Service, 1995, *Home and Garden Bulletin No. 157,* Washington, DC: USDA.

Value-Added Products

Today, chicken and turkey are sold as cuts rather than whole carcasses. Technically, dividing birds into cuts, with or without bones or skin, is the first step in processing. Even duck is now being sold in quarters or in boneless and skinless breast cuts. Once this division is accomplished, poultry cuts are further processed. They may be breaded, battered, fried, baked, barbequed, rotisseried or processed in other ways to meet customers' desires. Popular retail cuts of poultry are shown in Figure 12.5. For chicken and turkey, the white meat comes primarily from the breast and wing drumettes, and the dark meat from the thighs and drumsticks. A turkey cut directory is shown in Figure 12.6. Because of the size of the turkey, the breast can be divided into many different cuts not possible in smaller birds.

Figure 12.6.   Turkey cut directory.

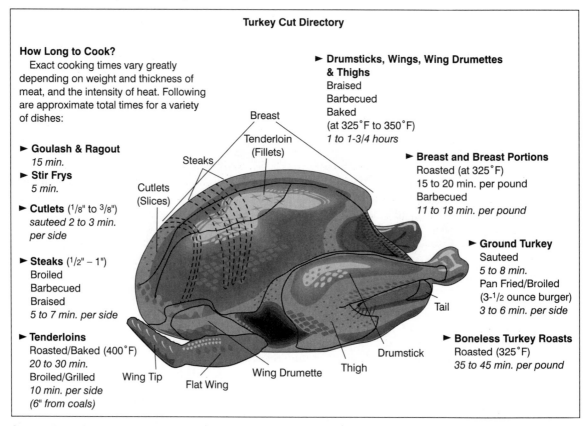

> **Turkey Cut Directory**
>
> **How Long to Cook?**
> Exact cooking times vary greatly depending on weight and thickness of meat, and the intensity of heat. Following are approximate total times for a variety of dishes:
>
> ► **Goulash & Ragout**
> *15 min.*
> ► **Stir Frys**
> *5 min.*
> ► **Cutlets** (¹/₈" to ³/₈")
> *sauteed 2 to 3 min. per side*
> ► **Steaks** (¹/₂" – 1")
> Broiled
> Barbecued
> Braised
> *5 to 7 min. per side*
> ► **Tenderloins**
> Roasted/Baked (400°F)
> *20 to 30 min.*
> Broiled/Grilled
> *10 min. per side*
> *(6" from coals)*
>
> ► **Drumsticks, Wings, Wing Drumettes & Thighs**
> Braised
> Barbecued
> Baked
> (at 325°F to 350°F)
> *1 to 1-3/4 hours*
> ► **Breast and Breast Portions**
> Roasted (at 325°F)
> *15 to 20 min. per pound*
> Barbecued
> *11 to 18 min. per pound*
> ► **Ground Turkey**
> Sauteed
> *5 to 8 min.*
> Pan Fried/Broiled
> (3-¹/₂ ounce burger)
> *3 to 6 min. per side*
> ► **Boneless Turkey Roasts**
> Roasted (325°F)
> *35 to 45 min. per pound*
>
> Breast, Tenderloin (Fillets), Steaks, Cutlets (Slices), Wing Tip, Flat Wing, Wing Drumette, Thigh, Drumstick, Tail

Source: From "Gobble Up Those Turkey Facts" by the National Turkey Federation, 1995. Used by permission.

Foodservice operations specializing in chicken menu items use either chill-pack or frozen poultry that can be prepared as specialty menu items unique to that operation. Some operators believe that freezing destroys some of the chicken's flavor. Operators known for other specialties might purchase frozen chicken products, for example, chicken kiev that only needs baking. Operations that have a minimum amount of labor use more convenience foods than those with a bigger staff. More frozen menu items that have poultry as the main ingredient are available than for any other product, including chop suey, tamales, noodles or dumplings, tetrazzini, a-la-king, and cacciatore. All of these have standards of identity and are listed in the Appendix.

Chicken also is canned, but canned chicken is used rarely in foodservice operations. Chicken soup is a popular menu item and comes in a can or frozen. Many chefs prefer frozen chicken soup because they believe the flavor is better. Of course, many chefs prefer to make chicken soup from scratch, especially if it is one of their signature items.

Purchasing

The poultry industry moreso than other food processors has made purchasing easier for foodservice operators. Less than 12% of all chickens are being sold as whole carcasses; the rest are marketed as value-added products. More than 50% are sold as parts and 36% as special processed products for quick-service operations. Turkey sales are following the same pattern. This has been a dramatic change from purchasing fresh whole carcasses. These changes are definitely responsive to the needs of foodservice operators for menu variety, convenience, and portion control. Through the Acceptance Service, USDA specialists can help foodservice buyers prepare explicit product specifications for purchasing and processing contracts.

USDA Regulations

Products delivered from the processor to the wholesaler must comply with all applicable federal and state requirements and regulations relating to the preparation, packaging, labeling, storage, distribution, and sales of the product. The products must originate and be produced, processed, and stored in poultry plants regularly operating under the **Poultry Products Inspection Regulations.** Quality assurance and specification requirements for the specified items are determined by the Poultry Division of the USDA Agricultural Marketing Service in accordance with USDA procedures. All raw poultry shall be fresh killed or frozen not more than 6 months.

All products to be delivered frozen must be frozen to 0°F within 72 hours of the beginning of the freezing process. At time of removal from holding facilities before shipment, the products must be at 0°F or lower as determined by the USDA. The product shall be preserved, packaged, and packed and cases marked in accordance with good commercial practice. Shipping containers shall comply with the National Motor Freight Classification or Uniform Freight Classification, as applicable. Each container of product must be identified as to contents and production date.

All items must be examined and accepted by a Poultry Division representative prior to delivery. The contractor arranges and pays for the necessary USDA service. All poultry products must be identified with the USDA contract compliance stamp. A USDA Poultry Grading Certificate must accompany each shipment to destination. Products not identified with the contract compliance stamp or not accompanied by the poultry grading certificate must be rejected.

Specifications

Because the USDA has developed detailed specifications for whole poultry carcasses and parts, writing specifications for a foodservice operation is not difficult (USDA Agricultural Marketing Association, 1991). The buyer needs to develop a specification based on USDA recommendations while meeting the needs of the foodservice operation. The buyer needs to include the kind of poultry, class, grade, style, size or weight, type, container or package, and temperature during transport and on delivery in the specification. A hospital keeps frozen boneless chicken breasts in the freezer at all times and, because they are a popular menu item, orders them often. The USDA detailed specification, shown in Figure 12.7, is used as a basis for this menu item, although it can be modified to meet the needs of a specific foodservice operation.

Figure 12.7. USDA detailed specification for chicken (broiler/fryer chicken), boneless breast halves with rib meat.

Type:	Frozen
Class:	Broiler/Fryer Chicken
Style:	Boneless Breast Halves with Rib Meat
Weight Range:	4.5 to 6.5 ounces (127.58 to 184.28 g) or otherwise specified in the invitation to bid.
Grade:	U.S. Grade A
Packaging and Packing:	Layer packed or packed in 4–10 pound (4.54 kg) 2 mil poly bags with cases completely lined with a 2 mil low density poly bag. Bag shall be securely closed by sealing or tying. Packed 40 pounds (18.1 kg) per master container.

Source: From "Specifications for Poultry Products" by the USDA Agricultural Marketing Service, 1993, Washington, DC: USDA.

Chicken Breast Fillets

Form: boneless, skinless, Cajun marinated breast halves with no rib meat

Use: grilled Cajun flavored chicken breast

Class: broiler/fryer

Preservation form: frozen, −10°F on delivery in refrigerated truck

Quality: U.S. Grade A

Weight: 3.5 to 4.5 ounces

Pack: 10-pound carton

Price: by the carton

Receiving and Storing

Fresh raw poultry must be handled carefully because it can easily become contaminated. Raw poultry has a limited shelf life and should be used as quickly as possible. It must be refrigerated immediately upon arrival in the foodservice operation. To be safe, the delivery person often takes the product from the refrigerated truck into the refrigerator and with the receiving person checks out the shipment. The receiver will count and weigh the products and determine if the quality is what was ordered. The delivery person should be able to tell the receiver when the poultry was killed. The truck and refrigerator temperatures are crucial and should be no more than 40°F.

Receiving frozen poultry is easier than receiving raw, but once again count, weight, and quality must be checked. Delivery temperature is very important and should be no more than 0°F. Frozen poultry needs to be stored in the freezer immediately.

EGGS

The Food Guide Pyramid suggests two to three servings each day of food from the meat group, the equivalent of 5 to 7 ounces of cooked lean meat, poultry, or fish. One whole egg can be counted as one-third serving. However, egg yolks should be limited to four per week.

"The incredible edible egg," the slogan developed by the American Egg Board, is known by anyone who watches television or reads newspapers. Another well-known saying, "which comes first, the chicken or the egg," has been debated by scholars for many years. There are those who think the chicken must come first because it lays the egg, but others argue that the egg comes first because without it, a chicken could never be hatched. The American Egg Board calls the egg one of nature's most nourishing foods, containing everything needed for life except vitamin C. However, food is not the original purpose of an egg; the primary purpose is reproduction. Built-in barriers in the egg protect the developing embryo from microbial contamination during its 21-day incubation. These same mechanisms protect the infertile egg on its journey from the hen to the kitchen. The foodservice buyer first must know the parts of an egg that in turn provide the buyer criteria for evaluating the quality of the egg and writing specifications. An egg has eight identifiable parts, as shown in Figure 12.8.

Purchasing Factors

Wholesomeness, nutritive value, size, grade, cost, and convenience should be considered when buying eggs. Safe handling of eggs also is crucial.

Wholesomeness

Packers who use the voluntary shell egg grading service have their facilities and procedures federally approved and monitored to ensure that they meet the rigid sanitary requirements established by the USDA. Federal inspectors check machines in packers' plants for critical sanitation, at issue when the egg shell touches the machine, and for noncritical sanitation, when the egg shell does not. Egg washing machines are considered critical and are therefore checked for water temperature, which must be 20°F higher than the plant temperature or a minimum of 90°F. In addition, spray nozzles must not be plugged, and an approved sanitizer must be added to the water. Eggs must be processed in a clean and safe environment, which is considered noncritical, including the sanitation of floors, shelves, and pallets in storage areas, and employee lavatories.

After the eggs are washed, they are put on an on-line belt and mass-scanned for defects. The eggs are passed over a light so that those with cracked shells or interior defects can be identified and removed. They are then packed in 30-pound cartons for most foodservice operations. A random sample of 100 eggs is taken from one carton and these eggs are hand candled. The shell and interior of each egg is carefully checked. The height of the white part of the egg is measured, blood in

Figure 12.8.   Parts of an egg.

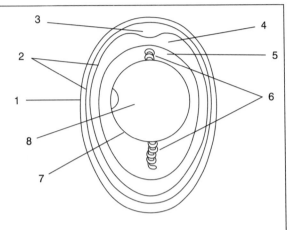

1—Shell
Outer covering of egg, composed mainly of calcium carbonate. May be white or brown depending on breed of chicken. Color does not affect quality, flavor, cooking characteristics, nutritional value, or shell thickness.

2—Shell Membranes
Two membranes — outer and inner — just inside the shell surrounding the albumen (white). Provide protective barrier against bacterial penetration. Air cell forms between membranes.

3—Air Cell
Pocket of air usually found at large end of the egg between shell membranes. Caused by contraction of contents while egg cools after laying. Increases in size with age.

4—Outer Thin Albumen (White)
Nearest to the shell. Spreads around thick white of high-quality egg.

5—Firm or Inner Thick Albumen (White)
Excellent source of riboflavin and protein. In high-quality eggs, stands higher and spreads less than thin white. In low-quality eggs, appears like thin white.

6—Chalazae
Twisted, cord-like strands of egg white. Anchor yolk in center of thick white. Prominent, thick chalazae indicate high quality and freshness.

7—Vitelline (Yolk) Membrane
Colorless membrane surrounding yolk.

8—Yolk
Yellow portion of egg. Color varies with feed of the hen; does not indicate nutritional content. Major source of vitamins, minerals, almost half of the protein, and all of the fat and cholesterol. Germinal disc; slight depression barely noticeable on side of yolk.

Source: From "How to Buy Eggs" by the USDA Agricultural Marketing Service, 1995, *Home and Garden Bulletin No. 144,* Washington, DC: USDA.

the yolks is noted, and the size of the air cell is checked because the larger the cell, the lower the quality. The shell is checked for cracks and any dirt that was not washed off.

Nutritive Value

Eggs provide protein, vitamin A, riboflavin, and other vitamins and minerals (USDA Agricultural Marketing Service, 1995b). The yolk contains all the fat, saturated fat, and cholesterol in an egg. In a large egg, the yolk contains 5 grams total fat, 2 grams saturated fatty acids, 213 milligrams cholesterol, and 60 calories. The yolk makes up just over one third of an egg, three fourths of the calories, all of the fat and Vitamins A, D, and E, most of the phosphorus, iron, and calcium, and almost half of the protein and riboflavin. The egg white contains only 15 calories.

Figure 12.9. Egg size.

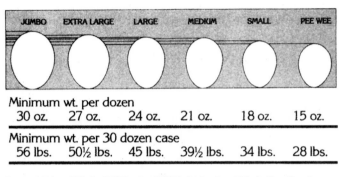

Minimum wt. per dozen
30 oz.   27 oz.   24 oz.   21 oz.   18 oz.   15 oz.

Minimum wt. per 30 dozen case
56 lbs.   50½ lbs.   45 lbs.   39½ lbs.   34 lbs.   28 lbs.

Source: From *This is AMS* by the USDA Agricultural Marketing Service, 1991, Washington, DC: USDA.

Size and Quality

The Food and Drug Administration (FDA) standards of identity for eggs are in the Appendix. Most eggs are packed according to official U.S. quality grade standards and size (USDA Agricultural Marketing Service, 1995b). The grade and size are printed on the egg carton. The USDA grade shield on the carton means the eggs were graded for quality and checked for weight under the supervision of a USDA grader. This grading service is voluntary and egg packers who request it pay for the service. Compliance with sanitary requirements is monitored by the USDA, which also monitors grade and size requirements. Egg packers who do not use the USDA grading service use terms such as "Grade A" without the shield on their egg cartons. Their compliance with size, grade, and other requirements is monitored by state agencies.

Size. Size refers to the minimum required net weight per dozen eggs (USDA Agricultural Marketing Service, 1995b). It does not refer to the dimensions of an egg or how big it looks. Eggs of any weight or size may differ in quality. Most published recipes are based on large size eggs. In Figure 12.9, egg sizes from Jumbo to Pee Wee and the minimum allowable weight per dozen and per 30 dozen case are listed.

Quality. U.S. Grade AA, A, and B are the three consumer grades for eggs (USDA Agricultural Marketing Service, 1995b). The grade is determined by the interior quality of the egg and the appearance and condition of the egg shell. Eggs of any quality grade may differ in size.

   U.S. Grade AA eggs have whites that are thick and firm; yolks that are high and round, and practically free from defects; and clean, unbroken shells with a ¼ inch or less in depth air cell.

   U.S. Grade A eggs have whites that are reasonably firm; yolks that are fairly high and round, and practically free from defects; and clean, unbroken shells with a ³⁄₁₆ inch or less in depth air cell. This is the quality most often sold in retail stores.

   U.S. Grade B eggs have whites that may be thinner and yolks that may be wider and flatter than eggs of the higher grades; the unbroken shells with a ³⁄₁₆ inch or

Figure 12.10. Characteristics of uncooked and poached egg quality.

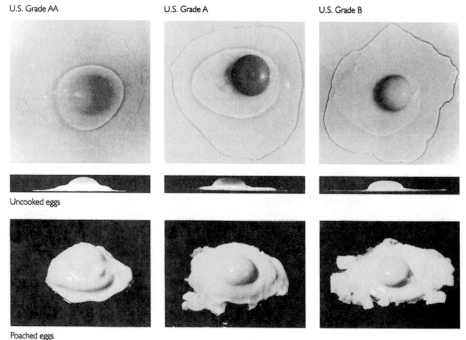

U.S. Grade AA U.S. Grade A U.S. Grade B

Uncooked eggs

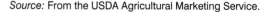

Poached eggs

Source: From the USDA Agricultural Marketing Service.

more in depth air cell must be unbroken and may show slight stains. This quality is seldom found in retail stores.

Graded broken-out raw eggs and cooked eggs are shown in Figure 12.10. U.S. Grade AA and A eggs are good for all purposes, especially for poaching and frying in which appearance is very important; U.S. Grade B eggs, if available, are fine for general cooking and baking.

Price

The price of an egg usually decreases as the grade goes down. But within each grade, prices may also vary, depending on the supply and demand of various sizes. Because the price relates to the size of eggs, the best value can be determined by calculating the price per pound. For example, one dozen large eggs weigh 1½ pounds. The buyer must remember that accurate comparisons can be made only between eggs of the same grade.

Eggs are really economical when compared with other sources of protein, such as meat. For the restaurant operator, eggs can be a good source of profit, and for the noncommercial operator, they can help cut costs. Eggs also are almost labor free, which adds to their value as an economical menu item.

Safety and Handling

Foodservice operators should be reassured to know that the egg industry, various government agencies, and state health regulators are working toward the same objectives in egg safety and handling. The industry maintains high production and quality assurance standards. The few problems that do arise often are traced back to improper handling and cooking. The FDA has identified shell eggs as a potentially hazardous food and recommends that foodservice managers refrigerate and cook them properly. Eggs are susceptible to bacterial growth and should be handled correctly.

Safety.   Salmonella infection is a common concern in eggs. Salmonella bacteria are sometimes found in the intestinal tracts of humans, animals, poultry, or seafood. These bacteria can be passed from the intestinal tract to the hands of cooks and then to food. The importance of washing hands cannot be emphasized enough.

Eggs must be washed in special detergents and sanitizing solutions before packing. This process should kill any bacteria on the shell of the egg. However, the shell can become contaminated from other sources. The washing process might not have been properly done or the shell could have become reinfected from other sources. Some bacteria may remain embedded in the shell. Care should be taken to avoid mixing the shells with the contents of the egg. Eating raw eggs—for example, in eggnogs or homemade ice cream—can be dangerous. Both of these products should be cooked to assure safety. Like all bacteria, salmonellae need food, moisture, a favorable temperature, and time for growth. All animal protein foods, including meat, milk, eggs, poultry, and fish, provide a good supply of food and moisture for bacterial growth.

Handling.   Shell eggs should be delivered to the foodservice operation in refrigerated trucks and should not be allowed to stand at room temperature for any length of time. They also should be kept in their case to prevent loss of moisture. Egg white cooks faster than yolks. In cooking a whole egg out of the shell, the white should be completely coagulated and firm and the yolk should begin to thicken.

Specifications

Writing specifications for eggs is not as difficult as for other food items because eggs packed according to U.S. grades are checked for quality and weight. USDA grade shields shown in Figure 12.11 certify that the eggs meet a specified quality and also

Figure 12.11.   USDA grade shields for eggs.

Grade Shields
Marks of Quality

are checked for size. The buyer knows that the eggs were produced and marketed under USDA's quality control program. Following is a sample specification for shell eggs.

Eggs

Form: shell

Use: breakfast items—fried, poached, soft cooked, omelets

Preservation form: 40°F when delivered in refrigerated truck

Quality: U.S. Grade AA

Color of shell: white

Delivery time: within 14 days of laying

Size: large, 24-oz. per dozen

Pack: 30-doz. moisture proof crate

Price: by crate

Egg Products

According to the American Egg Board (1990), the term *egg products* refers to processed and convenience forms of eggs for commercial, foodservice, and home use. More than 750 million pounds of all types of egg products are produced annually in the United States. Egg products are popular in foodservice operations because they are convenient to use and provide a cost savings from a decrease in labor required for cracking shells. They also require less storage space.

Types of Products

These products are refrigerated liquid, frozen, dried, and specialty items, which include prepeeled hard-cooked eggs, egg rolls or "long eggs," frozen omelets, egg patties, quiche mixes, and scrambled and fried eggs.

Refrigerated Liquid.   Refrigerated liquid egg products are distributed in 30-pound cans and in 4-, 5-, 8-, and 10-pound cartons. Egg whites, egg yolks, or variations of white and yolk blends may be purchased. These products should be transferred to refrigerators immediately upon delivery (40°F; do not freeze). Liquid egg products may be kept up to 6 days unopened in the refrigerator. Once opened, they should be used immediately. These egg products should be purchased directly from a local packer or egg processor because of their limited shelf life.

Frozen.   Frozen egg products are generally packed in 30-pound cans, 4-, 5-, 8-, and 10-pound pouches, or waxed or plastic cartons. Whole eggs, egg whites, and egg yolks are available as are salted or sweetened products. These products should be transferred to refrigerators or freezers immediately upon delivery. Frozen eggs should be stored at 0°F and never thawed at room temperature. Defrosting at temperatures higher than 45°F can cause curdling and off-flavors. Thaw only the amount needed. Use defrosted eggs promptly and refrigerate any left over for use within 1 to 3 days.

Dried.   Dried eggs are sold in 6-ounce pouches, No. 10 cans, and 3-pound and 25-pound poly-packs. Most dried egg products are produced by spray drying, although some egg white is dried on trays, which results in a flake or granule form. They are available as egg white, yolk, or whole solids. Dried eggs should be stored in a cool place, never above 70°F, away from light, and preferably in a refrigerator. After opening, the package should be sealed and stored at 50°F or below. Reconstitute only the amount needed.

Inspection

Continuous inspection of all processing plants that produce liquid, frozen, or dried eggs is required by the Egg Products Inspection Act (USDA Agriculture Marketing Service, 1991). Over 150 Agriculture Marketing Service inspectors across the country maintain records on the sanitation of all facilities and equipment, check the raw material used, and ensure proper processing and pasteurization of egg products. They check and analyze the products for salmonella; if contaminated, the products are not permitted to enter the consumer channel. Inspectors make sure that only clean, wholesome egg products are sold to food processors, bakers, restaurants, and others who buy bulk liquid, frozen, or dried eggs.

The law also controls the disposition of certain types of shell eggs, called *restricted eggs*, which include dirty eggs, leaking eggs, and incubator rejects. All of these can pose a health hazard to the public. Shell egg packers and distributors are checked periodically by the USDA and cooperating state agencies to see that they are following proper procedures. Restaurants and food processors are inspected by the FDA to ensure compliance with the law.

Specifications

Writing specifications for egg products is not difficult. The buyer can ask the supplier to help with the process. Once the buyer is satisfied with a product, ordering by brand name makes writing a specification easy.

Eggs

    Form: dried egg whites
    Use: baking, especially meringues and cakes
    Preservation form: spray dried, glucose removed
    Pack: 6/#10 cans per case
    Price: by case

SUMMARY

The term *poultry* is used to describe all domesticated birds, including chickens, turkeys, ducks, geese, and lesser known birds. Chicken is the most popular poultry primarily because it is cheap, readily available, and low in fat. Turkey, the leanest of all meat, is gaining in popularity and is eaten at times other than Thanksgiving. Modern technology has made poultry available all year. The poultry business is highly regulated by federal and state governments. The USDA is responsible for the wholesomeness and quality assurance of both raw and processed poultry. Inspectors assess the procedures and cleanliness of plants and the maintenance of equipment for all raw and processed poultry. A grading service also is available for a fee. The safety of poultry has been of great concern to consumers. Because salmonella bacteria have caused contamination of poultry, the USDA has developed some rules to follow after poultry is purchased. Most poultry is processed before it is purchased, and value is added to make it more attractive to the customer. Poultry is now portioned, skinned, boned, breaded, battered, fried, baked, barbequed, or rotisseried before it ever reaches the customer.

Eggs, usually the product of chickens, are part of the meat group in the Food Guide Pyramid because they are a good source of protein. The USDA is responsible for the wholesomeness and quality assurance of raw and processed eggs. The USDA grade seal on the carton means the eggs were graded for quality and checked for weight under the supervision of a USDA grader. Safety and handling of eggs are critical because salmonella infection can be a problem. Care should be taken to avoid mixing the shells with the contents of eggs. Processed egg products are being used more and more in foodservice operations. They are convenient to use and provide a cost savings by decreasing the amount of labor required for preparation; better portion control also is a cost saver. These products are refrigerated liquid, frozen, dried, and specialty items. Continuous inspection of all processing plants is required. The USDA maintains records on the sanitation of all facilities and equipment, checks the raw material used, and ensures proper processing and pasteurization of egg products. It also analyzes the products for salmonella.

REFERENCES

American Egg Board. (1990). *A scientist speaks about egg products*. Park Ridge, IL: Author.

Bennion, M. (1995). *Introductory foods* (10th ed.). Upper Saddle River, NJ: Merrill/Prentice Hall.

Frei, B. T. (1995). Poultry. *Restaurants & Institutions, 105*(26), 76.

Kramer, L. (1996). Rotisserie Gold plucked by KFC. *Restaurants & Institutions, 30*(9), 1, 77.

Lorenzini, B. (1994). Safe chicken checklist. *Restaurants & Institutions, 104*(11), 205.

National Restaurant Association, Educational Foundation. (1995). *Serving safe food, certification coursebook*. Chicago: Author.

Nation's Restaurant News Editorial Board. (1994). Industry plays the name game; What is home-meal replacement, *Nation's Restaurant News, 28*(41), 33.

National Turkey Federation. (1995). Gobble up these turkey facts. *Commodity Menu Alert.* Grand Rapids, MI, (8).

National Turkey Federation. (Undated). *Turkey cut directory, 4*(1), 5.

Rogers, M. (1994). New turkey temptations. *Restaurants & Institutions, 104*(11), 161–163, 166–168.

USDA Agricultural Marketing Service. (1995a). How to buy poultry. *Home and Garden Bulletin No. 157.* Washington, DC: USDA.

USDA Agricultural Marketing Service. (1995b). How to buy eggs. *Home and Garden Bulletin No. 144.* Washington, DC: USDA.

USDA Agricultural Marketing Service. (1993). *Specifications for poultry products.* Washington, DC: USDA.

USDA Agricultural Marketing Service. (1991). *This is AMS.* Washington, DC: USDA.

13

Dairy Products

Milk often is referred to as the perfect food because it contains many nutrients, especially protein and calcium. Note that in the Food Guide Pyramid, the milk, yogurt, and cheese group is on the same level as the meat, poultry, fish, dry beans, eggs, and nuts group highlighted in Figure 13.1. Two to three servings of this dairy group are recommended as the daily intake. Milk is almost a perfect food for human infants, and for other mammals, but as growth occurs, other foods are necessary. In different parts of the world, milk from various species of animals is used, including goats, buffalos, and camels, but in the United States, the cow furnishes almost all of the market milk (Bennion, 1995). A small amount of goat's milk also is available commercially. Milk and other dairy products make a significant contribution to the nation's supply of nutrients.

Fluid milk and cream products consumption in the United States has steadily decreased from 275 pounds per capita in 1970 to 226 pounds in 1993 (Putnam & Allshouse, 1994). At the same time, the amount of cheese consumed increased from 11.37 pounds per capita in 1970 to 26.25 pounds in 1993. Not surprisingly, American cheddar cheese consumption increased quite a lot, but the biggest per capita increase was mozzarella cheese. Many reasons for these consumption patterns explain these changes. As the population ages, less milk is consumed. People are eating out more and drinking soft drinks in place of milk. A noticeable change has been the decreased consumption of whole milk and increased consumption of fat free and

Figure 13.1.   Food Guide Pyramid with milk, yogurt, and cheese group highlighted.

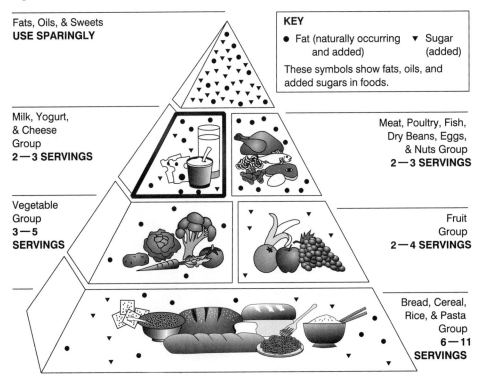

lowfat milks. The total consumption of fluid milk, however, still is much lower than in 1970. A fivefold increase in per capita consumption of yogurt since 1970 to 4.3 pounds per person in 1993 partially offset the decline in beverage milks. The increase in cheese consumption probably reflects the use of more convenient types of food, such as broccoli with cheddar cheese sauce or macaroni and cheese. Could the popularity of pizza and other Italian menu items be responsible for the increase in the amount of mozzarella cheese being consumed? Clearly, the dairy industry has been shaken up. A 30-year decline in milk consumption coupled with an increase in soft-drink sales has given the industry cause for alarm. A marketing war has been declared. Milk is up against companies trying to make their product the sexiest thing going. In the next few years, you will see the milk industry waking up. A real explosion of choices is going to make milk more fun.

Finally, Americans are buying more milk for the first time in 25 years (Sugarman, 1996). The National Fluid Milk Processor Promotion Board believes the celebrity-studded "milk mustache" advertising campaign may be behind that trend. The advertising campaign first set its sights on 25- to 44-year old women, teens, college students, and men. The next audience was men aged 18 to 34, targeted with pictures of white-upper-lipped Cal Ripken, Jr. (Figure 13.2), Spike Lee, Bob Costas, Frank Gifford, and Al Michaels in the magazines they read; teen-age girls saw Kristi Yamaguchi and Florence Griffith Joyner with milk mustaches.

Figure 13.2. Cal Ripken, Jr. with milk mustache.

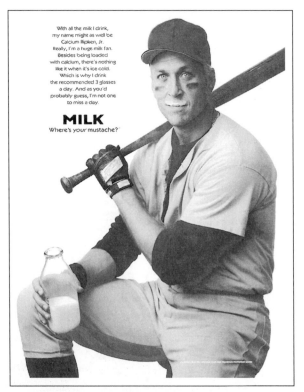

Source: Reprinted by permission of Bozell Worldwide, Inc.

What everybody really wants to know about the milk campaign is: Are the milk mustaches really milk? They are in fact a combination of dairy products—heavy cream thinned with a little milk and flavored with vanilla. Whatever it is, it has been a recipe for success. For the first 5 months of 1996, milk volume was up 0.7%. In 1995, Americans purchased 15% less milk than in 1974, and the milk industry lost sales of almost $1 billion. Most of that drop came from the decreased sales in whole milk because of fat content, even though lowfat and fat free milk sales have increased slightly.

The National Dairy Council (1993) defines **milk** as the lacteal secretion obtained by the complete milking of one or more cows. A tradition has been established by the dairy industry for minimal modification of milk as it is preserved and handled in market channels (Bennion, 1995). Dairy processors use simple processes for producing various dairy products that preserve their natural properties. Before dairy products can be discussed, milk, which is the basic ingredient of those products, must be considered in depth.

MILK QUALITY

Milk is one of the most perishable of all foods because of its nutritive composition and fluid form (National Dairy Council, 1993). Milk provides an ideal medium for bacterial growth; it may have many flavor changes unless it is protected against contamination and temperatures above 40°F. It also is an important source of many nutrients necessary for the development and maintenance of the human body. These nutrients must be retained as milk is processed, transported, and distributed in its various forms. Milk is the most legally controlled of all food items. Each state and many cities regulate veterinary inspections on farms and sanitary requirements throughout the entire chain of milk handling and processing. Milk also is highly regulated with respect to pricing structure and permissible marketing practices. The quality of milk should be the main factor in making it safe for consumption.

Quality milk is handled under rigid sanitary conditions that include a low bacterial count, good flavor and appearance, satisfactory keeping quality, high nutritive value, and freedom from disease-producing organisms and foreign constituents (National Dairy Council, 1993). The quality of milk is the responsibility of health officials, the dairy industry, and consumers. Dairy technology and public health advances assure the consumer that milk is nutritious and safe even if it is produced hundreds of miles away.

FDA Regulations

New Food and Drug Administration (FDA) regulations were issued in response to milk industry and consumer group requests to make it easier to identify lowfat and fat free milk (National Center for Nutrition and Dietetics, 1997). Use of the words *fat free, lowfat,* and *reduced fat* on milk labels will be consistent with other foods, such as crackers and cookies. As of January 1998, these terms have appeared on all milk

Table 13.1. A guide to new milk labels.

A Guide to New Milk Labels				
Current Name	**New Name**	**Calories**	**Fat**	**Nutrients**
Skim or Nonfat Milk	**Fat Free Milk,** Skim Milk or Nonfat Milk	80	0 g	300 mg calcium (30% DV) Eight other essential nutrients
1% Lowfat Milk	**1% Lowfat Milk*** Light Milk	100	2.5 g	300 mg calcium (30% DV) Eight other essential nutrients
2% Lowfat Milk	**2% Reduced Fat Milk***	120	5 g	300 mg calcium (30% DV) Eight other essential nutrients
Milk	Milk (unchanged)	150	8 g	300 mg calcium (30% DV) Eight other essential nutrients

Serving size—1 cup or 8 fl. oz.
*The milkfat percentages on labels would be optional
Source: Milk Processor Education Program. Used by permission.

labels. Skim milk is now labeled fat free milk; many consumers believed that skim milk was skimmed of nutrients instead of only fat. *Skim* and *nonfat* also may be used on milk labels in place of fat free, as shown in Table 13.1. Whether the milk is fat free, nonfat, or skim, it contains 0 grams of fat and 80 calories per cup. Most important, fat free milk offers the same amount of calcium, vitamin D, and other nutrients as whole milk.

Other types of milk also have a name change. Milk previously labeled 2% lowfat is now labeled reduced fat; 1% milk still is lowfat but also can be labeled *light*, a term used on other foods that provide at least a 50% reduction in total fat. The labeling for whole milk, often referred to as vitamin D or homogenized milk, remains unchanged.

Nutritive Value

Milk may be listed under beverages on menus, but it really should have a category of its own because it is much more than a beverage. It is an exceptional food! Milk is a high-quality protein and a rich source of calcium, which is as important for adults as it is for children because the body continually replaces bone throughout life. Milk contains the most usable form of calcium. It also contains other minerals, namely magnesium and phosphorus. The lactose, a carbohydrate, in milk helps in the absorption of calcium and other minerals from the intestine.

Many essential vitamins are found in milk in various quantities. Vitamin A, which is fat soluble, is in the cream of whole milk; by law, vitamin A must be added to lowfat and fat free milk. All milk is fortified with vitamin D, which is present in milk in small quantities. Thiamin occurs in moderate concentration in milk and riboflavin in higher concentration; both are water-soluble vitamins. Milk is a poor source of dietary iron and vitamin C, thus supporting the concept that a balanced diet is needed for good health.

Pasteurized Milk Ordinance

The Pasteurized Milk Ordinance (PMO) is one of the most effective ordinances for protecting the quality of the Grade A milk supply. It is a set of recommendations developed by the U.S. Public Health Service (USPHS) and the FDA for voluntary adoption by states. FDA standards of identity for milk and cream are in the Appendix. Legal responsibility for the quality of milk generally is assumed by state and local governments and is many times more stringent than the PMO. The PMO is periodically revised to reflect modern technology; the 15th revision took place in 1991.

Grade A Milk

The most rigid control occurs in the production and processing of Grade A market milk sold to consumers in its fluid state (National Dairy Council, 1993). Sanitary dairy practices outlined in the PMO include:

- inspection and sanitary control of farms and milk plants
- examination and testing of herds for the elimination of bovine diseases related to public health
- regular instruction on desirable sanitary practices for persons engaged in production, processing, and distribution of milk
- proper pasteurization, ultra-pasteurization, ultra high temperature processing of milk
- laboratory examination of milk
- monitoring of milk supplies by federal, state, and local health officials to protect against unintentional chemical, physical, and microbiological adulterants

Grade A pasteurized milk is obtained from dairy farms that meet the sanitation requirements of the PMO or its equivalent. The milk must come from cows tested and found free of disease. Raw milk is cooled immediately to the specified legal temperature and maintained at no higher temperature from the completion of milking until processing at a dairy plant that also conforms with state and local sanitation requirements. The milk is then analyzed for bacterial count and pasteurized, which is the only practical commercial process that destroys all disease-producing organisms that may be present in fluid milk. After pasteurizing, the milk is cooled again to the legal temperature that is maintained until sold.

Unintentional Micro Constituents

One side effect of the dairy industry's many technological changes is unintentional micro constituents in fluid milk (National Dairy Council, 1993). Because testing methods can now detect radioactive materials, pesticides, and antibiotics, research is being conducted to protect the consumer from possible adulterants in the nation's milk supply.

Radioactivity from environmental contamination may reach people in the future through the food supply. Milk, which is available all year and consumed by many people, has been used in research to establish guidelines for reducing exposure to radiation if the need arises.

Pesticides are needed to achieve maximum food production. The FDA, U.S. Department of Agriculture (USDA), and Environmental Protection Agency (EPA) have established pesticide limits. Dairy farmers must comply with the official policy to limit pesticides in milk.

Milk from dairy cows that are on antibiotics cannot be sold until the milk is shown to be free of the antibiotic or is below the established safe level. Almost every tanker truck of milk is tested for penicillin residues before it is unloaded at the processing plant. If a residue above the safe limit is detected, the milk is discarded, samples are used to trace back to the offending producer, and the state regulatory agency is notified.

New procedures and technologies are tested extensively before adoption by the dairy industry. Recently, the FDA approved recombinant bovine somatotropin (rBST) for commercial use on dairy farms (Mimberg, 1994). **Bovine somatotropin** (BST) is a natural protein hormone produced by cows that enables them to produce milk. **Recombinant bovine somatotropin** (rBST) is a synthetic version, mass produced under laboratory conditions, of the naturally occurring hormone found in a cow's pituitary glands. Supplementing a cow's natural BST increases the amount of milk she can produce. After 8 years of research, the FDA determined that milk and meat from BST-supplemented cows are safe for human consumption.

Pasteurization

The PMO has developed procedures for the proper pasteurization of milk and milk products to further safeguard consumers' health (National Dairy Council, 1993). Pasteurization is required by law for all Grade A fluid milk and milk products in interstate commerce. **Pasteurization** is the heating of raw milk in approved equipment at a sufficiently high temperature for a specified length of time to destroy pathogenic bacteria. Various time and temperature relationships can be used in pasteurization.

- Low-temperature longer-time (LTLT): Milk is heated to at least 145°F and held at that temperature for 30 minutes.
- High-temperature short-time (HTST): Milk is heated to at least 162°F for 15 seconds.
- Ultra-pasteurization process: Milk is heated to 280°F for 2 or more seconds and then cooled to 45°F or lower. This milk has a longer shelf life than LTLT and HTST.
- Ultra-high-temperature (UHT) processing: Milk is heat treated at temperatures higher than those used for pasteurization. This milk is called **long life** milk. Once it is pasteurized and aseptically packaged, it can be stored unrefrigerated and unopened for 6 months.

Temperatures and times for pasteurization are not high enough to change the constituents or properties of milk. Pasteurization makes milk bacteriologically safe and increases its keeping quality without changing significantly its nutritive value.

Homogenization

The fat in whole milk rises to the top unless it is broken down and dispersed permanently throughout the milk by a process known as **homogenization.** This process entails pumping milk under pressure of 2,500 pounds per square inch through very small openings of an homogenizer (National Dairy Council, 1993). Consequently, the size of the fat globules is reduced. Homogenized milk must be pasteurized to stop the action of an enzyme that causes the milk to taste rancid. Fluid milk is then cooled to 45°F. The nutritive value and shelf life are similar to those of nonhomogenized milk. Homogenization also aids digestion. Homogenized milk has increased viscosity and a more opaque or whiter color.

KINDS OF MILK

The customer is ultimately responsible for the many kinds of milk available on the market today (National Dairy Council, 1993). Many milk products have been developed to

- improve keeping quality,
- facilitate distribution and storage,
- make maximum use of by-products, and
- preserve surpluses on the market.

State and local governments have established standards of composition for milk and milk products, and the federal government developed standards of identity for products shipped in interstate commerce. Nutrition labeling is required for packaged foods, which include milk and milk products. Milk is classified as fluid, evaporated and condensed, dry, and acidified and cultured.

The United Dairy Industry Association administers a program for identification of real dairy foods. A **REAL Seal®,** as shown in Figure 13.3, on a carton or package identifies milk, cheese, and other qualified dairy foods made from milk produced in the United States that meet federal or state standards. The seal, a symbolic drop of milk enclosing the word "REAL," assures customers that the food is not an imitation or substitute.

Figure 13.3.   REAL Seal®.

Source: United Dairy Industry Association.

Fluid Milk

Fluid milk can be whole, lowfat, fat free or nonfat, or flavored milk. The milkfat content indicates if the milk is whole, lowfat, or fat free (National Dairy Council, 1993). Examples of the new milk labels are shown in Figure 13.4.

Whole Milk

According to federal standards, packaged whole milk cannot contain less than 3.25% milkfat and not less than 8.25% milk solids, mostly protein and carbohydrate and no fat. Milk from different farms is pooled and standardized by removing excess milkfat or adding it. Whole fluid milk shipped in interstate commerce is pasteurized. The addition of vitamin A or D to fluid whole milk is optional and must be mentioned on the label. Canned whole milk is available and is used on ships and for export. It can be stored at room temperature until opened, at which time it must be refrigerated.

Lowfat Milk

Milkfat contents of *lowfat milk* can be 0.5, 1.0, 1.5, or 2.0%, and the solids without fat must be a minimum of 8.2%. Lowfat milk that is shipped in interstate commerce is usually pasteurized, ultra-pasteurized, or UHT processed; this must be noted on the label. Also, vitamin A must be added because most of the cream that contains the vitamin has been removed. Milk-derived ingredients—for example, milk solids—are usually added to lowfat milk to increase its viscosity and opacity and to improve its palatability, appearance, and nutritive value.

Figure 13.4.   Examples of new milk labels.

Source: Milk Processor Education Program. Used by permission.

Fat Free or Nonfat Milk

The milkfat content of fat free or nonfat milk is less than 0.5%, and the milk solids without fat must be a minimum of 8.25%. It usually is pasteurized, ultra-pasteurized, or UHT processed if shipped in interstate commerce. The label must also contain information on homogenization, the addition of vitamins A and D, and the amount of milk solids, protein, and carbohydrates.

Flavored Milk

Flavors, color, and nutritive sweeteners may be added to whole, lowfat, and fat free milks. Nutritive content varies according to the amount of milkfat and the composition of added ingredients. The calories and amount of carbohydrate also vary, but the protein, mineral, and vitamin content of flavored milks is similar to that of whole, lowfat, or fat free milk. Chocolate is the favorite flavor. The calories in one cup of chocolate whole milk are 208, while chocolate nonfat milk has 158 calories.

Evaporated and Condensed Milk

Both of these milks are concentrated by the removal of water. They require no refrigeration until opened, although shelf life does depend on the storage temperature. Once the can is opened, the contents should be transferred to a clean opaque container and refrigerated.

Evaporated Milk

About 60% of the water in fluid milk is removed by concentrating it in a vacuum pan at 122°F to 131°F. The milk also is homogenized and standardized to the required percentages of components before vitamins are added. Evaporated milk is sealed in the can and then heat treated to sterilize it. A newer method is to process the concentrated milk in a continuous system by ultra-high temperatures and then canning it aseptically. The product has a lower viscosity and a whiter color than that produced by the first method and a flavor more similar to that of pasteurized milk. Federal standards of identity require that the milkfat be not less than 7.5% and the milk solids not less than 25%. Evaporated milk must be homogenized and vitamin D added; the addition of vitamin A is optional.

Evaporated fat free milk is concentrated, fortified, fat free milk containing not less than 20% milk solids and not more than 0.5% milkfat. Homogenization is optional, but addition of vitamin D is mandatory. Vitamin A also is optional.

Condensed Milk

Condensed milk is similar to evaporated milk in that water is removed from fluid milk. It is pasteurized and may be homogenized and fortified with vitamin D. The product contains not less than 7.5% milkfat and 25.5% total milk solids.

Sweetened condensed whole or fat free milk has 60% of the water removed from a mixture of milk and sugar. The amount of sweetener, about 40% to 45% of the condensed milk, is sufficient to prevent spoilage. Sweetened condensed fat free milk contains not more than 0.5% milkfat and not less than 24% total milk solids. Both products are pasteurized and may be homogenized. Sweetened condensed milk and evaporated milk cannot be used interchangeably in recipes.

Other Milks

Lactose free, organic, and fiber-enriched milks are available on the market. They represent only a small percentage of total milk sales, but these milks give customers more choices.

Lactose Free

Milk causes stomach distress for some consumers in the form of gas and bloating. **Lactose free milk** contains lactose that has already been broken down to make it easier to digest; some customers believe they can drink this milk with no ill effects. Lactose free milk has lactase, an enzyme, added for people who cannot digest and absorb the lactose in milk. The brand name for this milk is Lactaid. This product is not without controversy: some people believe that lactose intolerance is mostly in the minds of consumers.

Organic

Organic milk comes from cows that are raised in pastureland free of all chemical compounds. The cows have not been injected with growth hormones. Dairy farmers who produce organic milk say they have a strong interest in the environment and the humane treatment of animals. Consumption of organic milk is increasing even though the price is higher than regular milk.

Fiber-Enriched

Fiber-enriched milk is fat free milk with added dietary fiber, such as cellulose gel to enrich the texture. The product has a thicker consistency and a whiter color, through the addition of a natural coloring agent, than the watery, bluish-colored fat free milk. This milk has fewer calories than fat free milk and many more milligrams of calcium because it is enriched.

Dry Milk

Nonfat dry milk is prepared by removing water from pasteurized fat free milk (National Dairy Council, 1993). Federal standards of identity require that it contain not more than 5% by weight of moisture and not more than 1.5% of milkfat. It is fine textured and made by removing the water and then spraying the concentrated milk into a chamber of hot filtered air. It also can be made by spraying a jet of hot air into concentrated fat free milk; this process is known as foam spray drying.

Dry milk reconstitutes easily by mixing it in warm water. Instant nonfat dry milk made by a special process dissolves immediately in cold water. Because the low moisture content of dry milk inhibits the multiplication of microorganisms, it has a long shelf life. Nonfat dry milk can be fortified with vitamins A and D and conforms to the federal standards of identity. Dry whole and lowfat milk also are available. Dry whole milk and lowfat dry milk are made from pasteurized whole or lowfat milk from which water has been removed by spray drying. Dry whole milk contains between 26% and 40% milkfat, while lowfat contains between 5% and 20% milkfat.

Cultured Milk and Cream Products

Cultured milk products include yogurt, buttermilk, sour cream, and acidophilus milk (National Dairy Council, 1993). These products are produced under rigidly controlled conditions of sanitation, inoculation, incubation, acidification, and temperature. The word **cultured** as part of a product's name signifies that it was produced by souring milk or cream with an acid, usually lactic acid, with or without the addition of microbial organisms. In addition, flavoring ingredients, aroma- and flavor-producing microbial culture, and milkfat flakes may be added. The body, flavor, and aroma developed in the finished product vary with the type of culture and milk and the concentration of milkfat and solids. Many cultured and acidified dairy products are available on the market, but in foodservice operations yogurt, buttermilk, sour cream, and acidophilus milks are the most popular cultured dairy products.

Yogurt

During biblical times, people in the Middle East discovered yogurt. They found that when milk was left in a warm place, it thickened and developed a different, tart flavor. More importantly, it had better keeping qualities than fresh milk. Now yogurt is known in almost every part of the world. It met with limited success in the United States until flavors and fruits were added and healthy eating was emphasized.

Customers who do not like milk or have difficulty in digesting it often find that they can tolerate yogurt better than any other dairy product. **Yogurt** has the consistency of either a liquid or a gel and is processed from fresh whole, lowfat, or fat free milk. It is fermented by a mixed culture of specific bacteria that causes the milk sugar, lactose, to turn into lactic acid. Milk is pasteurized or ultra-pasteurized, inoculated, and incubated at 108°F to 115°F until the desired stage of acidity and flavor is reached. Then yogurt is chilled at 45°F. Federal standards specify that yogurt contains not less than 3.25% milkfat, lowfat yogurt from 0.5 to 2.0%, and nonfat yogurt not more than 0.5%. All yogurt must contain not less than 8.25% milk solids without fat.

Examples of specifications for Dannon flavored lowfat yogurt and Dannon plain fat free yogurt are shown in Figure 13.5. Many yogurts are flavored with fruit at the bottom of the container, which must be stirred to blend the ingredients. Sometimes the fruit is blended in the yogurt, giving a custard-like consistency known as Swiss or French-style yogurt. Soft or hard frozen yogurt has replaced many of the rich ice creams, although labels must be read to check fat and caloric count.

Note that these specifications are for a brand-name product and have been developed by the company. This is one reason for using brand products; the

Figure 13.5. Specifications for plain lowfat yogurt and plain nonfat yogurt.

Dannon® Flavored

[Based on 8oz. (227g) serving size]

VANILLA	101	
COFFEE	102	
LEMON	103	

		% Daily Value**	
Calories	210	Vitamin A	4
Calories From Fat	30	Vitamin C	4
Total Fat (g)	3	Calcium	40
Saturated Fat (g)	2	Iron	0
Cholesterol (mg)	15		
Sodium (mg)	160		
Potassium (mg)	510		
Total Carbs (g)	36		
Dietary Fiber (g)	0		
Sugars (g)	34-35		
Protein (g)	10		

Dannon Flavored Lowfat Yogurt is made from Grade A milk, skim milk, sugar, natural flavors, pectin and contains live and active yogurt cultures with *L. acidophilus.* Dannon Flavored Lowfat Yogurt is kosher O°.

cup size: 8 oz.　　case specifications: A

Dannon® Plain Fat Free

[Based on 8 oz. (227g) serving size]

PLAIN 8 OZ.	180	
PLAIN 16 OZ.	250	
PLAIN 32 OZ.	251	

		% Daily Value**	
Calories	110	Vitamin A	0
Calories From Fat	0	Vitamin C	4
Total Fat (g)	0	Calcium	40
Saturated Fat (g)	0	Iron	0
Cholesterol (mg)	5		
Sodium (mg)	150		
Potassium (mg)	550		
Total Carbs (g)	16		
Dietary Fiber (g)	0		
Sugars (g)	16		
Protein (g)	12		

Dannon Plain Fat Free Nonfat Yogurt is made from cultured Grade A nonfat milk, pectin and contains live and active yogurt cultures with *L. acidophilus.* Dannon Plain Fat Free Nonfat Yogurt is Kosher O°.

cup size: 8 oz.　　case specifications: A
cup size: 16 oz.　　case specifications: H
cup size: 32 oz.　　case specifications: I

Source: Dannon, Your Source For Healthy Profits, 1997. Used by permission.

buyer only has to specify the type of yogurt, size of the container, and number of cases. In large foodservice operations, the buyer might order by pallets. A **pallet** is a portable platform that holds a specified number of cases of food and usually is moved by a forklift from the distributor's warehouse to the buyer's facility.

Dannon light nonfat yogurt with aspartame and added calcium has 50% fewer calories than that with sugar (Figure 13.6). Some popular flavors are blueberry, strawberry kiwi, cappuccino, creme caramel, and white chocolate raspberry.

Buttermilk

Buttermilk is a cultured product made from fresh pasteurized or ultra-pasteurized lowfat or fat free milk with nonfat dry milk solids added. It also can be made from fluid whole milk, concentrated fluid milk, or reconstituted nonfat dry milk. During processing, *Streptococcus lactic* culture is added to the milk to produce acid and flavor components; the milk is incubated at 68°F to 72°F until the acidity is 0.8% to 0.9%. The result is a pleasantly tart milk with a characteristic buttery flavor and a smooth thick body.

Sour Cream

Cultured sour cream is made from pasteurized or ultra-pasteurized homogenized cream with *Streptococcus lactic* culture added at 72°F until the acidity is at least 0.5%. The result is an acid gel product known as cultured sour cream. Federal standards of identity provide that cultured sour cream contains not less than 18% milkfat. Fat free sour cream, which is labeled as a sour cream alternative because it does not meet the federal standard of identity for sour cream, is made from cultured fat free milk. Cholesterol-free sour cream alternative is made with fat free milk and vegetable oil.

Acidophilus Cultured Milk

Lowfat or fat free pasteurized milk is cultured with *Lactobacillus acidophilus* to digest the lactose and is incubated at 100°F until a soft curd is formed (Bennion, 1995). The product has a cooked and acid flavor. In a newer process, a concentrated culture is grown and added to pasteurized or ultra-pasteurized milk. Acidophilus bacteria are introduced into the intestine, where they are thought to help maintain a proper balance of microorganisms. The product is mixed, packaged, and held at 45°F or below. The natural flavor and consistency of the milk to which it is added are unchanged to maintain palatability.

Eggnog

Eggnog appears on the market most often from Thanksgiving through the New Year holidays. It contains milk products, cooked egg yolk, egg white ingredients, and nutritive carbohydrate sweetener. It also may contain salt, flavoring, stabilizers, and color additives; the color cannot simulate that of egg yolks, milkfat, or butterfat.

Figure 13.6. Specifications for light nonfat yogurt with aspartame and natural flavored lowfat yogurt.

Dannon® Light®

Nonfat Yogurt
with Aspartame
& Added Calcium

FLAVOR	UPC CODE
PEACH	620
STRAWBERRY BANANA	621
BLUEBERRY	622
RASPBERRY	624
STRAWBERRY	625
STRAWBERRY KIWI	626
CHERRY VANILLA	627
TANGERINE CHIFFON	628
VANILLA	660
CAPPUCCINO	661
LEMON CHIFFON	662
CREME CARAMEL	663
BANANA CREAM PIE	664
COCONUT CREAM PIE	665
WHITE CHOCOLATE RASPBERRY	667
BLACKBERRY PIE	668

NUTRITIONAL FACTS*
[Based on 8 oz. (227g) serving size]

		% Daily Value**	
Calories	100	Vitamin A	0
Calories From Fat	0	Vitamin C	0-10
Total Fat (g)	0	Calcium	35
Saturated Fat (g)	0	Iron	0
Cholesterol (mg)	5		
Sodium (mg)	115-130		
Potassium (mg)	340-380		
Total Carbs (g)	15-18		
Dietary Fiber (g)	0		
Sugars (g)	9-12		
Protein (g)	8		

INGREDIENT STATEMENT*

Dannon Light Nonfat yogurt with aspartame and added calcium may contain some or all of the following cultured, pasteurized Grade A nonfat milk, fruit, fruit puree, fruit juice concentrate, modified corn starch, whey protein concentrate, natural and artificial flavors and colors, sodium citrate, calcium lactate, calcium gluconate, kosher gelatin, aspartame, citric or malic acid, and contains live and active yogurt cultures with *L. Acidophilus*. Dannon Light Nonfat Yogurt is kosher K.

cup size: 8 oz.   case specifications: A

Source: Dannon, Your Source For Healthy Profits, 1997. Used by permission.

Federal standards specify that eggnog shall not contain less than 6% milkfat and 8.25% milk solids without fat. The egg yolk content may not be less than 1% by weight of the finished food. Eggnog must be pasteurized or ultra-pasteurized and may be homogenized.

Cream

Cream is a liquid milk product, high in fat, separated from milk with various amounts of milkfat. The amount can be adjusted by the addition of milk, concentrated milk, dry whole milk, fat free milk, concentrated fat free milk, or nonfat dry milk. Federal standards of identity require that cream contain not less than 18% milkfat. Several cream products are on the market, and those with federal standards of identity are:

- half-and-half—a mixture of milk and cream containing between 10.5% and 18% milkfat
- light cream—containing between 18% and 30% milkfat
- whipping cream or light whipping cream —containing between 30% and 36% milkfat
- heavy cream or heavy whipping cream—containing not less than 36% milkfat

Goat Milk

Even though the National Dairy Council defines milk as the product of a cow, goats also produce milk used the world over. The main differences between goat milk and cow milk are in the protein and fat structures. Goat milk contains only traces of a major protein of cow milk to which some people are allergic (Myenberg goat milk, Undated). Goat milk's easy digestibility results from its smaller, more evenly dispersed fat globules that soothe upset stomachs. Goat milk is usually sold evaporated in a can or dried. Ultra-pasteurized goat milk supplemented with vitamins A and D is now being sold in quarts. This milk has an unopened, unrefrigerated shelf life of up to 8 months. A new (1%) lowfat, ultra-pasteurized goat milk containing only 90 calories per 8-ounce serving is available.

CHEESE

According to the National Dairy Council (1992), cheese was discovered several thousand years before Christ was born. The legend is that a traveler starting on a journey placed milk in a pouch made of a sheep's stomach. During the day's journey, the action of the sun's heat and enzymes in the lining of the pouch changed the milk into a snowy white curd of cheese and a thin liquid now known as whey.

Definition

Cheese is a concentrated dairy product defined as the fresh or matured product obtained by draining the moisture, or whey, of the original milk after coagulation of the major milk protein, casein (National Dairy Council, 1992). Cow's milk is used most often in the United States. The yellow color of many cheeses comes from the addition of the pigment carotene. Most cheese is made from pasteurized milk.

Cheese-Making Process

Cheese ranges in texture from soft to hard and in flavor from mild to pungent and sharp. The basic art of cheese making has changed little. Milk is coagulated to produce curd by the action of lactic acid, which is produced by the breakdown of lactose by selected microorganisms and coagulating enzymes. Whey is removed from the curd, which is further treated to produce the many varieties of cheese.

Cottage cheese is a good example of the cheese-making process up to this point. **Cottage cheese** is classified as a soft cheese and is made from pasteurized fat free milk or reconstituted nonfat dry milk. It is coagulated by lactic acid until the curd is firm enough to cut into one-quarter-inch cubes for small curd cheese and three-quarter-inch cubes for large curd cheese. The whey is removed and the curd is washed with cold water to firm it and remove any remaining acid whey, thus producing a mild-flavored cheese. When the curd is firm and dry, it may be salted. For cottage cheese, a homogenized creaming mixture, such as cream and milk, is added to the dry curd to yield a cheese of not less than 4% milkfat. Federal standards of identity (see Appendix) state that this creaming mixture is to be prepared from safe and suitable ingredients including, but not limited to, milk and substances derived from milk. This soft, unripened cheese is packaged by automatic machines in moisture-proof containers. Because of its high moisture content and open texture, cottage cheese is a highly perishable product that must be kept under refrigeration.

Cream cheese, an unripened lactic acid coagulated type of cheese, is made in a similar way. Neufchâtel, often called cream cheese, is lower in fat, higher in moisture, and not as smooth.

The last step in cheese making is the ripening of the curd. **Ripening** refers to the changes of the chemical and physical properties, including aroma, flavor, and texture, when the cheese develops the desired characteristics for its type. Controlled scientific methods permitted U.S. cheese makers to make all types of foreign cheese, such as Swiss, camembert, limburger, blue, Parmesan, and mozzarella. They also created some distinctive original domestic varieties, such as brick, Colby, and Monterey.

Blue cheese, often referred to as moldy cheese, is characterized by the blue-green veins of mold throughout its interior and by its sharp, piquant flavor. Many people consider Roquefort cheese the best of all the varieties. It is made only in the Roquefort area of France from sheep's milk. All other blue-green veined cheeses are made from cow's milk and are called bleu cheese in other areas of France, blue in the United States, Stilton in England, and gorgonzola in Italy. Blue cheese usually is prepared from homogenized whole milk and may be inoculated with mold spores of *Penicillium Roquefort* or a similar mold that will result in blue-green veins in the cheese. Mold spores often are added to the fresh cheese to give a more uniform distribution of the blue-green mottling. The mold spores are responsible for the cheese's characteristic flavor. The usual ripening period for these cheeses is three to four months.

Classification

Several classification schemes have evolved because of the many varieties and names of cheeses, which number over 2,000. Some of the classifications are as follows:

- Origin: United States, Italy, France, Germany, England, Holland, Norway, Switzerland, Belgium, Greece, and others.
- Consistency and texture: soft, semisoft, hard; smooth, waxy, stringy, crumbly, mealy, moist, plastic; tiny eyes, round eyes, irregular-shaped eyes, large eyes.
- Color: creamy white, light yellow, slightly gray surface, white marbled with blue-green mold, white crust with creamy yellow interior, nearly white, brownish exterior, golden brown, light green.
- Shape: square, cylindrical, brick-shaped, distinctive shapes, varied shapes and styles, cuplike containers, flat loaves, flat wheels, small wheels, round, rectangular, cubical, spherical, various shapes (pear, sausage, salami) and sizes, cone-shaped.
- Coating: clear paraffin, black or brown paraffin, natural or red paraffin, red wax, shiny surface bound with cord, brown rind.
- Flavor: mild, piquant, sharp, robust, tangy, spicy, peppery, aromatic, smoked, pungent, salty, sweet caramel, nutlike, mellow, delicate, bland, semisweet.
- Basic ingredient: cow's milk, whole, lowfat, fat free, whole with cream, slightly soured with buttermilk, whey; goat's milk, whole, lowfat, whey; sheep's milk, whole, lowfat.
- Normal ripening period: Unripened, 4–5 days, 3–8 weeks, 2–12 months, 1 year.

Table 13.2 shows the name, origin, characteristics, and mode of serving of commonly used varieties of cheese (National Dairy Council, 1992). Figure 13.7 is a photograph of some popular kinds of cheese and a labeled drawing in which they are identified.

Popularity Trends

Chefs the world over are beginning to consider cheese as an indispensable secret weapon in a recipe (Straus, 1994). The right cheese used well turns basic dishes into bountiful delights. Cheese can turn a simple salad into something spectacular. Cheese is nutritious and, like all dairy products, is usually high in protein and calcium. However, most cheeses do contain high amounts of fat. An average slice of cheese contains as much fat, which is mostly saturated, as a cup of whole milk. Lowfat cheese is available, but it does not have the creamy, melting quality that regular cheese has. People are beginning to realize that they do not have to give up cheese; they just have to understand that they can have the same good flavor profile and texture by using a smaller amount of a sharp, aged cheese.

Cheese sales increase every year as Americans become more sophisticated about food. People still believe that a good, well-flavored cheese, a crusty loaf of bread,

Table 13.2. Name, origin, characteristics, and mode of serving of common varieties of cheese.

Name	Origin	Consistency and Texture	Color and Shape
American pasteurized process[b]	United States	Semisoft to soft; smooth, plastic body	Light yellow to orange; square slices
Asiago, fresh, medium, old	Italy	Semisoft (fresh), medium, or hard (old); tiny gas holes or eyes	Light yellow; may be coated with paraffin, clear or colored black or brown; round and flat
Bel paese	Italy	Soft; smooth, waxy body	Slightly gray surface, creamy yellow interior; small wheels
Blue[b], Bleu	France	Semisoft; visible veins of mold on white cheese, pasty, sometimes crumbly	White, marbled with blue-green mold; cylindrical
Breakfast, Frühstück	Germany	Soft; smooth, waxy body	Cylindrical, 2½ to 3 inches diameter
Brick[b]	United States	Semisoft; smooth, open texture; numerous round and irregular-shaped eyes	Light yellow to orange, brick-shaped
Brie[b]	France	Soft, thin edible crust, creamy interior	White crust, creamy yellow interior; large, medium, and small wheels
Caciocavallo	Italy	Hard, firm body; stringy texture	Light tan surface, interior; molded into distinctive shapes, typically spindle-shaped or oblong
Camembert[b]	France	Soft, almost fluid in consistency; thin edible crust, creamy interior	Gray-white crust, creamy yellow interior; small wheels
Cheddar[b]	England	Hard; smooth, firm body, can be crumbly	Nearly white to orange; varied shapes and styles
Colby[b]	United States	Hard but softer and more open in texture than Cheddar	White to light yellow, orange; cylindrical
Cottage, Dutch Farmers, Pot	Uncertain	Soft; moist, delicate, large or small curds	White; packaged in cuplike containers
Cream[b]	United States	Soft; smooth, buttery	White; foil-wrapped in rectangular portions
Edam[b]	Holland	Semisoft to hard; firm, crumbly body; small eyes	Creamy yellow with natural or red paraffin coat; flattened ball or loaf shape, about 4 pounds
Feta[b]	Greece	Soft, flaky, similar to very dry, high-acid cottage cheese	White
Gammelost	Norway	Semisoft	Brownish rind, brown-yellow interior with a blue-green tint; round and flat
Gjetost[b]	Norway	Hard; buttery	Golden brown; cubical and rectangular
Gorgonzola	Italy	Semisoft, less moist than blue	Light tan surface, light yellow interior, marbled with blue-green mold; cylindrical and flat loaves
Gouda[b]	Holland	Hard, but softer than cheddar; more open mealy body like edam, small eyes	Creamy yellow with or without red wax coat; oval or flattened sphere of about 10 to 12 pounds

Source: From *Newer Knowledge of Cheese.* Courtesy of National Dairy Council®, 1992. Used by permission.

Table 13.2. Continued.

Flavor	Basic Ingredient	Normal Ripening Period[c]	Mode of Serving
Mild	Cheddar, washed, colby, or granulated (stirred curd) or mixture of two or more	Unripened after cheese(s) heated to blend	In sandwiches; on crackers
Piquant, sharp in aged cheese	Cow's milk, whole or lowfat	60 days minimum for fresh (semisoft), 6 months minimum for medium, 12 months minimum for old (grating)	Table cheese (slicing cheese) when not aged; as seasoning (grated) when aged
Mild to moderately robust	Cow's milk, whole	6–8 weeks	As such (dessert); on crackers; in sand-wiches; with fruit
Piquant, tangy, spicy, peppery	Cow's milk, whole or goat's milk	60 days minimum; 3–4 months usually; 9 months for more flavor	As such (dessert); in dips, cooked foods; salads and dressings
Strong, aromatic	Cow's milk, whole or lowfat	Little or none (either)	As such (dessert); on crackers; in sandwiches
Mild but pungent and sweet	Cow's milk, whole	2–3 months	As such; in sandwiches, salads; Slices well without crumbling
Mild to pungent	Cow's milk, whole, lowfat, or skim	4–8 weeks	As such (dessert)
Sharp, similar to provolone	Sheep's, goat's or cow's milk (whole or lowfat) or mixtures of these	3 months minimum for table use, 12 months or longer for grating	As such; as seasoning (grated) when aged
Mild to pungent	Cow's milk, whole	4–5 weeks	As such (dessert)
Mild to sharp	Cow's milk, whole	60 days minimum; 3–6 months usually; 12 or longer for sharp flavor	As such; in sandwiches, cooked foods
Mild to mellow	Cow's milk, whole	1–3 months	As such; in sandwiches, cooked foods
Mild, slightly acid, flavoring may be added	Cow's milk, skim; cream dressing may be added	Unripened	As such; in salads, dips, on crackers
Mild, slightly acid, flavoring may be added	Cream and cow's milk, whole	Unripened	As such; in salads, in sandwiches, on crackers
Mild, sometimes salty	Cow's milk, lowfat	2 months or longer	As such; on crackers; with fresh fruit
Salty	Cow's, sheep's, or goat's milk	4–5 days to 1 month	As such; in cooked foods
Sharp, aromatic	Cow's milk, skim	4 weeks or longer	As such
Sweet, caramel	Whey from goat's milk	Unripened	As such; on crackers
Piquant, spicy, similar to blue	Cow's milk, whole or goat's milk or mixtures of these	3 months minimum, frequently 6 months to 1 year	As such (dessert)
Mild, nutlike, similar to edam	Cow's milk, lowfat but more milkfat than edam	2–6 months	As such; on crackers; with fresh fruit; in cooked dishes

(Continued)

369

Table 13.2. Name, origin, characteristics, and mode of serving of common varieties of cheese.

Name	Origin	Consistency and Texture	Color and Shape
Gruyere[b]	Switzerland	Hard, tiny gas holes or eyes	Light yellow; flat wheels
Limburger[b]	Belgium	Soft; smooth, waxy body	Creamy white interior, brownish exterior; rectangular
Monterey, Jack[b]	United States	Semisoft (whole milk), hard (lowfat or skim milk); smooth texture with small openings throughout	Creamy, white; round or rectangular
Mozzarella[b]	Italy	Semisoft; plastic	Creamy white; rectangular and spherical, may be molded into various shapes
Muenster[b]	Germany	Semisoft; smooth, waxy body, numerous small mechanical openings	Yellow, tan, or white surface, creamy white interior; cylindrical and flat or loaf shaped, small wheels and blocks
Neufchatel[b]	France	Soft; smooth, creamy	White; foil-wrapped in rectangular retail portions
Parmesan, Reggiano[b]	Italy	Very hard (grating), granular, hard brittle rind	Light yellow with brown or black coating; cylindrical
Port du salut, Oka[b]	Trappist Monasteries	Semisoft; smooth, buttery	Russet surface, creamy white interior; small wheels, cylindrical flat
Primost	Norway	Semisoft	Light brown; cubical and cylindrical
Provolone[b]	Italy	Hard, stringy texture; cuts without crumbling, plastic	Light golden-yellow to golden-brown, shiny surface bound with cord; yellow-white interior. Made in various shapes (pear, sausage, salami) and sizes
Queso blanco, White cheese	Latin America	Soft, dry and granular if not pressed; hard, open or crumbly if pressed	White; various shapes and sizes
Ricotta[b]	Italy	Soft, moist and grainy, or dry	White; packaged fresh in paper, plastic, or metal containers, or dry for grating
Romano[b]	Italy	Very hard, granular interior, hard brittle rind	Round with flat sides; various sizes
Roquefort[b]	France	Semisoft, pasty and sometimes crumbly	White, marbled with blue-green mold; cylindrical
Sap Sago	Switzerland	Very hard (grating), granular frequently dried	Light green; small, cone-shaped
Schloss, Castle cheese	Germany, Northern Austria	Soft; small, ripened	Molded in small rectangular blocks 1½" square by 4" long
Stirred Curd, Granular	United States	Semisoft to hard	Varied shapes and styles
Stilton	England	Semisoft-hard; open flaky texture, more crumbly than blue	White, marbled with blue-green mold; cylindrical
Swiss, Emmentaler[b]	Switzerland	Hard; smooth with large gas holes or eyes	Pale yellow, shiny; rindless rectangular blocks and large wheels with rind
Washed Curd	United States	Semisoft to hard	Varied shapes and styles

Table 13.2. Continued.

Flavor	Basic Ingredient	Normal Ripening Period[c]	Mode of Serving
Mild, sweet	Cow's milk, whole	3 months minimum	As such (dessert); fondue
Strong, robust, highly aromatic	Cow's milk, whole or lowfat	1–2 months	In sandwiches; on crackers
Mild to mellow	Cow's milk, whole, lowfat or skim	3–6 weeks for table use, 6 months minimum for grating	As such; in sandwiches; grating cheese if made form lowfat or skim milk
Mild, delicate	Cow's milk, whole or lowfat; may be acidified with vinegar	Unripened to 2 months	Generally used in cooking, pizza; as such
Mild to mellow, between brick and limburger	Cow's milk, whole	2–8 weeks	As such; in sandwiches
Mild	Cow's milk, whole or skim, or a mixture of milk and cream	3–4 weeks or unripened	As such; in sandwiches, dips salads
Sharp, piquant	Cow's milk, lowfat	10 months minimum	As such; as grated cheese on salads and soups
Mellow or mild to robust. Similar to gouda	Cow's milk, whole or lowfat	6–8 weeks	As such (dessert); with fresh fruit; on crackers
Mild, sweet, caramel	Whey with added buttermilk, whole milk or cream	Unripened	As such; in cooked foods
Bland acid flavor to sharp and piquant, usually smoked	Cow's milk, whole	6–14 months	As such (dessert) after it has ripened for 6 to 9 months; grating cheese when aged
Salty, strong, may be smoked	Cow's milk, whole, lowfat or skim or whole milk with cream or skim milk	Eaten within 2 days to 2 months or more; generally unripened if pressed	As such or later grated
Bland but semisweet	Whey and whole or skim milk or whole and lowfat milk	Unripened	As such; in cooked foods; as seasoning (grated) when dried
Sharp, piquant if aged	Cow's milk (usually lowfat), goat's milk, or mixtures of these	5 months minimum; usually 5–8 months for table cheese; 12 months minimum for grating cheese	As such; grated and used as a seasoning
Sharp, spicy (pepper), piquant	Sheep's milk	2 months minimum; usually 2–5 months or longer	As such (dessert); in salads; on crackers
Sharp, pungent, flavored with leaves; sweet	Cow's milk, skim, slightly soured with buttermilk and whey	5 months minimum	As such; as seasoning (grated)
Similar to, but milder than, limburger	Cow's milk, whole or lowfat and/or casein	Less than 1 month; less intensively than limburger	In sandwiches; on crackers
Similar to mild cheddar	Cow's milk	1–3 months	Usually used to make pasteurized process cheese
Piquant, spicy, but milder than roquefort	Cow's milk, whole with added cream	4–6 months or longer	As such (dessert); in cooked foods
Mild, sweet, nutty	Cow's milk, lowfat	2 months minimum, 2–9 months usually	As such; in sandwiches; with salads; fondue
Similar to mild cheddar	Cow's milk	1–3 months	Usually used to make pasteurized process cheese

371

Figure 13.7. Photograph and labeled drawing of popular kinds of cheese.

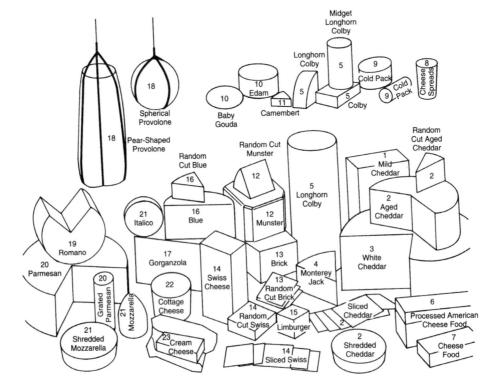

Source: USDA.

and a decent bottle of wine cement relationships among friends. Wine, cheese, and fruit have the same effect. Suggestions for combining these three are offered in Figure 13.8. Selection of cheese becomes an individual decision. Most cheeses are made by the same process. Differences occur in texture or in flavor. **Processed cheese** is a blend of natural cheese pasteurized to prevent further ripening. Substitute or imitation cheese is made from casein, vegetable oils, whey, color, flavor, and vitamins. **Natural cheese** is any cheese made by clotting milk to form a curd and then concentrating the curd by draining the whey (McWilliams, 1993). Cottage and cream cheese truly are natural cheeses because they are soft and unripened. Ripened cheese can be semisoft, such as fontina and liederkranz; blue-veined, such as gorgonzola, Roquefort, Stilton, and American blue; firm, including cheddar, Swiss, and provolone; or hard, for example asiago, Parmesan, and Romano.

Processed Cheese

More than half the cheese produced in the United States is made into processed cheese, which is sold as slices or spreads. It has a uniform color, flavor, and texture. McWilliams (1993) defined the following types of processed cheese currently on the market:

- Process cheese: made by heating natural cheeses with an emulsifier and then cooling in a brick form; moisture level is about 41%.
- Process cheese food: processed product with a moisture content of about 45%, which causes the cheese to be comparatively soft, yet firm.
- Process cheese spread: spreadable processed cheese with a moisture content of about 50%.
- Cold-pack (club) cheese: cheese product made by adding an emulsifier to a mixture of natural cheese.

Processed cheese products can be either cold-pack or heat-processed. Cold-pack cheese is made by grinding and mixing together one or more varieties without using heat. Salt, water, coloring, and chopped peppers, caraway seeds, chopped pineapple, or bacon are some of the additions that make each product unique. Cold-pack cheese is sold in containers or wrapped in moisture-proof packages. The moisture content can be no greater than that of the cheese from which it is made.

Heat-processed cheese also is a mixture of cheese varieties that are pasteurized and have water added to replace that which is lost by evaporation. An emulsifying agent is added to keep the fat from separating out of the cheese when it is melted. After melting, the cheese usually is poured into cardboard boxes that are lined with a transparent plastic material or metal foil. Some of the cheese is poured into glass jars or plastic containers. As it cools, the cheese clings to the plastic material or foil or to the jars, thus preventing mold on the surface. Pasteurization of the cheese destroys any enzymes or bacteria and at the same time stops ripening. Processed cheese also is sold in slices, sometimes individually wrapped.

Reduced-fat cheese usually is a processed cheese. Cheese consists of milk protein casein, nearly all of the fat and fat-soluble vitamins, minerals of the original milk, and varying amounts of entrapped moisture. Most commonly, the casein-to-fat ratio is regulated

Figure 13.8.   Crowd-pleasing wine, cheese, and fruit combinations.

CHEESES	APPETIZER WINES	WHITE WINES		RED WINES		SPARKLING WINES	DESSERT WINES	FRUITS
		Dry	Sweet	Dry	Sweet			
Blue, Gorgonzola—pungent, zesty; mold-veined	●			●	●	●	●	Pears, apples, melons
Brie—mild and creamy; edible white crust				●			●	Green grapes, pineapple, apples, melons, peaches
Brick—mild, sweet; yellow to orange		●	●	●	●		●	Apples, pineapple, melons, pears, green grapes
Camembert—mild to pungent; edible white crust				●	●	●	●	Green grapes, melons, apples, pineapple, pears
Cheddar—mild to sharp; white to orange	●			●			●	Apples, melons, pears, green grapes, pineapple
Colby—mild; firm; light yellow to orange	●			●			●	Pineapple, green grapes, melons
Cream cheeses—mild; white		●	●	●	●	●		Green grapes, pineapple, watermelon, strawberries, peaches

by the removal of fat or addition of casein, which can give the product off-flavors, bitterness, and a rubbery texture. If these are to be minimized, cooking temperatures are lowered in the processing of lowfat cheeses. In general, composition and processing controls must be more precise during the manufacture of lowfat cheese than for regular cheeses. lowfat cheese must rate a 3.0% fat content in the USDA melt test and meet FDA composition requirements for pasteurized processed American cheese.

FROZEN DESSERTS

Ice cream is one of America's favorite desserts. It is found on every foodservice menu from restaurants to hospitals to schools. It is sold to the foodservice operation in all kinds of forms, including pints, quarts, 5-gallon drums, chocolate-covered

Figure 13.8.   Continued.

CHEESES	APPETIZER WINES	WHITE WINES		RED WINES		SPARKLING WINES	DESSERT WINES	FRUITS
		Dry	Sweet	Dry	Sweet			
Edam, Gouda— mild, nutlike; soft texture; wax coating		●	●	●	●	●	●	Apples, green grapes, pears, pineapple
Monterey Jack— mild; creamy white	●	●	●	●	●	●	●	Apples, melons, pears, green grapes, pineapple
Muenster—mild to mellow; creamy white		●	●	●	●		●	Apples, melons, pineapple, green grapes, pears
Port du Salut—full flavor; creamy yellow; firm rind		●		●				Pears, pineapple, melons
Provolone—mild to sharp; white; light smoky flavor		●		●				Grapes, apples, pears, pineapple
Stilton—piquant, nippy; blue-veined, smooth	●			●	●		●	Pears, apples, melons
Swiss—sweet, nutlike; smooth, creamy white		●	●	●	●	●		Green grapes, pineapple, apples, pears, melons

Source: The Manhattan Mercury.

ice cream bars, and every flavor a customer might want. Ice cream is made from milk, often with cream added. By law, it must contain at least 10% milkfat by weight, which accounts for 48% of the calories (Margen, 1992). Super premium ice creams, which are very rich, can have up to 20% milkfat, accounting for approximately 60% of the calories.

Mixes are first prepared in the making of commercial ice creams by assembling, weighing, and mixing ingredients (Bennion, 1995). The mix is pasteurized to destroy pathogenic organisms. The mix then is homogenized to improve the texture and palatability of the ice cream. It is cooled and rapidly frozen while whipping the mix to incorporate air, thus making the mixture lighter and giving it extra volume; this process is called *overrun*. Overrun should be about 80% to 100% for ice cream, 40% for sherbets, and 25% for ices (Kotschevar & Donnelly, 1999). When the ice cream is partially frozen, it is drawn from the freezer into packages and transferred to cold storage rooms for freezing and hardening.

Today customers are looking for frozen desserts that are lower in calories or have less fat than the original products. Low-calorie, lowfat, and nonfat products are in high demand. Low-calorie frozen products are made with artificial sweeteners instead of sugar. Processors are trying to please the customer by producing modified fat products with the same rich, creamy, mouth-feel characteristics of fat in real ice cream (Benion, 1995).

Low-calorie, lowfat, and nonfat frozen yogurts are taking over a large share of the ice cream market. Iced milks have a 2% to 7% milkfat content and 10% to 30% total milk solids but are not as popular as they were a few years ago, because customers prefer other modified products. Sherbet usually contains some dairy products as well as fruit; sorbets, fruit ices, and fruit-juice bars usually do not contain dairy products and are most often free of cholesterol and fat.

Soft-serve ice cream is a big seller in many foodservice operations, especially in quick-service operations (Kotschevar & Donnelly, 1999). A regular ice cream mix can be used or a special one for soft ice cream. The mix is frozen and then whipped. When it reaches the "ribbon" stage, in which the product folds back and forth like a ribbon as it comes out of the freezer, the soft ice cream is ready to serve. It is not hardened in a freezer as traditional ice cream is. Soft ice cream mixes usually are sold in bulk containers that hold 3, 5, or more gallons. Some large operations have refrigerated tanks that are filled by delivery trucks. The tanks lead into the machines that freeze the soft ice cream, thus eliminating handling of the product.

BUTTER AND MARGARINE

According to the Food Guide Pyramid, fats should be used sparingly in the diet. Butter is classified as a dairy product because cream is its main ingredient, and because margarine is used as a butter substitute it often is considered a dairy product. Americans consumed 12 pounds more fats and oils per person in 1993 than in 1970 (Putnam & Allshouse, 1994). The average use of salad and cooking oils increased 58% during that time period and fell 6% for butter and margarine. The increase in oils probably is the result of increased consumer emphasis on unsaturated fats.

Butter

Federal standards require that butter contain no less than 80% milkfat. It may also contain salt and coloring. Approximately 18% of its weight is water dispersed in the fat. Cream, which can be sweet or sour, must be pasteurized for use in butter; butter made from sour cream has the most pronounced flavor. It can be naturally soured, or lactic acid bacteria may be added to the sweet cream. If the butter is colored, usually with carotene, the color is added before pasteurization. The cream then is churned to produce butter and buttermilk, which is drained off. The butter is then washed, salted, and worked to remove excess buttermilk and to distribute the salt. Some sweet-cream butter is not salted and is sold as sweet butter. Americans prefer salted butter, but Europeans use only sweet butter.

Figure 13.9. USDA grade stamps for butter and cheese.

The USDA has established grade standards based on quality scores for butter. Grade AA has a 93 score, Grade A a 92 score, Grade B a 90 score, and Grade C an 82 score. Flavor characteristics, which are determined by taste and smell, are the greatest part of the score. The rest of the score is based on body, color, and salt.

Butter is sold by the quarter pound, pound, and bulk. Most butter used in food-service operations is sold as pats, from 72 to 90 per pound, in 5-pound cartons. Today, with the emphasis on safe food, each pat usually is wrapped in plastic or foil or put into small plastic cups with covers. Grade stamps for butter are shown in Figure 13.9.

Margarine

Oleomargarine was first developed in 1869 by a French chemist who responded to an offer of a prize by Napoleon III for a palatable, nutritious, and economic alternative to butter (Bennion, 1995). Beef fat was used in the original margarine. According to standards of identity, margarine is a plastic food consisting of one or more approved vegetable or animal fats mixed with cream. Soybean and cottonseed oils are the primary ingredients in most margarines. Margarine should not contain less than 80% fat, 1% milk products, 9,000 international units of vitamin A, and not more than 15% moisture and 4% salt.

PURCHASING, RECEIVING, AND STORING

Proper purchasing, receiving, and storage procedures are essential for dairy products in a foodservice operation. Most of these products are perishable and spoil quickly if the temperature is not correct or if they become contaminated. Likely results of improper handling include increased costs, spoilage, customer dissatisfaction, and safety concerns.

Purchasing

Foodservice buyers need a thorough understanding of the daily census and menu when purchasing dairy products. Because of perishability, many operations require daily deliveries of milk, especially schools, colleges, universities, hospitals, and nursing homes. Daily deliveries add to the cost of milk, but most of these operations are not built with enough storage space for more than a few days' milk supplies (Gunn, 1995). In school foodservice operations, all milk is purchased on bid from one supplier. Can you imagine having one supplier deliver the lowfat unflavored milk, another the lowfat chocolate milk, and yet a third supplier for other milk types? Almost all school districts award milk bids on a bottom line, all-or-nothing basis.

If bids for milk are used, detailed specifications are required. Otherwise, brand names often are used. Butter, margarine, cheese, ice cream, and yogurt generally are purchased by a brand name that could be determined by an in-house and customer taste panel. A pricing plan under the authority of the Agricultural Marketing Act of 1937 has established prices for three classifications of dairy products. Each state has its own standards of identity for dairy products based on a federal code that is not regulatory.

Examples of specifications for dairy products follow.

Milk

Form: fluid milk, 2% reduced fat

Use: hospital individual patient service

Preservation form: fresh, 45°F or lower on delivery in refrigerated truck

Quality: U.S. Grade A, pasteurized

Milkfat: not less than 2.0%

Milk solids: not less than 8.25% not fat

Vitamin A: restored to not less than 2,000 I.U. per quart

Vitamin D: restored to not less than 400 IU per quart

Pack: half-pint cartons, 50/case

Price: by the half-pint carton

Yogurt

Form: plain nonfat yogurt

Use: salad dressings, Mexican menu items

Preservation form: 40°F or less on delivery in refrigerated truck

Brand: Dannon plain nonfat yogurt

Quality: meets National Yogurt Association criteria for live and active culture yogurt

Milkfat: not more than 0.5%

Milk solids: not less than 8.25% without fat

Pack: 32-ounce carton, 6 cartons/case

Price: by case

Cheese, American

Form: lowfat American pasteurized process

Use: hot entrées, salad bar

Preservation form: 38°F–40°F on delivery in refrigerated truck

Quality: must rate a 3 in USDA melt test and meet FDA composition requirements for pasteurized processed American cheese

Pack: 6/5-pound loaves per case

Price: by loaf or case

Butter

Form: sweet cream, unsalted

Use: customer service

Preservation form: 45°F or less on delivery in refrigerated truck

Quality: USDA Grade AA (score 93)

Milkfat: not less than 80%

Pack: 72 pats per pound individually wrapped in foil, 5-pounds/case

Price: by the case

Receiving

Receiving personnel should be trained what to check when receiving dairy products. This requires a visual check in addition to tasting and smelling the product. Unpasteurized milk and dairy products are a potential source of microorganisms that cause foodborne illnesses (National Restaurant Association, Educational Foundation, 1992). All cartons and bulk containers that enter a foodservice operation must carry the pasteurization label. Cream, dried milk, cottage cheese, Neufchâtel cheese, and cream cheese must be made from pasteurized milk. All market milk is Grade A quality. Local, state, and federal milk-control programs combine to assure consumers that the milk they buy is unadulterated, taken from safe cows, and processed using sanitary methods.

Milk that is used as a beverage must be packaged in individual containers, not larger than one pint, or may be served from a bulk dispenser. Milk used for cooking may be poured from commercially filled containers of less than one-half gallon capacity. Dried milk or milk in bulk containers of 5 to 10 gallons may be used for cooking and serving purposes, as local regulations permit.

Fresh milk has a sweetish taste. Sour, bitter, or moldy-tasting milk must be rejected. Many states' health departments require that milk be marked with a date. Milk that is delivered after the expiration date marked on the container should be rejected, along with milk with a temperature above 45°F on delivery. Milk with off-flavors may still be wholesome, but should be rejected because customers will complain.

The composition of cheese is regulated in the United States by a standard of identity specifying the ingredients that may be used, the maximum moisture content, the minimum fat content, and the requirements for pasteurization of milk to remove harmful bacteria. Cheese should be checked when purchased to determine if each type has its characteristic flavor, texture, and uniform color. The rind on cheese should be clean and not broken. Cheese with mold that is not natural to the product and is dried out should be rejected.

Butter should have a sweet, fresh flavor, uniform color, and firm texture. It also should be free of mold and dirt and should be in clean, unbroken containers. Butter that is rancid or has absorbed unpleasant odors should be rejected.

Storing

The storing procedure for dairy products is similar to that for most other perishable food products.

- Refrigerator temperature should be no more than 40°F. As the refrigerator temperature goes up, the storage life of dairy products goes down.
- "Sell by" dates on labels should be checked upon delivery and prior to use to ensure freshness.
- Open cartons or packages of milk, yogurt, or cheese should be returned to the refrigerator as quickly as possible. Be sure cheese is wrapped tightly in moisture-proof wrap. Strong flavored cheeses should be placed in storage containers with tight-fitting lids to prevent odor contamination of other foods. Store fluid dairy products, yogurt, and cottage cheese in original containers, tightly sealed.
- Both milk and cheese may be frozen, but the quality of the product will deteriorate, especially the texture and flavor. Frozen cheese will become crumbly and lose its flavor. Cheese that is being stored frozen should be cut in pieces weighing less than ½ pound and measuring less than 1-inch thick, then wrapped tightly. Frozen cheese should be thawed in the refrigerator for 24 hours and used as soon as possible.
- A large block of cheese can develop mold but is safe to use if you trim the cheese to ⅓ inch below the deepest mold-growth penetration. Do not let the mold touch the trimming knife, or the growth will spread.
- Recommended refrigeration storage life for opened dairy products, after which a loss of food quality occurs, is shown below (Storing dairy products, 1994).

Milk	5 days
Buttermilk	2 weeks
Ultra-pasteurized cream:	
opened	7–10 days
unopened	6–8 weeks
Butter	2–3 weeks
Sour cream	2–3 weeks

Yogurt	7–10 days
Cottage cheese	7–10 days
Cream cheese	2 weeks
Process cheese and cheese food products	3–4 weeks
Natural cheese	3–4 weeks
Grated Parmesan	12 months

- Dairy products should be stored at 38°F to 40°F with an 85% to 95% relative humidity.

SUMMARY

Milk is the basic ingredient in all dairy products. Milk is one of the most perishable of all foods because of its nutritive composition and fluid form. It is a high-quality protein and rich source of calcium. Rigid control occurs in the production and processing of Grade A fluid milk. Pasteurization is required by law for all Grade A fluid milk and milk products in interstate commerce. Nutrition labeling also is required for packaged foods, including milk and milk products. Fluid milk can be whole, lowfat, fat free or nonfat, or flavored milk. According to federal standards, packaged whole milk must contain at least 3.25% milkfat and 8.25% milk solids. lowfat milks can have between 0.5% to 2.0% milkfat and at least 8.2% milk solids. Fluid milk can also be concentrated to produce evaporated, condensed, and dry milk or cultured to produce yogurt, buttermilk, sour cream, and acidophilus milk.

Other dairy products include cheese, frozen desserts, and butter and margarine. Cheese is a concentrated dairy product made by draining the moisture from milk after coagulation of the major milk protein, casein. More than 2,000 varieties of cheese are classified by origin, consistency and texture, color, shape, flavor, and other criteria. Frozen dairy desserts, including ice cream and yogurt, are favorites of American customers.

Purchasing, receiving, and storing dairy products is a major responsibility for the foodservice manager. The perishability of these products makes food safety a top priority.

REFERENCES

Bennion, M. (1995). *Introductory foods* (10th ed.). Upper Saddle River, NJ: Merrill/Prentice Hall.

Dannon. (1997). *Your source for healthy profits.*

Gunn, M. (1995). *First choice, a purchasing systems manual for school foodservice.* University, MS: National Food Service Management Institute.

Kotschevar, L. H., & Donnelly, R. (1999). *Quantity food purchasing* (4th ed.). Upper Saddle River, NJ: Merrill/Prentice Hall.

Margen, S. A, and Editors of the University of California at Berkley Wellness Letter. (1992). *The wellness encyclopedia of food and nutrition*. New York: Rebus.

McWilliams, M. (1993). *Foods: experimental perspectives* (2nd ed.). New York: Macmillan.

Meyenberg goat milk. (Undated). *Help yourself to Meyenberg!* Santa Barbara, CA: Author.

Mimberg, K. (1994). BST & milk. *School Food Service & Nutrition, 48*(8), 44.

National Dairy Council. (1992). *Newer knowledge of cheese and other cheese products*. Rosemont, IL: Author.

National Dairy Council. (1993). *Newer knowledge of milk and other fluid dairy products*. Rosemont, IL: Author.

National Restaurant Association, Educational Foundation. (1992). *Applied foodservice sanitation* (4th ed.). Chicago: Author.

Nutrition Fact Sheet (1997). National Center for Nutrition and Dietetics of the American Dietetic Association.

Putnam, J. J., & Allshouse, J. E. (1994). Food consumption, prices, and expenditures, 1970–93. Food and Consumer Economics Division, Economic Research Service, U.S. Department of Agriculture. Statistical Bulletin No. 915.

Storing dairy products. (1994). *Restaurants & Institutions, 104*(14), 116.

Straus, K. (1994). Grate expectations. *Restaurants & Institutions, 104*(15), 133, 136, 138.

Sugarman, C. (1996, September 4). The milk-mustache campaign. *The Manhattan Mercury*.

Beverages

The small tip of the Food Guide Pyramid includes fats, oils, and sweets and is high-lighted in Figure 14.1. These are foods such as salad dressings, cream, butter, mar-garine, sugars, soft drinks, candies, and sweet desserts. Alcoholic beverages also are part of the group. These foods provide calories but few vitamins and minerals.

In general, customers are leaning toward ordering beverages infused with new fla-vors that often are more intense than established flavors (National Restaurant Association [NRA], 1994). Such is the case with flavored iced teas, noncola soft drinks, specialty coffees, single-malt liquors, and microbrewed beers now available in many foodservice operations.

NONALCOHOLIC BEVERAGES

Sales of nonalcoholic beverages have increased in the 1990s (NRA, 1994). The NRA reports that these beverages represented about 85% of the volume of all beverages consumed away from home in 1993 (Figure 14.2) compared to 81% in 1980. Though

Figure 14.1. Food Guide Pyramid with fats, oils, and sugars highlighted.

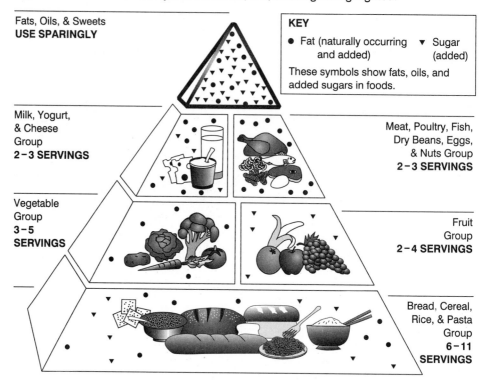

coffee consumption has decreased from the mid 1980s, sales of specialty coffees, such as cappuccino, espresso, and latte, have increased dramatically. Flavored iced teas introduced in the '90s could be responsible for the increase in sales. Diet and regular soft-drink sales have grown the greatest from 1980 to 1993. Noncolas, such as Sprite, Dr. Pepper, 7-Up, and Mountain Dew, were selling at a faster rate than the more traditional colas during that time period, as were hot and iced teas.

Coffee

The popularity of specialty coffees and the emergence of hip, new coffeehouses has helped reverse a 20-year downward trend in coffee consumption. The coffee craze is reborn! According to a *Restaurants & Institutions'* 1996 reader survey as shown in Figure 14.3, four of the ten top beverage-product demands are coffee-related: cappuccino (1), espresso (4), flavored coffee (5), and hot coffee (10). According to the U.S. Department of Agriculture (USDA), per capita consumption of coffee steadily decreased from more than 33 gallons per year in 1970 to 25.7 gallons in 1988. Since then, coffee consumption rebounded to 27.8 gallons in 1992. Coffee consumption at quick-service restaurants, according to the NRA (1994), has boomed in the last decade, increasing 36% since 1980.

One reason coffee sales are up at quick-service restaurants is that young people are behind the upswing in specialty coffee sales and youths are disproportionately

Figure 14.2. Percentage of all beverages consumed away from home, 1993.

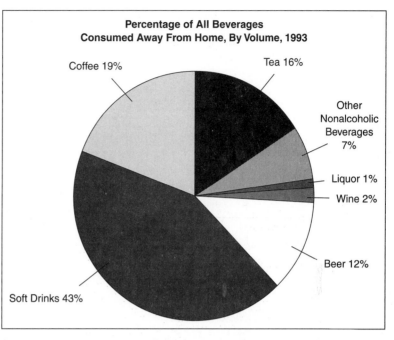

Percentage of All Beverages Consumed Away From Home, By Volume, 1993

Coffee 19%
Tea 16%
Other Nonalcoholic Beverages 7%
Liquor 1%
Wine 2%
Beer 12%
Soft Drinks 43%

Source: From "Soak Up the New Beverage Trends" by the National Restaurant Association, 1994. *Restaurant USA, 14*(10), p. 11–12. Used by permission.

heavy users of quick-service restaurants (Moomaw, 1994). An obvious reason for adding gourmet coffees to the menu is their profitability; specialty coffees are among the highest-margined menu items. The food cost for a cup of regular coffee selling for less than a dollar is about 6 cents; specialty coffees with a much higher selling price have a food cost of 13 to 15 cents.

Coffee Culture

A coffee culture has emerged throughout the world with a terminology all of its own. The International Coffee Organization calls it "java jive." For example, *joe* is another name for coffee, and *barista* is the name of the person serving at an espresso bar. Other terminology includes *The Drinks* and *The Lingo.*

The Drinks. A number of new coffee drinks are currently available in many food-service operations. Some of the most popular include:

- Espresso—a shot of hot, strong black coffee
- Macchiato—an espresso shot topped with a touch of foamed milk
- Cappuccino—a blend of espresso and steamed and foamed milk

Figure 14.3. Top 10 beverages in demand by *Restaurants & Institutions* readers.

TOP 10 BEVERAGES IN DEMAND BY OUR READERS

1. CAPPUCCINO
2. MINERAL WATER
3. LEMONADE
4. ESPRESSO
5. FLAVORED COFFEES
6. FRUIT BLENDS
7. BEER
8. FLAVORED WATERS
9. ICED TEA
10. HOT COFFEE

Source: *R&I Marketplace* research

Source: From "Coffee is King! Customers Clamor for Caffeine Creations. New Product Watch," 1996, *Restaurants & Institutions, 106*(24), p. 12. Used by permission.

- Caffe latte—same ingredients as cappuccino, but with more steamed and less foamed milk
- Caffe mocha—mostly steamed milk with a shot of espresso and mocha syrup

The Lingo.   Customers use unique terminology to order various coffee beverages. This lingo reflects the coffee culture, especially among the younger members of the population.

- Cup sizes are *short, tall,* and *grande.*
- Customers can order a single, double, or triple *espresso shot.*
- Coffee is no longer caffeinated or decaffeinated. In java jive, it is either *leaded* or *unleaded.*
- A half-leaded, half-unleaded cup of coffee is known as a *schizo.*
- Any coffee drink with skim milk is called a *skinny.*
- A coffee drink that is both decaffeinated and contains skim milk often is called a *no-fun.*

- A *thunder thigh* is one name for a quadruple grande whole-milk latte with chocolate syrup and extra whipped cream.
- Coffee to go is either *on wheels* or *with wings.*

History of Coffee

The origin of coffee can be traced to Ethiopia where beans grew wild. No one is quite sure how its use as a drink began. One legend tells of a goat herder who found his goats frolicking around a cluster of dark-leaved shrubs bearing red berries. The goat herder supposedly shared the discovery with local monks who found that if they boiled the berries when they were green and drank the broth, they could stay awake during evening prayers. About a thousand years ago, traders took the berries across the Red Sea into what is now Yemen, where Muslim monks began cultivating the shrubs.

The first coffeehouses in Italy and England opened around 1650. In the 1700s, coffee plants were taken to Paris, where Louis XIV apparently developed a fondness for the bitter drink. Some of the plants were stolen and made their way across the Atlantic Ocean to the New World. Coffee became a patriotic American beverage while the 13 colonies were still under English rule. Originally, colonists drank tea but later rebelled when the parliament of King George III imposed a stiff tax on tea imports, leading to the Boston Tea Party in which colonists dumped tea leaves into Boston Harbor and cast their votes for joe.

Interesting Coffee Facts

According to the *Restaurant & Institutions* menu census, regular coffee is the most common menu item overall and decaffeinated is the third most common (Straus, 1992). Interest in premium coffees and signature coffee drinks is at an all-time high. Even though a cup of coffee has two ingredients, ground coffee beans and water, a great deal of variation is possible in the final brew. Here are some facts about the popular beverage:

- Much of the flavor of coffee beans comes from growing conditions and production methods. In general, coffee is grown in an area ranging from 25° north of the equator to 25° south in a belt that runs around the world. Coffee growing regions include:

    Central and South America. Coffees are light- to medium-bodied with clean lively flavors.

    East Africa. Coffees have a unique floral and wine flavor and are typically medium- to full-bodied.

    Indonesia. Coffees are full-flavored with exotic elements.

    Hawaii. Kona coffee is the only coffee grown in the United States.
- Only a few of the 100 species of the plant genus *Coffea* are used to make coffee. The most popular is *Caffea arabic,* the most flavorful and aromatic bean. A cousin, *Robusta,* is less expensive.
- A coffee bush takes a minimum of five years to yield its first crop. On an average, each shrub produces 1 pound of coffee or 3,500 hand-picked coffee cherries annually during its productive years.

- Coffees are blended like wines to give a unique flavored brew.
- Coffee beans are often categorized by the degree of roasting. *Cinnamon roast,* also known as institutional roast, gives a tan color to the coffee beans; most grocery store coffee is cinnamon roast. *French roast* produces black beans with a smoky, pungent flavor.
- Decaffeinated coffee has the caffeine removed naturally by a Swiss water process method or by chemical extraction with solvents that disappear during roasting.
- The average yield of a pound of coffee is 40 six-ounce cups. Once the correct proportions of coffee to water are determined, they should be consistent regardless of the amount being made. Skimping by grinding the beans finer or using less coffee produces a thin brew.
- Coffee can be kept warm over a burner only about 20 minutes before the flavor deteriorates. An airpot or vacuum server keeps coffee hot and the flavor good longer.
- Coffee that is used within 2 weeks should be stored in an airtight container in a cool, dark place or a refrigerator. To keep it longer, store it in small airtight packages in the freezer.

Processing Coffee

The path to the coffee cup starts at coffee bushes from which the green beans are plucked. They must be roasted into an acceptable market form before they finally are made into a beverage. A good cup of coffee often sets the tone of customers' satisfaction with their meals. If customers begin and end a meal with a poor cup of coffee, that sets the tone for the entire meal. The quality of coffee is taking on a central importance in foodservice operations.

Coffee trees grow to about 15 to 30 feet at maturity but are pruned to a smaller height to permit easier picking. The tree is really an evergreen shrub with a double leaf like a bean. It grows best in a tropical climate and rocky soil, such as the volcanic soil in which Kona coffee is grown in Hawaii. The tree has white flowers from which red fruit smaller than a cherry develops (Figure 14.4).

Coffee Beans.   All coffee beans come from two basic types of plants: *arabicas* and *robustas*. **Arabicas coffee beans** are mild-tasting and primarily come from South America. **Robustas coffee beans** produce a strong, bitter, dark coffee from Africa and the Philippines. The red fruit is picked when fully ripe. Then the pulp is removed, leaving two oval beans with their flat sides together (Figure 14.5). The beans are either dried for 2 or 3 weeks in the sun or are soaked, depulped, washed, and dried by machine. The silverskin, parchment covering and pulp are removed, leaving cleaned beans which are either light green or blue green in color. When the green coffee reaches the United States, the green beans are classified into six different sizes and graded (Bennion, 1995). Imperfect beans and foreign objects, such as sticks and stones, are sorted out. The number of imperfections green beans have determines the grade.

After grading, **cuppers,** who are highly trained experts, check the product to determine its flavor quality. They start by roasting a small batch of beans in a gas or

Figure 14.4. Branch from coffee tree showing the white flowers of red fruit.

Figure 14.5. Coffee berry with two flat-sided beans.

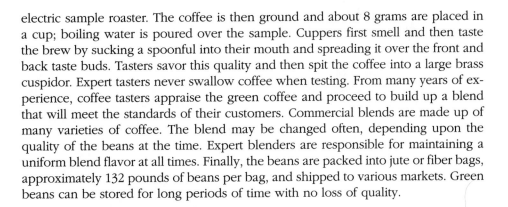

electric sample roaster. The coffee is then ground and about 8 grams are placed in a cup; boiling water is poured over the sample. Cuppers first smell and then taste the brew by sucking a spoonful into their mouth and spreading it over the front and back taste buds. Tasters savor this quality and then spit the coffee into a large brass cuspidor. Expert tasters never swallow coffee when testing. From many years of experience, coffee tasters appraise the green coffee and proceed to build up a blend that will meet the standards of their customers. Commercial blends are made up of many varieties of coffee. The blend may be changed often, depending upon the quality of the beans at the time. Expert blenders are responsible for maintaining a uniform blend flavor at all times. Finally, the beans are packed into jute or fiber bags, approximately 132 pounds of beans per bag, and shipped to various markets. Green beans can be stored for long periods of time with no loss of quality.

Roasting. After the green coffee is received at the roasting plant, it is stored until needed. Before roasting, the beans are cleaned to remove foreign materials that weigh less than the beans. Roasting causes the sugars in green coffee beans to caramelize, turning the beans a rich brown color. Roasts available in order of increasing darkness are: American, which is the most commonly used, Vienna, French, and espresso. Batch roasters operate at temperatures of 800°F to 1000°F and continuous roasters at 500°F. Regardless of the process, roasting is terminated when the beans reach between 390°F and 430°F. French and Italian roasted beans reach much higher temperatures, resulting in a black, oil-covered bean.

Beans are roasted in a revolving, perforated cylinder. As the temperature increases, the beans shrivel until about halfway through when they begin to puff up, increasing about 50% in size, and pop open. Although roasting results in an increased volume as the beans swell, they have about a 15% weight loss due to loss of moisture. When roasting is completed, the process is stopped quickly by means of a quench, cold water sprayed on the hot beans. The beans are put into a cooler bin to return them to room temperature. The most expensive brands of coffee are dry roasted.

Beverage Preparation

Grinds vary among coffees from coarse to very fine. Grinding exposes the bean's fibers; more flavor extraction is possible with more exposed fibers. All grinds contain particles of various sizes. A regular grind used for urns contains a higher proportion of coarse particles than any of the other grinds. The urn coffee maker used in large foodservice operations operates on the same principle as a drip-filter model. A drip or medium grind is used for a drip-filter coffee maker, as shown in Figure 14.6. The upper part of the coffee maker, through which cold water flows, has perforations covered with disposable thin parchment that holds the coffee grounds. Espresso uses a very fine or pulverized grind that produces a very strongly flavored brew. The larger the grind, the weaker the brew. Water temperature should be at least 185°F to extract a desirable amount of soluble solids but not more than 203°F to avoid bitter substances. Generally, the ratio of coffee to water is 1 ounce coffee to 2 ounces of water.

Market Forms

Coffee, like many foods, gives the consumer more choices than just plain coffee. Examples include decaffeinated, instant, flavored coffees, and espresso and cappuccino.

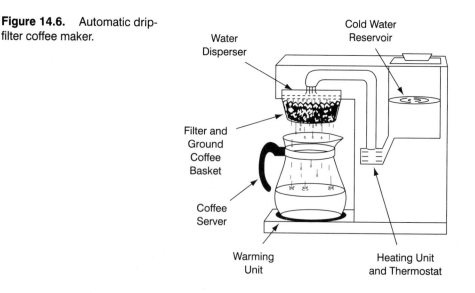

Figure 14.6. Automatic drip-filter coffee maker.

Water Disperser

Cold Water Reservoir

Filter and Ground Coffee Basket

Coffee Server

Warming Unit

Heating Unit and Thermostat

Decaffeinated.   **Caffeine** is a chemical compound that stimulates the body's central nervous system. Pharmacologists consider it one of the world's most widely used drugs (Margen, 1992). It is found naturally in coffee beans, tea leaves, cocoa beans, and cola nuts. To produce **decaffeinated coffee,** a chemical solvent is used to remove most of the caffeine from the green coffee beans. The Food and Drug Administration (FDA) sets the limit for the amount of solvent that can be used. A Swiss water-process method developed by Nestlé for removing caffeine is used in more expensive coffees.

Instant.   **Instant coffee** is a concentrated extract of a coffee brew. Hot water is passed through coarsely ground coffee beans and then the brew is passed again through fresh coffee grounds until the brew reaches the correct strength. The final product is then dehydrated into a powder by using the spray-drier method. This is a simplification of the commercial process in which sophisticated equipment is used to make instant coffee.

Liquid coffee is a freeze-dried instant coffee that is being used more and more in foodservice operations, such as hotels and restaurants and hospitals. It often is referred to as "coffee on demand." In many operations, coffee is available for customers 24 hours a day, but employees are not. The process used by Vitality Foodservice, Inc., a subsidiary of Lykes Pasco, Inc., for making this product is interesting.

- Approximately 450 pounds of ground coffee are placed in each of five brew canisters.
- Water at 330°F under 180 pounds per square inch pressure is used in the brew process.
- Coffee leaves the fifth canister in concentrated form, after 5½ hours of brewing.
- Heat exchanger brings temperature down to 40°F.
- The concentrated coffee is placed in plastic bottles.
- Bottles are sent through a freeze tunnel and held for 3 to 4 hours.

The bottle of frozen concentrate is put into a special dispensing machine in which a small amount of coffee is added to 190°F water into a cup. Vitality Foodservice sells the concentrated coffee to foodservice operations and provides the equipment and monthly service. Each bottle of coffee weighs 59.2 ounces and is packed three bottles to a case.

Flavored.   Many people are ordering flavored coffee to complement or replace dessert. Restaurants, coffee shops in hospitals, colleges and universities, and malls are featuring mouth-watering flavors that intrigue customers. Flavored coffees are found in most brands of coffee. Many of these coffees also are available decaffeinated. Customers can choose hazelnut, almond, chocolate, raspberry, or apricot. For example, Java Coast produces a tempting array of gourmet flavors.

- *Apricot Cordial.* Premium beans complemented by natural and artificial apricot cream flavor give this blend a smooth, cordial taste.
- *Bewitching Brandy.* The essence of fine cognac and premium arabicas create an elegant, sophisticated brew.

- *Chocolate Cherry Truffle*. Natural and artificial cherry flavor are combined with natural cocoa powder to create this treat.
- *Irish Cream*. This blend is flavored with chocolate, and the beans are dusted with natural cocoa powder. Irish Cream adds an Irish accent.

Espresso and Cappuccino.   Coffee-based drinks are among the beverages most quickly growing in popularity, according to the *Restaurants & Institutions* 1995 menu census (Bertagnoli, 1996). A foodservice manager faces many decisions before adding espresso and cappuccino to the menu. What you buy and how much you spend—anywhere from $2,000 to $17,000 for equipment—is directly related to how much time you must devote to training and how important you think espresso and cappuccino are to your menu.

Manual, automatic, or superautomatic machines are available. The buyer should conduct cost-effectiveness studies to determine which machine best serves the needs of the foodservice operation. These machines should be approved by the local health department because milk is used in most cappuccino drinks. Some European models only accommodate demi-tasse cups, which would not be adequate for the American mugs used for cappuccino. Also, if the machine breaks down, is a local service representative quickly available? Many operators lease the equipment and pay a monthly fee for its use. At the end of the lease, the equipment usually can be purchased for a low fee. Regardless of which machine is purchased, staff needs to be well trained in its use.

Specifications

Writing specifications for coffee is not difficult once the foodservice has determined which blend or brand its customers will most likely accept. In small foodservice operations, a retail brand name generally is specified. In larger operations, brands are still used, but if the volume of coffee is great enough, buyers might specify their own blend. An example is the coffee used in the foodservice operations in the Kansas State University (KSU) residence halls. Coffee is ordered through the state purchasing department, which has a contract with a specific distributor. KSU requests a variation of the state specification (Figure 14.7) to better meet the desires of its customers. Note the last sentence in which the buyer protects the university if the supplier does not meet the specification.

Tea

Hot tea service conjures up images of dowagers sipping Earl Grey tea from fine bone china cups while munching on watercress sandwiches, neatly trimmed of crusts, in some swanky hotel (Batty, 1994a). Coffee is extremely popular but a tea trend has been developing in the United States. Tearooms are opening and restaurateurs are beginning to realize that they need to know how to brew a proper pot of tea. According to the Tea Council of the USA, almost half of the population drinks tea every day.

Tea also has become popular in noncommercial foodservice operations. Hospitals serve a lot of tea as do nursing homes, probably because of the comfort factor. Colleges and universities also serve tea, especially iced tea, and canned teas are

Figure 14.7. Coffee specifications for Kansas State University residence halls.

> **Variations in State Specifications**
> **Requested by Kansas State University**
>
> *Blend:* Colombian coffees shall constitute 20% of the blend. The maximum Robustas permissible will be 5% of the blend. The remainder shall be Colombians, Central American Milds, or Brazils as defined by Fed Spec: HHH-C-571F.
>
> *Moisture:* The moisture content of the roasted ground coffee shall not exceed 3.5%.
>
> *Grind:* Bulk pack coffee shall be formulated and ground to meet the requirements of automatic drip coffee makers. Coffee should be of medium roast and have a cup quality of good or higher determined by the USDA.
>
> The roasted ground coffee should be packed in one (1) pound packages and have a minimum shelf life of sixteen (16) weeks after delivery.
>
> Coffee is subject to USDA inspection and supplier will pay for the inspection if any of the above requirements are not met.

stocked in the vending machines that are so commonplace on campus. Quite often in areas where iced tea is popular, glasses of iced tea are put on the table before guests are seated at banquets. This requires less labor than filling tea glasses and delivering them individually to guests when the waitstaff is the busiest.

History

Tea was known to man long before coffee was. Tea as a beverage has been traced back 5,000 years to ancient China. Zen Buddhist missionaries introduced tea to Japan where it soon became part of its culture as well. The Japanese Tea Ceremony literally became an art form. Tea finally entered Europe in the middle 1500s through a Portuguese Jesuit father. The Portuguese shipped their tea to Lisbon where Dutch ships transported it to France and Holland. Great Britain in the 1650s was the last country in Europe to use tea as a beverage. Its popularity led to an important social event, the afternoon tea, at which the ladies displayed their fine china and silver teapots. At the same time, Russia was trading with China and Japan, and tea was spreading throughout Russian society. The samovar, a vessel which holds enough boiling water and tea for 40 cups, was placed in most Russian homes.

English colonists in Boston began to use tea as a beverage at the end of the 17th century. When England imposed heavy taxes on tea and many other products, from newspapers to tavern licenses, American merchants smuggled in tea from other countries and began using herbal tea made by the Indians. Finally, American men dressed as Indians dumped hundreds of pounds of tea into the Boston harbor, and the Boston Tea Party heralded the beginning of the American Revolution.

Tea Plant

Tea comes from a tropical evergreen plant that usually grows 6,000 feet above sea level and is related to the camellia (Kotschevar & Donnelly, 1999). The plant is pruned and cultivated to produce many young shoots. The bud and next two leaves are the standard pluck. The bud has a delicate flavor that becomes stronger as the size of the leaf increases. The young unopened leaves at the top of the shoot are considered the highest quality.

Processing

Tea leaves are withered and then rolled over by a machine to break tissues and release flavorful juices and enzymes. They are then held and allowed to undergo oxidative changes identified as fermentation. After this, they are heated and dried, resulting in **black tea** with an amber color, a rich flavor and aroma, and a taste less bitter than green tea.

Green tea has a delicate, greenish yellow color and a fruity, slightly bitter flavor. It is produced by steaming the tea leaves, causing them to retain the original green color before rolling and drying them. **Oolong tea** is a partially fermented tea only slightly blackened and with a flavor and aroma between those of black and green teas.

Market Forms

According to the Tea Council of the USA, more than 127 million Americans, almost half the population, drink tea on any given day (Batty, 1994a). The tea market has almost doubled in the last 3 years.

Tea bags are the most popular method for making a cup of tea. They are convenient to use, and people can prepare the tea to meet their own desires of strength. Tea leaves contain soluble substances, some of which are bitter if the leaves are steeped too long. A pot of boiling, or near boiling, water accompanies the bag; the water should be poured over the tea bag for the best brew. An assortment of bag-in-the-box tea often is presented to customers who select their favorite tea.

More and more hotels and fine restaurants have gone to brewing loose tea of their customers' selection in a ceramic, stoneware, or silver pot. Then the waitstaff pours boiling water over the leaves that are in a little silver strainer, which can be removed when the brew is at the correct strength (Hochstein, 1996). Some customers seem to appreciate receiving "fresh" tea. Of course, this method requires more labor than tea bags, but when the pot of tea sells for $3.50 or more and the tea leaves cost from 4 to 7 cents a cup, tea is a high-profit menu item.

About 80% of all tea consumed in the United States is served over ice. The rise is mostly driven by new ready-to-drink iced tea products that are sweetened with corn syrup, sugar, or artificial sweeteners (Batty, 1994a). Iced tea has had some bad press about being a health risk because it contains bacteria (Kapner, 1996). However, it

Figure 14.8. Tea-brewing
guidelines.

The following are tea-brewing guidelines supported by the National Restaurant Association, the Food and Drug Administration, and the Tea Association of the USA:

- Brew tea using water 195°F or hotter.
- Let tea stand 5 minutes before cooling.
- Brew only enough tea for a few hours' service. Hold brewed tea at room temperature no longer than 8 hours.
- Wash, rinse, and sanitize all parts of tea equipment daily. Pay special attention to the dispensing valve, which must be disassembled for a thorough cleaning.
- Never pour fresh tea on top of old tea.

Source: From "Ice-Tea 'Brewhaha': CDC Says Drink OK" by S. Kapner, 1996, *Nation's Restaurant News, 30*(23). Used by permission.

may not be the harmful kind. The Centers for Disease Control and Prevention and most local health departments insist tea is safe when prepared and handled correctly. The NRA, FDA, and Tea Association of the USA have developed the tea-brewing guidelines shown in Figure 14.8.

Tea has about half the caffeine of coffee, and even that amount can be decreased by pouring a small amount of boiling water over the leaves and then discarding it. Pouring more water over the leaves will result in tea with almost no caffeine. **Decaffeinated tea,** like coffee, is made by using a chemical solvent to remove most of the caffeine from the tea leaves or by the water-process method. Lipton advertises that the caffeine in their tea is removed naturally by using pure, sparkling spring water.

Instant teas are dried products prepared from brewed teas and are used mostly in iced tea. Flavored teas like flavored coffees are becoming more popular. Celestial Seasonings offers flavored black teas, such as Misty Mango, Ceylon Apricot-Ginger, and Vanilla Maple; Bigelow has regular and decaffeinated flavored teas, including Constant Comment (flavored with orange rind and sweet spice), Lemon Lift, and Cinnamon Stick. These teas have either been treated with the fragrant and flavorful oils from fruit or spices or with bits of dried fruit.

Herbal teas are not really teas, but are naturally caffeine-free blends of dried herbs that produce a fragrant beverage once soaked. The most common herbs used are chamomile, rosehip, and verbena.

Types

According to the Tea Council of the USA, more than 3,000 different teas are available. About 93% of the tea sold in the United States is black tea. Green tea is extremely popular in the Orient but not as popular here (Batty, 1994a).

Purchasing

Writing specifications for tea is similar to writing them for coffee. Most buyers specify name brands; if the operation is large enough, it may specify its own blend. In foodservice operations that specialize in serving tea, buyers would be wise to purchase tea from suppliers who can train the waitstaff in the correct procedures for producing an excellent cup of tea. All teas need different steeping times. If serving quality tea is an objective, customers should not steep their own tea. This should be done by a trained person who knows that boiling water should be poured over the tea leaves and the length of time the tea should be steeped before removing the leaves.

For some tea drinkers, the teapot is almost as important as the tea itself (Batty, 1994b). The buyer for these operations not only must purchase tea and food but also teapots that are more than just vessels for serving tea. The type of teapot used to brew tea can enhance or detract from its flavor. Pots vary in the heat they hold. In some operations, each tea has its own type of pot, permitting it to become seasoned. Green teas taste better when brewed in glass or bone china pots. Flavored teas work best in the least porous pots, which do not absorb the aroma. A more porous pot, made of pottery or ceramic, should be used for oolong and lighter black teas. The heartiest black and smoky teas should be brewed in terra-cotta or clay pots, which are the most porous and actually absorb the tea's flavor. Metal pots, the least desirable for brewing tea, do not give the best flavor. Nor do they heat well.

Other Beverages

The volume of bottled water rose dramatically from 10% in 1980 to 16% in 1993 (Somerville, 1994). Soft drinks, the market leader, made up 43% of all beverages consumed in 1993 (Figure 14.2), an increase from 35% in 1980.

Profitable Choices

Many choices are available for customers who do not drink alcoholic beverages: nonalcoholic beers and wines; mocktails; fruit and vegetable juices; new-age beverages, such as flavored waters, all-natural sodas, and sparkling juices; bottled waters; hot and cold teas and coffees; frozen drinks; sports drinks; herb drinks; and even vitamin-charged "smart drinks" promoted as sparking an energy boost.

Many soft drinks are **carbonated,** or saturated with carbon dioxide to add unique zest to the beverage. Carbonation also protects against bacterial spoilage during storage (Bennion, 1995). Bottled mineral waters continue to be popular. Perrier, a natural sparkling, sodium-free, mineral water has been bottled in Vergeze, France, since 1863. Interestingly, bottled water is one of the fastest-growing categories; beer is down, coffee is down, and milk is down, but bottled water sales are up (Rhodes, 1996). Customers' thirst for water seems to be growing. The International Bottled Water Association reports that Americans drank 2.7 billion gallons of bottled water in 1995, an increase of 7.9% over the previous year. This brings the industry to a whopping 11.1% of the refreshment beverage market share.

The purpose of **sports,** or **isotonic, drinks** is to prevent dehydration during vigorous exercise and to give a quick energy boost. These beverages should have an osmotic pressure the same as human blood, permitting them to be rapidly absorbed. They have a low level of carbonation and a carbohydrate content of 6% to 8%, rather than the 10% to 12% found in regular soft drinks.

Nonalcoholic beers and wines have gained some popularity and are hard to distinguish by taste and appearance from alcoholic brews and spirits. They are stocked in many bars for customers who do not drink alcohol for a variety of reasons or who have been named the designated driver for the evening.

A common misconception among operators is that nonalcoholic beverages don't turn a profit (Somerville, 1994). Some foodservice operators think that these drinks should be priced lower than alcoholic beverages but are finding out that customers are quite willing to pay as much if the drink has style, taste, and panache.

Purchasing

Most nonalcoholic beverages are purchased by brand name and directly from specialized distributors. Because so many brands for each type of beverage are available, buyers might decide to conduct customer preference studies to determine which brands are most popular. In high volume operations, storage space, especially refrigerated, can be minimal, requiring more frequent deliveries. Accurate forecasting and inventory control need to be in place to keep customers satisfied. Stock turnover often is fast.

ALCOHOLIC BEVERAGES

The making of all alcoholic beverages involves the chemistry of fermentation. The process of **fermentation** is simple; yeast acts on sugar, converting it into alcohol and carbon dioxide gas. At this time, if the mixture is not protected from air, the alcohol turns into acetic acid, producing vinegar. Each type of alcoholic beverage has variances of this process, but the basic concept of fermentation is the same.

The total volume of alcoholic beverages consumed decreased from about 19% in 1980 to 15% in 1993 (Figure 14.2). Though Americans have been consuming fewer alcoholic beverages away from home, sales of wine have held steady. One third of the adult American population does not imbibe alcoholic beverages. The most popular beverage in the United States in 1960 was milk, with a per capita consumption of 38 gallons a year (Zraly, 1995). In 1990, soft drinks were the leading beverage at an annual per capita consumption of 50 gallons. Beer ranked second and milk third. Wine currently has a per capita consumption of 2 gallons each year in the United States, which ranks 30th in the world in wine consumption and fifth in production (Kolpan, Smith, & Weiss, 1996). Domestic American wines have improved considerably, in many cases matching or exceeding the quality of imported wines. The news that the consumption of wine could reduce the risk of heart disease could boost its popularity. Beer and liquor have been niched in the 1990s. Sales of specialty beers, such as microbrews, and specialty liquors, including single-malt scotches and single-barrel whiskeys, have countered the downward trend.

All beers, wines, and spirits are alcoholic beverages (Katsigris & Porter, 1991). An **alcoholic beverage** is any drinkable liquid that contains ethyl alcohol. Contrary to what many people think, beers and wines are not spirits. Beer, ale, and wine, including champagne, are not classified as spirits because they have different tastes, alcohol content, and ways of being served. An alcoholic beverage can have as little as 0.5% alcohol by volume to as much as 95%. The 0.5% level was set by the U.S. government at the time of the Prohibition Amendment in which an intoxication definition was required.

The **Bureau of Alcohol, Tobacco and Firearms** (ATF) is a law enforcement organization within the U.S. Department of Treasury with unique responsibilities dedicated to reducing violent crime, collecting revenue, and protecting the public. The amount of alcohol in a beverage is indicated either by proof or percent of alcohol. In the United States, **proof** is twice the percent of alcohol by volume. For example, W. L. Weller Kentucky Straight Bourbon Whiskey (Figure 14.9) is 45% alcohol by volume, or 90 proof. Another label on the bottle contains government warnings (1) to pregnant women who should not drink alcoholic beverages because of the risk of birth defects and (2) that consumption of alcoholic beverages impairs ability to drive a car or operate machinery. The ATF in 1986 issued new regulations for labeling; alcohol content must be indicated by percentage on the label because purchasers understand that number more readily. Note that the Beringer White Zinfandel wine la-

Figure 14.9. Whiskey labels indicating government warning and percent of alcohol by volume and proof.

bel in Figure 14.10 includes both the percent of alcohol by volume and the government warning. Both proof and percentage by volume may be used. Alcoholic beverages shipped out of the United States do not have the government warning label.

Wine

Purchasing wine is very challenging for foodservice buyers today. Wine has become part of the culture in many countries and is a major component of many meals. Restaurant managers have realized that including wine service in their operations helps boost the bottom line. In many finer restaurants, a **sommelier,** or wine steward, assists guests in choosing wines and opening and pouring them.

The Culinary Institute of America (CIA) has been America's center for culinary education since 1946 (Kolpan et al., 1996). Now in its 50th year, the CIA emphasizes wine appreciation as part of a fine meal in both its associate's two-year and bachelor's four-year degree curricula. In the associate degree program, students must complete a rigorous six-week course in the wines of the world. The curriculum in the bachelor's program includes the intellectual, historical, cultural, agricultural, and financial issues of the topic. Students are required to take a six-week wine and food

Figure 14.10. Wine labels indicating percent of alcohol by volume and government warning.

seminar, including four weeks at Greystone, the new campus in California's Napa Valley. The students learn about wines on a theoretical and practical level. In this text, wines are briefly discussed to give students some idea of the magnitude of the topic and to encourage them to attend seminars and workshops whenever possible.

Wines of the World

A minimum of 2,000 types of wine currently are on the market. Kolpan et al. (1996) categorize wines of the world as wines of the Old World and wines of the New World.

Old World.   French wines have long held the reputation of being among the best in the world. True French champagne is produced using one white grape variety, Chardonnay, and two red grape varieties, Pinot Noire and Pinot Meunier (Kolpan et al., 1996). German wines are gaining popularity. Bottles of Chianti, a full-bodied red wine, in straw-covered flasks were once thought of as cheap because those bottles hung over the bar in small local Italian restaurants; today, however, some Chiantis are aged for 3 years and are of high quality.

Spain is especially known for its sherry, a fortified wine in which the alcoholic strength is increased by the addition of grape brandy after fermentation. The wine is then oxidized by storing it in wooden barrels loosely covered to permit air to enter the wine. Other countries in the Old World that produce wine include Portugal; the central and eastern European countries of Switzerland, Austria, Hungary, Romania, and Russia; and the eastern Mediterranean region encompassing Greece, Turkey, Israel, Egypt, and northwest Africa.

New World.   North America and the Southern Hemisphere are considered the New World by Kolpan et al. (1996). The United States is the only country in the world that requires health warning labels on every bottle sold here; wines exported from the United States, however, cannot have these labels. It also is the only country where alcoholic beverages are regulated by the same federal organization that regulates firearms. A wine drinker in the United States is defined as a person who drinks a glass of wine a week; in Europe, however, a person who drinks a minimum of one glass of wine with dinner every day is considered a wine drinker.

Prohibition, an amendment to the U.S. Constitution, ruled the country from 1919 to 1933, but many states, counties, and towns still practiced it in some form for many years thereafter (Kolpan et al., 1996). An interesting bit of information is that more acres were planted with grapes in California before prohibition than are currently planted. California, Washington, Oregon, and New York are considered the major wine regions within the United States; most states that have growing conditions for grapes, however, have their own native wines. Wine makers and researchers have improved wine making since the 1950s and 1960s, and today America is considered to have very high quality wines.

California is the largest producer of U.S. wines, serving up more than the other states combined (Kolpan et al., 1996). Much of this wine comes in bulk or jug form, and the two most powerful producers are Gallo and Paul Masson. California's "lowliest" wines are as good or better than any wine in the world. Napa Valley produces some of the world's finest Cabernet Sauvignon and Chardonnay wines. Sonoma

Valley takes pride in its Chardonnay, Pinot Noir, Cabernet Sauvignon, Zinfandel, and some very fine sparkling wines.

New York, the second largest wine-producing state in the country, is a grape-growing area that produces fresh Rieslings, fuller Chardonnays, crisp sparkling wines, and full, dry Cabernet Savignons. The quality of New York wines is high enough to compete at a national and international level. The entire Great Lakes area, including New York, Pennsylvania, and Ohio, benefits from heavy snows that are beneficial to the grape vines by providing a layer of insulation against very low temperatures. Lakes Erie and Ontario stay cold longer than the ground in the spring and keep the air temperature low and the development of the buds slow. In the fall, the lakes stay colder than the ground and keep the temperature higher, permitting the grapes to continue ripening. Canada also produces wine, but few U.S. residents have ever tasted it.

The most important wine producing countries in the Southern Hemisphere are Chile, Argentina, Brazil, Australia, New Zealand, and South Africa (Kolpan et al., 1996). Australian wines are becoming quite popular in North America. Australia is the 11th largest producer of wines in the world despite the fact that half the continent is desert and many other areas have low rainfall and extremely hot weather. Shiraz, a robust and full-bodied red wine, recently has become popular in this country. The problem is that the Australian grape growers often cannot meet the demand, thus depleting the Shiraz stock in the United States.

Wine Production

Wine is available in many different colors, including white, red, and pink. It can have bubbles, be sweet or dry, be fortified with more alcohol, or have flavorings added. Fundamentally, the four major influences on the quality characteristics of wine are (Kolpan et al., 1996):

- grape variety
- climate, including weather conditions during the growing season
- vineyard soil
- decisions of the wine maker during the growing and processing of the wine

More wine makers are concentrating on the quality of wines. Kolpan et al. (1996) suggest that wine makers should emphasize these major considerations.

- Distinct taste and flavor characteristics typical of grape varieties should be evident.
- Place of origin of grapes should be reflected in the style, taste, and flavors of the wines.
- Aromas or flavors should be pleasant, not unpleasant.
- Pleasing the customer should have top priority.

Wine really is alcoholic grape juice, and the formula for making it is simple.

Sugar + Yeast → Alcohol + Carbon Dioxide

Wine is fermented fruit, usually grapes; the sugar in the grape juice is converted into alcohol by the action of yeasts. Most wines are a combination of many varieties of grapes because grapes have the exact proportion of sugar to liquid that other fruits do not have. In addition, grapes at harvest time have a bloom or dust on the skin that covers the fruit. This bloom is composed of microorganisms and contains special yeast cells that convert grape sugars to alcohol, releasing carbon dioxide into the atmosphere.

The color of the juice, which is almost clear with a slight yellow tint, is the same for white grapes and red grapes. The juice can be used to make white wine but if a fuller-bodied wine is desired, the juice is combined with the skins and lightly pressed for a short time. The juice then is drained off and put into either stainless steel or oak wooden barrels, and fermentation begins. The process of fermentation is quite simple. Yeast metabolizes sugar and creates in approximate equal proportions alcohol and carbon dioxide with heat as a by-product. If yeast were added to a sugar and water mixture, fermentation would produce only carbon dioxide, but when grapes and yeast are put together, the result is wine. Natural or added yeasts start the process that requires a carefully controlled temperature. Many white wines are made from red grapes that give the wine a fruity flavor but no red color because the skins are not pressed. In making a red wine, however, the skins need to remain in the wine during fermentation when the alcohol acts as a solvent by dissolving the color of the skin, thus making the juice red. Rosé wines are produced by permitting red grape skins to remain in the juice for a short time before fermentation starts. Rosé wine is a pink-colored grape juice.

Commercial wine making is based on these simple principles but of course the technology today is more sophisticated (Lipinski & Lipinski, 1989). Mechanical harvesting has replaced most of the hand picking of grapes in past centuries. A large and heavy piece of equipment moves down the rows of vines and shakes the trunks, causing ripe grapes at the top of the vines to fall into the machine below. The grapes travel on a conveyor past suction blowers which expel any leaves. The amount of grapes picked in one day by the harvester is equal to that of thirty manual laborers. Grapes are then crushed and sealed in a carbon dioxide atmosphere in tanks next to the mechanical harvester within minutes of picking.

The grapes are weighed and samples are taken for analysis before they are put into a crusher/destemmer that cracks the skin and permits the sugar juice to run freely. This equipment also separates the fruit and the stems. The stems exit on one side of the machine, and the grapes and juice exit through the bottom. The stems, a good source of nitrogen, are dumped between the vineyard rows to decompose in the soil.

The percentage of alcohol in wines is critical. The U.S. Treasury Department taxes 7% to 14% alcohol at one rate and 14% to 20% alcohol at a higher rate. In some countries, the amount of sugar is not high enough to produce enough alcohol to make the wine stable. By law, a limited amount of sugar can be added to the **must,** which is the unfermented grape juice that is fermented to make wine. This **chaptalization** results in a higher alcohol level for the wine, not a sweeter wine. Chaptalization originated in France and still is used there. It also is used in some areas where cool weather results in low sugar levels in grapes for wine. This practice is forbidden by law in Italy, Spain, Austria, and California where vineyards thrive in warm or even hot growing conditions.

The complexity of processing grapes into wine is illustrated in the red wine flow chart shown in Figure 14.11 (Kolpan et al., 1996). The flow chart is similar for white

Figure 14.11. Flowchart for producing red wine.

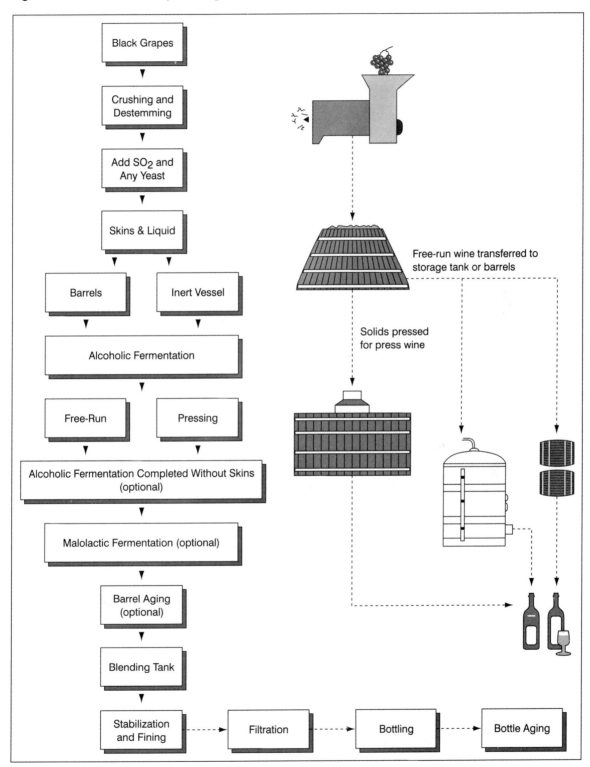

Source: From *Exploring Wine* by S. Kalpan, B. H. Smith, and A. W. Weiss, 1996, New York: Van Nostrand Reinhold. Used by permission. **403**

and rosé wines but has less emphasis on pressing the grape skins. Understanding all the processes grapes undergo to become wine is not in the scope of this text.

Food and Wine Pairing

In the book *Exploring Wine,* Kolpan et al. (1996) emphasize the importance of food and wine pairing. The authors developed a list of principles that should be considered in choosing wine for a specific meal.

- *Basic taste and sensations.* Our palates can only distinguish sweet, sour, bitter, and salt tastes. Sour, sweet, and bitter are the three basic tastes in wine because wines are not salty. Food has all four tastes and also the sensations of cold and heat. Wine should be matched with foods based on basic tastes and sensations, such as cold white wine with grilled salmon steak or with hot spicy Mexican food.
- *Food and wine matching: a learned response.* People do not automatically choose a perfect wine to go with a menu item. They make their choices based on experience and personal preference. Our personal tastes developed in adulthood; our food and culture experiences have broadened from canned tuna fish to grilled fresh tuna steak served rare. The same maturation process happens with wine, starting with beer at age 21 and growing to an appreciation of champagne at 51. Tastes change, and our palates are conditioned by life experiences.
- *Texture.* Food and wines have a texture, or mouth-feel, that is based on cultural and culinary experience. A filet mignon has a rich feel and a salad of baby greens with an oil and vinegar dressing has a light feel. Wine also has texture. An oak-aged Chardonnay creates a rich feeling in the mouth, while a fruity, young red wine creates a light feeling. The texture of both food and wine should be considered in making a selection.
- *Cooking methods.* Poached salmon requires a much different type of wine than grilled salmon. Cooking methods are of great importance when matching food and wine because flavor intensity changes rapidly. Compare, for example, the flavor of baked potatoes to french fries.
- *Matching power with power.* As food flavor intensifies, so should the wine flavor. Fish that is poached, panfried, deep-fried, broiled, or blackened will all take wines of different flavor intensities from Chenin Blanc, to Pinot Noir, to Cabernet Sauvignon. Neither the wine nor the food must be overpowered by the other.

In addition to these principles, the intensity of sauces and garnishes, complementing and contrasting flavors, and the dominant flavor in the menu item must be considered.

Beer

Today's beer lovers are not settling for just any old generic blend of barley, malt, hops, and water (Hampstra, 1996). Beverages have become sophisticated, and no longer are customers willing to settle for plain coffee, tea, wine, water, or beer.

Cappuccino, flavored teas, local wines, sparkling waters, and microbrewed beers have invaded the beverage market.

The bland, light-bodied beers produced by giant brewing companies have dominated the market for decades, but for several years imported beers and specialty beers have gained popularity in the United States. **Microbreweries,** defined as very small, independent companies with carefully controlled output of not more than 15,000 barrels of beer per year, and **regional breweries,** producing 15,000 to 500,000 barrels a year, are expanding their operations with new facilities and a diverse array of beer variations (Hampstra, 1996). Many restaurateurs are now adding microbreweries to their operations, which become **brewpubs.** Brewers are saying that the key to the popularity of microbrews is the fresh taste derived from the lack of preservatives and pasteurization in the brewing process. They also are brewing in quantities that ensure freshness and quality.

Beer Ingredients

Beer is the generic term used for all malted beverages made from malted grain, which is usually barley, hops, and water. The U.S. standard of identity uses the term **malted beverage** rather than beer and defines it as a "beverage made by the alcoholic fermentation in potable brewing water of malted barley with hops," and with or without various other commonly used ingredients such as malted or unmalted cereals and carbon dioxide (Katsigris & Porter, 1991).

The following four ingredients are required to make beer:

- **Water** is 90% of the beer and contributes certain minerals to the taste. Coors uses Colorado mountain spring water, which is essential to the taste of the brew.
- **Malt** is barley that has been soaked in water and allowed to germinate; occasionally wheat malt is used. Malt is the basic ingredient in brewing and contributes flavor, head, body, and color to the beer. It is roasted according to the specifications of the brewer. Roasting time and temperature affect the dryness or sweetness and the product's color, which intensifies with more roasting. In the United States a fifth ingredient, called a *malt adjunct,* often is added. It is another cereal, usually rice or corn, that gives beer a lighter color and milder flavor. The higher the proportion of barley to the adjunct, the more flavor and body and a better head is given to the beer. **Superpremium beers** usually have a higher proportion of barley malt. For example, Anheuser-Busch's Michelob has 95% barley malt and 5% rice, while its premium beer, Budweiser, uses 65% barley malt and 35% rice. **Additives** are other ingredients approved by the FDA that are used to stabilize the foam, prevent cloudiness, and lengthen the shelf life of beer.
- **Hops,** which are the dried, ripe blossoms of a perennial vine (humulus lupulus), are added to give beer a bitter flavor. Hops also possess antiseptic properties that inhibit the growth of bacteria, especially nonpasteurized draft beers.
- **Brewer's yeast** transforms sugars into alcohol and carbon dioxide and may affect the taste and hangover potential of the beer. It is a special laboratory product of each brewer and is constantly active and closely watched. If a

stray yeast from the air gets into the brew, the plant is shut down and cleaned and the equipment is sterilized. Another batch of beer must be started all over again.

Brewing Process

Brewing a great beer is truly an art because so many variations of the process are available. The moisture content of the barley at the time of drying and the time and temperature used in the process have a tremendous influence on the outcome of the malt and the ultimate flavor of the beer. The most lightly kilned malts are used in pilsner-style beers. Malt that is cured a little longer, but not toasted, is used for pale ales. Lightly toasted malts are suitable for Vienna-style beers. Increasing the moisture of the barley produces a caramel or Munich-style malt. Additional roasting produces chocolate malt and black malt, which have the character of burned toast. Each of these has many variations. Despite all these variations, however, brewing beer still is a four-step process.

- *Mashing.* Starches from the ground barley malt are converted into sugars and with hot water are fed into a container called a *mash tun* (Katsigris & Porter, 1991). Precooked adjuncts also are added to the mash tun and are cooked together at a low temperature for 1 to 6 hours. Malt enzymes are activated and turn starches into sugars. The grain residue then is strained out and the remaining liquid, identified as *wort,* flows into the *brew kettle.*
- *Brewing.* The wort is boiled with hops to extract the bitter hops flavor that is characteristic in beer. Huge copper or stainless steel brew kettles are used to boil the wort and hops for 1 to 2½ hours. This boiling also sterilizes the wort and protects the beer from spoilage. The hops are strained out after boiling, and the wort is cooled.
- *Fermenting.* Two major types of beer are made by using different strains of yeast and somewhat different methods of fermentation. **Lager beers** are fermented by yeast at the bottom of a cold tank (37°F to 49°F) by a process called *bottom fermentation* in which action starts from the bottom. The beer is then stored, or lagered, to mellow for several weeks before packaging. **Ale** is fermented at warmer temperatures (50°F to 70°F) by a yeast that rises to the top of the liquid; thus, the process is called *top fermentation.* It is stored only a few days.
- *Lagering.* After the primary fermentation, the wort is passed to lagering, or conditioning, tanks where it is allowed to age. During this period, brewers may add more hops to the brew to enhance its aroma. Lagering of beer takes place at near-freezing temperatures and can take several weeks. Ales are ripened, too, but for a much shorter time at warmer temperatures. At the same time, brewers may stimulate a second fermentation by adding a portion of unfermented wort to the brew, fresh yeast, or even sugar. This process is called *krausening,* or *natural carbonation.* All these methods create more buildup of natural carbonation and tend to convert fermentable sugars in the brew, giving it a more mellow flavor. Both beer and ale are matured in stainless steel or glass-lined tanks.

Once the beer is aged, it is either pasteurized or filtered before leaving the brewery. Most canned and bottled beers are pasteurized by exposing them in the container to 140°F to 150°F heat for 20 minutes to an hour to kill bacteria and any remaining yeast cells (Katsigris & Porter, 1991). Draft beers sometimes are flash-pasteurized with steam, but most are not, thus giving them a better taste. Draft beer is stored in metal containers that will withstand increased pressure that may come from continuing fermentation. Draft beer must be refrigerated at all times, including on delivery, to maintain its quality.

Some canned and bottled beers are not pasteurized. These beers are passed through very fine filters that remove yeast cells and other impurities but retain many of the characteristics of draft beer and may be labeled as draft beer. Coors beers are an example of unpasteurized beers that are made under hospital-clean conditions. Coors kegs, cans, and bottles are shipped and stored under refrigeration. Under federal regulations, pasteurized beers in cans or bottles may refer in advertising to "draft flavor" or "on-tap taste," but not draft beer, if the label states that the beer has been pasteurized.

Types of Beer

Lager beers and ales have many variations in the basic ingredients and modifications in the methods of brewing. While beer and brewing were an important part of American life since the days of the earliest colonists, brewing empires did not evolve until the late 1800s when German immigrants brought the technology to the United States. A number of breweries came into being at that time, including Anheuser-Busch, Miller, Stroh, Schlitz, Pabst, and Coors. After 126 years, the Pabst brewery was bought out by Miller, which is selling the famous Pabst Blue Ribbon beer. Currently, thousands of brands of beer—beer historians count more than 20,000—and more than 170 styles are on the world market.

Lager Beers.   Several kinds and styles of lager beers in many brands, each with its own flavor, are available. They are bright gold to yellow in color with a light to medium body and are usually well carbonated (Lipinski & Lipinski, 1989; Katsigris & Porter, 1991). Lagers are a bottom-fermented beer. About 90% of the beer made in the United States is lager. Some of the most popular lager beers include the following:

- *Pilsner.* The most popular style, rather than a distinctive type, of beer in the United States and the world. Pilsner includes the best-selling Budweiser, Miller's High Life, Busch, Coors, and the superpremium Michelob. These beers have a 3.2% to 4.5% alcohol content by weight, 4% to 5% by volume. The word *pilsner* is taken from the Czech town of Pilsen. Pilsner beer has a light golden color, distinctive hops flavor, and a delightful clean, crisp taste that leaves the palate clean.
- *Light beers.* These are a variant of the pilsner style and have one third to one half less alcohol and calories than other lagers—100 calories or less per 10-ounce serving compared to 135 to 170 for regular beer. These beers have a 2.3% to 2.8% alcohol content by weight, 3.2% to 3.9% by volume. The percentage of light beer sales is constantly increasing. Current favorites are Miller Lite, Bud Light, and Coors Light.

- *Bock beer.* This beer is usually dark in color but may be pale or amber with high alcohol content and a rich malt flavor. It comes mainly from Germany but also is made by some small U.S. brewers.
- *Steam beer.* This true American invention (Katsigris & Porter, 1991) was developed in California during the Gold Rush days. It is a combination of bottom fermentation of lager beer with, out of necessity, the warmer top-fermentation temperatures of ale. Ice was difficult to find in California in those days. The result is a beer with a good head and body and the taste of ale with an alcohol content of 4% by weight and 5% by volume. The name has no relationship with brewing; rather it comes from the "steam" released when the barrels are tapped. Steam beer is made by Anchor Brewing of San Francisco under the brand name of Ice. It has become very popular in America.

Ales.   The most distinctive styles of ale known today originated in Britain. They are top-fermented beers with a slightly darker color than lager beers. They also have more body and hops flavor than other beers and are usually lower in carbonation. Some styles include the following:

- *Cream.* This blend of ale and lager beer is highly carbonated, resulting in a rich foam. It is golden in color and mild and has a slightly sweet taste.
- *Pale.* It is translucent, rather than lighter in color. Pale ale is copper in color and has a stronger yeast and hops flavor than lager beer.
- *Bitter.* This British ale is usually bronze to deep copper in color and heavily hopped, resulting in a high degree of hops bitterness.
- *Porter.* This predecessor of stout has an intense dark color and bittersweet taste and aroma. Its alcohol content is lower than stout, and it is drunk by the pint in British pubs.
- *Stout.* It has a dark, almost black color due to highly roasted malt and a rich malty flavor usually combined with a strong, bitter hops taste. Stout is more alcoholic than porter, ranging from 3% to 7.5% alcohol. Guinness, made in Ireland, is the best-known bitter stout.

Serving Beer.   According to Katsigris & Porter (1991), a perfect glass of beer depends on the condition of the glass, the way the beer is poured, and the temperature of the beer. The glass must be grease-free, film-free, and lint-free because if it is not, the head of foam will break down leaving large bubbles and allowing carbonation to escape. The taste and odor of the beer also will be affected. The best solution may be a special glass washer in which nothing but glasses are washed using a special fat-free detergent. A three-compartment sink also can be used, but employees need to be trained in the technique.

Pouring draft, canned, or bottled beer into a glass correctly also is important in serving the customer. The size of the head depends upon the angle the beer is poured into the container and the length of time the angle is held. Tilting the glass at a 45° angle until it is about half-full and then holding the glass straight up and pouring the beer into the middle until the foam is slightly higher than the rim of the glass is the technique for pouring draft beer from a spigot. For canned or bottled beer, the beer is poured at a steep angle into the center of the container. Then the angle is lowered and the beer is poured until the foam rises just above the edge.

Temperature of the beer served to customers is crucial in serving the perfect glass of beer. American customers like beer at 40°F, ales at 45°F, and Guiness and bock beers lightly chilled. Frosted glasses or mugs are in vogue today and are used in many foodservice operations.

The key to success in serving beer that pleases customers is having a good supplier who will help train bar personnel. A good buyer and supplier relationship can be the answer to a profitable bar operation.

Spirits

The sugar in wine grapes breaks down into carbon dioxide, which escapes into the air, and alcohol, which is in the remaining liquid, resulting in a fermented beverage. Grains go through the same process when making beer and ale. However, spirits go through another process called *distillation*.

Distillation Process

The fermented liquid is heated in a still and the alcohol vapors rise and are carried off through a coil that goes through cold water, condensing the vapors into a liquid spirit (Katsigris & Porter, 1991). One of two types of stills, pot and column, are used for the distillation process. A **pot still** is limited in the degree of proof it can achieve, but it always has a lot of flavor, body, and aroma. A **column still** can be controlled to produce spirits at a wide range of proofs up to about 196. The alcohol is not the only ingredient that is vaporized at distilling temperatures; other substances also may vaporize. Water is one of them as are small amounts of other volatile substances that provide flavor, body, and aroma in the fermented beverage. These substances, called **cogeners,** are responsible for the smoky flavor of scotch or the rich aroma of bourbon.

A spirit that has been recently distilled is raw, sharp, and biting, not mellow and flavorful. Today, spirits that are less than 190 proof are aged in wooden barrels for 1 year for a light beverage to 20 years for a mellow brandy. The spirit changes as the congeners interact with air filtering through the wooden barrels, and new congeners absorbed from the wood add other flavors. Aging also adds color to the spirit.

Types of Spirits

The buyer of spirits needs to develop a basic understanding of spirits, especially if the restaurant manager doubles as the buyer. In foodservice operations with a large bar business, the bar manager needs a great deal of knowledge about the different types of spirits and which drinks customers prefer. Just keeping control of the inventory is a major task. In the last few years, a shift has occurred from drinking hard liquors to lighter liquors and wines. Taxes from the sale of alcohol, more than $5.5 billion annually, have increased and are ranked third among major sources of federal revenues; only personal and corporate income taxes bring in more (Fier, 1993).

Spirits most often are categorized as brown or white spirits and within each category, the product can be either straight or blended. **Straight spirits** on the label indicate that the product contains a minimum of 51% by volume of either corn, rye, barley, or wheat. **Blended spirits** indicate that the product contains less than 51% of different grains, batches, stills, or ages that are blended together. A brief description of the various types in each will follow. Detailed descriptions usually are covered in a bar and beverage course.

Brown Spirits.   **Brown spirits** are whiskeys that are brown in color usually because caramel, which is burnt sugar, has been added to the product. Examples include bourbon, scotch, rye, Irish, and Canadian. Whiskey has been declining in popularity but still has a prominent place in all bars. Whiskey can be either straight or blended. The most common straight whiskeys are bourbon, rye, and corn. A minimum of 51% by volume of a single whiskey must come from one of these grains.

- **Bourbon** is distilled at a minimum of 160 proof from a sour mash of at least 51% corn and aged for two years in charred new oak containers, which meet federal standards of identity. Bourbon is the most popular straight American whiskey on the market today (Katsigris & Porter, 1991). About 6 years of aging is needed to give it a strong flavor from the charred barrels and its familiar mellowness. It was named for Bourbon County in Kentucky and was first distilled by a preacher. Most bourbons are made from a sour-mash yeasting process; fresh yeast and leftovers from a previous distilling are added to the mash. Bourbon has a familiar and definitely sour flavor. Examples are Jim Beam sour mash and Old Grand-Dad Kentucky straight bourbon whiskey.
- **Scotch whiskeys** made in Scotland are blends of malt whiskeys and high-proof grain whiskeys that come entirely from fresh sprouted barley. They have a smoky flavor resulting from the barley being dried over peat fires. When malt scotch is blended with spirits from other grains, mostly from corn, the whiskey is known as *blended scotch* (Fier, 1993). Malt whiskeys are made in pot stills and grain whiskey in column stills. These two whiskeys are made and aged separately for many years and then blended. Sometimes as many as 30 or 40 different malt and grain whiskeys are blended in one brand of Scotch. Scotches are required to be at least 80 proof, but most are 86 proof. Popular brands include Chivas Regal, Dewar's White Label, and Johnnie Walker Red Label. Premium brands of Scotch have a longer aging time and are made with a higher quantity of malt. For example, the Johnnie Walker Black label reads that it is "extra special," aged 12 years, and distilled, blended, and bottled in Scotland. The popularity of blended scotches has waned lately, but the single malt is becoming popular (Katsigris & Porter, 1991). A single malt is one of the straight malt scotches that is used in making a blended scotch. It has a very distinctive flavor and is expensive. Some high-priced restaurants have collections of single malts and occasionally have tasting parties for selected customers. The best-known single malts are Glenlivet and Glenfiddich.
- **Rye whiskey** has a strong and distinctive taste of caraway seeds. It is produced from a mixture of various grains, 51% of which is rye to meet government regulations. Rye whiskey must be distilled at no higher than 160 proof, permitting it

to retain the congeners that contribute to its flavor. It must be aged in new charred barrels for a minimum of 2 years, although 4 years is the standard. Available top brands include Jim Beam and Wild Turkey rye whiskeys.

- **Irish whiskey** is a blend made from a mash of cereal grains, mostly wheat, oats, corn, and rye. It is most often produced in pot stills, which help give it a unique taste. It is an important ingredient in Irish coffee and is served in many bars, especially on March 17th, St. Patrick's Day. It is a product that is manufactured in compliance with the guidelines of Irish Distillers, Ltd. The main difference in Irish whiskey is that the taste does not have the smoky flavor of other whiskeys. Another difference is a triple distillation process through three pot stills instead of two. The traditional unblended Irish whiskey is smooth and mellow with a medium body. This Irish whiskey is not popular in the United States where it is blended with high-proof grain whiskey to create a lighter drink for today's customers. Jameson and Old Bushmill are examples of Irish whiskey sold in this country.

- **Canadian whisky,** spelled without the "e," is blended and made from corn, barley, rye, wheat, and other grains to give it a light taste. Canadian law requires that the cereal grains be aged a minimum of 3 years, but otherwise the formula is up to the distiller. Canadian whisky is distilled at 140% to 180% and aged a minimum of 8 years. Examples are Canadian Club, Crown Royal, and Seagram's V.O.

White Spirits.   The term **white spirits** refers to those spirits that are clear in color and usually are not aged in wood. They are lighter in taste than brown spirits. A word of caution is needed because they are not lower in alcoholic content. Like brown spirits, they are 80 proof or higher. Gin, vodka, rum, and tequila are examples of white spirits.

- **Gin,** according to U.S. standards of identity, is permitted to be produced from corn, rye, wheat, barley malt, and sugar cane. It was first produced in Holland and then London. It soon came to the United States as "bathtub gin" during Prohibition. It was the beverage of the poor because it was cheap and could be made at home. It often was called a lethal product. British officers began to drink gin and tonic, supposedly to prevent malaria, and the martini became the fashionable cocktail. The dominant flavor of gin comes from juniper berries with other herbs and spices. Bombay Sapphire distilled super-premium London Dry Gin has the following ten botanicals ingredients etched on its pale, blue glass bottle:

Angelica root from Saxony	Almonds from Spain
Coriander seeds from Morocco	Lemon peel from Spain
Casia bark from Indo-China	Liquorice from China
Cubeb berries from Java	Juniper berries from Italy
Grains of paradise from West Africa	Iris root from Italy

A real explosion, especially among younger drinkers, of interest in the old classic cocktails has occurred (Ursin, 1996). The martini, which is little more than gin or vodka with the merest hint of vermouth, is leading the comeback of the classic cocktail.

- **Vodka** is made from a fermented mash of grain, which is distilled at a high proof and, according to the U. S. standards of identity, is treated with charcoal to be without distinctive character, aroma, taste, or color. Now the most popular spirit in the United States, vodka was introduced commercially in 1934. Today more than 200 brands are available. Vodka mixes well with fruit juice, soft drinks, and other spirits. It is the alcoholic ingredient used in a Bloody Mary, screwdriver, Black Russian, and vodka martini. The most popular brand in the United States is Smirnoffs, in Russia Stolichnaya, and in Sweden Absolut. A variation of straight vodka are versions flavored with pepper, lemon, citrus, and other herbs or fruits. Bottles of premium vodka should be stored in the freezer, but they do not freeze because of the high alcohol content (Lipinski & Lipinski, 1989). They do become somewhat thick and syrupy and can be drunk neat (straight without ice) and downed in one gulp. Vodka goes well with caviar, pickled herring, anchovies, smoked salmon, and Russian rye bread.
- **Rum** is made from sugar cane molasses and is aged and blended. The color changes from white or silver rum to gold or amber depending upon how long it is aged. Puerto Rico, where sugar cane is grown, is the world's leading rum producer. Rum is a popular ingredient of mixed drinks; it can be mixed with juice or soft drinks. It is the spirit used in the daiquiri, rum and coke, piña colada, mai tai, and zombie.

Other Spirits.   American and French brandies and liqueurs and cordials belong in this classification. These after-dinner drinks are usually served in small quantities and sometimes sipped while puffing a cigar.

- **Brandy** is made from grapes and aged at least 2 years. In the United States, brandy comes from California. It is made in column stills up to 170 proof and aged in white-oak barrels a minimum of 2 years and usually longer. Most American brandies are sweetened and flavored. Brandies are served straight in a **brandy snifter,** a large rounded short-stem glass that is held in the palm of the hand to warm it slightly and rolled around to release the rich aroma. Korbel, Paul Masson, and Christian Brothers are popular American brands. **Cognac** from the Cognac region of France is the most prestigious and famous of all cognacs. **Liqueurs,** also called **cordials,** are distilled spirits sweetened with 2.5% or more of sugar and flavored with a variety of ingredients: fruits, herbs, spices, flowers, nuts, and cream. They are very trendy and usually served after dinner with coffee. The most popular are usually imported and include Amaretto with an almond and apricot base; Bailey's Original Irish Cream with a chocolate, coffee, coconut taste; and Drambuie made in Scotland with a scotch base and a delicate mixture of herbs and honey.

Purchasing

The alcohol industry is probably the most regulated industry in the United States (Kotschevar & Donnelly, 1999). Federal legislation and control comes mostly from the **Federal Alcohol Administration Act** that closely controls the production and marketing of alcoholic beverages. Standards of identity are available for specific types of beverages. In addition to these regulations, state and local laws also are in action. The **Dram Shop Law** in force in many states makes servers of alcoholic beverages partly responsible for the actions of those they serve. Heavy fines and court awards for damages have been levied against operators. The NRA's "Bar Code: Serving Alcohol Responsibly" is a program designed to train restaurant staff about these critical issues.

Buyers have many decisions to make before purchasing alcoholic beverages. According to Katsigris & Porter (1991), buyers must decide what, where, and how much to buy and how much to pay.

What to Buy

The buyer must make two decisions before purchasing alcoholic beverages (Katsigris & Porter, 1991): the quality of the beverage and the variety desired by customers. What quality do customers want and how much are they willing to pay for a drink? The quality desired by customers on a limited budget may be quite different from that expected by customers in an expensive restaurant. Many low- or moderate-priced brands are available on the market as are high-priced brands. The buyer needs to decide on brands that are acceptable to customers, and the restaurant needs to serve those brands consistently. Customers are quick to complain if prices are increased but quality decreases or remains the same.

Because so many brands are on the market, the buyer has to determine how many are needed to keep customers happy. A bottle of liquor standing on a shelf does not earn profit. Experienced bartenders quickly figure out the good sellers and keep them in stock. Many bars stock well-known brands that can be substituted for the ones requested as long as customers agree. Never try to fool customers! Buying beers and spirits usually requires the selection of a brand. Buying wines, however, is much more difficult. Customers purchase wines by the name of the wine maker, vintage (year the grapes were harvested and the wine began), or age. The wise wine buyer needs to have a good relationship with salespeople who know which wines customers currently are requesting most often.

Where to Buy

Buyers do not always have a choice of where to purchase alcoholic beverages. Some states, known as **control states,** control sales through state stores, thus establishing a monopoly. Control states publish lists of all available brands with prices and addresses of state stores. Other states and the District of Columbia, known as **license states,** regulate by licensing wholesalers; some of these states also license distributors and processors. In most of these states, a list of names of wholesalers, brands, and prices is published monthly. The quickest way to determine what to buy in license states is through sales representatives, who quite often cannot sell directly to the buyer but can suggest where to buy their products. They also have information on sales and promotions of brands.

How Much to Buy

Determining the amount of alcoholic beverages to buy at one time is a difficult question for the buyer (Katsigris & Porter, 1991). The objective is to have enough on hand to meet customer needs but not so much that it stands on the shelves and ties up money that could be used for other purposes. Establishing a **par stock** from detailed sales records is the starting point. The par stock generally includes enough of each type and brand to meet one and a half times the amount used on the busiest day of the week. Par stock also can be used to measure the daily consumption and to determine the popularity of brands. From par stock needs, the amount of each item in the storeroom for back-up is easily figured. Par stock for the storeroom then becomes the normal inventory.

Regardless of buying intervals, a good idea is to set minimum and maximum stock levels for each item to maintain the storeroom inventory. A reorder point provides lead time and prevents the stock from dropping below the minimum before replenishing. Stealing is a big problem in operations that carry a large inventory. Also, the larger the inventory, the more difficult record keeping and taking a physical inventory can be. Suppliers sell mostly in case lots, although some will sell a broken case that is made up of several brands to meet the buyer's specification. Some will sell one bottle or three bottles of a wine. Of course, the price is higher for any items not sold in case lots.

What to Pay

In control states, prices usually are fixed by law and will be the same in all state stores (Katsigris & Porter, 1991). Occasionally, the buyer can take advantage of a special or quantity discount. In license states, buyers often shop around to find the best price. Seldom are large price differences found because state laws are designed to avoid price wars. However, buyers should study price lists and talk to salespeople because sometimes prices are lowered. Buyers must decide whether tying up money in inventory is more profitable than purchasing a labor-saving piece of equipment, such as a microwave oven or food processor.

Receiving, Storing, and Inventory

Once the quantity of alcoholic beverages is determined, the order is placed by telephone or fax, through a salesperson, or by a purchase order. Telephone or fax seems to be the easiest method for most buyers. Whatever the method is, the order should be written down or entered into a computer.

Receiving

If someone other than the person who placed the order receives the shipment, the delivery can be confirmed and checked by comparing the supplier's invoice against the purchase order on file. Each item should be checked for quantity, brand, vintage, and anything else in the specification. Bottles in open cases should be checked for breakage, missing or broken stamps, or loose corks. Unopen cases should be examined for leaking containers or weighed; the weight is printed on the case. Expiration dates on beer need to be carefully checked, along with the temperature when delivered. Items that are unacceptable should be returned to the delivery person and deducted from the bill. A credit memo, discussed in Chapter 5, or a notation on the invoice should be noted by the delivery person. Only when the buyer is satisfied that all the items are the ones ordered at the prices quoted should the receiving person sign the invoice that transfers ownership from the supplier to the buyer.

Storing

Once delivered, the liquor supply becomes potential profit, and proper storage is essential (Fier, 1993). Treat inventory like gold! The manager needs to keep track of it from the time it is accepted from the delivery truck to when it is poured into a drink and paid for. Inventory control helps the manager determine how much money is earned daily and longer term from liquor.

Any storeroom must be protected from theft, but the liquor storeroom needs protection more than any other. This storeroom needs to be wired to the security and alarm system if the foodservice operation has one. The number of people who enter this room should be minimal, and key locks should be changed often in case someone makes duplicates or personnel changes. If combination locks are used, they should be reset frequently and only two people need to know the combination. The back door of the operation must be kept locked at all times; a buzzer installed outside the storage area door can be pushed by the delivery person, thus alerting the manager that a delivery is being made. If a storeroom has windows, and most do not, they should be barred.

A well-organized storeroom is considered a security measure because each type of liquor has an area on a shelf and a vacant space indicates that something is missing (Katsigris & Porter, 1991). Cases need to be opened immediately and the bottles placed on a designated shelf. The empty cartons should be flattened and removed from the area; otherwise, bottles could be put into the cartons and carried out with the trash. Shelving must be heavy and sturdy because of the weight of liquor bottles. Unopened cases are usually stacked and stored on palettes until opened.

The FIFO (first in, first out) inventory system should be used in storing liquors; the oldest needs to be used first. Wine, including champagne, and beer must be stored in a cool, dark, dry place in an area that has a constant temperature. Temperature for wine storage is between 55°F and 60°F; the bottles never should be exposed to bright sunlight or constant movement. Corked bottles should be stored on their sides on special tilted racks with the cork end lower than the bottom of the bottle to keep the cork moist. The only exception to horizontal storage is for bottles sealed with plastic corks or metal screw caps, which are stored upright.

Beer, even pasteurized beer, has the shortest shelf life of any alcoholic beverage (Katsigris & Porter, 1991). Beer should be kept cold and used within 3 to 4 months. Some brewers put a pull date on the containers to indicate when the beer should be pulled off the shelves. Other brewers put the brewing date on the container.

Canned and bottled beers are stored between 40°F and 70°F to protect flavor and aroma. Unpasteurized beer needs to be kept cold, below 70°F at all times. Light destroys the taste of beer quickly. Most bottled beer is stored in brown bottles, but even then, it should not be subjected to light and heat. The temperature of draft beer needs to be kept between 36°F and 38°F at all times; it has a shelf life between 30 and 45 days. Good quality draft beer requires a good beer system that consists of a cylinder of carbon dioxide gas under pressure, a tap or faucet, lines running from the cylinder to the keg and from the keg to the tap, and a refrigerated beer box. The astute buyer of draft beer purchases from a supplier who understands and sets up the process. The thermometer and pressure gauge need to be checked constantly and the lines to transport the beer to the glass need to be clean. A good relationship between the buyer and supplier is essential to keep customers satisfied.

Inventory Control

A perpetual inventory is necessary for controlling the costs of alcoholic beverages (Fier, 1993). Using computer inventory control software or index cards is a standard practice. Most operations are using inventory software. In large operations, the bartender at the end of each shift fills out a daily beverage requisition sheet that indicates how many bottles of liquor were used and need to be replaced. **Breakage,** or empty liquor bottles, can be replaced at the end of each shift or when the bar opens the next day. The cost of each bottle of liquor can be taken from the invoice bill. By dividing the cost of the liquor by the total sales for the day, the manager can determine what percentage of the price charged for the drinks was for liquor. By keeping these daily records, the manager can spot trouble and make price or inventory corrections.

On the last day of the month, a physical inventory needs to be taken. Each visible bottle in the storeroom and bar must be counted, as well as those in closed cartons. The amount of liquor in each open bottle needs to be estimated; for example, a half-full bottle would be recorded as 0.5 on the inventory sheet. The end of the month total for each type and brand of liquor should be figured and checked with the daily, or perpetual, inventory to determine if they match. Daily and monthly inventories make year-end figures easy to calculate. Over years of good inventory control, patterns in the operation surface, not only in how much and what kind of liquor needs to be ordered, but also how many employees will be needed to serve customers during busy and slack seasons.

SUMMARY

Nonalcoholic beverages have increased in popularity in the last few years. Specialty coffees served in coffeehouses have increased the consumption of coffee among young people. Tea also has been increasing in popularity, especially ready-to-drink products sold in cans or bottles. Soft drinks make up almost half of all nonalcoholic beverages consumed. The volume of bottled waters sold has also increased dramatically. Most of these drinks are carbonated. Nonalcoholic beers and wines have gained some popularity, especially since drunk driving laws have been tightened. Nonalcoholic beverages usually are purchased by brand names.

The total volume of alcoholic beverages consumed in the United States has decreased steadily since 1980. All are made by the process of fermentation; yeast acts on sugar, converting it to alcohol and carbon dioxide gas. Beers, wines, and spirits are alcoholic beverages. They all taste different, have different amounts of alcohol, and are served differently. The Bureau of Alcohol, Tobacco, and Firearms issued new regulations for labeling; percent of alcohol by volume must be indicated on the label. Previously in the United States, proof, which is twice the percent of alcohol by volume, was used more often.

More than 2,000 types of wine are on the market. French wines were always considered the best in the world, but currently some California, New York state, and other U.S. wines are considered to be as good. Wine can be white, red, or pink; all wines come from white, including pale green, and red grapes. All have clear juice, but pressing white skins a short time produces a pale yellow wine and pressing red skins for a longer time produces red wine. Many white wines are made from red grapes.

Beer is a malted beverage made from malted grain, usually barley, hops, and water. It is classified as lager beer or ale. Pilsner is the most popular lager beer in the United States and is light in color with a distinctive hops flavor and a crisp taste. It is bottom fermented. Ale is most often made in Europe and is top fermented. It is darker in color than lager beer and has more body and hops flavor.

Spirits go through another process, distillation, after fermentation. They are categorized as brown or white spirits. Whiskey is a brown spirit and can be straight or blended. Bourbon is the most popular straight whiskey and Scotch the most popular blended whiskey in the United States. White spirits refer to those that are clear and lighter in taste. They still have the same alcoholic content as brown spirits. White spirits include gin, vodka, rum, and tequila. Other spirits are brandy, cognac, and liqueurs.

Alcoholic beverages are purchased by brand names. Tight controls must be used in receiving and storing products, primarily because of theft. Managers need to keep track of these beverages from the time they are accepted from the delivery truck to when they are poured into a drink and paid for. Inventory control is mandatory; a daily perpetual inventory must be kept.

REFERENCES

Batty, J. (1994a). Demand is brewing for tea, Part one. *Restaurants USA, 14*(6), 13–17.
Batty, J. (1994b). Demand is brewing for tea, Part two. *Restaurants USA, 14*(7), 18–21.
Bennion, M. (1995). *Introductory Foods* (10th ed.). Englewood Cliffs, NJ: Prentice Hall.
Bertagnoli, L. (1996). Espresso concerns. *Restaurants & Institutions, 106*(7), 88.
Coffee is king. Customers clamor for caffeine creations. New product watch. (1996). *Restaurants & Institutions, 106*(24), 12.

Fier, B. (1993). *Start and run a money-making bar* (2nd ed.). New York: McGraw-Hill.

Hampstra, M. (1996). Casual themers hop into future with sophisticated beers. *Nation's Restaurant News, 30*(2), 31, 34, 36.

Hochstein, M. (1996). Be a tea-totaler: Economical brew good for health, profits. *Nation's Restaurant News, 30*(19), 49.

Kapner, S. (1996). Ice-tea 'brewhaha': CDC says drink OK. *Nation's Restaurant News, 30*(23), 1, 145.

Katsigris, C., & Porter, M. (1991). *The bar and beverage book.* New York: John Wiley & Sons.

Kolpan, S., Smith, B.H., & Weiss, A.W. (1996). *Exploring wine.* New York: Van Nostrand Reinhold.

Kotschevar, L. H., & Donnelly, R. (1999). Quantity food purchasing (4th ed.). Upper Saddle River, NJ: Merrill/Prentice Hall.

Lipinski, R. A., & Lipinski, K. A. (1989). *Professional guide to alcoholic beverages.* New York: Van Nostrand Reinhold.

Margen, S. & Editors of the University of California at Berkeley WELLNESS LETTER (1992). *The wellness encyclopedia of food and nutrition.* New York: Rebus.

Moomaw, P. (1994). Gourmet coffee gaining ground in fast food. *Restaurants USA, 14*(10), 13–16.

National Restaurant Association, (1994). Soak up the new beverage trends. *Restaurants USA, 14*(10), 11–12.

Rhodes, L. (1996). Bottled water works for restaurants. *Restaurants USA, 16*(11), 16–18.

Somerville, S. (1994). Buoy business with a bevy of nonalcoholic beverages. *Restaurants USA, 14*(10), 35–38.

Straus, K. (1992). All about coffee. *Restaurants & Institutions, 102*(24), 66.

Ursin, C. (1996). Classic cocktails shake up beverages sales. *Restaurants USA, 16*(9), 26–31.

Zraly, K. (1995). Windows on the world. New York: Sterling Publishing.

Purchasing Nonfood Products

The two chapters in Part 4 contain information about production equipment and service equipment. Equipment is the most expensive expenditure in the foodservice operation.

- **Chapter 15, Production Equipment.**   Production equipment is required in a foodservice operation to produce menu items that satisfy the customer. Foodservice design consultants not only have the expertise to choose the right equipment but also can help managers make good equipment purchasing decisions.

- **Chapter 16, Service Equipment.**   Service currently is being emphasized in foodservice operations. Good customer service requires the buyer to seek out equipment that is practical but also attractive to customers. The foodservice equipment supplier is in a position to help the manager make good service equipment decisions.

15

Production Equipment

Production equipment is probably the highest cost item in a foodservice operation budget. *Restaurants & Institutions* (Equipment Purchasing Outlook, 1994) estimated that the foodservice industry would spend $5.5 billion on equipment and supplies in 1996. In today's bottom-line business climate, shopping for the lowest priced equipment is critical (Frable, 1996a). In our competitive environment, shopping for a few extra dollars often yields far less savings than does finding the best value. This is often referred to as the **sweet spot** in pricing: the size or capacity of equipment from which the buyer gets the best value and lowest cost per menu item produced. Much of the cost is for the labor required to make the equipment; downsizing standard size models often yields far less savings than expected. A half-size convection oven is priced only 10% to 15% less than a full-sized unit. Value should be considered in terms of performance or capacity per dollar invested. Selecting equipment based on that criterion can offer far more savings than just the lowest price. Foodservice managers need to be aware of trends in the industry before figuring the cost effectiveness of purchasing a specific piece of equipment.

TRENDS

Trends in equipment for commercial and noncommercial foodservice operations should be carefully studied along with other industry trends. A **trend** can be defined as a straight or curved line showing the tendency of some function to grow or decline over time.

Foodservice Operations

Foodservice managers should note these important trends before buying equipment (Equipment Purchasing Outlook, 1994).

- Most equipment will be purchased by large-volume operations, such as quick-service chains.
- About two thirds of the purchases will be made to replace existing equipment rather than for new installations.
- More small wares will be purchased than large pieces of equipment.

Commercial

Managers of commercial foodservice operations constantly face new challenges and opportunities. They must keep an eye on business conditions while seeking new opportunities for growth that often require the purchase of new equipment (Equipment Purchasing Outlook, 1994). Equipment manufacturers need to project the changes in and type of equipment needed to meet these trends.

- *International growth.* Overseas markets have great potential, but decisions on the type and price of equipment must be studied carefully.

- *Miniaturization.* Because of costs, smaller units of restaurants, especially quick-serve, require smaller and more multifunction equipment.
- *Menu-driven equipment.* To satisfy customers, more multifunction equipment, such as open spit roasters, rotisseries, and expresso brewers, is needed to give them what they want.

Noncommercial

No longer is a straight line cafeteria being used in the various noncommercial food-service operations. Universities, schools, hospitals, and other noncommercial operations are moving to more of a marketplace ambience by cooking food in front of the customer or using kiosks on wheels to sell such items as coffee, frozen desserts, and sandwiches. The customer is participating in the process. Dining areas have changed from green walls and long tables that seat 12 or more customers to cheerful places conducive to relaxation and fun. Special equipment is needed to create this ambience. Each segment of noncommercial operations has its own demands that affect equipment purchases (Equipment Purchasing Outlook, 1994).

- Health care foodservices are facing staff reductions and pressures to increase revenue while improving foodservice options.
- Universities and schools are saving on labor at the same time they are doing more exhibition cooking and increasing the use of the cook/chill concept with a central kitchen to serve many operations.
- Business and industry are questioning the use of brand menu items with franchise restrictions and looking at developing their own brands.
- Prisons with increasing populations are involved in new construction and renovation of outdated facilities. Better food delivery systems and increased security in kitchens and dining areas are part of their plans. Accomplishing those goals entails lowering the seating capacity in dining areas.

New health, sanitation, and environmental regulations from local, state, and federal governments also are affecting purchase plans, all in the name of public safety.

Foodservice Trends

Steel Edge, the Newsletter of Low Temp Industries, looks at "what's hot, what's not in foodservice" (1996). Attempts at gazing into the complicated future of purchasing equipment requires an understanding of changes in the profile of customer needs and desires, current food safety and environmental regulations, and labor problems. The consensus for what's hot includes reengineering, convenience foods, branding, self-serve, labor reductions, and consolidation of departments. The challenge is to purchase the correct equipment to accomplish these hot items while increasing the bottom line of the foodservice operation.

- *Reengineering.* Managed care is here to stay and will affect every healthcare facility in the country. The trend toward fewer inpatients and more outpatients demands a new look at the distribution of tasks, number of employees, and type of service. An emerging major trend is transporting food, such as coffee, soft drinks, snacks, fruits, and sandwiches, on mobile carts to hospital outpatients and families. Foodservices are enhanced by this trend and at the same time can establish a broader revenue base.

- *Convenience foods.* Menus are being changed from selective to nonselective, or restaurant style, to streamline production and enhance customer satisfaction. Because skilled labor is limited, the focus is to ensure quality by selecting popular menu items, many of which are convenience foods produced and cook-chilled in the facility, delivered from a commissary, or purchased commercially.
- *Branding.* Self-branding or commercial branding helps increase hospital cafeteria checks 3% to 5% and outside nonemployee sales. Quality is a key reason why customers are brand loyal; they know they can depend on the quality and are willing to pay more.
- *Self-serve.* To reduce labor and enable customers to portion control their own prices, serving lines are being converted to self-serve operations. Existing sneeze guards can be modified on site as shown in Figure 15.1.
- *Labor reductions.* Today, labor must be cost justified. Managers are streamlining tasks and number of personnel and diversifying services. Prepared food items, branding, self-service, mobile carts, self-leveling dispensers, and refrigerated and nonrefrigerated storage above and below workstations are streamlining operations and reducing labor costs. To diversify, foodservice operators are providing takeout, room service, display cooking, home-baked bakery items, and catering, thus generating revenue and cost justifying the operation.
- *Consolidation of departments.* Administrators are promoting foodservice directors to head many departments, including housekeeping, central supply, or purchasing. Top management is eliminating positions for middle management, streamlining operations, and reducing costs.

Times are changing, and resources are limited. Purchasing the correct equipment is necessary to meet these challenges related to customer satisfaction while increasing the bottom line in a foodservice operation.

Figure 15.1. Conversion of serving from employee-serve to self-serve.

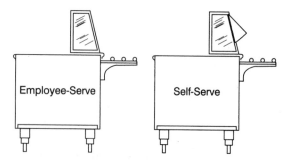

Source: From *Steel Edge, The Newsletter of Low Temp Industries, Inc.,* 1996. Used by permission.

PURCHASING EQUIPMENT

Restaurants & Institutions asked foodservice managers about purchasing equipment as part of its exclusive Business Confidence Index (Wallace, 1996). Foodservice equipment buying intentions are about as strong as they have ever been. The 2.5% growth rate in foodservice operations in 1995 and 1996 apparently is strong enough to convince buyers of equipment to invest in the future. When business is not good, the manager often decides that the old piece of equipment will last another year.

In commercial operations, hotels lead in replacement with 45% planning purchases, followed by full-service restaurants at 35%. Quick-service operations are not replacing equipment, but about 20% are buying it for expansion. Only 38% of all commercial operations planned to purchase new equipment in 1996 compared to 63% of noncommercial foodservices. About 60% of colleges planned to replace equipment, however, and about 60% of schools planned to buy equipment for expansion. Public schools, correction institutions, and nursing homes are three hot growth markets.

In many foodservice operations, the manager purchases equipment in conjunction with the administrator's guidance. Capital investment is required for most equipment. In a well-established operation, replacement of existing equipment might be all that is needed. In a commercial operation, the owner gives final approval for the purchase. In noncommercial operations, the foodservice manager explains to the administrator what is needed to improve the foodservice; if the administrator agrees, the proposed purchase and costs are presented to the board of directors for approval. Once the need has been determined in both types of operations and a budget is agreed upon, an architect is hired if structural changes are required and a foodservice design consultant is contracted to design and equip the operation.

Architect and Consultant

Historically, the **architect** is responsible for producing a structure that meets the needs of the customer (Miller, 1996). For example, the architect designs a school that meets the educational goals of the school board, administrators and teachers, students, and community; the architect then hires specialists, technical advisers, and consultants, including a foodservice design consultant, to make the design a reality. In addition, the architect often hires engineers, roofing contractors, interior designers, and safety specialists to oversee design and construction.

The first step in purchasing equipment is to seek the advice of a **foodservice design consultant,** who is responsible for understanding and communicating the entire process of foodservice from the moment the food comes into the operation until it is served to the customer. The consultant should be a member of the **Foodservice Consultants Society International** (FCSI), which promotes client usage of services, encourages free exchange of ideas between members, and promotes ethical industry practices. The consultant also should attend the biannual meetings of the National Association of Food Equipment Manufacturers (NAFEM), which has a mission to develop and promote cooperative programs and activities to improve the level of professionalism of its members and to provide a vehicle for broadening knowledge of members within the global foodservice and supplies industry.

These consultants communicate the specific needs of the foodservice manager to the architect and design team (Miller, 1996). These consultants have been planning commercial and noncommercial kitchens for many years and therefore keep up-to-date on equipment. They write specifications for the equipment that best meets the needs of the operation and send them out for bids. Consultants are very knowledgeable about the plumbing, ventilation, and electrical requirements of modern quantity food production equipment. They also know area fire, health and safety, and building codes and are current on HACCP regulations.

Consultants are paid by the architect. They are reimbursed for expenses, such as travel and telephone, and receive a fee for services. This can be an hourly rate or a fixed fee for a well-defined amount of work, or a certain percentage of the cost of the equipment. The five phases of consulting services include:

- schematic design—rough drawing indicating flow of work
- design development—plan of the new or renovated operation to scale, usually including a set of mechanical plans
- construction document—detailed drawings to be used by the architect, builder, and others
- bid—evaluation and recommendation of the bids that meet the needs of the operation
- construction administration—shop drawing review and approval response to Requests for Information (RFI) on job site inspection and start-up demonstration of equipment by company representatives for employees and management

Often after a designated time, a reinspection of the foodservice operation, especially the equipment, is scheduled with the consultant, architect, and client. Because these phases might take 2 or more years, consultants usually are paid at the end of each.

Consultants do not come cheap, but in the long run they save their clients money and time. They can identify state-of-the-art equipment and recommend efficient placement. Foodservice equipment is more sophisticated and expensive than ever before; consultants assume responsibility for all the equipment details and their placement in the kitchen area. Accurate designs reduce the number of adjustments that need to be made during construction.

Marketing Channel

The marketing channel, discussed and illustrated in chapter 3, is the basis for Figure 15.2, a modification for foodservice equipment. The producer of the raw materials can be either the farmer or rancher for food products or the miner for metals or manufacturer of nuts and bolts for equipment. These raw materials are then sold to processors or manufacturers who make food items or equipment used for menu items, such as canned fruits and vegetables or an oven for roasting meat. Once the equipment is manufactured, it can be sold directly to the end user. In most cases, however, a distributor usually hired by the manufacturer, such as a manufacturer's wholesaler or representative, is responsible for the sale to the supplier. The major

Figure 15.2. Marketing channel for foodservice equipment.

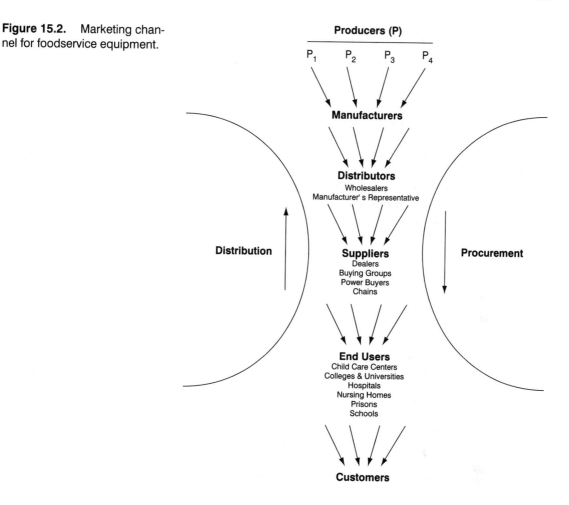

types of equipment suppliers are listed below. Remember that in the marketing channel, the producer exchanges products for money, and this exchange occurs all the
way down the channel to the ultimate customer.

- *Dealer.* This is the most direct route for procuring foodservice equipment. The
  dealer directly purchases the equipment from the manufacturer and is the
  owner of that equipment until someone buys it. The dealer assumes responsibility for the equipment until it reaches the facility; then ownership is transferred to the end user. Installation of the equipment, when it is taken off the
  truck, usually is the responsibility of the end user. Some dealers install the
  equipment or give the user the name of someone who will do it for a fee. If,
  however, a design consultant has been hired, that person will be sure the
  equipment is properly installed.

- *Buying group.* A group of similar operations, such as hospitals, do their purchasing together. The group members negotiate with the manufacturer for discounts because of the volume of equipment purchased. Joint decisions are

made on specifications and services. The most widely used contracts are for medical/surgical supplies and pharmaceuticals in healthcare facilities. The largest U.S. group purchasing service has more than 3,700 healthcare accounts and 40 field staff to service accounts and open new ones.

- *Power buyer.* Individual companies, such as Sysco Food Services, Inc., have thousands of accounts and, like group purchasing buyers, have power in numbers, thus receiving large discounts based on volume from manufacturers. Sysco started out as a supplier of food products but has expanded to selling other products, including foodservice equipment.
- *Chain buyer.* Many large restaurant chains with many units, such as McDonald's, Burger King and Wendy's, have set up companies to handle their purchasing. These companies are big enough to purchase directly from the processor or manufacturer and therefore receive large discounts.

New or Used

Without question, the best way to purchase equipment is to buy it new. Going to a reputable supplier with a thorough understanding of the type of equipment you want makes the purchase much easier. The supplier can help the buyer decide which equipment will meet the needs of the operation and often will come to the foodservice to measure the space needed and check whether additional wiring, gas pipes, or venting will be required. Used equipment sales and rebuilding are a large and profitable part of the foodservice equipment industry. Some suppliers sell only used equipment and others sell both new and used. Equipment coming off a lease also is another possibility as leasing becomes more popular.

Often when a facility undergoes renovation, most equipment, especially if it was new when purchased and has been well maintained, can be used again (Frable, 1994a). If the equipment has not been well maintained, perhaps steam cleaning, minor repairs, and the replacement of knobs, handles, and other hardware can make the equipment look like new. Equipment that is moved from another operation must be carefully examined to see if compressors, motors, gaskets, seals, and other parts might have broken during the move. Used equipment that is almost new and has a warranty from a reputable company usually is a good purchase. However, if it is the only piece of equipment in the foodservice operation of that type, such as a freezer, purchasing a used one might be risky. Nonmechanical equipment, such as used pots, work tables, counters, and shelving, often is a good value. It should have the National Sanitation Foundation® (NSF) seal and meet NSF standards; local codes also should be met.

Temperature control in refrigerators is emphasized in HACCP programs. Most old refrigerators cannot meet the temperature standards. If the equipment is menu critical—if a grill is needed for grilled chicken breast, for example—it should be purchased. Equipment must protect the safety of employees; product liability awards over the last 10 years have forced manufacturers to redesign safety devices on slicers and mixers. If the equipment is mechanically or electronically complex, buy new. Outdated ice machines, microwave ovens, and conveyor toasters seldom are good buys because new models have better design and reliability.

Scheduling Purchases

Expectations and reality often are far apart when owners purchase new or renovated equipment, especially as part of a move or major renovation (Frable, 1994b). Many owners cannot estimate a timetable for finishing a project and miss the completion date by 3 or 4 months. Scheduling is particularly critical when projects need to be completed for a special event or a specific date. Equipment manufacturers usually are busiest during the summer to make up lost time on projects that are started late but must be opened in fall. Equipment installations for renovated schools or colleges or for fall openings of restaurants all converge in July and August when summer vacations and factory shutdowns occur. Even if equipment is available, only a limited number of experienced fabricators, installers, and electricians are available, and custom fabrication suffers.

Many foodservice operations open late and lose significant revenues. Others open anyway without checking the equipment, correcting defects, or training staff. Expenses occur by having to pay overtime to installation and building trades. The owner is frustrated and poorer because realistic expectations and timetables were not planned. Some common problems are preventable:

- *Most kitchen equipment is not stocked.* Manufacturers are using the same just-in-time inventory trend that other businesses have embraced. They buy parts and materials from many different suppliers that buy them from other manufacturers. Because of drops in sales, plants and warehouses sometimes close. In addition, skilled workers in stainless steel fabrication and installation take years to develop. Even if manufacturers want to stock equipment, the wide variety of options and accessories precludes doing so.
- *Shop drawings require time for review and approval.* Special order equipment requires shop drawings that often take several weeks for approval. This equipment includes custom stainless and millwork fabrication, ventilators, large dishwashers, and walk-in refrigerators. Manufacturers refuse to make a product without approved drawings.
- *Rough-in drawings need to be prepared and checked.* Dimensioned rough-in drawings are required for setting floor drains before pouring concrete floor slabs, which determine wall locations. Contractors like to have this information 3 to 4 weeks before equipment is delivered. Utility requirements are specific for each piece of equipment, but the contractor cannot start on rough-ins before the contract is awarded. A delay in this phase makes the project 3 or 4 weeks late.
- *Delivery delays and freight damage are not uncommon.* The more critical the timetable, the more potential there is that the equipment will be assigned the slowest freight routing or that it will arrive damaged, sometimes beyond use or repair.
- *Local approvals are required.* Local building officials, fire marshals, and health inspectors currently enforce much more stringent codes and standards than they did a few years ago. They focus on the kitchen because it is usually the most hazardous and complex part of all buildings. Code officials do not hesitate to stop construction or delay approval for opening if they find defects or

violations. Obtaining health department approval and a certificate of occupancy can be an experience for owners trying to open a new facility. Expediting approvals can take weeks or months. A minimum of 2 or 3 weeks for the code compliance process should be scheduled before opening.

- *The punch list must be checked.* Near the end of a project, a detailed checklist, known as a punch list, should be prepared by a qualified person. This list should be prepared a few weeks before the opening to allow time for corrective action before the equipment is put into service and the staff is trained.

National Sanitation Foundation

The **National Sanitation Foundation® (NSF),** organized by a group of industrial leaders and public health officials, is a nonprofit, noncommercial organization dedicated to public health safety and protection of the environment by developing standards and providing education and third-party assessment services (NSF Listings, 1997). Standards are developed and revised with the active participation of public health and other regulatory officials, users, and industry. Standards must be accepted by the **Council of Public Health Consultants,** a group of people from all levels of government, academia, and private consulting firms with expertise in health and environmental issues. Only after acceptance by a joint committee and the Council of Public Health Consultants may proposed standards or revisions be adopted by the NSF Board of Trustees.

The NSF set out to serve its customers more effectively in the 1970s by building an international network of partner organizations to provide global service in support of its public health mission (The Standard of Excellence, 1997). In 1991, the foundation changed its name to NSF International. Today, with clients in more than 60 countries and offices in the United States and Belgium, NSF International has emerged as one of the world's leading environmental and public health service organizations.

Products tested by NSF must conform to all NSF requirements before a company is authorized to use the foundation's mark denoting certification. Eight product certification programs, one of which is Food Equipment, are available. Certified equipment must bear a blue laminated foil mark with an identifying number and data plate or label (Figure 15.3). Companies authorized to use the mark have signed a contract agreeing that the mark will be placed only on products fully complying with the relevant standard.

Underwriters Laboratory

Underwriters Laboratories Inc.® is an independent, not-for-profit organization that has been evaluating products in the interest of public safety since 1894. The UL mark, as shown in Figure 15.3, is the most widely recognized and accepted safety mark in the United States. The familiar UL symbol is well known to building officials, electrical inspectors, public health officials, and consumers. UL has over 70 years experience evaluating commercial gas and electric cooking appliances, refrigeration, and food preparation and processing equipment for manufacturers seeking safety

Figure 15.3. National Sanitation Foundation® international certification mark and Underwriters Laboratory® certification mark on foodservice equipment.

and sanitation certification and energy-efficiency evaluations. UL staff members are experts at carrying out a variety of product investigations of foodservice industry equipment. In addition, UL has developed nearly 20 safety standards for the commercial foodservice industry (Underwriters Laboratories Inc.®, 1993).

Equipment Maintenance

Keeping records on equipment maintenance often is a manager's headache; rising costs of these services add to the headaches (Frable, 1996b). Most foodservice managers have few records of the age, condition, service history, or maintenance requirements for equipment in their operations. Records for the number of repairs and cost of each provide crucial information when considering whether to repair or replace equipment. Another benefit of keeping inventory and service records is tracking warranties. The manager who has no records might be paying for parts and labor that are covered by extended warranties purchased with the equipment.

Some type of electronic database can help track this warranty information. An equipment maintenance program is a good way of documenting age, condition, and reliability of all equipment and mechanical systems. Some database software permits an unlimited amount of equipment to be entered, which allows for scheduling of periodic maintenance and repairs while keeping notes on each. Sometimes those who can benefit the most from computers don't have access because of the cost of the hardware. For some business applications, like maintaining databases, a high-powered processor is not needed. When new models are introduced, the older computer models are sold at substantial reductions. Also, a wide variety of business and personal software, usually one version behind the current release, is available at substantial price breaks. At those prices, anyone who needs a computer should be able to afford one.

HACCP Program

In an HACCP program, temperatures must be monitored and recorded. Placing deep containers of hot foods, especially soups and stocks, in refrigeration units is one of the most often-cited causes of food safety risk. Not only does hot food not reach recommended safe temperatures within the specified time frame, but the heat from the containers can raise the temperatures in refrigerators. Hot foods should be put into shallow pans before refrigeration. Walk-ins can now be purchased with alarms that are triggered when the temperature exceeds a certain range; the alarms also can dial programmed phone numbers to alert an off-duty manager that something is wrong.

An HACCP program in a foodservice operation minimizes the risk of acquiring a foodborne illness. By charting the flow of food through the operation, points can be identified where contamination or growth of microorganisms occur. This program is responsible for making thermometers more sophisticated than they have ever been. The same thermometer often was used for finding out the temperature in a refrigerator or an oven, and results were seldom analyzed. Currently, thermometers are becoming very specialized; for example, some models are designed for ovens, deepfry, and coffee. (Remember the scalding coffee served in a quick-service restaurant that ended up in court?) All potentially hazardous foods should be prepared according to specific HACCP guidelines. The minimum number of thermometers needed in a foodservice operation are the digital pocket test (Cooper model DFP450), refrigerator/freezer/dry storage (Cooper model 25HP), hot holding (Cooper model 26HP), and meat (Cooper model 323) thermometers shown in Plate 5. The following types of thermometers should be available and used in most foodservice operations. The fifth one, the HACCP Manager (Cooper model HT3000) is excellent but expensive; it is used primarily in processing plants and large foodservice operations.

- Model DFP450—digital pocket test thermometer with sensors in the tip of the probe; ideal for testing hamburgers.
- Model 25HP—a refrigerator/freezer/dry storage thermometer with a temperature range of −20°F to 80°F; NSF certified.
- Model 26HP—a hot holding thermometer with a temperature range of 100°F to 175°F, NSF certified.

- Model 323—a meat thermometer with specific HACCP temperature ranges for a variety of popular meats; temperature range of 130°F to 190°F.
- Model HT3000—designed to record temperature, time, and location for any manufacturing or food preparation process that requires accurate record keeping; downloading feature allows the user to graph and chart data to review and analyze for corrective action or required record keeping.

Many foodservice operations have supplemented the use of thermometers with a disposable product called T-Sticks offered through ECOLAB®, the world's largest supplier of cleaning and service for the foodservice industry. T-Sticks are multipurpose sensor sticks used to monitor food temperatures and the temperature in the dishwasher's final rinse section. They help promote food safety in restaurants and other foodservice operations. They are not expensive, costing 20 cents or less per T-Stick, and employees who might not take the time to track down a thermometer find them easy to use. T-Stick 140 Plus is used for monitoring food temperatures on hot lines or steam tables; food must be held at 140°F or higher to stop growth of harmful bacteria. It turns green at 142°F to 144°F for a margin of safety. T-Stick 160 monitors the cooking temperature of hamburger, ground meat, fish, pork, and eggs, as well as verifying temperatures in the final rinse section of the dishwashing machine. It turns black if the temperature reaches 160°F. An illustration of how to use the T-Stick 160 for cooking hamburgers is shown in Figure 15.4.

Equipment Categories

Types of foodservice equipment are often categorized as cooking, refrigeration, warewashing, and other equipment, including food machines, carts, and fabricated.

Figure 15.4. Monitoring the temperature of hamburgers with a T-Stick 160 while cooking.

1 Insert white plastic-coated end of T-Stick into the center of the hamburger to be tested. **Do not remove the protective plastic coating. Wait 5 seconds.**

2 Remove T-Stick from hamburger. If plastic-coated end has turned black, temperature of food has reached 160°F (71°C). T-Stick can be discarded.

3 If plastic-coated end still white, food has yet reached 160°F (71°C). Cook further and repeat steps 1 and 2, using the same T-Stick in the same hamburger.

Source: ECOLAB®. Used by permission.

Each category has many models available for purchase. These can be standard or specialty models depending on what is needed to do a specific task. Currently, multifunction equipment is being emphasized. A variety of new equipment and accessories has been developed that can perform more than one task at different times, especially in small operations (Frable, 1996b). This multifunction equipment also can become a backup in large operations, especially when the primary equipment is overloaded or not working. With limited budgets and space, equipment that can provide more than one function is a sound purchase.

Each piece of equipment has many models, and suppliers cannot keep them all in stock. If they do not have the equipment in stock, most suppliers will special order it. This chapter provides an overall view of the various types of equipment available on the market, but an in-depth discussion with the foodservice consultant and the supplier will be necessary before a purchase is made. The consultant also will write the specifications, take care of the installation, and make sure employees are trained to operate the equipment.

COOKING EQUIPMENT

Up until the last few years, cooking methods were classified only as moist heat and dry heat, and equipment was purchased to perform these functions. Steamers still are manufactured to provide moist heat and broilers, fryers, and ovens to provide dry heat. Regardless of the type of cooking equipment, the buyer should be aware that exhaust hoods are required over all cooking equipment; if new equipment cannot be put under the same hood as all other equipment, another hood must be purchased and installed. Before discussing the types of equipment available on the market, the buyer needs to have some idea about how heat is transferred from a gas flame or an electric coil to food.

Heated Equipment

Heat causes many reactions to occur in food, and the type and amount of heat greatly affects the resulting product. Buyers who understand heating sources and heat transfer from the equipment to the food can better make the right purchase.

Heat Source

Relative costs of the heating source in the foodservice operation should play an important part in the decision to purchase equipment for cooking (Bendall, 1997). Most cooking equipment is available as either gas-fired or electric units. The choice depends upon preference and utility costs. Many chefs prefer gas because the heat is immediate and can be controlled instantly. An open gas flame heats food in pans that are placed on a grate. The electric equivalent is a coil burner, which generally is used for sautéing or fast cooking. The electric hot top plate uses a sealed burner that is easier to clean than the coil and has even heat distribution, but it is not as efficient for fast cooking. The disadvantage of the hot top is that it wastes more heat than an open burner because the burners need to remain on to keep the top hot.

Gas open burners on heavy-duty ranges vary from 20,000 BTUs (British thermal units) to 40,000 BTUs of input. These are heavy-duty burners made for high production. The average household ranges have burners rated as 8,000 BTUs to 10,000 BTUs; commercial ranges have a lot of power. The style of the burner and the pan used for cooking influence the effectiveness of the equipment. Many options are available on all heated equipment, and buyers need to take the time to determine exactly what is best for their foodservice operations. When purchasing gas equipment, be sure to specify electronic ignition, which eliminates pilot lights, for safety.

Heat Transfer

Heat is transferred in four ways: conduction, convection, radiation, and induction (Spears, 1995).

- **Conduction** is the transfer of heat through direct contact of one object or substance with another. In cooking by conduction, the heat is first transferred from a heat source, either gas or electricity, through a cooking vessel to food. Metals are good conductors, and different metals conduct heat at different rates. For example, copper, iron, and aluminum are effective conductors for cooking pans; stainless steel, developed from iron, is not as effective. Conduction is the best way to transfer heat in grilling, boiling, frying, and to some degree baking and roasting. In broiling or grilling a steak, heat is transferred from the source to the pan or grill and then directly to the meat.
- **Convection** is the distribution of heat by the movement of liquid or vapor. It may be either natural or forced. Natural convection occurs from density or temperature differences within a liquid or vapor. The temperature differences cause hot air to rise and cool air to fall. Thus, in a kettle of liquid or a deep fat fryer, convection keeps the liquid in motion when heated. Forced convection is caused by a fan that circulates the heat, which is transferred quickly to the food, causing faster cooking. As a general rule, the temperature should be set 25°F lower than required for a radiant oven and the time a little less as well.
- **Radiation** pertains to the generation of heat energy by wave action within an object. The waves do not possess energy, but they induce heat by molecular action upon entering food. **Infrared waves** are a type of radiation used in food production that have a longer wavelength than visible light. Broiling is the most familiar example of infrared cooking. Infrared lamps are commonly used in foodservice operations for holding food on the counter before the waitstaff picks it up. **Microwaves** have a very short length and are generated by an electromagnetic tube. Microwaves penetrate partway into the food and agitate water molecules. The friction resulting from this agitation creates heat, which in turn cooks the product. Most microwaves penetrate only about 2 inches into food and heat is transferred to the center of large masses of food by conduction. In foodservice operations microwave ovens are used primarily for heating prepared foods for service.

• **Induction** is the use of electrical magnetic fields to excite the molecules of metal cooking surfaces. An induction-heat cooktop is one of the hottest new innovations in ranges. Although induction units use electricity, magnetic friction is used rather than an element for heating (Bendall, 1997). A magnetic field is created along the ceramic cooktop and when magnetic cookware is placed on the top, the molecules in the pan start moving so rapidly the pan gets hot. As soon as the pan is removed, it cools down. The actual surface of the cooktop never gets hot. The cooktop has no open flame, making it safer, and needs no thermostat for control. Energy is saved because all the heat goes into the pan; no warm-up time is required and the unit can be turned on only when needed. Temperatures are determined by specific alloys in four removable grills, which also allow a single grill to be divided into four different cooking zones. According to foodservice operators, induction heating is faster and more even than any other method of cooking. It also is cleaner and easier to ventilate and does not require gas piping.

Moist Heat Equipment

The most common moist heat methods of cooking are boiling, simmering, stewing, poaching, blanching, braising, and steaming. These methods are similar, with only slight differences. To boil, simmer, stew, or poach means to cook a food in water or a seasoned liquid. The first five methods generally are done by using a steam-jacketed kettle, which technically is not a steamer. These kettles are either self-contained or direct steam models (Handbook of Steam Equipment, Undated). Self-contained kettles are closed systems that generate their own steam, recycle condensate, and operate without water or drain plumbing connections. Direct steam kettles operate with steam provided by a remote steam source that can be the main steam-heating boiler for the facility or a boiler for the kitchen. Today, however, most steam-jacketed kettles are self-contained.

The **steam-jacketed kettle** is placed into a larger kettle, and steam is introduced between the two in an open space, or jacket. The steam entering the jacket condenses on the inner wall, transferring its heat to the inner kettle's metal, which in turn transfers the heat to the food being cooked. The steam does not actually touch the food. The kettle size ranges from 20 to 150 gallons. Groen model DEE/4T (Plate 6) is a stainless steel steam-jacketed unit, operating with an electric heated steam source contained within the unit. The enclosed support base contains a self-locking tilt mechanism. Steam-jacketed kettles are relatively easy to keep clean and shining, but a handy floor drain for larger kettles and a sink/drain for tabletop kettles are needed. A kettle-mounted faucet with hot-and-cold water is necessary for making soups and stews as well as for washing the kettle after it is used.

To steam is to cook foods by exposing them directly to steam. **Pressure steamers** work by trapping and removing air that causes steam pressure to build. The pressureless convection steamer, Cleveland Range Inc. model 24-CEM-24 (Plate 6), literally has replaced the old pressure steamers that cooks were afraid to use because a gust of steam shot out whenever the door was opened. Because the cavity is not under pressure, a pressureless steamer's door may be opened at any time during the process to check cooking progress or to remove or add food. In a **pressureless convection steamer,** heat transfer from steam to food is accomplished by forced convection caused by a fan inside which encircles the food, thus cooking it without pressure. Because of a continuous venting system in pressureless steamers, the result is fast, gentle cooking at a low temperature, 212°F. Pressureless steamers are well suited for a wide variety of foods, from fresh to loose pack frozen or frozen block vegetables. Because the steam is continuously vented, unwanted flavor transfer from one food to another is eliminated.

Dry Heat Equipment

The major methods of cooking without liquid are roasting, baking, oven frying, broiling, grilling, barbecuing, and frying, including sautéing, pan frying, and deep fat frying. Some foodservice managers contend that including foods cooked in oil as dry cooking does not make sense because oil is wet. Perhaps three methods of cooking should be recognized: cooking in liquids, cooking in dry heat, and cooking in fat. In this text, however, frying in oil will be included under dry heat.

Broilers

A **broiler** has its heat source above the rack that holds the food, usually meat, poultry, and seafood. The food is placed 3 to 6 inches from the heat, depending on the type and intensity of the heat (Spears, 1995). The temperature required depends on the amount of fat, tenderness, or thickness of the food item. Traditional broilers lack precise temperature controls, and foods must be closely monitored during the cooking process. Some equipment, such as conveyorized infrared broilers, give more flexibility and control over the broiling process by varying the conveyor speed.

Charbroiling has become popular in many foodservice operations, especially in steak houses and quick-service hamburger establishments. A **charbroiler,** U.S. Range model 0836-36A, as shown in Plate 7, is either gas or electric equipment with a bed of ceramic briquettes above the heat source and below the grid. Because the heat source in charbroiling is from below, it technically is a grilling and not a broiling method.

Grilling, griddling, and pan broiling are all dry heat cooking methods that use heat from below (Spears, 1995). Grilling is the culmination of a chef's culinary experience. Grilling is taking on an international flavor that is exciting customers. Asian teriyakis, Tex-Mex fajitas, Middle Eastern kebabs, and all-American cowboy-grilled steaks are highlights. **Grilling** is done on an open grid over a heat source, which may be an electric or gas-heated element, ceramic briquettes, or exotic woods and flavored chips.

Eighteen years ago, Lang Manufacturing Company introduced double-sided cooking technology with the Clamshell®. This model is being phased out. It is being replaced by the Lang Add-On Clamshell hood that uses the customers' existing equipment, thus eliminating the purchase of a griddle and/or charbroiler. The Lang Add-On **Clamshell®** is a broiler hood that fits directly into existing griddles and broilers at a fraction of the cost of the original doubled-sided cooking equipment.

The Add-On can be easily connected to the back of a grill or broiler. The add-on Clamshell hood shown in Plate 7 is made of stainless steel and has comfortable grip handles. The new model also has a patented burner design that cooks food evenly regardless of where it is located. Rapid cooking action from the hood's infrared broiler and the grilling heat from below drives the natural juices in the food to the center and decreases food shrinkage, resulting in juicy meat in half the time. Menu items cook faster; for example, New York steaks that take 7 minutes to broil can be served after only 4 minutes and chicken that takes 6 minutes to broil takes only 3½ minutes. These cooking times may vary depending on the thickness and weight of the raw product.

Deep Fat Fryers

A **deep fat fryer,** Frymaster FPH-350C, is a tank of oil heated by gas or electricity into which foods are immersed. Tremendous improvement has been made in gas and electric deep fat frying equipment for foodservice operations (Spears, 1995). Today, solid state electronics monitor the cooking cycle and control cooking temperature in deep fat fryers (Plate 7). Two of the most important developments in frying technology are precise thermostatic control and fast recovery of fat temperature, permitting foodservice operations to produce consistent quality fried food rapidly. Improvements for deep fat fryers have centered on fat filtration and automatic controls. The easy-to-use filtration operation is an integral part of the equipment. A built-in filter features automatic washdown and an instant change filter. Control functions range from a simple indication of elapsed time to presetting times for more than one product per basket, lift controls, holding time indication, adjustment of frying time for lower temperatures, and automatic shutdown.

Ovens

Roasting or baking uses a combination of all three modes of heat transfer: conduction, convection, and radiation. Heat is conducted through the pan to the food, and natural or forced convection circulates the air. Heat also radiates from the hot walls of the cooking chamber.

A wide range of oven types is used in foodservice operations. The three main categories are hot-air ovens, infrared broilers, and microwave ovens. Several types of hot-air ovens are in use: range, deck, forced convection, conveyor, reel ovens, and low-temperature roasters.

The first questions to ask before buying an oven are "What are we cooking?" and "Where are we cooking it?" Many ovens worked fine for a specific type of food 15 or 20 years ago, when most menu items were prepared from scratch. Today in many foodservice operations, more prepared foods and frozen ingredients that require a different type of preparation are being used.

Many types of ovens are available, and finding the right one for a foodservice operation takes many hours of research (Plate 7). Again, a foodservice consultant or a knowledgeable supplier can help the foodservice manager make the right purchase decision.

- **Range oven.** The **range oven** is part of a stove and is located under the cooking surface. Today it is used primarily in small operations. For many years, stoves were the only cooking equipment in commercial and noncommercial kitchens. Cooks complained about their backs because they had to bend and lift heavy pans of food many times each day. Many accidents occurred in kitchens, especially if the floors were slippery.
- **Deck oven.** The **deck oven** has traditionally been the standby of hot-air ovens in foodservice operations. It is so named because pans of food usually are placed directly on the stacked metal decks (Plate 7). They vary in size, depending on their function, either roasting meat or baking breads, cakes, and cookies. Deck ovens come in basic sections, each with two shelves that may be stacked on each other. Blodgett model 962 (Plate 7) has two sections, each with its own source of heat, and four shelves. Most deck ovens have a separate heat source under each shelf.
- **Convection oven.** The **convection oven** (Blodgett model DFG 100) has a fan on the back wall that creates currents of air within the cooking chamber (Plate 7). This process eliminates hot and cold air zones, thereby accelerating the rate of heat transfer. The convection oven has three major advantages over the range oven. It has more space and holds two to three times as much food, reduces cooking time by 30%, and cooks at 25°F to 35°F lower temperatures, thus conserving energy. The standard convection oven is the square cabinet type that holds from 6 to 11 full-size baking pans and can be double-stacked to conserve floor space. Another type of convection oven is the roll-in rack oven that holds 16 to 20 full-size baking pans that can be rolled into the oven on a special rack on casters.
- **Conveyor oven. Conveyor ovens** are called pizza ovens in quick-service operations and can be either gas or electric. They range in size from 55 inches wide by 31 inches deep that bake 10 to 15 16-inch pizzas an hour to 55- by 77-inch models that bake 60 to 65 pizzas or 13 full-size sheet pans an hour. When buying a conveyor, be sure that the cooking time and temperature can be easily adjusted and that it is easy to clean. The **impinger,** Lincoln Foodservice Products model 1130, is a conveyorized gas-fired or electric oven that toasts the bottom of the pizza crust and makes it flaky (Plate 7). Most sold are mobile and can be single, double, or triple impingers, making them very versatile in the kitchen. Air impingement permits heating, cooking, baking, and crisping of foods two to four times faster than conventional ovens, depending on the food product.
- **Microwave oven.** Microwaves are generated by an electromagnetic tube which produces microwaves that penetrate partway into the food and agitate water molecules. The friction resulting from this agitation creates heat, which in turn cooks the product. Because microwave radiation affects only water molecules, a waterless material will not become hot in a microwave oven. Thus disposable plastic or paper plates can be used for heating or cooking some foods. Most microwaves penetrate only about 2 inches into food, and heat is transferred to the center of large masses of food by conduction. Foodservices should not try to save money by purchasing a home model for

$100 instead of a commercial-grade microwave for $300. Commercial microwave ovens have to pass two primary tests for Commercial UL and NSF approval. A home style microwave has to be opened and closed 100,000 times with no appreciable wear on the hinge; a commercial unit must be able to withstand 250,000 openings and closings. When purchasing a commercial microwave oven, size is important if counter space is at a premium. Even a microwave with a narrow width should be able to accommodate a half-size pan. Most of the better and most powerful ovens are made of stainless steel both inside and out. Speed is in direct relation to power; if the food takes 3 minutes to cook in an 800-watt oven, it will be done in under 90 seconds in a 1,700-watt model. In Plate 7, a 26-inch wide microwave oven (Panasonic model NE-2680) holds two full-size pans of lasagna that cook in 20 minutes, 6 pounds of fresh vegetables done in 6 minutes, and 1¼ pounds of lobster. Microwave is not a predominant method for cooking in foodservice operations; microwave ovens are used more for heating prepared foods for service. They are used in hospital galleys for heating chilled or frozen individual portions and in vending operations for heating sandwiches and soups.

- **Smoker oven.** The **smoker oven,** Cookshack model 150, shown in Plate 7, is an electric, compact-size oven with racks to smoke up to 100 pounds of meat at a time. The smoker oven uses 1½ pounds of wood chips to produce a mild, medium, or heavy smoke. In many areas, hoods or vents are not required. The dry rub of spices and barbecue sauce unique to an operation add a piquant flavor to the meat.
- **Low-temp cooking and holding oven.** Cooking temperatures in a **low-temp cooking and holding oven,** Alto-Shaam model 750-TH-III, are from 100°F to 325°F, and holding temperatures are from 60°F to 200°F. The increased product yield of meats roasted at low temperatures over longer than usual periods of time has led to the development of these ovens (Plate 7). Yield of meats can be increased up to 25% and energy consumption reduced by 30% to 50% (Spears, 1995). Mobile low-temp ovens are flexible because they can also be used as warmers. Low-temp ovens stacked on casters are frequently used in catering operations.

Multifunction Equipment

Cutting down on the square footage of a foodservice is a goal in both commercial and noncommercial operations today. The range, often referred to as a stove, probably was the first multifunction foodservice equipment.

Space is expensive and should be used to increase revenue rather than for production. The amount of labor hours required to prepare food can be decreased if employees do not have to walk miles every day. Three pieces of cooking equipment are manufactured to alleviate many of the space and labor problems in a foodservice operation: the combination convection oven/steamer or combi-oven, the tilting fry or braising pan, and the convection/microwave oven.

- **Combi-oven.** The **combi-oven** directs the flow of both convected air and steam through the oven cavity to produce a super-heated, moist internal atmosphere. Blodgett model COS-101S has five stainless steel wire shelves and an attached pan-holding rack on casters underneath it. Combi-ovens (Plate 8) are considered the "hottest" foodservice equipment on the market today (Spears, 1995). Industry insiders call them a revolution in cooking. Foodservice design consultants predict that they will replace most ovens and steamers in foodservice operations in the future. Meat, seafood, poultry, vegetables, and even delicate meringues, pastries, and breads with a crusty surface can be prepared in this oven. Four cooking methods are combined in one unit: convection, steam, convection plus continuous steam, and convection plus cycled steam. The advantage of this combination is its versatility, which permits menu expansion with a single piece of equipment, conservation of valuable floor space, and faster cooking with minimal shrinkage and maximum retention of flavor, color, and nutrients. "Combis" can be either electric or gas. A foodservice design consultant suggests that when steam is added to convection-cooked roasts, the meat stays more moist (Fellin, 1996). In addition to versatility, these ovens offer quick cooking time and low operating costs and have greater capacity than a convection oven (Fellin, 1996). A combi is significantly higher priced than a single convection oven but if the cost is compared to the total cost of the pieces of equipment it replaces—two convection ovens and a steamer—the cost is about the same. Combis are available in full widths accommodating 18-by-26-inch pans. Combis can be purchased as single- or two-deck or roll-in models in which racks of pans are rolled into the oven; and when the food is baked or roasted, the racks can be rolled into a holding cabinet before serving.

- **Tilting skillet.** The **tilting skillet,** Groen model NHFP, is a floor-mounted rectangular pan with a gas or electric-heated flat bottom, pouring lip, and hinged cover (Plate 8). It is considered the most versatile of all kitchen equipment, because it combines the advantages of a range, griddle, kettle, stock pot, and frying pan. These skillets can cook batches of food such as pasta, stew, gravies, sauces, and multi-ingredient entrées as well as individual orders of bacon and eggs, hamburgers, or steaks. They are available in many sizes, from 20 gallons to 40 gallons, and are operated by gas or electricity. An optional pilotless ignition is available on gas models. A smooth operating motorized or manual tilt mechanism is available, and an easy-pour lip design provides speed and precise control when removing cooked foods. The counter-balanced cover directs condensate back into the skillet even when open. The open base makes floor care easy. Cleanup is fast and easy and fewer pots are used; it really is a labor-saving piece of equipment.

- **Convection/microwave oven.** This **convection/microwave oven,** Amana model CMA2000, called the *Amana®* Convection Express™, is multifunction equipment (Plate 8) with convection and microwave capabilities. It can use convection air alone, microwave energy alone, or a combination of the two. It really is a convection oven that browns, bakes, and roasts and a microwave that steams and cooks foods. Hot air jets from a convection oven (note the fan in the back of the oven in Plate 8) provide surface color and texture and microwave energy provides the major thawing and heating of the product. One of the biggest complaints about microwave cooking is that the food never browns. By combining these two functions, a turkey or roast can be cooked in a much shorter time than usual and the product will be juicy on the inside and brown on the outside. A beautiful brown, juicy, broiler chicken can be ready to serve in 18 minutes. Amana introduced microwave cooking a number of years ago. The Convection Express™ is NSF and UL approved and is the first commercially approved oven of this type in North America.

REFRIGERATED EQUIPMENT

Refrigerated equipment is among the most important equipment in a foodservice operation. Without refrigeration, the world's food supply would be very limited. Before discussing the types of refrigerated equipment used in a foodservice operation, we will review the 1997 FDA Model Food Code and its effect on the HACCP program.

FDA Model Food Code

In the 1997 FDA Model Food Code, the "safe" temperature for cold food was lowered from 45°F to 41°F (Industry Council on Food Safety, 1997). That means refrigeration temperatures must be lower than 41°F to ensure the food reaches an internal temperature of 41°F. State and local health departments are revising rules to incorporate these new temperature recommendations. In 1997, industry, regulatory agencies, and consumers made recommendations that would allow foodservice operations some leeway in meeting HACCP rules. Foods refrigerated at 41°F can be stored for 10 days, but those refrigerated at temperatures up to 45°F can be kept for only 3 days. Foodservice operations have 5 years to meet the new standard.

Types of Equipment

Refrigerators and freezers are the most important pieces of equipment in the refrigerated equipment category. They are essential to serving customers safe food. The comparatively new blast freezers are becoming essential in foodservice operations. Ice machines have an important role, too, but for a different reason—customer satisfaction. Iced beverages have become extremely popular, especially in restaurants. Consider how quickly contaminated ice could ruin a foodservice operation.

Refrigerators and Freezers

Equipment manufacturers are meeting the challenge of the FDA Model Food Code by building prep tables with refrigerated cabinets underneath, counter tops with refrigerated rails for sandwich prep, and special units that chill pans (Industry Council on Food Safety, 1997). Because storage walk-ins often are not designed to cool large loads quickly, more foodservice design consultants are using small blast chillers and adding more refrigerated storage close to both prep areas and cooking lines, including under-counter drawers, reach-ins, and walk-ins that can hold rolling carts.

The major types of refrigerators and freezers are either walk-ins or reach-ins. In most operations, both types are used. Instead of purchasing a specific model like those in homes, refrigerators for foodservice operations usually are assembled from specific modules to meet the needs of the operation.

Once again, a foodservice design consultant can assist the buyer in choosing the best refrigerator and freezer for a specific operation. Basic purchasing decisions need to be made for all types of refrigerators, freezers, blast chillers, and ice machines.

Basic Purchasing Decisions

The buyer should

- determine the amount of refrigerated space needed.
- specify the temperature that should be maintained for each piece: 36°F to 38°F for refrigerators; 0°F for reach-in freezers and −10°F for walk-in freezers.
- choose type of metal finishes, such as stainless steel, aluminum, or painted galvanized for exterior and interior.
- choose type of thermometer, such as dial or digital.
- check standard accessories and order desired features.
- check manufacturer's warranty on the compressor and on other parts of the unit, such as hinges and latches.
- check standards and testing agencies, especially NSF and UL.
- analyze prices of several bids before making a decision.

Specific Purchasing Decisions

In addition to basic purchasing decisions for all refrigerated equipment, specific features must be considered. The purchase of walk-in refrigerators, freezers, or combination units requires different purchasing decisions than those for reach-in refrigerators and freezers.

Walk-In.   The buyer should

- figure required space in cubic feet or lineal footage of shelf space in 18-, 21-, or 24-inch widths.
- have ramps built to the walk-in door for easy access by carts and dollies if an insulated floor set on a building floor is desired.
- specify size and finish of door, a heated window, a built-in heat strip around the perimeter to reduce frost and condensation, hinges for self-closing, and a sweep gasket at bottom to close the gap.
- specify a key lock, padlock, or both, if needed. The door must have an inside safety release.
- determine number of inside incandescent or fluorescent lights to be installed. Light fixtures must be vapor sealed.
- specify a drain outside the door to remove condensate from the evaporator coils and location of air- or water-cooled condensing units that produce heat.
- decide with the supplier before signing a purchase agreement who will deliver the walk-in, put it in place, and make the refrigeration, plumbing, and electrical connections.

Reach-In.   An example of these units is the McCall model 4-4045 (Plate 9). To make this purchase, the buyer should

- figure the required space in cubic feet or square footage of shelf space. Refrigerators and freezers come in one, two, or three sections and are approximately 20 to 25 cubic feet per section.
- ask the manager whether long full or half doors or solid or glass doors are preferred. Type and number of hinges must be determined.
- specify a key lock or padlock, if needed.
- ask the manager whether standard wire shelves or pan slides are preferred.
- ask the manager if 6-inch legs with adjustable feet for leveling or casters are preferred.
- decide if the reach-in should have a cord and plug or be wired directly. The reach-in can be wired for low voltage (120 volt–60 cycle–1 phase) or high voltage (208 volt–60 cycle–1 or 3 phase) depending on the electrical power available.
- specify a condensate evaporator, thus eliminating a need for a drain.
- check the overall size of the reach-in to make sure it can be brought into the building and placed where desired.
- decide with the supplier before signing a contract if the reach-in is to be delivered, uncrated, and set in place or if it is to be drop shipped at the dock or door.

Blast Chillers

Foodservice consultants are adding more prep sinks, separate prep areas for meat and poultry to prevent cross-contamination, more storage areas for utensils and cutting boards, and blast chillers in their design plans (Industry Council on Food Safety, 1997). The cook-chill method for preparing menu items and rethermalizing them at the time of service has been used for a number of years in hospital foodservice. It has also been adopted by school foodservices and other operations. The cook-chill method is referred to as cooking to inventory rather than to serve immediately. Blast chiller equipment, such as Whirl-Wind model BC-250-UR (Plate 9), has been improved and its use expanded. This equipment can be either a reach-in or under-counter model.

Many foodservice operators are now scrutinizing food safety procedures within their kitchens and are implementing HACCP programs (Industry Council on Food Safety, 1997). Increased cooking temperatures for potentially hazardous foods, such as meat, poultry, eggs, and seafood, have been suggested in the FDA Model Food Code. However, the code allows for lower cooking temperatures as long as these foods hold those temperatures for a longer time. For example, a beef roast cooked to an internal temperature of 145°F must hold that temperature for 3 minutes. It can be cooked to an internal temperature of 130°F as long as it maintains that temperature for 121 minutes. Refrigeration is needed to keep foods cold in storage but also to rapidly lower temperatures in cooked foods that are being stored. Walk-in refrigerators are not designed to cool down large amounts of food quickly. Therefore consultants are suggesting small under-counter or single-door blast chillers and more refrigerated storage close to both prep areas and cooking lines. They are working more closely with architects to be sure the kitchen environment is safe, including properly tempered airflow for food safety and minimal potential for cross-contamination between prep, cooking, and dishwashing areas.

Blast chilling means to utilize cold convected air for the purpose of rapidly cooling cooked foods to prepare them for refrigerated storage. It is an excellent and reliable way to cool hot foods safely if the right equipment is available. Chilling 250 pounds of hot food through the danger zone to 34°F to 36°F in 2 or less hours is possible. The **blast chiller** is used to extend the quality and safe storage life of menu items that are cooked, chilled, and then held in refrigerated storage for a limited amount of time. It looks like a reach-in refrigerator but, instead of having shelves, has slides that hold shallow pans are on each side of the interior (Figure 15.5). Users slide regular-sized pans of hot cooked food into it, and a high velocity directed airflow is turned on to pull hot foods through the danger zone fast.

The pattern of airflow in a Whirl-Wind blast chiller also is illustrated in Figure 15.5. Note that the chilled air comes from a 3-horsepower compressor on the left and goes

Figure 15.5.   Pattern of airflow in a blast chiller.

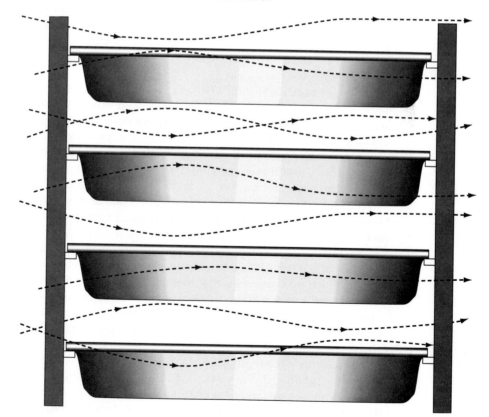

Source: Whirl-Wind Corporation. (Undated). Used by permission.

horizontally across the cabinet straight through the product, which is in the center. The fan on the right side pulls the air through. The temperature is held at 37°F, and the high velocity directed airflow prevents freezing of food products. Blast chillers are available in various sizes; most hold 20, 40, or 60 12-by-20-by-2½-inch pans of food at one time. The processing time usually is from 75 to 120 minutes, depending on density, composition, initial temperature, and type of container. Many foods are chilled in less than 30 minutes. In other blast chillers, the chilled air coil with a fan behind it is placed in the center of the cabinet. A 5-horsepower compressor is required because the whole cabinet must be chilled to bring the food temperature to the correct level. For foodservice operations on a tight budget, a blast chiller conversion kit that transforms any walk-in cooler or freezer into a reliable, efficient blast chiller is available. The purchase price is low and installation is quick.

Ice Machines

The ice machine is considered a basic piece of equipment in every foodservice operation. Unlike consumers elsewhere, most American customers expect ice water with a meal. Customers in other countries often are charged for water. Ice machines have improved tremendously over the last few years. Older models broke down and were often out of ice. Health inspectors were nervous about the potential that bacteria might be rampant in the machines. Today, however, some models have built-in self-cleaning systems that keep the machine's water distribution system free of mineral scale and lime deposits and air filters that protect the condenser from lint, dust, and grease.

The buyer needs to decide whether cubed, flaked, crushed, or cracked ice is preferred. The buyer must know how much is needed over a 24-hour period, because ice machines are rated by the amount of ice produced during that time. Small or large cubes generally are used for icing beverages. Many foodservice operations use a minimum of 150 pounds of ice through the lunch period. Flake ice molds to any shaped object and therefore is used primarily in display counters. It cools more quickly than any other form of ice and is ideal for displaying salads and desserts.

An ice machine consists of an ice-making compartment, which includes a condenser, and a bin for storing ice. The bin is larger than the ice-making compartment and serves as a reserve for emergencies. Self-service operations can order a dispenser, either push-button or lever type. The lever type is more acceptable to the NSF. One of the best-selling ice machines is the Scotsman model TDE-550 (Plate 9). It has a touch-free dispenser that uses infrared sensors to determine when to dispense ice and water. With no levers or push buttons, the risk of cross-contamination is greatly reduced, because physical contact does not occur. This ice machine meets the most stringent requirements of the NSF and complies with the Americans with Disabilities Act.

The mechanics of serving iced carbonated beverages is interesting. Containers of beverage syrup mixed with carbon dioxide usually are stored near the loading dock of the foodservice operation because if they drip, the area can be easily hosed down. The syrup is piped into the dispenser and mixed with carbonated water before being dispensed with ice into the glass or cup held by the customer or server. Getting the ice into the dispenser is a concern because one of the big problems with ice machines has been the amount of space required for the equipment; large ones can be 7 feet tall. To alleviate this problem, compact, self-contained under-counter cubers, only 39 inches high, are available for locations where space is at a premium. Beverage dispensers that sit on a counter either are tall, because all the ice is made and stored above the dispenser, or much shorter. Shorter dispensers have a small bin on top to hold ice that has been augured up through a plastic tube from a storage bin located near the dispenser.

WAREWASHING EQUIPMENT

According to Webster's Dictionary, *ware* refers to manufactured articles that include silverware, glassware, and tableware. **Warewashing** is the process of washing and sanitizing dishes, glassware, flatware, and pots and pans either manually or mechanically (Spears, 1995). Sinks, dishwashers, and pot-washing machines are the most common equipment for this process. Specialized equipment, such as flatware washers and glassware washers, also are available. Probably the biggest equipment expenditures in a foodservice operation are dishwashers used to keep these wares clean, free of contamination, and acceptable to the customer. Serving food on a greasy plate, from a water-spotted tray, or in a dull and streaked glass turns away customers quicker than mediocre food. Purchasing a dishwasher requires a team approach, including the owner of the operation, architect, foodservice design consultant, supplier, foodservice operation manager, dishroom manager, and sanitation supervisor. Many purchasing decisions must be made to narrow the selection down to the best machine for the operation. Before making the final decisions, however, the buyer must be sure that the selected dishwasher has the UL and NSF seal of approval.

Purchasing Decisions

Energy conservation must be kept in mind at all times. Dishwashing costs make up 7% to 10% of the operating budget, but good planning can keep those expenses under control. Different decisions must be made if the operation is in a new construction, in a renovated building, or in a kitchen that is being remodeled. The location of the dishroom in the operation and the plan for its operation must be studied.

Location of Dish Room

Before purchasing warewashing equipment, the place where it will be installed should be analyzed. The floor, ceiling, and walls must be checked. Ventilation, lighting, and noise level are important because they can affect the efficiency of the entire dishwashing operation. Also, the area must be accessible, within acceptable dimensions. A surprise for a manager may be the returning of a dishwasher because it will not fit through the building door. Utilities, including water lines, pressure, and temperatures, must be checked. Since energy conservation must be kept in mind at all times, the type of heat—be it electric, natural or LP gas, or steam—needs to be monitored. Also, good ventilation in the dishroom is required not only for employees' comfort but also to keep the humidity under control, thus permitting the dishes to air-dry. How to dispose of trash and waste also must be planned in advance. Preserving the environment has become a top priority in the last decade.

The owner, architect, chef, and foodservice manager must supply this information about the operation before a plan can be drawn up.

- menu food items
- number of customers per meal (for commercial foodservice, the number of customers per seating, how often the seats are turned over, and peak periods; for noncommercial foodservice, the number of people eating at one time)
- type of dishes—for example, china or plastic—and number of pieces per person
- tray sizes, if used
- method of busing dishes
- decision about where dining and bar glassware will be washed

The Plan

The foodservice staff should devise a master plan for dishwashing. If only a dishwasher will be purchased, a knowledgeable supplier could help the foodservice manager choose the best machine model. Usually, however, the dishroom needs to be redesigned at the same time. The flow of work is extremely important, and many managers hire a foodservice design consultant to develop this plan. A step-by-step procedure for designing a new dishroom or renovating an old one follows:

- Make a preliminary sketch of the dishwashing area, with complete and accurate measurements.
- Consider how to alleviate traffic congestion, which becomes a big problem as employees work hard and fast, with a great volume of dirty dishes in a short period of time, to produce enough clean ware for the next meal.
- Carefully calculate dishwasher size to handle the load. The rule of thumb is that the machine should be 30% oversized.
- Fit clean and soiled dish tables into the flow of work design for an efficient operation.
- Calculate aisle space to give employees enough room to move around and to permit the use of carts.
- Determine how to ventilate hot, moist air in the dishroom, even though the dishwasher is ventilated.
- Keep in mind these goals of a good dishroom design: clean dishes and glasses; reduction of breakage, labor hours, and detergent and rinse additive costs; an efficient flow pattern from the kitchen to the dishroom; conservation of energy; and ultimately satisfied customers.

Warewashing equipment includes dishwashers, pot washers, and food waste disposals.

Dishwashers

Many different brands of dishwashers are on the market today, and the buyer should not scrimp on research before purchasing a specific model. Most manufacturers have a series of machines starting with simple models to very sophisticated equipment. The dishwashing process, whether manual or machine driven, consists of scrapping, prewashing, washing, sanitizing, and air-drying.

In choosing the size of a dishwasher to purchase, check the manufacturer's data chart that gives the maximum mechanical capacity of the machine. A factor of 70% should be used to determine what actually happens in the dishroom. Seldom is the maximum attainable. Production of clean dishes will vary depending on the type and efficiency of the dishroom layout, traffic flow, type and length of time the food soil has remained on the dishes, relative hardness of water, skill of the dishwasher operator, and fluctuations in flow of soiled dishes. Suppliers might contend that dishwasher sizing and layout is an art, not pure science.

To illustrate some of the differences in dishwashers, the Hobart brand, one of many good brands, will be used as an example. Dishwashing machines are generally classified by the number of tanks they have. Door, rack conveyor, and flight type continuous racking automatic conveyor dishwashers are the major categories, and are shown in Plate 10.

- **Door.** The Hobart model AM-14C is designed for a corner installation and has two doors that can be manually or automatically opened and one combined wash-and-rinse tank (Plate 10). It holds a rack of dishes that does not move. Dishes are washed by a detergent and water from below. **Scrapping** is a dishwasher term used for disposing of fragments of discarded or leftover food. Recent models also have a rotating wash arm in the top of the machine. Optional accessories include a utility or heavy-duty prerinse spray and a booster heater because the NSF requires a final hot water rinse of 180°F for sanitizing. Chemical sanitization approved by the NSF also is available on some models, thus eliminating the need for a booster. A prerinse table with a source of water and a drain should be purchased and attached to the dishwasher on one side; a long drying table is needed on the other side to air-dry the dishes. Enough racks should be available to eliminate unnecessary handling and contamination of the dishes. In door and rack conveyor dishwashers, each rack can hold approximately

    16 to 18 9-inch plates, or
    25 water glasses, or
    16 coffee cups, or
    100 pieces of flatware (forks, knives, spoons)

    The racks are unloaded at serving time when food is put on plates. Under no circumstances should dishes be dried with bacteria-laden towels; health departments are adamant about this regulation.
- **Rack conveyor.** Dishes are still racked in the C-series models. All of the Hobart C-line automatic rack conveyor dishwashers are listed by the NSF and UL and bear their seals. After dishes are scrapped and sorted, they are placed

in racks designed for plates, cups, or glasses. The racks with soiled dishes are put on a conveyor and come out at the other end clean and dry. The machine has one (Hobart model C-44A, Plate 10), two (Hobart model CPW-80A, Plate 10), or three tanks (Hobart model CPW-100A); the two-tank machine has pre-wash and power-wash tanks, and the three-tank machine has a 36-inch, heavy-duty power prewash, power-wash, and power-rinse. The prewash tank has powerful jets that use overflow detergent water from the power-wash tank to quickly strip soil from the dishes. This model is used in many hospitals because the bacterial count on the clean dishes is very low. A blower-dryer option for the C-line can be added to improve drying of difficult to dry dishware, such as plastic and airline ware, by using high temperature and velocity air.

- **Flight type continuous conveyor.** This dishwasher is especially popular in high-volume operations; Hobart has upgraded its model FT-800 to FT-900. With these machines, plates and trays are placed between rows of plastic pegs on a conveyor; smaller items such as glasses, cups, and flatware are racked before sending them through the machine. The racks are placed directly on the pegs of the conveyor. Flatware usually is presorted, and forks, knives, and spoons are put in separate compartment flatware baskets or plastic cylinders to eliminate extra handling of clean utensils. The machines have an exposed loading section in which the dishes are manually put on the conveyor, an enclosed washing and power-rinsing section, and an exposed unloading section that is longer than the loading end to give the clean dishes more time to dry. A blower-dryer option is available for either a 9- or 11-foot unloading section and is often added to flight-type dishwashers in school foodservice operations that have plastic hard-to-dry compartment trays.

Pot and Pan Washers

Many smaller pots and pans can be washed in a dishwashing machine. The scrapping with a knife or spatula and soaking required for burned-on food particles are usually done at the pot and pan sink close to the production areas. A common procedure is to transport pots and pans that have been prerinsed to the dishwashing machine for washing and sanitizing after the bulk of the dishwashing has been completed.

In large-volume operations, special pot- and pan-washing machines are used for this labor-intensive task. The machines are heavy duty and capable of cleaning cooked-on foods off pots and pans. Pot washing is quite different from dishwashing because pressurized hot water is sprayed directly on the soiled surface.

A piece of equipment called Power Soak (Plate 10) is considered the easiest way to clean pots and pans. Introduced a few years ago, **Power Soak** capitalizes on the natural scouring abilities of high-turbulence, heated water. Maintaining an optimum cleaning temperature of 115°F loosens soil while powerful jets blast clinging particles away. Dirty pots and pans are literally water-blasted clean, thus eliminating handscrubbing. It is so powerful that it can clean dirty hood filters and oven parts. The "power" behind Power Soak is in its recirculating wash pump that dispatches more than 300 gallons of water every minute. At the beginning of the first shift of employees, the tank is filled with warm water and detergent is added. Because the pans are prerinsed and scrapped, the water and detergent will successfully perform for an entire shift. A heating element keeps the temperature at 115°F; the heating element automatically turns on with the presence of water and turns off when the wash tank is emptied.

Power Soak is available in nine basic models with many options. All feature the totally enclosed 1½ HP, fan-cooled motor and powerful industrial wash pump. They are made from 14-gauge, number 304 stainless steel and come in three sizes, all of which have the NSF seal of approval. All models can be ordered for right-to-left or left-to-right operation. A left-to-right model for a small operation is shown in Plate 10. A portable scrapping basket is used in this model. However, in a large operation, the first sink is used to scrap and rinse pans and has a built-in disposal as an option. The second sink, the Power Soak or cleaning tank, is double the size of the others. After a quick prerinse, 10 to 12 pans are put in and thoroughly scoured for 10 to 15 minutes. The third sink is the rinse tank and the fourth the sanitizing tank. The pans are then put on the drain board, which is optional, to air-dry.

This is a fantastic piece of equipment now in use in big foodservice operations, such as large barbecue and pizza restaurants. The Power Soak is a very expensive piece of equipment, but over time the amount of labor saved makes up for the cost. Pot washer employee jobs are probably the most difficult to fill, and the turnover rate is high. The Power Soak full-line system costs between $13,000 and $15,000; however, a number of large hospitals, schools, and colleges are using them. The smaller junior line is sold to restaurant chains for individual stores; Taco Bell, KFC, and Boston Market restaurants currently are using this line, which is more compact and cheaper than the full line.

Food Waste Disposals

Mechanical devices are used in most foodservice facilities to assist in garbage and trash disposal. At a minimum, garbage disposal units should be available in prepreparation, dishwashing, and pot- and pan-washing areas. A **food waste disposal** is a piece of equipment with sharp blades that fits into a sink because a source of water is needed to wash the ground garbage down into a sewer. Not all operations can use disposals, especially if water consumption and sewage use are concerns in the community. Disposals come in various sizes based on the number of meals served per day; different models can handle anywhere from 200 to 4,000 meals per day.

A **pulper** works somewhat like a garbage disposal except it dehydrates the product into a slurry by a shredding device, and then water is pressed out of it. The waste becomes a semidry, degradable pulp ready for disposal; the excess water is recycled in the pulping tank for reuse. Solid waste can be reduced by 85%, which means less space is used in a landfill. Pulpers are a good alternative when disposals cannot be used. Pulpers can handle paper trays, foam, foil, corrugated boxes, bones, food scraps, and some plastics. Pulpers are expensive, costing from $25,000 to $75,000, but manufacturers are beginning to downsize them for use in restaurants and small institutions (Frable, 1996c). Hobart, Champion, Somat, and National Conveyor have developed lower-cost pulpers for around $10,000. Pulpers require a lot of maintenance and cleaning. At the end of the night, the pulper must be broken down and cleaned; otherwise the wad of garbage would be harder than a rock. When considering disposals or pulpers, buyers should check the latest water/sewer department regulations.

Mechanical trash compactors are used for dry bulky trash, such as cans and cartons. Compacting reduces the volume of trash to one fifth of its original bulk.

OTHER EQUIPMENT

Up to this point, only large power-driven equipment—mostly for the production, or kitchen, area—has been discussed. However, nothing would happen in the kitchen if other types of equipment were not available, such as mixers, slicers, tables, knives, and stirring spoons. The receiving area also requires special equipment, including scales, unloading platforms, dollies and hand trucks, short-blade knives for opening cartons, thermometers, file cabinets, and desks, to name a few. Storage, distribution, and service areas require other types of equipment. The buyer would be wise to find local foodservice equipment dealers that have many of these items in stock or can get them quickly. Only some of these are discussed in this text. Production machines, carts, scales, and thermometers are cited used as examples.

Production Machines

Small machines available on the market are mixers, cutter mixers, food cutters, choppers, food processors, and slicers. Vegetable peelers were once popular as well but have become almost extinct in most foodservice operations because potato processors have taken over that task. The mixer with many attachments is the best example of the production machines category. A mixer is as essential as an oven or refrigerator. A foodservice operation could not function without at least one mixer. Hobart mixers have been on the market for more than 75 years. They come in 11 sizes, measured by the capacity of a standard bowl in quarts. The smallest has a 5-quart bowl and the largest a 140-quart bowl. Motors are anywhere from ⅙-horsepower for the 5-quart size to 5-horsepower for the 140-quart. They all have a standard metallic gray polyurethane enamel finish unless a "deluxe" finish is specified. Smaller mixers with 5- to 30-quart bowls have a full range of mixing capabilities and are sold to restaurants, delicatessens, and small bakeries. The 20-quart mixer Hobart model A-200 (Plate 11) is the industry standard and the most popular mixer in the world. The heavy-duty Hobart model D-330 is a small floor model with a 1¼-horsepower motor that handles every application including tough dough-mixing chores. It is a powerful machine. The big 60-quart Hobart model H-600 has been labeled as the kitchen and bakery workhorse.

Heavy-duty stainless steel Bowl Guards are on all models to protect the operator's fingers. Many different kinds of agitators, including flat beaters, wire whips, dough arms, pastry knives, and bowl scrapers, are optional. The bowl scraper improves productivity because the operator does not have to stop the machine three or four times per batch to scrape the food from the sides of the bowl. Hobart mixers have **planetary action:** the agitator revolves around the bowl as it twirls rapidly. Other optional attachments are a vegetable slicer, chopper, and dicer. Mixers of up to 30 quarts are bench models and those from 40 to 140 quarts are floor models.

Carts

Carts have literally taken over foodservice operations. From the time food comes into the building until it reaches the customer, carts are the only mode of transportation in this cycle. Carts are categorized by their functions. Utility carts usually are found in the back of the house, or kitchen; service carts are used in the front of the house, or dining area. Meal delivery carts are used primarily in hospitals, nursing homes, and other noncommercial foodservice operations (Plate 12).

Utility Carts

Utility carts, or back-of-the-house carts, most often are made of 14-gauge stainless steel. They have four 3½- or 4-inch diameter swivel-type rubber casters with brakes on two of them that provide easy maneuverability in limited space aisles, especially if the load is heavy. These carts require limited maintenance. Many utility carts today are made with a polyethylene exterior, and heavy-duty casters bolted to molded metal plates that create quiet, durable carts, such as the Cambro Manufacturing Company Model BC2354-S (Plate 12). They also come in various colors, such as dusty rose, slate blue, and dark brown.

Service Carts

Four types of carts are used in the front of the house for their merchandising appeal. These carts also can be heated or refrigerated. Service carts generally have 5-inch rubber casters, two of which swivel and two with brakes. The buffet cart most often is used as a salad bar or buffet line for breakfast or lunch and then rolled away to the back of the house during full-service dinners. Display carts usually hold a tasty array of desserts to tempt customers. They also may display fresh fruit, wine, or after-dinner drinks. The service cart is wheeled to the table, and the food is served from it. The most common service cart is the carving cart, where the turkey during the holiday season or the ham or roast beef is carved to order at tableside. The fourth type is the preparation cart in which cherries jubilee are flambéed or a Caesar salad is prepared, giving customers a ringside view of the magic of custom preparation. Customers enjoy watching waiters or captains prepare special menu items at the table. The appeal of such showmanship draws customers and upgrades meal checks and tips for the serving personnel. To use carts for effective tableside merchandising, however, means that space must be available between tables and for parking them when not in use. The parking space should be in or near the kitchen to permit loading and replenishment without disturbing patrons.

A whole new line of carts has been introduced. Stainless steel still is the most durable, but it lacks pizzazz. Materials for making service carts attractive to customers have expanded. Serving carts are available in many different colors with frames covered by colored or traditional wood grain vinyl or formica. Carts that are used outside often have umbrellas or canopies over them, such as the Carts of Colorado (Plate 12). Mobile food bars have become very popular at business luncheons, in food courts, on patios, or for poolside service or happy hours. Tough polyethylene surfaces resist scuffs and scratches, while full polyurethane insulation adds strength and excellent temperature retention. These also have a clear full-length breath guard, formerly called a sneeze guard, with end panels that mount directly to the food bar. The Vollrath Company, Inc., which makes smallwares and light equipment, has developed a seven-step Signature Server® program to build mobile servers to operators' individual specifications. Foodservice operators choose the base of the cart, color, breath guards, lights and heating, electrical, accessories, and add-ons. This custom-built equipment is delivered in the same time as most stock items.

Meal Delivery Carts

Meal delivery carts are used mainly in healthcare and correctional facilities (Friedland, 1995). Several types of carts are available, and choosing the right one requires an analysis of the entire meal delivery program, including transportation needs, menu flexibility, and the time that lapses between serving the first and last tray. Some carts only rethermalize, while others offer refrigeration as well. Others can be rolled into refrigerators and connected to an outlet that will allow rethermalization to begin at a preset time, while maintaining proper temperatures for cold foods.

The tray delivery cart in Plate 12 (Seco® model TDCH-1418-28), is a low-profile cart designed for delivery of patient or resident meals on trays to decentralized locations within the facility. This model holds 36 trays. A unitized plastic molded base which holds two bright stainless steel plates sandwiching a patented wax core provides insulation. Initial heat-up time in a base heater is about 2 hours. A dinner plate of hot menu items is placed on the base with a dome over it. The holding time with a noninsulated dome is 140°F for 1 hour; an insulated dome extends holding time another half hour. If cold temperatures are desired, the base can be placed in the freezer for 1 to 2 hours prior to meal time.

A committee with representatives from foodservice, administration, purchasing, and other applicable departments should visit other operations using the equipment to be sure their institution understands and supports the purchase of these carts. The buyer should insist on testing a cart for several days to determine if it fits into the operation. Choosing the appropriate cart should be based upon which options work best for the operation. Just transporting heated and refrigerated carts to another facility poses problems, including size constraints, loading docks, freight elevators, and traveling distance. Other concerns include how quickly foods need to be rethermed, how long the carts must maintain a specific temperature, what type of serviceware is used, and how flexible the menu is. The challenge is to deliver food at the proper temperature. Carts usually are made of stainless steel with removable tray slides of the same material for easy cleaning. Carts usually have four heavy-duty, 6-inch, polyurethane casters, two swivel and two rigid.

Fabricated

Fabricated equipment is defined as a piece of equipment that is designed and made for a specific foodservice operation. Most of this equipment is stainless steel and includes work tables, sinks, dish tables, and any other equipment that makes the flow of work in the operation easier. Quality fabrication means (Steel Edge, 1996):

- tables don't sag
- doors don't warp
- shelves don't bow
- sinks don't leak
- legs don't rust
- kitchen noise isn't deafening

Here are specifics to help ensure that the foodservice operation receives quality fabricated equipment.

- *Gauge.* The higher the gauge of the stainless steel, the lighter the metal. For example, 20-gauge stainless steel is ideal for cabinet doors that do not need to support weight; 14-gauge stainless steel is heavier and is used for work table tops to help ensure stability.
- *Bracing.* Properly bracing the top of the work table, as shown in Figure 15.6, around the full perimeter in addition to the 4-inch-wide, 12-gauge galvanized or stainless steel channel bracing down the center of the underside of the table top eliminates bowing or sagging. Note also the gussets welded to the corners of the framework rather than to the table top. Cross bracing with a sheet of metal welded to the legs eliminates table wobble when heavy pieces of equipment are placed on top.
- *Edges.* Many different types of edges, illustrated in Figure 15.7, can be fabricated on stainless steel table and countertops. For example, a V-edge, referred to as a marine edge, keeps cutting boards from sliding off. A rolled splash edge keeps moisture from running on the floor, while a square edge can be sealed to a wall or another piece of equipment. The type of edge often is a matter of preference.
- *Legs.* To save money, some operations substitute painted steel legs for stainless steel ones. Painted legs do not hold paint well and will become mottled,

Figure 15.6. Bracing a fabricated table top.

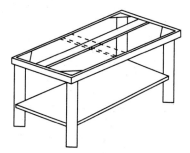

Source: From *Steel Edge, The Newsletter of Low Temp Industries, Inc.,* 1996. Used by permission.

Figure 15.7.   Types of edges on fabricated tables and counter tops.

V or Marine Edge   Square Edge   Rolled Splash Edge

Source: From *Steel Edge, The Newsletter of Low Temp Industries, Inc.,* 1996. Used by permission.

scratched, and pitted from high moisture and acidity and from carts bumping into the legs.

- *Height.* The American Disabilities Act mandates work tables and counters be adjustable from 32 inches and 36 inches to accommodate the handicapped. Unless specified, standard stainless steel bullet feet can only be adjusted 1 inch. Specify a minimum of 4-inch adjustable legs.
- *Warranty.* Insist on a warranty from the fabricator of 1 year for parts and 90 days for additional labor, if needed, for each piece of fabricated equipment.
- *UL listed.* Specify that the fabricated equipment be UL listed to be sure of its safety and quality. The highest quality fabricators are now using UL for their sanitation approval under the UL classification program to NSF standards. This program has been approved by all 50 state sanitation agencies.
- *Service.* Check to see whether the fabricator provides full-time factory field welders who properly finish the job or if that work is subcontracted. How long has the fabricator been in business? Request a list of references for similar facilities that have used the fabricator under consideration.

Since the 1940s and '50s foodservice planning and engineering has developed into a professional and academic discipline (Frable, 1996d). Some of the major components of this new field are the study of human engineering, time motion studies, and work flow design. Today, equipment manufacturers and facility planners are paying attention to human factors engineering and workplace **ergonomics,** which is the application of biological and engineering data to mutual adjustment of man to machine. Ergonomic planning is a requirement in the tray or plate assembly and soiled dish-scrapping areas. In the past few years, a trend in elementary school foodservice counters has been to decrease 36-inch counters to 30 inches for children. Unfortunately, this simple change has been difficult for adults who dip up and serve food at that height. Back problems can occur for tall servers who often must serve for 2 hours at a time. In some operations, stools are provided to workers who are physically challenged and those who are more productive sitting than standing.

SUMMARY

Production equipment is as critical to cost control and profit generating as any other expense in a foodservice operation. Buyers must analyze trends in the foodservice business to choose the best equipment for making menu items that will keep customers satisfied and profits high. They must know more than a model number to purchase production equipment. In most operations, a foodservice design consultant is hired to help the manager make decisions about what to buy. The consultant can work with the architect and foodservice manager and assume the responsibility of seeing that the best equipment at the lowest price is purchased. The consultant also is very knowledgeable about choosing equipment that meets HACCP regulations.

The production equipment buyer needs to know how the equipment operates, how to maintain it, how cost effective it is, and what options are needed. In the cooking equipment category, buyers need to understand the source of heat and how heat is transferred from the equipment to the food. Steam-jacketed kettles and steamers are used in moist cooking most often in noncommercial operations. Dry heat equipment is necessary for broiling, frying, roasting, and baking and produces the most popular menu items. Just purchasing an oven can be quite a chore because range, deck, convection, conveyor, microwave, smoker, and low-temp cooking and holding ovens are available on the market. Because they conserve expensive space, multifunction equipment is becoming more popular. As a result, combi-ovens, tilting skillets, and convection/microwave ovens are showing up in more foodservice operations.

Refrigerated equipment is among the most important equipment on the market today, especially as equipment manufacturers meet the challenge of the 1997 FDA Model Food Code. Manufacturers are producing smaller refrigerators that can be placed in various units of the kitchen rather than in one or two large refrigerators. The number of blast chillers on the market today has increased greatly because food temperatures can be lowered in less than 2 hours, which is impossible in large refrigerators. Ice machines were always difficult to clean but have been improved to meet HACCP requirements.

Warewashing includes dishwashers, pot and pan machines, food waste disposals, and pulpers. The biggest equipment expenditure is the dishwasher to clean dishes, glasses, and eating utensils. Much research is required before purchasing this long-term investment. Special equipment is available for pot and pan washing.

Power-driven production machines, especially mixers, are a requirement in foodservice operations. Mixers come in various sizes with different motor sizes. A variety of carts are being used more and more. Fabricated equipment, including work and dish tables, counters, and sinks, usually is custom designed to fit into a specific area of the operation.

REFERENCES

Bendall, D. (1997). Ranges and griddles. *Food Management, 32*(3), 89, 91, 94.

Equipment purchasing outlook: A supplement to Restaurants & Institutions. (1994).

Fellin, T. A. (1996). Oven overview. *School Foodservice and Nutrition, 50*(9), 63, 66.

Frable, F. (1994a). Is purchasing used equipment a wise decision? *Nation's Restaurant News, 128*(40), 36, 62.

Frable, F. (1994b). Timing is key to new, renovated kitchens. *Nation's Restaurant News, 28*(41), 24, 28.

Frable, F. (1996a). Finding the 'sweet spot' in equipment pricing. *Nation's Restaurant News, 30*(27), 26, 28.

Frable, F. (1996b). Manage equipment maintenance, replacement with software. *Nation's Restaurant News, 30*(1), 58, 63.

Frable, F. (1996c). New, low-cost pulpers merit a rethinking of waste disposal. *Nation's Restaurant News, 30*(5), 39, 51.

Frable, F. (1996d). Enhance operational efficiencies with improved ergonomics. *Nation's Restaurant News, 30*(32), 92, 95.

Friedland, A. (1995). Rethermalization carts. *Food Management, 30*(1), 44.

Handbook of steam equipment: A guide to understanding steam cooking equipment. (Undated). North American Association of Food Equipment Manufacturers Publication 94.11.

Industry Council on Food Safety. (1997). The Education Foundation of the National Restaurant Association. Chicago, IL.

Miller, L. (1996). Healthy meals by design. *School Foodservice and Nutrition, 50*(11), 35–38.

NSF listings—Food equipment and related products, components, and materials. (1997, March 27). National Sanitation Foundation.

Spears, M. C. (1995). *Foodservice organizations: A managerial and systems approach* (3rd ed.). Upper Saddle River, NJ: Merrill/Prentice Hall.

The standard of excellence. (1997). NSF International.

Underwriters Laboratories Inc.® (1993). *Foodservice equipment.* Northbrook, Illinois.

Wallace, J. (1996). Is new equipment in your future? *Restaurants & Institutions, 106*(5), 48.

What's hot, what's not in food service. (1996). *Steel Edge, The Newsletter of Low Temp Industries, 1*(1), 1–4.

16

Service Equipment

Production equipment is required in a foodservice operation to produce menu items that satisfy customers, but if the food is not served in an attractive atmosphere, customers are not likely to return. Foodservice managers need to concentrate on making the dining experience a pleasant one. Elegant china, beautiful glassware, and polished silver create a decor for a fine dining restaurant. An attractive hospital tray of food can perk up the appetite of a patient who might not feel like eating if the food were served on a chipped heavy white or tan speckled china plate. School and college foodservice operations have much better participation when managers put some thought into presentation of the food. They don't need to switch to china when plastic products today look so much like finer tableware. If meals are attractively presented and the dining area is exciting, students will return.

This chapter covers the purchasing of china, glassware, flatware, disposables, smallwares, detergents, uniforms, and service contracts. These are just a few of the many items available to improve the decor of a foodservice operation. The manufacturers of tableware typically hire manufacturer's representatives who do not take title, bill, or set prices but serve as a go-between for the manufacturer and supplier. The supplier often doubles as the foodservice equipment dealer. The best source for many end users, or foodservice managers, is a local foodservice equipment dealer with a large showroom and displays. If managers cannot find exactly what they need, the dealer has catalogs and can suggest sources for purchasing those products. A good example of this chain-of-command is the Sweetheart Cup Company, Inc., in Baltimore. The company has 150 manufacturer's reps all over the country who call on foodservice operations and help managers with decisions about which products would best meet their needs. Offices and expenses for the reps plus a salary and a percentage of sales are paid by the manufacturer.

TABLEWARE

Choosing the right tableware for a particular foodservice operation is no simple task. Webster's Dictionary defines **tableware** as "china, glassware, silver, and other utensils used for setting a table or serving food and drink." Tableware sets the tone for what is to come. Will the dining experience be "gourmet" with fine china, crystal, and sterling silver flatware? Will it be served family-style on pottery dishes, heavy glass tumblers, and stainless steel flatware? Or is it quick service, with a disposable insulated food container or grease-resistant french fry paper bag, 32-ounce jumbo "big drink" paper cup with a lid and drinking straw, and plastic cutlery?

Another example of a foodservice tableware supplier is World Tableware, Inc., with headquarters in Dallas and warehouse locations in Honolulu, Laredo, Texas, Los Angeles, Toronto, and West Chicago, Ill. World Tableware roots go back to 1847, when it became one of the first U.S. manufacturers of silverplated flatware. The company also manufactures other products to specifications. Its products are sold to foodservice equipment dealers, such as Edward Don, Sysco, and Rycoff-Sexton. World Tableware promotes its Total Tabletop® as the only complete line of tabletop products in the world (Figure 16.1). What the company does not manufacture, it purchases from other manufacturers. It offers a wide selection of products for every price range, including:

Figure 16.1. Total Tabletop®
logo.

Source: World Crisa, 1996. Used by permission.

- fine porcelain dinnerware, from the exquisite to the economical
- complete assortment of quality glassware and specialty items
- flatware settings from elegant silverplate to budget-conscious stainless steel
- complete line of holloware, buffetware, and accessories to suit every occasion

Dinnerware

Most china used in U.S. foodservice operations is made right here. The biggest competitor is the Orient, where fine china is made cheaper than it is in the United States because workers' salaries are much lower. U.S. companies making china dinnerware are located primarily in Ohio, West Virginia, New York, and Pennsylvania because of the quality of the clay in these states. The Syracuse China Company in Syracuse, N.Y., the Hall China Company in East Liverpool, Ohio, and the Homer Laughlin China Company in Newell, W.V., are three well-known U.S. manufacturers of china.

Types

China is a clay-like product that is blended with other compounds and molded or formed into the required shape. Fine and foodservice china, pottery, and plastic are the major types of dinnerware used in commercial and noncommercial foodservice operations. Each type is manufactured differently.

China.   **Fine china,** usually purchased for the home, is a term applied to a thin, translucent, vitrified body, generally fired twice: first at a relatively high temperature to mature the clay and other materials and secondly to develop the high gloss of beautiful glaze. To **vitrify** china is to change the raw materials into glass crystals by increasing the temperature of firing to bring them closer together to give a glasslike finish. This process gives American vitrified china its strength. Sometimes, china intended for home use finds its way into a restaurant where it too quickly becomes a pile of broken pieces in the rough and tumble atmosphere of a commercial kitchen (Durocher, 1992).

Foodservice China.   Purchasing china for a foodservice operation should not be an impulsive or last-minute decision. Restaurateurs can expect to lose 15% to 20% of their china stock each year, and losses can be significantly higher when noncommercial china is used. Even though the look of bone china or porcelain might be appealing, buying it could be an expensive mistake. The type and thickness of the glaze on restaurant china will drastically affect durability. China should be covered with abrasion-resistant glazes that do not crack or craze. **Crazing** is caused by a difference in the expansion characteristics of the china body and the glaze. Astute restaurant managers purchase china that is glazed on the top and base, called the foot, of the plate. Otherwise, a stack of plates will wobble on a rolling dishcart. If the base is not glazed, it will quickly abrade the glazed top of the plate below it. Buyer also should take a close look at the handles of cups to examine their thickness and how they attach to the bowl. If the joint appears to be rough or cracked, the chances of losing a handle are increased.

Some colors can be applied before the final glaze coat is applied and fired. Other colors, such as gold, are applied over the glaze and thus are prone to deterioration with use. Buyers should be aware of the composition of colors, particularly those that are applied over the glaze. Lead is the most common concern, but other heavy metals and chemicals also should be checked. Purchasing china with underglaze colors makes the chance of lead release almost impossible.

The Syracuse China Company has been a leader in the manufacture of chinaware products in North America since 1871. Like most other dinnerware companies, the company has established a network of over 60 manufacturer's representatives who support more than 300 suppliers in the United States and Canada. The export division sells to more than 100 countries worldwide. The Syracuse Company has three categories of commercial china: Hospitality Express, Syracuse Select, and made-to-order Standard Custom patterns. Hospitality Express has 32 patterns ready to ship anywhere in the world within 36 hours of the order. Syracuse Select patterns are shipped in 30 days or less, and made-to-order Standard Custom patterns are shipped as soon as the artists have them ready.

Trends.   The trend in the '90s has been toward simplicity. Most restaurants are using basic white china with a rim and maybe a little line on it; the Greyson pattern is shown in Plate 13. Note that the rim holds the pasta on the plate, preventing it from sliding off. Oversize plates, 11 to 12 inches in diameter, are popular partly because of the value message they send to customers. Hotels usually select a simple, fine white china that often is custom-made with the hotel's logo. The china usually has rolled edges and rims embossed with a simple pattern. Chefs often prefer to let the food do the talking, but managers want to bring some color to the table. They have found that using a few attention-getting pieces of china for signature menu items adds style without detracting from the food.

Purchasing.   Purchasing dinnerware for a foodservice operation entails many choices. As the stock of dinnerware diminishes, either it needs to be replenished or new china must be purchased. A problem might be that the dinnerware is no longer available. When it was first purchased, it was open stock. Technically, **open stock** means that the product is always available, but for various reasons even open stock has some time limitations. Perhaps, sales of a particular type of dinnerware have declined drastically and the cost effectiveness of manufacturing more is low. The foodservice manager must choose another type; perhaps the foodservice equipment dealer will buy back the old when the manager purchases new china. If the manager does not feel secure in making the decision alone, he or she can solicit assistance from other people. The foodservice design consultant is more a back-of-the-house expert, but the foodservice equipment dealer from whom the manager would be buying the dinnerware, glasses, and flatware might be an excellent resource. Many dealers have a decorator or designer on staff or available to consult, thus relieving the manager from making the decision alone.

Determining how much china is needed for an operation depends on the number of people who would be eating at one time. China manufacturers and foodservice dealers have developed a formula that indicates the quantity of each item needed by restaurant, quick-service, cafeteria, banquet/catering, and noncommercial operations. To determine the quantity of each item, multiply the number of seats by an ordering factor as shown in Table 16.1. For example, a 5½-inch bread and butter plate for a 125-seat cafeteria = 6 × 125 = 750 plates, rounded to 63 dozen. The foodservice equipment dealer has similar information on quantity to purchase for glassware and flatware.

To keep up with the competition, manufacturers are giving warranties on some products. The foodservice buyer would be wise to check warranties on expensive dinnerware. A **warranty** is a written guarantee given to the buyer that states the manufacturer will for a period of time be responsible for the repair or replacement of the defective product. The Syracuse China Company warrants products against edge chipping for 3 years from date of purchase and will replace or provide equivalent substitutes one-for-one at no charge for any piece found to be defective. Libbey, Inc., has a commitment to quality when it guarantees that if any glass covered by the Safedge® warranty chips, Libbey will replace or refund the price of the glass when it is returned to the dealer from whom it was originally purchased. Of course, this warranty does not cover breakage.

Most tableware is sold by the dozen: 1 dozen plates, 1 dozen tumblers, or 1 dozen teaspoons. All of these are packed in cases; for example, 7½-ounce coffee cups are packed 3 dozen to a 1.1-cubic-foot carton weighing 21 pounds, and 12½-inch platters are packed 1 dozen to a 0.8-cubic-foot carton weighing 32 pounds. Seldom will dealers sell fewer than a dozen pieces. Most are reluctant to break a case.

Pottery.   The Hall China Company was founded in 1903 in East Liverpool, Ohio. The first chinaware to bear the trade name Hall China were combinets, a lidded pot known as a chamber pot, and spittoons. Robert Taggart Hall experimented with the possibility of developing a glaze that would withstand the heat required for bisque firing, making possible single-fire ware without cracking. **Bisque** is unglazed ceramic ware that is not glazed but is hard-fired and resembles glass. Finally, in 1911, the first successful leadless glazed chinaware was produced by the single-fire process at a firing temperature of 2400°F. At this same time, Hall China also demonstrated the capability of producing chinaware not only in standard white but in a variety of colors.

Hall China is proud of its Super Express Service, which guarantees every item in the catalog is in packed stock and available for immediate shipment. Hall China is designed to be the most chip resistant in critical wear areas such as the rim, bottom, and side walls. It can go from freezer to oven to table. Hall's Chinaware is

Table 16.1.   Amount of china needed for various foodservice operations.

Item	Suggested Use	Restaurant Dining	Fast Dining	Cafeteria	Banquet/ Catering	Institutional
5½"-6⅝" Plate	Bread & Butter, Deserts, Bowl or Bouillon Underliner	1½	2	6	2	2
7½"-7⅞" Plate	Sandwiches, Salad, Desserts, Underliner for Grapefruit, Salad Bowls	1½	2	•	2	•
8½"-9⅛" Plate	Luncheon, Entree, Tray Dinner Plate, Pastries, Underliner for Salad Plate	1½	2	2	2	2
9¾"-10" Plate	Dinner, Breakfast, Luncheon, Steaks, Underliner for Salad	1½	3	2	1½	•
10¼"-10⅜" Plate	Entree, Steaks, Prime Ribs, Fish, Mexican Dishes, Service Plate, Fowl	2	2	•	2	•
Coffee/Tea Cup	Coffee, Tea, Hot Chocolate, Soup	3	3	2	2	2
Mug	Hot & Cold Beverages	3	3	2	2	2
Coffee/Tea Saucer	Underliner for Cups, Bouillon, Tray Fruit	3	3	2	2	2
4¼"-5" Fruit	"Monkey" Dish for Vegetables, Fruits, Puddings, Desserts, Bake & Serve	2	3	6	2½	3
8⅞"-9¼" Rim Deep Soup	A la Carte Soup, Salad, Pasta, Chili, Oyster Stew, Bouillabaisse	½	½	•	½	•

Source: Syracuse China Company, 1997. Used by permission.

microwave-proof and oven-proof to 450°F. It is thermal shock resistant and retains heat and cold, assuring that hot entrées stay hot and cold salads stay fresh and crisp. Because it is made of dense raw materials, the industry's highest firing temperature (2400°F) is used. This results in stronger china bodies and glazes. Lead-free glazes bond with the china body and protect it from chipping, crazing, and color loss, resulting in clean, brilliant colors that do not fade or wear away.

In addition to place-setting china, Hall Chinaware includes **pottery,** which is dense china. Elegant shapes are combined with practical portion control, such as soup, salad, and pasta bowls, cook-and-serve entrée bowls and bakers (Plate 13), and ramekins and custard cups. It also is made into center-of-the-table and accessories, including a complete selection of colored flower vases, salt and pepper shakers, sauce boats, butter warmers, butter dishes, jelly dishes, and more in a wide variety of colors, shapes, and sizes. Colorful sugars, creamers, teapots, coffee pots, and pitchers help add excitement to beverage presentations. Latté cups, cappuccino cups, expresso cups, and more also are available to complement specialty coffee service.

The Homer Laughlin China Company started out as a two-kiln pottery in East Liverpool, Ohio, in 1871. In 1907, it was moved across the Ohio River to West Virginia. A noted ceramist was hired and in 1936 Fiesta® became the best-selling line of pottery in the country. It remains today one of the most collected china products in the world. Until 1959, Homer Laughlin made only semivitrified earthenware products, but with a new fully vitrified product, the company entered the restaurant/hotel markets. The reintroduction of Fiesta® in 1986 as a high-fire, fully vitrified, lead-free product redefined the standard for both foodservice and retail products. New contemporary colors, shown in Plate 13, are used, and all shapes are cast from original molds. The rimless plates' shape allows maximum food plating surface, and sculpted concentric rings highlight and frame the food presentation. All Fiesta® shapes and colors are lead-free as a result of much research, major capital investments, and new manufacturing methods. The new and improved china of the Homer Laughlin China Co. meets the most stringent health and safety laws now in existence or proposed.

Plastic.   The Cambro Manufacturing Company in California makes all kinds of attractive and practical plastic dinnerware for school lunch programs, healthcare facilities, and outdoor catering parties. Camware dinnerware, which is approved by the National Sanitation Foundation (NSF), is available in a variety of shapes, configurations, and colors. The products are made from polycarbonate plastic, which is tough and virtually unbreakable. It is not, however, microwavable, which is true for most dinnerware plastics. Cambro does have plastic H-Pans™ that are designed for extreme temperatures ranging from −40°F to +375°F and are perfect for the microwave oven or steam table. They also are easier to clean than stainless steel and are quiet and do not bend or dent.

Melamine plastic dishware is considered some of the best on the market. Melamine starts out as four components: melamine crystal, formalin, alpha cellulose, and water. The four ingredients are processed by a melamine molding compound manufacturer. Once these ingredients are processed, they are then ready for molding. The product is shaped by a steel mold. The material is placed in the mold, and through a process of intense pressure and temperature, the chemical structure of this product is altered and a dinnerware piece is produced. In 1997, Carlisle Foodservice Products acquired the Plastic Manufacturing Company's Foodservice Division, including all its melamine products.

Melamine plastic resists breaks, stains, and scratches and is dishwasher safe. Durus®, Texas Ware®, Dallas Ware®, and Epicure® are the four types of melamine dinnerware on the market today. Durus® is the highest quality and heaviest weight melamine dinnerware available. It also is the highest priced of the four types. It looks and feels like china and has minimum scratch and stain problems because of a unique glaze. It has a quick drying time because of the advanced vented foot design, which raises the plates and cups higher than the counter, and a slick water-sheeting glazed surface. The color of the dinnerware has been the traditional bone, ivory, and sand, but Carlisle has just introduced the Durus® Caribbean line that has four fun new colors: honey yellow, meadow green, ocean blue, and sunset orange.

Dallas Ware® is considered the "workhorse" of the industry. It is durable, has superior stain and scratch resistance, and is NSF listed. It comes in pastel green and yellow, ivory, tan, and white colors. Cafe blue has recently been added. Texas Ware® comes in the same colors and is the cheapest of all four brands. Epicure® comes only in white and is a little more expensive than Texas Ware®. All four of these melamine products are NSF listed.

One of the biggest sellers of melamine is the compartment tray used in most of the school lunch programs. The foodservice director of a large Texas school district noted that "the trays really take a beating from the kids, but they are the most durable trays that I have ever used. On top of that, the trays also resist stains and maintain their appearance." The trays are designed with greater sloping compartment walls and stacking lugs on the bottom for easy draining and fast drying (Plate 14). The NSF-listed trays have a smooth shiny surface that resists bacterial growth.

Carlisle gives a two-year warranty for breakage of melamine dinnerware. Most plates, small bowls, cups, and saucers are packed 48 pieces to a case; pasta/soup/chef salad bowls are packed 24 to a case. Platters and compartment plates, which are much larger than other dinnerware, are packed 12 to a case. Price by the piece is quoted to the customer. A word of caution about washing melamine products: The foodservice manager should ask the detergent salesperson what kind of solution should be used, and employees should be told to avoid abrasive or copper and brass scouring pads when removing stains. A woven plastic pad or soft brush will give the best results without dulling the lustrous finish. Do NOT put melamine dishes in a microwave oven because one of the components of melamine is water, which has a tendency to dissipate and create a brittle part in the dish that is more apt to shatter than is a dish that is not microwaved.

Glassware

For over 175 years, Libbey® has been North America's leading designer, manufacturer, and marketer of high-quality glass tableware for the foodservice industry. Today, Libbey is the leading producer of glass tableware, with more than 800 items to fit customers' needs. Most glassware manufacturing companies are located in lower Michigan and upper Ohio because these states have silicon sand and gas wells. The silicon sand and other materials are fused together in gas furnaces to produce a glassy substance that cools down to a rigid condition, which can be blown or pressed. The Libbey glass factory is in Toledo, Ohio, and the Anchor Hocking factory is in Lancaster, Ohio.

Pressed glassware and blown glassware are being manufactured today. **Pressed glassware** is given its shape by pouring melted glass under pressure into a mold, thus making it resistant to thermal and mechanical shock. It is recommended for quick-service operations. **Blown glassware** is shaped by forcing air into a ball of melted glass. Glassblowing was a profession for many years, but today the process has been mechanized.

Types

Glassware might be fine stemware, heavy, shatterproof tumblers, or plastic. Two basic types of glass are used in foodservice glassware: lead crystal and lime glass. Several different types of transparent plastic are used in permanent and disposable plastic glasses.

Lead Crystal.   Crystal, because of its expense, is used mostly in hotels, white tablecloth restaurants, and private clubs. **Lead crystal** is glass with lead oxide added to give the product brilliance and clarity. Lead crystal is noted for a pleasant ringing tone when struck lightly with a fingertip. Today the glass-making art produces lime glass stemware that is so similar to crystal that the untrained eye cannot distinguish one from the other. Some lime glass will ring as well instead of just clinking.

Lime Glass.   **Lime glass** contains a substantial proportion of lime, which is used in most commercial glass products, such as bottles, tumblers, and windows. Foodservice operations use it almost exclusively.

Standard lime glassware is **annealed,** or slowly cooled to room temperature after it has been formed. It tends to chip easily and, when broken, will shatter into large, sharp pieces. A typical annealed glass tumbler will withstand about 250 to 300 dishwashings, and stemware will take less wear. **Tempered** lime glass is cooled quickly after it is formed. It is more resistant to chipping and, when it breaks, it tends to form smaller, pebble-like pieces, which are not so dangerous. However, tempered glass is not more resistant to thermal shock than other types of glass. **Thermal shock** is caused by sharply heating or cooling a glass, as when pouring cold liquid into a hot glass. A thick-walled tumbler is more subject to thermal shock than a thin-walled glass because the thick glass cannot dissipate heat as quickly. Both tempered and annealed glass scratch at about the same rate. In fact, scratching is the main reason after breakage for removing glassware from service.

Should you use tumblers or stemware? The decision should be based upon the cost and the impression you wish to give your customers. Fine dining restaurants often choose stemware, as shown in Figure 16.2. The choice generally is tumblers in coffee shops and family restaurants, although stemware is used when wine is served. A compromise found in moderate-priced operations is the **footed goblet,** which has a bowl like stemware, but the bowl attaches directly to the disklike base. The footed goblet generally has thicker walls and is far more sturdy than stemware.

Plastic.   Plastic "glassware" is obviously a misnomer because it is made of plastic, not glass. Permanent and disposable types are available on the market. Permanent plastic glasses usually are called tumblers. Plastic is softer than glass and is therefore more easily scratched. For that reason, plastic tumblers are pebbled, which tends to hide these surface scratches. They are usually stackable, which

Figure 16.2.   Types of glass-ware.

Source: Libbey, Inc., 1997. Used by permission.

requires that they have **lugs,** a projection or ridge either inside or outside the tumbler to prevent jamming when stored. Plastic tumblers come in many colors and are dishwasher safe.

Purchasing

How much glassware should be in stock? Most glassware manufacturers provide charts that give average quantities for different types of operations. For example, one chart lists 24 dozen water glasses for a 100-seat restaurant that has from one and a half to two turns per meal period. A 100-seat coffee shop with three turns an hour during peak periods could require as many as 36 dozen. However, a fine dining restaurant with 100 seats that has only one turn or less per hour might require only 15 to 18 dozen. Individual needs may vary from the charts.

Some managers believe that the supply should be large enough to wash glasses during slack periods. However, bartenders who must wash glasses during peak periods cannot wait on customers, and refill business could be lost. The stock level for bar glasses should be kept up to a point where a shortage will not occur. Thus, ordering glassware should be an automatic procedure. Glasses, like food, are a consumable item used up in normal operations. Even when glasses are not broken, constant handling will eventually scratch them; at that time, they should be removed from service. Employees should be taught how to handle glassware properly.

Flatware

Flatware usually refers to forks, knives, spoons, and other eating utensils. Flatware does not have to look as if it were designed for restaurant or hospital use. In the wide range of different styles and shapes is everything from elegant pieces to heavy, solid designs that might have been used in pubs throughout the early days of our country. In selecting flatware, the foodservice manager must decide what would look best with dinnerware and glassware already chosen. Flatware has a longer life than either and therefore should be versatile enough to go with different china and glass patterns.

Composition

Composition is important in choosing flatware. Cost also is a factor. Flatware can be silver-plated or stainless steel.

Silverplated. The finest restaurants still use silverplated flatware that actually becomes more beautiful and durable with use. Oneida® Foodservice in Oneida, N.Y., considered America's leading tabletop supplier to the foodservice industry, plates the base metal with nickel before plating with silver. This hard intermediate plating gives the silverplate extra resistance to damage from scratches. Nickel also acts like a primer to give the silverplate a stronger silver bond that will not chip or peel. After nickel plating, a special "balanced" plating of extra silver is deposited on the back of each piece for longer wear. Not all silverplating companies use such a thorough process; therefore, their products cost less than Oneida® flatware.

Stainless Steel. Stainless steel flatware is used in many foodservice operations; the top quality often is identified as silverplate. Oneida® manufactures the finest 18/8 (18% chrome, 8% nickel) stainless that has a warm, silver-like appearance. The rich blend of chrome and nickel gives maximum protection against corrosion and attacks by food and cleaning chemicals. The 18% chrome stainless provides excellent resistance to corrosion and attacks by food, even in the most demanding commercial applications. In addition, it costs less than the 18/8 stainless. Also, a 13% chrome stainless product has an adequate chrome content to guard against rust and corrosion. This is the best choice when low initial investment is the overriding factor.

Holloware

Holloware is a metal container that usually holds a food product. Even though it is not flatware, Holloware is usually manufactured from the same materials. Coffee servers, teapots, water pitchers, sauce boats, creamers, and sugar bowls are examples of holloware (Plate 15). The most elegant holloware is molded from solid, heavy gauge nickel silver alloy. All mounts and attachments are hard soldered with silver solder to eliminate breakage. The finest heavyweight 18/8 stainless steel holloware is built to withstand many years of use. It is bright mirror polished and also available in a silverplated finish.

Purchasing

Flatware is sold as place settings or individual pieces. A **place setting** usually consists of a dinner fork, knife, and teaspoon plus a salad fork and a soup spoon or another teaspoon. The most common additions to the basic place settings are a butter spreader, cocktail fork, cream soup spoon, and iced teaspoon. Each of the basic pieces has many variations. For example, a fork has a minimum of seven

Figure16.3. Fork identification guide.

Source: World Tableware Inc., 1996. Used by permission.

types from dinner fork to salad fork to pastry fork (Figure 16.3). A knife has 10 types from dinner knife to steak knife to butter knife (Figure 16.4). And a spoon has eight types from a teaspoon to a round bowl soup spoon to a tablespoon or serving spoon (Figure 16.5). Note the number of serrated knives in Figure 16.4. Today, most knives have serrated blades because customers want a knife that can cut through menu items.

Flatware may be stamped with a name or logo on either the front or back, as permitted by the pattern. Most stamping jobs require at least two dies and usually three because the lettering needs to be in proper proportion to handle sizes. A **die** is a device used to stamp initials or a seal on the handles of flatware. For example, a teaspoon, fork, and knife each need a different size die because the handles are different sizes. Die charges are invoiced according to the following approximate list prices:

Letter die (any style)	$340.00
Monogram or crest die	$390.00
Hollow handle knife die (any type)	$450.00

Ownership of the stamping dies remains with customers who order and pay for them.

Figure 16.4. Knife identification guide.

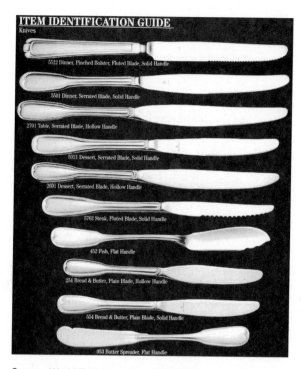

Source: World Tableware Inc., 1996. Used by permission.

Figure 16.5. Spoon identification guide.

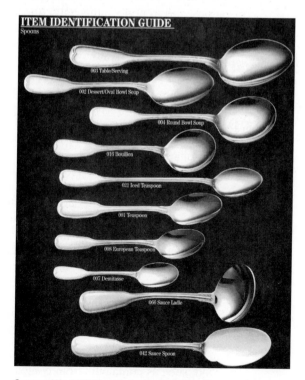

Source: World Tableware Inc., 1996. Used by permission.

FOODSERVICE DISPOSABLES

"Foodservice disposables are indispensable!" (Figure 16.6) is the trademark slogan of the **Foodservice & Packaging Institute** (FPI), founded in 1933. It is the material-neutral trade association for manufacturers, raw material suppliers, machinery suppliers, and distributors of foodservice disposable products. The FPI's mission is to promote the sanitary, safety, functional, economic, and environmental benefits of single-use foodservice containers and packaging. FPI supports the environmentally responsible manufacture, distribution, use, and disposal of these products.

Single-use foodservice and packaging products include:

- cups, plates, bowls, bags, wraps, cutlery, trays, and hinged-lid "clamshell" containers used for salads and sandwiches
- containers for use in microwaves and conventional ovens
- nested containers for packaging ice cream, cottage cheese, sour cream, yogurt, and other food products
- meat, produce, and other prepackaging trays
- egg cartons
- doilies and placemats

Foodservice disposables typically are used at home; in commercial foodservice, including quick-service, convenience store, take-out, home-delivery, and concession operations; and in noncommercial settings, such as school cafeterias, hospitals, corporations, nursing homes, and correctional facilities.

Environmental Benefits

FPI supports the environmentally responsible manufacture, distribution, use, and disposal of these products. The 1993 Food Code of the Food and Drug Administration (FDA), which serves as a model for state and local public health standards, spells out the sanitary and health advantages of foodservice disposables: "In situations in which the reuse of multiuse items could result in foodborne illness to consumers, single service and single-use articles must be used to assure safety." If cups, glasses, plates, flatware, and other reusable items cannot be properly cleaned and sanitized due to inadequate facilities or equipment, the FDA specifically directs foodservice operators to use disposables.

Two environmental misconceptions are that single-use foodservice containers contribute disproportionately to the municipal solid waste stream and that ozone-depleting chlorofluorocarbons, or CFCs, are used to produce polystyrene foam foodservice containers (Foodservice and Packaging Institute, 1995). In fact, single-use foodservice containers make up less than 1% of the total solid waste stream in the United States, and most of the products were never manufactured using CFCs. In general, FPI members have entered into environmental conservation programs that include recycling, source reduction, energy recovery, composting, and litter reduction.

- *Recycling programs.* Internally, FPI members recycle everything that is not food, such as containers from company cafeterias, packaging, plastic bags, bottles, cans, and other items. Externally, FPI members have programs that collect and recycle egg cartons, school lunch trays, and cups and plates.

Figure 16.6. Trademark of Foodservice and Packaging Institute.

Source: Foodservice and Packaging Institute, Inc., 1997. Used by permission.

- *Source reduction programs.* Reduction occurs in weight or volume of materials used in a package without changing its capacity. FPI members have decreased materials used in packaging while maintaining the strength and protective function of the container through technological advances and package redesign.
- *Energy recovery programs.* Some FPI member companies use combustible waste to produce energy that reduces the amount of waste sent to landfills and the amount of natural resources used to produce energy. Since foodservice containers do not have toxic materials, inks, or dyes, burning them in waste-to-energy incinerators does not harm the environment.
- *Composting programs.* FPI member companies are composting foodservice organic wastes, including difficult-to-recycle paper.
- *Litter reduction programs.* FPI members sponsor and participate in many litter reduction and prevention programs and also have developed materials to educate the community about litter, the environment, and waste management.

Materials that come in contact with food are regulated under the Federal Food, Drug, and Cosmetics Act and Food Additive Amendments. Under these provisions a food additive, including materials used to manufacture food-contact packaging, may not be marketed without prior FDA approval. Before materials are improved, manufacturers must submit scientific and technical data through a formal petition process.

Manufacturing

The manufacturing of disposables begins in the factory where raw materials, such as polystyrene sheet, paper stock, and molded pulp are handled with attention to cleanliness throughout every step of the production process as they are made into hundreds of types of disposable foodservice items. Manufacturers are careful to safeguard foodservice disposables from all sources of contamination. Disposables are tested and then packaged to protect them during shipment to foodservice operations.

Once the disposables are received, the buyer needs to be sure that they are properly stored. According to the FDA Food Code:

- Store cartons at least 6 inches above the floor in a clean, dry location where they will not be contaminated.
- Keep them away from pesticides, detergents, and cleaning compounds.
- Do not touch the eating surfaces of unwrapped containers, cups, or plates.
- Remove only disposables that are needed and keep the rest in the original storage container that is reclosed immediately.

Employees should be trained to

- Handle containers as little as possible by working off the top of the stack of disposable plates, bowls, cups, and containers.
- Hold cups and bowls by the side or bottom, keeping fingers away from any food-contact surface.
- Pick up forks, knives, and spoons by the handles only. Individually wrapped utensils eliminate this problem.

Purchasing

As previously mentioned, most foodservice disposables are purchased through foodservice dealers. Using the Sweetheart Cup Company, Inc., as an example of a manufacturer, the number of products on the market is unbelievable. The company has strategically located plants, a network of warehouses, and state-of-the-art computerized operations that assure customers of fast, dependable, just-in-time delivery. Much emphasis has been placed on Sweetheart Cup's total quality management style. The company has the largest sales force in the industry, consisting of well-trained sales representatives who consult with foodservice managers on how their products and programs can make the operation more profitable.

Buyers for operations that use disposables should request a catalog from their foodservice dealer before making decisions on what to buy. Sweetheart is the largest manufacturer and supplier of single service products, offering the broadest range of paper, plastic, and foam products. Using cups as an example:

- Paper cups are made from paper stock, the weight of which increases with size of the cup, that is either untreated or coated with wax inside and outside for cold drinks or lined with plastic for hot drinks.
- Plastic cups are made from clear, durable soft plastic that is strong and shatterproof or from strong, lightweight, translucent polystyrene.
- Foam cups are made of tough, lightweight, and foamlike materials that insulate liquids, keeping them hot or cold. They are the cheapest disposable cup and often are used for giving samples of coffee to customers.

Table 16.2.   Specifications for hot drink cups.

Stock Number	Description	Packing		Lbs. Per Case	Case Cube	Referral Page
		Bag	Case			
Paper Cups						
Hot Drink Cups						13
P504	4 oz.	20/50	1,000	9.0	1.3	
HP504	4 oz. Handled	20/50	1,000	10.0	1.3	
P506	6 oz.	20/50	1,000	17.0	2.3	
HP506	6 oz. Handled	20/50	1,000	19.0	2.3	
P508	8 oz.	20/50	1,000	20.5	2.7	
HP508	8 oz. Handled	20/50	1,000	22.5	2.7	
P510	10 oz.	20/50	1,000	25.0	2.9	
PS510	10 oz. Squat	20/50	1,000	26.0	3.9	
P512	12 oz.	20/50	1,000	28.0	3.2	
P516	16 oz.	20/50	1,000	36.5	4.2	
P520	20 oz.	20/50	1,000	41.5	4.4	

Source: Sweetheart Foodservice Products and Merchandising, 1995. Used by permission.

The major classifications of cups are paper; vending, which are specially tapered for low, even nesting and easy dispensing and with a broad base for nontip landing; trophy, which are the finest foam cups, beautifully printed, thin-walled, and super insulating; and plastic, which are durable soft plastic, strong, and shatterproof or strong, lightweight, and translucent. Under the paper cups classification, the buyer must decide which of the 11 types would best meet the needs of the foodservice operation. Would water cups or soda cups or big drink cups or hot drink cups or conical soda cups or pleated cups be best? Once the type is chosen, buyers must specify size, anywhere from 4 to 20 ounces, and other choices, such as plain or handled, or squat or tall. Finally, a specification, as shown in Table 16.2, is needed. The company has developed specifications for each of the 11 types that include the stock number, description, and packing, such as 20 bags with 50 cups each or 1,000 cups per case. An illustration of Sweetheart hot cups and lids is shown in Figure 16.7. Through electronic ordering, the stock number and number of cases is all that the buyer must specify. The manufacturer's representative will help the buyer make all these decisions and with just-in-time delivery, business will go on as usual.

SMALLWARES

Smallwares is a coined foodservice word that means any type of light equipment, including cooking and serving utensils. Smallwares generally are purchased from a food-service equipment dealer and can include pots and pans, steam table pans, kitchen accessories, table service, and buffet equipment.

The Vollrath Company, L.L.C., is the world's largest manufacturer of smallware, with world headquarters in Wisconsin, Scotland, the United Kingdom, and Canada. It was founded in the middle of the nineteenth century by Jacob Johann Vollrath, who moved his family from Germany to the United States. Vollrath was more than a manufacturer,

Figure 16.7. Illustrations of hot cups and lids.

Source: Sweetheart Foodservice Product and Merchandising, 1995. Used by permission.

he also was a visionary. By the end of the century, the name *Vollrath* had been stamped or cast on the bottoms of hundreds of thousands of pots and pans. The Vollrath name was recognized across the nation. Vollrath started out by manufacturing enamelware but soon replaced it with stainless steel. Today, health departments do not permit the use of enamelware in foodservice operations because the enamel can chip into the food. Vollrath now produces products made from stainless steel and aluminum to molded plastics and fabricated steel. Its motto is that the company makes more than cookware, kitchen and serving accessories, and plasticware: "We make satisfied customers."

Cookware

Cookware refers to pots that set on top of a range. They are used most often in restaurants because customers can choose what they want from a menu. Most menu items are prepared individually by the chef after choices are made. Pots and pans can be made of easy-cleaning stainless steel or even-heating aluminum and laminated stainless. They should have double-thick rims because they are easier to clean than rolled rims. Tapered rivet heads securely bond handles to cookware, eliminate food traps, and make cleanup easy.

Aluminum cookware conducts heat much better than stainless steel. Vollrath has developed a Tri-Ply stainless steel stock pot by bonding an inner and outer layer of stainless over a core of highly conductive carbon steel that ensures superior transfer of heat by spreading heat evenly across the bottom and up the sides for complete cooking without hot spots. Tri-Ply stock pots perform equally well on induction cooktops and traditional gas and electric ranges. Vollrath also has developed a nonstick coating with microparticles of stainless steel to give the pan its long-lasting, easy-cleaning performance. SteelCoat surfaces brown and sauté with minimum cooking oil.

Bakeware

Bakeware consists of pans, usually aluminum and without covers, that are filled with raw food baked in an oven. Aluminum roasting pans, some with covers, heat so evenly and efficiently that the oven temperature should be lowered by 25°F. The pans can have a polished or satin finish. Basic pieces of bakeware, such as cookie sheets, pie plates, cake pans, and bun pans, are sold to meet the increasing demand for new and different desserts.

Steam Table Pans

Steam tables are essential pieces of equipment in many foodservice operations, such as cafeterias in restaurants, supermarkets, industries, schools, colleges, and hospitals. Most of these serve three meals a day, while others, such as schools, serve only lunches and operations with night shifts, including hospitals and factories, serve a minimum of four meals. Cafeteria serving equipment needs to be strong to prevent denting. Except for special pieces of equipment, 18 parts chrome nickle and 8 parts type 304 stainless steel should be used for steam tables and pans. All steam table equipment must be NSF approved.

Steam table pans fit into steam table wells. Specific criteria need to be checked before purchasing the pans, including the design of corners, storage stacking ability, safe temperatures of food, fit of covers, and number of portions in the pan. They come in all sizes from full size, 20¾ inches by 12¾ inches, to one-ninth size, 6⅞ inches by 4¼ inches; the depth can be from 2½ to 6 inches. The diagram in Figure 16.8 illustrates the variety of sizes. Note the sample specifications at the bottom of the diagram.

Serving Utensils

As foodservice managers know, portion control is necessary if the operation's goal is to stay within the bottom line. Many portion control utensils, such as dishers, "spoodles," and ladles, are on the market to help foodservices meet this goal. A number that specifies the number of servings per quart when leveled off is commonly used to indicate the size of these utensils. For example, a level measure of a number 8 disher yields eight servings per quart, each portion measuring about ½ cup. Dishers are used during production to ensure consistent size for such menu items as meatballs, drop cookies, and muffins and during service to ensure correct serving size. Spoodles® combine the ease of serving with a spoon and the portion control of a ladle into one handy utensil. Vollrath has developed a color coding system to help employees choose the right size (Plate 16). If the menu calls for 2-ounces of corn, the manager can tell the employee to use a blue Spoodle or for ½ cup of ice cream to use a gray disher.

Because these utensils are subject to hard usage, they need to be good quality and NSF listed. They should be made of 18-8, Type 304 stainless steel to prevent corrosion, ensure long-lasting service, and be dishwasher safe. The handle of a disher should be one piece and extended to provide a sure grip for comfortable use. An ergonomically approved thumb tab to reduce operator fatigue should be specified for natural hand movement. Spoodles need handles that are designed for hours of comfortable use and should remain cool to the touch up to 230°F and up to 180°F for ladles.

Other types of serving and cooking equipment include spoons, tongs, hamburger and pancake turners, and spatula/scrapers. They all need to be carefully selected because they last for a long time. For example, spoons should be made of 18 gauge, Type 304, stainless steel and can be solid, perforated, or slotted. Many have plastic handles that resist heat to 230°F. Many other types of small equipment must be purchased according to menu requirements.

Table Service

From steak knives and serving bowls to cheese shakers and coffee decanters, specialty table service items are a stylish addition to the dining room. The buyer should be looking for items that are elegantly designed, functional, and durable.

Steak houses need to have steak knives for all customers who order steaks. If plain stainless steel knives are the only cutlery available in a restaurant, the manager is likely to hear complaints that the steak is tough. Most steak knives are **hollow ground,** defined as a concave surface behind the cutting edge of the blade that is notched, or serrated (Figure 16.9). They can have **laminated** plastic or wood handles that are made of thin layers of paper or wood which are bonded together with

Figure 16.8. Steam table pan sizes and specifications.

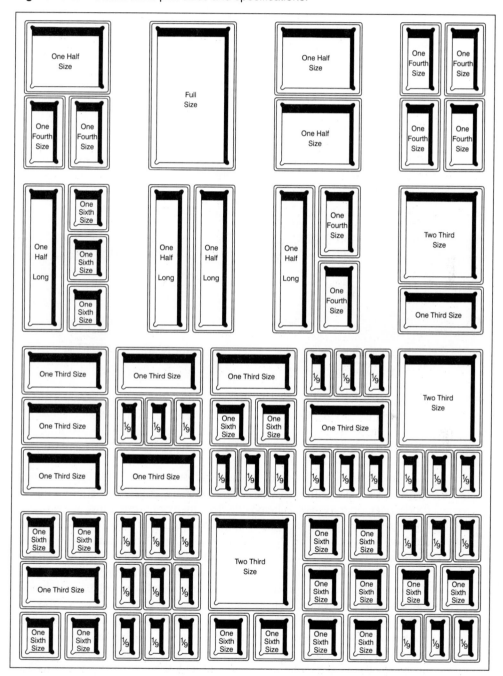

Specifications Super Pan II® item no._____, size, _____, shall be _____gauge (specify medium, standard, of heavy) 18-8, Type 304 stainless steel. Top outside corners shall be designed with built-in concave diagonal groove, i.e. reinforcer for impact resistance. All depths of solid pans shall have anti-jamming design to prevent pans from sticking together. Reverse formed edge shall be buff polished and flattened for consistent tangent to well opening and for hand comfort. Pan capacity and portion yield to be stamped on pan. NSF listed.

Source: Vollrath Company, L.L.C., 1995. Used by permission.

Figure 16.9.   Steak knife with a hollow ground blade with wave serrations and laminated plastic or wood handle.

Source: Vollrath Company, L.L.C., 1995. Used by permission.

Figure 16.10.   Chafers heated by special fuel or electricity.

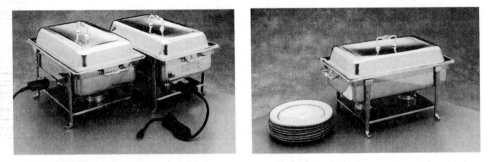

Source: Vollrath Company, L.L.C., 1995. Used by permission.

glue and compressed under heat. Only steak knives with solid plastic handles are dishwasher safe.

Airlines, cruise ships, fine hotels, and clubs often use 18-8, Type 304, heavy gauge stainless steel for coffee servers, water pitchers, sugar bowls, and creamers. Other foodservice operations use heavy glass for many of these items. A heat-resistant glass coffee server, or decanter, is used in many restaurants. A black plastic band and handle have always been on these decanters but now some have orange plastic bands to indicate that the coffee is decaffeinated. Other small service equipment includes glass salt and pepper shakers, cheese shakers, sugar pourers, and syrup dispensers, all with stainless steel or chrome tops, and stainless steel napkin holders, butter melters, and most of the bar utensils.

If buffet service is used, special equipment is needed to keep food warm and safe. Chafers are used on most buffets for that purpose. A **chafer** consists of a cover and two pans, one for the food, which is set into the second holding water, which is heated by a can of special fuel set into a fuel holder, as shown in Figure 16.10. Some operations do not permit fuel because it could cause a fire. Electric chafers are available. They have thermostatic control and a grounded plug and must be UL listed. This equipment is very expensive but lasts a long time. Special serving utensils, preferably stainless steel, also are needed on a buffet.

UNIFORMS

The days of formal uniforms are over for now. Remember, we're talking fashion here. If the 1960s hippie look can come back, so can the formal tuxedo, white shirt, and bow tie. But as restaurants dress down and become more casual, so do staff uniforms.

Trends

Baggy pants and big shirts are being replaced with trim pants or shorts and either above-the-knee or calf-length skirts, along with tucked-in sport shirts, usually a 65% poly/35% cotton washable blend. The shirts usually are in a color that coordinates with the decor of the operation. Baseball caps are very popular today, and one size fits all because they have a tab adjustment in the back. In addition to style, they have another function; they control the hair and keep it out of the food, which eliminates a potentially serious problem.

Customers like to see a chef who looks like a chef and dresses like a chef. Because many people have chosen to go to a culinary school to become chefs, the traditional uniforms consisting of a white jacket, checked pants, and a **toque,** which typically is a soft hat with a full crown pleated into a snug headband, as illustrated in Figure 16.11, have become very popular. These uniforms are made from a 65% polyester/35% cotton washable blend.

The black and white combination is a perennial favorite because it provides overall consistency in image and appearance and, with fabric quality and styling, gives the staff a look of polished perfection. The staff can be focused on the business of serving the customer. The unisex black tuxedo is in vogue again, not only in fine dining restaurants, but also in noncommercial senior living services communities. The tuxedo often has a signature look by adding a dashing distinction, such as a burgundy or white jacket, a patterned vest or lapels on the jacket, or a patterned tie. Again most of these outfits are 65% polyester/35% cotton washable, but 100% wool, which must be dry cleaned, is available.

Purchasing

Foodservice managers decide about the type of uniform needed for the operation. In addition, managers must decide who pays for the uniform and its upkeep. More and more,

Figure 16.11.   A chef's toque.

Source: Angelica Image Apparel,
a division of Angelica Corporation,
1997. Used by permission.

foodservice operations assume the responsibility for purchasing or renting uniforms and for their upkeep. Occasionally, the employee must purchase the uniform, which often is no more than black pants and a white shirt, and keep it clean. The manager must decide if the uniforms should be purchased or rented from a uniform company. Will the laundry and cleaning of the uniforms be contracted out or done on premises? Then the manager must select the uniform, remembering that employees come in different sizes and shapes. The cost effectiveness of various decisions must be studied.

The largest uniform and commercial laundry in the nation is Angelica® with headquarters in St. Louis. It is a $500 million per year business. The company has 40 manufacturing and laundry plants throughout the United States and other plants in Canada and England. Angelica® also has a laundry division. Customers can purchase the uniforms and take care of the laundry on-premise; currently, however, most customers are using area laundries. With the emphasis on cost controls in hospitals and other healthcare operations, many have closed down their laundries and are using commercial cleaners. The same procedure applies in restaurants, schools, and other facilities with uniforms and linens that need to be laundered. The charge for this service is figured by the pound or piece.

Angelica® has a separate rental division for uniforms and linens, such as bar towels and aprons. A contractual agreement is made between Angelica® and the facility. Within a radius of so many miles, soiled garments and linens are picked up, washed, pressed, and returned to the facility. Damaged uniforms or linens are replaced immediately.

Protective Clothing

A major factor contributing to foodborne illness is cross-contamination resulting from poor cleaning and sanitizing practices or from the personal hygiene of employees (Best Practices, 1997). A growing number of states and municipalities are implementing new FDA sanitary codes requiring the use of gloves and related barrier protection products by workers. Foodhandler® offers the widest range of products and sizes designed specifically for foodservice safety. This company specializes in high-quality gloves, aprons, and headwear in addition to training and educational materials and support services.

Gloves

Gloves can be purchased in various lengths; some cover the wrist and others are elbow length, depending upon the task the employee is performing. They also are made of different materials, and most are disposable. The following glove types are available:

- Regular or elbow-length gloves are low-cost, loose-fitting gloves recommended for light tasks that require changing gloves often. They are used for mixing salads, making sandwiches, and bagging bagels.
- Silky touch poly gloves are softer, more comfortable, and more form-fitting than regular poly gloves and extremely easy to put on. They are ideal for light tasks that require frequent glove changing.
- Vinyl gloves are more durable and closer fitting than poly gloves. They are recommended for food processing and medium duty foodservice tasks where tactile sensitivity is important. They can be used by people who are allergic to latex. They are perfect for quick-serve and busy kitchen operations.

- Blue vinyl gloves are used in food processing and preparation areas where color coding is used to prevent cross contamination. For example, in a raw poultry plant, employees wear blue gloves to indicate the potential for salmonella contamination.
- Latex gloves are ultra form fitting and offer the ultimate in dexterity. They are used for delicate work where maximum fingertip sensitivity is needed (Food Handlers, 1997).

Aprons and Headwear

Disposable aprons, headwear, and beard covers also are made by Foodhandler®. The aprons are made of regular and heavyweight plastic that resists tearing; they are inexpensive enough for frequent changing. Aprons are protection for food and clothing and can be worn over uniforms. Head caps are sanitary protection against food contamination from hair and can be purchased in three sizes. Cooks and chefs are required to wear them in many kitchens, and most employees prefer them to hair nets. Beard covers prevent facial hair from contaminating food and should be worn by bearded men who handle food.

CLEANING SUPPLIES

In most foodservice operations, employees are responsible for cleaning and sanitizing their work areas, but heavy cleaning, including walls, floors, restrooms, and other big jobs, often are done by an in-house cleaning crew or are contracted out to a company specializing in cleaning kitchens and dining rooms. In too many operations, however, cleaning is not well organized and inadequate. Often in small operations, all-purpose cleaning materials are purchased at the local supermarket and used for cleaning everything without considering food safety.

Products made for cleaning specific pieces of equipment, such as ovens and mixers, for washing and sanitizing walls and floors, or for washing dishes can be purchased from companies that make them or from foodservice dealers. These products were sold in bulk a number of years ago, and employees would dip into them and take out what they thought was enough to get a job done. Today, sophisticated dispensing systems are used; these systems eliminate waste and misuse, improve safety, save time, and control costs. Many use color and numerical product coding to ensure proper use.

ECOLAB® is the largest stock-owned company in the United States and Canada and expects to become number one in Europe. ECOLAB® was founded in 1923. Customers include hotels and restaurants; foodservice, healthcare, and educational facilities; quick-service units; commercial laundries, light industry, dairy plants, and farms; and food and beverage processors around the world. It has approximately 3,000 sales representatives and 172 district managers in the North American institutional division, which includes restaurants, hotels, hospitals, nursing homes, and schools. ECOLAB® is product based but service oriented and promises to meet customer's cleaning and sanitation needs. Sales representatives are on call 24 hours a day, 7 days a week, in case of an emergency. All sales employees, including the president of the company, must go through the same training program and are promoted from within. Once an operator has purchased an ECOLAB® product, the sales representative visits the operation once a month to check out the equipment and replace any parts that are not functioning. The operation is charged for the part but not the labor.

Discussion of all the products available on the market is outside the scope of this textbook. ECOLAB® categorizes cleaning and rinsing products under machine warewashing, manual warewashing, and specialty cleaning. Types of products in each of these categories follow.

Product Types

Products required for machine warewashing of dinnerware, glassware, and flatware include solid or liquid detergents and rinse additives. Solid detergents are 100% concentrated to eliminate waste and misuse, increase safety, last longer, and take less room than liquid detergents in storage. They yield the best possible results at the lowest use cost. Liquid detergents are excellent for bar glass washing. Solid rinse additives eliminate film and reduce drying time on all types of dinnerware, even plastic; they also promote rapid sheeting and spot-free drying. Liquid rinse additives have the same characteristics. Manual warewashing is done mostly on pots and pans and requires a maximum strength formula that cuts grease and baked-on greasy food soil. Presoak products, which remove the dulling protein film and restore the original sheen, are available for detarnishing stainless steel and silver flatware.

Many specialty products are on the market, such as grease and lime removers, germicidal detergents, and sanitizers. Cleaners and polishes that are safe on brass, copper, chrome, silver, and bronze require a completely organic, biodegradable formula that will not degrade silver or stainless steel and will restore sheen to all metals.

Purchasing

No matter how small or large the foodservice operation is, purchasing the best cleaning and sanitation materials is a crucial task. Certainly, household supplies are not adequate or potent enough to protect foodservice customers from foodborne illnesses. One incident of customer illness can destroy an operation. The buyer should conduct research on available products to determine which are the best for a specific foodservice. The safest method for selecting one product over another is to check out the services each company provides and whether those services are dependable in emergency situations. Automatic dispensers are available for some products, and inventory control has been automated. Foodservice managers often are surprised to find that the cost of the product is lower if the product is automatically dispensed because some employees believe that if the product is good, it might be better if more is used.

All materials must have easy-to-read labels; many are color-coded, which helps people who have difficulty reading. Once the materials have been delivered, they need to be stored in a separate area to prevent employees from mistaking them for a food product. Material safety data sheets (MSDS) must be provided to the buyer by the federal Occupational Safety and Health Administration (OSHA) Hazard Communication Standard or any corresponding state or local worker right-to-know rule by the company that sells the product.

CONTRACTS

A **contract** is an agreement after negotiation between two or more parties. Purchasing **negotiation** is the art of arriving at a mutual agreement with suppliers by means of bargaining on the essentials of a purchasing contract, such as specifications, quality assurance, price, payment terms, and delivery schedules. As such, the effectiveness of purchasing negotiation depends largely on a buyer's ability to establish bargaining strength.

Contract law was discussed in chapter 5. Buyers should be certain that each contract bearing their signature is legally sound. An offer is made by the buyer and then accepted by the supplier, and money is exchanged for a material or service. Once it has been accepted by a supplier, a purchase order becomes a legally enforceable contract. Technically the buyer is purchasing a product or a service.

Product

More and more products are being contracted in a foodservice operation. Six-month or annual contracts for such food products as milk, canned products, bread, and other items are made between buyers and suppliers. Buyers submit specifications to suppliers who decide what prices they will charge. Negotiations occur between buyers and suppliers; buyers start out offering a very low price for the product while suppliers try for a much higher price. Before an agreement is reached, buyers might have to modify the specifications to raise the price, while suppliers might have to bring down the price to sell the product. After bargaining, both sides finally come to an agreement in the form of a purchase order, which is a contract. Once the contract is signed by the two parties, the document becomes legal.

Service

Contract management is big business today. Cleaning the operation often is contracted out to a cleaning and sanitation company. Doing the yard work, especially for restaurants, generally is handled by a landscape and maintenance company. Repair and maintenance services can be contracted for a flat fee that provides routine maintenance and emergency service when needed, such as when a freezer breaks down. Mechanical equipment generally comes with a guarantee usually for only major repair problems. Equipment dealers sell warranty coverage for repair and maintenance responsibilities, and many are willing to extend the coverage again for a price. Often foodservice operators do not want to purchase service contracts and would rather pay for what they need.

Whether or not to buy a contract is not an easy decision; the price usually is not negotiable. The foodservice manager usually has to pay for next year's service immediately. If a contract is purchased, the buyer should make sure that the service is available 24 hours a day and on weekends. Foodservice managers know from experience that equipment breaks down on weekends and holidays, at night, and when the operation is the busiest.

Contract Foodservice Operations

The emphasis on managed care in the healthcare industry is a good example of what is going on in many foodservice operations. The philosophy that the function of a hospital is to improve the health of patients, not to run a foodservice operation, is increasingly accepted. Hence, many foodservice operations are being contracted to outside firms. Because each operation is unique, contracts between a contract company and the facility receiving the services must be tailor made. The two largest contract companies in the United States are Aramark and Marriott Management Services. Both of these companies have gone far beyond just contracting for foodservice. For example, Aramark has divisions that include uniforms; clinical, emergency, food, and maintenance services; child care; and many other services. Marriott Management Services are into healthcare, foodservice, and housekeeping operations. Marriott has a unique service for its accounts. The company sends its clients' managers, chefs, and dietitians from across the country to meet twice a year with corporate nutrition and field marketing representatives, suppliers, and chefs from American culinary schools to develop menus for the next 6 months. The teams create recipes for new ethnic dishes and regional and seasonal specialties.

Morrison Health Care Inc. has decided to focus its energies on central food production as a way to gain more hospital accounts. The company understands that hospital administrators must drive down costs. As more and more hospitals consolidate or become part of regional healthcare systems, Morrison promotes central food production for a group of hospitals as a way to reduce costs. Morrison takes buyers through a series of questions before a contract for providing food and nutrition services to the dietetics departments of hospitals is drawn up.

- What foodservice operations are in the hospital, such as patient, cafeteria, vending, and convenience store?
- Who is responsible for the maintenance and repair of the facilities and equipment in use?
- Who is responsible for providing and paying for such items as food, office supplies, in-service training materials, and telephone service?
- Who is responsible for daily cleaning of walls, floors, ceilings, vents, and other tasks?
- What are the financial arrangements for payments, interest, investments, and fees?
- What happens if the contract is terminated before the end of the term?
- What provisions are made to comply with laws and regulations related to health and sanitation?
- Are the standards in the Joint Commission on Accreditation of Health Care Organizations being followed?
- What insurance and security protection against loss of items or damage to property are available?
- What kind of mediation and arbitration provisions is available?

FLOWERS

Though restaurants do not have to use fresh flowers, doing so enhances the decor and atmosphere. Using fresh flowers in restaurants has been a tradition in Europe, and it has become more popular in the United States. Supplying fresh flowers to restaurants on a regular basis may sound like a relatively easy way for a retail floral shop to make a profit, but marketing fresh flowers to restaurants has its own unique set of conditions. Restaurants generally require three different types of flowers: table flowers, an arrangement for a public area or lobby, and party or banquet flowers.

Most retail florists provide fresh flowers once a week. Restaurant managers should understand that flowers will not look the same at the end of the week as they did at the beginning. If the restaurant is open 7 days a week, the florist usually replaces flowers right before the weekend so they will be the freshest at that time. Fresh flowers with a good vase life are expected to last the entire week. Flowers that stay fresh longer can be purchased from a wholesaler at a good price; examples are various types of lilies and miniature carnations. Roses and spring flowers, such as iris, tulips, and snapdragons, should be avoided because they wilt within a couple of days. The manager often places a standing order with the florist assuming that the florist will always provide the same quality at the same price.

The restaurant staff usually is responsible for arranging and keeping the flowers in good condition during the week. After the account is obtained, one of the florist's staff trains a restaurant employee to arrange the flowers in a vase. Explicit instructions are given to the employee to refrigerate the flowers each night in a beverage or wine cooler, to change the water each day, and to add preservatives. The restaurant typically is charged by the number of tables or by the number of flowers, referred to by the florist as the number of stems. Often the markup is lower on the flowers because arranging is not involved. The florist is responsible for processing, wrapping, and delivering the flowers to the restaurant. The cost of flowers per table averages about $8 to $10. For an additional charge, many wholesalers service the flowers once a week and replace wilted with fresh flowers.

Arrangements for the lobby cost about $100 each, depending upon the flowers and the size of the finished product. The florist can make arrangements of artificial flowers that will look as good as fresh flowers. Another option is to make a dried and silk arrangement that can be changed every month or two with the stipulation that the flowers go back to the shop. Silk flowers should not be used for table flowers because customers have a tendency to handle them, and "vase life" is only a couple weeks.

If the florist has all the business for a restaurant, he or she might give a restaurant a 10% discount on banquet flowers. A discount is seldom given for arrangements below $35. Unless a restaurant manager has a true appreciation for flowers, knows what they cost, and understands the restaurant's duties in flower upkeep, the manager may place unrealistic demands on a florist. Good business sense, a firm hand in dealing with restaurants, and good quality flowers can make marketing to restaurants a profitable business.

SUMMARY

Even though the objective of a foodservice operation is to prepare food that satisfies customer needs, the way food is served is just as important. Choosing the correct tableware helps to make the dining experience a pleasant one and at the same time increases profit. A local foodservice equipment dealer with a large showroom with displays and many catalogs serves as a go-between for the manufacturer and supplier.

Choosing the right tableware for a particular foodservice operation is difficult. The amount of tableware required for a foodservice operation is based on the number of turns per hour during peak periods multiplied by the number of seats in the operation. The buyer also should check warranties on expensive tableware.

Dinnerware includes china, pottery, and plastic. China is a claylike product blended with other compounds and formed into plates, cups, and saucers. Fine china seldom is used in foodservice operations, which opt instead for more durable foodservice china. Pottery, or dense china, comes in various shapes and colors and enhances the tabletop. Plastic, usually polycarbonate, dinnerware is tough, durable, and virtually unbreakable, but usually not microwavable. School, prison, and nursing home foodservice operations are the primary users of plastic dishes and trays. Glassware can be fine stemware, heavy, shatterproof tumblers, or plastic. The basic types of glass used in foodservices are lead crystal and lime glass. The use of permanent and disposable plastic glasses is increasing. Flatware includes eating utensils and can be silverplated or stainless steel sold as place settings or individually by the dozen. Many foodservices use top-quality stainless steel flatware that look like silverplate. Holloware is made from the same materials as flatware.

Foodservice disposables are used in many operations in which speed of service is a requirement. Members of the Foodservice and Packaging Institute have entered into environmental conservation programs that include recycling and other programs.

Smallwares, any type of light equipment that includes cooking and serving utensils, can become a major expense in the foodservice equipment budget. Most of these are purchased through a foodservice equipment dealer. They include pots and pans used on top of the range, oven baking pans, steam table pans, serving utensils, steak knives, and buffet equipment.

Uniforms for employees are usually purchased or rented. Most foodservice operations assume responsibility for their purchase and upkeep, including laundry, which is usually contracted out. Protective clothing, such as disposable gloves, aprons, and hair coverings, is purchased in bulk quantities.

Cleaning supplies and contracts also are included in this chapter. An all-purpose household detergent is not potent enough to protect customers from foodborne illnesses. Cleaning supplies for foodservice operations are made for various tasks. Buyers must ascertain the range of products and reliability of cleaning supply companies. Automatic dispensers are available for some products, and inventory control has been automated.

REFERENCES

Durocher, J. (1992, June 10). Fashion plate. *Restaurant Business,* 188, 190.

Foodservice and Packaging Institute, Inc. (1995). Environment. Arlington, VA.

Foodservice and Packaging Institute, Inc. (1997). Environmental stewardship report (2nd ed.). Arlington, VA: Author.

Industry Council on Food Safety. (1997). The Educational Foundation of the National Restaurant Association. Chicago, IL.

Appendix

FOODS WITH STANDARDS OF IDENTITY

Milk and Cream

Sweetened condensed milk
*Sweetened condensed skim milk
Milk
*Nonfat dry milk
Light cream
Heavy cream
*Lowfat milk
*Skim milk
Acidified sour cream
Sour cream
Half and half
Evaporated milk
*Evaporated skimmed milk

Canned Fruits

Applesauce
Apricots
Berries
Cherries
Figs
Fruit cocktail
Seedless grapes
Grapefruit
Peaches
Pineapple
Pears
Plums
Prunes

*As of November 20, 1996, the FDA eliminated standards of identity for these products.

Canned Fruit Juices

Cranberry juice cocktail
Lemon juice
Grapefruit juice
Orange juice and orange juice products
  *also frozen concentrate
Prune juice
Pineapple juice

Fruit Butters, Jellies, Preserves, and Related Products

Fruit butters: apple, apricot, grape, peach, pear, plum, prune, quince
Fruit jelly: apple, apricot, blackberry, black raspberry, boysenberry, cherry, crabapple, cranberry, Damson, Damson plum, dewberry, fig, gooseberry, grape, grapefruit, Greengage, Greengage plum, guava, loganberry, orange, peach, pineapple, plum, pomegranate, prickly pear, quince, raspberry, red raspberry, red currant, currant, strawberry, and youngberry
Artificially sweetened fruit jelly
Fruit preserves and jams: blackberry, black raspberry, blueberry, boysenberry, cherry, crabapple, dewberry, elderberry, grape, grapefruit, huckleberry, loganberry, orange, pineapple, raspberry, red raspberry, rhubarb, strawberry, tangerine, tomato, yellow tomato, youngberry
Artificially sweetened fruit preserves and jams
Frozen cherry pie

Canned Vegetables

Corn
Field corn
Peas
Dry peas
Tomatoes
Tomato concentrates
Catsup
Mushrooms
Certain other canned vegetables: artichokes, asparagus, bean sprouts, shelled beans, lima beans, butter beans, beets, beet greens, broccoli, brussel sprouts, cabbage, carrots, cauliflower, celery, collards, dandelion greens, kale, mustard greens, okra, onions, parsnips, black-eyed peas, field peas, green sweet peppers, red sweet peppers, pimentos, potatoes, rutabagas, salsify, spinach, sweet potatoes, swiss chard, truffles, turnip greens, turnips

Canned Juices

Tomato

Frozen Vegetables

Peas

Fish and Shellfish

Canned oysters, all sizes
Canned Pacific salmon

Canned shrimp
Frozen raw breaded shrimp
Frozen raw lightly breaded shrimp
Canned tuna

Nutritive Sweeteners and Table Syrups

Dextrose anhydrous
Dextrose monohydrate
Glucose syrup
Dried glucose syrup
Lactose
Cane syrup
Maple syrup
Sorghum syrup
Table syrup

Raw Meat Products

Chopped beef, ground beef
Hamburger
Beef patties
Fabricated steak
Partially defatted beef fatty tissue
Partially defatted pork fatty tissue

Tree Nut and Peanut Products

Peanut butter
Mixed nuts
Shelled nuts

Food Dressings and Flavorings

French dressing
Mayonnaise
Salad dressing
Vanilla extract
Concentrated vanilla extract
Vanilla powder

Eggs

Eggs
Dried eggs
Frozen eggs
Liquid eggs
Egg whites
Dried egg whites
Frozen egg whites
Egg yolks

Dried egg yolks
Frozen egg yolks

Cacao Products

Cacao nibs
Chocolate liquor
Breakfast cocoa
Cocoa
Lowfat cocoa
Sweet chocolate
Milk chocolate
Buttermilk chocolate
Skim milk chocolate
Mixed dairy products chocolate
Sweet cocoa and vegetable fat coating
Sweet chocolate and vegetable fat coating
Milk chocolate and vegetable fat coating

Cheese and Related Products

Blue cheese
Brick cheese
Cheddar cheese
Low-sodium cheddar cheese
Colby cheese
Low-sodium colby cheese
Cold pack and club cheese
Cold pack cheese food
Cold pack cheese food with fruits, vegetables, or meats
Cottage cheese
Dry curd cottage cheese
Lowfat cottage cheese
Cream cheese
Cream cheese with other foods
Edam cheese
Gouda cheese
Grated Cheese
Monterey cheese
Mozzarella cheese
Part-skim mozzarella
Pasteurized process cheese
Pasteurized process cheese food
Swiss cheese
55 other varieties of cheese

Frozen Desserts

Ice cream and frozen custard
Ice milk
Mellorine
Sherbet
Water ices

Cereal Flour and Related Products

Flour
Enriched flour
Self-rising flour
Enriched self-rising flour
Whole wheat flour
Corn grits
Enriched corn grits
Quick grits
White cornmeal
Enriched corn meals
Self-rising white corn meal
Yellow corn meal
Farina
Enriched rice
15 other variations

Macaroni and Noodle Products

Macaroni products
Enriched macaroni products
Whole wheat macaroni products
7 other variations of macaroni
Noodle products
Enriched noodle products
3 other variations of noodles

Bakery Products

Breads, rolls, and buns
Enriched bread, rolls, and buns
Raisin bread, rolls, and buns
Enriched raisin bread, rolls, and buns
Whole wheat breads, rolls, and buns

Cooked Meats

Barbecued meats
Roast beef parboiled and steam roasted

Cured Meats, Unsmoked and Smoked

Corned beef
Corned beef brisket
Corned beef round and other corned beef cuts
Cured beef tongue
Cooked ham, loin
Cooked shoulder, butt, picnic
Uncooked cured shoulder, butt, picnic
Ham patties, chopped ham, pressed ham, spiced ham,
    and similar products

Country ham, country style ham, dry cured ham, country pork shoulder, country-style pork shoulder, and dry-cured pork shoulder

Bacon

Sausage: Fresh, Smoked, Cooked

Fresh pork sausage

Fresh beef sausage

Breakfast sausage

Whole hog sausage

Smoked pork sausage

Frankfurter, hotdog, wiener, vienna, bologna, garlic bologna, knockwurst, and similar products

Cheesefurters and similar products

Braunschweiger and liver sausage or liverwurst

Luncheon Meat, Loaves, Jellied Products

Luncheon meat

Meat loaf

Meat Specialties

Scrapple

Bockwurst

Canned, Frozen, or Dehydrated Meat Food Products

Chili

Chili con carne with beans

Hash

Corned beef hash

Meat stews

Tamales

Spaghetti with meatballs and sauce, spaghetti with meat and sauce, and similar products

Spaghetti sauce with meat

Tripe with milk

Beans with frankfurters in sauce, sauerkraut with wieners and juice, and similar products

Lima beans with ham in sauce, beans with ham in sauce, beans with bacon in sauce, and similar products

Chow mein vegetables with meat, and chop suey vegetables with meat

Pork with barbecue sauce and beef with barbecue sauce

Beef with gravy and gravy with beef

Meat pies

Pizza

Pizza with meat

Pizza with sausage

Fats, Oils, Shortenings

Margarine or oleomargarine

Mixed fat shortening

Lard, leaf lard

Rendered animal fat or mixture thereof

Meat Salads and Spreads

Deviled ham, deviled tongue, and similar products
Potted meat food product and deviled meat food product
Ham spread, tongue spread, and similar products

Poultry

Canned boned poultry
Baby or geriatric food
Poultry dinners (frozen) and pies
Poultry rolls
Burgers and patties*
A la Kiev*
Steak or fillet*
Baked or roasted*
Barbecued*
Barbecued prepared with moist heat*
Breaded products

Other Poultry Dishes and Specialty Items

Ravioli**
Soup**
Chop suey with**
Chop suey**
Chow mein without noodles**
Tamales**
Noodles or dumplings with**
Stew**
Fricassee of wings**
Noodles or dumplings**
With vegetables**
Gravy with sliced**
Tetrazzini**
Chili with beans**
Creamed**
Cacciatore**
Fricassee**
A la King**
Croquettes**
Slice with gravy and dressing**
Salad**
Chili**
Hash**
Sliced with gravy**
Minced barbecue**

*Kind of poultry must be specified on label
**Kind of poultry must be stated at the appropriate place in the name

Raw Poultry Products

Broiler or fryer
Roaster or roasting chicken
Hen, fowl, or baking or stewing
Turkeys
   fryer roaster turkey
   young turkey
   yearling turkey
   mature turkey or old turkey
Breasts
Breast with ribs
Wishbones (pulley bones)
Drumsticks
Thighs
Legs (kind must be specified)
Wings
Backs
Halves
Quarters
Breast quarter
Breast quarter without wing
Leg quarter
Thigh with back portion
Legs with pelvic bone
Wing drummette
Wing portion
Cut-up poultry
Giblets

Glossary

ABC inventory method Technique to keep the desired quantity of products in storage and maintain assets at desired levels.

Additives Other ingredients approved by the Food and Drug Administration used to stabilize the foam, prevent cloudiness, and lengthen the shelf life of beer.

Adulterated Food that contains substances injurious to health, usually prepared or held under unsanitary conditions, or filthy, decomposed, or containing portions of diseased animals.

Aerobic microorganism Organism of microscopic size that requires oxygen to grow.

Affective sensory test Preference, acceptance, and opinions of a product evaluated by an untrained panel of consumers.

Aging Method of holding beef at refrigerated temperatures for an extended period of time to maximize flavor and tenderness that occur through natural enzymatic processes.

Agricultural Marketing Act (1946) Law providing for the issuance of official U.S. Grades by the USDA to designate different levels of quality.

Agricultural Marketing Service Official federal grading agency with services offered in cooperation with state agencies for inspecting quality of processed dairy products, poultry and eggs, fresh and processed fruits and vegetables, and meat and meat products.

Agent Individual authorized to act on behalf of another party, known as the principal.

Agency Business relationship between the agent and principal.

Air-blast freezing Air at −31°F is forced through a tunnel or chamber in which food moves through on belts or carts.

Ale An alcoholic beverage fermented at warm temperatures (50°F to 70°F) by a yeast that rises to the top of the liquid.

Anaerobic microorganisms Organisms that grow only if oxygen is not present.

Analytical test Differences and similarities of quality and quantity of sensory characteristics evaluated by a trained panel.

Annealed glass Lime glassware, which tends to chip easily, slowly cooled to room temperature after it has been formed.

Approved brand specifications Quality is indicated by designating a specific product by known desirable characteristics.

Aquaculture Elegant name given to fish farming, the practice of growing fish and shellfish in tanks or in ponds.

Arabicas Mild-tasting coffee beans that come primarily from South America.

Architect Professional responsible for producing a structure that meets the needs of the customer.

As purchased (AP) Amount of food purchased before processing to give the number of edible portions required to serve a specific number of customers.

Audit Final report following a formal examination of the books of account.

Audit trail   Organized flow for source documents, including the requisition, purchase order, and invoice.

Baker's percent formula   Recipe for bread products in which weights of all ingredients except flour are converted into a percentage of the weight in pounds of the total amount of flour in a recipe.

Bakeware   Pans, usually aluminum and without covers, used to bake raw food in an oven.

Barrier bag   Bag made of four layers of see-through plastic that prevents air from entering and water from leaving.

Beer   Generic term used for all malted beverages made from malted grain, usually barley, hops, and water.

Benchmark   Point of reference in measuring or judging quality or value that gives purchasing professionals the objective standard they need to evaluate their own performance.

Best-if-Used-By   Date that is intended to tell the buyer how long the product will retain the best flavor or quality.

Bid buying   Selecting a supplier based on who gives the best price quote on the specification.

Bisque   Unglazed ceramic ware that is hard-fired and resembles glass.

Black tea   Tea with an amber color and a rich flavor and aroma; less bitter than green tea.

Blast chiller   Equipment used to extend the quality and safe storage life of menu items that are cooked, chilled, and then held in refrigerated storage for a limited amount of time.

Blended spirits   Alcoholic beverages containing different grains, batches, stills, or ages that are blended together.

Blown glassware   Glasses shaped by forcing air into a ball of melted glass.

Bourbon   Alcoholic beverage distilled at a minimum of 160 proof from a sour mash of at least 51 percent corn and aged for 2 years in charred new oak containers.

Bovine somatotropin (BST)   Natural protein hormone produced by cows that enables them to produce milk.

Boxed meat   Primal cut of meat placed inside a barrier bag in a box to be shipped to wholesale distributors.

Brandy   Alcoholic beverage made from grapes and aged for at least 2 years.

Brandy snifter   Large balloon-shaped short-stem glass held in the palm of the hand to warm brandy slightly while releasing the rich aroma.

Breakage   Bar term used for empty liquor bottles.

Brewer's yeast   Ingredient in beer that transforms sugars into alcohol and carbon dioxide, which may affect its taste and hangover potential.

Brewpub   Microbrewery added to a restaurant operation.

Brix hydrometer   An instrument that measures the percent of sucrose, or sugar, in a syrup.

Broiler   Equipment with its heat source above the food rack, which is placed 3 to 6 inches from the heat.

Broker   Independent sales and marketing representative who contracts with manufacturers, processors, or prime source producers to both sell and conduct local marketing programs with wholesalers, suppliers, or foodservice operators.

Brown spirits   Whiskey colored by caramel, which is burnt sugar, added to the product; examples include bourbon, scotch, rye, Irish, and Canadian.

Budget   Plan for operating a business expressed in financial terms or a plan to control expenses and profit in relation to sales.

Bulgur   Processed form of cracked wheat.

Bureau of Alcohol, Tobacco and Firearms (ATF)   Law enforcement organization within the U.S. Department of Treasury with unique responsibilities dedicated to reducing violent crime, collecting revenue, and protecting the public.

Business ethics   Self-generating system of moral standards to which a substantial majority of business executives gives voluntary assent.

Buttermilk   Cultured product made from fresh pasteurized or ultra-pasteurized lowfat or fat-free milk with nonfat dry milk solids added.

Buyer   A purchaser responsible for the selection and purchasing of products.

Caffeine   Chemical compound that stimulates the body's central nervous system; considered one of the world's most widely used drugs by pharmacologists.

Canadian whisky   Blended alcoholic beverage, spelled without the "e," made from corn, barley, rye, wheat, and other grains to give it a light taste.

Canning   Highly mechanized food industry with washing, sizing, grading, peeling or shelling, trimming, and putting into cans done by machine.

Capon chicken   Surgically unsexed male chicken.

Carbonated   Beverage saturated with carbon dioxide to give it a unique zest.

Cash discount   Percentage reduction in the price of a product if the bill is paid within a specific time period; for example, before, at the time, or shortly after the product is delivered.

Centralized purchasing   Purchasing by one person or department.

Cereal   Not limited to breakfast, including a large group of products made from grains, such as flours, breads, meals, and pastas.

Chafer   Buffet equipment consisting of a cover and two pans, one for the food that is set into another pan containing water heated by a can of special fuel set into a holder.

Charbroiler   Either gas or electric equipment with a bed of ceramic briquettes above the heat source and below the grid.

Chaptalization   Process of adding sugar to grape juice before or during fermentation to achieve a higher alcohol level in the wine.

Cheese   Concentrated dairy product obtained by draining moisture, or whey, from the original milk after coagulation of the major milk protein, casein.

China   Claylike product blended with other compounds and molded or formed into the required shape.

Clamshell®   Broiler hood that fits directly into existing griddles and broilers at a fraction of the cost of the original double-sided cooking equipment.

Clean   Free of visible soil.

Code   Set of rules for standards of professional practice or behavior established by a group.

Code of ethics   Major emphasis is on the relationships within professional organizations and businesses that are influenced by personal codes.

Cogeners   Flavor, body, and aroma in fermented beverages responsible for the smoky flavor of scotch or the rich aroma of bourbon.

Cognac   Most prestigious and famous of all brandies made in the Cognac region of France.

Combi-oven   Flow of both convected air and steam through oven cavity producing super-heated, moist, internal atmosphere.

Column still   Piece of equipment used in the distillation process that can be controlled to produce spirits at a wide range of proofs up to about 196.

Commercial segment   Usually a restaurant that is concerned about the bottom line because profit is required to keep the business operating.

Competition   Act of winning out over other suppliers.

Complex carbohydrates   Carbohydrates that break down slowly during digestion, giving the body a time-released source of energy.

Concentrated foods   Products preserved by drawing water from microbial cells with concentrated solutions of sugar or salt.

Condition   Any physical change that might occur in a product before or after harvest, thus detracting from its acceptability.

Conduction   Transfer of heat from the gas or electric source through a cooking vessel to food.

Consumer panel   Group that evaluates acceptance of, or preference for, a food product.

Contract   Agreement after negotiation between two or more parties.

Control states   State stores that control liquor sales, thus establishing a monopoly.

Controlled atmosphere storage   Nonchemical process requiring airtight rooms and special equipment to maintain desired atmospheric conditions.

Controlling   Process of ensuring that plans are being followed.

Convection   Distribution of either natural or forced heat by the movement of liquid or vapor.

Convection/microwave oven   Multifunction equipment that can use convection air alone, microwave energy alone, or a combination of the two.

Convection oven   Oven with a fan on the back wall that creates currents of air within the cooking chamber.

Conveyor oven   A gas or electric oven, often called a pizza oven in quick-service operations, with a belt running through a hot chamber on which products are baked.

Cookware   Pots that cook on top of a range.

Cooperative purchasing   A large organization owned by and operated for the benefit of those using its services.

Cordials   Distilled spirits sweetened with 2.5% or more of sugar and flavored with a variety of ingredients: fruits, herbs, spices, flowers, nuts, and cream.

Corn   Native American plant that produces a cereal grain.

Cost center   Department that is expected to manage expenses but not generate profits for the organization.

Cost effectiveness   Technique that provides a comparison of alternative courses of action in terms of their cost and effectiveness in obtaining a specific objective.

Cost plus fixed fee   Buyer reimburses the supplier for the actual cost of a product and freight and pays a predetermined set fee for delivery, warehousing, inventory costs, and profit to the supplier.

Cottage cheese   Soft cheese made from pasteurized fat free milk or reconstituted nonfat dry milk.

Council of Public Health Consultants   Group of people from all levels of government, academia, and private consulting firms with expertise in health and environmental issues.

Crazing   Cracking caused by a difference in the expansion characteristics of the china body and glaze.

Cream   Liquid high fat milk product separated from milk that has various amounts of milkfat.

Critical control points   Procedures by which a preventive or control measure can be applied to prevent hazards.

Crustaceans   Type of seafood with a soft outer shell and jointed appendages.

Cryogenic freezing   Most rapid freezing method that uses condensed gases, which cause very small ice crystals to form, resulting in minimal damage to the tissue.

Cultured   Part of a product's name that signifies it was produced by souring milk or cream with an acid with or without the addition of microbial organisms.

Cultured sour cream   Pasteurized homogenized cream with *Streptococcus lactic* added at 72°F until the acidity is at least 0.5%.

Cuppers   Highly trained experts who check the coffee beverage to determine its flavor quality.

Customer   Anyone who is affected by a product or service.

Cutability   Amount of salable meat obtained from the carcass as boneless or semi-boneless trimmed retail cuts from the round, loin, rib, and chuck.

Cycle menu   Series of menus offering different items daily on a weekly, biweekly, or some other basis.

Daily bid   Method of pricing perishable products that last only a few days.

Dark cutting   Condition occurring in animals suffering from stress or severe weather conditions that causes meat to turn dark or black.

Decaffeinated coffee   Chemical solvent is used to remove most of the caffeine from green coffee beans.

Decaffeinated tea   Chemical solvent is used to remove most of the caffeine from tea leaves.

Deck oven   Ovens that come in basic sections, each with two shelves and its own source of heat, and that may be stacked on each other.

Deep fat fryer   Tank of oil heated by gas or electricity in which foods are immersed; fryer has thermostatic control and fast recovery of fat temperature.

Dehydration   Drying foods, usually fruits and vegetables, to preserve them by decreasing bulk and weight and eliminating water that could be used by microorganisms for growth.

Die   Device used to stamp initials or a seal on the handles of flatware.

Direct costs   Costs that can be specifically and accurately assigned to a given unit of production, usually the menu item served to the customer.

Distribution   Process of transporting food from the production unit to the service area.

Distributor   Wholesaler responsible for transferring products from the processor or manufacturer to the supplier.

Dram Shop Law   Legal requirement that servers of alcoholic beverages in many states are partly responsible for the actions of customers.

Dry aging   Beef carcasses or wholesale cuts are held at refrigerated temperatures with no protective covering.

Dry food storage   Place where food not requiring refrigeration or freezing can be protected from the elements, insects, rodents, and theft.

Economic Order Quantity (EOQ)   Concept that is derived from a sensible balance of ordering cost and inventory holding cost.

Edible portion (EP)   Weight of a menu item without skin, bones, and fat available for eating by the customer after it is cooked.

Emergency Permit Control   Regulations that require processing plants to be registered and their processes to be filed with the Food and Drug Administration.

Ergonomics   Application of biological and engineering data to mutual adjustment of man to machine.

Ethics   Principles of conduct governing an individual or a business.

Expert systems   Computer programs that build knowledge bases for making decisions.

Exponential smoothing method   Popular time series model in which an exponentially decreasing set of weights is used, giving recent values more weight than older ones.

Fabricated equipment   Equipment designed and manufactured for a specific foodservice operation.

Fair Packaging and Labeling Act   (1967) Federal law requiring consumers to obtain accurate quantity or content information from a food label, thus permitting value comparison.

Fair price   Lowest price that ensures a continuous supply of the proper quality where and when needed.

Farmer's market   Place for selling products, mostly fruits and vegetables, raised by local growers.

Federal Alcohol Administration Act   Law closely controlling production and marketing of alcoholic beverages.

Federal Food, Drug, and Cosmetic Act   Law requiring that foods other than meat, poultry, and fish are pure and wholesome, safe to eat, and produced under sanitary conditions and that packaging and labeling accurately report the contents.

Federal Meat Inspection Act   Rules requiring inspection of all meat crossing state lines.

Fermentation   The action of yeast on sugar, converting it into alcohol and carbon dioxide gas.

Fiber   General term for the indigestible part of plant foods.

Fiber enriched milk   Fat free milk with dietary fiber, such as cellulose gel to enrich the texture, added to it.

Field heat   Heat from the field, which is removed as quickly as possible from harvested fruits and vegetables to prevent deterioration of quality prior to shipping or storage.

File   Collection of logically arranged related data or records.

Fine china   China term applied to a thin, translucent, vitrified body, generally fired twice: first at a relatively high temperature to mature the clay and other materials and secondly to develop the high gloss of the beautiful glaze.

Finnan haddie   Famous Scottish smoked haddock specialty cured in brine, to which carotene pigment has been added, and later smoked.

Firm price   Contracts limited to one-time delivery or short-term.

FIFO (first in, first out)   Order of using inventory, based on the assumption that current prices will be higher than older ones.

Fixed bid   Monetary offer for purchasing large quantities over a long period of time that cannot be changed.

Flatfish   Type of fish with a flat, oval body and both eyes on one side of its head because it swims parallel to the ocean floor.

Flatware   Term used for forks, knives, spoons, and other eating utensils.

Food acceptance service   USDA program for grading and inspection of foods that provides impartial evaluation and certification of purchases to determine if they meet contract specifications.

Food danger zone   The temperature range in which bacteria multiply rapidly, between 40°F and 140°F.

Food Guide Pyramid   Complex illustration with many different food and nutrition messages.

F.O.B. destination   Place where the product is going.

F.O.B. origin   Place from which the product is originally transported.

Food product flow   Alternative paths within the foodservice operation that menu items may follow, beginning with receiving and ending with service to the customer.

Food Safety and Inspection Service (FSIS)   USDA agency responsible for ensuring that meat and poultry products destined for interstate commerce and human consumption are wholesome, unadulterated, properly labeled, and not hazardous to health.

Foodservice & Packaging Institute   Organization that promotes sanitary, safety, functional, economic, and environmental benefits of single-use foodservice containers.

Foodservice Consultants Society International (FCSI)   Professional organization that promotes client use of services, free exchange of ideas between members, and ethical industry practices.

Foodservice design consultant   Professional responsible for understanding and communicating the entire process of foodservice from the moment the food comes into the operation until it is served to the customer.

Foodservice Purchasing Managers (FPM)   Group of buyers formed under the auspices of the National Restaurant Association in 1977 that is dedicated to purchasing professionalism through industry communication and education.

Food standard   Standards of identity developed by the Food and Drug Administration for the most commonly used foods, including characteristics for a specific product and providing a quality reference, usually indicated by a grade.

Food waste disposal   Piece of equipment with sharp blades that fits into a sink because a source of water is needed to wash the ground garbage into the sewer.

Footed glass   Drinking glass with a bowl attached directly to a short stem on a disklike base.

Forecasting   Art and science of estimating events in the future that provide a database for decision making and planning.

Forecasting model   Mathematical formula to predict future needs used as an aid for determining quantity.

Free on board (F.O.B.)   Delivery of products to a specified point, or place, with all transport charges paid.

Freeze-dried instant coffee   Coffee extract that is frozen and then dried by vaporization in a vacuum.

Freeze drying   Process of drying food from a solid frozen stage to prevent shrinking.

Freezer burn   Loss of moisture on the surface of a frozen food that causes it to burn.

Fruit   Botanically the flesh, or ovary, of a plant that surrounds or contains the seeds.

Fruit butters   Pastelike consistency caused by cooking fruit down and then putting it through a sieve to make it spread like butter.

Full or broadline wholesalers   Generally, wholesalers who carry large amounts of stock permitting the buyer to purchase everything from frozen and canned products to kitchen equipment and furniture.

Generally Recognized as Safe   (GRAS) List of safe substances, authorized by trained scientific experts, that may be added to foods.

Genetically engineered food   Food that can be altered to reduce spoilage and improve flavor by splicing in new genes or eliminating existing genes.

Gill net fishing   Catching fish by the gills in nets, a practice that is outlawed in many coastal states.

Gin   Alcoholic beverage that is permitted to be produced from corn, rye, wheat, barley malt, and sugar cane according to the U.S. standards of identity.

Grade   Sum of characteristics of the product at the time it was graded, not sold.

Grains   Seeds of the grass family, often referred to as the foundation of healthy eating.

Green tea   Type of tea that has a delicate, greenish yellow color and a fruity, slightly bitter flavor.

Grilling   Cooking on an open grid over a heat source, which may be an electric or gas-heated element, ceramic briquettes, or exotic woods and flavored chips.

Group purchasing   Bringing together foodservice managers from different operations, most often noncommercial, for joint purchasing.

Hazard   An unacceptable contamination.

Hazard analysis   Studying specific foods and their locations in the food product flow to determine where adulteration from mishandling is likely to occur.

Heat processing   Most often used method for preservation of fruits and vegetables done to decrease the number of microorganisms in a food, thus extending the shelf life while keeping the product palatable and acceptable in flavor, color, and texture.

Herbal tea   Naturally caffeine-free blends of dried herbs that produce a fragrant liquor, not really tea, once soaked.

Herbs   Stems and leaves of low-growing plants.

Historical records   Written accounts of previous events, such as purchase orders, census sheets, and inventory statements, that become the base for most forecasting processes.

Holding cost   Total of all expenses in maintaining an inventory, including the cost of capital tied up in inventory, obsolescence of products, storage, insurance, handling taxes, depreciation, deterioration, and breakage.

Holloware   Metal container that usually holds food.

Hollow ground   Concave surface behind the cutting edge of the knife blade that is notched, or serrated.

Homogenization   Process in which fat in whole milk is broken down and dispersed permanently throughout the milk.

Hops   Dried, ripe blossoms of a perennial vine (humulus lupulus), which are an essential ingredient added to beer to give it a bitter flavor.

Immersion freezing   Very expensive process of submerging food in a liquid refrigerant or spraying the liquid on the product, usually shrimp or scallops.

Impinger   Conveyorized gas-fired or electric oven that toasts the bottom of pizza crust and makes it flaky.

Independent purchasing   A separate purchasing unit in an organization that is authorized by management to purchase for all departments.

Indirect contact freezing   Packaged food placed between freezer shelves for 1 to 2 hours.

Indirect costs   Costs incurred in the foodservice operation that cannot be related directly to production, such as costs of the facility and its operation.

Induction   Heat transfer method in which electrical magnetic fields are created along the ceramic cooktop; when magnetic cookware is placed on the top, the molecules in the pan start moving so rapidly the pan gets hot.

Infrared waves   Type of radiation used in broiling that has a longer wave length than visible light.

Ingredient room   Area in which ingredients from storage are measured or weighed according to a recipe before being sent to production.

Instant coffee   Concentrated extract of a coffee brew.

Instant tea   Dried product prepared from brewed tea used mostly in iced tea.

Institutional Meat Purchase Specifications (IMPS)   Accurate description of standardized cuts of meat.

Internal control   Plan to coordinate methods within a business to safeguard assets, check the accuracy and reliability of its accounting data, promote operational efficiency, and encourage adherence to prescribed managerial policies.

Inventory   Record of food and supply assets owned by the foodservice operation.

Inventory control   Technique of maintaining items in storage at desired quantity levels.

Invertebrate shellfish   Shellfish with no backbone that is covered with some type of shell.

IQF products   Individually quick-frozen in air products used almost exclusively in foodservice operations.

Irish whiskey   Blend made from a mash of cereal grains, usually wheat, oats, corn, and rye, most often produced in pot stills which help give it a unique taste.

Irradiation   Low levels of gamma rays or radiant energy used to inhibit growth, maturation, and infestation by insects of fresh fruits, vegetables, and mushrooms.

Isotonic drinks   Sports drinks that prevent dehydration during vigorous exercise and give a quick energy boost.

Issuing   Process used to supply food to production units after it has been received.

Jaccarding   Special instrument used to tenderize meat by piercing it with multiple, thin needles and making small holes visible only in the raw meat.

Jam   Jelly with mashed fruit added.

Jelly   Product made from fruit juices and sugar that is the clear color of the fruit with a sparkling appearance.

Just-in-time (JIT)   Philosophy and strategy that has effects on inventory control, purchasing, and suppliers.

Just-in-time purchasing   Products purchased as needed for production and immediate consumption by the customer, eliminating the need to record it in inventory.

Kosher meat   Meat processed under the supervision of a specially trained rabbi who performs the ritual slaughter and drains the blood from the animal.

Lactose free milk   Milk in which hard-to-digest lactose has already been broken down.

Lager beer   Beer fermented by yeast at the bottom of a cold tank (37°F to 49°F) by a process called *bottom fermentation* in which action starts from the bottom.

Laminated   Plastic or wood made of thin layers of paper or wood bonded together with glue and compressed under heat.

Latest purchase price   Method using the latest purchase price in valuing the ending inventory.

Law of agency   Buyer's authority to act for the organization is defined, as well as the obligation each owes the other and the extent to which each may be held liable for the other's actions.

Law of contract   Agreement between two or more parties.

Law of warranty   Guarantee by the supplier that an item will perform in a specified way.

Lead crystal   Glass with lead oxide added to give the product brilliance and clarity.

Lead time   Interval between initiation of a requisition and receipt of the product.

Leading   Human resource function particularly concerned with individual and group behavior.

Leakers   Packages that have lost their vacuum because of poor seals or mishandling during shipping.

License states   States and the District of Columbia that regulate liquor sales by licensing wholesalers and, in some states, distributors and processors.

LIFO (last in, first out)   Method of using inventory based on the assumption that current purchases are largely, if not completely made for the purpose of meeting current demands of production.

Lime glass   Substantial proportion of lime used in most commercial glass products, such as bottles, tumblers, and windows.

Liqueurs   (also called **cordials**) Distilled spirits sweetened with 2.5% or more of sugar and flavored with a variety of ingredients: fruits, herbs, spices, flowers, nuts, and cream.

Local markets   Products from local farms or processors sold to customers in a specific geographic area.

Long life   Milk pasteurized at UHT temperature and aseptically packaged so it can be stored unrefrigerated and unopened for 6 months.

Low-temp cooking and holding oven   Oven with cooking temperatures from 100°F to 325°F, giving a 25% yield increase for meat, and holding temperatures from 60°F to 200°F.

Lug   Projection or ridge either inside or outside a tumbler to prevent jamming when stored or on the bottom of trays for easy draining and fast drying.

Macerator   Equipment used by retail stores and restaurants to make cubed steaks cut from less tender cuts of meat, such as chuck or bottom round.

Maintenance   Act of keeping the facility and equipment in a state of repair or efficiency.

Make-or-buy decision   Procedure for deciding whether to purchase from oneself (make) or purchase from suppliers (buy).

Malt   Barley soaked in water and allowed to germinate; occasionally wheat malt is used.

Malted beverage   U.S. standard of identity uses this term rather than beer and defines it as a "beverage made by the alcoholic fermentation in potable brewing water, of malted barley with hops."

Management   Process whereby unrelated resources are integrated for accomplishing organizational goals.

Manufacturer's representative   Distributor who does not take title, bill, or set prices and usually represents small manufacturing companies, including foodservice equipment manufacturers.

Market   Medium through which a change in ownership moves products from producer to customer.

Marketing channel   Exchange of ownership of a product from the producer through the manufacturer or processor and the distributor to the customer.

Marmalades   Jellies with slices, including the peel, of citrus fruits, usually orange or lemon.

Materials handling   Movement and storage of materials as they proceed through the foodservice operation.

Materials management   Unifying force that gives interrelated functional units a sense of common direction.

Meat Buyers Guide   Pictorial representation of items in the *Institutional Meat Purchase Specifications* published by the North American Meat Processors (NAMP).

Meat Inspection Act   Federal act that provides for the destruction of diseased and unfit meat, regulates sanitation in meat plants, requires stamping of inspected meat, prevents addition of harmful substances in meat products, and prohibits false or deceptive labeling.

Mechanical trash compactors   Equipment that compacts dry bulky trash, such as cans and cartons, to one fifth of its original bulk.

Melamine   Four chemical ingredient compound, including water, molded into dinnerware that is break resistant, stain and scratch resistant, and dishwasher safe.

Menu   List of food items that serves as the primary control and core of everything happening in the foodservice operation.

Microbreweries   Very small, independent companies with carefully controlled output of not more than 15,000 barrels of beer per year.

Microwaves   Very short wave lengths that penetrate partway into food and agitate water molecules, causing friction to create heat.

Milk   The National Dairy Council defines milk as the lacteal secretion obtained by the complete milking of one or more cows.

Mini-max method   Method requiring a safety stock be maintained at a constant level both on the inventory record and in storerooms.

Mollusks   Animals with no backbones and soft bodies that usually have a shell; mussels, clams, oysters, and scallops are examples.

Morals   Individual's personal belief about what is right or wrong.

Moving average method   Method using a time series model that is a repetitive process for developing a trend line.

Municipal solid waste (MSW)   Refuse collected routinely from households, commercial institutions, offices, and light industry by municipal or private haulers or carried to dumpsters or disposal areas by individuals.

Must   Unfermented grape juice that must be fermented to make wine.

National Association of Food Equipment Manufacturers (NAFEM)   Organization of manufacturers that make equipment for the foodservice industry.

National Association of Purchasing Management (NAPM)   Association committed to providing national and international leadership in purchasing and materials management education and research.

National Marine Fisheries Service   U.S. Department of Commerce agency that offers a voluntary seafood grading and inspection program for a fee.

National Sanitation Foundation® (NSF)   Nonprofit, noncommercial organization dedicated to public health safety and protection of the environment by developing standards, providing education, and offering third party assessment services.

Natural cheese   Cheese made by clotting milk to form a curd and then concentrating the curd by draining the whey.

Negotiation   Art of arriving at a mutual agreement with suppliers by bargaining on essentials of a purchasing contract, such as specifications, quality assurance, price, payment terms, and delivery schedules.

NSF International   Nonprofit, noncommercial organization that seeks solutions to problems involving cleanliness and sanitation of foodservice equipment.

Nutrition Labeling and Education Act   (1990) Act responsible for food labeling regulations agreed upon by FDA and USDA; it took effect in 1994.

Ocean Trust   Country's only national foundation dedicated to protecting the oceans as a food source for humanity.

Olive   Botanically a fruit because it has a single stone or pit; either green or black in color.

Oolong tea   Partially fermented tea that is only slightly blackened and has a flavor and aroma between those of black and green teas.

Open stock   Product is always available.

Operational resources   Resources essential for the functioning of a foodservice operation: money, time, utilities, and information.

Ordering cost   Cost of total operating expenses of the purchasing and receiving departments, expenses of purchase orders and invoice payment, and data processing for purchasing and inventory.

Organic milk   Milk from cows that are raised in pasture land free of all chemical compounds and that have not been injected with growth hormones.

Organizational purchasing   Usually handled by a committee authorized to purchase food and supplies for many foodservices within a specific category of foodservice operations.

Organizing   Process of grouping activities, delegating authority to accomplish activities, and providing for coordination of relationships, both horizontally and vertically.

Palatability   Overall taste appeal, tenderness, juiciness, and flavor of cooked lean meat.

Pallet   Portable wooden or metal platform for handling products by a forklift truck, used for storage of materials in warehouses.

Par stock   Average amount of each type and brand of a product needed in storage to meet one and a half times the amount used on the busiest day of the week.

Pasta   Dough in various shapes and forms often referred to as a paste; the word *pasta* means paste in Italian.

Pasteurization   Heating of raw milk in approved equipment at a sufficiently high temperature for a specified length of time to destroy pathogenic bacteria.

Performance specifications   Quality measured by the effective functioning of small or large equipment, disposable paper and plastic items, or detergents.

Perpetual inventory   Continuous record of all purchases and products in stock.

Personal ethics   Ethics based on a person's religion or philosophy of life and derived from definite moral standards.

Physical inventory   Periodic actual counting and recording of products in stock in all storage areas.

Pilferage   Stealing in small quantities, often referred to as inventory shrinkage.

Place setting   Number of different pieces of dinnerware or flatware needed for each person served.

Planetary action   Revolving of an agitator in a mixer around the bowl as it twirls rapidly.

Planning   Determining in advance what should happen in the future.

Policy   General guide to organizational behavior developed by top-level management.

Pot still   Piece of equipment used in the distillation of spirits that is limited in the degree of proof it can achieve while preserving flavor, body, and aroma.

Pottery   Dense china.

Poultry   All domesticated birds that are intended for human consumption.

Power Soak   Pot and pan washing equipment that capitalizes on the natural scouring abilities of high-turbulence, heated water.

Preserves   Jellies that have identifiable pieces of fruit.

Pressed glassware   Glassware shaped by pouring melted glass under pressure into a mold, thus making it resistant to thermal and mechanical shock.

Pressure steamers   Equipment that works by trapping and removing air from its cavity, causing steam pressure to build.

Pressureless convection steamer   Equipment in which heat is transferred from steam to food by forced convection caused by a fan inside that encircles the food, thus cooking it without pressure.

Primal cuts   Chuck, rib, loin, and round of beef, lamb, veal, and pork.

Principal   Person who needs an agent to work on his or her behalf.

Processed cheese   Blend of natural cheeses pasteurized to prevent further ripening and produce a uniform color, flavor, and texture.

Processed meat   Meat that has been changed by any mechanical, chemical, or enzymatic treatment, altering taste, appearance, and often shelf life.

Procurement   Managerial process of acquiring material, both food and nonfood items, for production.

Producers   Farmers or ranchers who produce raw food to sell to processors who sell to distributors or directly to the foodservice operation.

Production   Process after procurement in which menu items and services are created.

Profit center   Any department assigned both revenue and expense responsibilities.

Promotional discount   Reduction in the price of a product to feature it in the operation.

Pulper   Equipment similar to a garbage disposal except that it dehydrates the product into a slurry by a shredding device and then presses water out of it.

Purchasing   Activity concerned with the acquisition of goods, often described as obtaining the right product in the right amount at the right time and at the right price.

Purchasing cooperative   Large organization owned by and operated for the benefit of those using its services.

Quality   Features and characteristics of a product or service that focus on their ability to satisfy a customer's given needs.

Quality control   Continuous process of checking to determine if standards are being followed and, if not, taking corrective action.

Quality grading service   Voluntary service directed by the USDA available to foodservice operations for a fee to check products for wholesomeness measured by standards for each grade.

Quantity   Part of the decision process when the ability to produce in the desired amount is required.

Quantity discount   Percentage reduction in the price of a product if the amount ordered exceeds the amount established by the supplier.

Radiation   Generation of heat energy by wave action within an object.

Range oven   Part of a stove located under the cooking surface.

Ready-to-serve meat   Precooked meat that only needs thawing or heating; a convenience item or a backup for underproduction of menu items.

REAL Seal®   Special seal on a carton or package of milk, cheese, and other qualified dairy foods indicating that these products are made from milk produced in the United States that they meet federal or state standards.

Rebates   Another form of discounting for quantity.

Receiving   Process ensuring that products delivered by suppliers are those that were ordered by the buyer.

Recombinant bovine somatotropin (rBST)   Synthetic version of the naturally occurring hormone found in a cow's pituitary glands, mass produced under laboratory conditions.

Reorder point   Lowest stock level that can safely be maintained to avoid a stock-out or emergency purchasing.

Recycling   Act of removing materials from the solid waste stream.

Regional breweries   Companies that produce 15,000 to 500,000 barrels of beer in a year.

Ripening   When cheese develops desired characteristics for its type, changes occur in chemical and physical properties, including aroma, flavor, and texture.

Risk   Chance that a condition in foodservice will lead to a hazard.

Robustas coffee   Dark coffee beverage made from special beans grown in Africa and the Philippines.

Rock Cornish game hen   5- to 6-week-old plump-breasted bird named for the cross-bred White Plymouth Rock chicken with the Cornish game cock.

Roundfish   Fish with a bullet-shaped body and a spine that lies deep in the rounded flesh.

Rum   Alcoholic beverage made from sugar cane molasses that is aged and blended.

Rye whiskey   Alcoholic beverage that has a strong and distinctive taste of caraway seeds and is produced from a mixture of various grains, 51% of which must be rye to meet government regulations.

Safety stock   Backup supply of products to ensure against sudden increases in usage rate, failure to receive products on schedule, receipt of products not meeting specifications, and clerical errors in inventory records.

Sanitarian   Health official or inspector who is trained in sanitation principles and methods and in public health.

Sanitary   Free of harmful levels of contamination.

Sanitation   Use of heat or chemicals to destroy 99.99% of the disease-causing microorganisms on a food-contact surface, as defined by the FDA.

Saturated fat   Fat that usually is solid at room temperature, such as butter and lard.

Scotch whiskey   Alcoholic beverage made in Scotland that is a blend of malt whiskey and high-proof grain whiskey that comes entirely from fresh sprouted barley and has a smoky flavor resulting from the barley being dried over peat fires.

Scrapping   A dishwasher term for disposing of fragments of discarded or leftover food.

Seafood   General term for all edible aquatic organisms whether or not they come from an ocean or sea.

Seasonality   Time when the quality of raw food products is highest and price is usually the lowest.

Semolina   Coarsely ground flour from durum wheat and the principal ingredient in pasta.

Sensory analysis   Science that measures texture, aroma, flavor, and appearance of food products through human senses.

Service   Wide variety of many intangible factors that influences buyer's satisfaction.

Simple carbohydrate   Sugar found in table sugar, molasses, honey, lactose (in milk), and fructose (in fruits).

Smallwares   Coined word in foodservice that means any type of light equipment, including cooking and serving utensils.

Smoker oven   Electric, compact oven with racks to smoke up to 100 pounds of meat at a time.

Sommelier   Wine steward who assists guests with choosing wines and then opens and pours them.

Source reduction   Goal of the U.S. Environmental Protection Agency to retain strength while reducing weight of minimum toxic packaging materials, thus giving the product a longer useful life.

Special breed distributors   Purchasing and product movement specialists that purchase food directly from processors and hire a distributor to deliver the products to their restaurant chain clients.

Specialty wholesalers   Distributors that specialize in a particular product category, such as meat, produce, dairy, paper, or detergent.

Specification   Statement readily understood by both buyers and suppliers of required qualities of a product, including the allowable limits of tolerance.

Spices   Seeds, bark, roots, and fruit or berries of perennial plants used to flavor foods.

Spirits   Alcoholic beverages most often categorized as brown or white spirits; within each category, the product can be either straight or blended.

Staffing   Recruitment, selection, training, and development of employees who will be most effective in helping the foodservice operation meet its goals.

Standards   Basis for monitoring performance of the foodservice operation and taking corrective action deemed necessary.

Standards of fill   FDA regulations on how full a container must be to avoid a charge of deception.

Standards of identity   FDA regulations on what a given food product must contain.

Standards of quality   Quality levels established by the FDA for canned fruits and vegetables; if not met, the can must be labeled "Below Standard of Quality."

Static menu   Menu in which the same items are offered every day.

Steam-jacket kettle   One kettle in a larger kettle with an open space, or jacket, between the two into which steam is introduced.

Steam table pans   Containers that fit into steam table wells.

Storage   Holding goods under proper conditions to ensure quality until time of use.

Straight spirits   Alcoholic beverage that contains a minimum of 51% by volume of either corn, rye, barley, or wheat.

Strategic planning   Determining in advance the decisions that must be made.

Subprimal cuts   Small cuts of meat derived from primal cuts.

Supplier   Fourth component of the marketing channel, often identified as a seller or vendor; the person who offers products for sale.

Supply and demand   Basic economic concept that greatly influences the price paid for a product.

Superpremium beer   Beer that usually has a higher proportion of barley malt.

Sweet spot   Size or capacity of equipment from which the buyer gets the best value and lowest price per menu item produced.

Tableware   China, glassware, silver, and other utensils used for setting a table or serving food and drink.

Technical specifications   Type of specification that is written for products in which quality can be measured objectively and impartially by testing instruments.

Tempered glass   Lime glassware that is more resistant to chipping than annealed glassware because the glass is cooled quickly after it is formed.

Theft   The act of stealing; in a foodservice, the term denotes a greater loss than in pilfering.

Thermal shock   Sharply heating or cooling a glass, such as pouring cold liquid into a hot glass, which can cause it to crack.

Tilting skillet   Floor-mounted rectangular pan with a gas or electric-heated flat bottom, pouring lip, and hinged cover.

Time series model   Most often used foodservice forecasting model that assumes actual occurrences follow an identifiable pattern over time.

Toque   Soft hat worn by chefs with a full crown pleated into snug headband.

Trend   Straight or curved line showing the tendency of some function to grow or decline over time.

Ultra-high-temperature (UHT) milk   Milk heated to 280°F for 2 or more seconds and then cooled to 45°F; identified as long-life milk that can be stored unrefrigerated and unopened for 6 months.

Underwriters Laboratories Inc.® (UL)   Independent, not-for-profit organization that has been evaluating products in the interest of public safety since 1894.

Uniform Commercial Code   Law pertaining to business transactions in eight areas, identified as articles.

Universal Product Code (UPC)   System for uniquely identifying thousands of different suppliers and millions of different products that are warehoused, sold, delivered, and billed throughout retail and commercial channels of distribution.

Unsaturated fats   Fats that usually are liquid at room temperature.

Urimi   Processed seafood that is minced and usually salted.

Usage rate   Amount of time a product is used determined by past experience and forecasts.

USDA poultry voluntary grade stamp   Stamp that is used to indicate that the poultry has been graded by the Agricultural Marketing Service (AMS) according to quality factors established by grade standards.

U.S. Department of Commerce   Federal department established to promote American businesses and trades with responsibility to expand U.S. efforts throughout the world.

Vacucooling   Dry method for cooling produce by putting it in shipping cartons and then into a tightly sealed chamber in which pressure is reduced by exhausting air, resulting in rapid evaporation and cooling.

Value   Relationship between the price paid for a particular item and its use in the function it fulfills.

Value-added   Increase in value caused by processing, manufacturing, marketing, or distributing, exclusive of the cost of materials, packaging, and overhead.

Value analysis   Methodical investigation of all components of an existing product or service with the goal of discovering and eliminating unnecessary costs without interfering with effectiveness.

Vegetable   Any edible portion of a plant that either accompanies or is the entrée of a meal.

Vertebrate fish   Fish with a backbone, fins, and scales.

Vitrified china   Raw materials changed into glass crystals by increasing the temperature of firing to bring them closer together and produce glasslike finish.

Vodka   Fermented mash of grain, which is distilled at a high proof and, according to federal standards of identity, is treated with charcoal to be without distinctive character, aroma, taste, or color.

Warehouse club   Retailer offering self-service, cash and carry, and wholesale prices.

Warewashing   Process of washing and sanitizing dishes, glassware, flatware, and pots and pans either manually or mechanically.

Warranty   Written guarantee given to the buyer that states the manufacturer will for a period of time be responsible for the repair or replacement of the defective product.

Wet aging   Storage of wholesale beef carcasses at refrigerated temperatures in a vacuum package bag.

White spirits   Those spirits that are clear in color and usually not aged in wood.

Wholesalers   Distributors that purchase from various manufacturers or processors, provide storage, sell, and deliver products to suppliers.

Wholesome Meat Act of 1967   Law requiring inspection of all meat if it is moved within or between states and inspection of foreign plants exporting meats to the United States.

Wholesome Poultry Products Act   Requirement that inspectors assess procedures, cleanliness of plants, and maintenance of equipment.

Wild game   All animals and birds that are hunted.

Wine   Fermented fruit, usually grapes, in which sugar in the juice is converted into alcohol by the action of yeasts.

Yield   Amount of product resulting at the completion of the various phases of the procurement/production/service cycle that usually is expressed as a definite weight, volume, or serving size.

Yield grades   Grades based on the amount of external fat, internal fat, size of the ribeye area, and carcass weight of the animal.

Yogurt   Cultured milk product with the consistency of either a liquid or a gel and processed from fresh whole, lowfat, or fat free milk.

Index

Note: Italicized page references indicate information located in figures or tables.